Marketing Management

Fourth Edition

Russell S. Winer
New York University

Ravi Dhar
Yale University

Boston Columbus Indianapolis New York San Francisco Upper Saddle River
Amsterdam Cape Town Dubai London Madrid Milan Munich Paris Montréal Toronto
Delhi Mexico City São Paulo Sydney Hong Kong Seoul Singapore Taipei Tokyo

Editorial Director: Sally Yagan
Editor in Chief: Eric Svendsen
Director of Marketing: Patrice Lumumba Jones
Executive Editor: Melissa Sabella
Senior Marketing Manager: Anne Fahlgren
Director of Editorial Services: Ashley Santora
Editorial Project Manager: Meeta Pendharkar
Senior Managing Editor: Judy Leale
Production Project Manager: Ann Pulido
Senior Operations Supervisor: Arnold Vila
Creative Director: Christy Mahon
Senior Art Director/Design Supervisor: Janet Slowik
Interior Designer: Karen Quigley
Cover Designer: Jodi Notowitz
Manager, Visual Research: Karen Sanatar
Photo Researcher: Cindy Durand
Media Project Manager: Lisa Rinaldi
Media Editor: Denise Vaughn
Full-Service Project Management: Elm Street Publishing Services
Composition: Integra Software Services Pvt. Ltd.
Printer/Binder: Quebecor World Color
Cover Printer: Lehigh-Phoenix Color/Hagerstown
Text Font: 9.5/11.5 Melior

Credits and acknowledgments borrowed from other sources and reproduced, with permission, in this textbook appear on appropriate page within text.

10 9 8 7 6 5 4 3 2 1

ISBN 10: 0-13-038792-4
ISBN 13: 978-0-13-038792-9

Dedication

R.W.: With much love to Toby, Jessica, and Andrew
R.D.: To Lilia and my parents, Jaya and Pearey Lal Dhar.
This book is for all of you.

Brief Contents

Contents

Preface

Overview: The Landscape of Marketing in 2010

The field of marketing was relatively stable up to the mid-1990s. Before then, marketing managers in charge of products and services could develop their marketing strategies by focusing on some selected groups of customers with controlled messages about how their brand was superior to the competition in a number of ways. This message would be delivered through television, newspapers, radio, magazines, and billboards, and, sometimes, through personal selling. People shopped in stores, in catalogues, or through the telephone. Price was pretty much the same for all customers with some exceptions such as senior citizen discounts or for matinee movies.

Then, the Internet was developed and the marketer's world changed substantially, until today, where the job of a marketing manager is very different from what it was only 15 years ago, even five years ago. Rapid changes in digital and mobile technology have enabled companies to deliver targeted, customized communications to individuals rather than one message to large groups of customers. Customers now can communicate much more easily with each other through e-mail and social networking sites like Facebook, making word-of-mouth a critical marketing tool. Customers are more involved than ever with the companies that are producing the products and delivering services. Many customers are helping companies develop new products, for example, or creating their own ads and putting them on YouTube. It is now possible to purchase products virtually anywhere, whether at home, at work, or on the commuter train. In general, control of the image of the brand that the marketing manager wants to project is increasingly in the hands of customers rather than being fully controlled by the company.

Additionally, global markets continue to increase in importance. The rise of the middle class in India and China as well as the other BRIC countries (Brazil and Russia) have created new, large markets for consumer durables such as automobiles, flat-screen TVs, and washing machines as well as for global brands in supermarket and drug categories. Also, given the rapid changes in technology mentioned previously, anyone in the world can order a product from anyone's Web site independent of geographical location.

Changes from the Third Edition

In developing this fourth edition, we have been careful to retain the best-liked aspects of the previous three editions—the easy-to-follow writing style, the integration of information technology into the appropriate topics, and the coverage of new and important areas of marketing, such as customer relationship management. But we have also listened to adopters, students, and reviewers in working to make this fourth edition an even more effective teaching and learning tool. Major changes include:

- An entirely revamped look and feel. Marketing is a visual discipline, so along with updated text, advertisements, photos, and graphics, the book has a decidedly twenty-first century appearance.
- There are many new illustrations. Here is a partial listing:
  - Chapter 1: The new opening example for the book is the Segway highlighting the difficulty of the job of the marketing manager.
  - Chapter 2: There is a new illustration of the Gillette Fusion razor demonstrating physical product differentiation.
  - Chapter 3: A new illustration of Splenda artificial sweetener shows the importance of marketing research.
  - Chapter 4: A Hyundai example focuses on understanding consumer behavior.

- Chapter 5: There is an illustration of HSBC bank and its approach to B-to-B segmentation.
- Chapter 6: An illustration of the growth of "telepresence" (long-distance video conferencing) demonstrates how airlines and other forms of transportation have new competition.
- Chapter 7: The new Heineken Draught Keg shows the importance of innovative product design.
- Chapter 8: Many companies are "inviting" their customers to help design new products. An example of this is Levi's 501 jeans.

- The most obvious change is the addition of Professor Ravi Dhar of Yale University as a co-author. Ravi brings a different perspective to the text. His academic field of interest is behavioral decision making in which he is one of the leading scholars in the world. He is also the director of Yale's Center for Customer Insights. Ravi's knowledge of consumer behavior and global teaching and consulting experience add significantly to the chapters.

Marketing Management: A Strategic Perspective

To understand fully what has happened in this new digital and global environment and to give prospective marketing managers guidelines on how to be effective in their jobs, we need a marketing management textbook that goes beyond an explanation of basic concepts—it must present a strategic, integrative perspective that incorporates information on how to utilize these new technologies. After teaching a core marketing management course for more than 25 years at the time of the first edition, Russ Winer wrote *Marketing Management* because he came to understand how important the strategic perspective is and he observed that no textbook provided it. Readers of this book will find a strategic framework set up in Chapter 2, which is used throughout the rest of the text. Using strategy as a framework for the entire course is the chief distinguishing feature of this book.

Showing how changes in digital technology have changed the marketing manager's job is interwoven into the text as it is with the day-to-day life of the manager. The strategic framework in this fourth edition of *Marketing Management* promotes understanding of the second distinguishing feature of this text: its emphasis on the rapid changes thrust upon marketing managers by information technology in general, and the Internet in particular. Today every marketing textbook includes numerous references to the Internet, and despite the crash in the Internet stock bubble in 2001, it remains the most fundamental change in marketing in the last decade or so. As noted above, the Internet is a place where products and services are sold, it is a communications and information medium, it facilitates customer service, and it provides other benefits and opportunities to marketing managers and customers. The fundamental nature of this new, information-intensive technology is *interactivity*, the ability of customers to be active participants in the exchange between consumers and companies (for more than money for goods). This book also discusses at length the many ways that companies' investments in information technology have changed the marketing manager's job, in areas such as information gathering, communications, pricing, and product development.

While looking at the transformations that information technology has brought, this fourth edition of *Marketing Management* also integrates the issues involved with marketing technology-based goods and services. In discussions with business students at a variety of schools, I have found that many are interested in careers in software, biotechnology, semiconductors, and other technology-based industries. While the basics of marketing are the same across all industries, there are some features of high-technology markets (for example, short product life cycles) that make being a marketing manager for high-tech companies a somewhat different experience than being a brand manager for, say, Procter & Gamble's Crest toothpaste.

We have also included illustrations of global contexts by weaving foreign examples throughout the text to convey to the reader that thinking about global markets is a natural part of the job for many marketing managers. In many companies, developing a global marketing strategy is no longer a separate activity from developing a U.S. strategy, since an important task is to develop a unified, global brand image.

Another unique feature of the book is the chapter on customer relationship management (Chapter 14). No other marketing management book covers this topical and vitally important area of marketing in this depth. Few aspects have received as much attention in recent years as the question of how to maintain and enhance long-term relationships with customers. Considerable research has shown that it is less expensive and more profitable to retain customers than it is to try to get customers to switch from competitors. A good example of this recent emphasis on customer retention is the proliferation of loyalty programs. We discuss these programs in Chapter 14 and also provide several examples. It is also covered in Chapter 13 in the context of direct marketing.

Organization of the Book

This book is divided into three parts, the contents of which follow this sequence: (1) introduction to the philosophy of marketing, the marketing manager's job, and the complete marketing strategy that forms the backbone of the book; (2) analyses that marketing managers must perform to develop a strategy; and (3) marketing-mix decision-making.

The key benefit of this sequence is that it shows very clearly that strategic decisions must be made before tactical decisions. The marketing strategy chapter appears early in the book (Chapter 2) because we do not believe that a discussion about pricing, for example, can take place before you get a sense of how price must fit into the product's positioning and value proposition or be suitable for the particular market segment being pursued. In other words, marketing managers cannot make pricing decisions without clear direction from the strategy. This is an important feature of the book and distinguishes it clearly from comparable texts. In addition, Chapters 3 through 13 repeat the figure (Figure 2.1) describing the overall strategic structure with indications of "where we are" in the development of a complete marketing strategy. This approach continually reinforces the strategic perspective.

Part 1: Marketing Philosophy and Strategy. These two chapters provide a general overview of marketing and the "behind-the-scenes" work that marketing managers do in framing the specific decisions that are ultimately made, such as what price to charge. In addition, the elements of a complete marketing strategy are described. This is a unique aspect of the book since, as noted previously, we cover this material earlier in the discussion than other textbooks.

Chapter 1, "Marketing and the Job of the Marketing Manager," covers the basics of marketing: what it is, why it is important, the importance of a customer/competitor orientation, and the controversy over being led by the customer versus leading the customer. In addition, this chapter covers topics such as marketing organizations, the marketing plan, and how technology is changing marketing management and the marketing manager's job. *Key benefit:* This chapter gives you an understanding of the importance of being customer-oriented as well as an understanding of the organizational environment within which marketing decisions are made. In addition, some common marketing terminology is introduced.

Chapter 2, "A Strategic Marketing Framework," introduces a basic strategic framework that ties together the rest of the book. Topics include the development of a complete marketing strategy, differentiation, product positioning, developing a value proposition, the product life cycle, and product line management. We have put much of the traditional material on one of the "four Ps"—product—in this chapter to show that my emphasis in the book is on how product decisions must fit within an overall strategic framework. *Key benefit:* This chapter provides readers with the backbone of the book, a practical guide to the development of a marketing strategy that is a key takeaway from reading this chapter.

Part 2: Analysis for Marketing Decisions. Behind the development of every marketing strategy is a set of analyses that form the basis for decision making. Chapters 3 through 6 are used to show the reader what kind of information is necessary to develop a marketing strategy and how to organize this information.

Chapter 3, "Marketing Research," shows how market research is fundamental to customer insights and hence, the development of a marketing strategy. This chapter covers primary and secondary data collection, electronic sources of information, forecasting, and methods of estimating market potential. *Key benefit:* This chapter introduces you both to the general point that research is critical to the marketing management function and to some specific pointers about how to conduct a marketing research study.

Chapter 4, "Analyzing Consumer Behavior," covers the basics of understanding how and why consumers (individuals) make purchasing decisions. We discuss market segmentation and special attention is given to secondary sources of information that are useful for developing segmentation strategies. *Key benefit:* An understanding of consumer behavior is crucial to the development of a marketing strategy.

Chapter 5, "Organizational Buying Behavior," highlights the differences between consumer and organizational (business-to-business) buying behavior. *Key benefit:* This chapter provides the background for developing marketing strategies targeting business-to-business (B2B) customers.

Chapter 6, "Market Structure and Competitor Analysis," covers competitor definition (against whom are you competing?), competitor analysis, and where information about competitors can be obtained. We also introduce a game-theoretic approach to competitive strategy. *Key benefit:* You will obtain a "hands on" approach and concrete methods for determining competitors and analyzing their strengths and weaknesses. The simple game-theoretic illustrations are generally not included in other texts.

Part 3: Marketing Decision Making. These chapters cover the actual decisions marketing managers have to make. This is the section instructors would consider to be the four Ps, although, as noted earlier, some aspects of "product" are integrated into the strategy discussion in Chapter 2. In addition, we consider decisions related to customer relationship management to be an integral part of the marketing "mix" today.

Chapter 7, "Product Decisions," covers major decisions related to the product. These include developing and maintaining brand equity, product positioning, product line management, and some issues in packaging and product design. In addition, we place these topics in both technology and global contexts. *Key benefit:* You will gain knowledge about two key strategic parts of the marketing manager's job: branding and product positioning.

Chapter 8, "New-Product Development and Marketing," discusses various approaches to new product development, for example, the classical linear process versus the "rugby," cross-functional approach versus target costing. New product forecasting and issues such as how to decrease time to market receive special attention. The chapter logically follows Chapter 7 to show that new product policy should be integrated with an overall product strategy. *Key benefit:* New-products are the lifeline of any business; students will better appreciate the complexities of developing and introducing new products.

Chapter 9, "Pricing," focuses on how to measure customer value and how to use it to make pricing decisions. We also cover specific pricing issues such as EDLP (everyday low pricing) and private label competition. *Key benefit:* You should understand that pricing decisions can be made systematically versus the *ad hoc* approaches that are commonly used in practice.

Chapter 10, "Communications and Advertising Strategy," covers the basic communications model and the importance of integrating all communications activities to deliver a uniform message and image to customers. In addition, we emphasize how managing communications and making communications decisions have changed due to the Internet and the Web. After reviewing the elements of the communications mix, the chapter covers advertising decision making, including new approaches to advertising on the Internet. *Key benefit:* You will have a better understanding of integrated marketing communications (IMC) and advertising's role in the communications mix.

Chapter 11, "Sales Promotion," covers the essentials of sales promotion (different types, objectives, trade versus retailer promotions) as well as budgeting and Internet applications. *Key benefit:* You will better appreciate how sales promotion complements other elements of the communications mix.

Chapter 12, "Channels of Distribution," covers channel structure and management with an emphasis on managing indirect channels, that is, independent channel members. In addition, we discuss using the Internet as a channel, multilevel marketing, and current issues in supermarket retailing. *Key benefit:* You will better appreciate the wide variety of channel options that exist today as well as some of the management problems involved with channels.

Chapter 13, "Direct Channels of Distribution: Personal Selling and Direct Marketing," introduces personal selling as a mixture of communications and distribution. We position personal selling as a channel—that is, a way for customers to gain access to the company's products and services. We discuss the basics of sales management, with an emphasis on the impact of information technology on the salesperson's job. *Key benefit:* Readers will gain an understanding of how personal selling fits into the marketing mix.

Chapter 14, "Customer Relationship Management," is a unique part of the book in that other marketing management texts do not cover it extensively. We introduce a conceptual approach to developing CRM programs that can be used to establish such programs in organizations. This chapter covers various topics in customer retention including loyalty programs, mass customization, and information technology used to create customer databases. *Key benefit:* The reader will understand how to develop a CRM program for his or her company and the various issues involved with implementation.

Chapter 15, "Special Topic: Strategies for Service Markets," discusses what makes services marketing different from marketing manufactured goods. Topics covered include the service quality model, strategic and tactical issues, and the impact of technology on service markets with special attention paid to financial services. *Key benefit:* Given that about 80 percent of the U.S. economy is service-based, you must understand how marketing services is different from marketing physical goods.

Acknowledgments

No project like this one can be completed without help from a great number of people. Russ Winer is indebted to many of the colleagues at my current and previous institutions for their influence on my thinking about marketing management. These include Don Lehmann, Mac Hulbert, and the late Bill Brandt at Columbia; Al Shocker at San Francisco State University; and Dave Aaker, Rashi Glazer, and Debu Purohit at Berkeley (now at Duke University). Former students at Columbia, Vanderbilt, Berkeley, and NYU and in various executive and MBA programs around the world have forced him to think and rethink how to present this material, and they have provided valuable insights from their work and life experiences. Ravi Dhar is indebted to the students at the Yale School of Management who have helped shape my thinking and especially to Jennifer Danilowitz who provided feedback. Ravi would also like to thank the many different corporations he has collaborated with as the Director of the Yale Center, for customer insights that have shaped his thinking about marketing.

As any author knows, the production of a book is a team effort. Our editor at Prentice Hall, Katie Stevens, and the entire Prentice Hall team, including Ashley Santora, Ashaki Charles, Christine Ietto, and Peter Snell deserve substantial credit for assisting us. And, of course, thank you to the reviewers who had the thankless task of reading rough manuscripts and giving valuable advice.

Finally, we would be remiss if we did not acknowledge the people to whom this book is dedicated. Russ Winer: The love and support given to me by my family: Toby, Jessica, and Andrew. Ravi Dhar: My parents, Jaya and Pearey Lal Dhar. This book is for all of you.

Russell S. Winer
New York University
Rwiner@stern.nyu.edu

Ravi Dhar
Yale University
Ravi.Dhar@Yale.edu

About the Authors

Russell S. Winer is the William Joyce Professor and Chair of the Department of Marketing at the Stern School of Business, New York University. He received a B.A. in Economics from Union College and an M.S. and Ph.D. in Industrial Administration from Carnegie Mellon University. He has been on the faculties of Columbia and Vanderbilt universities and the University of California at Berkeley. Russ has been a visiting faculty member at M.I.T., Stanford University, Cranfield School of Management (U.K.), the Helsinki School of Economics, the University of Tokyo, École Nationale des Ponts et Chausées, and Henley Management College (U.K.). He has written three books, *Marketing Management, Analysis for Marketing Planning* and *Product Management*, and a research monograph, *Pricing*. He has authored over 60 papers in marketing on a variety of topics including consumer choice, marketing research methodology, marketing planning, advertising, and pricing. Russ has served two terms as the editor of the *Journal of Marketing Research*, he is the past co-editor of the *Journal of Interactive Marketing*, he is an Associate Editor of the *International Journal of Research in Marketing*, he is the co-editor of the *Review of Marketing Science*, and he is on the editorial boards of the *Journal of Marketing*, the *Journal of Marketing Research*, and *Marketing Science*. He is the most recent past Executive Director of the Marketing Science Institute in Cambridge, Massachusetts. He has participated in executive education programs around the world and is currently an advisor to a number of start-up companies and non-profit institutions. Russ is a founding Fellow of the INFORMS Society for Marketing Science.

Ravi Dhar is the George Rogers Clark Professor of Management and Marketing and the Director of the Yale Center for Customer Insights at the Yale School of Management. Ravi also has an affiliated appointment as Professor of Psychology in the Department of Psychology, Yale University. His research awards include the William F. O'Dell Award and the AMA Doctoral Dissertation Award (Honorable mention). His other research papers have also been a Finalist for the Paul Green Award, and Finalist (twice) for the O'Dell award. He has written more than 40 articles and serves on the editorial boards of leading marketing journals, such as the *Journal of Consumer Research* (Associate Editor), *Journal of Marketing, Journal of Marketing Research* (Area Editor), and *Marketing Science* (Area Editor) and other journals. Ravi is an expert in consumer behavior and branding, marketing management, and marketing strategy. His research involves using psychological and economic principles to identify successful consumer and competitive strategies in the offline and online marketplace. He has worked on collaborative research with leading corporations such as General Mills, Hewlett-Packard, IBM, Procter & Gamble, Samsung, PepsiCo, VISA, and other leading companies. He has led marketing seminars for senior executives in Asia, Europe, and North and South America.

part one Marketing Philosophy and Strategy

Key Learning Points

The purpose of this chapter is to introduce what marketing is, to discuss how marketing managers and the marketing environment are being buffeted by major changes in the business environment, and to clarify the job of the marketing manager. Key areas of learning are:

- The marketing concept
- Different organizational philosophies about marketing
- The importance of being customer focused
- The job of the marketing manager
- Typical marketing organizational forms
- How marketing is changing
- The focus of this book

Marketing the Segway presents numerous challenges.
Source: Hermann J. Knippertz/AP Wide World Photos

Marketing and the Job of the Marketing Manager

Chapter Brief

Inventor Dean Kamen's idea was to change the world by inventing a futuristic, upright scooter. The motorized scooter uses microchip-driven gyroscopes and sensors that permit its riders to stand upright. It can go up to 12.5 miles per hour and travel 10 to 15 miles on a single charge of its batteries. Controlling it involves leaning forward to go forward and leaning backward to reverse.

Introduced in 2001, Kamen's vision was that at $5,000, the Segway would satisfy a need for a clean, energy-efficient vehicle that would replace automobiles in the world's cities and could coexist with pedestrians.

The Segway was subjected to more hype and speculation than probably any product in history. Famed technology investor John Doerr, together with venture capital firm Kleiner Perkins Caufield & Byers, predicted that the Segway would hit $1 billion in sales faster than any other startup in history. Doerr also said that entire cities would be redesigned around it. It was introduced with so much excitement that the public relations firm retained to introduce it still uses it as a case study in how to create a media frenzy.

Through 2006, sales had hit only 23,500 units despite a factory that had the capacity to produce up to 40,000 per month. Some cities such as San Francisco banned them from their sidewalks. Priced at $4,950 and sold through Amazon.com, the Segway required a two-hour training class to learn how to use it. The company found that the largest adopters are warehouse workers who can easily get around a vast space quickly. In addition, people with physical disabilities used it to more easily navigate outdoors.

Fast forward to 2010. The company has expanded the product line considerably. From the initial single-product offering in 2001, the company now has nine models for different market segments:

- The i2 for normal consumer use
- The x2 for consumer use on uneven terrain
- The i2 Commuter designed for running errands
- The i2 Cargo for carrying loads
- The i2 and x2 Patrollers for police and security guards
- The x2 Golf
- The x2 Turf with tires that are gentle on any terrain
- The RMP, a Segway-based mobile platform

However, it is clear that the Segway is still not a hit. After investing $100 million and building factories that could produce 480,000 units per year, only 50,000 units have been sold since its introduction. Some cities are still making it difficult to use the Segway. For example, St. Louis requires a permit that costs $300 to use it. It is still very much a curiosity rather than a pandemic solution to urban crowding and pollution. However, the company is hoping that the periodic large swings in gasoline prices will get more consumers to consider it for short trips. In addition, the company has been talking with General Motors about a joint venture called Puma to create a tiny, two-wheeled, two-seat car based on the Segway platform.[1]

As the marketing manager for Segway, how do you gain customers for your products? Is it possible that the technology is great but that customers will not be willing to pay the price? How will the introduction of new low-priced cars from China and India affect the sales of Segways? How much of your communications should be for the basic concept versus the Segway brand? How do you educate the channels of distribution to sell Segways over the alternatives such as bicycles, motor scooters, motorcycles, and small cars?

In an attempt to answer these questions and many others, this book has been written to help marketing managers in organizations (in both the commercial and the nonprofit sectors), to develop better marketing strategies, make better decisions, and ultimately create more successful products and services in the markets in which they compete.

Marketing is difficult to define. Many organizations, such as the American Marketing Association, and many authors struggle to pin down what marketing is and what marketers do. A faulty concept is the ubiquitous marketing department in many organizations. In some of these organizations, managers think that marketing is what the people in the marketing department do—creating brochures, developing advertisements, organizing promotional events, and performing similar activities. This concept is dangerous because it gives people who are not in marketing the sense that those who work in the traditional marketing department are the only people charged with performing marketing activities.

Consider the following example. The customer newsletter for a small community bank in California contained an article about a teller at a branch in a small town outside of San Francisco. This article described how a customer was frustrated at being unable to balance her checkbook—not an unusual situation. This customer called the branch several times seeking assistance until the teller took it upon herself to drive to the customer's home (about 30 minutes from her own home) and help her balance the checkbook. Naturally, the customer was delighted with this level of personal service and will probably be a long-term customer of the bank.

From an organizational perspective, the teller was not in the marketing department. However, she had a significant impact on the short- and long-term likelihood that the customer would maintain her accounts at the bank. In addition, the teller was not performing what might normally be considered marketing activities. She did not talk about price, communicate any of the benefits of using her bank, or try to persuade the customer to do anything.

The point is that what marketing is and who is involved with marketing are difficult to determine. It could be argued that *any* employee of an organization who either has or could have contact with customers is actually in a marketing job, whether it is in his or her title or not. Any person who can potentially win or lose customers is in marketing. Of course, this creates a very broad set of marketers in organizations, from the receptionist who greets customers, to the actual marketing managers making strategic decisions about the products, to the people on the manufacturing line attempting to ensure that the product is made at the level of quality consistent with the marketing strategy.

marketing
the set of activities designed to influence choice whenever an individual or organization has a choice to make
Source: Copyright (c) 2010 by American Marketing Association. Reprinted with permission

And what about the definition of marketing? It is not really worth struggling over a definition of what it is. Instead it is more useful to describe when one would use the marketing tools and techniques described in this book. **Marketing** is involved and necessary *whenever an individual or organization has a choice to make*. This is obviously a broad definition, but it is intended to be. It includes what are normally thought to be marketing situations (e.g., "What brand of toothpaste should I buy?") and personal situations (e.g., "Should I take a vacation in Europe or visit my family in Los Angeles?"). Marketing is involved in both situations because there is a choice to be made *and* some individual, organization, or institution has or is attempting to have an influence on the decision. Marketing is the set of activities that attempt to influence choice.[2]

The reason marketing is such an exciting field is that choices are made in a wide variety of contexts and the influences and influencers can vary from context to context, and also from each other in the same situation. The archetypical marketing situation is the brand manager at Coca-Cola trying to persuade you to buy Diet Coke rather than Diet Pepsi. Similarly, Dell spends a considerable amount of money trying to persuade personal computer customers to purchase its brand rather than Hewlett-Packard, Toshiba, Apple, or some other competing brand. In Japan, the marketing manager at Kao is interested in consumers buying its brands of disposable diapers rather than Procter & Gamble's. Visa wants you to use its card rather than MasterCard and American Express. Continuing our Segway example, the company is trying to get you to buy a ecologically beneficial form of transportation among a number of others.

However, these situations are only a subset of the applications of marketing concepts. Consider the U.S. government's attempts to reduce the incidence of smoking. Similarly, the leaders of China have succeeded in reducing their country's population by marketing the importance of having only one child. What about the local art museum's attempts to draw people away from staying at home or a baseball game? Students graduating from business schools must convince corporate recruiters to pick them from a large number of qualified candidates. Churches, synagogues, and other religious groups must increase their congregations and keep their current members. Even the local utility that has a monopoly is often interested in convincing customers to cut back on their consumption of electricity to reduce the need to add expensive new capacity.

Thus, most kinds of organizations need to understand marketing and use marketing techniques to increase the number of "customers" that choose their options instead of others. That is why marketing is pervasive in most developed economies: there are simply too many choices that customers can make, including doing nothing. Therefore organizations that want to be sustainable successes and achieve their organizational objectives cannot ignore marketing and what it can do for them.

At the same time, marketing is also very difficult. The correct decision rarely (if ever) pops out of a formula such as a net present value calculation, as it might in accounting or finance. An infinite number of combinations of market segments, positioning statements, advertising budgets, prices, and other factors could make up a marketing strategy for a product. Although most of these combinations can be eliminated because of financial constraints, the product or service characteristics, what the competition is doing, or other reasons, the marketing manager still must consider a large set of options. Usually there is no obvious answer.

That marketing is difficult is clear when one views the vast graveyard of marketing mistakes and products that have gone from greatness to sadness: New Coke, Sony Betamax VCRs, Lotus 1-2-3, the Newton personal digital assistant, videodiscs, Pan American Airlines, Iridium (the brick-sized global cell phone), 3Com's Audrey Internet appliance, Webvan (and most other dot-coms), Kmart, Toshiba's HD DVD disc players, Pontiac (by the end of 2010), and many others.[3] Although some of these products still exist and have a loyal base of customers, they all have either disappeared or have significantly lower sales than they once had. Product failures and depressed sales do not always result from poor decisions made by marketers. Although Apple is a very strong company now, the company was in decline in the early 1990s. John Sculley, the CEO (chief executive officer) of Apple at the time, was widely blamed for its decline although he had a reputation as one of the world's best marketers when he was at PepsiCo. Besides organizational failures, such as not spending any money on marketing research, some of the reasons that marketing is difficult are:

- Unlike successful corporate financial, accounting, or production personnel, a marketing manager cannot be successful without spending a considerable amount of time talking to customers.
- At the same time, customers are not always able to tell you what products they want.

Strong technology does not guarantee market success as 3Com found with its Internet appliance.
Source: Stuart Ramson/AP Wide World Photos

- Competitors' actions are difficult to predict, particularly those of new competitors from other countries.
- Changes in customer tastes and general societal trends occur frequently.
- Changing economic conditions can have a large impact on consumer disposable income and corporate budgets (as has been seen in the past year or so).
- Implementing strategies precisely as they are written in the marketing plan is difficult.

In other words, the environment in which marketing and marketers operate is dynamic and outside the full control of marketing management. The fact that the environment is so dynamic is perhaps the greatest threat to successful implementation of marketing strategies and tools. For example, with corporate purchasing budgets on hold during the global economic slump of 2009–2010, purchasing Segways to improve the movements of personnel in factories seems like a luxury.

Although marketing is difficult, some organizations consistently produce winning products and services. These include McDonald's (fast food), Johnson & Johnson (baby and medical supplies), Nestlé (food products), Procter & Gamble (household products), General Electric (diversified consumer and industrial products and financial services), and Emerson Electric (motors). Although some of their success has resulted from nonmarketing factors, these companies are all lauded for their marketing capabilities.

Table 1.1 shows some interesting data on brand leadership from 1923 and 2005 for a variety of consumer products. Of the 25 leaders in 1923, 20 were still first in 2005! This is strong evidence that although marketing is very much a creative activity, some things clearly can be taught and passed down through the fabric of an organization. Much like a sports team with great natural talent, a marketing team still needs strong training in the fundamentals to be a winner. One of the goals of this book is to provide the fundamentals that will lend a marketing structure to the reader's natural creative abilities.

Marketing Philosophies

As noted earlier, many businesspeople feel that marketing is restricted to areas such as the development of marketing communications, promotions, and so on—often referred to as the tactical aspect of marketing. However, marketing is much broader than that. Marketing-thought leaders have developed a number of overarching philosophies of marketing that are important for any student in the field to understand.

The Marketing Concept

marketing concept
the importance of having a customer focus (i.e., organizing the resources of the firm toward understanding customers' needs and wants and then offering products and services to meet those needs)

One of the most pervasive ideas in marketing is what is known as the **marketing concept**. In its simplest terms, this concept emphasizes a customer focus or organizing the resources of the firm toward understanding customers' needs and wants and offering products and services that meet those needs.

Although many definitions of the marketing concept exist and a number of people are credited with originating the concept,[4] perhaps the best way to describe the importance of a customer focus has been stated by the late management guru Peter Drucker:[5]

> *There is only one valid definition of business purpose: to create a customer.*

According to Drucker, the focus of a business is not profits but customers: one generates profits by serving customers better than competitors do.

This was elegantly restated by the late marketing theorist Theodore Levitt:[6]

> *The purpose of a business is to create and keep a customer. To do that you have to produce and deliver goods and services that people want and value at prices*

Table 1.1

Market Share Rank of Brands: 1923 and 2005

Brand	1923 Rank	2005 Rank
Swift's Premium bacon	1	1
Kellogg's corn flakes	1	3
Eastman Kodak cameras	1	1
Del Monte canned fruit	1	1
Hershey's chocolates	1	1
Crisco shortening	1	1
Carnation canned milk	1	1
Wrigley chewing gum	1	1
Nabisco biscuits	1	1
Eveready flashlight batteries	1	2
Gold Medal flour	1	1
Lifesavers mint candies	1	1
Sherwin-Williams paint	1	1
Hammermill paper	1	1
Prince Albert pipe tobacco	1	1
Gillette razors	1	1
Singer sewing machines	1	1
Manhattan shirts	1	top 5
Coca-Cola soft drinks	1	1
Campbell's soup	1	1
Ivory soap	1	2
Lipton tea	1	1
Goodyear tires	1	1
Palmolive toilet soap	1	2
Colgate Toothpaste	1	1

Source: Jack Trout (2005), "Branding Can't Exist Without Positioning," *Advertising Age*, March 14, 2005, p. 28. Reprinted with permission from *Advertising Age*. Copyright Crain Communications, Inc. 2005.

and under conditions that are reasonably attractive relative to those offered by others to a proportion of customers large enough to make those prices and conditions possible.

Therefore, the marketing concept not only embraces the notion of being customer focused. As is less often perceived, it is also consistent with being competitor focused and making a profit.

This latter point is particularly important because sometimes the marketing concept is interpreted as "serving all customer needs at all costs" and "the customer is always right" (i.e., there is no such thing as a bad customer). This is simply not true. The marketing concept is entirely consistent with serving only segments of the consumer population and is also consistent with turning away customers and customer segments that are unprofitable to serve.[7] Some customers cost more in time, money, and morale than they add in terms of profit to the company. For example, companies such as ING Direct USA and Citibank attempt to drive away customers who cost more to serve than the revenues they generate by offering them fewer services than those who are profitable to serve.

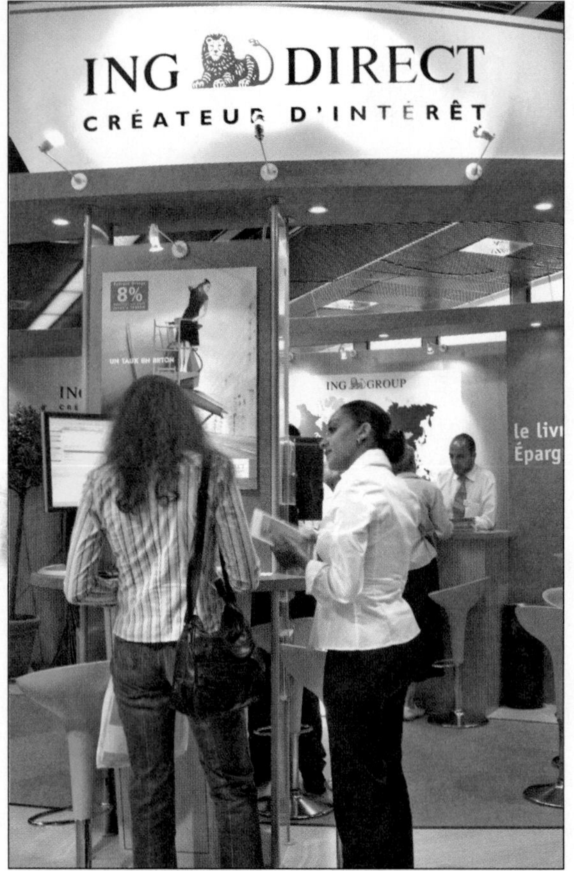

ING Direct USA is one of the fastest-growing online banks in the world.
Source: Directphoto.org/Alamy Images

Application | ING Direct USA

ING Direct USA is one of the fastest-growing retail banks in the United States and the world. It opened for business in September 2000 as a purely online operation. Since then, it has attracted more than 2 million customers and $30 billion of assets in the United States and 20 million customers in nine countries with $300 billion in assets worldwide. The company took more than 104,000 customers and $1.4 billion in assets in late 2007 when the online bank NetBank folded. It is a unit of the Dutch bank, ING Groep. Although an Internet-based savings bank (www.ingdirect.com), customers can use the phone or mail as well. There are no ATMs and no branches (although there are a few ING Cafés used for brand-building); there are also no fees, minimum deposits, and few products: their Orange-branded savings accounts, some certificates of deposit, some mutual funds, mortgages, and home equity loans. This keeps their costs low, as much as one-sixth of the costs of a conventional bank in some areas. This means that they can offer higher rates on deposits, as much as four times as high as competitors. The bank's mission is to encourage Americans to save and invest rather than spend, so it does not offer car loans, for example.

Relevant to our point, ING Direct rejects customers it does not want to serve. In 2004, it "fired" more than 3,500 customers who cost too much (e.g., made too many calls to customer service) or who wanted some exceptions from standard operating procedures. Thus, ING is clearly not interested in serving all customers, only those who are the most profitable to serve.[8]

The marketing concept and customer focus are core concepts, not only in marketing but in general business practice today. Marketing does not have proprietary claim to customer orientation. Organizations have found that it is simply not enough to produce excellent products and services. To be successful and ultimately achieve their goals, they have to figure out what customers want and offer it in a better way than their competitors. As noted earlier, this is not easy to do. However, from preachers of the total quality management (TQM) trend in the 1980s to today's business writers exhorting companies to concentrate on the long-term value of customer relationships, the customer has been and should be the focus of attention.

Different Organizational Philosophies

Although it may seem obvious that it is important to focus on the customer in order to be successful, a casual inspection of marketing practices shows that this is not always done. Figure 1.1 shows four different strategic approaches to the marketplace, three of which are not consistent with the customer-focused marketing concept.

One kind of organization is what might be called sales driven. In such an organization, the philosophy is "what we make, we sell." This is usually a very aggressive, push-the-catalogue approach to marketing. In these organizations, the sales function is the leader and marketing usually acts in a supporting role through the production of

Figure 1.1

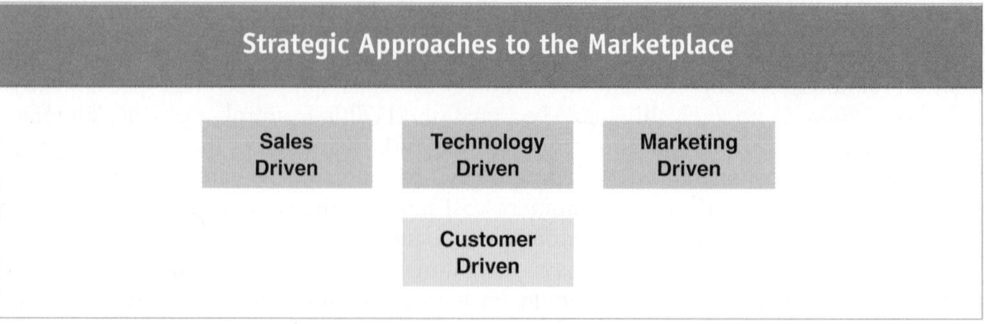

Source: Gary Hamel and C. K. Prahalad (1994), *Competing for the Future* (Boston: Harvard Business School Press).

collateral material (e.g., sales literature) and coordination of promotional events. Little effort usually is expended in listening to what the customer is saying or even attempting to understand what the customer wants. The main focus is on selling and meeting sales targets, not marketing. The sales organization is interested in volume, not profits; sells to all comers; and uses flexible price, credit, and service policies in order to close the deal (i.e., give the customer everything she wants even if it is not in her long-term best interests).

Every reader of this book has undoubtedly been exposed to an organization like this. When your dinner is interrupted by a telemarketer selling stocks or some other opportunity that you simply cannot pass up, you clearly understand this approach to the marketplace. Retail salespeople who obviously are participating in sales contests or trying to cash in on manufacturers' promotions give the impression that they are not looking out for the customer's welfare. Sometimes this impression reflects a lack of investment in training. However, it is a clear signal of the company's attitudes toward customers. For example, the database software company Oracle has a reputation for having "strong-armed" salespeople who try to convince customers to purchase more software than they need. The opposite approach is shown by this Ace Hardware illustration.

Application | Ace Hardware

When the Ace Hardware store in Cape Coral, Florida, gets very busy, its "customer quarterback" swings into action. Ace, with $3.8 billion in sales, started adding this position to all of its 4,600 U.S. stores in 2008. The idea is to focus on helping customers when the store traffic gets heavy. The customer quarterback talks to incoming shoppers, analyzes their body language, and decides whether each one is browsing, seeking a particular product with little time to spare, or trying to get a large project off the ground. Then, she or he "calls the play" by calling ahead to the appropriate department so that the right expert is waiting. As a result, Ace has created a very customer-oriented experience in its competitive battle against the "big-box" hardware chains like Home Depot and Lowe's.[9]

A second common approach to the marketplace is the technology or product-driven organization. Here, the focus is on the research and development (R&D) group as well as sales. In these companies, R&D develops products and "throws them over the wall" for marketing and sales to sell. The next technology (i.e., a newer and better mousetrap) will be even better. The problem with this kind of focus is not that the technology is bad, but the technology may not solve anyone's problem.

A good example of a product category developed under this kind of philosophy is personal digital assistants (PDAs). The term was introduced by Apple in 1992 when it introduced the Newton, a handheld computer that had a pen-based interface and could send faxes, take notes, and organize your life. Many other large companies, such as Motorola, AT&T, Sony, and Casio, saw tremendous potential in this market and invested large amounts of money in product development. However, the Newton was a flop. Why? Most customers are not interested in technology for technology's sake. There was a basic problem with the Newton: although it was cute, it did not provide enough benefits to customers to make them want to pay more than $500 for it. The Newton was not the only flop in this market. Prior to the introduction of the Palm Pilot in 1996 and its subsequent raging success, many other companies launched unsuccessful handheld devices.

The reason can be summarized by one of the pioneers in the PDA market, Jerry Kaplan, who founded GO (which became EO when AT&T invested in them), a company that predated the development of the Newton:[10]

> *In looking back over the entire GO-EO experience, it is tempting to blame the failure on management errors, aggressive actions by competitors, and indifference on the part of large corporate partners. While all these played important roles, the project might have withstood them if we had succeeded in building a useful product at a reasonable price that met a clear market need.*

It is clear that having a great technology does not guarantee that a company will have customers. This is a critical risk that the Segway faces.

Application Sony Betamax

One of the best-known cases of a technologically excellent product that did not meet customer needs was the Sony Betamax. Although the home video market emerged in 1971, the current standard playing format, VHS, was not introduced until 1976. Other technologies promoted besides VHS and Betamax were Ampex's InstaVideo and Sony's U-matic formats. Betamax followed U-matic and was introduced in 1975, a full year before VHS. Not only was it introduced earlier, but Betamax was also considered to be a superior technology. How could it fail?

When Sony introduced the Betamax format following the U-matic failure, it was the first compact, lightweight, and inexpensive VCR taping format (InstaVideo and U-matic tapes were bulky and expensive). A strength of the Betamax format was a broader carrier signal bandwidth than VHS. Videophiles considered Betamax to have superior picture quality. Also contributing to the better picture quality was Beta's higher signal-to-noise ratio. Although some commentators questioned whether consumers could tell the difference in picture quality, it was generally conceded that Beta was the higher-quality format.

However, a key difference between the two was playing time. Beta tapes had recording capacities of only one hour, whereas VHS tapes could record up to six hours of material. Sony's product development process focused on the technical aspect of the product and ignored customer preferences. RCA, considering an alliance with Sony, conducted its own research and discovered that consumers required a minimum tape capacity of two hours. As a result, RCA did not enter into an agreement with Sony, instead waiting to find a partner that could produce a tape format with greater capacity.

However, Sony launched the format in 1975. Although RCA and other companies such as Matsushita had a one-year disadvantage, Beta's market share slumped from 100 percent in 1975 to only 28 percent in 1981. Extending the Beta format to longer playing times did not revive it because VHS had already become the *de facto* standard. Few Betamax machines survive today. After 27 years and 18 million machines, Sony stopped making the Betamax in 2002.

The Betamax experience was traumatic for Sony. The failed attempt to set a product standard that did not meet customer needs was so crushing that the company reportedly gave serious consideration to abandoning consumer products altogether. This is another illustration of the fact that the best mousetrap does not always lead to market success.

Alternatively, engineers love to overengineer products with features customers do not need or want and underappreciate products that are simple but meet a need. Palm's Pilot PDA is a perfect example. The two main functions customers wanted in a handheld device were a calendar and an address list. That is what they got in the Palm in a small, inexpensive, and easy-to-use package. The mobile phone company Vodafone introduced a model called the Simply that has no camera, no browser, and very few icons. The phone is large and ordinary-looking, not sleek like many of the newer models. However, it is easy to use, which is a key benefit to older consumers.[11] This over-engineering phenomenon where more product features are added to products than customer really want has been termed "feature fatigue."[12]

The third type of strategic approach to the marketplace is what might be called market*ing* driven. This kind of organization embraces marketing, but to excess. Much money is spent on marketing research and test marketing until the product is finely honed. These companies are great customers for the marketing research industry because they have large budgets and use every new and old technique that exists. They rely on customers to tell them what they want rather than take risks and anticipate customer needs. They typically have brand managers, associate brand managers, assistant brand managers, and multiple layers of decision making.

This overmarketing approach has been historically associated with the large consumer packaged-goods companies, such as Procter & Gamble and Kraft Foods. Those companies have been more successful introducing line extensions (i.e., new flavors of Jell-O) than establishing new product categories. This had been such a problem for Procter & Gamble (P&G) that a former CEO, A. G. Lafley, made it a point to focus on speed-to-market when he assumed the position. He was very successful in making P&G more innovative and responsive to the market. However, this overmarketing approach is not limited to consumer packaged-goods companies. Gap Inc. has been accused of making decisions based upon extensive marketing research rather than instinct and emotion favored by clothing merchandisers.[13]

The main problem with this kind of organization is its speed of response to changes in the marketplace: it is dreadfully slow. The company Coca-Cola had been around for about 100 years before it attempted to introduce a new product with the Coke name, the very successful Diet Coke. However, the diet cola category had been around for many years before Diet Coke entered. Because of corporate downsizing, the introduction of multidisciplinary new product teams and a general slimming down of marketing organizations within companies, the marketing-driven organization is more difficult to find today.

What Is Customer Orientation?

We described three organizational attitudes toward the marketplace in the previous section. But how would we describe an organization that is customer oriented? It is important to start with a statement about what customers do not want:

> *Customers do not inherently want to buy products. Products cost money and, for corporate buyers, reduce profits. Customers buy products for the benefits that the product features provide.*

This is a critical distinction in understanding how you and your organization can become customer oriented. Companies sell automobiles; customers buy transportation, prestige, economy, and fun. Companies sell local area networks; customers buy the ability for their employees to easily share documents and send e-mail. Companies sell laundry detergent; customers buy clean clothes that smell nice. Banks sell mortgages; customers buy homes.

Customer-oriented organizations understand that there are differences between the physical products that engineers often describe and the products customers buy. Companies sell product attributes such as microprocessor speed, interest rates, the ability to detect the phone number of the person who is calling you, and antilock brakes. Customers buy the ability to get work done more quickly, the ability to finance a new car, security, and safety. The job of marketing is to understand what benefits customers are seeking, translate them into products, and then retranslate the physical products or services back into benefit terms the customers can understand.

We can also describe the customer orientation of an organization in terms of whether it views customer relationships as long or short term. Marketing is often criticized for making customers buy things that they do not really want. We have all purchased something under those conditions. However, the keys are whether we repurchased the product or brand and what we said about it to other people. As noted earlier, the marketing concept involves creating *and* recreating customers. It is the rare product that can be successful creating unhappy customers. Companies, particularly those whose shares are traded on stock exchanges, have also often been criticized for being short-term oriented in order to post attractive quarterly earnings reports. That kind of activity is not consistent with a customer orientation. Marketers should be and often are in conflict with financially oriented managers.

A good example of the conflict between finance and marketing is the leveraged buyout of R.J. Reynolds by Kohlberg, Kravis, and Roberts (KKR) in 1987. In the 1980s and even through the 1990s, companies were bought and sold and their brands and product lines considered assets in a financial sense. The problem from a marketing perspective is that concern for customers rarely plays a role in takeovers. In the case of R.J. Reynolds, the tobacco company suffered tremendously under KKR's management. If a company is taken private through a leveraged buyout, generating cash flow to pay down debt becomes of primary importance. Spending money investing in brands in terms of understanding changing customer needs and benefits sought becomes much less important. Through 1995, their leading brands (Winston, Camel, and Salem) all suffered disastrous market share losses against Philip Morris's Marlboro, Brown & Williamson's Kool, and the new low-price brands. It is difficult to be customer oriented and market driven when the main objective is to sustain profit margins and generate cash. Another indicator of whether the company is customer oriented and maintains a long-term focus on its customers is how it reacts to a crisis.

An example of a failure of a company to be customer oriented is Bridgestone-Firestone. As you might recall, in 2000, some owners of Ford Explorers suffered fatal accidents when their Firestone tires blew out. As a result, Ford recalled all of the 15-, 16-, and 17-inch

Firestone Wilderness AT tires on all of its cars and also changed suppliers. Bridgestone-Firestone was heavily criticized for initially denying the problem, blaming drivers (i.e., customers) for the problem by underinflating their tires, and generally being unresponsive to the public outcry. The result was the firing of its CEO, a $1.7 billion loss in 2001, and speculation that the venerable Firestone brand could die. Although the latter has not happened, the company's response was (and is) a textbook example of lack of customer orientation, both to Ford and to Ford's customers.

More recently, a number of toy companies recalled products made in China due to their excessive lead content. Well-known companies like Mattel were caught unaware that some of their products were dangerous to children, even though their brand images were based on being family friendly. One of these companies, RC2 Corporation, makes Thomas the Tank Engine based on the children's books of that name. However, the company handled the situation very badly, bringing its customer orientation into question. First, it asked customers to pay the shipping costs to return the contaminated toys. Then, top executives did not explain what happened nor did they apologize. Finally, the company sent replacement trains plus an additional train as a free gift to customers who asked for refunds on the recalled trains rather than giving them their money back. Incredibly, the additional train was also later recalled![14]

One last, but important, example is the problems that Toyota had with its defective accelerator pedals in early 2010. Toyota's speed to market, lean manufacturing, and technological advances helped to make it a legend in the industry and the leading auto manufacturer in the world. Many leading business commentators were highly critical of how Toyota handled the pedal problem as well as the brake problem found in the Prius. Importantly, many Toyota owners were left wondering if their car was safe and, critical to Toyota in the long term, whether they should trust Toyota again.

Finally, it is useful to examine an organization's attitudes toward marketing expenditures. Is advertising considered a way of investing in the brand and providing value to customers, or is it simply an expense? What about investments in customer service? FedEx has invested billions of dollars in its customer service operation, from its initial telephone-based system to the current PowerShip terminals, FedEx Ship software, and Web site that permit customers to track their own packages. Most observers credit the company's success in differentiating itself from its competitors (UPS, DHL, Emery, U.S. Postal Service) to its higher level of customer service.

To summarize:

- Customer-oriented organizations understand that customers buy benefits, not products. The job of marketing is to translate these benefits into products and services that satisfy enough customers better than competitors to make a profit.
- Customer-oriented organizations make their key investments in their customers and their customers' long-term satisfaction.

How does an organization achieve this kind of customer orientation? One writer suggests the following:[15]

- Information on all-important buying influences should be distributed to every corporate function. Marketing research information should not be restricted to marketers and the sales force, but should be disseminated to production, R&D, application engineers, and everyone else in the organization with customer contact.
- Make strategic and tactical decisions cross-functionally and cross-divisionally. Often, marketing managers in a division are competing for companywide resources. It is important to be able to get key conflicts out on the table in order for each to be maximally successful. In addition, it is important for a variety of corporate functions to be involved with key processes such as new-product development. Today, it is common for marketing, R&D, and customer service employees to work together on developing new products.
- Divisions and functions should make coordinated decisions and execute them with a sense of commitment. For example, the decision to serve customer needs better with a sophisticated information system based on the Internet is not just a one-product decision but also one that could be adopted throughout the organization.

Table 1.2

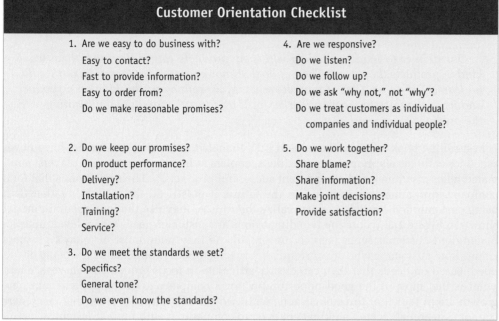

Customer Orientation Checklist

1. Are we easy to do business with?
   Easy to contact?
   Fast to provide information?
   Easy to order from?
   Do we make reasonable promises?

2. Do we keep our promises?
   On product performance?
   Delivery?
   Installation?
   Training?
   Service?

3. Do we meet the standards we set?
   Specifics?
   General tone?
   Do we even know the standards?

4. Are we responsive?
   Do we listen?
   Do we follow up?
   Do we ask "why not," not "why"?
   Do we treat customers as individual companies and individual people?

5. Do we work together?
   Share blame?
   Share information?
   Make joint decisions?
   Provide satisfaction?

Source: Benson P. Shapiro (1988), "What the Hell Is 'Market Oriented'?" *Harvard Business Review*, 88 (November–December), pp. 119–25 Copyright © 1988 by the President and Fellows of Harvard College. Reprinted by Permission.

Table 1.2 provides a checklist for determining whether your organization is customer oriented.

An interesting perspective on customer orientation is taken by reversing Michael Porter's famous value chain.[16] In Figure 1.2, both the traditional and the new versions of the value chain are displayed. The traditional version of the value chain dictates that the company starts with its core competencies and assets to decide what products to make or services to sell. This then dictates the selection of inputs (e.g., labor) and raw materials, which are then made into a product and sold through channels to the end customer. While this does not imply that the customer's needs have been ignored, it is clearly a company-centric approach. The alternative is to change the thought process by starting with the customer rather than the firm. This will result in a company that is structured around the customer. A good example of this reversed value chain is Dell Computer. It started with a customer that wanted a high-quality, technically up-to-date computer or server at a good price, with excellent customer service, having just the features he or she wanted. Michael Dell then built the company around these needs and created the Web-based, mass-customized company that you see today.

Figure 1.2

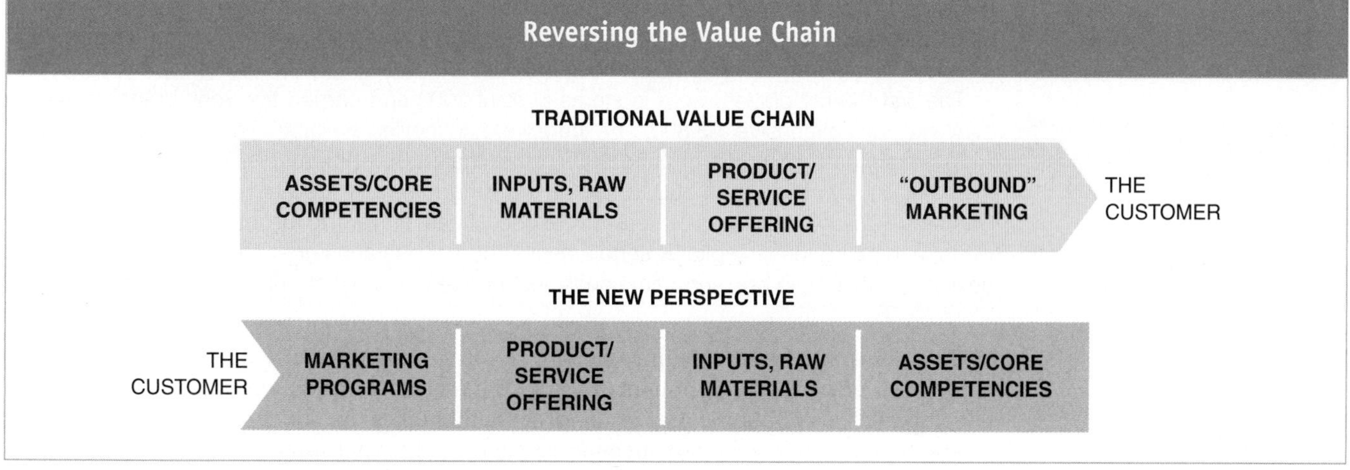

An Alternative Perspective

Given the Sony Betamax example cited earlier in this chapter, readers will not be surprised by the following quote from Akio Morita, the late CEO and visionary leader of Sony:

> *Our plan is to lead the public with new products rather than ask them what kind of products they want. The public does not know what is possible, but we do. So instead of doing a lot of market research, we refine our thinking on a product and its use and try to create a market for it by educating and communicating with the public.*

A best-selling book by Gary Hamel and C.K. Prahalad noted that consumers have never asked for cellular telephones, fax machines, copiers at home, compact disc players, automated teller machines, and other recent successful products.[17] Their position is that for a company to dominate its industry in the future, it must lead the customer rather than being customer led. To help conceptualize their ideas, they use the four-quadrant model shown in Figure 1.3, where the two dimensions are customer needs (articulated, unarticulated) and customer types (served, unserved). As they note, most of today's business comes from customers who are currently being served with products that are being developed, based on needs that they can clearly articulate in focus groups and surveys. Their point is that most of the good opportunities for a company to develop significant new growth are in the other three quadrants, with two-thirds of them in areas that customers cannot conceptualize well and that are open to competitors with more foresight.

The laws of probability dictate that some products will be successful and more will fail, despite any amount of money spent on research. However, the point being made is more important. The marketing concept and a strong customer orientation will not produce true innovations. If the concept is useful only for marginal product improvements (i.e., line extensions), then how useful is it? How do we reconcile these seemingly opposing points of view? Let's first consider the example of Blu-ray high-definition disc technology.

Application Blu-ray HD Discs

Commercial high-definition (HD) TV sets started selling globally in 1998. However, at the time, there was a lack of complementary players to both record and playback prerecorded material in the HD format. While DVDs and their players were enormously successful, there was no market yet for HDTVs much less players.

However, research proceeded with the expectation (and hope) that a market for both the TVs and players would emerge. While it seems eminently sensible today, back in the late 1990s, the ultimate market for HDTV was very unclear because the prices were very high and there was no government mandate in the United States for TV stations to begin sending out HD signals. Consumers were pretty happy with cable TV and were not expressing any significant needs for either HDTVs or the players.

A Japanese researcher, Shuji Nakamura, invented the basis for the blue-violet laser (hence the name, Blu-ray) used to write and read optical discs. Although the discs are the same size as DVDs and CDs, they can hold much more data. A Blu-ray disc can store almost six times as much data as the equivalent DVD. A rival technology, HD DVD pushed by Toshiba, attempted to compete with Blu-ray but was abandoned in 2008.

The first Blu-ray players were in stores in April 2003 and carried the Sony brand. However, they were very expensive ($3,800) and there were no movies available. The final standards were still several years away. As of June 2009, more than 1,000 Blu-ray disc titles are available in Australia, 2,500 in Japan, 1,500 in the United Kingdom, and 2,500 in the United States and Canada. Consumer electronics retailers expect these players to be big hits in the next few years; according to the Digital Entertainment Group, the total number of Blu-ray Disc playback devices (both set-top box and game consoles) had reached 9.6 million by the end of 2008.[18]

Thus, one way to address this question about how to reconcile the two points of view is to consider the two components of R&D. These are the basic research component and development, which is the part of the process that takes the concept and develops actual products. Basic scientific advancements, such as the microprocessor developed at Bell

Figure 1.3

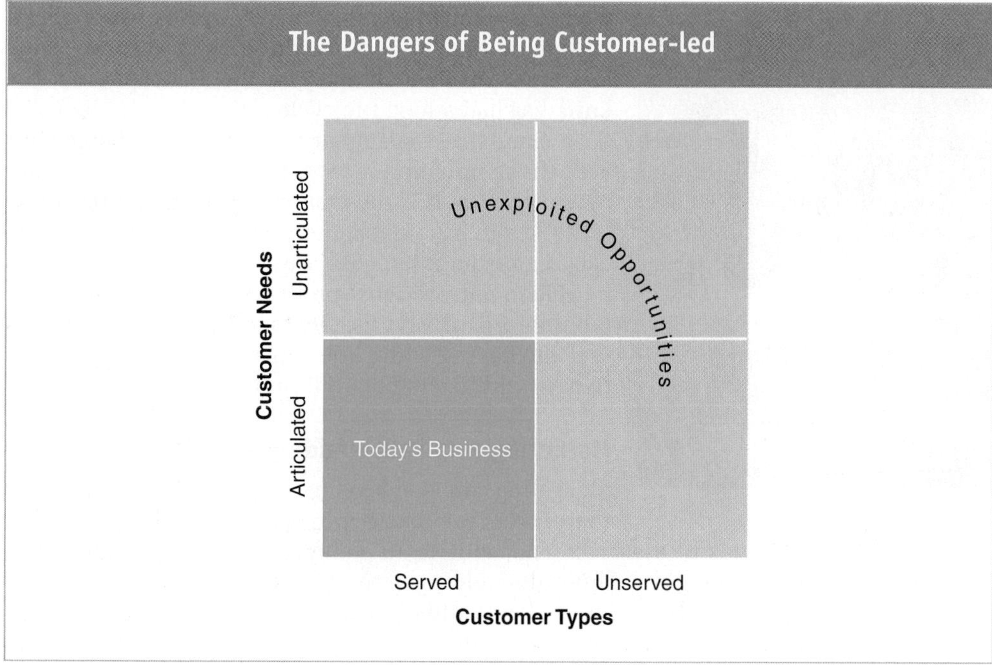

Source: Gary Hamel and C.K. Prahalad (1994), *Competing for the Future* (Boston: Harvard Business School Press). Copyright © 1994 by the President and Fellows of Harvard College. Reprinted by Permission.

Labs, a better understanding of DNA patterns, flat-panel display technology, HDTV, and Blu-ray technology will be researched whether customers can see benefits from them or not at the point in time when basic research is beginning. However, a customer orientation is critical to development and someone within the organization must have the foresight to see that there are commercial prospects for what has been developed. At that point, a company should say, "OK, we have the ability to develop high-resolution TV pictures that look like photographs; now, how do we make the products that customers will buy?" Customer input is absolutely essential in moving from research to development.

In other words, the marketing concept is not limited to *current, expressed* needs.[19] The research must be translated into developed concepts. If a marketing manager sees a new product concept that has the potential to meet customer needs and is willing to develop this product while attempting to satisfy the customer, then the marketing concept is being applied.

Finally, you will be disappointed if you expect customers to be able to express what they want to see in products, particularly for newer technologies. As Morita said, you cannot ask consumers what kind of products they want because they do not always know what is possible to make. However, customers can always express their feelings in terms of needs or benefits. As Hamel and Prahalad noted, customers never did ask for cellular phones or fax machines. However, if you asked people whether they would like to be able to call their children at home from their cars when stuck in traffic, they would probably say, "Yes." If you asked people whether they would like to be able to transmit nonconfidential documents instantly from one place to another, again, they would say, "Yes." New Coke failed, not because people lied about how much they liked it, but, because Coke's marketing research did not place people in the context of having only the New Coke, with the original Coke pulled from the market. What is critical is not only what question is asked but also *how the question is asked.*

An interesting (but probably apocryphal) story revolves around the development of the electric knife by General Electric in 1948. GE's new-product evaluation committee liked the concept because it was electric and fitted with its other electrical appliances. It would only cost $10 retail, it cut almost as well as a real knife, and it was easy to use. GE did its marketing research and asked people whether they liked the idea of an electric knife. Most said "No" and the project was shelved. In 1954, a new small appliance general manager looked at some past product ideas that did not make it to market. He immediately loved the concept of an electric knife because he saw it as the ideal gift for

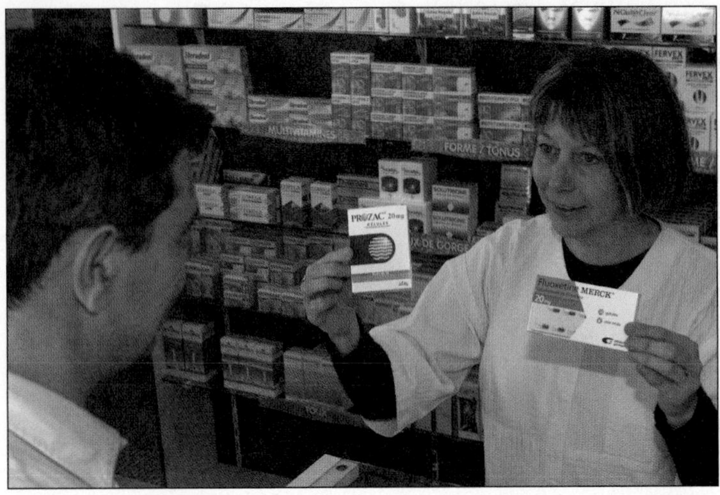

Eli Lilly adds value to Prozac through the brand name.
Source: BSIP/Photoshot Archive Creative

weddings and in-laws. Why? The price was right, it was unobtrusive, and would hardly ever be used. Research strongly supported the concept and the knife has had a long life cycle.

In summary, a customer orientation and being market driven are not inconsistent with revolutionary new products. It is the marketing manager's responsibility to put the concepts in terms so that customers can understand: benefits. Customers will not always be able to tell you what products they want and need, but they will always be able to tell you what problems they are having with current products and the benefits they would like to obtain from new ones.

Marketing as a Value-Adding Activity

Marketing can also be viewed generally as an activity that takes the basic physical characteristics of a product or the attributes of a service and adds to its value, to some segment or segments of the buying population. This value-adding activity could be a brand, customer service, packaging, or anything the marketer adds to differentiate it from what might be called the "commodity" version of the product. For example, bottled waters are chemically indistinguishable from tap water. When a company puts a brand on it, it can mean safety, purity, taste, or whatever the company has decided to emphasize. Aquafina by Pepsico and Dasani by Coke are tap water that has been branded. However, the marketer must not only figure out how to *create* value but also how to *capture* value, that is, find the customers who appreciate the value-added benefits imbedded in the product or service.

Application Outsourcing

In the business environment of the early 2000s, it is common for companies to outsource much of the production of their products to contract manufacturing companies. In such cases, the firms become mainly marketing companies by taking the physical product and finding the appropriate marketing strategy and implementation. Well-known brands such as Baskin-Robbins ice cream, Samuel Adams beer, Calvin Klein jeans, Motorola cell phones, and Dell computers are not made by the companies but by third parties. In the area of technology products, two companies—Solectron and Flextronics International—have become successful in becoming contract manufacturers for companies such as Cisco and Handspring. Korex makes laundry detergents such as Oxydol and Biz for Procter & Gamble and for others. This growth in outsourcing production and focusing on marketing has been attributed to three reasons: Investors value "intangibles" like branding more than physical assets such as plant and machinery, global sources have lower labor costs and high skill levels, and the overhead associated with large factories is a headache when demand slows.

Finally, besides creating and capturing value, marketers must also be concerned about *sustaining* value by making sure that their products and services retain a competitive advantage. This implies that the value-adding aspect of marketing is not a one-shot activity when the product is launched. A marketing manager must be continually concerned about adding new value when competitors enter and when customers change.

The Job of the Marketing Manager

The title *marketing manager* is purposefully vague because usually a large number of people in an organization are managers involved with marketing. It is difficult to characterize the main job of the marketing manager because it depends on how the organization is structured, what industry is represented, and on what level in the organization we are focusing.

Figure 1.4

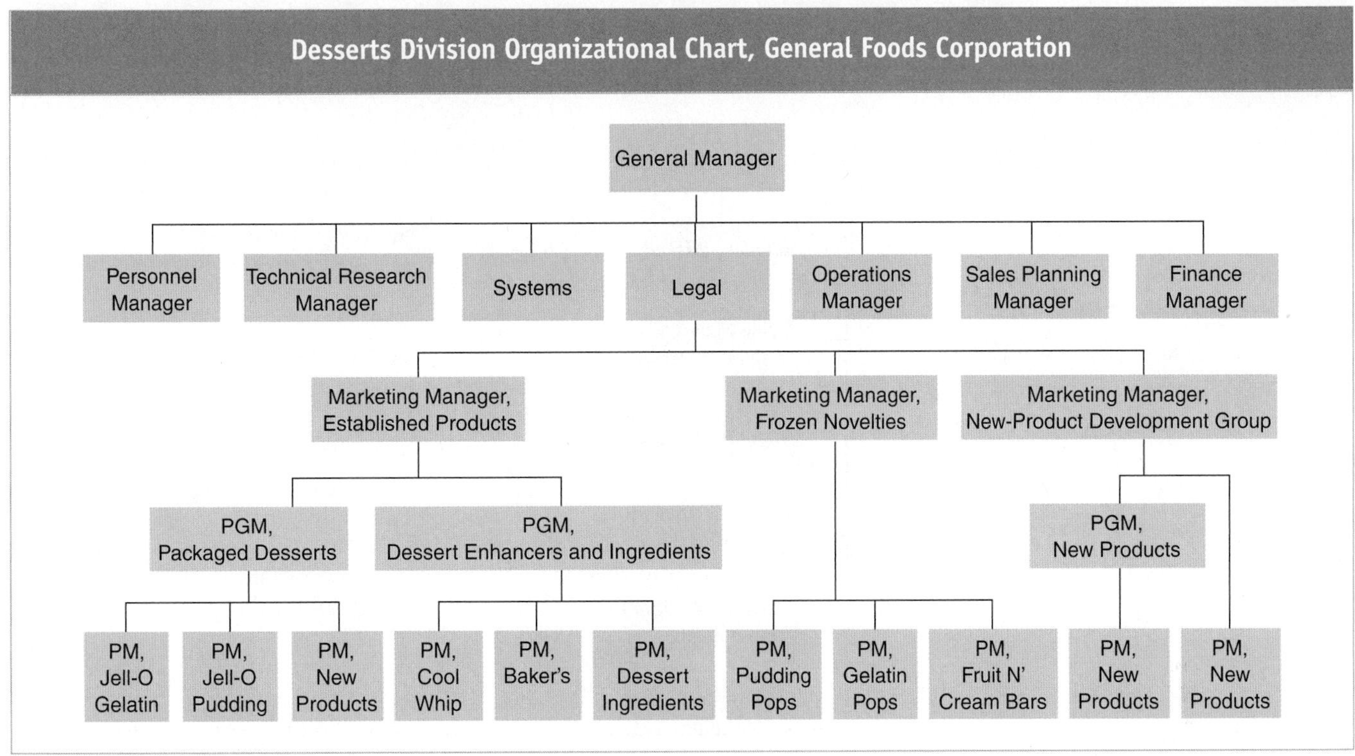

Source: Adapted from John A. Quelch and Paul W. Farris (1985), "General Foods Corporation: The Product Management System," Harvard Business School case #9-586-057, p. 27.

Perhaps the best way to show how varied the marketing manager's job can be is to describe the most common marketing organization: the product-focused organization. This is sometimes called the classic brand or product management system, pioneered by Procter & Gamble in the 1930s.[20] Figure 1.4 illustrates a typical brand management system from the former General Foods Corporation's (now part of Kraft Foods) Desserts Division in 1984.

In this organization, four different kinds of managers are involved with marketing. At the lowest level of the chart (not necessarily the lowest level of the organization), product managers (PMs) have responsibility for the success of individual brands such as Jell-O and Cool Whip. They develop marketing strategies for their brands and coordinate marketing activities such as advertising and sales promotion.[21] Above them, group product managers (or product group managers [PGMs]) are responsible for closely related clusters of brands (e.g., packaged desserts and dessert enhancers). They look at the marketing strategies and programs of the PMs and make sure that they will attain the objectives of the cluster or group. Above the group product managers are what General Foods called marketing managers, who are essentially super-group product managers because they manage larger clusters of brands such as established products, frozen novelties, and new products. Finally, at the top of the organization, the general manager of the division has the ultimate responsibility for dessert marketing. Thus, four levels of managers and four different job titles have marketing responsibility in this organization.

An internationally focused organizational structure for Grasse Fragrances SA, one of the world's largest producers of fragrances, is shown in Figure 1.5.[22] Like General Foods, this company has product managers for its four major product lines: fine fragrances, toiletries and cosmetics, soaps and detergents, and household and industrial applications. These managers report to a marketing director, who acts like the group and marketing managers in General Foods to coordinate the marketing strategies of the product managers and to achieve the organization's objectives. However, these activities are limited to France. At the same level as the marketing director, reporting to the company's managing director, are country managers, who are responsible for all company activities in each country. These country managers have diverse responsibilities, including marketing.

Figure 1.5

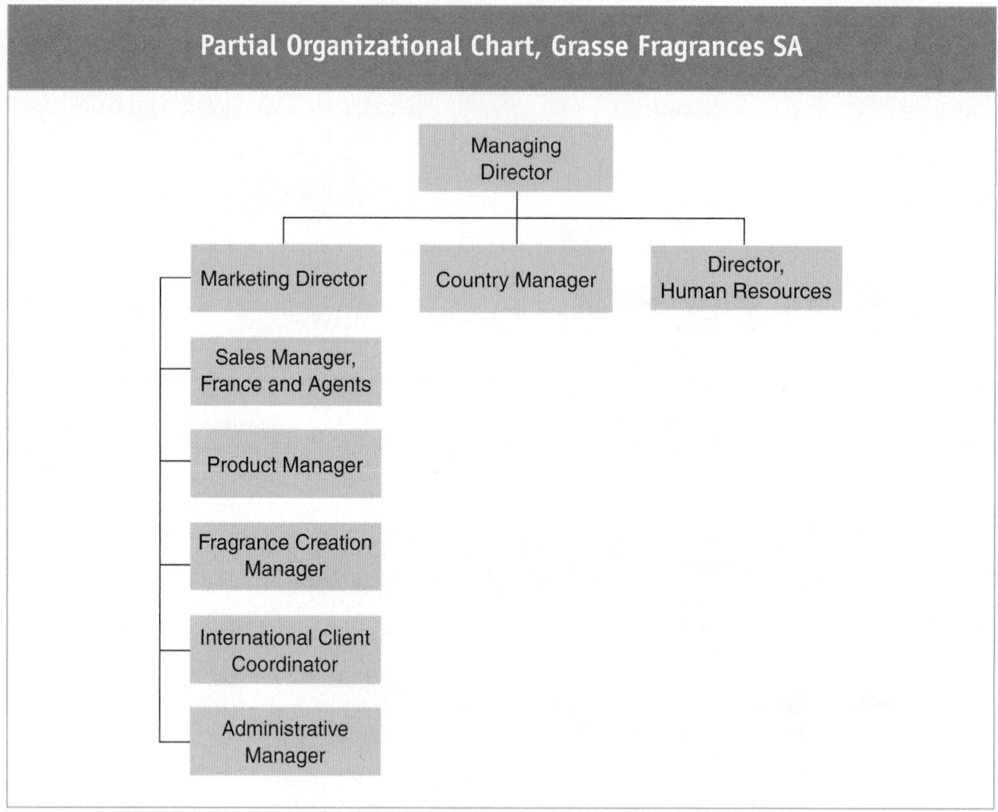

Source: Adapted from Michael Hayes (1989), "Grasse Fragrances SA," IMD International case #M-369, p. 13.

An alternative to the product-focused organizational structure is a market-based structure. In some industries, particularly industrial or business-to-business products (the customer is an organization rather than a consumer or family), it would be awkward to have several people selling different products or services, calling on the same customer. In addition, a market-based organization puts more emphasis on understanding particular customers or market segments than the product management organization does.

Figure 1.6 shows the marketing organization of a large telecommunications company. This organizational chart divides marketing into three large groups: consumer, business,

Figure 1.6

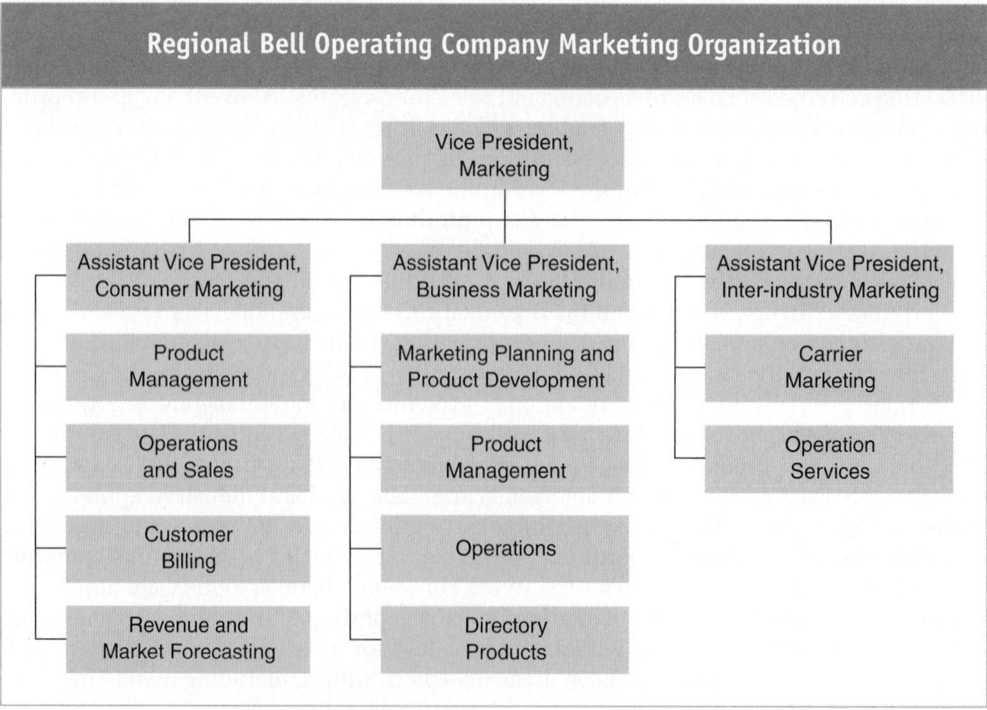

and inter-industry (business with other carriers, such as Verizon). Each business market includes different operational functions and product management. For example, the consumer sector includes product managers for custom-calling features such as call waiting and special phone directory listings. The business sector includes product managers for pay telephones, central office phone services, local area network planning services, and many other services. Unlike the purely product-focused marketing organization, this type of organization does not give managers full profit/loss responsibility for their products. Product managers are more like coordinators who implement marketing programs developed by the staffs of the three marketing managers.

A marketing organization is dynamic and must adapt to internal (company) and external (competition, environment) changes. For example, several of the U.S. auto companies adopted a brand management system in the 1990s when they realized that little effort was being made to differentiate the brands sold by the divisions, which resulted in consumer confusion. By having a manager in charge of each brand of, say, Chevrolet, the marketing of each brand became more distinct. In 2005, the new Chief Marketing Officer at Intel changed its marketing organization from a broad overall brand image structure to a system that assigns a brand manager to products such as Centrino and Pentium. This was due to his feeling that more focus was needed on individual products to fight off increased competition from AMD.[23]

Although it is difficult to generalize about the precise duties of marketing managers, *the main job of anyone in marketing is to create or implement a marketing strategy for the product or service that meets the needs of the targeted customers better than the competitors' offerings and achieves the objectives set by the organization.* That is, anyone with a marketing or marketing-related title (or, as argued earlier, possibly anyone in a company) is either setting and monitoring the strategic direction of the product or performing some activity such as serving customers, implementing a promotion, working with the advertising agency, or selling to a large customer account.

More specifically, based on the organizational charts shown earlier and this strategic orientation, the marketing manager's job can be described by a large number of interactions both within and outside of the organization. Figure 1.7 shows many of these interactions.

Figure 1.7

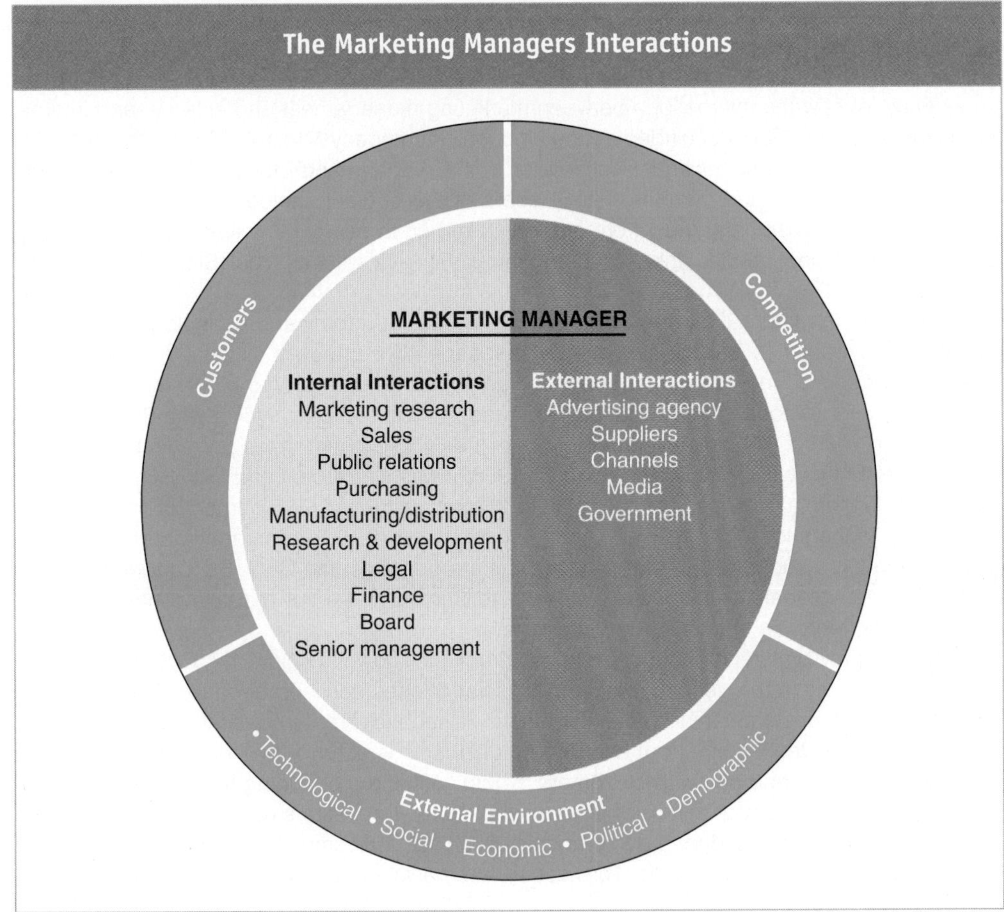

Within the box, the interactions may or may not occur, depending on the level of the position, the type of product, and the particular company. *External* interactions include working with the company's or brand's advertising agency, dealing with suppliers (e.g., raw materials, consultants), improving relationships with members of the channel of distribution system, talking about the firm's prospects with members of the media (e.g., business press, trade journals), and interacting with government agencies for export/import licenses. *Internal* interactions are with the parts of the firm that help the marketing manager to develop the marketing strategy and achieve success within the company. These people include marketing researchers, the sales force management organization, public relations, purchasing (raw materials), manufacturing and distribution logistics, and research and development (new products). Many marketing managers also interact with the legal department, financial management, senior management, and board of trust.

These internal and external interactions are somewhat within the control of the marketing manager. The manager can make his or her own decisions about how much time to spend in the field with the channel members or with the advertising agency. The manager can also determine how much time he or she should spend with marketing researchers, sales, purchasing, and other personnel.

However, the three areas outside the box (Figure 1.7) affect the marketing manager's job greatly and are beyond the manager's control. In addition, they are dynamic and can determine whether the product or service and, therefore, the manager are successful. *Customers*' needs are constantly changing, as are many other aspects of their buying behavior, such as the underlying process. *Competitors* are also changing, not only in who they are but also in what strategies they use in the marketplace. The five key factors in the *external environment* must be monitored closely. As will be noted later in this chapter, *technology* is having a profound impact on marketing. *Social* factors such as income distributions and birth rates in different countries affect marketing strategies. *Economic* factors such as exchange rates have significant effects on raw materials and labor prices. Similarly, as we have seen in the aftermath of September 11, 2001, shifts in *political* situations affect global and domestic markets. Finally, *demographic* changes such as aging populations create new market segments and opportunities for growth.

Application Motorola

An example of how the interactions between marketing management and external and internal forces must be managed is provided by the electronics company Motorola.[24] In the early 1990s, Motorola was the trendsetter and clear leader in the global market for cellular phones. From 1992 through to 1998, the number of U.S. users of the original analog technology (calls are broadcast like radio signals) grew from around 11 million to nearly 66 million. Motorola consistently developed new phones ahead of competitors. For example, its small StarTAC phone was a winner.

However, in the late 1990s and into the early 2000s, the dominant technology was and is digital, which transmits calls in the binary language of computers. Digital communication brings better sound, more security, and more advanced features. Who is the market leader? Unfortunately for Motorola, the global leader is the Finnish company Nokia with 39 percent of the market in 2008 vs. 14 percent for Motorola. In 1996, 53 percent of the portable phones sold in the United States were cellular (analog). By 1998, it was 41 percent and today, of course, it is about zero. Motorola is the leader in the United States, with about 35 percent of the market—due largely to the success of its Razr, a very stylish product. The company is currently struggling to develop a successor to that product; the struggle cost the CEO, Ed Zander, his job in 2008. The "hot" global companies are Nokia and Samsung. As the marketing has moved to smart phones, Motorola has continued to struggle.

Motorola's problems related directly to the interactions shown in Figure 1.7. One problem was that the growth rate in the general market for cellular phones declined because of market saturation. This is a customer–manager interaction. A second problem was that the company missed the shift in technology from analog to digital. This is actually two interactions, one with technological forces and one with customers, whose tastes are changing from analog to digital along with the technology. A third problem was that some competitors use semiconductor chips already developed and produced by companies such as Qualcomm. Motorola's slower production of chips delayed response time. This was an internal interaction with manufacturing.

What emerges from Figure 1.7 and the Motorola illustration is a picture of the marketing manager interacting with both internal and external forces, some of which can be controlled and many which cannot. Returning to the Segway illustration, the company's managers can control the products being offered but cannot control what the city council of St. Louis wants to do in terms of requiring owners to purchase permits. In this kind of environment, how does the marketing manager create the strategies for which he or she is responsible? The mechanism for accomplishing this is the marketing plan.

The Marketing Plan

One activity with which all marketing managers become (or should become) involved is marketing planning. The kind of involvement varies with the level of the manager. Product managers typically write and execute the plans, whereas more senior marketing managers take the plans from the individual product managers, give feedback and suggest revisions, and ensure that the specific objectives stated in the plans achieve the desired goals. In addition, the senior marketing personnel evaluate the product managers based on their abilities to execute the plan.

The definition of a marketing plan is as follows:[25]

> *A **marketing plan** is a written document containing the guidelines for the product's marketing programs and allocations over the planning period.*

marketing plan
a written document containing the guidelines for a product's marketing programs and allocations over the planning period

Thus, a key feature of the marketing plan is that it is written. This may seem obvious but many plans exist only in the manager's head. A written plan is easy to communicate throughout the organization because it provides a concrete history of the product's strategies over a period of time. This helps educate new managers and pinpoints responsibility for achieving particular results by a specified date.

The major benefit of the written marketing plan is that because it forces the marketing manager to analyze the external environment as well as internal factors, the customer and competitor orientations mentioned earlier in this chapter are automatically enforced. This disciplined thinking helps ensure that before any marketing strategies or programs are developed, the manager first analyzes customer and competitor behavior and the general climate in the product category or industry. Market-focused decisions are more likely to emerge under this scenario than with a more random approach to decision making.

Because planning can occur at various levels of an organization, it is important to pinpoint where marketing planning most often takes place. Figure 1.8 shows a hierarchy of planning. More general strategic planning occurs at the corporate and group levels. These kinds of plans typically have broad objectives (e.g., return on investment) and focus on decisions such as which products or businesses to emphasize and what acquisitions should occur. Marketing plans are constructed at the strategic business unit

Figure 1.8

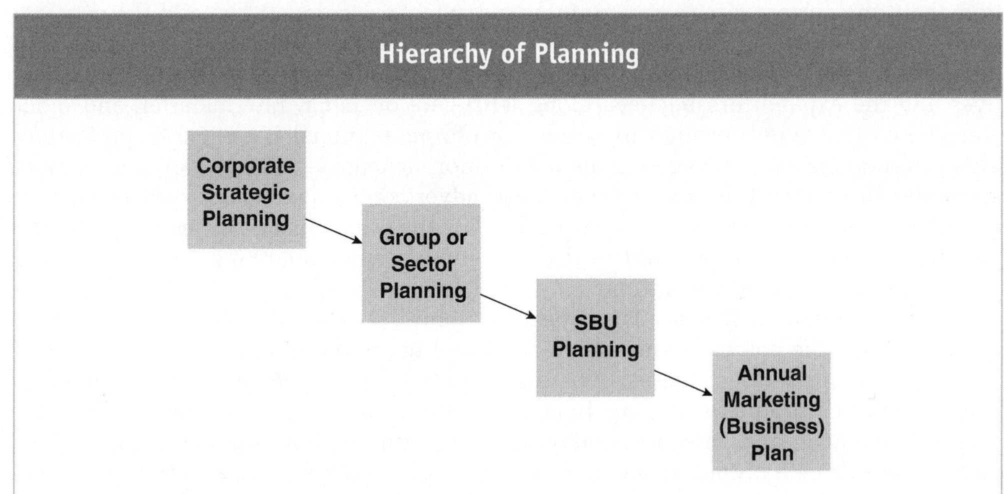

Figure 1.9

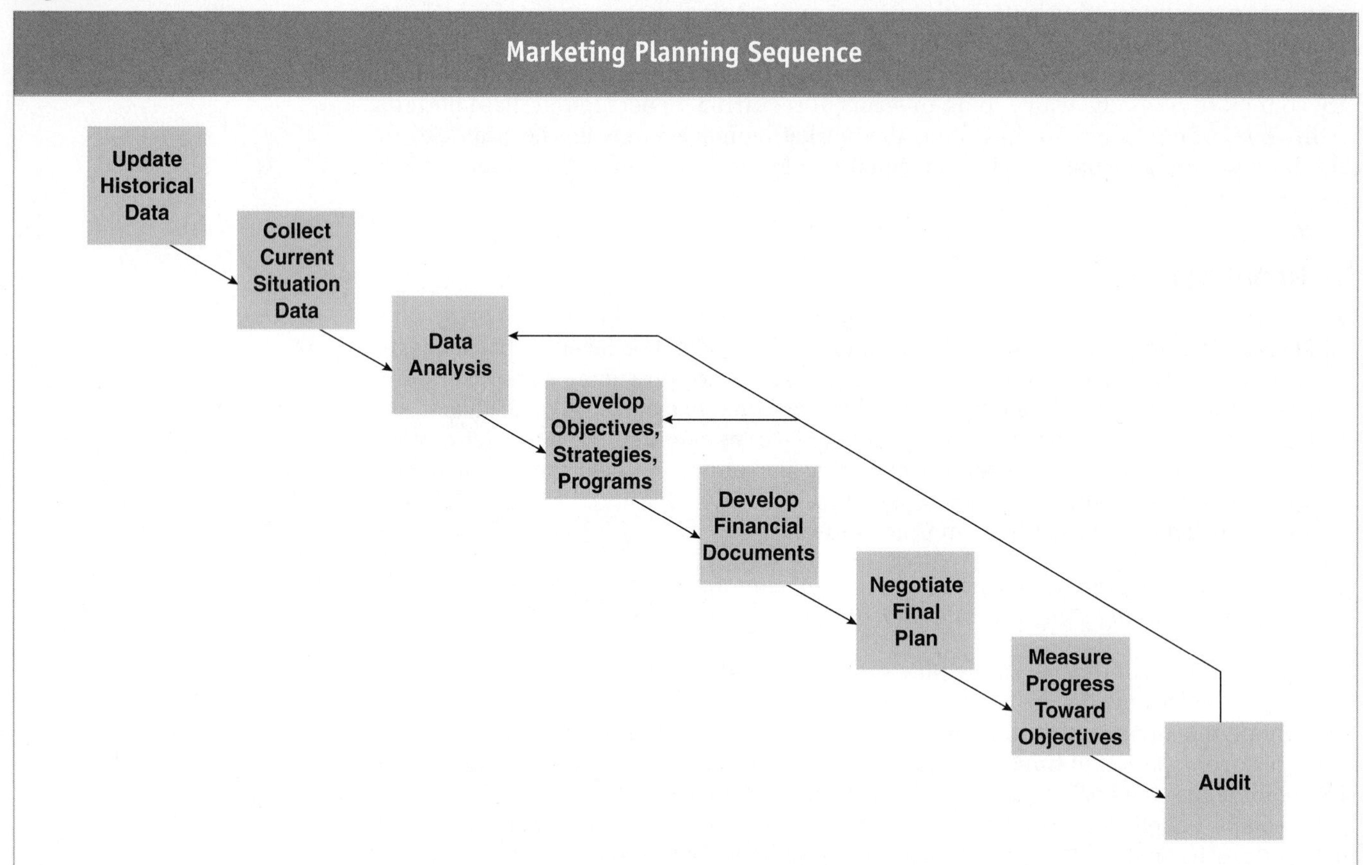

(SBU) and, of course, on the product levels (the focus of the annual marketing plan). An SBU might be desserts or personal computers (PCs) for the home and the product or brands would be Jell-O and the Hewlett-Packard Pavilion line of home PCs. In some cases, a marketing plan might be developed for a particular customer segment. For example, the toy manufacturer Lego is beginning to focus on girls rather than boys and has developed special marketing strategies to reach that target.

A typical marketing planning sequence followed by product or other marketing managers is shown in Figure 1.9. In this process, the marketing manager first updates some of the facts (e.g., market shares) contained in the old plan. Because planning is always forward-looking, a plan to be implemented in 2011 would be developed in 2010. Thus, the most recent facts might be from 2009 or, depending on the industry and the quality of data available, even earlier. The next major activity is to collect and analyze information about the current situation pertaining to customers, competitors, and the category environment. Based on this analysis, the manager develops objectives, strategies, and programs for the product, product line, or closely related group of products. The objectives and the expenditure budgets, along with data on labor, raw material, and other assigned costs, are put together to create a pro forma financial statement or projection. This projection is used in negotiations with senior management. They may want a more aggressive profit result, for example, or lower advertising expenditures. When the plan is finally implemented, progress toward achieving the goals must be measured. After the planning period is over, an audit of the plan reveals why something went wrong and what can be improved the next time.

A basic outline of a typical plan appears in Table 1.3. There are three major parts to the plan. First, the marketing manager conducts a background assessment, the "homework" part of the plan. In this part, the historical data are collected and updated, often being stored in a product fact book. In addition, the manager analyzes the current competitive, customer, and category situation and determines how the firm's capabilities match these three external elements (i.e., he or she performs the situation analysis).

Table 1.3

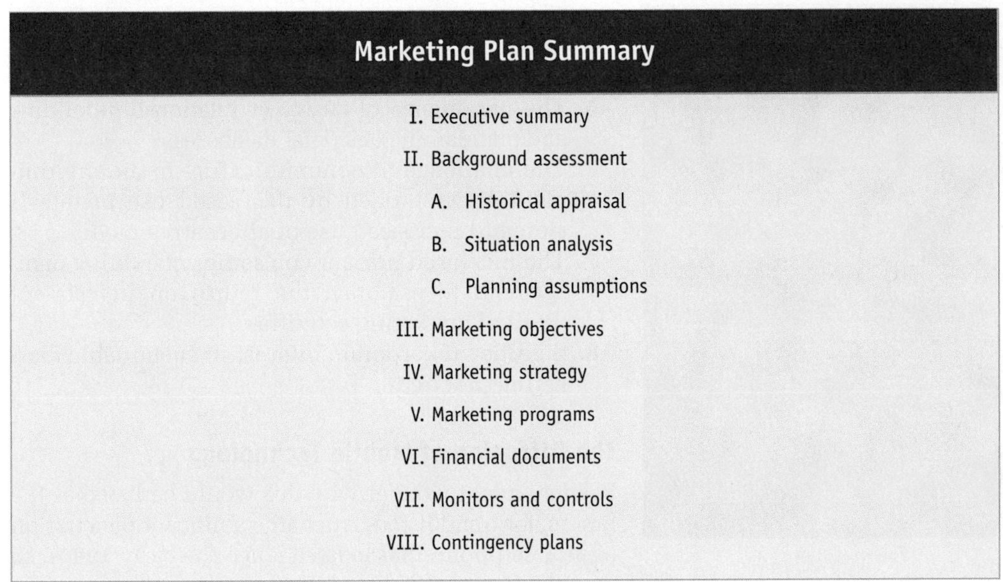

Marketing Plan Summary

I. Executive summary
II. Background assessment
    A. Historical appraisal
    B. Situation analysis
    C. Planning assumptions
III. Marketing objectives
IV. Marketing strategy
V. Marketing programs
VI. Financial documents
VII. Monitors and controls
VIII. Contingency plans

Finally, forecasts, estimates of market potential, and other assumptions that must be made about the market environment are collected and put into a section called the planning assumptions. The second major part is the strategy section, which is composed of the product's or service's objectives (e.g., increase market share by *x* share points), the marketing strategy itself, and the implementation of the strategy (i.e., the marketing mix of price, advertising, and personal selling effort). Finally, the plan includes the financial implications, the monitors and controls used to assess the progress being made toward the plan's objectives, and contingency plans.

Therefore, the overall purpose of the marketing plan is to enable the marketing manager to stay in touch with the three key parts of the business environment crucial to his or her success: customers, competitors, and factors outside the control of both customers and competitors. By doing this, the manager should be able to adapt the marketing strategies to changes in customer tastes, competitor strategies, and external factors such as exchange rates or global politics. That is the theory, at least. In practice, however, the problems facing a marketing manager and a particular product or brand cannot be solved so easily.

The Changing Nature of Marketing

Even in the short time since the previous edition of this book, a number of major changes in the business environment have significantly affected the practice of marketing and the development of marketing strategies and programs. Some of these changes are related primarily to a particular aspect of strategy or program development. For example, there has been a dramatic increase in the use of "new" media such as social networking sites (e.g., Facebook, MySpace), online video (YouTube), and new messaging systems (Twitter) for customers to talk to each other and to develop their own marketing campaigns for brands. We discuss this issue in Chapter 10. In addition, significant changes in basic technologies continue to spur development of new products and improved business processes in many industries, including biotechnology, communication, and robotics. The economic slump of 2008–2010 has had a serious impact on a number of industries (e.g., financial services, automobiles) as some trusted brands such as Lehman Brothers have disappeared, others have been acquired (e.g., Chrysler by Fiat), and consumers have significantly reduced their spending.

However, eight issues represent such fundamental change that they have created ripple effects across many aspects of marketing. As a result, the implications of the following issues permeate this textbook:

1. The diffusion of mobile technology.
2. The new era of customer power.

Investments in information technology are critical in retail today.
Source: kolvenback/Alamy Images

3. The increased adoption of interactive marketing.
4. The impact of the two largest countries, China and India, on business and marketing.
5. The importance of customer relationship-building and maintaining customer databases.
6. The challenge of communicating in an environment characterized by decreased use of television and increased use of alternative media.
7. The increased pressure on senior marketing management to establish the return on investment (ROI) of marketing activities.
8. Significant corporate interest in sustainable marketing practices.

The Diffusion of Mobile Technology

Readers might wonder why this would be listed as the first major trend listed. After all, significant penetration of mobile phones has existed since the early 1990s, so mobile technology is not exactly new. Why then is this listed first?

There are at least three reasons that the state of mobile phone technology ca. 2010–2011 is given first priority on the list:

1. The increasingly sophisticated technology available in such a small package is representative of the significant advances made in digital technology for all applications. As noted in the earlier Motorola illustration, cellular technology for many years was analog, which severely limited the number of applications available on the phone and its physical size. With the movement to digital technology, mobile phones pack an incredible amount of computing power and features. The typical high-end phone today (e.g., Apple's iPhone, BlackBerries, Android-based phones) can surf the Web, get e-mails, take pictures, store music, send messages, provide directions, and, oh yes, send and receive phone calls. It is not really a mobile phone but a portable digital device. Figure 1.10 shows the way that phones are being used today, by age group. Note the heavy use of phones to visit Internet sites, play games, take pictures, etc.—activities that have little to do with the basic idea of a phone.
2. Because of the extensive capabilities of today's digital phone, it is basically a mobile marketing platform capable of receiving communications about products, allowing

Figure 1.10

Mobile Device Usage: Anywhere, Any Time

Use of mobile phone or PDA to do the following by age group, %, 2007

	18–29	30–49	50–64	65+
Send or receive text messages	85	65	38	11
Take a picture	82	64	42	22
Play a game	47	29	13	6
Play music	38	16	5	2
Record a video	34	19	8	3
Access the internet	31	22	10	6
Send or receive e-mail	28	21	12	6
Send or receive instant messages	26	18	11	7
Watch a video	19	11	4	2
At least one of these activities	96	85	63	36

Source: Pew Research Center

customers to talk to or message each other about brands, facilitating the collection of information about products, and making purchases. In addition, with most phones having GPS (global positioning) capabilities, marketers potentially can locate customers when they are geographically proximate to a retail outlet. While the communications and transactions capabilities of mobile phones are not utilized much in the United States, this is not the case globally. Consumers in South Korea, Japan, China, India, and many European countries are already making purchases and receiving ads via their phones.

3. Mobile phones are available to almost every socioeconomic stratum. While certain countries like North Korea prohibit individual ownership, this is rare. From the rural areas of India and China to Iran and other less-developed countries, mobile phones have become one of the necessities of life and a "flattener" in terms of access to information and the ability to communicate.[26] Global companies like Nokia and local companies like Bharti Airtel in India have developed low-cost phones and specially priced service plans so that even remote villages can have a community phone. While many of these lack the functionality noted earlier, it is only a matter of time for costs to come down of the most technologically advanced models. The actions of these companies have paid off. As of late 2009, there were almost 4.6 billion mobile phone subscribers out of about 6.5 billion inhabitants of the planet.[27]

It is highly likely that the mobile phone is the most important device of the early part of the 21st century from the perspective of the marketer. While it may not be fully utilized for a number of years, any forward-thinking marketing manager has to be considering how to include it in his or her marketing plans.

The New Power of the Customer

Because of the increased penetration of the Internet, the development of Web sites and services that allow customers to interact with companies and each other easily and frequently, and the mobile revolution noted previously, customers are seizing more power in their relationships with their suppliers. Specifically, customers are becoming more powerful for the following reasons:

- Customers have access to information about a company and its products from a number of sources, many of which are online. This includes product reviews and comments from other customers.
- Customers can find information about competing products more easily using the same sources.
- Due to the Internet, customers can buy from anywhere independent of physical location and easily compare prices.
- Customers can determine if companies have mistreated former customers from customer postings and blogs.
- Word-of-mouth has been amplified due to technology and the adoption of "buzz marketing" methods.
- Customers can avoid marketing efforts.
- Customers can "co-create" marketing campaigns by satirizing TV commercials and posting them on video sites like YouTube.
- Customers are increasingly using recommendations by other consumers posted on companies' and independent Web sites.

In a speech, the former CEO of Procter & Gamble, A. G. Lafley, summarized the situation nicely:[28]

> *Consumer expectations are changing. Consumers used to "lean back" as passive recipients of one-way broadcast messages. Today, they "lean forward." Consumers want a conversation, to dialogue, to participate, to be more in control. Consumers expect more personal attention—communication, products and services that are tailored to their wants and needs. Consumers will expect customization, so products and services reflect their unique wants and needs. Marketing is being re-defined.*

solutions
products or services that solve a particular customer's problem at a given point in time

experiences
the interactions that a customer has with a company

relationships
meaningful relationships between an individual and his or her brand.

We're going from one-dimensional, product-myopic marketing to three-dimensional marketing—that offers better ***solutions****—product and/or service solutions—more delightful* ***experiences****—shopping, usage, total brand experiences... and the opportunity for on-going* ***relationships****—meaningful relationships between an individual and his or her brand.*

As a result, more companies are trying to figure out how to partner with their customers in the development of new products, communications programs, and in developing mutually beneficial and satisfying relationships. Ultimately this leads to greater profits or the achievement of other organization goals.

Some writers refer to this as the era of customer "advocacy."[29] In this era of transparency, companies need to become true representatives of customers' best interests. This implies that in order to gain a customer's trust, a company must be open and honest with information about its products and services. If a company tries to fool a customer, the information is quickly disseminated throughout the Web. Dishonesty is quickly punished. One well-known marketing professor puts it this way:[30]

> Marketers no longer rule the market.
>
> They are invited guests.
>
> If they are provocative, pertinent, and entertaining, they get to stay.
>
> If they try to dominate and control, there are ways to shut them out.

Interactive Marketing

In the late 1990s, some writers were saying that the "Internet is everything." In 2001–2002, some said that the "Internet is dead." Today, it has become clear that the Internet and the Web have become integral and indispensable tools of the marketing manager. The impact has been particularly pronounced in the major areas of decision-making:

- **Communications:** Through a combination of keyword advertising (think Google), banner ads, advertising on social networking sites, and a variety of other media, online advertising spending is projected to $50 billion by 2012.[31] The Internet is not being tested any more as a potential medium, but has become an essential part of the media mix. In addition, the Web is a key source of information for buyers. According to J.D. Power & Associates, two-thirds of new car shoppers use the Internet in some way when shopping for a new car.[32] As noted earlier, M-commerce (or mobile commerce) is growing rapidly with cell phones and other mobile devices being used as a platform to deliver advertising messages and make purchases through their use as a digital "wallet."
- **Price:** The ability of marketers to change prices dynamically online, based upon supply/demand conditions and the nature of the customer, gives marketing managers using the online channel more pricing flexibility than they ever had. The booming success of eBay has introduced the auction format into the lexicon of business.
- **Distribution channels:** The "bust" of the Internet was largely concentrated on Internet "pure plays," that is, those companies that were only online entities. Today, the buzzword is "multichannel" or "clicks and mortar" in that retailers and manufacturers often have multiple channels of distribution that include the Internet. The U.S. Department of Commerce reported that about $130 billion worth of goods were sold on the Internet in 2008, 3.6 percent of all U.S. retail sales.

This represents only a small part of the impact that the Internet has had on marketing. A key characteristic of this book is how advances in information technology and increased use of the Internet are affecting marketing management.

Globalization and the Impact of China and India

It is virtually impossible to market a product today and not be concerned about markets outside the manager's home market. Even in the United States, which has the largest economy in the world, marketing managers are thinking about how to launch their products in some foreign countries or are concerned about foreign competitors entering their markets. Often the way to be successful is through joint ventures. An excellent example of such a partnership is the more than 40-year relationship between Xerox and Fuji Photo Film Company; the latter distributes the former's copiers in Japan.

The availability of better information through improved communications and increased exposure to marketing tools such as advertising, has caused the worldwide consumer population to rise, thus increasing the demand for goods and services. Therefore, when a home market matures and little growth potential is left, market opportunities abroad must be exploited. Although there are debates about how marketing should approach global populations with different cultures and histories, there is little question that marketing management is a global topic. Consider the following quote from a Yahoo! executive making a speech to company employees on the importance of being global: "Don't think about 'international' as being *part* of our business. It *is* our business!... It's not a department. It's not a business unit. It's the whole business! The full schmear!"[33] Thus, like the Internet, the global aspects should be woven into any aspect of marketing.

The need to be concerned about global marketing issues comes at a time when nearly every sector of the world is undergoing a dramatic political or economic shift, creating new opportunities for global companies who are attuned to these shifts and willing to take advantage of them:

- The smooth introduction of the euro in 2002 has facilitated the flow of goods and services across borders and the improved economies in some of the former Eastern Bloc countries such as Hungary and Poland. Despite some of the political issues involved in adding countries such as Turkey to the European Union (EU), taken together with an already large and sophisticated industrial base in traditional economies led by Germany, the United Kingdom, and France, this is the second-largest market in the world and demands attention.
- The breakup of the Soviet Union and increased democratization of Russia are creating new market opportunities. Many entrepreneurs are establishing businesses and a financial infrastructure that will help the country modernize its distribution and communication systems, if there is no further social and political upheaval.
- Latin America is an emerging market. Although the Mexican economy has had its ups and downs, its large population and industrial base make it an attractive market and a competitor in many international markets. Strong economies in Chile, Brazil, and a potentially strong one in Argentina also create attractive opportunities, as long as there is political stability.
- Layered on top of all of this are geopolitical events such as September 11, 2001, and the Iraq war. These events had several impacts on the global business environment. First, companies such as McDonald's that have spent considerable sums creating global brands and linkages to the United States now find their companies under attack in some countries. Labels such as "Made in the U.S." or "Made in Pakistan" became more salient in customers' decision-making processes. Second, from the slump in travel and tourism and the ensuing global economic slump, it became much clearer how interrelated the global economy had become.

Perhaps the largest global stories are the emergence of the BRIC countries (Brazil, Russia, India, China) as competitors, suppliers, and customers of global companies. The main focus of companies has been on China and India, in that order.

China

Is the 21st century China's era? Like Japan in the late 1980s to early 1990s, the world is looking to China as the next emerging global economic power. Here are just a few of the areas in which China is having an impact:

- China is potentially a monstrous market. With 1.3 billion people and a fifth of the world's population, it has 20 percent of the world's cell phone users and consumes 35 percent of the world's cigarettes, 51 percent of the world's pork, and one-third of the world's fish. Also, it is a very young market and technologically savvy.[34]

- Due to low wages, China can undercut the prices of most of the rest of the world's companies. For example, in machine molds, a Chinese supplier bid 50 percent of the price offered by XCel Mold. Some beds made in China retail for 40 percent less than the equivalent bed made in the United States.
- Although China is not a major supplier (yet) of global brands, it has become a buyer of these brands. In 2004, the Chinese computer manufacturer Lenovo bought IBM's personal computer division and its well-known Thinkpad brand. In mid-2005, the Chinese appliance company Haier bid more than $1 billion for Maytag, and CNOOC (China National Offshore Oil Corporation) bid nearly $20 billion for Unocal. Chinese consumers enjoy brands from all major global manufacturers such as Revlon, L'Oreal, Procter & Gamble, and General Motors. The 2008 Olympic Games in Beijing gave Chinese companies a greater opportunity to promote its own brands.

It is thus clear that the impact of China on the global economy is significant and will continue to increase.

India

India's impact has been different. With 1 billion people, it has the potential to have the kind of impact that China has had. Different government and economic systems, culture, and English-language facility have made India's contributions to the global economy unique:

- The largest impact and the one with the most visibility is outsourcing. India has successfully built companies that handle computer programming, customer service, brain scan analyses, tax preparation, and a number of other processes remotely. The high education level, low wage rates, and English-language capabilities combined with 21st-century information technology have made India a global outsourcing powerhouse.
- For some time, India has been a significant market for consumer goods, particularly inexpensive, frequently purchased products such as shampoo, soap, and the like. However, with the growth of the middle class due to the increased jobs available from outsourcing and other industrial growth, India has also started to become a significant market for automobiles, consumer durables, financial products, and other, more expensive goods.
- An area of similarity with China is that India is a huge market for buying global brands but few Indian brands are well-known outside of the region. Tata's purchase of Jaguar and Rover automobile brands in 2008 show that Indian companies can be major acquisition players, but this is different from successfully marketing an Indian brand.

India will continue to grow in importance as a consumer market. The high level of education and the quality of its engineers may ultimately create a source for technological innovation as well.

The Value of the Customer Base

Many studies have shown that it costs more to get a new customer than to keep an existing one. That should be fairly obvious. Current customers are familiar with your products, are satisfied with their performance (ideally), and know your brand name. To convince a customer to leave a competitor and buy your product or service, it takes either a financial inducement (lower price through a price promotion) or a particularly convincing communication program targeted at that group, both of which are expensive to launch.

What is new then? Marketers are discovering not only that pursuing their current customers is more efficient but also that over the long term it pays to do this more proactively than has been done before. Much has been written about a concept called **lifetime customer value**, that is, the present value of a stream of profits that can be produced by a customer. Many marketers have traditionally focused on the *transaction* as the consummation of their marketing efforts. Today, marketing managers have to focus on the *relationship* between the organization and the customer as the end result of a

lifetime customer value
the present value of a stream of revenue that can be produced by a customer

successful marketing strategy. Marketers who can retain more customers by satisfying them better than competitors will have profitable products in the long run, not just in the short run.

In other words, one way to quantify the value of a product or service is the lifetime value of the customer base. Two products with identical 2010 sales levels can have different lifetime values. One brand with customers who often switch brands (low brand loyalty) has a much lower lifetime value of its customer base than a competitor with high brand loyalty.

The era of relationship marketing involves a number of different activities, each one helping to improve customers' lifetime values:

- **Database marketing:** If a company is not actively creating a customer database and extensively using it to target products to customers and offer overall better service, it is definitely behind the competition. Databases are created through transactions, surveys, warranty cards, and a number of other ways. The purpose is mainly to take products that are traditionally mass marketed and make them appear to be targeted to you—hence the term **mass customization**. For example, at its Web site, www.nikeid.com, customers can produce a set of running shoes to their specifications and style. Andersen Windows does this for its customers by permitting them to design their own windows at their retailers through computer-aided design. The design is automatically routed to the plant where the windows are produced. The growth in database marketing is highly related to the information technology revolution that is reshaping marketing.
- **Customer satisfaction:** A major area of emphasis of many organizations is continuing to satisfy customers, even when the physical product or service is identical to competitors' offerings. Some of this is done through extraordinary customer service, and we cover this in Chapter 14. Achieving high levels of customer satisfaction also occurs through product and service quality. The TQM movement alluded to earlier in this chapter has been successful in increasing the average level of product quality in many product categories, such as automobiles. This has led to increased rates of customer satisfaction.

mass customization
also called one-to-one marketing, a new marketing process whereby a company takes a product or service that is widely marketed and develops a system for customizing it to each customer's specifications

As a result, a key goal of a marketing manager today is to leverage the existing customer base by creating high degrees of brand loyalty and, therefore, high rates of repeat purchasing into the future. This is done generally with an increasing focus on *personalization* or the attempt to increasingly focus on customers one at a time.

The New Communications Environment

Traditionally, in most of the world, consumer products companies have used TV advertising to reach large numbers of consumers efficiently. This worked for many years. However, a number of factors have changed the environment:

- Media usage continues to decline, driven by the consumer movement to digital alternatives for news, information, and entertainment, which requires less time investment than traditional media such as magazines, newspapers, and TV.
- The rise of digital video recorders in the United States has resulted in an increased number of ads skipped by households, resulting in a loss of control of when and if ads are seen.
- As noted earlier, the Internet has continued to increase in popularity as a medium to reach households that are spending more and more time online. Likewise, the use of other media and electronic devices has fragmented viewing audiences.
- Although the U.S. population is increasing, this fragmentation has resulted in the number of households watching TV in the "prime time" period declining precipitously.
- Young audiences, particularly those in the 18- to 24-year age bracket, are becoming increasingly difficult to attract to TV as they spend more time both online and using video games. They also multitask by often listening to MP3 devices, watching TV, talking on the telephone, sending text messages, and reading at the same time.

Figure 1.11

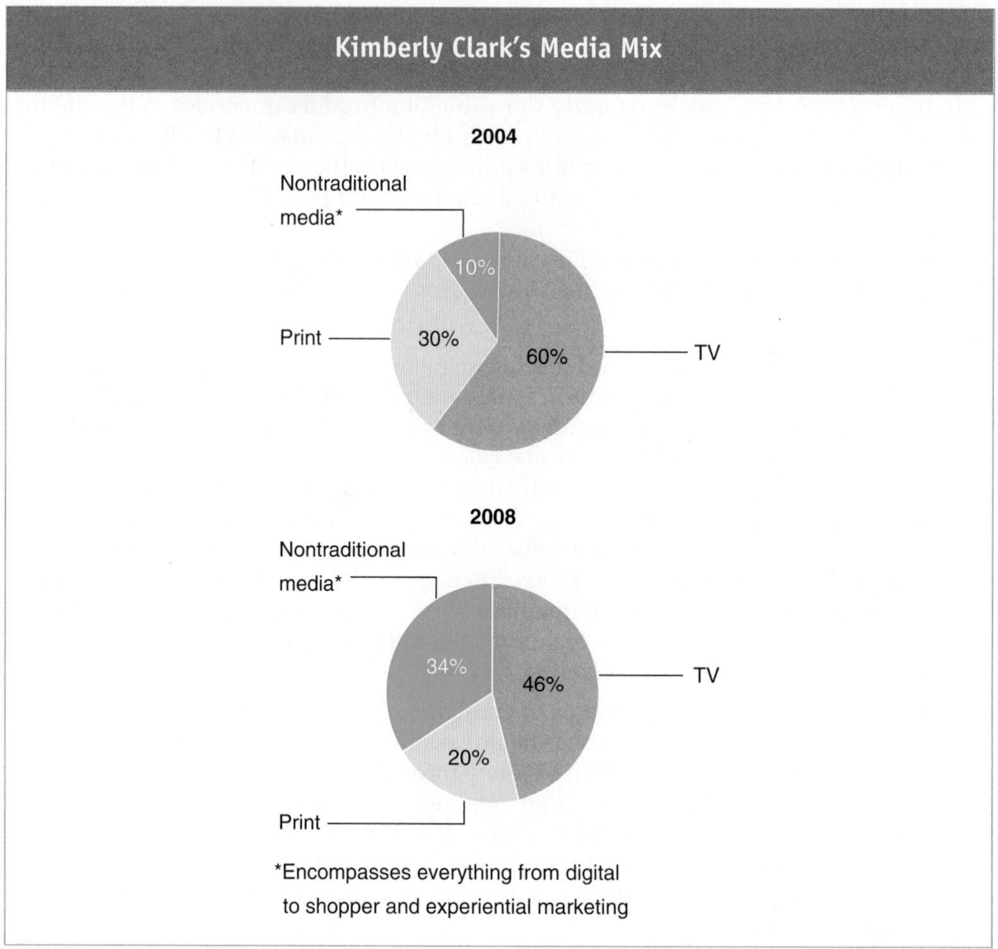

Source: Jack Neff (2008), "K-C Unilever Turn Down TV to Ramp Up ROI," *Advertising Age,* February 28, 2008. Reproduced with permission of Crain Communications Inc in the format Textbook via Copyright Clearance Center.

As a result of these factors, there has been a large shift in how companies are spending their advertising money. Figure 1.11 shows some data from 2008 on how Kimberly-Clark (Kleenex, Huggies) has changed its media mix from 2004 to 2008. As can be seen, the company has reduced its percentage spending on TV from 60 to 46 percent and print from 30 to 20 percent in favor of nontraditional media, including digital, in-store, sponsored events, and a number of other programs. General Motors spent half of its $3 billion advertising budget in 2008 on digital and other personalizable communications.[35]

In addition, marketers are looking to new ways of reaching audiences. There has been significant growth in the use of "branded entertainment," also known as product placements, in TV, movies, and videogames where the actors or characters are shown using brand-name products and services. Companies are shifting money into grassroots or "buzz marketing," attempting to generate strong word-of-mouth among potential users. Marketers are using MP3 devices to "podcast" and the Internet to sponsor blogs. We will go into this important trend in more detail in Chapter 10.

ROI and Marketing

Chief marketing officers (CMOs) are under pressure from CEOs and corporate boards to assess the returns from marketing investments. It is not just a matter of the difficulty of determining whether or not, say, advertising is paying off. It is also the case that consumers are becoming more skeptical about marketing. For example, a Yankelovich survey showed that 65 percent of consumers felt that they are constantly bombarded with too much advertising, Sixty-nine percent are interested in products and services that would help skip or block marketing, and 54 percent report avoid buying products that overwhelm them with marketing and advertising.[36] In addition, measuring the financial impact of marketing expenditures has been a key research priority identified by the Marketing Science Institute for several years.

Marketing management is thus under more pressure to not only develop better strategies and programs to make these strategies successful, but to also develop measurement programs to assess whether the programs are accomplishing both strategic and financial objectives. Fortunately, some books have been written to help CMOs.[37] In addition, marketing academics and consultants have worked to develop sophisticated quantitative models to aid in assessing marketing program performance. In this book, where appropriate, measurement tools to help marketing managers will be described.

Sustainable Marketing Practices

In leading companies in the United States, Europe, and other countries, significant corporate resources are being expended on the notion of sustainability. Priorities in these companies are being set to reduce the amount of packaging, cutting fuel consumption, and developing products and services for customers that are produced and delivered in an ethical and environmentally friendly fashion.

For example, April 2008 was "Earth Month" at Walmart, not a company that most consumers would link with these kinds of practices. During this month, customers could buy eco-friendly lightbulbs and detergents and choose among organic, Fair Trade, or Rainforest Alliance-certified coffee. The chairman of Walmart says that he wants the company to move toward becoming a major purchaser of renewable energy, to create no waste, and to sell products that sustain the Earth's resources and environment.[38]

The implication is that marketing managers in many industries are going to have to start thinking about this issue, particularly if consumer demand for sustainable and environmentally friendly products continues to increase.

The Focus of This Book

Readers of this book should expect to be able to answer the following questions:

- What is the marketing manager's job? How is the marketing function organized? How is marketing changing (Chapter 1)?
- What are the components of a marketing strategy? How can I develop a strategy that differentiates my product or service from competition to improve my position in the marketplace (Chapter 2)?
- What information do I need to collect to make marketing decisions? How and where do I collect information about customers, competitors, and the external environment (Chapters 3, 4, 5, and 6)?
- What are the important decisions that have to be made concerning products? These include such decisions as positioning, branding, and packaging (Chapter 7) and new products (Chapter 8).
- How do I make the key marketing decisions of price (Chapter 9), communications (Chapter 10), sales promotion (Chapter 11), indirect (outside of the direct control of the marketing manager) channels of distribution (Chapter 12), and direct channels such as sales force and direct marketing (Chapter 13)?
- What are the considerations for building strong, long-term customer relationships (Chapter 14)?
- What are the novel issues in marketing services (Chapter 15)?

Overarching Themes

The eight themes noted in the section "The Changing Nature of Marketing" will be interwoven throughout the text where appropriate. Growth in mobile technology, customer "advocacy," interactive marketing, globalization, customer relationship management, communications, marketing ROI analyses, and sustainability affect marketing strategy and tactics in a variety of ways. In addition, there is an overall "flavor" of technology because many of the examples and illustrations are based on products and services that are heavily technology based, sometimes referred to as "high-tech." One definition of a high-technology product market is one in which both market (e.g., customer reaction, market size) and technology (e.g., product performance) uncertainty are high. High-tech products such as computer servers and optical networks share many of the same marketing problems as disposable diapers. However, the unique aspects of marketing high-tech products and services will be highlighted. At the same time, this is not a text on the marketing of high-technology products so there will be many examples from consumer products and services and "low-tech" industries as well.

Executive Summary

Key learning points in this chapter include the following:

- Marketing is pervasive; it is involved whenever a customer has a choice to make between alternatives, including a decision not to buy (or act, depending on the context).
- Marketing is a difficult area of decision making because of the dynamics of the external market: customers, competitors, and general societal and technological conditions change constantly.
- The purpose of marketing is to AQUIRE and KEEP a customer forever.
- The marketing concept involves being customer and competitor focused and making a profit as a result.
- Customer-oriented organizations understand that customers buy benefits, not products, and these companies make their key investments in their customers and their customers' long-term satisfaction.
- Being customer oriented is not inconsistent with being technologically innovative.
- Key changes in the marketing environment affecting every marketing manager's job are the rapid diffusion of mobile communications technology, the new era of customer power, the growth of the Internet and interactive marketing, the importance of customer relationship-building and the value of the customer database, the challenge of communicating in an increasingly fragmented market, the increased pressure on CMOs to understand the return on marketing investments, and the ability to develop and market sustainable and environmentally friendly products and services.
- The main job of anyone in marketing is to create or implement a marketing strategy for the product or service that meets the needs of the targeted customers better than the competitors' offerings and achieves the organization's objectives.
- A marketing plan is a written document containing the guidelines for the product's marketing programs and allocations over the planning period.

Chapter Questions

1. Compare the situation facing Segway with the problem of selling videocassette recorders in the late 1970s when they were a brand new technology. From the consumer perspective, what are the similarities and differences?
2. What are some other examples of companies that have reversed the value chain, as shown in Figure 1.2?

3. Give an example of a company or service provider that has treated you well (i.e., one that appears to be customer focused). What particular steps has it taken to achieve this success? How do you feel about the company? Do you recommend it to friends and relatives? Do you pay a higher price for its products than you would for a competitor's?
4. Find a company or product that has recently suffered a disaster, such as those suffered by Mattel and Bridgestone-Firestone discussed in this chapter. How did the company handle the situation? Would you say that it was a customer-focused approach?
5. Marketing has often been criticized for forcing people to buy things they do not really want or need, or cannot afford. Discuss.
6. Given the kinds of interactions shown in Figure 1.7, what kind of educational background is appropriate for a marketing manager? What skills are needed?

Key Learning Points

The purpose of this chapter is to provide a framework for the rest of the book. That framework is the key part of the marketing manager's job: the development of a marketing strategy. Key learning points include:

- The elements of a complete marketing strategy
- Developing a value proposition
- Developing a sustainable competitive advantage
- Positioning products and services
- The product life cycle and how it affects marketing strategies

Developing a competitive marketing strategy is a critical task for Miller High Life's marketing manager.
Source: Charlie Neibergal/AP Wide World Photos

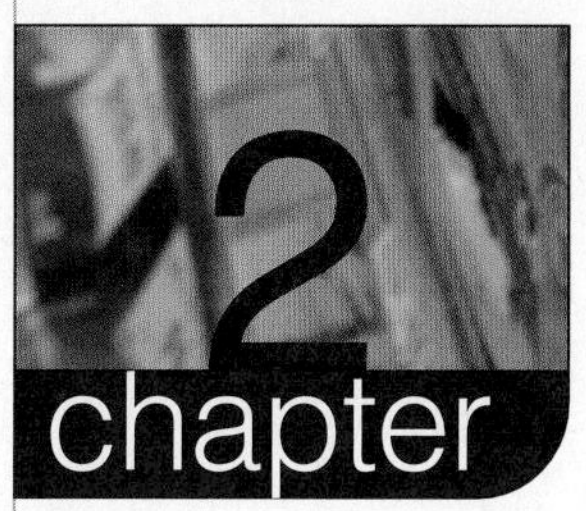

A Strategic Marketing Framework

Chapter Brief

One of the largest global businesses is the beer industry. More than 30 billion gallons of beer are sold annually.[1] One brand, Heineken, is consumed in 170 countries around the world. The two largest selling brands in the world, Budweiser and Bud Light, sell nearly 70 million barrels in the United States alone. However, the global beer market is fragmented—the top 20 beer brands account for only 25 percent of the market.

One of the major U.S. brands is Miller with its two flagship products, Miller High Life and Miller Lite. Until 2002, Miller Brewing Co. was owned by the diversified food and tobacco company Philip Morris.[2] In the late 1970s and early 1980s, with the surprise success of Miller Lite (due largely to its "Tastes great, less filling" advertising campaign), Miller's U.S. market share was around 20 percent, competitive with Bud's roughly 25 percent share of the market. However, by 2007, Miller's share had decreased sharply to only around 11 percent (High Life and Lite), while Bud's had risen to 31 percent (Budweiser and Bud Light brands).

Miller's critics say that the brand does not resonate with a new generation of beer drinkers. In a market where real product differentiation is difficult to achieve, these drinkers have been seduced by great Bud advertising, the classic 2000 "Whassup" being one example and the highly entertaining croaking frogs being another. In addition, Budweiser outspends Miller on advertising. Bud's annual advertising budget (Bud and Bud Light combined) of $288 million in 2007 was substantially higher than Miller's annual budget of $174 million (Miller and Miller Lite combined). In addition, Miller has lost some share to hot-selling malt-based drinks like Smirnoff Ice and to imported beers like Corona, which have been increasing at nearly 20 percent per year, and to flavored vodkas and mixed drinks concocted with other beverages such as Red Bull.

A variety of industry and global trends also buffet the company. First, the sales growth rate of beer is relatively flat and is projected to be so for several years. The low-carb craze hurt regular beers in the early 2000s, dragging down the whole industry. Volume bounced back in 2004 when they grew 0.8 percent, but volume decreased in 2005 and has remained basically flat since then. Second, due to a historically fragmented industry with many competitors (Budweiser is the leading global brand with a market share of only 4 percent) and the high costs of marketing and product development, there has been considerable global consolidation among brewers. Besides the Miller acquisition by SAB, Belgium's Interbrew SA, Heineken NV, Anheuser-Busch, and Adolph Coors made significant acquisitions in the early 2000s. InBev was created in 2004 when the Belgian company Interbrew and the Brazilian company AmBev merged, creating the world's largest brewer at that time. In 2008, InBev agreed to buy Anheuser-Busch for a total value of $52 billion, which would create a new company to be named Anheuser-Busch InBev. Third, all brands have been affected by the growth of alternative alcoholic beverages such as flavored vodkas. Finally, an important problem is that the coveted 21- to 29-year-old male drinker considers beer to be boring compared with alternatives. Industry consultants and retailers also complain that the major brands are undifferentiated in that they all rely on humor and entertainment in their advertising to try to capture customers.

Miller has not helped itself by its marketing. One of its minor brands, Miller Genuine Draft (referred to as MGD) has been ridiculed in the press for changing advertising agencies and taglines frequently. One of the key attributes of strong brands is consistent messaging over time. Bud Light became the number one beer by using "frat-boy" humor for 30 years. Corona's "vacation in a bottle" theme has been successful, as has Coors with its Rocky Mountain allusions. None of Miller's brands could be characterized as having a strong, consistent theme over time.[3]

Thus, the marketing managers at Miller Brewing faced the following problems:

- What are reasonable sales and market share goals for Miller?
- To which customers should Miller High Life and Lite market? Should they be defined by age and gender as is the current custom or by other variables such as income and similar descriptors, or even other kinds of variables such as life style?
- In a market where the brands are physically similar, how should Miller differentiate its products from competitors' offerings? Can Lite's new taste differentiation from Bud Light be sustained?
- Over time, how should the company adapt its marketing to changes in competition, customer awareness and usage of the alternative brands of beer, and also to other changes in the environment?

In Chapter 1 we stated that the central job of the marketing manager, or anyone involved with marketing, is to develop or implement a marketing strategy for a product or service, based on the marketing plan. The key task facing Miller Brewing marketing managers, in 2010 and beyond, was to develop a marketing strategy for their brands and adapt that strategy over time to changes in the market environment. This chapter describes the basics of developing a marketing strategy for a product or service (Sections III and IV of the marketing plan outline shown in Table 1.3).

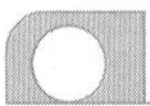

Complete Marketing Strategy

objective
the criterion by which the success or failure of the strategy is to be measured

customer targets
a more specific statement by customers (e.g., income over $40,000, small businesses with revenues under $10 billion), which the marketing manager wants to entice to buy the product or service

competitor targets
the brands or companies that offer the most likely competition for that customer

core strategy
designed by the marketing manager, a statement that communicates the reason to buy to a specific customer group

The marketing strategy framework used in this book is shown in Figure 2.1. The components of a strategy are:

- The **objective** to be achieved. This is the criterion by which the success or failure of the strategy is measured.
- The **customer targets**. This is a more specific statement of which customers (e.g., income over $40,000, small businesses with revenues under $10 million) the marketing manager wants to persuade to buy the product or service.
- For each customer target, **competitor targets** must be identified. These are the brands or companies that offer the most likely competition for that customer.
- The marketing manager must target the customer group with the **core strategy**. The most important component of the core strategy is crafting the **value proposition**. This summarizes the customer and competitor targets, defines the product category, and makes a succinct statement of how the product/service is differentiated in the market, that is, the key reason that a customer should buy this product rather than a competing offering. The value proposition is operationalized and represented in the customers' minds through **product positioning**.
- The **marketing mix** is the set of decisions about price, channels of distribution, product, communications, and customer relationship management that implements the marketing strategy. These are often referred as the "4Ps" of marketing ("price," "place," "promotion," and "product"). This aspect of the marketing strategy is covered in later chapters.

Figure 2.1

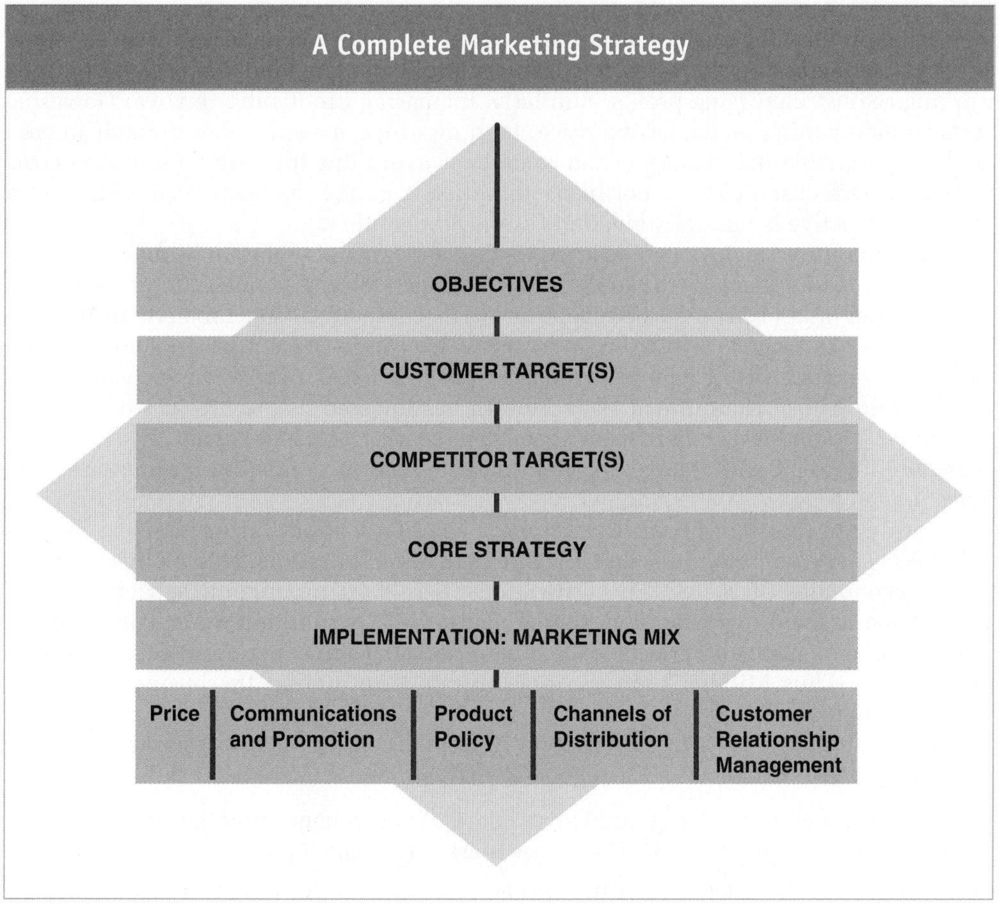

A Complete Marketing Strategy

OBJECTIVES

CUSTOMER TARGET(S)

COMPETITOR TARGET(S)

CORE STRATEGY

IMPLEMENTATION: MARKETING MIX

Price	Communications and Promotion	Product Policy	Channels of Distribution	Customer Relationship Management

This marketing strategy framework follows the flow of decision making. The marketing manager first decides what the goal is and then how to get there. The key decision is which customer groups to target; other decisions then flow from that crucial one. The customers' needs, an analysis of the competitors, and an understanding of the industry environment lead to a core strategy that is tailored to each customer target. Finally, the marketing mix or implementation of the strategy is customized for each target, with an additional understanding of the key reasons to buy. Of course, this is a simplified model. In practice, the marketing manager often moves back and forth between steps of the strategy as new information about customers, changes in competitors' actions, and other changes emerge.

Many new products are developed with the target market in mind a priori. For example, the toy company Mattel developed a line of construction and activity toys called Ello, targeting young girls. In such a case, the strategy may be developed in concert with the product development. However, strategies for new products evolve over time. For example, if Ello is a success, Mattel may decide to market the line outside of the United States. Additionally, a major competitor, Lego, may adapt its product positioning to Ello, causing Mattel to rethink its own positioning for the product.

Objectives

Many different kinds of objectives are set in an organization. A company's **mission statement** usually describes in general terms its major business thrusts, customer orientation, or business philosophy. For example, Honda's mission statement is listed as "Maintaining a global viewpoint, we are dedicated to supplying products of the highest quality, yet at a reasonable price for worldwide customer satisfaction." The corporate objective is an overall goal to be achieved, usually stated in financial (return on sales, margins, etc.) or stock price terms. Business units or divisions also have objectives, which might be stated in terms of sales growth or profitability. Brands or products have specific objectives, usually stated in either growth in volume-related measures (sales, market share) or profits. Finally, specific programs such as advertising can have objectives in terms that are relevant to the particular activity (e.g., awareness).

value proposition
a one-paragraph summary of a product or service's differentiation strategy and positioning to each target customer group; in short, a statement of why the customer should buy that product or service rather than the competitor's

product positioning
considering the alternative differentiation possibilities and determining what differential advantages are to be emphasized and communicated to the target

marketing mix
the set of decisions about price, channels of distribution, product, communications, and customer relationship management that implements the marketing strategy

mission statement
a general statement describing a company's major business thrusts, customer orientation, or business philosophy

There is often tension between objectives such as increasing market share and increasing profits. Obviously, some of the activities required to increase share (e.g., lowering price, increasing the sales force) lower profit margins and increase costs, thus working against increasing profits. Similarly, increasing profitability involves lowering costs or maintaining or increasing price, both of which make it more difficult to gain market share. Although managers can sometimes avoid this trade-off by lowering costs in areas where customers are not likely to notice (e.g., the thickness of the metal of a can), one objective is normally given priority over the others.

Two illustrations vividly demonstrate the trade-off that often has to be made between increasing market share (or a similar growth objective) and profits. Floturn Inc. is a manufacturer of laser-printer cartridge drums. The company decided more than 10 years ago that the best way to win in its industry was to forgo present profits and focus on market share. As a result, when its after-tax profit margins rise above 10 percent, the company drops its prices. Since 1988, Floturn has lowered its drum prices to just over $1 from $2.85 and has a +70 percent share in its market.[4] In 2007, then-CEO Ed Zander changed Motorola's corporate goals from market share to profits due to pressure from investors.[5]

Returning to the Miller Beer illustration, a key to a manufacturing business is sales volume because volume often has a significant negative relationship with unit costs due to economies of scale.[6] The utilization of existing production capacity is also critical due to fixed overhead and maintenance costs. In addition, in consumer-goods industries, increased sales are critical to keep shelf space in supermarkets and distribution in bars. Thus Miller's short-run objective to turn around the business must be market share focused.

It is not sufficient to state an objective in terms such as "increase market share" or "increase profits." Characteristics of good objective statements include:

- Objectives should have a quantified standard of performance. In other words, an improved statement would be "increase market share by 5 points."
- Objectives should have a clear time frame, that is, a period within which it should be achieved. To further improve the objective, it would be "increase market share by 5 points by the end of calendar year 2011."
- Objectives should be stated in measurable terms. Although there is some variation between industries and companies, market share, profitability, and sales volume are easy to measure. Less tangible objectives such as quality need to be put into verifiable terms.
- Objectives should be ambitious enough to be challenging. One of the purposes of an objective is to stretch management to improve its performance. Objectives that are not challenging do not test the management team and are therefore poor measures of the quality of the personnel. At the same time, the objectives should be realistic, taking external and internal constraints into consideration.

Customer and Competitor Targets

target market
group of customers or segment on which the marketing manager has decided to focus a marketing strategy

Once the objective for the brand or product line has been established, the next major decision is on which customer groups to focus. Although the motivation and methods for making this focus or **target market** decision are elaborated on in Chapter 4, the primary reason to think about the market in terms of groups or segments is market heterogeneity. Simply put, customers have different personal values, are looking for different benefits from products and services, and respond differently to the marketing-mix variables. As a result, even if the manager decides to pursue all potential customers in the market, it is still important to consider the market as being composed of distinct segments for which alternative marketing strategies must be developed.

market penetration strategy
one possible strategy in segmenting the market; the decision to target current customers of a product or service

Because there are many ways to segment a market, a useful first step is to consider the strategic alternatives shown in Figure 2.2. The strategic alternatives divide the total potential market into two general strategies:

1. A **market penetration strategy** targets current customers of the product or service. These are customers who are buying your product or a direct competitor's (often both).

Figure 2.2

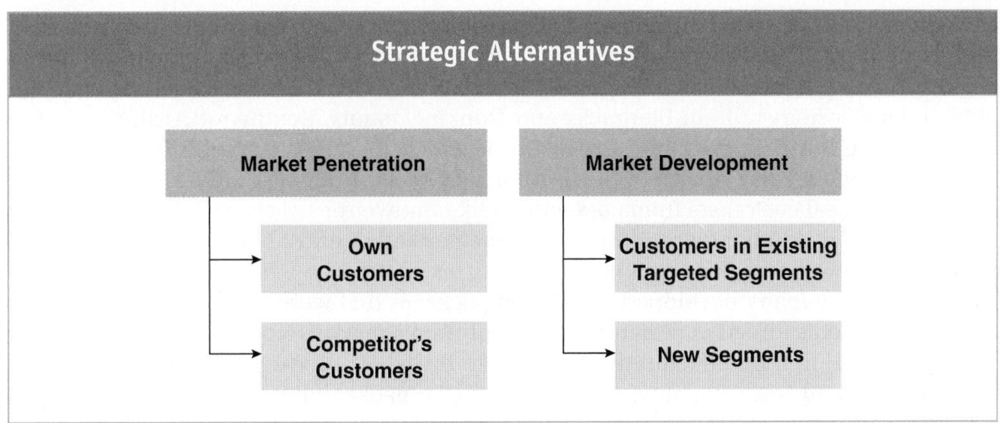

2. A **market development strategy** targets customers who either have been targeted by you or your competitors but simply have not been persuaded to buy; or they could be customers in segments that have not been pursued by you or the competitors in your product category.

market development strategy one possible strategy in segmenting the market; the decision to target customers who have not yet purchased the product or service

The market penetration strategy targeting current customers should always be a high priority for the marketing manager. Clearly, customers who have purchased your product or service are familiar with its benefits. Assuming that a high percentage of your customers enjoyed the consumption experience, there is often potential left in the market from the current customers who could be persuaded to buy more. For example:

- In an organizational buying or industrial marketing setting, where products or services are marketed to companies rather than households, it is often possible to get the organization to adopt the product more widely throughout the organization. This can be done at a particular location or, if the company has multiple locations throughout the country or the world, at other sites. Computer software programs used for applications such as inventory control can be applied in a plant in Europe and then, if found to be useful, applied to the U.S. plants.
- Per capita consumption of consumer products can be increased by using larger package sizes or showing how the product can be used on other occasions or in other ways. American Express has attempted to get consumers to use the card even for small purchases. DeBeers wants women to think of the other fingers on their left hand, besides the fourth finger, where they could buy themselves a diamond. The U.S. Golf Association is working on programs to get existing golfers to play more rounds each year. PepsiCo would like you to drink Pepsi at breakfast or in the morning as a substitute for coffee.[7]

A more difficult strategy that also focuses on customers who have purchased the product is to target competitors' customers. This strategy is riskier and more expensive because it involves persuading customers—who may be satisfied with their current supplier or brand—to switch. This is often done in markets in which the growth rate is slowing, usually called a *mature* market. Because new customers are unlikely to enter the market, competitors try to convince customers to switch brands. Often this is done through price or price-related promotions. Customers often use reduced-price coupons delivered in magazines or by direct mail for frequently purchased grocery items. A point-of-purchase machine developed by Catalina Marketing Corporation can be programmed to print coupons for a particular brand when a competitor's brand is scanned at the checkout. Cellular phone service providers, such

Coupons are often used to shift consumers to larger package sizes or to switch brands.
Source: Carsten Reisinger/Alamy Images Royalty Free

as Verizon and at&t, spend millions of dollars each attempting to get people to switch from their current provider. Computer software companies often offer reduced prices if a user of a competitor's product sends in a proof-of-purchase. McDonald's started selling coffee in 2008 to take customers from Starbucks and Dunkin' Donuts. Southwest Airlines is interested in more business travelers, a segment in which the other major airlines dominate. Given the relatively flat growth of the beer market, Miller Brewing's only hope to increase its sales is to steal customers from competitors like Budweiser.

A market development strategy expands the marketing effort beyond the current segments into new ones. This can be done with or without product modifications. The Burpee Seed Company developed small seed packages that were sold with plastic watering cans and tools aimed at penetrating the children's market. Kodak and Fuji have also focused on children by developing programs to link their products with school photography classes and featuring movie tie-ins on special packaging for their cameras. Private banking companies such as U.S. Trust have reduced the net worth threshold to obtain special services that are usually offered only to people with net worth of at least $1 million. The National Football League has stated its interest in attracting more women to its TV broadcasts. Manischewitz is attempting to go beyond is traditional kosher/Jewish segment by marketing to Muslims as well as to non-Jews, to whom "kosher" connotes high standards of production and quality. Harley-Davidson has developed programs to woo female motorcycle buyers.

Application | Wii

Nintendo is an example of how a company founded 118 years ago as a maker of playing cards in Kyoto came to be pummeling Microsoft and Sony. The answer has something to do with reinvention. From industry-changing arcade machines to handhelds, three-dimensional (3-D) graphics to immersive game play, Nintendo has shown a knack for leapfrogging its industry.

Videogame controllers generally feature a bewildering array of buttons, and watching an avid gamer work the device, thumbs pattering across plastic, can be intimidating. By contrast the Wii's wireless, motion-sensitive remote often requires no button manipulation whatsoever. While game consoles typically attract youngish males with an antisocial streak, the Wii is pursuing a market development strategy by bringing people of all demographics together: in nursing homes, for Wii bowling leagues, on cruise ships, at coed (!) Wii-themed parties and, of course, in lines—as hordes of consumers clamor to buy the impossible-to-find $250 machine.[8]

Market development can also involve working harder to attract customers in segments that are already being targeted. In this case, the marketing manager has to assess whether it is profitable to do so. For example, a customer who fits the description of a targeted group may be located in a region of the country that makes the cost of attempting to gain the sale too high. Alternatively, the strategy may address some systematic reason (e.g., insufficient production or retail sites) that potential customers are not buying. For example, Peter Gelb, the head of the Metropolitan Opera, has been successful in luring younger opera fans in their 20s and 30s. While there were always some people in that group attending, Gelb has developed new distribution strategies like showing operas in movie theaters around the country to help build more interest in these age groups.[9]

The marketing manager uses these four groups (existing customers, competitors' customers, nonbuying customers in currently targeted segments, and segments that have not been previously targeted) to give more focus to the market segment decision. Once you have decided to target current customers, for example, your next task is to precisely define who these customers are (women between ages 20 and 40, mid-sized companies, etc.). These specific, actionable definitions are necessary in implementing a marketing strategy. Following Figure 2.1, these targeted customer groups become the basis for the rest of the marketing strategy.

The strategic alternatives chosen also help determine the competitor targets. For example, if a penetration strategy of stealing competitors' customers is chosen, the exact competitors must be specified. Even a decision to continue to pursue current customers should result in a set of competitors who may be trying to steal them from you.

Application Grey Poupon

The Grey Poupon brand of Dijon mustard, now owned by Kraft Foods, featured one of the most memorable advertising campaigns ever developed: the "Pardon Me" campaign with the Rolls-Royce cars.[10] In this campaign, the marketing managers sought to give an element of prestige to a brand that cost more and brought an element of distinction to any dish in which it was used. The advertising developed a high level of awareness and was parodied in different media, from the *Tonight Show* to the movie *Wayne's World*. It was so successful that it persuaded millions of consumers to pay $3.99 instead of $1.49 for eight ounces and created the gourmet mustard section of the supermarket.

However, at some point every advertising campaign gets tired and must be replaced. In addition, the "special occasions" theme limits the perception of when it can be used and thereby reduces the purchase volume. Therefore, in 1998 the brand's managers decided to focus on persuading current customers to buy more (penetration strategy) by encouraging them to use Grey Poupon for everyday use. A suggested advertising theme was "Pamper your family, not just your guests." The managers were also trying to attract new users, mainly by getting new customers in the targeted segments (development strategy). This was attempted through coupons with price discounts, recipes, and premiums, such as measuring spoons that were obtained with purchases of the brand.

There is a risk in attempting to broaden the occasions when Grey Poupon can be used. By extending into everyday use, the brand may lose its prestigious image and start to look more like lower-priced brands such as Gulden's. As a result, it could be priced higher than the normal brands of mustards and less prestigious than the upper-end brands (i.e., stuck in the middle, which is discussed further later in this chapter). Therefore, it is risky to expand into other strategic alternatives because increasing the segments you are trying to attract may be inconsistent with the brand's image.

Market Development Strategies: Entering Foreign Markets

A special case of a market development strategy is when a firm originating in a particular country decides to market its product or service in another country. Normally, companies enter foreign markets slowly at first, testing to see whether there is demand for the product outside of the home market. Thus, important decisions at early stages in this hierarchy of foreign involvement are:

- The choice of which country or countries to enter.
- The timing of the entry.
- How to operate in these countries.

Although obviously important, the first two decisions are beyond the scope of this book.[11] Once the decision has been made to enter a country, from a marketing perspective, the most important decision is the mode of entry (i.e., whether to export using a local importing firm, license the product to a company, establish a joint venture, or use some other approach).

As shown in Figure 2.3, five sets of factors should be considered when deciding on how to enter a new foreign market.[12] Three of these factors—country characteristics, trade barriers and government regulations, and product market characteristics—are external to the firm and cannot be affected by you. The other two—the management's objectives and country selection strategy—are internal to your company.

Country Characteristics

A key characteristic is the market size and growth. Larger countries and those with higher growth rates are more likely to be seen as good places to make significant investments. Therefore the idea of a wholly owned subsidiary or sales force in such a country would make more sense than one in a smaller country with lower growth prospects. In these latter markets, lower-cost approaches or those that are mainly variable costs (e.g., licensing, where payments must be made only when products are sold) are normally preferable.

One measure of market size is purchasing power. Table 2.1 gives year 2007 indices for the purchasing power of the highest and the lowest 20 countries in the world.[13]

Figure 2.3

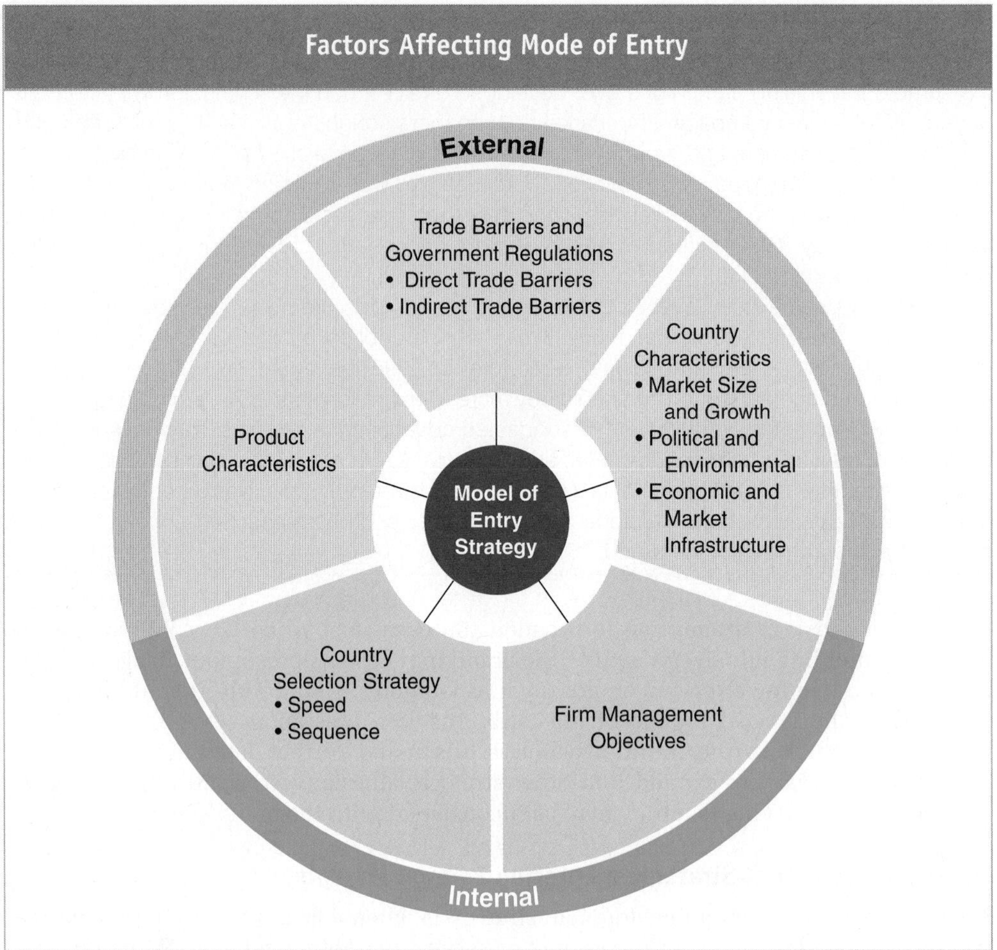

Source: Susan P. Douglas and C. Samuel Craig (1995), *Global Marketing Strategy* (New York: McGraw-Hill), p. 147. Reproduced with permission of the McGraw-Hill Companies.

Obviously, purchasing power is positively related to the potential sales of products. However, it does not account for population size. So while Luxembourg has the highest purchasing power of 176.3, it has only 425,000 people. Argentina has a purchasing power index of only 33.5 but has 39 million people.

A second country factor is the political and environmental risks. Companies are understandably reluctant to make substantial investments in countries with high levels of political instability. Although many emerging markets have governments that are increasingly hospitable to business in general, it is unknown how long this attitude will last. For example, although Russia is a large, tempting market on most dimensions, communist candidates for president consistently receive large numbers of votes. That is a matter of concern to managers considering making significant investments in the country.

The third country factor is the economic and market infrastructure. Using Russia as an example again, the internal telecommunication, road, and airline structures are much weaker than in developed countries. This is another drawback to making substantial investments in Russia and would lead to more joint or other lower-risk arrangements.

Trade Barriers and Government Regulations

The government of India used to restrict the percentage of an Indian firm that could be owned by a foreign-based company to 49 percent. Coca-Cola withdrew from India in 1977, stating that it would not operate in a country where it could not control the marketing and production of its products. When the Indian government loosened this regulation, Coke reentered India.

Countries often have laws that place restrictions on the abilities of companies to operate freely, with some of these regulations targeting foreign companies. In some cases, tariffs or quotas on the importation of foreign products and components make establishing local facilities more attractive. This is part of the reason many non-U.S.

Table 2.1

Global Purchasing Power Indices (U.S. = 100)

Highest	Lowest
Luxembourg (176.3)	Somalia (1.2)
Bermuda (174.5)	Sierra Leone (1.4)
Channel Islands (156.0)	Malawi (1.6)
United States (100.0)	Burundi/Tanzania (1.7)
Ireland (97.9)	Congo-Kinshasa (1.8)
Norway (96.9)	Ethiopia (1.9)
Iceland/Switzerland (83.3)	Afghanistan/Niger (2.0)
Cayman Islands (81.5)	Madagascar/Yemen (2.2)
Austria (81.3)	Liberia (2.3)
Denmark (80.4)	West Bank and Gaza (2.4)

Source: The Economist Pocket World in Figures, 2007 Edition (London: Profile Books, Ltd.) Used by permission, courtesy of Profile Books

companies such as Nissan, Toyota, BMW, and Mercedes have opened large manufacturing plants in the United States.

In some instances, the trade barriers are more subtle. Many foreign companies complain about the restrictions of the Japanese market. For example, NTT, the Japanese telecommunication giant, claims that it has had open competition for suppliers for many years. However, the reality (at least according to potential non-Japanese suppliers) is that design specifications and other elements of the bidding process favor Japanese companies. When there is a serious problem with these informal barriers, it is often useful to enter a new market with a local partner that knows the ropes.

Product Market Characteristics

The physical characteristics of the product or service can affect how entry should be accomplished. Where it is expensive to ship a product, local licensing or manufacturing arrangements are usually made rather than direct exporting. This is usually the case with soft drinks and beer, especially when the sales volumes are high. More expensive goods such as computers and watches are usually exported.

Management Objectives

An internal factor is the company's commitment to international expansion. Often companies, with little interest and those that are risk averse, develop joint partnerships to minimize that risk. Those with more aggressive expansion objectives make larger investments in new markets.

Throughout the rest of this book, issues germane to marketing products globally will be discussed as they relate to the topics covered.

The Core Strategy: The Value Proposition

The basic component of the core strategy is the value proposition. In one paragraph, the customer and competitor targets are summarized and the customer's reason to buy your product or service rather than the competitor's is clearly stated. The advantage of developing a succinct summary of the relative value of your product to the customer is that it forms the basis on which the programs (marketing mix) can be developed because the key point of differentiation is clear.

The following is a model for a value proposition:[14]

> *For (target segment), the (product/brand name) is a (product category) that unlike (competitor targets), (statement of primary differentiation).*

For example, as readers know, Amazon.com sells books (and other things) through its Web site. Although the company faces strong competition from other sites, it is one of the most successful Web-based businesses because it has a very sound value proposition:

> *For World Wide Web users who enjoy books, Amazon.com is a retail bookseller that, unlike traditional book retailers, provides a combination of extraordinary convenience, low prices, and comprehensive selection.*

A second example comes from the global soft-drink industry. In 1993, Coca-Cola bought an Indian brand of cola, Thums Up, from its local bottler. It outsells Coke in some parts of India by a 4-to-1 margin. It has a somewhat spicier taste and, according to some sources, tastes better warm than Coke, an important trait in a country where many people lack refrigerators. The brand's value proposition could be stated as follows:

> *For men aged 20 to 29, Thums Up is a cola that unlike Coke and Pepsi, has Indian heritage, tastes spicier, and tastes just as good warm as it does cold.*

Some of the best value propositions are timeless. The advertising tag line for George Eastman's original Kodak camera built in the late 1800s communicated the customer value simply by saying, "Anybody can use it. No knowledge of photography is required."

The Core Strategy: Differentiation

competitive advantage
the strategic development of some basis on which customers will choose a firm's product or service over its competitors'

differential advantage
one of the three components of a core strategy, a statement of how a particular product or service is better than the competition

The value proposition statement discussed previously requires one of the most important strategic decisions you make: the basis on which customers will choose your product over the competitors'. This is called developing a **competitive** or **differential advantage**. When customers cannot discriminate among products, they consider the products to be similar, and the main determinant of which product is purchased is their relative price. Such competition is not necessarily bad if you are the low-cost producer or supplier. In fact, as we discuss later in this chapter, you might choose to compete on that basis. However, if you are not the low-cost producer and you are unable to differentiate your product on any basis other than price, you are unlikely to succeed.

The search for a competitive advantage, particularly a sustainable one, is one of the basic jobs of the marketing manager. Such an advantage may allow you to charge a higher price than the competition or gain more share at the same price. Fortunately, there are many possible ways to develop competitive advantage. A successful basis for developing such an advantage should have three characteristics:[15]

1. *It should generate customer value.* In other words, it should improve some characteristic or be relevant to some aspect of the product or service that is valued by the customer. For example, you could paint your mainframe computers red to differentiate them from the competition, but the color of the computer probably does not matter to the key decision makers. Low price, speedy delivery, and Internet access are product dimensions that generate value to some sets of customers. Thus, a point of difference is a competitive advantage only if, from the customer's perspective, your product delivers better value than the competition.
2. *The increased value must be perceived by the customer.* In other words, even if your product is better than the competition, if the customer cannot discern this point of difference, it is not a competitive advantage. For example, Intel felt that its ×86 line of microprocessor chips delivered superior value to customers. However, microprocessors are invisible to the user. By branding the Intel name with the "Intel Inside" advertising campaign, the company attempted to make the value visible and more tangible to personal computer buyers.
3. *The advantage should be difficult to imitate.* Clearly, a successful competitive advantage adopted by one product is going to be emulated by others, if at all possible. Although American Airlines was the first airline to offer a frequent-flyer program, few people remember this because of the flood of imitators. A competitive advantage is more likely to be sustainable if it is difficult to copy because of unique organizational assets and skills that can be brought into play or because of patents. For example, FedEx has developed a sustainable competitive advantage over UPS, DHL, and other package delivery companies in the area of customer service. This is because of its pioneering use of information technology and the company's continued investments in such technology, which the other companies have been unable or unwilling to match.

There are three general approaches to developing competitive advantage:

1. Cost- or price-based advantage.
2. Quality-based or differentiation advantage.
3. Perceived quality or brand-based advantage.

Another advantage, particularly in a global context, are "hard" barriers when companies are protected by their governments. For example, China does not allow foreign competitors in certain industries. Since this varies from country to country, we will not discuss this in detail below.

Cost- or Price-Based Competitive Advantage

One of the most difficult approaches to competitive advantage is the cost-based approach. It is difficult for the following reasons: you need to know the competitors' costs to be sure that you can compete on this basis by matching price cuts, if necessary. Because of improvements in technology, it is possible to be leapfrogged in terms of low costs, and only one supplier or producer can be the low-cost competitor in a market. As a result, it is not surprising that most marketing managers choose to compete on the other two bases (actual and perceived quality), while exercising as much cost control as possible.

It has been argued that there are two ways to attain the low-cost position in an industry or product category. One of these is by simply being the largest producer and taking advantage of **economies of scale** (sometimes called economies of size). The rationale behind economies of scale is that larger sales mean fixed costs of operations can be spread over more units, which lowers average unit costs. Originally developed for manufacturing plant construction, the economies of scale concept also applies to marketing, distribution, and other expenditures. For example, scale is critical to fast-food profitability. A fast-food chain has to spend the same amount on regional advertising whether it has 1 or 50 stores in the area. With more stores against which the advertising can be leveraged, revenues go up while advertising costs remain constant, thus increasing profits.

economies of scale
also called economies of size, the rationale that larger sales mean that fixed costs of operations can be spread over more units, which lowers average unit costs

One of the major ways to achieve the low-cost position is to take advantage of a phenomenon called the **experience curve**. Simply put, costs fall with cumulative production or delivery of a service and, after some observations based on the first few years of a product's life, the continued decline in costs is predictable. The experience curve phenomenon has been observed in a wide variety of industries, from semiconductors to airline transportation to life insurance administration. As a product is produced over time, companies learn how to make it better and more efficient through changes in the production process, work specialization, product standardization, and redesign. According to the proponents of the experience curve, a product that has more cumulative production (i.e., greater sales aggregated over time) is in the best cost position in the industry or product category and has the most flexibility for using price as a differential advantage.

experience curve
the notion that costs fall with cumulative production or delivery of a service and that, using the first few years of a product's life as a yardstick, the continued decline in costs is predictable

Figure 2.4 shows learning curves for the computer software and semiconductor industries. The vertical axis is cost per unit, adjusted for inflation; the horizontal axis is time.[16] The costs for semiconductors are given in cost per transistor. For software they are given in terms of cost per software function point, a measure of the number of inputs, outputs, and internal and external files manipulated by the program. As can be seen, the experience curve is much steeper for semiconductors than for software. The figure implies that costs per transistor have declined 48 percent per year while costs per function point have declined only 4.5 percent per year.

Although using these two effects (scale and experience) to develop marketing strategies has been popular, it is possible to be the low-cost producer and use a low-price competitive advantage even if you are not the industry leader, or do not have the greatest cumulative experience. In today's manufacturing environment, flexible manufacturing systems make it possible to have short production runs of different models of products tailored to segments and to simultaneously have low costs. What is perhaps most important in attaining a low-cost–low-price advantage is to focus all the company's controls on costs. In other words, it is possible to compete on price without being the largest.

For example, Southwest Airlines, JetBlue, and other, smaller regional airlines in different parts of the world such as EasyJet and Ryanair, always compete on price and are not nearly as large as their international competitors, nor do they have as much experience. They succeed by having a maniacal approach to cost control. Southwest's

Figure 2.4

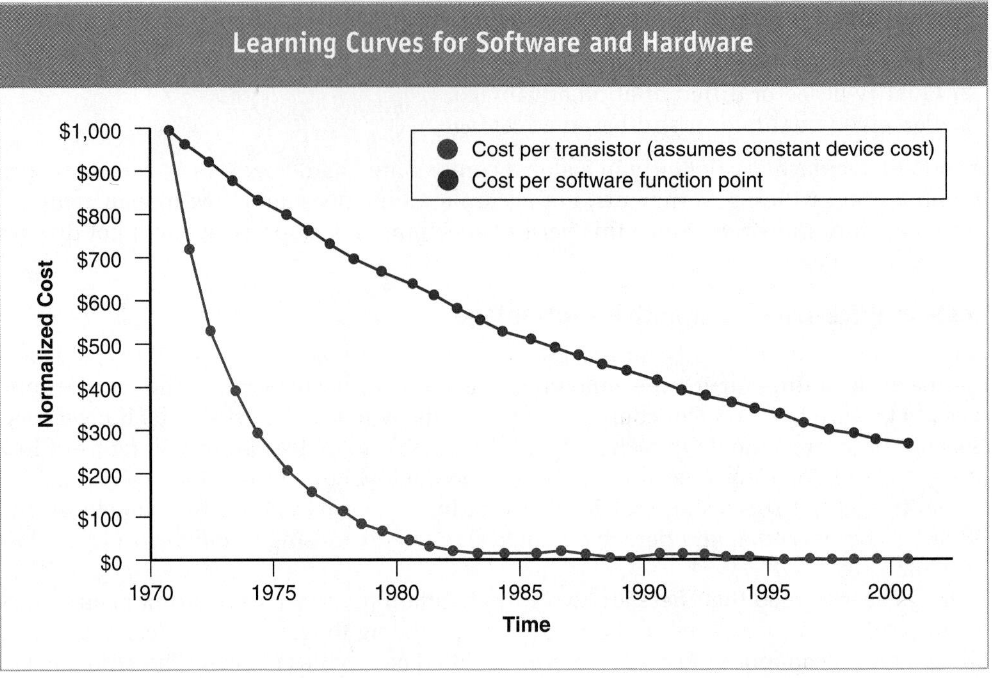

Source: Upside (1996), March, p. 68.

approach includes no meals (just peanuts and soft drinks), not much investment in baggage handling equipment, no fancy computerized reservation systems (mainly ticketless, no reserved seats, no agents to whom they have to pay commissions, and greater use of the Web), standardized planes for easier maintenance (Boeing 737s), and one class of seating. Also, flexible work rules keep their costs way down. Many small airlines also lease their planes and subcontract out maintenance to further reduce costs.

Here are some other examples of successful low-price competitive advantages:

- IKEA, the Swedish furniture retailer with stores around the world, keeps its prices down by emphasizing self-service, low-cost modular designs, and customer pickup and delivery.
- Jiffy Lube International focuses on one area of automobile maintenance—lubricants—and does not do any other work.
- Mutual fund marketer, the Vanguard Group, is known for its index funds and has fund managers who keep trading levels low to keep costs down, as well as a low-cost approach to managing distribution, customer service, and marketing.
- Walmart became the low-price leader in retailing by having the best information technology in the industry. It is supplied directly by manufacturers rather than distributors, using satellite-based links to track inventory. The suppliers provide Walmart with inventory that is ready to be put directly on the shelves.

There are many other examples, and most product categories have at least one product attempting to obtain a price-based advantage. The key to successful price competition is having the lowest costs.

Quality-Based Differentiation

A second approach to creating a competitive advantage is to develop an observable difference that is valued by the target customers. This approach is distinctly different from the low-cost–low-price competitive advantage because it usually implies higher costs but a concomitant higher willingness to pay by consumers—and often higher margins. You can think of this approach as a search for some point of difference that customers value and for which they are willing to pay a price premium. Thus, this approach is often called **differentiation**.[17]

differentiation
an approach to creating a competitive advantage based on obtaining an observable point of difference that customers will value and for which they will be willing to pay

Some readers may argue that for some products it is impossible to differentiate based on quality. This is sometimes referred to as a commodity mentality. The problem is that if you are not the low-cost producer and you cannot differentiate on the basis of quality, real or perceived, then your product will be unsuccessful, or "stuck in the middle."[18] This is because other products in your category or industry are (or can be) priced lower and have better perceived or actual quality (recall the Grey Poupon illustration earlier in this chapter). Think of the most commodity-like products (e.g., gasoline, long-distance phone service, bulk chemicals). The challenge to the marketing manager is to find the dimensions of the product or service that differentiate it from the competition.

Sun Microsystems differentiates its products by having its own operating system, Solaris.
Source: Phillip Elberling/Alamy Images

Because increased competition, greater customer product knowledge, and slow growth markets tend to cause products to be perceived similarly by customers, it is important to realize that even so-called commodities can be differentiated. A chemical company believed that it was in the commodity chemical business selling bulk chemicals at the lowest possible price. However, marketing research showed that 70 percent of its largest customers rated customer service and quality higher than price in importance. The company subsequently segmented its customers by needs and developed different products. King Arthur is a premium brand of flour, yes, flour. Its whole wheat flour is prized by professional bakers and serious cooks for the consistent baking results obtained. Cemex, one of the world's largest producers of cement, invested heavily in information technology to place GPS (global positioning satellite) technology in its trucks. This reduced delivery time from 3 hours to 30 minutes, even in traffic-choked Mexico City, and allowed the company to charge a premium price for what had previously been considered a "commodity."[19]

One way to differentiate is through what might be called a real difference, that is, one not built solely on the basis of perceptions. For example, Caterpillar markets the most reliable farm and construction equipment in the industry. This is an actual difference that can be supported with data on intervals between equipment breakdowns. For industrial and highly technical products and services, this kind of differentiation is common. However, for consumer products, it is often more difficult to differentiate on the basis of an actual quality difference, which presents a greater challenge to the marketing manager.

One approach to conceptualizing ways to differentiate is the traditional value chain introduced in the top part of Figure 1.2. The value chain concept emphasizes that differentiation can be obtained through efforts of the whole corporation, not just marketing. One way to differentiate is through inbound logistics, that is, through the selection of the highest-quality raw materials and other inputs, including technology. Bottled waters, for example, often use their natural water sources as a point of difference. For years, supercomputer company Cray had a significant technological edge on other companies. A second way to gain competitive advantages is through operational advantages. One of the ways McDonald's has remained the fast-food market leader throughout the world is by significant investments in training programs that maintain consistency in service and product quality. Outbound logistics provides a third basis for differentiation. This can be through speedy and on-time delivery, such as the FedEx promise of being there "absolutely and positively overnight." A company called Premier Industrial Corporation distributes nuts and bolts, seemingly a commodity, but differentiates itself from competition (and has higher margins) by agreeing to ship in any quantity desired by the customer. Marketing and sales also differentiate. The IBM sales force has historically been a major asset to the company, enabling IBM to satisfy customer needs better than competitors. Finally, as will be discussed further in Chapter 14, service can be an important differentiator, as the retailer Nordstrom has found. Therefore, one way you can attempt to differentiate is by seeking advantage in one or more of the five dimensions of the value chain.

Chevron is using two of the elements of the value chain to differentiate itself from other major brands such as Shell and ExxonMobil, as well as from low-price brands such as Arco and other local brands. One way is through a proprietary additive, Techron (inbound logistics). This is an advantage if Chevron can convince customers that Techron actually enhances performance as claimed. Chevron is also developing a joint venture with McDonald's that will differentiate it from the other leading brands (marketing and sales), which often have mini-marts selling food and sundry items.

Other examples are:

- Anheuser-Busch puts a "Born On" date on its beer labels to indicate when the product was brewed (operations).
- Marks & Spencer, the British retailer known for its own brands of clothing and food, maintains tight quality control standards that produce some of the highest-quality private label products in the world (inbound logistics).
- Perkin Elmer Applied Biosystems Division developed a polymerase chain reaction thermal cycler (used in DNA analysis) that has a smaller footprint (takes up less space on the researcher's table), a better user interface, and higher reliability than currently exists in the industry (inbound logistics/operations).
- Oral-B differentiated its toothbrush by introducing a patented blue dye in the bristles of its toothbrushes, thus communicating to the consumer when the toothbrush is no longer effective.
- Although it was heavier and offered lower-quality picture resolution than competitors' products, Sony's Mavica digital camera was the market leader when it was introduced because it was the only one that stored the pictures on a conventional 3.5-inch disk. This permitted the user to download the pictures easily and conveniently on to a PC.
- Snap-on Tools, a manufacturer of tools for auto mechanics, differentiates its product based on quality, the 6,000 salespeople who travel to the repair shops door-to-door in their distinctive white trucks, and by letting the customers—usually, the auto mechanics themselves—pay on an installment basis.
- Apple Computer differentiates on product design and features designed to be user-friendly and to appeal to creative activities.

Application Shaving with Five Blades

Gillette began selling its five-blade Fusion in 2006. Is the fifth blade really a sharp turn in shaving technology? Some dermatologists say the five-blade design smacks of overkill, because more blades mean more friction, and friction irritates the skin. "When you add more blades, there's a greater chance of nicks and razor burn," said Dr. Ezra Kest, a dermatologist in Beverly Hills. "I always tell my patients not to use more than two blades." But some early testers of the new razor say they like it. And given how many consumers have come to accept three-blade razors—Gillette's M3Power is the number-one-selling razor in the United States, according to Information Resources Inc., a market research firm, and the Quattro is number 2—it may turn out that for some men five blades is not too many. Selling the new razor will mean persuading men to spend $9.99 on the model; $1.50 more than the Quattro and $2 more than the Mach 3 and the two-bladed Gillette Sensor Excel. A four-pack of replacement cartridges will cost $12 to $13. Procter & Gamble maintains that Fusion continues to gain market share, and now holds 36 percent of the U.S. shaving-systems market in 2008.[20]

Perceived Quality or Brand-Based Differentiation

It is often said that in both marketing and politics, "The perception *is* the reality." Many products and services differentiate themselves from competitors by doing a better job of giving customers the perception that they are of higher overall quality or better on a particular product characteristic (part of the marketing and sales portion of the value chain shown in Figure 1.2). Good examples are "taste," "freshness," or just "quality." Marketing managers might also attempt to differentiate their products in terms of image ("cool," "young," "sumptuous"). Perceptual differential advantages are often used when actual product differences are small, hard to achieve, or difficult to sustain. Although you might think that this would characterize only consumer products and services, many industrial and high-tech marketing managers attempt to develop perceptual differences in addition to the actual differences that their customers usually demand. For example, some high-tech companies try to differentiate by being on the leading edge of the technology they use.

Perceptual differential advantages can be conveyed using all elements of the marketing mix. High price can communicate high quality for product categories in which consumers perceive a price–quality correlation. Electronic and print advertising is an excellent vehicle for delivering images and feelings. Exclusive distribution channels can be used to provide the potential customer with the feeling that the product is rare and expensive.

The dimensions of a perceptual differential advantage are the same as for an actual one. You can use the value chain shown in Figure 1.2 to develop alternative ideas for how to deliver unique perceptions to customers. For example, you might want to deliver the image that your customer service is the best in the industry. Alternatively, you can tell customers that you use the best ingredients. Although you would clearly want to do this if you have a real or actual advantage in terms of that characteristic, the difference between this approach to competitive advantage and that based on real differences is that in this case, the claims are more difficult for customers to verify. Thus, categories that rely heavily on this approach to differentiation are beer, cosmetics, and many services such as airlines and banks. The point is that perceptual differences can be created even when physical differences are small.

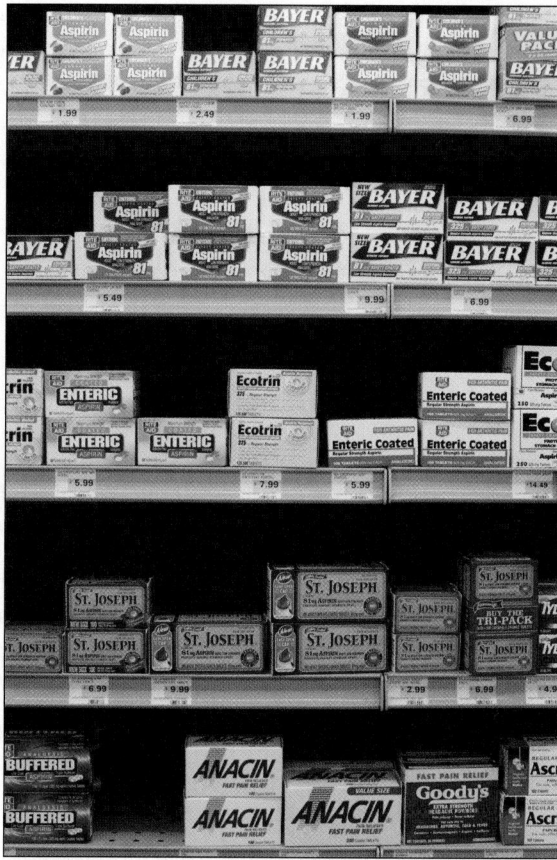

Bayer's strong brand name provides differentiation against generics and private labels.
Source: Jonathan Nourok/PhotoEdit Inc.

An important tool in understanding how your brand or product is perceived is marketing research that measures customers' perceptions of your product on a variety of attributes. Although it is covered in more detail in Chapter 6, one way to conceptualize the output of this kind of research is a **perceptual map**. A perceptual map based on retail banks is shown in Figure 2.5. This provides the marketing manager with information about how the bank is perceived on attributes or dimensions that customers consider important in choosing among competitors. The two key attributes in this example are courteous service and good interest rates offered (higher for deposits, lower for credit). The dimensions cannot be interpreted quantitatively; differences, whether horizontal or vertical, cannot be translated into actual rate differences or waiting times for a teller. In addition, the location of the axes is arbitrary because what counts are the relative distances between the banks. However, the map gives you information about perceptions of your brand relative to

perceptual map
a map, based on marketing research from customers, that measures perceptions of competing products on a variety of attributes

Figure 2.5

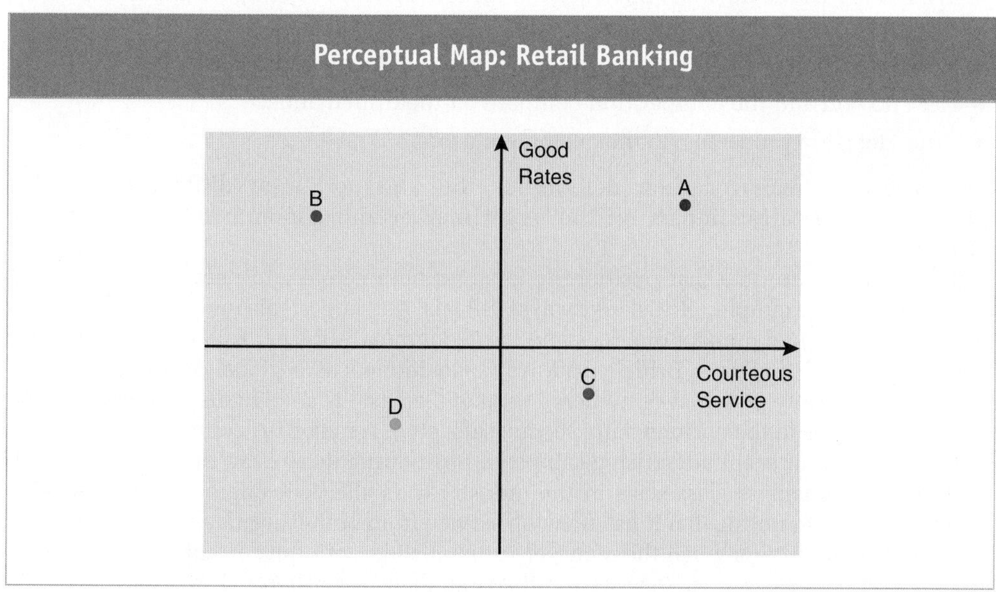

brand positions
customers' perceptions of one brand in relation to its competitors

competitors, or the **brand positions**. Customers are asked to provide ratings of how similar the banks are overall as well as supplemental information about how important different characteristics are in their bank selection process. The map indicates:

- Bank A is perceived to have the best rates and the most courteous service.
- Banks D and C are roughly comparable in terms of rates, but C is perceived to offer better service.
- Bank B is well perceived on the rate dimension but is the poorest on the service dimension.

Note that this is valuable diagnostic information, particularly to banks B, C, and D, who may have had little idea of the customers' perceptions about them. In addition, what is most interesting is that the perceptions could be at variance with reality; perhaps Bank C spends as much money as Bank A on teller and manager training, has the same hours, and so on. However, Bank C's position is inferior to A's on the service dimension.

One of the key ways to define a perceptual differential advantage is through the brand name. The value of a brand name in communicating quality or other aspects of the product is called **brand equity**.[21] Brand names by themselves are powerful communicators of product quality that form an important part of the product's differential advantage. In some cases (e.g., prescription drugs), brand names are the sole source of advantage, in many others (e.g., Nike in running shoes), they are the key source. In all cases, brands can add (e.g., Nestlé, Mercedes) or subtract (e.g., Firestone, Enron) from the actual quality of the products and services. How to create and sustain brand names will be covered in more detail in Chapter 6.

brand equity
the value of a brand name in communicating quality or other aspects of a product

Core Strategy: Product Positioning

At this point in the development of the marketing strategy, you have established:

- The product's objective.
- The customer targets.
- The competitor targets for each customer target.
- The possible ways to differentiate your product, based on either real or perceived (or both) advantages, in your target groups.

The next task is to consider the alternative differentiation possibilities and determine what differential advantages are to be emphasized and communicated to the target customers. In other words, you need to take the value proposition and put it to work in the marketplace. This is called *product positioning*.[22] Positioning takes the competitive advantage and plants it in the mind of the customer so that it is clear what the product stands for and how it is different from the other offerings in the product category.

To make a good positioning decision, we need to know:

- What dimensions do consumers use to evaluate product offerings in the industry or category?
- How important is each of these dimensions in the decision process?
- How do you and the competition compare on the dimensions?
- What decision processes do the customers use?

The marketing manager then determines the key points of differentiation that will have the greatest impact on the target market and communicates them to the customer.

It is important to note that positioning involves both actual and perceived differential advantages. For example, British Airways (BA) is the largest airline in the world, as measured by the total number of passengers carried annually. Recent advertising campaigns have emphasized that fact: British Airways is positioned as a global airline that is the world's largest. How potential customers interpret "largest" is ambiguous, as it could mean a variety of things to them (financially secure, safe, etc.). A major BA competitor, Singapore Airlines, has run a recent advertising campaign positioning itself as an innovator, trumpeting the largest business class seats in the industry. It is also focusing on the trans-Pacific market with the ad noting that it has nonstop service from both Newark and Los Angeles.

Repositioning occurs when the manager is dissatisfied with the current positioning and seeks a new perceived advantage. While this sounds easy in theory, it can be difficult to execute if the product has a high awareness level of the former image. For example, La-Z-Boy reclining chairs have a "Joe Six-Pack" image from the target audience (blue collar) and the product line (one of its best-selling recliners comes with a built-in ice chest). The company is trying to change its target to affluent professionals in their 30s and 40s with sleeker designs, but one consultant describes the effort similar to "McDonald's trying to sell health food."

repositioning
seeking a new perceived advantage in order to improve on a product's current positioning

Summary

What constitutes a marketing strategy for a product or service is a combination of a strategic objective, one or more customer segments or targets, an understanding of the competition for each one of those targets, a value proposition that incorporates all of these elements, and positioning that communicates the value proposition. Sometimes this is referred to as the "3Cs" of marketing strategy: customers, competitors, and the company (what the company can deliver as a competitor advantage to the customers). Thus, in marketing "jargon," we have 3Cs and 4Ps (to follow).

The Marketing Mix

Often, steps 2 (choosing the customer targets) and 4 (setting the core strategy) shown in Figure 2.1 are called the marketing strategy. However, the "complete" marketing strategy reflects the importance of making decisions about all three major components—the objective, the strategy, and the marketing mix or tactics—in concert and in the appropriate sequence. For example, it is impossible to determine what price to charge unless you know how price sensitive your customer target is or whether your core strategy is to position the product as one with a premium image. Similarly, you cannot make advertising copy decisions without knowing the target market's media habits and what reason to buy must be communicated. Therefore, both the components of the strategy and the order in which they are completed are critical.

The marketing mix, or the 4Ps, is often referred to as the implementation stage of the strategy. Steps 1 to 4 are conceptual in nature, because the marketing mix is how the manager makes the strategy operational. The Singapore Airlines example given earlier shows how print advertising can work to implement the value proposition. It also shows how the marketing mix must be consistent with the strategy. A value proposition stating a differential advantage of high quality cannot be successfully executed with a low price. A high-quality value proposition must be implemented with the appropriate channels of distribution, advertising, product features, a commensurate price, and customer service and other relationship activities consistent with the desired image.

Application | Clorox Aims to Show That "Green Works"

Can a major consumer packaged goods company with a name indelibly associated with household bleach become a leading light in the green marketplace? That's the hope of Clorox, the Oakland-based company, which this week is launching its first new brand in 20 years: Green Works, a line of cleaning products that are, in the company's words, "at least 99 percent natural"—made from coconuts and lemon oil, formulated to be biodegradable and nonallergenic, packaged in recyclable bottles, and not tested on animals. The initial launch included five products: an all-purpose cleaner, a glass cleaner, a toilet bowl cleaner, a dilutable cleaner, and a bathroom cleaner. It's an intriguing moment. Green Works enters the marketplace with a near-perfect storm of market conditions: growing mainstream consumer demand for green products that don't require compromise or sacrifice; significant interest from Walmart and other big retailers in pushing greener products to the masses; a product that seems competitive with the leading green brands; and endorsement from Big Green. That last item comes in the form of an "alliance," just announced, with the Sierra Club, which has endorsed Green Works and whose logo will appear on Green Works labels starting around Earth Day.[23]

One way to help ensure consistency of the strategy and the marketing mix is to conceptualize the problem using Figure 2.6. Different target groups may require different core strategies and marketing mix. Returning to the Miller example from the beginning of this chapter, the positioning that works for the core drinking market, males 21 to 29, will

Figure 2.6

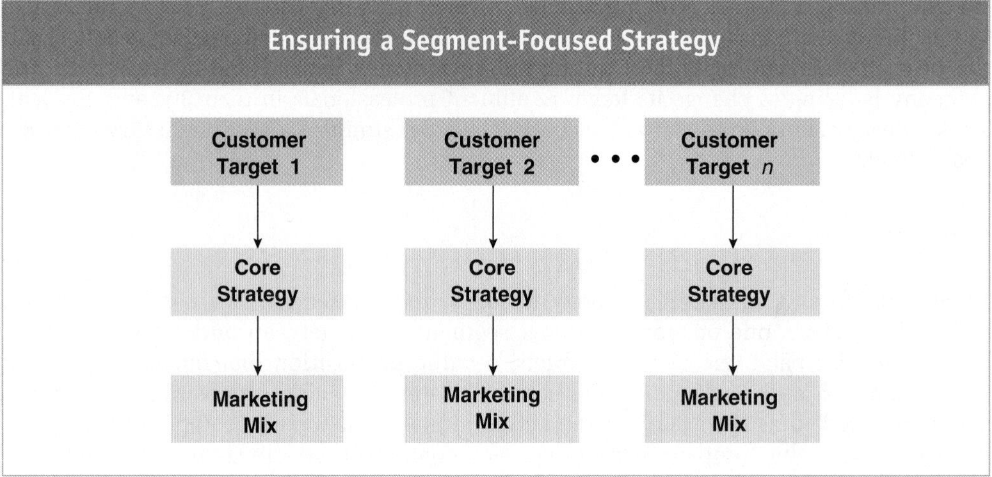

probably not work for older consumers or for women. Thus, the best approach is to consider what is necessary for different target markets and if there is overlap, fine. Figure 2.6 also highlights the difficulties with having multiple customer targets. Not only could customers become confused with multiple messages for the same product, but having different advertising executions and promotional programs becomes expensive.

Marketing Strategies Over the Product Life Cycle

This chapter has covered the basics of developing a complete marketing strategy. These basics hold at any given point in time; that is, the marketing manager has to follow Figure 2.1 whether it is a new or an old product.

product life cycle (PLC) a sketch of the sales history of a product category over time; used as a strategic tool because the importance of various marketing mix elements and strategic options available to the marketing manager vary over the life cycle

However, specific decisions about the strategy can and will change over time. A major factor in how these changes occur is in which stage of the **product life cycle (PLC)** the product or service occurs. The PLC is defined for a product category[24] and sketches the sales history of the category over time. The importance of the PLC is as a strategic tool. The strategic options available to the marketing manager vary over the life cycle, as does the importance of various marketing-mix elements. Although the PLC should not be followed religiously because category characteristics can vary widely, it is a useful conceptual tool.

Figure 2.7 shows a theoretical PLC. As can be seen, the curve is normally *S*-shaped and breaks down product sales over time into four discrete segments: introduction,

Figure 2.7

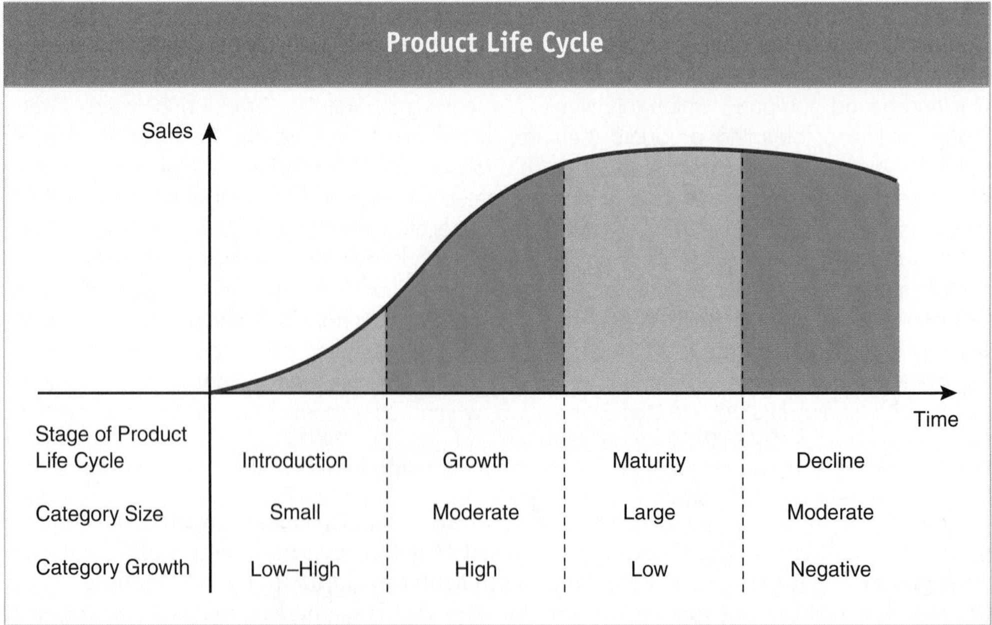

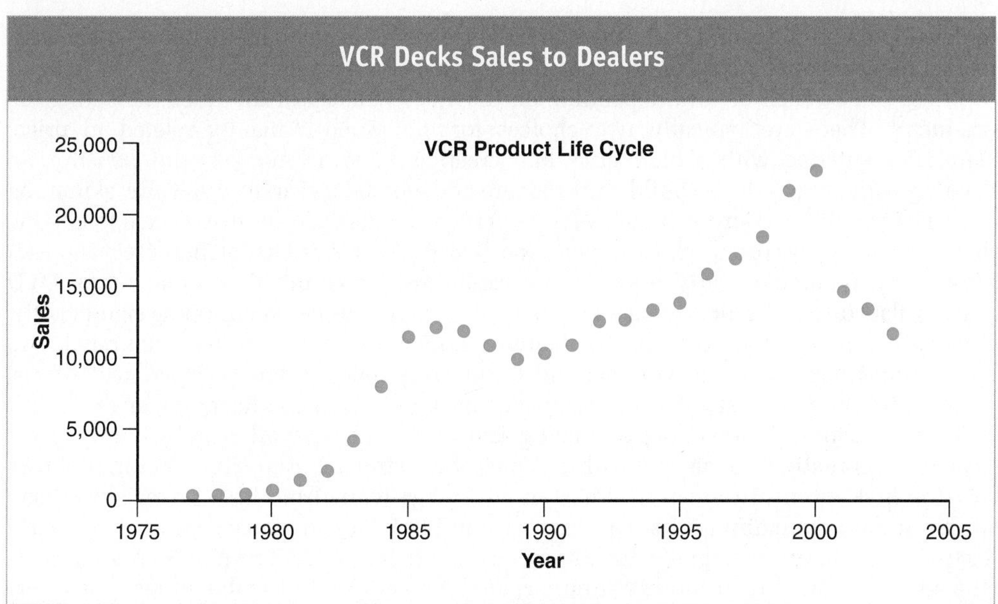

Figure 2.8

growth, maturity, and decline. In the introductory phase, the growth rate and the size of the market are low. At this stage of the PLC, there is normally one company, the pioneer of the category. For example, MTV was the pioneer in the music television category and Cray in the supercomputer category. If the pioneer is successful in building demand or the category appears attractive to other companies, the sales in the category will increase, thus creating the growth stage. During this stage, the market grows rapidly at first and then begins to slow down. When the market growth becomes flat, the maturity phase has been reached. This is usually when competition is most intense, as some of the earlier entrants have dropped out, and the ones that are left normally have substantial resources and are attempting to steal market share from each other (e.g., Miller vs. Budweiser). At some point, the market begins to decline. Firms must decide whether to continue investing in the category or to withdraw.

The PLC is a theoretical model because categories do not follow Figure 2.7 perfectly (or even closely, in some cases). Sometimes, the curves go through several cycles. For example, Figure 2.8 shows the PLC for videocassette recorders through 2003. It has the general shape characteristic of the theoretical PLC through 1990, with sales increasing through 1986, a short flat period in 1986–1987, and then a decline through 1990. However, in this case, sales increased linearly again between 1990 and 1999. Clearly, the market for VCRs had a "second wind," perhaps due to price declines that have been sufficient to spur households to have several. The growth of the sales of DVD players probably caused the flattening seen in 2000 and then the subsequent precipitous drop, which has continued to this day. A second point is that there is no standard time interval for each stage. Some product categories, particularly for frequently purchased products such as beer and cigarettes, have maturity phases that can last for 20 or 30 years or more. In some cases, maturity and then decline are reached quickly. Witness the fast cycles for different classes of microprocessors such as the 286 (three years to being technologically leapfrogged by the next-generation product), 386 four years), and 486 (four years). Finally, it is not always easy to define the product. For example, should the PLC be defined by the sales of all personal computers, or should there be separate life cycles depending on the microprocessor inside?

Strategies for the Introductory Phase

In the **introductory phase**, because the product is new, sales volume increases slowly because of lack of marketing effort (only one or a very small number of firms) and the reluctance of customers to buy it. Selling and advertising focus on the *generic* product, that is, the basic concept. Customers must be convinced that the benefits from this new product provide an improvement over the product or service that is being replaced. Distributors usually have power in the relationship with manufacturers or service suppliers because the product is still unproven with customers. This is a risky stage as profits for pioneers have been lower in the long run than for followers, due to the high levels of investment required

introductory phase
in the product life cycle, the stage in which the product or service is new; sales volume increases slowly because of a lack of marketing effort and the reluctance of customers to buy the product

to develop the product and build the market.[25] However, as the data in Table 1.1 showed, market pioneers often retain their leadership positions for decades.

Prices can be high or low, depending on the entry strategy of the firms marketing the product.[26] There are typically two choices for the pioneer, mainly related to price: *skimming*, entering with a high price and creating a narrow market, and *penetration*, entering with a low price to build market share and a broader market. Typically, skimming strategies are employed by technology-based products, where prices are expected to fall due to the technology becoming cheaper over time. It is also employed to obtain those customers most likely to purchase early, normally a price-insensitive group. Thus, camcorders, DVD players, flat-screen TVs, and so on all started with high prices before dropping significantly. Penetration strategies are used by companies who want to build market share quickly to keep competitors out, build volume, and lower costs quickly due to experience effects. Texas Instruments has used this approach effectively in its semiconductor business.

There are strategic advantages to being first in the market and establishing a strong position, a situation consistent with a penetration strategy. Empirical research shows that the first entrant in a category has an advantage (called the first-mover advantage) in that it tends to maintain its lead through the PLC. The advantage results from early access to distribution channels, locking in customers for products where *switching costs* (the costs of switching to another supplier) are high and products where there are strong *network* effects (where the value of the product to customers increases with the number of customers buying, such as for fax machines). Also, the first mover establishes awareness of its product as the prototype against which later entrants must be compared.

However, some evidence indicates that this first-mover advantage is not as strong as was once believed.[27] The Internet boom of 1995–2001 popularized the first-mover advantage. The subsequent bust brought out many articles giving persuasive evidence that second movers and the use of other strategies could be successful.[28] Some famous first movers that did not survive are Visicalc (PC spreadsheets), Osborne (portable PCs), and Mosaic (Web browser).

Growth Strategies

growth phase
in the product life cycle, the stage immediately following the introductory phase, in which product category sales are growing, competitors are increasing in number, and market segmentation begins to be a key issue

The **growth phase** of the PLC actually encompasses two different kinds of market behavior: early growth (the phase just following the introductory phase) and late growth (the phase in which the rapid increase in sales begins to flatten out). In general, the growth phase has several features beyond the obvious fact that product category sales are still growing. First, the number of competitors is increasing. This puts pressure on marketing managers to keep distribution channels and changes the focus of sales and communications to emphasize competitive advantage. As customers become more knowledgeable about the product and the available options, they put more pressure on price. Finally, with the increased competition, market segmentation becomes a key issue.

The general strategic options relate to the product's position in the market, whether it is a leader (the brand with the leading market share) or a follower (the second or later entrant in the market). The leader can choose to fight, keeping the leadership position, or to withdraw/exit, ceding market leadership to another product. If the leader chooses to fight, the manager can attempt to simply maintain the current position or to keep enhancing the product or service. Why would the leader choose to flee? It is possible that the new entrants in the market are just too strong and raise the stakes for competing to a level that the incumbent cannot sustain. For example, Minnetonka established the liquid soap category. When Unilever and Procter & Gamble entered with their own versions, Minnetonka sold out. Thus, exit is always an option. The other option implies an attempt to reposition the product so that it can be a strong number-two or number-three brand.

In many cases, the market leader is a small company that develops a new technology and a small market and faces the prospect of larger companies taking over. In 1997, Storm Technology Inc. developed software and hardware that let users drop photos into computer documents. Their chief product was a mousepad-sized scanner called the EasyPhoto Reader. The user feeds in a snapshot and pushes a button and the photo appears on the screen. You can then touch up the image, put the photo in a document, or send it over the Internet. That is the good news—the bad news is that by 2002, there were many solutions developed by large software producers Adobe and Hewlett-Packard, among others. It is difficult for a small company to fight in such circumstances. A similar story can be told for Web browsers, where the first one was Mosaic introduced in 1992. It was soon eclipsed by Microsoft's Internet Explorer.

However, a clear success story for a leader is the home finance software product, Quicken. The manufacturer, Intuit, chose to enhance its product rather than flee. Although other large software companies, including Microsoft, have attempted to gain a large presence in this category, Intuit has done an excellent job in enhancing its product and developing an outstanding customer service operation to maintain its leadership position.

The follower has a number of options depending on the strength of the leader, its own strength, and market conditions. One option is to simply exit quickly and invest in some product that has better long-term potential. A second option is to imitate the leader by developing a "me-too" product at perhaps a lower price. The follower can also be content as a strong number two or three by fortifying its position. Finally, the riskiest move is to try to leapfrog the competition. Some companies do this with pure marketing muscle and an imitative product. For example, in over-the-counter yeast infection drugs, Schering-Plough established the market and Johnson & Johnson followed with its Monistat 7 brand, which quickly obtained more than half of the market. America Online leapfrogged Prodigy in the at-home electronic services market through more creative marketing and product features that appealed to consumers. Microsoft leapfrogged both Mosaic and Netscape to where it currently has about 60 percent of the Web browser market.

Strategies for Maturity

The maturity stage of the PLC is characteristic of most products, particularly consumer products and services. Product categories exhibiting fierce battles for market share, access to distribution channels, large amounts of money spent on trade and consumer promotion, and competitive pricing policies are probably in this stage of the PLC.

In the **maturity phase**, the sales curve has flattened out and few new buyers are in the market. Market potential usually remains, but it is either difficult or expensive to reach non-buyers. Customers are sophisticated and well versed in product features and benefits. Where differential advantage can be obtained, it is through intangible or perceived product quality or from other innovations such as packaging, distribution, or customer service. Market segments are also well defined, and finding new ones that are still untapped is difficult.

maturity phase
in the product life cycle, the stage in which the sales curve has flattened out and few new buyers are in the market

The general strategies in mature markets are similar to those in growth markets in that they depend on the relative market position of the product in question. In this case, however, leaders sometimes look at the time horizon for cashing out the product. If the manager is committed to the product for an extended time period, the objective is usually to invest just enough money to maintain share. An alternative short-term objective is to "harvest" the product, that is, set an objective of gradual share decline with minimal investment to maximize short-run profits. The followers have some interesting alternatives that depend on the leader's strategy. If the leader is harvesting the product, the number-one position may be left open for an aggressive number-two brand. If the leader is intent on maintaining that position for a long time, the follower may choose to be a profitable number two or exit the category.

Strategies for Decline

You need not accept the fact that a market is in **decline**. Most strategies for reviving mature markets also can be used to revive declining markets. In addition, serendipity may come to your rescue. Witness the recent surge in demand for cigars in the United States. This was not caused by anything the manufacturers did. There was simply a revival in cigar smoking among certain higher-income segments of the population. Such changes in customer tastes, not stimulated by marketers, cannot always be explained but can profitably be exploited.

decline
stage of the product life cycle where product category sales are decreasing

If the market is truly dying, it can be very profitable to be the "last iceman." By being last, a product gains monopoly rights to the remaining customers, which results in the ability to charge high prices. For example, Lansdale Semiconductor is the last firm making the 8080 computer chip introduced by Intel in 1974.[29] Although most applications of computer chips are well beyond the 8080, it is still used in military systems that are typically built to last 20 to 25 years, such as the Hellfire and Pershing 2 missiles and the Aegis radar system for battleships. Where does the Department of Defense go when it needs 8080s? Lansdale. There are now only a few companies that make computer punch (also known as Hollerith) cards. One of these is Cardamation Company, from which you can purchase or rent the machines.

Using the PLC

Keep in mind that the PLC is a conceptual framework of how product or service strategies can shift with changes in the market. However, the life-cycle model should not be followed mindlessly. As was noted earlier, life cycles can be rejuvenated by marketing or product innovation (the VCR example in Figure 2.8). Thus, the fact that a market appears to be maturing or declining does not mean it is time to abandon ship. It can also mean that other managers will treat the market as a mature market, which creates a competitive opportunity. And there is always opportunity for a creative manager. In addition, the marketing manager has to be cognizant that the appropriate strategy at each stage of the PLC is affected by changes in the 3Cs noted earlier (customers, competitors, and company strengths). For example, a company in weakened financial condition may not be able to compete at the maturity stage where significant battles are often fought with advertising and promotion resources.

How can you develop this creative perspective? One way is to exploit the PLC by always looking ahead to the next stage and planning the product's evolutionary change. This helps you keep the product profitably alive and avoid profit margin squeezes at the maturity phase. This is called stretching out the life cycle.

How can you do this? You can consider using the strategic alternatives shown in Figure 2.2 as a guide:

- Promote more frequent use of the product by current users (market penetration).
- Promote more varied use of the product (market penetration).
- Create new users by expanding the market (market development).
- Find new uses (market penetration).

Or, as Campbell Soup CEO David Johnson said, "There are no mature markets, only tired marketers."[30]

For example, DuPont's Nylon was originally developed for military uses (parachutes, thread, rope). They stretched the PLC to hosiery (new use); tinted hosiery (varied usage); and rugs, ties, and other products (new uses). 3M's Scotch tape was extended through the use of new dispensers (more usage), colored and waterproof varieties (varied usage), commercial applications (new users), and reflective and double-sided tape (new uses).

Global Aspects of the PLC

The unit of analysis for the product life cycle is a particular product category in an individual country. A mature product or service in one country could be a growth product in another. Figure 2.9 shows the stages of the PLC with respect to the development of the beer industry across a variety of countries and regions around 1994.[31] As can be seen, there are significant differences between parts of the world. Beer is a highly developed category in the United States, north/central Europe, and Australia, but it is in its infancy in Africa. Today, the growth rates are significantly different in Latin America, with Mexico being a relatively mature market (with only 1.1 percent growth forecasted through 2009) and Colombia and Peru at an earlier stage of the PLC (with more than 4 percent growth).[32] Thus, you should not assume that the PLC strategies developed for one market can be applied to another.

Executive Summary

Key learning points in this chapter include the following:

- A complete marketing strategy features a statement of the product's objectives, customer targets, competitor targets, a core strategy (value proposition and positioning), and the marketing mix used to implement the strategy.
- The value proposition concisely summarizes the customer target and positioning, that is, the segment's reason to buy.

Figure 2.9

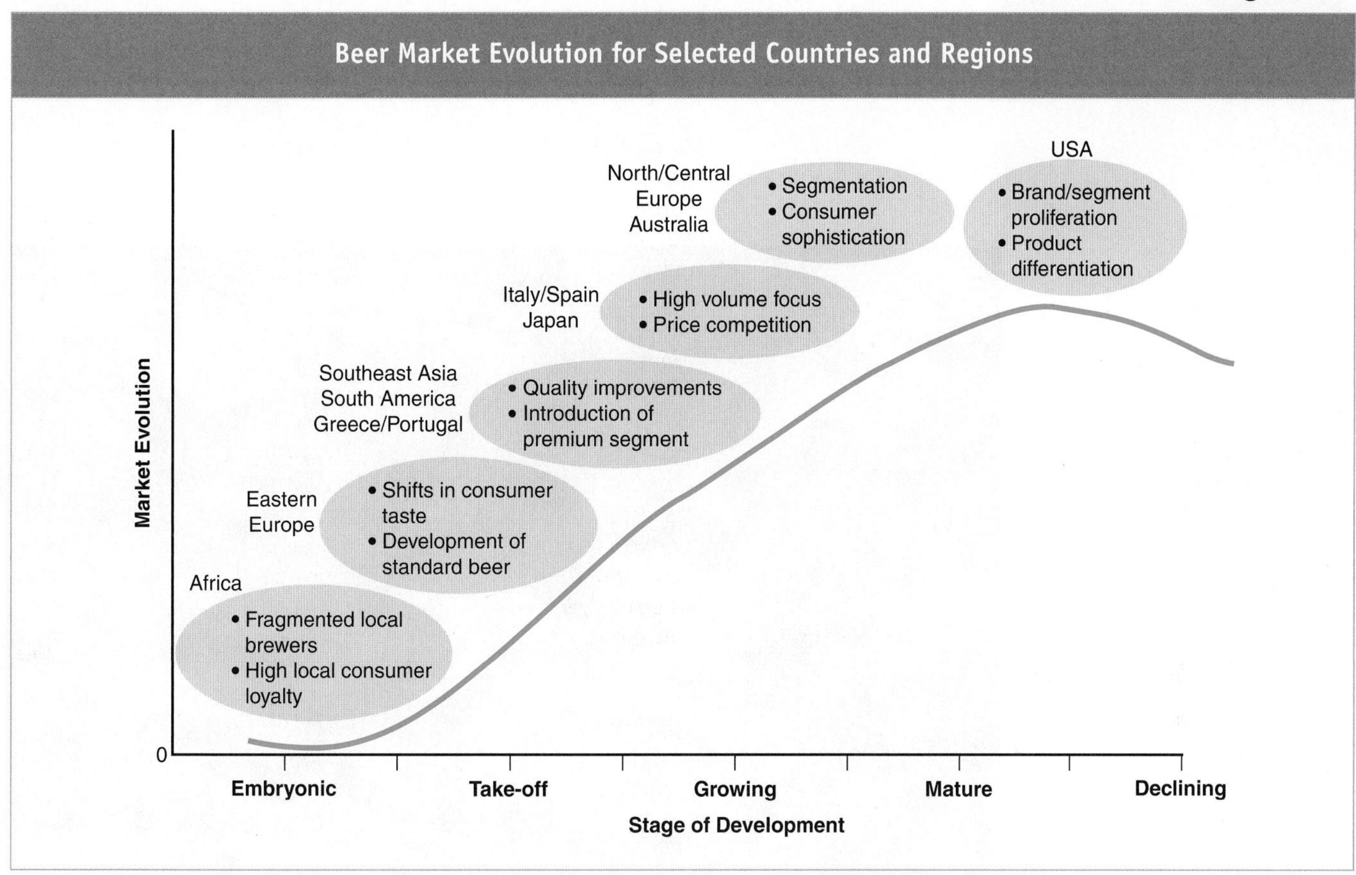

- Differential advantages can be obtained in three ways: low cost with concomitant low price, objective quality differences, and perceived quality differences.
- Product positioning involves developing an image in the mind of the customer about how you want him or her to perceive your product.
- The product life cycle consists of four stages determined by the market's growth rate: introduction, growth, maturity, and decline. The strategic options available to the marketing manager vary over the life cycle.

Chapter Questions

1. Suppose that a marketing manager first develops an advertising campaign before the marketing strategy. How could this potentially create problems for the product?
2. Choose a consumer product or service. How can you get current customers of the product or service to buy more? Do the same for a business-to-business product or service.
3. Assume that you inherited a company that makes and sells packaged ice. Traditionally, the company has sold in bulk to industrial users. You want to sell to consumers. Develop a marketing strategy for your packaged ice that includes a value proposition.
4. Select several magazine advertisements. How are the companies positioning their products?
5. Pick a product that is in an early stage of the product life cycle and then pick one that you believe is a mature product. How is the marketing different for the two products?
6. What is a possible value proposition for your school?

part two Analysis for Marketing Decisions

Key Learning Points

The purpose of this chapter is to provide insights into marketing research. After studying the chapter, the reader should be familiar with:

- The scope of marketing research activities
- Where to find secondary sources of information
- Primary sources of marketing research information
- Developing estimates of market potential
- Developing sales forecasts
- The impact of the Internet on marketing research

The Toyota Scion has become a success in part due to extensive prelaunch marketing research.
Source: Mark Lennihan/AP Wide World Photos

Marketing Research

Chapter Brief

Toyota Motor Corporation is one of the largest automobile manufacturers in the world, selling more than 9 million cars annually.[1] Everyone is familiar with its highly reliable and reasonably stylish products that have resulted in significant sales slumps at both General Motors and Ford. The company has been innovative as well. In 1989 it developed a luxury car brand, the Lexus. This car was marketed totally separately from Toyotas, in terms of both strategy and implementation, in areas such as distribution (different dealers). Toyota was one of the first companies to successfully market a car with a hybrid engine, the Prius. Also, it was an innovator in being the first automobile company to completely adopt total quality management techniques into its manufacturing policies.

However, in the late 1990s, Toyota was concerned that it had lost touch with the youth market, particularly in the United States, its largest market. Due to its emphasis on reliability, the average age of a Toyota buyer is 48. The company was particularly interested in a group called the Millennials, the generation of Americans born between 1980 and 1994. This group has also been referred to as Generation Y or echo boomers (the latter term due to their status as children of baby boomers). The Millennials number more than 71 million in the United States, and 63 million of them will either have or be eligible for a driver's license by the year 2010. Although the youth market was crowded with inexpensive models from Kia, Hyundai, and other manufacturers, the company hoped to be able to develop an innovative car that would establish its reputation in this target group.

To target this young age group, Toyota developed the Scion. It appointed a group of six people to better understand this market. Focus groups (small groups of potential customers) and product clinics discovered that Millennials wanted a brand separate from Toyota (i.e., Lexus). The team parked a bB minivan (sold only in Japan) outside a southern California rave. Attendees at the party filled out marketing surveys in exchange for free bottles of water. Members of the team also observed their customer targets in their natural environment, such as at high school football games, record-release parties, and custom-car shows known as Hot Import Nights.

From these data, Toyota discovered that the Scion had to be inexpensive (around $15,000) and the show rooms needed to look like a scene from MTV's Real World program. There was to be a no-haggling pricing policy, the product line should be dominated by mini-vans (they noticed that today's high school students like to hug each other), and it had to look distinctive, not like their parents' cars. The accompanying photo provides an idea of the styling.

The Scion was initially a smashing success. Nearly 100,000 Scions were sold in 2004, and in 2008 when gas prices hit more than $4 per gallon, sales of the Scion xB increased more than 60 percent over the previous year. Although Toyota was targeting 18- to 24-year-olds, the median age of purchasers is 35, with more than 80 percent of them new to the Toyota brand. Interviews conducted about the Scion brand indicate that it is considered to be "urban" and "cool." The company is continuing to mine this positioning by partnering with Kitsune, a French boutique with a clothing line and music label that are very sophisticated about how it manages its brand and by producing the show by the band Motorhead at the 2008 South by Southwest music festival in Austin, Texas. However, with the slump in the economy in late 2008, Scion sales dipped, and the company engaged Roman Coppola, son of the famous director Francis Ford Coppola, for a live-action, nine-episode puppet series called "The Fist of Oblivion" that appeared on its marketing Web site, Scion Broadband.

This illustration shows how critical the information from customers is in the new-product development process. In general, such research is essential for the marketing manager to stay on top of changes in customer needs. Chapter 1 emphasized the need for constant contact with the business environment. Indeed, such contact is essential to the situation analysis and planning assumption steps in the marketing plan (Table 1.3). Developing a marketing strategy that targets the right customers and competitors (see the marketing strategy diagram) also requires data collection from the environment, and analysis. The mechanism for maintaining this contact is **marketing research**. The American Marketing Association defines marketing research as follows:

marketing research
the function that links the consumer, customer, and public to the marketer through information used to identify marketing opportunities and problems, generate and evaluate marketing actions, monitor marketing performance, and improve understanding of marketing as a process
Source: Copyright © 2010 by American Marketing Association. Reprinted with permission

> *Marketing research is the function which links the consumer, customer, and public to the marketer through information—information used to identify and define marketing opportunities and problems; generate, refine, and evaluate marketing actions; monitor marketing performance; and improve understanding of marketing as a process.*

Also consider the mission statements of the market research departments at Thomas J. Lipton, Marriott Corporation, and Coca-Cola:

> *The mission of the Market Research Department is to gather, analyze, and interpret marketing and other relevant information needed for decision making at all levels of management. These activities are to be carried out in a cost-effective manner consistent with high professional standards.*[2]

Note that in this latter statement, the companies emphasize that marketing research information is not just for marketing managers, but for all managers in the organization.

Table 3.1 shows the three major functions of marketing research:

1. **Scanning for opportunities and threats.** A good research operation collects and analyzes information about customers, competitors, technology, global economic conditions, and other factors. It provides input to marketing managers that they can use to find new markets for existing products, uncover new market segments (see the marketing strategy diagram in Figure 2.1), and anticipate competitors' moves. These data are used in the situation analysis of the marketing plan and the development of a marketing strategy.
2. **Risk assessment of future programs.** When considering alternative marketing strategies, the marketing manager should test them against different scenarios. For example, if the manager is considering entering an international expansion into India, the variations in government attitudes toward business over time would increase the importance of creating different strategies contingent upon which party is in power.
3. **Monitoring of current programs.** Marketing research plays a key role in monitoring the progress of the plan toward its objectives. For example, to raise awareness of your brand from 60 to 70 percent in the target market, you need to develop a plan to measure customer awareness.

Table 3.1

Marketing Research Functions	
Major Functions	**Targets**
Scanning (for opportunities and threats)	Markets Competitors Technology Environment Economic • Regulatory • Political • Social • Cultural
Risk assessment (of future programs)	Own customers Competitors' customers Nonusers
Monitoring (of current programs)	Tracking performance evaluation among all intended segments, including: • Own customers • Competitors' customers • Nonusers

Source: Used by permission from Eli Seggev (1995), "A Role in Flux," *Marketing Management*, 4 (Winter), p. 37.

More specifically, marketing research is most commonly used to:

- Forecast the sales of existing and new products.
- Refine new product concepts.
- Develop a new strategy for an existing product.
- Understand competitors.
- Identify market segmentation opportunities.
- Understand how customers in different market segments make buying decisions.
- Evaluate how customers in the target audience react to various advertising messages and executions.
- Determine what price to charge.
- Understand how satisfied customers are with the product and the company.

This is only a subset of the many valuable ways marketing research helps the manager develop a better marketing plan and, ultimately, a better, more competitive marketing strategy. Marketing research is so valuable that companies invest more than $16 billion worldwide on it annually.

The Research Process

The standard approach to marketing research is shown in Figure 3.1. The research process can be condensed into six steps:

1. **Problem definition.** A key to any kind of research is to establish the problem to be addressed. "Evaluation of advertising" is too vague to be operational. "Measuring current awareness levels of our current advertising theme" is better.
2. **Information needs.** The marketing researcher needs to establish what kinds of information are most appropriate for solving the problem.

3. **Type of study or research.** Many kinds of studies can be performed, ranging from exploratory ("We do not know much at this time, so we are just trying to establish some basic facts"), to descriptive ("We think that the major users of personal digital assistants are businesspeople on the road, and we need to collect some information establishing that relationship"), to causal ("We need to establish that our recent price reduction caused the increase in sales we observed"). Many different kinds of research data can be collected, which we describe later in this chapter.
4. **Data collection.** At this stage, depending on the kind of information needed, the researcher must establish the specific data sources, including the sample of people or organizations studied, if appropriate.
5. **Data analysis and conclusions.** Some person, either internal to the organization or external (e.g., a marketing research firm), must analyze the data and draw conclusions that address the stated problem.
6. **Reporting.** If appropriate to the research problem, a report is usually written to communicate the findings to the marketing organization and other relevant groups (e.g., manufacturing, customer service).

secondary information sources in market research, sources of information that already exist and were not developed for the particular problem at hand

primary information sources in market research, sources of information that are generated for the particular problem being studied by the marketing manager

Particularly relevant to this book are the different kinds of research information available to the marketing manager. Table 3.2 shows the different types. It is important to distinguish between secondary and primary sources of information. **Secondary information sources** are those that already exist and were not developed for the particular problem at hand. For example, U.S. government sources such as the census are secondary sources of information. **Primary information sources** are those that are generated for the specific problem under study. The Scion survey is an example of primary data collection.

Although we will go into further detail about these sources of information later in this chapter, one useful generalization is that marketing managers almost always consult secondary sources before embarking on primary data collection. Because secondary

Figure 3.1

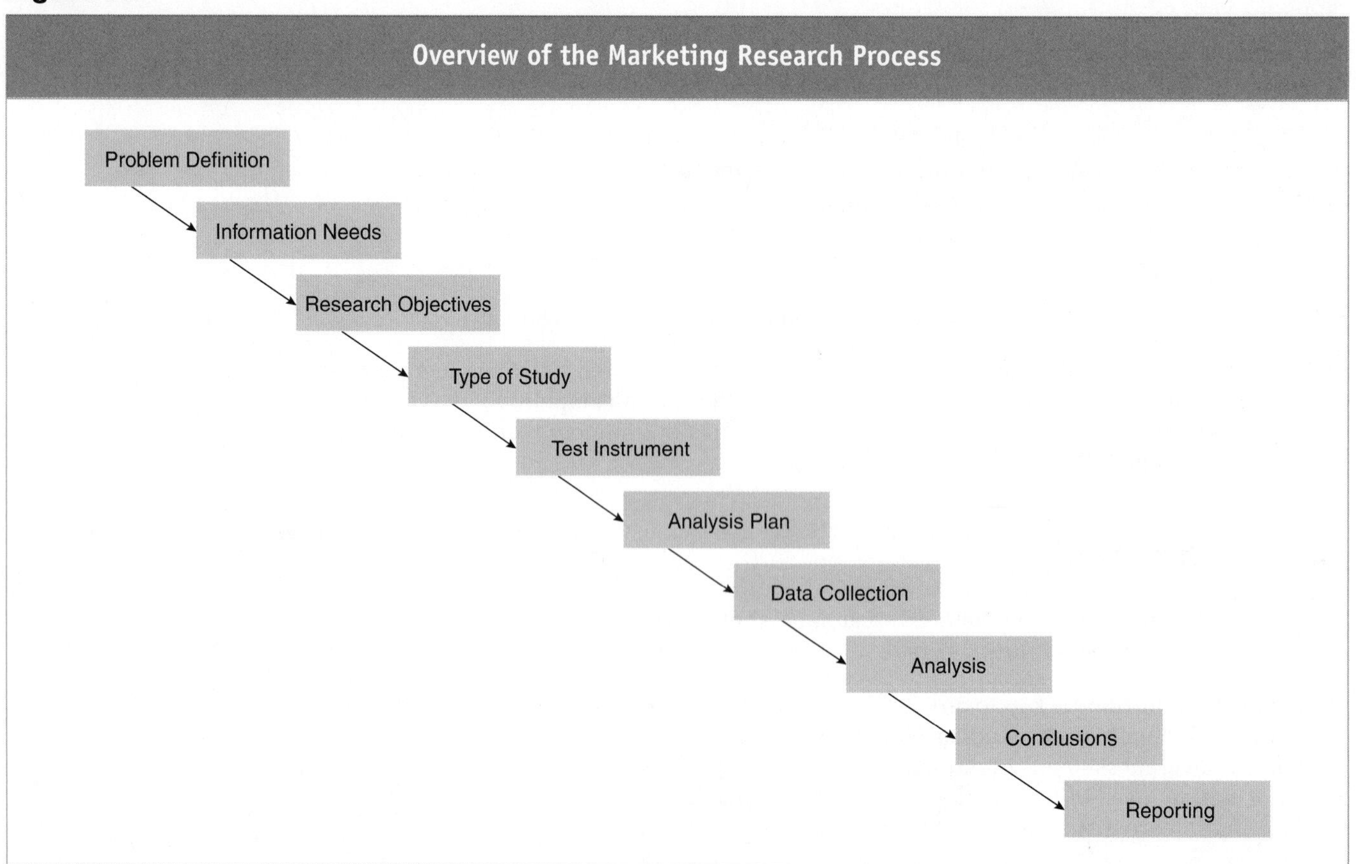

Source: Donald R. Lehmann, Sunil Gupta, and Joel H. Steckel (1998), Marketing Research (Reading, MA: Addison-Wesley), p. 59.

Table 3.2

Marketing Research Data Sources		
Secondary	Observations	Experiments
Internal	Surveys	Laboratory
External	Personal	Field
Public domain	Phone	Models/simulations
Private	Mail	
Primary	Internet	
Informal	Panels	
Qualitative	Continuous reporting	
Introspection	Special purpose	
Depth interviews	Scanner	
Focus groups		

Source: Donald R. Lehmann, Sunil Gupta, and Joel H. Steckel (1998), *Marketing Research* (Reading, MA: Addison-Wesley), pp. 79, 88. Electronically reproduced by permission of Pearson Education, Inc. Upper Saddle River, New Jersey.

sources are usually less expensive (particularly with advances in information technology), marketing managers are well advised to consult existing data before doing special-purpose surveys. These secondary sources can be either internal to the organization (e.g., past marketing plans) or external (e.g., computer databases).

As can be seen in Table 3.2, there are many ways of obtaining primary data. The advantage of primary data collection is that the study is tailored to the manager's needs. Other than cost, the disadvantages of primary data collection are the time it takes to collect the required information and the fact that expertise for this kind of marketing research often lies outside the organization. Unless the manager has a list of trusted research suppliers based on past experience and performance, he or she must go through a vendor selection process.[3]

In this chapter, we focus on primary and secondary marketing research. In addition, two applications of secondary and primary research—market potential estimation and forecasting—are also discussed. The marketing manager must understand basic marketing research methods to better understand customers (Chapter 4), competitors, and the external environment (Chapter 5).

Secondary Data Sources

As noted in Table 3.2, there are two kinds of secondary data sources: internal and external.

Internal

A good place to start collecting information is within your own organization. There is much more information here than you might expect. For example:

- In the marketing organization, past marketing plans are invaluable sources of statistical information (e.g., market shares) as well as strategic information (e.g., past marketing strategies). As noted in Chapter 1, analyzing the marketplace is a significant part of the marketing plan, so if your organization has a history of developing plans that roughly adhere to the outline presented, you are in luck.
- The sales organization should have information based on call reports submitted by the salespeople. These reports not only indicate what happened during the call but also often contain valuable information about competitor activities (e.g., a special promotion or price cut) and changes in attitudes and behavior by the channels of distribution. Salespeople also have direct customer contact and are thus an

invaluable (although sometimes biased) source of information about customer attitudes toward your products and services.

- The accounting department collects a considerable amount of detailed information on transactions. If you market a line of products with a large number of stock-keeping units (SKUs), each representing a particular combination of size, color, flavor, and other attributes, the accounting department can tell you which sizes, for example, are selling better than others. Catalogue marketers, retailers, and distributors that carry large numbers of SKUs, are particularly interested in this kind of sales analysis.
- Research and development departments not only focus on bringing your company's product ideas to market, but may also analyze competitors' products or services. This kind of analysis, called reverse engineering for manufactured products (taking the products apart to better understand their costs, technology, etc.) or benchmarking in service businesses, provides excellent information about the competitors' costs, technology, and quality.
- The IT department has information about the number of hits to the company's Web site, customer visit information (known as log files), and so on. If products can be purchased at the site, more detailed information is probably available, such as shopping cart abandonment rates (the percentage of visitors who put something in the virtual basket but do not consummate the purchase).

These are only some of the sources available within the organization that can help marketing managers get a better picture of the environment. Often, larger companies have their own libraries with information specialists who are particularly focused on the industry in which the firm competes. In addition, many companies use intranets to make internal data available online to managers around the world. For example, salespeople now routinely file their call reports electronically via a notebook computer and a broadband connection. The information in these reports is instantaneously available to marketing managers.

A major problem facing marketing managers with internal sources of information is getting them in a useful format. The accounting department's information system may be incompatible with the marketing system, for example. Similarly, a database established for direct-mail purposes might not be appropriate for storing the broad range of information about customers provided by the sales force, marketing research studies, and other sources. Marketing management should be involved in the design and implementation of information systems to ensure that they provide the maximum value. Perhaps surprisingly, a second problem is getting other departments in an organization to share the information with marketing management.

External

With the growth of the Internet as an information source and the concomitant ability of the marketing manager to access a large amount of information, it is sometimes difficult to distinguish between external and internal sources, because so much information is available from your desktop. However, there is a clear distinction between sources that the company has collected for the manager's use and those that are collected by external organizations for public use.

The general categories of external secondary information are the following:[4]

- **Trade associations.** These industry organizations often collect information about their member companies, particularly on sales and profits.
- **General business publications.** Magazines such as *Bloomberg Businessweek, Fortune,* and *Forbes* often include useful information about company product introductions and strategies. Newspapers such as *The Wall Street Journal* and its various global editions (Europe and Asia) are similarly valuable.
- **Trade publications.** Even better than general business publications for specific data about product categories, are publications such as *Advertising Age, Twice* (consumer electronics), *PC Magazine* (computers), and *Progressive Grocer* that target managers in particular industries. These media often provide detailed sales and share information along with personnel changes, new-product announcements and strategies, promotional plans, and other useful data.

- **Academic publications.** Although these journals tend to target academic audiences, the *Harvard Business Review*, the *California Management Review*, the *Sloan Management Review*, and the *Journal of Marketing* do a good job of translating academic material for practitioners. They enable managers to keep abreast of new concepts being developed in universities. More academic journals, such as the *Journal of Marketing Research*, are methodologically oriented and better for marketing research professionals or managers who are academically inclined.
- **Corporate reports.** These include annual reports, 10K statements (detailed financial reports of publicly held companies), and other releases that are mandated by the Securities and Exchange Commission for publicly held firms.
- **Government publications.** These are some of the most commonly used sources of information. Almost every government in the world collects information about commerce in its own country. The U.S. Department of Commerce/Bureau of the Census publishes the *Statistical Abstract of the United States*, containing a large amount of data about the economy and various business sectors. Much of the government data are collected by North American Industrial Classification (NAIC) codes rather than product categories. These codes range from broad two-digit codes (e.g., number 31 is Manufacturing) to more detailed six-digit codes (e.g., number 312111 is soft-drink manufacturing).
- **Internet discussion groups.** Marketing researchers are scouring social networking sites such as Facebook, blogs, recommendations, and other user-generated media for information about brand usage and attitudes. This information not only covers your brands but also the competition as well. Nielsen's BuzzMetrics and TNS's Cymfony scan the Web for discussions and mentions of brands to develop measures of "buzz" indicating how "hot" or "cold" a brand is.

Table 3.3 shows a partial list of the data sources typically available in a well-equipped "virtual" business library such as the Stern School of Business, New York University. For

Table 3.3

ABI/INFORM Dateline

Business, Economics: local and regional business publications

Search a unique resource focusing on hard-to-find local and regional business news coverage of large corporations, privately held companies, local startups, executive profiles, marketing, finance, and industry news. Provides access to business information not typically found in national news sources. Contains news and analysis, information on local markets, and more gathered from major business tabloids; magazines; daily newspapers; wire services; and city, state, and regional business publications.

ABI/INFORM Global

Business, Finance, Economics: journals, company profiles, *The Wall Street Journal*

Most scholarly and comprehensive way to explore and understand business research topics. Search nearly 1,800 worldwide business periodicals for in-depth coverage of business and economic conditions, management techniques, theory, and practice of business, advertising, marketing, economics, human resources, finance, taxation, computers, and more. Expanded international coverage. Fast access to information on 60,000+ companies with business and executive profiles. Now includes *The Wall Street Journal*.

ABI/INFORM Trade & Industry

Business, Economics: trade and industry periodicals and newsletters

Search more than 750 business periodicals and newsletters with a trade or industry focus. Provides users with the latest industry news, product and competitive information, marketing trends, and a wide variety of other topics. Contains publications on every major industry, including finance, insurance, transportation, construction, and many more.

Alt-Press Watch (APW)

A full text database comprised of the newspapers, magazines, and journals of the alternative and independent press.

(*continued*)

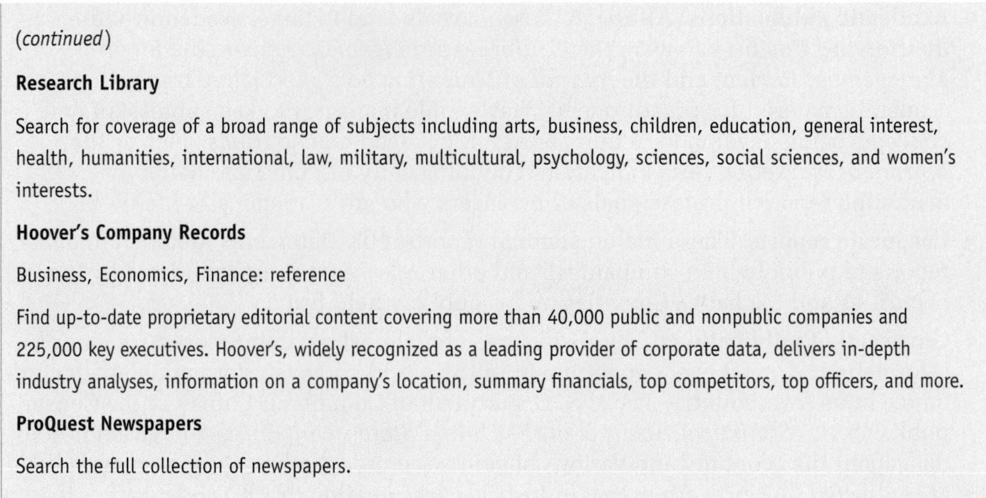

(continued)

Research Library

Search for coverage of a broad range of subjects including arts, business, children, education, general interest, health, humanities, international, law, military, multicultural, psychology, sciences, social sciences, and women's interests.

Hoover's Company Records

Business, Economics, Finance: reference

Find up-to-date proprietary editorial content covering more than 40,000 public and nonpublic companies and 225,000 key executives. Hoover's, widely recognized as a leading provider of corporate data, delivers in-depth industry analyses, information on a company's location, summary financials, top competitors, top officers, and more.

ProQuest Newspapers

Search the full collection of newspapers.

example, ABI/Inform indexes more than 1,000 business, trade, and economic publications. Managers and students should not hesitate to ask the professional staff in these libraries to help locate the appropriate sources. However, much of this information is available on the Internet, including all U.S. Census statistics. General searches for business information can be conducted using the various search engines available on the Web. For example, many people now use the search engine Google for fast, efficient searches. Figure 3.2 shows the results from a search using the keywords "toy industry." As can be seen, a number of good sources of information about the industry emerge. Figure 3.3 shows a page from the Web site of Groupe Danone, a French company perhaps best known for its fresh dairy products (Dannon) and bottled water (Evian) brands. You can quickly and easily find financial information (see the link to its 2008 annual report), Danone's product line, information about its global orientation, and other useful information.

Figure 3.2

"Toy Industry" Google Search Results

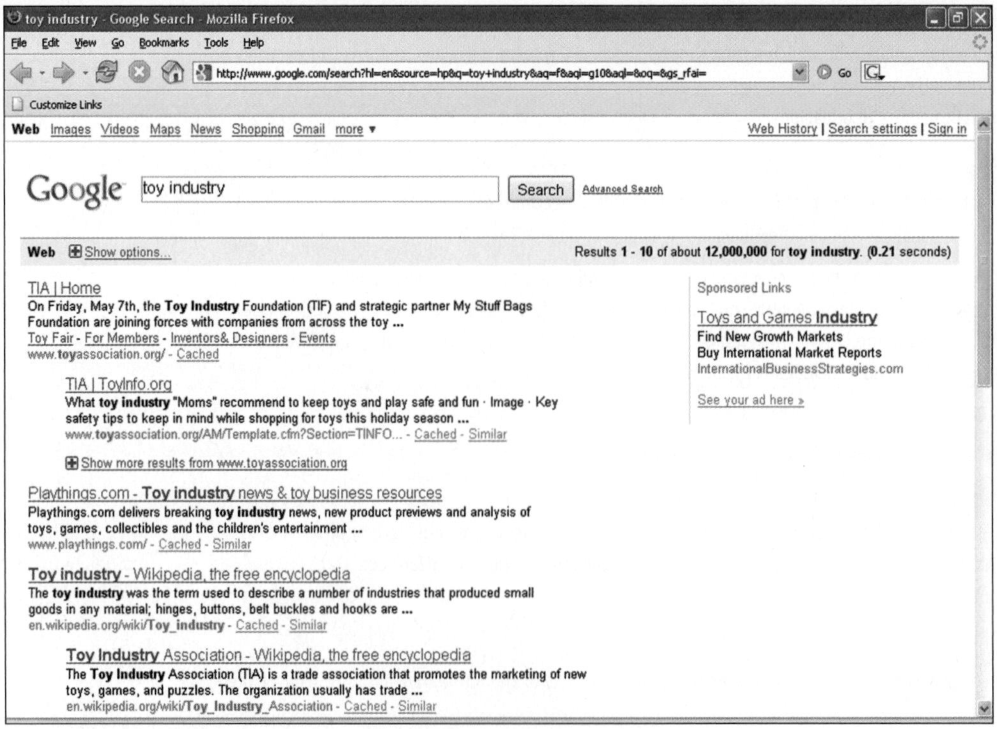

toy industry - Google Search - Mozilla Firefox

Web Images Videos Maps News Shopping Gmail more ▾ | Web History | Search settings | Sign in

Google toy industry Search Advanced Search

Web Show options... Results 1 - 10 of about 12,000,000 for toy industry. (0.21 seconds)

TIA | Home
On Friday, May 7th, the Toy Industry Foundation (TIF) and strategic partner My Stuff Bags Foundation are joining forces with companies from across the toy ...
Toy Fair - For Members - Inventors& Designers - Events
www.toyassociation.org/ - Cached

TIA | ToyInfo.org
What toy industry "Moms" recommend to keep toys and play safe and fun · Image · Key safety tips to keep in mind while shopping for toys this holiday season ...
www.toyassociation.org/AM/Template.cfm?Section=TINFO... - Cached - Similar

Show more results from www.toyassociation.org

Playthings.com - Toy industry news & toy business resources
Playthings.com delivers breaking toy industry news, new product previews and analysis of toys, games, collectibles and the children's entertainment ...
www.playthings.com/ - Cached - Similar

Toy industry - Wikipedia, the free encyclopedia
The toy industry was the term used to describe a number of industries that produced small goods in any material; hinges, buttons, belt buckles and hooks are ...
en.wikipedia.org/wiki/Toy_industry - Cached - Similar

Toy Industry Association - Wikipedia, the free encyclopedia
The Toy Industry Association (TIA) is a trade association that promotes the marketing of new toys, games, and puzzles. The organization usually has trade ...
en.wikipedia.org/wiki/Toy_Industry_Association - Cached - Similar

Sponsored Links

Toys and Games Industry
Find New Growth Markets
Buy International Market Reports
InternationalBusinessStrategies.com

See your ad here »

Figure 3.3

Group Danone Screen Capture

Primary Data Sources

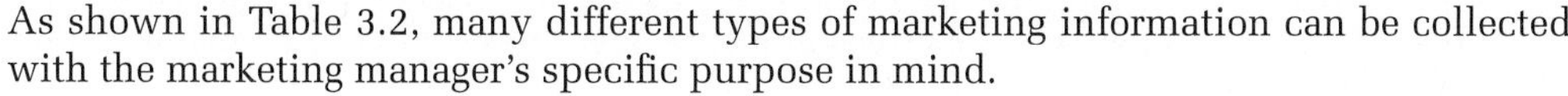

As shown in Table 3.2, many different types of marketing information can be collected with the marketing manager's specific purpose in mind.

Informal

It is often useful to collect information from friends, relatives, customers, and informal observation. Although these sources may not be representative samples, such information can help you form hypotheses about the quality of a competitor's product, your own marketing strategy, and so forth. For example, a marketing manager for a product that is sold through a retailer would find it useful to simply browse the store, looking at the point-of-purchase displays, talking with customers at the displays, and speaking with the store or department managers. Useful insights about channels of distribution relationships can be obtained. Manufacturers of farm equipment should talk to farmers who actually use the equipment. You can do this as a "mystery shopper" (i.e., posing as a real customer) or with full disclosure of your identity. Managers often "lurk" in online chat rooms or browse bulletin boards to see what people are saying about their products as well as those of competitors.

Qualitative Research

A large portion of marketing research budgets is spent on what is generally called **qualitative research**. Qualitative research is sometimes defined in terms of what it is not: "not good enough, not large enough, not comprehensive enough to serve as a benchmark or a basis for statistical projection."[5] This definition may seem overly negative, but qualitative research usually involves small samples of customers and produces information

qualitative research market research that usually involves small samples of customers and produces information that by itself does not directly lead to decisions but is valuable as an input for further research

Table 3.4

Qualitative versus Quantitative Research

Subtypes	Knowledge	Examples
Quantitative Research		
Descriptive	General	Nielsen, Starch, Burke
Scientific	Causal	Quantitative techniques that test hypotheses
Qualitative Research		
Phenomenological	General	Focus groups
Exploratory	Precausal	Open-ended interviews
Clinical	Causal	Depth interviews

Source: Adapted from Bobby J. Calder (1977), "Focus Groups and the Nature of Qualitative Marketing Research," *Journal of Marketing Research*, 14 (August), pp. 353–364.

that does not lead directly to decisions but is valuable as an input for further research. In addition, qualitative research can produce insights into customer behavior that other kinds of research cannot.

quantitative research
market research that typically involves statistical analysis of data, where the intent is to provide descriptive results or explicitly test a hypothesis

Table 3.4 illustrates the difference between qualitative research and **quantitative research**. Quantitative research typically involves statistical analysis of data (not necessarily just primary) in order to provide descriptive results such as the relationship among variables such as age, income, country, and purchasing behavior, or to explicitly test a hypothesis, such as "Our product's advertising has a significant impact on its sales." Qualitative research may be of three types:[6]

1. **Phenomenological.** Often the marketing manager is interested in understanding how customers use products in everyday life. For example, a marketing manager for Toshiba might be interested in all the ways a businessperson uses a laptop computer (report writing, communicating with the home office, etc.). Phenomenological research elicits this kind of information.
2. **Exploratory.** This kind of qualitative research generates hypotheses for further research, often quantitative. For example, a marketing manager would use qualitative research to test advertising campaigns at an early stage of their development. The manager would then develop hypotheses about which campaign does the best job at achieving the stated objectives and then test these hypotheses using further research.
3. **Clinical.** In this kind of qualitative research, the manager explores the reasoning behind customer purchasing behavior. The methods used are often psychoanalytic, including in-depth interviews and other techniques such as metaphors to understand customer motivations.

focus group
small groups of people, typically recruited through their membership in various target groups of interest, who are brought together in a room to discuss a topic chosen by the marketing manager and led by a professional moderator

Focus groups are a major source of marketing research information.
Source: PhotoEdit Inc.

Focus Groups

There are many kinds of qualitative research methods, but the best known and most widely used is the **focus group**. Focus groups are small groups of people typically chosen for their membership in various target groups of interest. The people could be consumers, influencers of buying decisions in organizations, former customers, or noncustomers; or they may be chosen for their personal characteristics (e.g., teenagers). These people are usually brought together in a room to have a discussion about a topic chosen by the marketing manager, which is led by a professional moderator. The focus group is often observed by members of the marketing group (through a one-way mirror), and a videotape and transcript of the proceedings are made. The moderator usually develops a report on his or her conclusions.

Table 3.5

Characteristics of Focus Groups			
Key Questions	**Exploratory**	**Clinical**	**Phenomenological**
Should results be generalized with further study?	No	No	Yes
When should each type be used?	Support prior research; before quantitative research	When you need an indirect approach	When management needs to better understand customers
How many groups?		As many as deemed needed	
Interaction within the group?	Unnecessary	Considerable, but moderator is detached	Considerable, but moderator is involved
Homogeneity of the group?	Heterogeneous	Either	Homogeneous
Moderator expertise is important?	Yes, scientific	Yes, psychological	Yes, personal
Management observation?	Unnecessary	Unnecessary	Essential

Source: Adapted from Bobby J. Calder (1977), "Focus Groups and the Nature of Qualitative Marketing Research," *Journal of Marketing Research*, 14 (August), pp. 353–364.

The different kinds of focus groups are compared in Table 3.5. Probably the most popular use of focus groups is for phenomenological research, a basic understanding of how customers use the product or service in question. As noted in the table, these kinds of groups must not be used to develop generalizations and should be followed up with further research, usually quantitative. Because clinical focus groups are used to explore the psychological underpinnings of the customers through in-depth questioning, the results cannot be generalized so follow-up research is unnecessary. Likewise, the purpose of exploratory focus groups is to generate research hypotheses for further study. They are not intended to produce generalizable, actionable results.

The focus group is probably the most misused of all marketing research methods. This is because most marketing managers do not understand the various kinds of groups (exploratory, clinical, phenomenological), the purposes of each, and how to structure the group to achieve different kinds of results. The marketing manager must develop an objective for the focus group research, match it with the kind of group needed, and then structure the process accordingly. The most common misuse of focus groups is attempting to use them to draw general conclusions. This may be an inexpensive way to do research, but because the groups are small and not all behaviors are generalizable, the results can be misleading. Focus groups are a valuable source of information for keeping in touch with customers, but they have their limits.[7]

Improvements in technology have changed focus group research. Videoconferencing is being used as a way to reduce costs and to make it more convenient for customers to participate. Videoconferencing also enables managers at different locations to observe sessions. The use of telephone focus groups is also expanding. Respondents are recruited from various geographic locations and asked to call a toll-free number at a prearranged time to participate in the group. Greater use is being made of the telephone as a way to conduct in-depth qualitative research as well.

As you might expect, more companies are offering Web-based focus group services (it is estimated that about 10 to 15 percent of all groups are being conducted on the Web). Using a moderator, the focus groups are conducted in an instant messaging format or with video mini-cams providing visual, on-screen pictures of respondents. The advantage of the latter is that other members and the moderator can observe facial expressions and body language, which are often interpreted by observers of the groups. Companies offer clients tools to engage customers in online discussions, often about new-product concepts. Visiting the Web site of a client and hitting the "Help Us Create New Products Link" (for example), you get involved in a conversation with other customers. Simultaneously, the research firm is analyzing the responses in real time. Other companies like Keynote offer clients more focused, Internet-based qualitative research through a panel of customers it has recruited, who can be selected by predetermined variables (e.g., men ages 18 to 25) to test different aspects of the client's Web site, such as customer service.

Application Splenda

The managers of the sweetener brand, Splenda, developed a prototype of a new product called Splenda Mist, a pocket-size spray form of the sweetener.[8] In cases like this, most marketers would use traditional focus group or product sampling (giving away free samples) to solicit feedback on the concept. However, Splenda instead used Facebook. The company used ads to its target group, women aged 25 and older, to drive them to a Splenda Mist Facebook page where they could sign up for a "first look" at the new product. Through the sign-up process, the company obtained names, shipping and e-mail addresses, and demographic data. After sending out 16,000 free samples, the company received valuable feedback from many of the users that it is using to further develop the concept. While many companies have used Facebook to offer free samples or other promotions, the Splenda Mist use of Facebook as a new-product feedback mechanism was unique.

A new approach to focus groups has been developed called the Zaltman metaphor elicitation technique (ZMET), named after its developer, Jerry Zaltman.[9] The theory behind ZMET is that while traditional focus groups force customers to think rationally by giving their top-of-mind responses to the moderators' questions, most of thought, emotion, and learning occurs in the unconscious mind. In ZMET focus groups, subjects are asked to explain their true feelings with images, not words. Many major companies have used the ZMET approach to better understand the subliminal appeal of their products.

Observations and Ethnographic Research

Not all observational research is informal. A common observational technique is to set up a one-way mirror in a supermarket or other retail outlet. In this way, the marketing manager or researcher can observe the behavior patterns of shoppers in different demographic groups. The observer might count the different items examined, calculate how much time is spent considering a purchase in a product category, or evaluate the interactions with a salesperson (if appropriate). Another observational approach is to go through a household's pantry to see what brands are being purchased and measure their consumption rates. Other observational methods are more intrusive and involve measuring the dilation of a person's pupil to measure attention to an advertisement or measuring the electric impulses transmitted through the skin to determine the subject's excitement level.

Application In-Store Video Monitoring

Two specific examples highlight how in-store video monitoring is becoming more popular as a marketing research tool.

A retail store in Minneapolis, Once Famous, is both a real store and a source of information about how people shop.[10] It is run by the branding agency, Fame. When a young woman shops in the boutique, each move she makes is recorded by ceiling-mounted video cameras, and her conversations are monitored by concealed microphones. There is also a two-way mirror for real-time observation. The company also interviews customers after each purchase. Customers are informed that they are being studied and must sign a waiver to enter the shop.

Many of these observations of shoppers, however, occur without the customer's knowledge or consent. Envirosell, founded by Paco Underhill, a pioneer in the field of observational customer research, uses hidden cameras to better understand, for example, whether a retail display is more appealing to men or women. In addition, the cameras can monitor how long sales clerks took to approach customers to improve a store's customer service. Privacy advocates, however, are not entirely happy with this kind of monitoring and view it as an invasion of privacy.[11]

Many companies are looking for qualitative methods to help develop brand strategies that go beyond what focus groups and quantitative research can deliver. A San Francisco–based company called Tattoo Marketing Inc. has employees hang out on sidewalks with video cameras and ask people on the street for their impressions of a brand. In a project for a clothing retailer, researchers looked through people's closets and asked them to tell on-camera stories about their wardrobes, such as how they feel when they wear certain outfits. Consultants try to decode the male-bonding rituals of 20-something Miller Lite drinkers. Microsoft has created an in-house team to better understand how households use MSN, the company's Internet service. This kind of research is referred to as **ethnographic research** and requires people with a variety of skills beyond marketing research, including anthropology.

ethnographic research in-depth study of consumer consumption through interviews and observing behavior

Application Campbell Soup

Since 2002, Campbell Soup has been running a popular series of advertisements for its "Chunky" soup that feature National Football League stars and their mothers calling them inside for dinner and serving them soup. However, starting with the fall 2008 season, the company is putting the "moms" on the "bench." The company has found through its research that the target group—men in their 30s—have achieved soup "independence" from their mothers.

How did the company's managers determine this? In 2007, as part of the research for the campaign, members of the Campbell's marketing team visited more than 100 customers in Baltimore, Detroit, Seattle, and Milwaukee. They went into their homes and collected information about their relationships with the product. This depth research found that customers were ready for a more empowering message than the one sent by images of grown men listening to their mothers. However, the moms haven't totally disappeared—a number of them will speak on behalf of the company to raise food donations for Feeding America, a nationwide network of food banks.[12]

A new technology incorporating computer graphics and three-dimensional modeling allows marketing managers to observe how consumers choose between different brands in a virtual reality–like setting. In **virtual shopping**, the consumer can use the simulation to view (on a screen) shelves stocked with any kind of product. The shopper can choose a package on the virtual shelf by touching its image on the screen. The product can be rotated and examined on all sides. The consumer can also "purchase" the product by touching the image of a shopping cart. Unlike the artificial environment in a focus group, the shopper can choose simulated brands in a realistic setting. New-product concepts can be tested easily and quickly.

virtual shopping a new technology incorporating computer graphics and three-dimensional modeling that allows marketing managers to observe how consumers choose between different brands using a virtual reality setting

Borrowing from cognitive neuroscience, marketers are adopting new technologies that study consumers' cognitive and affective response to marketing variables. These technologies include the use of fMRI (functional magnetic resonance imaging) to observe brain activity in response to advertising, price discounts, packaging, etc. and sensors that measure consumer's physiological response to determine a response. Although in its infancy, these techniques are very expensive and likely to be useful when consumers may not be able to articulate a response or inhibited to be completely frank in their response.

Application Campbell's Soup

Following up on the earlier illustration from Campbell's, the company is also on the forefront of using neurological sciences to better understand consumer behavior. For years, Campbell's researchers asked consumers whether they remembered an ad and whether it made them more likely to buy a product. However, in 2005, a study by the company showed that survey-based measures of ad effectiveness had little relation to sales changes.

In 2008, the company hired Innerscope Research to measure bodily responses to their marketing programs. Researchers interviewed 40 people in their homes and later in stores. Vests that the testers wore captured skin-moisture levels, heart rate, depth and pace of breather, and posture. Video monitors also tacked eye movements and pupil width.

The company found that warmth and other positive attributes associated with Campbell's soup disappeared in the store. As a result, the company developed ways to trigger more emotional responses in stores. On many soup can labesl, steam rises from larger, more vibrant pictures of soup in more modern, white bowls. Also, soup spoons have disappeared as consumers did not have strong emotional responses to them.[13]

Surveys

A major portion of many research budgets is devoted to survey research, performed by administering questionnaires to people. This is a form of quantitative research and, as Table 3.4 shows, the major purposes of survey research are either descriptive, such as attempting to understand various market segmentation approaches, or scientific, such as testing a marketing manager's hypothesis that women consume more of a product than men. The two primary issues for the manager to consider are the sample from which the responses are taken and the various survey approaches that can be used.

Survey development and analysis are complex, and a full description is beyond the scope of this book. For example, the construction of useful survey questions is much more difficult than you might expect. The wording of a question may be biased, leading the respondent to a particular answer. In addition, the possible responses can be open-ended (e.g., "How many times did you go to the movies last month?") or fixed (e.g., "Check off from the following list how many times you went to the movies last month"). Each of these styles has different implications for analysis and opportunities for inaccurate responses. In addition, many questions on opinions and attitudes use scales (e.g., "On a 1 to 7 scale, where 1 is very bad and 7 is excellent, please rate the quality of service you received at the hotel during your recent stay"); the number of points on the scale and whether it should be an even or odd number must be considered carefully.

Sampling Considerations

An important concept in marketing research is the population or universe from which the sample should be drawn. In this context, *universe* means the entire population of the target group. Suppose you are marketing a computer software product used in local area networks. One target audience is the population or universe of network managers in a country. Few companies can afford to administer a survey to every member of a population. As a result, we would draw a sample from the network managers and assume that the results could be extrapolated to the population. Using statistical analysis, you can determine the range of results within which the "true" or population results would fall. An exception is when the universe is small. For example, if you are working with an aircraft manufacturer, the universe of airlines is sufficiently small that you could survey each potential customer.

The results of any survey are only as good as the sample taken. If the sample is biased, then the results cannot be considered representative of the population and any analysis of the survey results would be misleading without some adjustment. It is usually assumed that samples are taken randomly; that is, every member of the population has a nonzero probability of being chosen for the sample. Note that this does not imply that every member of the population has an equal chance of being selected. Some random sampling approaches give more weight to subgroups or segments within the population. Samples in which some members of the population have a zero probability of being chosen are nonrandom and are sometimes called convenience samples because they are used for expediency rather than scientific reasons. Thus, one important characteristic of a survey is how the sample is taken. The marketing manager should always ask about the characteristics of the sample before using the results of the survey.

Note that any sampling process in which the customers can self-select to return a survey is not random. For example, it is common for hotels, restaurants, and other service organizations to give customers short surveys to complete about the service quality. Obviously, many customers do not return them. Those that are returned are not a random sample of customers, most likely representing the views of customers who are highly satisfied or highly dissatisfied.

Samples are usually pulled from lists of customers obtained from company records, industry associations, or companies that specialize in developing lists. In some cases, such lists are unnecessary because the universe is readily observable. For example, a researcher who wants to study the dishwashing habits of German households could use government records to randomly sample cities and blocks within cities, and then randomly choose houses within the blocks.

However, there is often a large difference between the original random sample and the final group of surveys obtained. Those who respond, even if randomly chosen, may not ultimately represent a random sample of the target population. This is called nonresponse bias: the people who did not respond may feel differently about the issue being surveyed than those who did. It is important for the marketing manager to make sure the sample has been inspected for nonresponse bias by examining the answers to some of the other questions on the survey (e.g., income, age) or the geographic distribution of the responses.

Survey Types

The three main approaches to collecting survey data are personal interviews, telephone interviews, and mail, although the Internet is becoming more popular as a survey tool as the number of users grows. The trade-offs between these four approaches are highlighted in Table 3.6.

The main criteria for evaluating the survey alternatives are the following:

- **Cost.** Most marketing managers have a fixed budget for research, so cost considerations are important. Personal interviews are the most expensive choice.
- **Control.** This refers to how much control the data collector has in the data collection process. For example, because mail surveys are completed at a location distant from the organization collecting the data, there is no opportunity to answer clarification questions. In addition, there is no opportunity to prod the respondent to fill out the survey.
- **Response rate.** This is the percentage of surveys completed.
- **Potential for interviewer bias.** The inability of the data collector to interact with the respondent is not necessarily a bad thing. Personal interactions with survey respondents could lead to answers that would not be given otherwise.
- **Time to obtain data.** The marketing manager may need the data within two weeks or two months.
- **Flexibility.** This characteristic describes how many different kinds of survey formats and question types can be used. For example, with personal interviews flexibility is high because a large variety of question-and-answer formats can be used, including video, and the surveys can be long.
- **Nonresponse bias.** A serious problem with survey research is that the people who choose to respond to the survey may be significantly different from those who do not. The different survey methods offer the marketing researcher varying ability to control and correct for this bias.

Table 3.6

Trade-offs with Different Kinds of Surveys

Criteria for Evaluation	Personal Interview	Phone	Mail	Internet
Cost	High	Medium	Low	Low
Control	High	Medium	Low	Low
Response rate	High	Medium	Low	Low
Potential for interviewer bias	High	Medium	Low	Low
Time to obtain data	Long	Short	Long	Short
Flexibility	High	Medium	Low	Medium
Nonresponse bias	Low	Low	High	High

The trade-offs noted in Table 3.6 are not surprising. If the manager needs a quick response, telephone surveys are the way to go, although the Internet is also usually quick. If budget limitations are critical, mail surveys are the least expensive. In survey research, you get what you pay for.

Technology is also affecting survey research. Besides the Internet, fax and e-mail approaches have been used. A study on the use of fax surveys showed that the response time was about 40 percent faster than for mail surveys, but response rates and quality of information were the same.[14] The small number of fax machines in the home limits this approach, however. A similar study compared e-mail surveys to mail surveys. This study found a greater response rate and a much faster return rate for e-mail than for mail.[15] Of course, the problem with this approach is that not all (80 percent) U.S. households (and fewer in other countries) own personal computers (PCs). Easy-to-use and inexpensive online survey tools such as SurveyMonkey and Zoomerang make it easy to collect and analyze information quickly from online samples of respondents.

Some companies take surveys at fixed time intervals (e.g., every three months) in order to monitor advertising awareness, product usage, or strategy-related measures such as product positioning over time. These are called tracking studies.

Application Net Promoter Surveys

A number of companies are using a relatively simply survey to better understand how customers feel about their products. Called Net Promoter (www.netpromoter.com), only one question is asked: "Would you recommend this product to friends and family?" Subtract negative responses from positive and neutral ones and you get a net promoter score that is an overall measure of customer satisfaction. Popularized by the consulting firm Bain and Company, the net promoter approach is being used by companies like Intuit, General Electric, Symantec, and *The Wall Street Journal*. While touted as superior to other measures such as customer satisfaction and customer retention in predicting firm growth, some studies have questioned this assertion.[16]

panel
a set of customers enlisted to give responses to questions or to provide data repeatedly over a period of time

Panels

A **panel** is a set of customers who are enlisted to give responses to questions or to provide data repeatedly over a period of time. A panel is different from a tracking study. Both take measures from a set of respondents over time, but a panel uses the same set of respondents, whereas a tracking study selects a new random sample at each measurement period. The main benefit of a panel is the ability to observe changes in behavior caused by changes in marketing variables or other factors in the marketplace. Conventional surveys and focus groups are called cross-sectional data because they provide a slice of life at one point in time. Panels provide both cross-sectional data and time-series data. When correlated with other factors, panel data can provide useful longitudinal results that cross-sectional data cannot match.

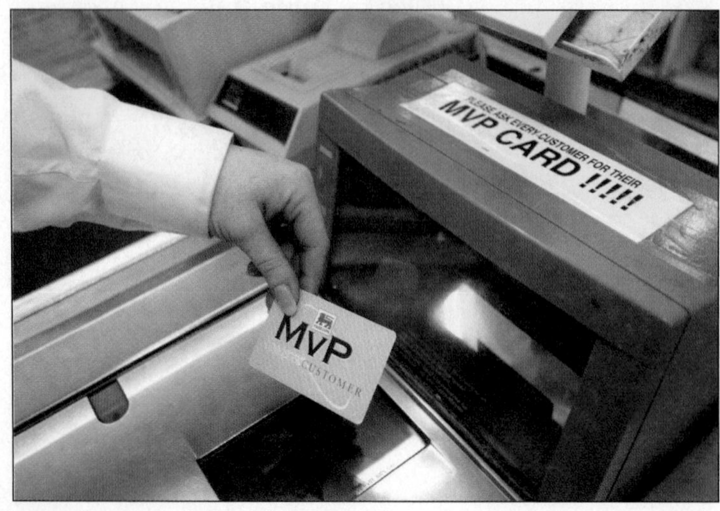

Loyalty programs such as this one at Food Lion stores provide valuable information on household purchasing behavior.
Source: Neil Redmond/AP Wide World Photos

There are several problems with panels, however. The most important is panel dropout (also called mortality). It is difficult for a marketing researcher to keep panel members sufficiently interested to remain on panels. Because panels often involve a fair amount of work answering a detailed survey multiple times, a second problem is that people who agree to be on panels are not always representative of the underlying population. This can particularly be a problem with Internet-based panels, which may draw a particular group of "fanatics." Finally, the researcher must ensure that being on a panel does not change the member's behavior, a problem sometimes called panel conditioning.

There are many types of panels:

- **Continuous reporting panels.** Some panels require the members to report all their purchases in certain product categories or to report other kinds of behavior as it occurs. An example is the Nielsen TV panel, which provides the ratings for the network and local shows. NFO Worldwide is the largest panel operator in the world. Through its prerecruited consumer panel and other specialized databases, NFO offers access to more than 550,000 U.S. households (more than 1.4 million people) and some 100,000 European households. Another example is comScore Media Metrix's panel of more than 2 million people whose Internet usage is monitored at home and at work.
- A special kind of continuous panel in a grocery-purchasing context is a **scanner panel**. Consumers are enlisted to allow A.C. Nielsen and Information Resources Inc. (IRI) to track their supermarket purchases through the electronic checkout scanners. The consumer scans in his or her bar-coded ID card, and all of the purchases following are put into a data file. When combined with in-store data, such as the existence of point-of-purchase displays, coupon usage, price paid, and, for some panels, TV advertising exposure, Nielsen and IRI can track consumer reaction to promotions, price changes, and new-product introductions. Scanner panels eliminate several of the problems typical of panels. In particular, conditioning and the nonrepresentativeness of the panels are mitigated because of the unobtrusive nature of the data collection process.

scanner panel
a collection of supermarket/drug store purchasing data of individual households obtained from electronic scanners in the stores

- **Special-purpose panels.** A company may want to set up a panel for a particular reason. For example, software companies often engage potential customers to be beta testers for new versions in late stages of development. A panel of users can be established only for this development period and then disbanded. The panel provides feedback to the company on bugs in the program, the clarity and accuracy of the operating manuals, and other product characteristics.

Experiments

In science, an experiment is the only true way to determine cause and effect. Marketing managers can track the sales response to a new advertising campaign. However, without controlling for other factors that could have also caused a sales change, it is impossible to determine how much of the change resulted from the advertising. The purpose of an experiment is to allow the marketing manager to conclusively show that a change in *x* produced *y*.

A marketing experiment has several important features:

- A **manipulation.** This is the marketing variable that is of central interest. It is called a manipulation because different levels or values of the variable are controlled by the researcher. For example, a company interested in finding out whether increasing its advertising budget by 25 percent would be profitable would choose some geographic areas in which to increase spending (the manipulation) and others in which to maintain the current level.

manipulation
in an experiment, the marketing variable that is of central interest and is experimentally controlled by the researcher

- A **control group.** A control group is a set of respondents or experimental units (e.g., cities) that receive the "normal" level of the manipulation. In other words, they are not subject to the experiment. The control group is used as a base against which the experimental group can be compared. Continuing the advertising example, the geographic areas receiving the current level of spending would be the control.

control group
in an experiment, a set of respondents or experimental units who receive the normal level of the manipulation and against which the experimental group is compared

- **External validity.** A key issue in evaluating experimental results is validity. One kind of validity, external validity, is the degree to which the results can be generalized to the real world or, more generally, to the target population. For example, if a marketing researcher tests different advertising copy targeted to a broad audience on undergraduate students only, the experiment may not be externally valid.

external validity
the ability to generalize experimental results to the real world or, more generally, the target population

- **Internal validity.** A second kind of validity, internal validity, is the degree to which the results found are actually caused by the experimental manipulation. For example, suppose a company increases advertising in one city (the manipulation) and maintains the same level in another (the control). Let us assume that the cities

internal validity
the degree to which experimental results are caused by the experimental manipulation

are perfectly matched in terms of buying habits, demographics, and other relevant characteristics and that the results would be externally valid. If the company also launches a promotional campaign in the test city but not in the control city, then the results of the advertising experiment are not internally valid because the increased sales could result from the advertising or the promotional campaign.

laboratory experiment
an experiment run in an artificial environment

field experiment
an experiment that takes place in a realistic environment

Experiments can be conducted in a laboratory or in the field. A **laboratory experiment** is run in an artificial environment such as a classroom or movie theater. The advantage of lab experiments is that they generally have high internal validity because the experimenter can control the environment easily. However, they usually have low external validity because the controlled environment does not replicate the real world. **Field experiments** take place in realistic environments such as an actual city. The advantage of field experiments is that they generally have high external validity, but they suffer from potential internal validity problems because the experimenter cannot control events in the real-world business environment.

Application Drug Advertising

The U.S. pharmaceutical industry spends nearly $5 billion on direct-to-consumer (DTC) advertising. The spending is controversial as shareholders wonder whether they are getting their money's worth and consumer advocates worry that patients will ask for prescriptions from their doctors that they do not need or, worse, are inappropriate. A group of Harvard Medical School researchers compared the drug-prescribing behavior of a control group in Quebec with very little exposure to U.S. TV exposure with Canada's English-speaking provinces where residents are estimated to spend about 30 percent of their watching time on American channels. The researchers analyzed two major ad campaigns for Amgen's Enbrel arthritis treatment and Schering Plough's antiallergy drug Nasonex and found no change in the difference in per-capita usage between the control and test groups from before the ad campaigns started. A third drug, Novartis's Zelnorm, briefly showed an increase in English-speaking provinces relative to Quebec, but the difference soon disappeared. While this study does not rule out the possibility that DTC advertising can generate prescriptions, it is an interesting example of a field experiment.[17]

Models and Simulations

Very different from focus groups are mathematical models developed to simulate a particular marketing problem. These are normally abstractions of the actual complexity of what is being modeled. For example, a researcher might develop a model assuming a mathematical relationship between two controllable marketing variables (such as price and advertising) and brand sales. The researcher knows that although these may be the main two variables affecting sales, several other factors (e.g., the weather, the salesperson's attitude toward the brand) also affect sales. Because these factors are not controllable, they are omitted from the model. Normally, a statistical method such as regression analysis (discussed later in this chapter) is used to estimate the assumed relationships.

Global Considerations

The general types of market research data and the set of techniques available obviously do not vary by country. However, particular sources will depend upon, for example, the quality of data collected by the relevant government. In addition, the application of certain approaches will be determined by local technological capabilities, cultural attitudes toward providing information, legal restrictions, and so on. For example, Internet-based surveys are common in the United States and other countries with high penetration rates of PC ownership. In Italy, where the penetration rate is only about 30 percent, online surveys would clearly be biased (unless the relevant population was PC owners who use the Internet).

Despite the tendency to feel that knowledge from one market can be transferred to another, you should ignore assumptions and hearsay about a market and find out for yourself. Following the general prescription noted earlier in this chapter, secondary sources should be consulted first, followed by primary research. Often companies will employ consultants or firms knowledgeable about the local market and facile in the language to ensure that questionnaires are translated properly. A good, low-cost approach is to use a local business school and sponsor projects for which students can obtain course credit. While it usually does not provide the final answer, such a study can be used to obtain a basic understanding of the market before hiring professional marketing researchers.

Some general issues that arise in global marketing research are:[18]

1. **The complexity of the research design.** Conducting research in different countries implies that you have to spend more time defining relevant units of analysis. For example, are you interested in Germany or western Europe? Market segments within Germany? Country boundaries may be the most convenient due to data availability, but they may not be appropriate for defining your problem.
2. **Difficulties in establishing comparability and equivalence.** Motor vehicle registrations, for example, may provide different data in different countries. Also, in some countries where companies provide cars to their executives, private ownership data may understate auto usage.
3. **Coordination of research and data collection across countries.** Surveys and data collection methods being used across countries and regions need to be standardized. This can add considerable cost and time to the execution of the work.
4. **Intrafunctional character of international marketing decisions.** The decisions involving which countries to enter involve manufacturing, finance, legal, and other parts of the business beyond marketing. This affects the nature of the research being done. Because pricing decisions may involve risk of currency fluctuations, for example, the research should consider customer decision making with respect to desired currency of transaction and sensitivity to short-term swings.

Potential and Forecasting

Two important applications of marketing research information are the calculations of **potential** and the development of **forecasts**. These quantities aid the marketing manager in setting quotas for the sales force, setting product objectives, and performing a number of other tasks. These calculations depend on both primary and secondary research information and are themselves used as foundations for marketing decision making.

potential
the maximum sales reasonably attainable under a given set of conditions within a specified period of time

forecasts
a prediction of a future quantity such as sales extrapolation Extending a line based on existing data outside the range of the data

market potential
the maximum sales reasonably attainable under a given set of conditions within a specified period of time

The terms *forecast* and *potential* are used in many different ways and are often confused. We use the following definitions:[19]

- **Market potential:** the maximum sales of a product category reasonably attainable under a given set of conditions within a specified period of time.
- **Market forecast:** the amount of sales of a product category expected to be achieved under a set of conditions within a specified period of time.
- **Sales potential/forecast:** the same concept but at the brand level.

Thus, potential is an upper limit or ceiling on category sales, whereas a forecast is what you expect to sell. Both are circumscribed by the assumptions that the market conditions remain stable (what economists call the *ceteris paribus* condition, or "all else remaining equal") and that the numbers produced are good only for a specified period of time (e.g., a forecast for the year 2011). Returning to the example at the beginning of the chapter, the managers at Toyota would be very interested in the potential market for automobiles (market potential), the potential for the Scion brand (sales potential), forecasted sales of automobiles (market forecast) and forecasted sales for the Scion brand (sales forecast). The two potential estimates give them some estimate of how large the market is for cars and its brand in its size/price category, whereas the forecasts help them plan manufacturing and distribution as well as estimate market share.

Market Potential: Basic Calculations

Market potential is one of the most difficult quantities to estimate because of the problems in developing a concrete number that people can agree on. Part of this difficulty results from the mechanics of the calculation, but part of it results from confusion over the notion of a ceiling or maximum amount that can be sold. Because estimates of market potential often bear little resemblance to current sales figures, these numbers are often viewed with skepticism.

However, market potential estimates have considerable value to marketing managers. They can be used to allocate resources over a product line so that products with the greatest potential receive more money for their marketing efforts. This may make more sense than allocating simply on the basis of current sales, which is a myopic approach. Products with higher estimated levels of market potential may also be given more aggressive objectives to achieve. As we will see in Chapter 13, estimates of market potential assist the sales manager in developing sales territories, assigning salespeople to those territories, and setting appropriate quotas. Depending on the situation, it may make more sense to develop territories that have equal potential so that the salespeople have equivalent chances of performing well and earning bonuses. An important use of market potential is strategic—when there is a large gap between actual and potential sales, the marketing manager should ask, "Why is there such a big difference?" Often such ruminations can lead to innovations in packaging, choosing new segments, or other activities that narrow the gap between a product category's actual and potential sales.

The general approach for estimating market potential has three steps:

1. *Determine the potential buyers or users of the product.* Using either primary or secondary marketing research information or judgment, the marketing manager must first establish who are the potential buyers of the product. These potential buyers should be defined broadly as any person or organization that has a need for the product, the resources to use the product, and the ability to pay for it. In fact, it might actually be easier to start with all end-buyer "units" and then subtract those who cannot buy the product. For example, apartment dwellers are not potential buyers of lawnmowers, diabetics are not potential customers for food products containing sugar, and law firms are not potential customers for supercomputers. This part of the analysis can be done judgmentally and often relies on the expertise and experience of the marketing manager.
2. *Determine how many individual customers are in the potential groups of buyers defined in step 1.* At this stage, the manager must use basic data such as how many households there are in a particular country, how many people live in apartments, and what percentage of the population has diabetes.
3. *Estimate the potential purchasing or usage rate.* This can be done by taking the average purchasing rate determined by surveys or other research or by assuming that the potential usage rate is characterized by heavy buyers. This latter approach assumes that all buyers of the category could potentially consume as much as heavy buyers.

The estimate of market potential is simply the product of step 2 times step 3, that is, the number of potential customers times their potential buying rate.

Application Disposable Diapers

An illustration of this method applied to the market for disposable diapers for babies in the United States is shown in Table 3.7. The answer to step 1 begins with all babies between the ages of 0 and 2.5 years (the average age of toilet training). Babies who are allergic to the lining should be subtracted from this total. Assume that research shows that 5 percent of all babies have such an allergy. Data obtained from the National Center for Health Statistics show that there were 4.3 million births in the United States in 2009 (precise figures are not necessary for potential calculations). The current infant mortality rate in the United States is about 1 percent, leaving about 4.26 million babies who can potentially wear disposable diapers. Subtracting another 5 percent leaves about 4.04 million babies. Data from Mediamark Research show that the heaviest users go through 9 or more diapers per day (assume 10), the heaviest medium users 7, and the heaviest light users 3. Assuming that the heaviest users are 0 to 1 year old, the medium users are 1 to 2 years old, and the light users are 2 to 3 years old (and only half the children 2 to 3 years old will need diapers at all), then the total market potential is 75 million diapers per day, or 27.4 billion diapers per year. This compares to actual sales of more than 19 billion units.[20] Thus, while there is some market potential left, the category has reached about 70 percent of its potential.

Table 3.7

Market Potential Illustration

Disposable Diapers in the United States

Step 1: Who are the potential consumers?

Babies 0–2.5 years old, minus those who are allergic to the liner and other materials

Step 2: How many are there?

Facts: 4.3 million births annually, an annual 1% mortality rate, and 5% allergic incidence, or 4.04 million 0–1 year old, 4.00 million 1–2 years old, and 3.96 million 2–3 years old

Step 3: How much can they consume?

0–1: 10 diapers per day

1–2: 7 diapers per day

2–3: 3 diapers per day

Market potential:

0–1 year old	4.04 m × 10	= 40.4 m
1–2 years old	4.0 m × 7	= 28.0 m
2–3 years old	(3.96 m × 3)/2*	= 6.6 m
Total/day		= 75 m
or		= 27.4 billion diapers per year

*Assumes one-half of the children 2–3 years old are toilet-trained and therefore do not need diapers.

Note that in calculating the market potential for disposable diapers, you do not subtract out the number of babies using cloth diapers. Unless they are allergic to the lining, they are part of the potential market for disposables because their parents *could* buy them but they are not. It is up to marketing managers to induce the switching.

The important insights from the calculation of market potential come from the steps of the analysis. In the first stages, the marketing manager must consider who the potential customers are. This activity creates a broadened perspective that often carries beyond the current boundaries of the target marketing efforts of the major competitors. For example, by considering that children might be potential consumers of seeds, Burpee developed a program aimed at creating young gardeners. The second insight comes from step 3, a consideration of the potential purchasing rate. One way to increase sales is to get customers to buy more. As we noted in Chapter 2, this market penetration strategy can be done with innovative and larger package sizes, promotions, or product enhancements. For example, when DVD players were first introduced, who suspected that families would eventually own two, three, or more of them? Therefore, the benefit from going through the market potential exercise is that the marketing manager often obtains a better understanding of two new routes to sales growth—new, untapped segments and greater per-capita purchasing quantities.

Sales Potential

As noted earlier, sales potential is the potential market size but at the specific brand level. Thus, one approach to estimating sales potential is to take the market potential estimate and multiply it by an optimistic prediction of the brand's market share for the relevant year.

An alternative way of thinking about potential is to work with two quantities that are commonly used by marketing managers in frequently-purchased product categories. These are called the Category Development Index (CDI) and the Brand Development Index (BDI). The CDI and BDI are defined for a particular geographic area. The CDI is defined in the following way:

$$\text{CDI} = \frac{\text{percentage of the category sales in a geographical area}}{\text{percentage of the country's population in the area}} \times 100$$

For example, assume that a particular city in a country accounts for 5 percent of its population. Assume next that that city accounts for 6 percent of the sales of a product

Table 3.8

Cellphone Sales/Price Data			
Year	Phone sales	Growth	Avg Price
2000	52.6	56.1	171
2001	53.4	1.5	162
2002	58.7	9.9	138
2003	70.5	20.1	130
2004	84.6	20	125
2005	104.5	23.5	130
2006	121	15.8	138
2007	134	10.7	143

(e.g., laundry detergent). The CDI is then 120 (6/5 × 100). The CDI thus shows whether the sales of a category are more or less proportionate to the population. A CDI over 100 demonstrates a greater propensity to buy the product relative to the population size. The BDI is computed similarly, but the numerator of the formula contains the sales of a brand rather than the category.

Although we cannot develop a specific number for sales potential, the relationship of BDI to CDI can tell us something about the sales potential in a market. A market with a high CDI but low BDI indicates that the category is selling better than the brand. This indicates that there is potential for the brand to perform better. If both the CDI and BDI are high, this is a very successful situation for the brand, but you have to question how much growth is left. A situation where the BDI is high but the CDI is low is obviously a good situation for the marketing manager in terms of the brand's performance. This situation may have potential if the low CDI can be increased through product development or new marketing strategies. The low–low combination might have potential if the CDI can be increased or if the marketing manager can obtain a disproportionate number of customers in the market by improving the BDI.

Forecasting

Consider the data shown in Table 3.8 on sales of cellular telephones in the United States from 2000–2007. Assume these data were available to a marketing manager in 2008, as there is often a lag from when final category sales are computed to when they are available for use. The data are plotted in Figure 3.4. As can be seen, the double-digit growth in the market starting in 2003 has slowed significantly in 2007 but was still a healthy 10.7 percent.

Figure 3.4

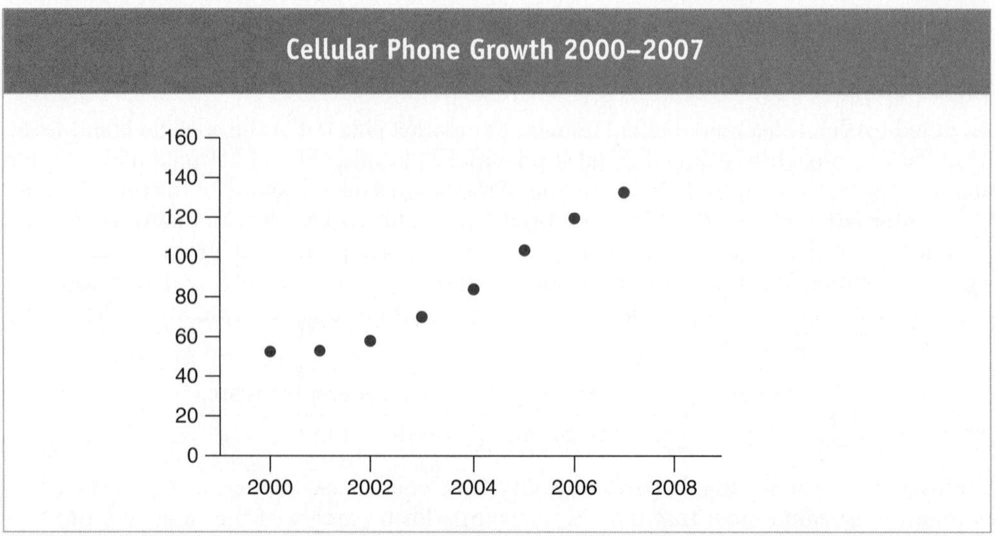

At this stage of the product life cycle, if you are a marketing manager for one of the major brands in the category (Apple, Nokia, etc.), market forecasts are important to understand whether growth in sales is going to go back to the 15 to 20 percent range or decline to single digits or less and to answer questions such as, "How much should we invest in advertising or promotion?" "How many should we produce (or purchase from a third party)?" The marketing plan you must create to answer these questions and others is outlined in Chapter 1. A key part of the situation analysis is developing some predictions or forecasts for a variety of market conditions that will exist in the U.S. market for 2010 and beyond. These include the following:

- A forecast of the likely consumer trends in adopting technology in the home.
- A forecast of the actions competitors will take.
- Predictions about the kinds of products that are substituting for traditional cellular phones such as the BlackBerry and iPhone.
- Predictions about the economic climate. Because cell phones are relatively inexpensive, a downturn in the economy might help sales.
- Predictions about the regulatory climate on issues such as eliminating the tying of phones to carriers in favor of allowing customers to choose phones they wish and then the carrier.

These important questions must be addressed for 2010 and every year for which marketing plans are developed. In addition, the marketing manager is interested in forecasts of specific quantities such as sales, market share, and profits. Sales forecasts are essential for production planning. Producing too few units results in retail shortages and opportunities for potential customers to buy competitors' products. Producing too many units increases inventory holding costs and often results in price cutting, thus lowering profit margins. Sales forecasts are also important for budgeting purposes. Part of the marketing plan is to develop a pro forma income statement. The top line of the statement, sales revenue, is produced from forecasted sales. Managers also like to do **scenario planning**, asking "what-if" questions. As a result, forecasts of alternative outcomes based on different assumptions about advertising spending, price levels, and competitor actions are important parts of planning.

scenario planning
planning that involves asking "what-if" questions to produce forecasts of alternative outcomes based on different assumptions about advertising spending, price levels, competitor actions, and other variables

Therefore, forecasting in general and market/sales forecasting in particular are important marketing research activities. Many different forecasting methods are available.[21] As Table 3.9 shows, we divide the methods into four types:

1. **Judgment methods,** which rely on pure opinion.
2. **Counting methods,** which use customer data.
3. **Time-series methods,** which use the kind of sales data shown in Table 3.8.
4. **Association/causal methods,** which try to develop statistical models relating market factors to sales.

judgment methods
sales forecasting methods that rely on pure opinion

counting methods
sales forecasting methods that rely on customer data

time-series methods
sales forecasting methods that rely on historical sales data

association/causal methods
a sales forecasting method that tries to develop statistical models relating market factors to sales

The remainder of this chapter focuses on further defining and describing these various forecasting methods.

Judgmental Methods

Naïve Extrapolation

Naïve extrapolation simply takes the most current sales and adds a judgmentally determined *x* percent, where *x* is the estimated percentage change in sales. For example, given the cell phone sales level of 134 million in 2007, the manager would have to determine what percentage to add to/subtract from it to predict sales in 2008. This could be the most recent growth rate from 2006 (15.8 percent), the average of the last three years (19.8 percent), or a percentage based on the recent sales change figures modified by some other information.

Naïve extrapolation
a judgment method of sales forecasting that takes the most current sales and adds a judgmentally determined x%, where x is the estimated percentage change in sales

Sales Force

In the **sales force method of forecasting**, a marketing manager would ask the salespeople calling on retail and corporate accounts to form their own forecasts of the sales in their territories. These would be summed to provide an overall forecast. This approach is

sales force method of forecasting
a judgment method of sales forecasting in which salespeople form their own forecasts of the sales in their territories and the marketing manager sums them up to provide an overall forecast

Table 3.9

Summary of Forecasting Methods						
	Judgment				Counting	
Dimensions	Naïve Extrapolation	Sales Force	Executive Opinion	Delphi	Market Testing	Market Survey
Time span	Short/medium term	Short/medium term	Short/medium term	Medium/long	Medium	Medium
Urgency	Rapid turnaround	Fast turnaround	Depends whether inside or outside company	Needs time	Needs time	Needs time
Quantitative skills needed	Minimal	Minimal	Minimal	Minimal	Moderate level	Yes
Financial resources	Very low	Low	Could be high if outside experts used	Could get high	High	High
Past data needed	Some	Not necessary	Not necessary	Not necessary	Not necessary	Not necessary
Accuracy	Limited	Highly variable	Poor if one individual; better if a group	Best under dynamic conditions	Good for new products	Limited
	Time Series				Association/Causal	
Moving Average	Exponential Smoothing	Extrapolation	Correlation	Regression	Leading Indicators	Econometric
Short/medium	Short/medium	Short/medium/long	Short/medium/long	Short/medium/long	Short/medium/long	Short/medium/long
Fast turnaround	Fast turnaround	Fast turnaround	Fast turnaround	Moderately fast	Moderately fast	Needs time
Minimal	Minimal	Basic skills	Basic skills	Basic skills	Basic skills	High level
Low	Low	Low	Moderate	Moderate/high	Moderate	High
Necessary	Necessary	Necessary	Necessary	Necessary	Necessary	Necessary
Good only in stable environment	Good in short run	Good for trends, stable time series	Highly variable	Can be accurate if explained variance is high	Moderately accurate at best	Best in stable environment

Source: David M. Georgoff and Robert G. Murdick, "Manager's Guide to Forecasting," *Harvard Business Review*, January–February 1986, pp. 110–20. Copyright © 1996 by the President and Fellows of Harvard College. Reprinted by permission.

usually justified by the fact that the sales force is close to customers and is therefore in a good position to understand buying habits. On the other hand, salespeople might underestimate sales if their quotas are based on forecasts, or they might be overly optimistic to impress the sales manager.

executive opinion method of forecasting
a judgment method of sales forecasting in which the marketing manager relies on his or her own opinion to predict sales, based on his or her experience and knowledge or consultations with internal or external experts

Executive Opinion

In the **executive opinion method of forecasting**, the marketing manager might simply rely on his or her own opinion to predict sales based on experience and other qualitative knowledge gained from reading trade publications and talking to industry representatives at trade shows. Alternatively, the manager might consult with internal or external experts. There are consultants who specialize in different industries and provide a variety of forecasts (such as the Gartner Group and Millward Brown Intelliquest for computers).

Delphi method of forecasting
a judgment method of sales forecasting that relies on a jury of experts formed from a diverse population to provide individual estimates of forecasted sales, which then are collated and refined in order to produce a final number

Delphi Method

The **Delphi method of forecasting** is implemented by forming a jury of experts from a diverse population. For video games, this might include consultants, marketing managers, and distributors or retailers. These people are sent a questionnaire and asked to provide an estimate of 2008 sales and a justification for the number. The answers are collated by the company or a research firm and the information redistributed to the panel members. Given the other members' responses and their reasoning, the members are asked to revise their estimates. Usually, the second round produces convergence on a number. This method is also useful to forecast the demand for new products and technologies for which there are no available data.

Counting Methods

Market Testing

The **market testing method of forecasting** uses primary data collection methods to predict sales. Focus groups, in-depth interviews, or other methods are used to estimate the likely demand for a product. This method is often used in new-product forecasting. A marketing manager would be unlikely to use this approach to forecast market or brand demand but might use it for a new model that was being launched.

market testing method of forecasting
a counting method of sales forecasting that uses primary data collection methods, such as focus groups and in-depth interviews, to predict sales

Market Surveys

In many cases, companies use the **market survey method of forecasting**, using purchase intention questions, for example, to attempt to predict demand. The surveys often use a 10-point scale, with 1 meaning nearly certain not to purchase and 10 meaning nearly certain to purchase. The company or research firm must estimate the cutoff for counting the response as a forecasted sale. The Motorola cell phone marketing manager could administer this survey to a sample of households to estimate consumer demand, to purchasing agents in companies to estimate corporate demand, and to retailers and distributors to estimate sales through various channels.

market survey method of forecasting
a counting method of sales forecasting that relies on surveys to predict demand

Time-Series Methods

Moving Average

The **moving average method of forecasting** is a simple method for taking the data shown in Table 3.8 and using averages of historical sales figures to make a forecast. The researcher must decide how many years (or, in general, periods) of data will be used to form the forecast. Assuming a three-year moving average, the forecast for 2008 would use the average of sales from 2005, 2006, and 2007: 119.8 million units. The forecast for 2009 would drop the 2005 sales figure and add the 2008 sales figure when it became available. Obviously, the merits of the method are its ease of implementation and low cost. On the downside, any sales series must adjust for trends or the forecasts will always be too low (such as in this case of a rising trend) or too high (falling trend).

moving average method of forecasting
a time-series method of sales forecasting that uses the averages of historical sales figures to make a forecast

Exponential Smoothing

The **exponential smoothing method of forecasting** also relies on the historical sales data and is slightly more complicated than the moving average. The formula for a simple exponentially smoothed forecast is

$$PS_{t+1} = aS_t + (1 - a)\mathrm{PS}_t$$

where *PS* is the predicted sales in a period and *S* is the actual sales. In other words, an exponentially smoothed forecast for period $t + 1$ is a combination of the current period's sales and the current period's forecast. The smoothing parameter a is between 0 and 1 and can be empirically determined from the historical sales data. Exponential smoothing is close to moving average forecasting, but it includes exponentially declining weights on the past sales values, as opposed to the latter's equal-weighted scheme. Assuming a high value of $a = 0.9$ (because of the rapid increases in sales, making recent sales more important) and the moving average forecast for 2006 of 86.5 million units (based on 2003–2005 sales), the 2008 forecast would be 0.9 × 134.0 million (2007 actual sales) + 0.1 × 86.5 million (2006 forecasted sales) = 129.3 million units. This number would then be updated to create forecasts for 2009, 2010, etc.

exponential smoothing method of forecasting
a time-series method of sales forecasting that relies on historical sales data, like the moving averages method, but also uses exponentially declining weights based on past sales values

Extrapolation

It is basic human nature to linearly extrapolate data. When a baseball player has an outstanding early season, announcers and writers always say, "At this pace, he will hit..." The assumption is that he will keep up the same pace. The same holds for sales forecasting. Consider Figure 3.4, the graph of the cell phone sales data over time. Time-series

extrapolation
extending a line based on existing data outside the range of the data

extrapolation simply extends the line into the future. Alternatively, if you are familiar with regression analysis, you could analyze the following simple regression:

$$S = a + b\text{Time}$$

where Time is simply the numbers 1–8 for each time period 2000–2007. The parameter b is the slope of the line through these data observations. If this calculation is done for all eight years of the cell phone data (using an Excel spreadsheet), the estimate of b is 12.6, or an average increase of 12.6 million units per year. The estimate of a, the spot where the line crosses the y-axis, is 28.2. Therefore, the forecast for 2008 would then be 12.6×9 (the value of Time for the year 2009) plus 28.2, or 144.3 million units, a 6.9 percent increase in sales over the 2007 figure. Note, however, that the estimate of b is an average over the whole time series of sales. As you can see in Figure 3.4, the sales of cell phones have had periods of both rapid and slow growth over the length of the data. More sophisticated forms of extrapolation could be used, such as a variety of nonlinear approaches that could account for all eight years of data without the averaging problem. As we have seen, linear extrapolation can be dangerous, particularly in a category with various ups and downs.

Association/Causal Methods

Correlation

A correlation is a number between -1 and $+1$, indicating the relationship between two variables. If one variable is sales, the correlation would indicate the strength of the association between sales and the other variable chosen. A high positive correlation (near 1) indicates that as the variable changes, sales change at approximately the same rate. Although the correlation itself does not produce a forecast, the **correlation method of forecasting** can be useful for detecting variables that are indicators of changes in sales.

correlation method of forecasting
an association/causal method of sales forecasting in which a correlation between two variables is used to indicate the strength of the association

Regression Analysis

Regression analysis is a generalization of the time-series extrapolation model that includes independent variables other than time. Normally, the marketing manager selects variables that he or she believes have a causal effect on sales, such as price, advertising, demographic, and macroeconomic variables. For example, in the cell phone market, the variables predicting market demand might include average price, the number of models available, and marketing effort such as advertising and the number of distribution channels.

regression analysis
an association/causal method of sales forecasting in which the time-series extrapolation model is generalized to include independent variables other than simply time

Leading Indicators

Economists use certain macroeconomic variables to forecast changes in the economy. When changes in these variables occur before changes in the economy and they are thought to cause those changes, they are called **leading indicators**. Because replacement phones in particular are discretionary purchases, one such indicator for cell phones might be unemployment. Other leading indicators might be measures of the general health of the U.S. economy.

leading indicators
an association/causal method of sales forecasting in which certain macroeconomic variables are used to forecast changes in the economy, based on the fact that changes in these variables occur before changes in the economy

Econometric Models

Econometric models are large-scale, multiple-equation regression models that are rarely used in product forecasting. They are often used to predict the performance of a country's economy or a particularly large business sector such as the demand for all manufactured goods.

econometric models
an association/causal method of sales forecasting that involves the use of large-scale, multiple-equation models most often used to predict the economic performance of a country or a particularly large business sector

A Tip

It has been found that taking the average of a set of forecasts using disparate methods outperforms any one approach. This finding is intuitive: diversification of forecasts, as in a portfolio of stocks, reduces the unique risk associated with any one approach. Because most forecasts are judgment based, checking a forecast with some other method is a good idea. For example, using expert judgment, Jupiter/Media Metrix, a well-known Internet research firm, forecasted that consumers would spend more than $400 million buying clothing online by the year 2000. The reality was that they spent about $5 billion according to Forrester Research. This was probably one of the few conservative forecasts made about the Internet in 1999.

Executive Summary

Key learning points in this chapter include the following:

- Marketing research is critical to developing a marketing plan and, therefore, to an understanding of the market in which your product or service competes. It is impossible to develop a sound marketing strategy without some form of marketing research.
- There are two kinds of marketing research information. Primary data are those that are collected specifically with your research topic in mind; secondary data were initially collected for some other reason.
- It is always advisable to begin a marketing research project by searching for useful secondary sources of information.
- Secondary sources of information can be internal or external to the organization. A significant amount of useful external information can be found on the Internet.
- Primary data sources include informal sources; qualitative sources such as focus groups; and quantitative sources such as surveys, panels, and experiments.
- Market potential is the maximum amount of sales obtainable in a product category at a point in time. Estimates of market potential guide the marketing manager in exploring potential new segments and new ways to increase consumption rates.
- Forecasts are made for expected sales, profit, market share, technology, or other data of interest. A variety of methods for developing forecasts include judgmental, counting (customer data–based), time series (historical sales data), and association/causal (identifying key factors affecting sales). It is always useful to take the average of a set of forecasts developed using disparate techniques.

Chapter Questions

1. Suppose that McDonald's was considering bringing a new kind of hamburger to its stores. What kind of research would it need to do in order to have some confidence that the new product would sell well?
2. I am interested in finding out if the demand for this book (new, not "pre-owned" copies) is sensitive to higher or lower prices. Design an experiment that you could run in the campus bookstore to determine this.
3. Pick a product that is used in everyday life. Observe your roommate, spouse, or some other person's use of this product. Ask him or her questions about his or her brand loyalty, what he or she likes/dislikes about it, and anything else you want to know. How does the information obtained differ from what you would get if you administered a survey?
4. Microsoft is planning to introduce a new PC operating system to replace Windows 7. What kind of research would it need to do in order to have confidence that the new software would sell well?
5. What are the trade-offs among all the kinds of research described in this chapter? Suppose you worked for a small startup company with a small research budget. Which of these kinds of research would be the most valuable?
6. Other than forecasting sales, what other uses are there for forecasting methods?

Key Learning Points

In this chapter, the reader will learn how to analyze buyers in consumer markets. The key learning points include:

- The concept and activity of market segmentation
- Issues in implementing market segmentation strategies
- Understanding why consumers make purchase decisions, that is, the motives that drive buying behavior
- Understanding how consumers make purchase decisions, that is, the mechanism used to make purchases
- The importance of understanding where and when consumers purchase
- Implications for global and technology-based markets

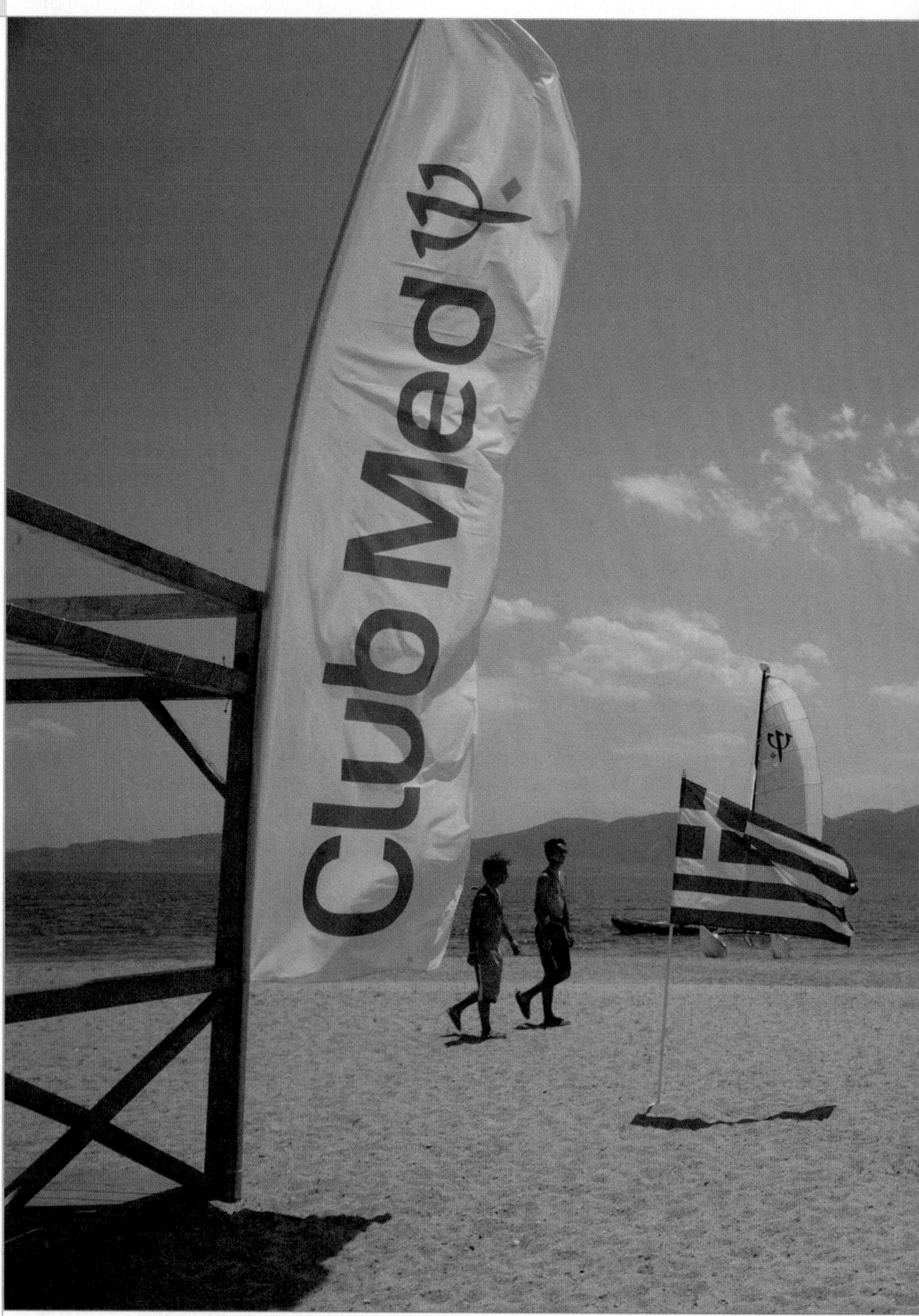

Club Med needs to study its customers intensively to keep up with changing tastes in vacations.
Source: Yannis Kontos/Getty Images, Inc–Liaison

Analyzing Consumer Behavior

Chapter Brief

Club Méditerranée, better known as Club Med, began as a sports association in France in 1950.[1] Founded by a former member of the Belgian Olympic team and some of his friends, the first Club Med was a vacation village in Majorca, Spain, with an initial membership of 2,500. It was a village of tents where members slept in sleeping bags and assisted in cooking meals and cleaning. There was a staff of five sports instructors.

A vacation at a Club Med was planned to be a unique experience. It allowed vacationers, generally city dwellers, to escape from the routine of their daily lives. Each Club Med location offered its own society free of the need for money, with casual dress and no telephones, radios, or newspapers. People could mingle freely without the societal and class barriers that often separated them in their normal lives. The employees were also unusual, called *gentil organisateurs* (GOs), or "nice organizers." They provided service to the vacationers (*gentil membres* [GMs], or "nice members") and acted as sports instructors, entertainers, and confidants, generally behaving as GMs. No tipping was allowed. Because of this free and open atmosphere, Club Med became closely identified with a swinging, hedonistic lifestyle.

By the mid-1970s, Club Med operated 77 villages in 24 countries, with 19 ski villages, 35 summer villages, 26 year-round villages, and 2 winter seaside villages (some villages served several purposes) and was the largest vacation organization of its kind. More than 500,000 people visited the villages yearly; nearly half were French, 18 percent were from North and Central America, and about 25 percent were from other western European countries. By the late 1980s, visitors had increased to 1.8 million each year, and there were 114 villages in 37 countries.

However, problems arose in the 1980s and have continued to this day. Vacationers who went to Club Med in the 1970s as singles had children in the 1980s. The Club Med image, firmly etched in prospective customers' minds, was inconsistent with what families were looking for. When Club Med changed many of its locations to be more hospitable to children, they were not what singles were looking for. Increased concern about AIDS, more competitors (e.g., cruises), and significant demand for more intellectually oriented vacations also contributed to Club Med's financial losses in the 1990s. To add to its miseries, post-9/11 reductions in travel resulted in the closure of 17 of its now 120 resorts.

To improve its market position, Club Med clearly needs to study its customers. Marketing research has shown that while awareness continues to be high (92 percent in the United States), the company has changed its positioning several times within the last few years by attempting to find the "right" approach. In 2002, with the "Wanna play?" campaign, it emphasized the "de-stressing" benefit of a Club Med vacation. In 2005, the theme changed to an emotional one building on the concept that Club Med is a vacation resort where people travel great distances to get closer. In addition, the company is opening a line of deluxe hotels beginning with the Riad in Marrakesh, Morocco. In 2008 Club Med launched a new advertising campaign, "Where Happiness Means the World," reflecting Club Med's upmarket experience and a value strategy over a volume strategy.

The company needs to understand:

- Who are the customers visiting its various locations? Who are the customers who are not going to Club Med but taking vacations? Who are the customers who have gone to Club Med once but have not returned?
- What benefits are the various types of customers looking for when they take vacations in general and at Club Med in particular?
- What criteria do people use in choosing vacations?
- What are the perceptions that potential consumers have of Club Med and its competitors?
- Do customers use travel agents or make the reservations themselves?
- Which types of customers travel at different times of the year?

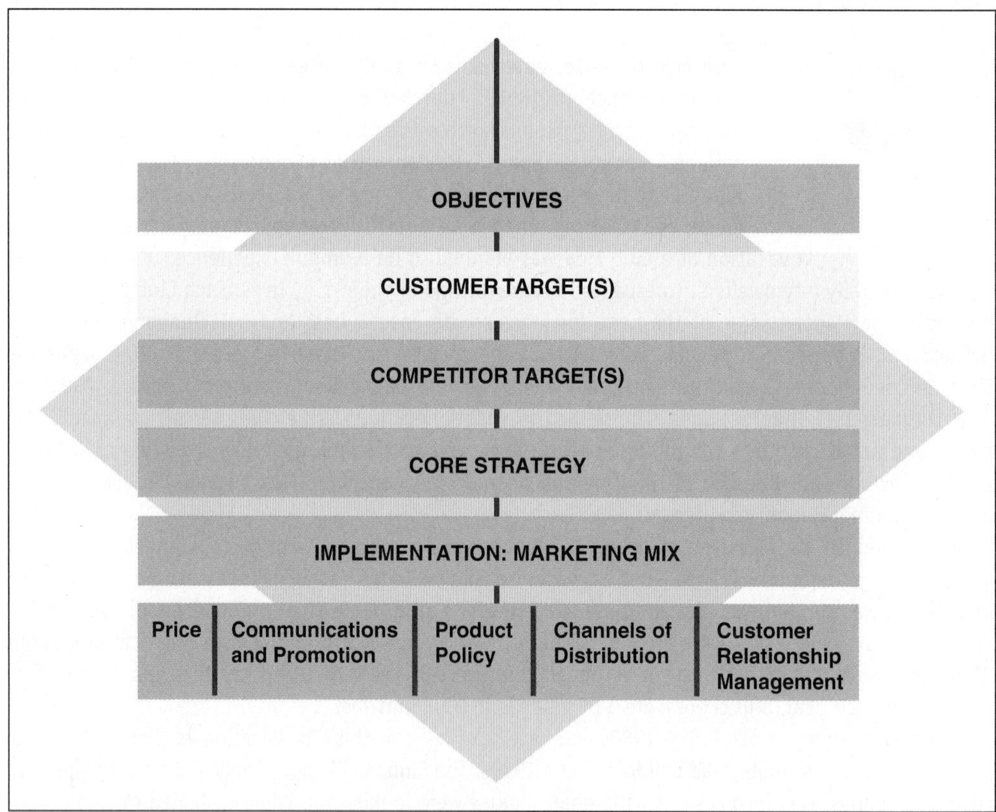

The marketing research methods described in Chapter 3 are used to analyze one of the key external constituents a marketing manager must consider in developing a marketing plan and strategy—customers. Customer analysis is one of the key building blocks on which the strategy rests. No strategy can be developed without an up-to-date understanding of customer behavior. Besides being essential to applying the customer targets, part of the strategic framework developed in Chapter 2 (see the marketing strategy diagram), a customer analysis is fundamental to the market and customer orientations described in Chapter 1.

A customer analysis addresses five questions that are the focus of this chapter:

1. *Who* are the current and potential customers for the product or service?
2. *Why* do they buy?
3. *How* do they make purchasing decisions?

4. *Where* do they buy the product or service; that is, what channels of distribution are used?
5. *When* do they buy? What time of day, month, year etc. do they purchase?

The objective is to develop a complete picture of customer behavior in the relevant product category or market.

Keep in mind that a customer analysis should include more than just current customers. Although it is certainly important to understand your current customer base as well as you can, several other groups are important as well:

- Analyzing competitors' customers may help you understand why they are buying competitors' products instead of yours and provides some ideas for stimulating brand switching.
- Analyzing former customers helps you understand weaknesses in your product or service operations.
- Analyzing people who have never purchased the product helps you understand how to expand the market and achieve sales closer to market potential.

Thus, in this chapter we use the term *customer* in a general sense, to refer to the four possible types of customers and all the concepts developed apply to all potential customers. In addition, we focus on analyzing consumers, individuals, and households purchasing products and services.[2] Note that understanding consumers is important even if you are in an industrial product or service business, because your demand is derived from underlying consumer demand. For example, if you are a plastics manufacturer and the auto industry is a major customer, it is important for you to understand consumer behavior (or your customers' customers) toward autos, in order to develop products that meet your customers' needs, such as child-proof cupholders.

Who Are the Consumers?

The analysis required to answer this question addresses one of the key principles in marketing: **market segmentation**. Market segmentation breaks mass markets into segments that have different behaviors or needs. In grouping customers by many different variables or characteristics, the aim is to group customers that differ from one another but show considerable similarity within the group. Therefore, they should be treated differently in terms of marketing variables, such as advertising, and often in terms of product attributes. In other words, there are two questions that help to determine whether a particular segmentation scheme is useful:

market segmentation breaking mass marketing into segments that have different buying habits; also refers to the decision about which customer groups a company will pursue for a particular brand or product line

1. Do the people in different segments behave differently toward the product or service?
2. Would we use different marketing elements (marketing mix such as price, communications, etc.) with the different segments?

There are many examples of how segmentation is applied in marketing. Diet cola brands such as Diet Coke and Diet Pepsi exist for consumers who want the attributes of a cola but also want a low-calorie drink. Special prices are often used as inducements for particular market segments. For example, matinee movie prices attract customers during the lower-volume daytime period. Airlines in Asia offer special prices by age, race, and gender. Air India has a "ladies' fare" program offering 33 percent discounts to women traveling between India and shopping destinations such as Dubai, Hong Kong, and Singapore. Procter & Gamble introduced Tide Basic in 2009 that lacks some of the cleaning capabilities but costs 20 percent less that addresses the needs of a specific customer segment. Thus, the concept of market segmentation has become ubiquitous in marketing.

It is important to separate the act of segmenting the market from the act of choosing which segment or segments to pursue actively. The former, the topic of this part of this chapter, is where the marketing manager considers the many possible ways to segment the market for the product. In doing this, the manager often uses both secondary and primary marketing research (discussed in Chapter 3) to develop profiles of the customers and their buying habits. The act of choosing which segments to pursue is called selecting the target market and is part of the marketing strategy covered in Chapter 2.

The concept of segmentation is important because it implies an understanding that customers are heterogeneous. The idea that only some customers might be interested in your product and are worth targeting is also important because it has implications for marketing efficiency and effectiveness. A segmentation approach to the market rather than a mass-marketing approach (i.e., marketing to all customers and letting the purchasers self-select) is efficient because money is spent only on those whom the manager has determined are potential customers. Thus, less money is wasted on customers who have a low probability of buying the product, which is important in an era when budgets are being tightened.

At the same time, segmentation is more effective than mass marketing because of the tailored nature of the programs. For example, toothpaste users tend to seek decay prevention, teeth whitening, or social (breath-related) benefits. A mass-marketing approach would develop one product and one communications program that attempted to bundle all benefits simultaneously. As a result, none of the segments would necessarily be satisfied because the typical consumer in each would not feel that the product was right for him or her. A segmentation approach would develop separate advertising campaigns focusing on each benefit in media used by the members of each segment. Although this approach can be expensive, the overall response in terms of sales will be better. The sum of the three segments' responses to communications that are tailored to their needs will be greater than if the same amount is spent on a mass-market campaign.

Interestingly, in some situations, single-customer segments make sense. The first situation is one in which the number of customers is small. For example, Airbus's marketing of its new A380 jumbo jet considers each potential customer individually, given how few there are. The second situation is the current trend toward **one-to-one marketing** and **mass customization**.[3] In this case, even when there are too many customers to treat each one separately, companies attempt to give the customer the perception that he or she is being treated as a unique segment through sending individualized communications (one-to-one marketing) or personalized products and services (mass customization). This trend toward personalization is due to the fact that many marketers feel that even well-defined market segments are heterogeneous and customers are lumped together with similarities on one or two dimensions but quite different buying behavior. Personalization is implemented through investments in information technology. For example, it can be through an information technology link to a manufacturing facility, such as Lands' End's system for custom-fitting men's chino pants. Alternatively, some companies create a database of information from previous transactions and use that information to create a custom-tailored feel for the next transaction. For example, Ritz-Carlton hotels keep electronic files on customer tastes and use the information to make the experience feel unique. Note that even in the context of personalization it is still necessary to understand how the segments are different. For example, Nike's personalization site, Nikeid.com, offers some choice in basic styles but not styles that would suit everyone's tastes.

one-to-one marketing
also called mass customization, a marketing process whereby a company takes a product or service that is widely developed and develops a system for customizing it to each customer's specifications

mass customization
also called one-to-one marketing, a new marketing process whereby a company takes a product or service that is widely marketed and develops a system for customizing it to each customer's specifications

Segmentation Variables

In an ideal world, marketers would segment based on consumer needs or benefits sought. However, in practice, marketers typically describe segments based on customer characteristics. Hence, the task facing the marketing manager is to identify variables that describe the customers in terms of their inherent characteristics, called **descriptors**, and to link those variables to customer behavior toward the product or service. Both kinds of information are needed. For example, it is insufficient to note that 50 percent of the population are women and 50 percent are men. What is useful is to know that *50 percent of the purchasers of your product* are women and 50 percent are men. This information links characteristics to behavior.

descriptors
variables that describe customers in terms of their inherent characteristics

The kinds of variables that usually serve as descriptors are shown in Table 4.1. As can be seen, they fall into three major categories:

1. **Geographic.** The underlying rationale is that tastes vary by part of the world, part of a country, or even between cities and rural areas.
2. **Demographic.** Income, age, occupation, education, race, and other variables have all been found to influence different kinds of consumer buying habits.
3. **Psychographic.** These variables characterize the psychological differences among people in terms of lifestyles, personalities, and social class. People with identical demographic profiles can have quite different personalities and lifestyle interests and hence different interests in products and services.

Table 4.1

Consumer Market Segmentation Variables	
Descriptor Variables	
Geographic	
Region	Pacific, Mountain, West North Central, West South Central, East North Central, East South Central, South Atlantic, Middle Atlantic, New England
City or metro size	Under 4,999, 5,000–19,999, 20,000–49,999, 50,000–99,999, 100,000–249,999, 250,000–499,999, 500,000–999,999, 1,000,000–3,999,999, 4,000,000 or over
Density	Urban, suburban, rural
Climate	Northern, southern
Demographic	
Age	Under 6, 6–11, 12–19, 20–34, 35–49, 50–64, 65+
Family size	1–2, 3–4, 5+
Family life cycle	Young, single; young, married, no children; young, married, youngest child under 6; young, married, youngest child 6 or over; older, married, with children; older, married, no children under 18; older, single; other
Gender	Male, female
Income	Under $9,999, $10,000–$14,999, $15,000–$19,999, $20,000–$29,999, $30,000–$49,999, $50,000–$99,999, $100,000 and over
Occupation	Professional and technical; managers, officials, and proprietors; clerical, sales; craftspeople; forepersons; operatives; farmers; retired; students; homemakers; unemployed
Education	Grade school or less; some high school; high school graduate; some college; college graduate
Religion	Catholic, Protestant, Jewish, Muslim, Hindu, other
Race	White, Black, Asian
Generation	Baby boomers, Generation X
Nationality	North American, South American, British, French, German, Italian, Japanese
Social class	Lower lowers, upper lowers, working class, middle class, upper middles, lower uppers, upper uppers
Psychographic	
Lifestyle	Straights, swingers, longhairs
Personality	Compulsive, gregarious, authoritarian, ambitious

Source: Philip Kotler and Kevin Lane Keller (2009), *Marketing Management,* 13th ed. (Upper Saddle River, NJ: Prentice Hall), p. 214. Electronically reproduced by permission of Pearson Education, Inc.

For example, Club Med would use country of origin (United States, Europe, etc.), demographics (young marrieds without children, single, families), and psychographics (hedonists, extroverts) to help target likely prospects.

The kinds of behavioral variables that can be used to form segments are shown in Table 4.2. The most popular variables are benefits and usage rate. Usage rate or quantity is obviously important to a marketing manager because it measures how the consumer is actually behaving. Each purchasing level generates its own set of questions. Are heavy users already saturated, or is there more potential in that group? Can medium users be bumped up to the heavy group? Are light users simply brand switchers? Benefit segmentation is a useful way to segment because it relates fundamentally to why people buy products and recognizes the fact that consumers buy the same product for many different reasons.

Table 4.2

Consumer Market Segmentation Variables	
Behavioral Variables	
Occasions	Regular occasion, special occasion
Benefits	Quality, service, economy, speed
User status	Nonuser, ex-user, potential user, first-time user, regular user
Usage rate	Light user, medium user, heavy user
Loyalty status	None, medium, strong, absolute
Buyer readiness stage	Unaware, aware, informed, interested, desirous, intending to buy
Attitude toward product	Enthusiastic, positive, indifferent, negative, hostile

Source: Based on Philip Kotler and Kevin Lane Keller (2009), *Marketing Management,* 13th ed. (Upper Saddle River, NJ: Prentice Hall), pp. 223–225. Electronically reproduced by permission of Pearson Education, Inc.

Examples of how the descriptor and behavioral variables can be linked are shown in Tables 4.3 and 4.4. The table relates different stages in the family life cycle and geography (Table 4.1) to usage of dental accessories (e.g., dental floss, oral rinse, denture products). The numbers in the table are index numbers, where 100 equals average consumption. As can be seen, households with young children less than 6 years old (Startup Families) in Cosmopolitan Centers are not good customers for dental accessories (index = 43), while Senior Couples tend to be heavy consumers in nearly every geographic territory. Table 4.4 examines product penetration rates by household size. The first column, Item Penetration, is the percentage of households purchasing the product (e.g., 69.9 percent of households purchase dough products). The other entries are indexes that again give relative penetration information. So, for example, two-person households are about

Table 4.3

Consumption Index: Dental Accessories

Behavior Stage	Cosmopolitan Centers	Affluent Suburban Spreads	Comfortable Country	Struggling Urban Areas	Modest Working Towns	Plain Rural Living	Total
WITH CHILDREN:							
Startup Families HHs with young children only (<6)	43	99	53	56	46	22	54
Small-Scale Families small HHs with older children (6+)	96	82	66	92	86	67	78
Younger Bustling Families large HHs with children (6+), OH < 40	83	51	71	210	60	67	86
Older Bustling Families large HHs with children (6+), OH 40+	81	87	76	78	91	62	79
NO CHILDREN:							
Young Transitionals Any size HHs, no children <35	60	34	27	30	33	33	37
Independent Singles 2-person HHs, no children, 35–64	139	107	77	64	82	91	94

Continued							
Behavior Stage	Cosmopolitan Centers	Affluent Suburban Spreads	Comfortable Country	Struggling Urban Areas	Modest Working Towns	Plain Rural Living	Total
Senior Singles							
2-person HHs, no children, 65+	152	147	130	110	107	74	112
Established Couples							
2-person HHs, no children, 35–54	123	105	88	73	99	103	99
Empty Nest Couples							
2-person HHs, no children, 55–64	207	167	159	131	174	116	157
Senior Couples							
2-person HHs, no children, 65+	208	228	233	104	210	143	193
Total	120	115	105	86	97	82	100

Very High Consumption (150+) High Consumption (120–149) Average Consumption = 100

Source: Progressive Grocer by Nielsen. Copyright 2009 by Nielsen Business Media. Reproduced by permission of Nielsen Business Media in the format Textbook via Copyright Clearance Center

twice as likely to buy dairy products as single-person households (31.9 percent versus 15.7 percent).

Demographic variables cover a wide variety of household descriptors. A currently popular age-related type of segmentation, called **cohort analysis**, develops profiles of

cohort analysis
an analysis that develops age-related profiles of each generation to segment the market

Table 4.4

Product Preferences by Stage in Family Life Cycle					
Item Penetration and Lifestage Index	Item Penetration	Household Size 1 Member	2 Members	3–4 Members	5+ Members
Total Food and Beverages	**100.0%**	**16.3%**	**32.8%**	**36.5%**	**14.4%**
Alcoholic Beverages	**62.4**	**22.3**	**42.7**	**26.9**	**8.1**
Beer	41.8	21.6	38.2	30.8	9.4
Coolers	15.0	11.6	34.4	36.7	17.3
Liquor	29.8	24.4	45.2	23.5	6.9
Wine	38.6	21.8	46.5	24.8	6.9
Dairy	**99.6**	**15.7**	**31.9**	**37.3**	**15.1**
Butter and margarine	93.6	16.5	35.5	34.8	13.3
Cheese	96.7	14.2	32.0	38.3	15.5
Cottage cheese, sour cream, toppings	82.1	17.0	35.5	34.3	13.2
Dough products	69.9	10.8	29.2	42.6	17.4
Eggs	93.0	15.8	33.9	35.4	14.8
Juices, drinks—refrigerated	77.5	19.1	32.7	35.4	12.8
Milk	97.2	15.4	30.0	38.2	16.4
Pudding, desserts	26.8	19.1	36.2	33.9	10.8
Snacks, spreads, dips	56.0	19.1	34.7	34.7	11.5
Yogurt	75.6	16.7	30.8	37.6	14.9
Deli—Refrigerated (dressings, salads, prepared foods)	**94.8**	**16.5**	**31.5**	**37.9**	**14.1**
Grocery (Food)	**100.0**	**15.9**	**32.4**	**37.0**	**14.7**
Baby food	15.8	3.1	20.0	55.7	21.2
Baking mixes	82.0	13.7	31.2	38.6	16.4

(continued)

Continued

Item Penetration and Lifestage Index	Item Penetration	1 Member	Household Size 2 Members	3–4 Members	5+ Members
Baking supplies	88.5	14.1	32.5	38.0	15.3
Bread and baked goods	99.0	15.9	32.5	36.6	14.9
Breakfast food	75.0	12.2	26.3	43.1	18.4
Candy	97.3	17.9	33.2	35.3	13.7
Carbonated beverages	96.6	15.7	32.5	37.9	13.9
Cereal	95.5	14.7	29.3	38.3	17.6
Coffee	73.1	18.6	39.4	30.8	11.1
Condiments, gravies, sauces	97.7	13.2	31.3	39.0	16.5
Cookies	93.1	16.4	31.6	37.0	15.0
Crackers	93.7	17.1	32.3	36.6	14.0
Desserts, gelatins, syrup	83.7	14.6	29.9	39.1	16.4
Flour	55.8	15.8	36.3	34.1	13.8
Fruit—canned	81.7	19.1	35.7	32.4	12.8
Fruit—dried	67.1	13.5	27.2	40.3	19.0
Gum	63.3	14.0	30.2	40.6	15.3
Jams, jellies, spreads	86.8	18.6	33.3	34.0	14.0
Juices, drinks	94.3	14.1	27.2	41.0	17.7
Meal starters	1.4	13.7	30.1	37.2	19.0
Nuts	81.9	21.0	40.3	29.7	9.0
Packed milk and modifiers	77.5	15.7	32.7	36.2	15.4
Pasta	85.6	12.7	30.5	39.7	17.0
Pet food	71.0	19.9	39.8	30.9	9.4
Pickles, olives, relish	81.8	16.8	34.6	35.0	13.5
Prepared food—dry mixes	90.6	10.5	26.6	43.3	19.6
Prepared food—ready-to-serve	92.8	16.8	30.9	37.0	15.3
Salad dressings, mayonnaise, toppings	93.5	16.1	34.5	35.6	13.8
Seafood—canned	76.6	20.5	33.9	32.6	13.0
Shortening, oil	85.4	15.3	35.5	34.9	14.3
Snacks	98.5	15.2	30.7	38.8	15.4
Soft drinks—noncarbonated	62.5	13.9	28.1	39.3	18.6
Soup	94.5	17.6	33.4	35.2	13.7
Spices, seasonings, extracts	90.1	16.5	29.1	34.5	13.9
Sugar, sweeteners	82.9	15.7	33.9	35.1	15.3
Table syrups, molasses	62.3	13.9	29.1	39.2	17.8
Tea	74.8	17.3	33.9	35.8	13.0
Vegetables—canned	93.4	15.1	35.0	35.6	14.2
Vegetables and grains—dried	66.4	14.1	31.3	37.3	17.3
Water bottled	79.5	15.5	31.8	39.3	13.4

Source: Progressive Grocer, July 1, 2007, p. 36.

each generation. This type of analysis is illustrated in Figure 4.1. As can be seen, U.S. consumers can be divided into "mega" segments of six types of consumers, ranging from the oldest (the GI Generation born between 1901 and 1924) to the Millenials (born between 1982 and 2002). While this kind of analysis is popular, it is more useful for trend-spotting than for developing segments for individual brands that usually target one or two of these groups.

Also consider Table 4.5, which shows the differences in purchase incidence of a variety of products between African Americans, Hispanics, and Asian Americans. Some product categories such as ready-to-eat cereal, frozen vegetables, deodorants, and canned soups show some remarkable differences, giving only partial information about how heterogeneous the U.S. population is.[4] These differences also go down to the brand level. Studies show that Latin families prefer Kimberly-Clark's Huggies disposable diapers over

Figure 4.1

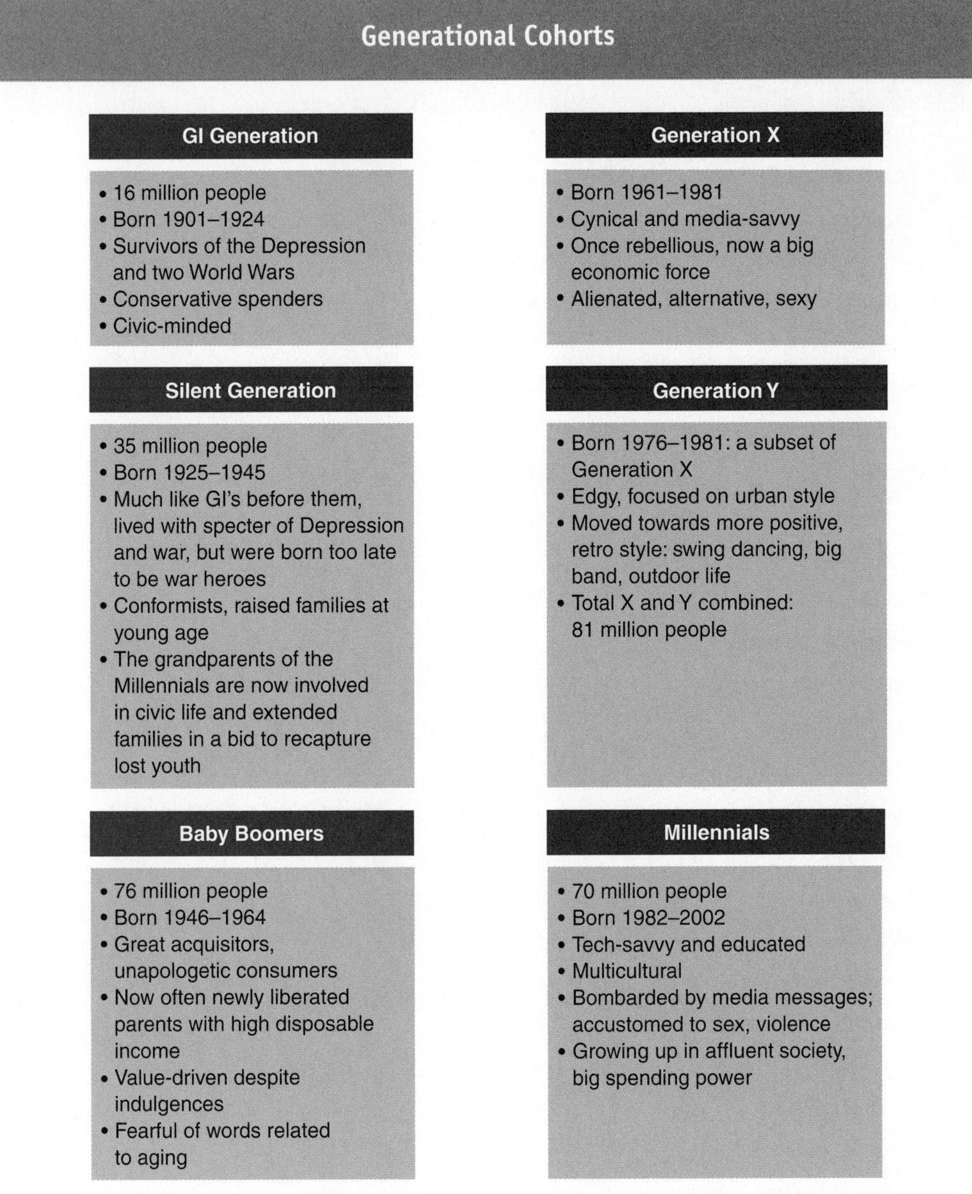

Generational Cohorts
GI Generation
• 16 million people
• Born 1901–1924
• Survivors of the Depression and two World Wars
• Conservative spenders
• Civic-minded
Generation X
• Born 1961–1981
• Cynical and media-savvy
• Once rebellious, now a big economic force
• Alienated, alternative, sexy
Silent Generation
• 35 million people
• Born 1925–1945
• Much like GI's before them, lived with specter of Depression and war, but were born too late to be war heroes
• Conformists, raised families at young age
• The grandparents of the Millennials are now involved in civic life and extended families in a bid to recapture lost youth
Generation Y
• Born 1976–1981: a subset of Generation X
• Edgy, focused on urban style
• Moved towards more positive, retro style: swing dancing, big band, outdoor life
• Total X and Y combined: 81 million people
Baby Boomers
• 76 million people
• Born 1946–1964
• Great acquisitors, unapologetic consumers
• Now often newly liberated parents with high disposable income
• Value-driven despite indulgences
• Fearful of words related to aging
Millennials
• 70 million people
• Born 1982–2002
• Tech-savvy and educated
• Multicultural
• Bombarded by media messages; accustomed to sex, violence
• Growing up in affluent society, big spending power

Source: Advertising Age, January 15, 2001, pp. 14–16.

Procter & Gamble's Pampers and that Hispanic women prefer L'Oreal's Maybelline to P&G's Cover Girl.[5]

There are several well-known approaches to developing psychographic profiles of consumers. Psychographics divide the total market in a geographic area (usually a country) into segments based on a combination of psychological and demographic characteristics using statistical procedures.[6] The most popular is the VALS™ system developed by SRI International and currently run by Strategic Business Insights. Based on questions like those shown in Figure 4.2, the VALS groups are:

- **Innovators** (10 percent of the U.S. population). These are successful, sophisticated, and active people with high self-esteem and significant resources. Image is important to these people not as evidence of power or status, but as an expression of taste, independence, and character. They are change leaders and are the most receptive group to new products and ideas.
- **Thinkers** (11 percent). Mature, satisfied, comfortable people who value order, knowledge, and responsibility. Most are well educated and are in or have recently retired from professional occupations. They are conservative, practical consumers.

Table 4.5

Ethnic Differences in Consumption

Product	African American	Hispanics	Asian American
Regular coffee	54%	72%	49%
Decaffeinated coffee	19	20	13
Regular carbonated soft drinks	71	77	70
Diet carbonated soft drinks	23	20	12
Fruit juice/nectar	68	78	73
Ready-to-eat cereal	72	78	44
Shampoo	76	93	89
Conditioner	52	61	59
Toothpaste	92	95	93
Frozen vegetables	40	21	17
Bath soaps	95	97	89
Deodorants	84	89	26
Dishwashing detergent	86	88	79
Canned soups	53	32	36
Powdered cleansers	57	53	46
Fabric softener	67	81	51
Liquid cleaners	61	57	43
Toilet paper	95	95	93
Bleach	76	73	57
White rice	73	89	90
Packaged cheese	53	65	39
Packaged sliced meats	39	55	43
Potato chips	52	36	41
Underwear	63	66	66
Packaged cookies	46	42	44
Analgesics/headache remedies	60	80	48
Peanut butter	54	31	51
Beer	31	38	44
Condoms	16	9	12

Source: Brandweek (1995), July 17, p. 28.

- **Experiencers** (13 percent). These people are young, vital, enthusiastic, impulsive, and rebellious and seek variety and excitement. They are avid consumers and spend much of their money on clothing, fast food, music, movies, and video.
- **Achievers** (14 percent). They are successful career people who feel in control of their lives. They are committed to work and family and buy established, prestige products and services. They live conventional lives and are politically conservative.
- **Believers** (16.5 percent). These are conservative, conventional people whose beliefs revolve around family, church, community, and their country. They are conservative consumers favoring national products and established brands.
- **Strivers** (11.5 percent). Trendy and fun-loving, they are striving to find a place in life. They are unsure about themselves and low in socioeconomic status. They feel

Figure 4.2

Sample VALS Questions

We are interested in the attitudes that describe you as a person. For each of the following statements, please indicate how much you agree or disagree with that statement as a description of you. There are no right or wrong answers—just answers that describe you best.

7. I am often interested in theories.
○ Strongly disagree ○ Slightly disagree ○ Slightly agree ○ Strongly agree

8. I like outrageous people and things.
○ Strongly disagree ○ Slightly disagree ○ Slightly agree ○ Strongly agree

9. I like a lot of variety in my life.
○ Strongly disagree ○ Slightly disagree ○ Slightly agree ○ Strongly agree

10. I like to make things I can use every day.
○ Strongly disagree ○ Slightly disagree ○ Slightly agree ○ Strongly agree

11. I follow the latest trends and fashions.
○ Strongly disagree ○ Slightly disagree ○ Slightly agree ○ Strongly agree

12. Just as the Bible says, the world literally was created in six days.
○ Strongly disagree ○ Slightly disagree ○ Slightly agree ○ Strongly agree

13. I like being in charge of a group.
○ Strongly disagree ○ Slightly disagree ○ Slightly agree ○ Strongly agree

14. I like to learn about art, culture, and history.
○ Strongly disagree ○ Slightly disagree ○ Slightly agree ○ Strongly agree

15. I often crave excitement.
○ Strongly disagree ○ Slightly disagree ○ Slightly agree ○ Strongly agree

16. I am really interested only in a few things.
○ Strongly disagree ○ Slightly disagree ○ Slightly agree ○ Strongly agree

17. I would rather make something than buy it.
○ Strongly disagree ○ Slightly disagree ○ Slightly agree ○ Strongly agree

18. I dress more fashionably than most people.
○ Strongly disagree ○ Slightly disagree ○ Slightly agree ○ Strongly agree

19. The federal government should encourage prayers in public schools.
○ Strongly disagree ○ Slightly disagree ○ Slightly agree ○ Strongly agree

20. I have more ability than most people.
○ Strongly disagree ○ Slightly disagree ○ Slightly agree ○ Strongly agree

that they do not have enough money. They purchase products to emulate people who are more successful.

- **Makers** (12 percent). These are practical people who have constructive skills and value self-sufficiency. They experience the world by working on it (e.g., fixing their cars). Makers are politically conservative, suspicious of new ideas, and resentful of government intrusion on individual rights.
- **Survivors** (12 percent). They are poor, ill-educated, low-skilled, and elderly, with concerns about security and safety. They believe the world is changing too rapidly and are most comfortable with the familiar. They are cautious consumers.[7]

When matched against purchasing and media habits, psychographics can provide useful information about the consumers of a product or service that goes beyond demographic information. For example, an analysis of usage of two brands of pain relievers, Nuprin and Advil, by VALS types versus the U.S. average index of 100 showed that Achievers are heavy users of Nuprin while Advil has more appeal to Experiencers.

A final illustration is the segmentation scheme devised by Forrester Research Inc., a well-known technology consultant. They divide consumers into 10 groups through the use of what they call Technographics.[8] As can be seen in Figure 4.3, the groups range from Fast Forwards, who are early adopters of technology for a wide variety of uses, to Sidelined Citizens at the other end of the technology adoption spectrum.

Marketing managers are interested in behavioral variables such as usage rate and degree of loyalty. However, Enterprise Rent-A-Car segments its markets based on another behavioral variable—occasion. It may be a surprise to learn that Enterprise is larger than Hertz in the United States in terms of the size of its fleet and the number of locations. Enterprise specializes in renting cars to people whose cars have been wrecked or stolen and does not emphasize the airport rental business. Thus, it has focused much of its business on a market segment that is supported by insurance companies. The rest is focused on another occasion segment ignored by the major companies: the local business for customers who need a car for errands or short trips.

Traditionally, the first two descriptor categories, geographic and demographic variables, plus behavioral data on usage, have been used to form segments. However, marketing managers are increasingly combining psychographics and a variety of usage measures to better understand their target groups. These new kinds of segments cut across broad demographic groups. For example, Colgate-Palmolive introduced its new Total brand of toothpaste in the United States in 1997. In addition to the usual cavity-fighting and breath-freshening properties, the product has an ingredient, triclosan, that combats gingivitis. This unique combination of benefits also comes with a higher price tag. The prime target for the product is "orally aware" consumers who have an above-average interest in their oral health (psychographic), are heavy users of toothcare products in general, and visit their dentists regularly (both behavioral). This segment is very broad in terms of income and age, traditional demographic groups.[9]

Figure 4.3

How Tech Customers Stack Up

	Career	Family	Entertainment
Optimists	**Fast Forwards** These consumers are the biggest spenders, and they're early adopters of new technology for home, office, and personal use.	**New Age Nurturers** Also big spenders, but focused on technology for home uses, such as a family PC.	**Mouse Potatoes** They like the on-line world for entertainment and are willing to spend for the latest in techno-tainment.
Optimists	**Techno-Strivers** Use technology from cell phones and pagers to on-line services primarily to gain a career edge.	**Digital Hopefuls** Families with a limited budget but still interested in new technology. Good candidates for the under-$1,000 PC.	**Gadget-Grabbers** They also favor on-line entertainment but have less cash to spend on it.
Pessimists	**Hand-Shakers** Older consumers, typically managers, who don't touch their computers at work. They leave that to younger assistants.	**Traditionalists** Willing to use technology but slow to upgrade. Not convinced upgrades and other add-ons are worth paying for.	**Media Junkies** Seek entertainment and can't find much of it on-line. Prefer TV and other older media.
Pessimists	**Sidelined Citizens**: Not interested in technology.		

More affluent / Less affluent

Source: Forrester Research, Inc.

Segmenting in Technology-Based Markets: The Diffusion of Innovations

Customers react to the characteristics of innovations and perceived risk differently. Some customers are risk takers and some are risk-averse. Some customers have the vision to see the relative advantage of a technological innovation earlier than others. In other words, some customers will adopt an innovation sooner than others. In addition, the rate of adoption of new technologies is highly dependent on how many customers are in this early adopter group. If this group grows, the technology is likely to be adopted by a large fraction of the potential user group. If the group stays small, the technology is not likely to be a successful product category. In technology-based markets, the marketing manager must understand who are the different customers that will purchase the product at the introductory stage of the product life cycle and as the product category matures.

Everett Rogers developed a popular framework for understanding this process: the diffusion of innovations.[10] Figure 4.4 illustrates the sizes of different customer cohorts that typically buy new innovations at different stages of the innovation's product life cycle. As can be seen in the figure, Rogers's model assumes that innovativeness, like many other human traits, is distributed normally throughout the population.

The basic idea behind the diffusion of innovations is that, like a disease or a new idea, the spread of the innovation is affected by the amount of "inoculation" that occurs from the first buyers. These first buyers, the **innovators**, try the product first. If they like it, they spread positive word-of-mouth about the product to later users who, in turn, also talk about it. Combined with the marketing efforts of the companies involved, the product then spreads through the population. The success of the product is ultimately determined by how favorable the word-of-mouth is. That is, information from innovators and other early buyers about the product may reduce later buyers' perceived risk.

innovators
one type of adopter in Everett Rogers's diffusion of innovations framework; the first buyers of an innovation

The symmetric decomposition of the complete life cycle shown in Figure 4.4 is an ideal picture and applies mainly to completely new products. The percentages in each group may be different for each new technological development. However, a considerable amount of research has verified that there are five types of adopters:

1. As we noted previously, the earliest customers for a new technology are called innovators. These customers have a high utility for being on the leading edge, are often technologists, are eager to try new ideas, and are generally venturesome. In addition, because they are most interested in being the first to own a new technological product, they are price insensitive. They are valuable to companies because they help get the bugs out of new products. In 2000, people buying TiVo, the first digital video recorder, were innovators.
2. The next group of customers to adopt new products are **early adopters**. These customers are generally not interested in technology for its own sake, but are good at

early adopters
one type of adopter in Everett Rogers's diffusion of innovations framework; buyers who are not the first to purchase an innovation but who follow innovators

Figure 4.4

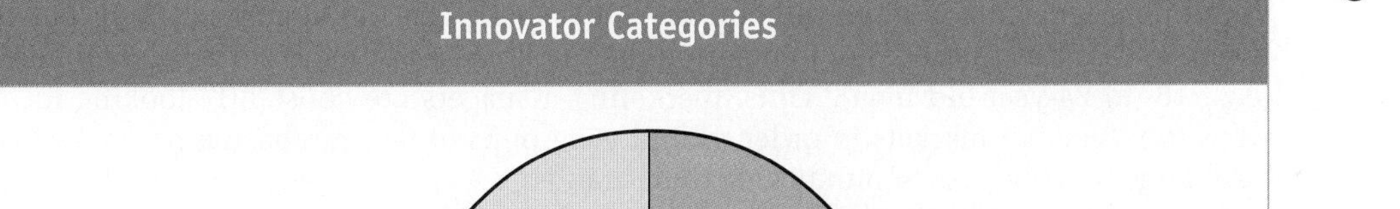

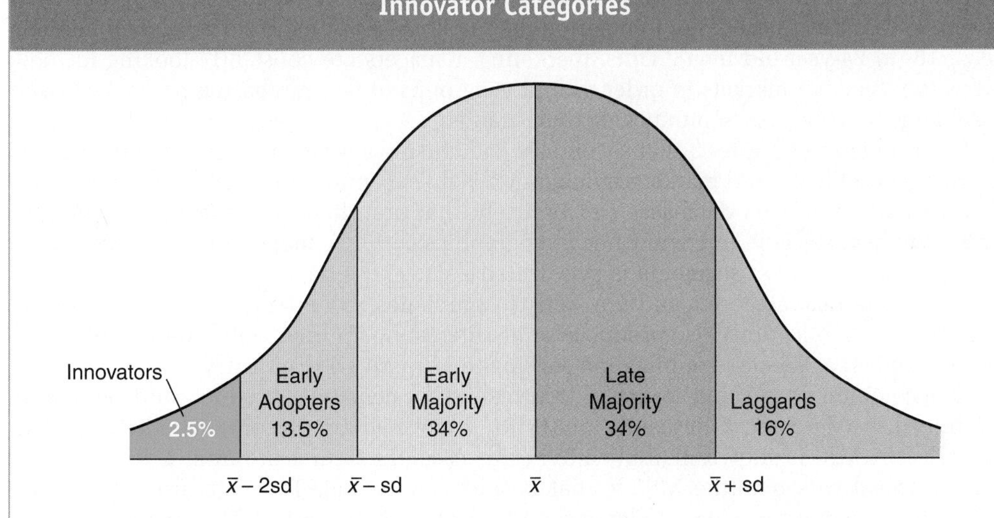

Source: Everett M. Rogers (1995), *Diffusion of Innovations,* 4th ed. (New York: Free Press).

detecting the value of a new product and how it will enhance their lives or their businesses. Their value in high-technology markets is their vision in how the technology can actually satisfy customer benefits. Thus, this group is critical in making a new technologically based product successful. In 2010–2011, the digital e-book reader industry is trying to attract these buyers.

early majority
one type of adopter in Everett Rogers's diffusion of innovations framework that follows early adopters; buyers who are interested in new technology and gadgets but who wait to see whether an innovative product is just a fad

late majority
one type of adopter in Everett Rogers's diffusion of innovations framework; buyers who are conservative in terms of how much of an industry infrastructure must be built before they will buy an innovative product

laggards
one type of adopter in Everett Rogers's diffusion of innovations framework that follows the late majority; buyers who are generally not interested in new technology and are the last customers to buy, if they ever do

3. A larger portion of the market is the **early majority**. These buyers are interested in new technology and gadgets but take a wait-and-see attitude to determine whether the product is a fad; they are basically pragmatists. The value of this group of customers is obvious. It is a large group and it is necessary to attract them for the product to be commercially viable. MP3 player manufacturers are targeting this group.
4. The **late majority** are similar to the early majority but are more conservative in terms of how much of an industry infrastructure must be built before they will buy. They want the product to be an established standard and require substantial levels of product support. DVD players are still being purchased by this group of consumers, as are cell phones.
5. **Laggards** generally are not interested in new technology and are the last customers to buy, if they ever do. These are the technology skeptics. Even the penetration rates of televisions and telephones in the United States are not 100 percent!

Like the product life cycle curve shown in Chapter 2, the diffusion curve shown in Figure 4.4 is a stylized version of how markets actually evolve. Not only do the actual percentages in each buyer group differ by product category, but also at a given point in time, it is not necessarily clear which stage you are in. However, from the marketing manager's perspective, it is important to understand the characteristics of the buyers who are the largest group at a particular stage in the technology product's life cycle. It is fairly obvious that the particular group purchasing a product at a given point in time varies among different kinds of technologically based products, depending on where they are in their product life cycles. Early technologies such as satellite television are appealing to a different group than microwave ovens. However, even for one product, the innovator group can vary across markets. Sony is marketing its digital cameras to early adopters in the United States, to the early majority in Japan, and to the innovators in India.

Marketing Research Implications: Data Collection

To collect information of the type described in this section, the marketing manager can use either primary or secondary data. It is common for the manager to use a survey designed in-house or by a marketing research firm to better understand the customer base. Although the questions would cover a range of topics, these surveys include requests for descriptive information that falls into the categories shown in Table 4.1. In addition, the surveys try to obtain behavioral data indicating quantities purchased and other information. However, developing segments is more difficult than it seems given the large number of potential variables that can be used, not to mention the possible two or more variable combinations (e.g., 18- to 24-year-old men). Thus, marketing managers are constantly looking for new ways to resegment markets in order to find subgroups of the purchasing population who have large probabilities of purchasing their brands.

It was noted in Chapter 3 that secondary data are always a good place to start to solve marketing problems, and market segmentation is no exception. Demographic information from countries' census databases can be useful but are often too general to be helpful (e.g., www.census.gov and www.freedemographics.com). A major source of secondary information on market segments is syndicated data. These data cover a large number of different product categories and are sold to companies requesting the reports. Reading professional publications also produces some interesting findings. Table 4.4 was obtained from *Progressive Grocer,* a publication serving the supermarket industry.

One common syndicated source of information for consumer products and services is produced by Mediamark Research Inc. (MRI, www.mediamark.com). The kind of data supplied by MRI is shown in Table 4.6. In this case, the figures are from 1998 MRI data on the travel category (the MRI format is the same today). The data are obtained by administering questionnaires to large samples of U.S. households. The responses to the surveys are extrapolated to the general population. As can be seen, the rows represent

Table 4.6

MRI Travel Data

		Go to Beach				General Sightseeing				Attend a Specific Event				Scuba Diving			
Base: Adults	Total U.S. '000	A '000	B % Down	C % Across	D Index	A '000	B % Down	C % Across	D Index	A '000	B % Down	C % Across	D Index	A '000	B % Down	C % Across	D Index
All Adults	195,192	15,667	100.0	8.0	100	2,349	100.0	12.0	100	7,320	100.0	3.8	100	2,923	100.0	1.5	100
Men	93,553	7,388	47.2	7.9	98	10,784	46.0	11.5	96	3,159	43.1	3.4	90	1,526	52.2	1.6	109
Women	101,639	8,278	52.8	8.1	101	12,655	54.0	12.5	104	4,161	56.9	4.1	109	1,398	47.8	1.4	92
Household heads	118,644	8,937	57.0	7.5	94	13,630	58.1	11.5	96	3,928	53.7	3.3	88	1,816	62.1	1.5	102
Homemakers	121,504	9,702	61.9	8.0	99	14,519	61.9	11.9	100	4,660	63.7	3.8	102	1,835	62.8	1.5	101
Graduated college	42,453	6,522	41.6	15.4	191	10,086	43.0	23.8	198	2,710	37.0	6.4	170	1,179	40.3	2.8	185
Attended college	51498	4,294	27.4	8.3	104	6,082	25.9	11.8	98	2,142	29.3	4.2	111	837	28.6	1.6	109
Graduated high school	64,868	3,810	24.3	5.9	73	5734	24.5	8.8	74	1,920	26.2	3.0	79	626	21.4	1.0	64
Did not graduate high school	36,372	1,040	6.6	2.9	36	1,538	6.6	4.2	35	*548	7.5	1.5	40	*282	9.7	0.8	52
18–24	24,842	1,682	10.7	6.8	84	1,908	8.1	7.7	64	970	13.3	3.9	104	442	15.1	1.8	119
25–34	40,972	3,767	24.0	9.2	115	4,561	19.5	11.1	93	1,799	24.6	4.4	117	826	28.3	2.0	135
35–44	43,561	4,318	27.6	9.9	123	5,568	23.8	12.8	106	1,617	22.1	3.7	99	819	28.0	1.9	126
45–54	32,521	3,166	20.2	9.7	121	5,074	21.6	15.6	130	1,393	19.0	4.3	114	473	16.2	1.5	97
55–64	21,227	1,606	10.3	7.6	94	3,090	13.2	14.6	121	764	10.4	3.6	96	*230	7.9	1.1	72
65 or over	32,069	1,128	7.2	3.5	44	3,239	13.8	10.1	84	777	10.6	2.4	65	*133	4.5	0.4	28
18–34	65,815	5,449	34.8	8.3	103	6,469	27.6	9.8	82	2,770	37.8	4.2	112	1,268	43.4	1.9	129
18–49	127,841	11,682	74.6	9.1	114	14,941	63.7	11.7	97	5,210	71.2	4.1	109	2,339	80.0	1.8	122
25–54	117,054	11,251	71.8	9.6	120	15,203	64.9	13.0	108	4,809	65.7	4.1	110	2,119	72.5	1.8	121
Employed full-time	107,605	10,834	69.2	10.1	125	15,058	64.2	14.0	117	4,538	62.0	4.2	112	2,149	73.5	2.0	133
Part-time	19,881	1,841	11.8	9.3	115	2,605	11.1	13.1	109	862	11.8	4.3	116	*292	10.0	1.5	98
Sole wage earner	35,254	2,628	16.8	7.5	93	3,604	15.4	10.2	85	1,015	13.9	2.9	77	650	22.2	1.8	123
Not employed	67,705	2,992	19.1	4.4	55	5,776	24.6	8.5	71	1,920	26.2	2.8	76	483	16.5	0.7	48
Professional	19,522	2,994	19.1	15.3	191	4,591	19.6	23.5	196	1,409	19.3	7.2	193	576	19.7	3.0	197
Executive/administrative/managerial	18,220	2,915	18.6	16.0	199	4,200	17.9	23.1	192	1,099	15.0	6.0	161	494	16.9	2.7	181
Clerical/sales/technical	37,144	3,531	22.5	9.5	118	4,676	19.9	12.6	105	1,399	19.1	3.8	100	698	23.9	1.9	125
Precision/crafts/repair	14,111	1,010	6.4	7.2	89	1,245	5.3	8.8	73	346	4.7	2.4	65	*261	8.9	1.8	123
Other employed	38,490	2,225	14.2	5.8	72	2,951	12.6	7.7	64	1,148	15.7	3.0	80	412	14.1	1.1	71
H/D income $75,000 or more	38,349	6,497	41.5	16.9	211	9,561	40.8	24.9	208	2,733	37.3	7.1	190	1,113	38.1	2.9	194
$60,000–74,999	20,921	2,288	14.6	10.9	136	3,390	14.5	16.2	135	925	12.6	4.4	118	467	16.0	2.2	149
$50,000–59,999	18,782	1,410	9.0	7.5	94	2,481	10.6	13.2	110	749	10.2	4.0	106	*188	6.4	1.0	67
$40,000–49,999	22,135	1,760	11.2	7.9	99	2,473	10.5	11.2	93	731	10.0	3.3	88	*349	11.9	1.6	105
$30,000–39,999	25,204	1,545	9.9	6.1	76	2,304	9.8	9.1	76	898	12.3	3.6	95	*325	11.1	1.3	86
$20,000–29,999	27,129	1,243	7.9	4.6	57	1,785	7.6	6.6	55	823	11.2	3.0	81	*250	8.5	0.9	62
$10,000–19,999	26,824	7,39	4.7	2.8	34	1,203	5.1	4.5	37	*358	4.9	1.3	36	*191	6.5	0.7	47
Less than $10,000	15,846	*185	1.2	1.2	15	*244	1.0	1.5	13	*103	1.4	0.7	17	*40	1.4	0.3	17
Census region: North East	39,302	4,061	25.9	10.3	129	5,749	24.5	14.6	122	1,720	23.5	4.4	117	664	22.7	1.7	113
North Central	45,475	3,271	20.9	7.2	90	4,908	20.9	10.8	90	1,767	24.1	3.9	104	550	18.8	1.2	81
South	68,341	4,076	26.0	6.0	74	6,304	26.9	9.2	77	1,838	25.1	2.7	72	928	31.8	1.4	91
West	42,074	4,260	27.2	10.1	126	6,479	27.6	15.4	128	1,996	27.3	4.7	126	782	26.7	1.9	124
Marketing region: New England	10,432	790	5.0	7.6	94	1,333	5.7	12.8	106	437	6.0	4.2	112	*108	3.7	1.0	69
Middle Atlantic	33,414	3,535	22.6	10.6	132	4,857	20.7	14.5	121	1,405	19.2	4.2	112	588	20.1	1.8	117
East Central	25,623	1,859	11.9	7.3	90	2,805	12.0	10.9	91	1,034	14.1	4.0	108	368	12.6	1.4	96
West Central	29,279	2,177	13.9	7.4	93	3,463	14.8	11.8	99	1,021	13.9	3.5	93	*398	13.6	1.4	91
South East	38,021	2,155	13.8	5.7	71	3,340	14.2	8.8	73	972	13.3	2.6	68	579	19.8	1.5	102
South West	21,996	1,377	8.8	6.3	78	2,073	8.8	9.4	78	592	8.1	2.7	72	*244	8.4	1.1	74
Pacific	36,427	3,774	24.1	10.4	129	5,568	23.8	15.3	127	1,860	25.4	5.1	136	639	21.9	1.8	117
County size A	79,981	8,199	52.3	10.3	128	11,843	50.5	14.8	123	3,919	53.5	4.9	131	1,392	47.6	1.7	116
County size B	58,438	4,910	31.3	8.4	105	7,189	30.7	12.3	102	2,164	29.6	3.7	99	1,103	37.7	1.9	126

(*continued*)

Continued

		Go to Beach				General Sightseeing				Attend a Specific Event				Scuba Diving			
	Total	A	B	C	D	A	B	C	D	A	B	C	D	A	B	C	D
	U.S.		%	%			%	%			%	%			%	%	
Base: Adults	'000	'000	Down	Across	Index	'000	Down	Across	Index	'000	Down	Across	Index	'000	Down	Across	Index
County size C	27,978	1,457	9.3	5.2	65	2,361	10.1	8.4	70	776	10.6	2.8	74	*272	9.3	1.0	65
County size D	28,795	1,101	7.0	3.8	48	2,047	8.7	7.1	59	*461	6.3	1.6	43	*156	5.3	0.5	36
MSA central city	64,706	5,092	32.5	7.9	98	7,546	32.2	11.7	97	2,356	32.2	3.6	97	1048	35.9	1.6	108
MSA suburban	92,438	9,013	57.5	9.7	121	13,099	55.9	14.2	118	4,176	57.1	4.5	120	1614	55.2	1.7	117
Non-MSA	38,047	1,562	10.0	4.1	51	2,795	11.9	7.3	61	788	10.8	2.1	55	*261	8.9	0.7	46
Single	45,144	3,310	21.1	7.3	91	4,158	17.7	9.2	77	1,758	24.0	3.9	104	710	24.3	1.6	105
Married	112,383	10,367	66.2	9.2	115	16,090	68.6	14.3	119	4,852	66.3	4.3	115	1850	63.3	1.6	110
Other	37,664	1,989	12.7	5.3	66	3,192	13.6	8.5	71	710	9.7	1.9	50	363	12.4	1.0	64
Parents	68,208	5,757	36.7	8.4	105	7,650	32.6	11.2	93	2,465	33.7	3.6	96	1024	35.0	1.5	100
Working parents	53,687	5,010	32.0	9.3	116	6,628	28.3	12.3	103	2,059	28.1	3.8	102	931	31.9	1.7	116
Household size: 1 person	25,024	1,234	7.9	4.9	61	2,074	8.8	8.3	69	574	7.8	2.3	61	299	10.2	1.2	80
2 persons	63,398	5,509	35.2	8.7	108	9,021	38.5	14.2	118	2,627	35.9	4.1	110	1005	34.4	1.6	106
3 or more persons	106,780	8,924	57.0	8.4	104	12,345	52.7	11.6	96	4,119	56.3	3.9	103	1620	55.4	1.5	101
Any child in household	81,339	6,732	43.0	8.3	103	8,965	38.2	11.0	92	2,880	39.3	3.5	94	1147	39.2	1.4	94
Under 2 years	14,305	1,272	8.1	8.9	111	1,575	6.7	11.0	92	579	7.9	4.0	108	*231	7.9	1.6	108
2–5 years	29,745	2,170	13.8	7.3	91	2,571	11.0	8.6	72	930	12.7	3.1	83	*324	11.1	1.1	73
6–11 years	38,480	3,060	19.5	8.0	99	4,219	18.0	11.0	91	1,209	16.5	3.1	84	485	16.6	1.3	84
12–17 years	37,713	3,105	19.8	8.2	103	4,407	18.8	11.7	97	1,288	17.6	3.4	91	458	15.7	1.2	81
White	164,831	13,991	89.3	8.5	106	21,188	90.4	12.9	107	6,380	87.2	3.9	103	2606	89.1	1.6	106
Black	22,686	802	5.1	3.5	44	1,020	4.4	4.5	37	461	6.3	2.0	54	*168	5.7	0.7	49
Spanish-speaking	19,624	1,715	10.9	8.7	109	1,991	8.5	10.1	84	744	10.2	3.8	101	*285	9.8	1.5	97
Homeowner	133,858	12,237	78.1	9.1	114	18,894	80.6	14.1	118	5,509	75.3	4.1	110	2245	76.8	1.7	112
Daily newspapers: read any	102,590	9,051	57.8	8.8	110	14,381	61.4	14.0	117	4,267	58.3	4.2	111	1400	47.9	1.4	91
Read one daily	82,641	6,792	43.3	8.2	102	10,959	46.8	13.3	110	3,244	44.3	3.9	105	1024	35.0	1.2	83
Read two or more dailies	19,949	2,259	14.4	11.3	141	3,422	14.6	17.2	143	1,023	14.0	5.1	137	375	12.8	1.9	126
Sunday newspapers: read any	120,791	11,146	71.1	9.2	115	17,336	74.0	14.4	120	5,303	72.4	4.4	117	1970	67.4	1.6	109
Read one Sunday	107,388	9,622	61.4	9.0	112	14,842	63.3	13.8	115	4,469	61.0	4.2	111	1737	59.4	1.6	108
Read two or more Sundays	13,403	1,524	9.7	11.4	142	2,494	10.6	18.6	155	834	11.4	6.2	166	*233	8.0	1.7	116
Quintile I—outdoor	39,038	3,980	25.4	10.2	127	5,942	25.3	15.2	127	1,777	24.3	4.6	121	735	25.1	1.9	126
Quintile II	39,038	3,747	23.9	9.6	120	5,454	23.3	14.0	116	1,651	22.6	4.2	113	610	20.9	1.6	104
Quintile III	39,039	3,665	23.4	9.4	117	5,256	22.4	13.5	112	1,780	24.3	4.6	122	742	25.4	1.9	127
Quintile IV	39,038	2,366	15.1	6.1	76	3,643	15.5	9.3	78	1,209	16.5	3.1	83	467	16.0	1.2	80
Quintile V	39,038	1,908	12.2	4.9	61	3,145	13.4	8.1	67	903	12.3	2.3	62	*370	12.7	0.9	63
Quintile I—magazines	39,038	3,725	23.8	9.5	119	5,342	22.8	13.7	114	1,838	25.1	4.7	126	704	24.1	1.8	120
Quintile II	39,037	3,461	22.1	8.9	110	5,464	23.3	14.0	117	1,658	22.7	4.2	113	488	16.7	1.3	83
Quintile III	39,040	3,484	22.2	8.9	111	4,984	21.3	12.8	106	1,536	21.0	3.9	105	677	23.2	1.7	116
Quintile IV	39,038	2,791	17.8	7.2	89	4,334	18.5	11.1	92	1,228	16.8	3.1	84	691	23.7	1.8	118
Quintile V	39,039	2,205	14.1	5.6	70	3,315	14.1	8.5	71	1,060	14.5	2.7	72	*363	12.4	0.9	62
Quintile I—newspapers	39,033	3,749	23.9	9.6	120	6,248	26.7	16.0	133	1,824	24.9	4.7	125	573	19.6	1.5	98
Quintile II	39,037	3,245	20.7	8.3	104	5,303	22.6	13.6	113	1,540	21.0	3.9	105	494	16.9	1.3	84
Quintile III	39,056	3,212	20.5	8.2	102	4,590	19.6	11.8	98	1,399	19.1	3.6	95	610	20.9	1.6	104
Quintile IV	39,028	3,384	21.6	8.7	108	4,421	18.9	11.3	94	1,556	21.3	4.0	106	756	25.9	1.9	129
Quintile V	39,037	2,077	13.3	5.3	66	2,878	12.3	7.4	61	1,001	13.7	2.6	68	491	16.8	1.3	84
Quintile I—radio	39,038	3,233	20.6	8.3	103	4,375	18.7	11.2	93	1,531	20.9	3.9	105	560	19.2	1.4	96
Quintile II	39,038	3,076	19.6	7.9	98	4,628	19.7	11.9	99	1,552	21.2	4.0	106	544	18.6	1.4	93
Quintile III	39,039	3,602	23.0	9.2	115	5,238	22.3	13.4	112	1,609	22.0	4.1	110	715	24.5	1.8	122
Quintile IV	39,038	3,517	22.4	9.0	112	5,423	23.1	13.9	116	1,521	20.8	3.9	104	619	21.2	1.6	106
Quintile V	39,038	2238	14.3	5.7	71	3776	16.1	9.7	81	1107	15.1	2.8	76	485	16.6	1.2	83

*Indicates where the sample size was too small to draw a reliable inference to the U.S. population.

demographic and geographic variables and the columns represent behavioral variables—in this case, ownership of a particular credit card. The numbers in the Total U.S. column represent the total number of adults in the United States in that particular row. For example, in 1998, there were 24,842,000 18- to 24-year-old adults in the United States. The numbers in column A represent the number of people participating in various vacation activities in the row segment. Thus 1,682,000 18- to 24-year-old adults went to the beach during a vacation in 1998. Column B (% Down) indicates what percentage of the people in the column group are in the particular segment. Thus, 10.7 percent of all people who went to the beach while on vacation are 18 to 24 years old. The number in column C indicates the percentage in the segment who went to the beach, thus 6.8 percent of all 18- to 24-year-old adults went to the beach on vacation. An important column is labeled Index. This gives the relative incidence of people who went to the beach while on vacation in the segment compared with the overall percentage who went to the beach (similar to the index used in Figure 4.3). In this case, because 8.0 percent of all adults went to the beach (the top number in column C) and 6.8 percent of 18- to 24-year-old adults did the same, the index is 6.8/8.0 multiplied by 100, or 84. A quick glance in the Index column shows which segments have a disproportionately greater tendency to go to the beach on vacation than does the overall U.S. population. So good segments for beach resorts (like many Club Med locations) are people holding professional and executive jobs (Index = 191 and 199, respectively) and those with a household income of $75,000 or more (Index = 211). The scuba diving results are similar.[11]

A second kind of syndicated data links together census data and purchasing data to form psychographic-like segments. Perhaps the best known of these systems is Nielsen's PRIZM NE system (www.claritas.com). Using the most recent census data from 2000, Claritas analyzes several dozen demographic variables, including household composition, income, employment, education, ethnicity, and housing, and has developed 67 separate segments, each with a distinctive name that describes its members.[12] Figure 4.5

Figure 4.5

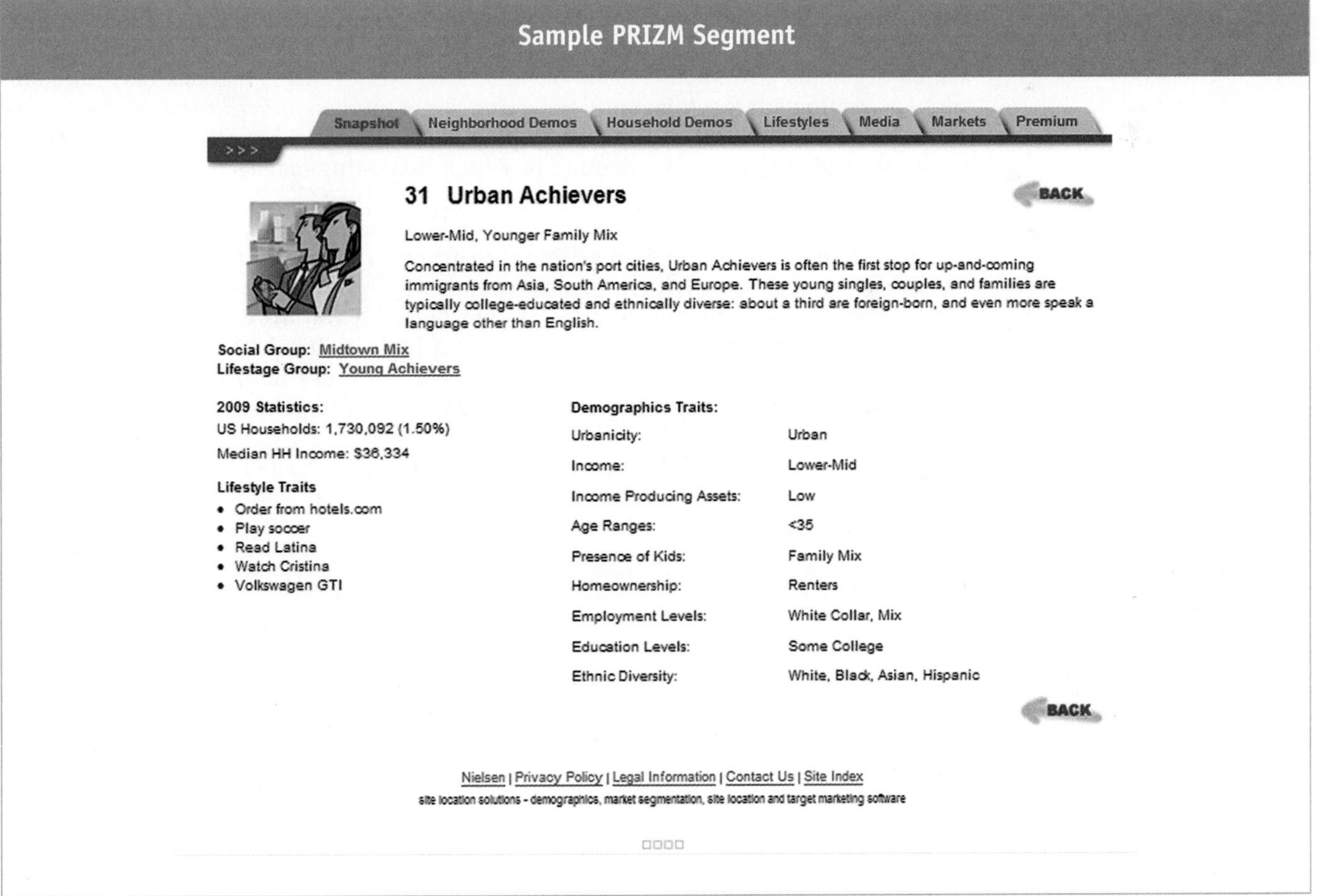

shows one such group, the Urban Achievers segment. More detailed descriptions of the people in this segment are given in the figure.

What is interesting is how the groups vary in terms of consumption of various products and services. As a result, Claritas offers a service that links membership in a descriptive segment to actual purchasing behavior. Because the data are known by ZIP codes (no individual household data are used), PRIZM can be useful for a direct-mail campaign. Similar services are offered by NDS/Equifax's MicroVision, Strategic Mapping's ClusterPLUS 2000, and Strategic Business Insight's GeoVALS, which develops geographic maps of the locations of the members of the different VALS2 groups. When new census data become available after 2010, all these approaches will be updated.

Club Med could use such services in the following way. The company could take the demographic data it already collects about its customers and overlay it on, say, the PRIZM clusters. Because PRIZM clusters are identified by ZIP codes, very targeted direct-mail catalogs can be constructed and mailed to appropriate households. For example, urban singles with high disposable income levels can be mailed brochures highlighting only the sites most appealing to singles.

It should be noted that the syndicated research studies can show only what has happened in the past. It may be inaccurate to extrapolate from these data to the potential of a particular segment because the segments may reflect only historical marketing patterns of the companies in the market. For example, the fact that Table 4.6 shows disproportionately high scuba diving propensity among households with income of $75,000 and over may reflect the fact that marketing efforts have targeted that group. Primary research is more capable of determining potential by asking appropriate questions that probe possible future behavior.

Marketing Research Implications: Developing Target Markets

Market segmentation is an intuitively appealing process, and it makes a great deal of sense to try to find different segments of the market that are more interested in your product than others or to develop products specifically for those segments. At the same time, given the myriad ways of segmenting markets, the task of determining which segments are better than others is daunting. This is the job of determining which segments you should focus on—the selection of target markets (see the complete marketing strategy diagram). Selecting target markets moves segmentation away from the purely descriptive (i.e., developing what are called buyer/nonbuyer profiles) to the strategic aspects of marketing, in which marketing managers pursue particular groups of customers.

One criterion that should always be applied is *parsimony.* Although having a large number of segments sounds appealing, because you can capture most of the differences between customers, it is expensive and inefficient to pursue too many segments. If the segments are different in terms of their behavior toward your product and they should receive different levels of marketing, a budget stretched over too many segments results in an insufficient concentration of resources in any one segment. It is very expensive to develop advertising and promotion programs for a large number of different target audiences.

Although it is not possible to generalize about the appropriate number of segments to pursue, the following criteria can be applied to a particular scheme or way to segment the market:

- Does the segmentation scheme explain differences in purchasing behavior or some other related variable (e.g., membership in different loyalty groups)? The basic issue to explore is whether the segmentation variable (say, income) explains purchasing behavior better than another variable (say, VALS groups). This can be done by considering the behavior as a dependent variable and the segmentation variables as independent variables in a framework like the following:

  $$\text{Behavior} = f(\text{segmentation variables})$$

  Several statistical approaches can be used to determine the strength (in a statistical sense) of the relationship between the variables and purchasing behavior. The marketing manager could then choose that variable (e.g., income) and particular levels of that variable (e.g., households earning $75,000 or more per year) that have the strongest association with the behavioral variable of interest.

For example, the MRI data shown in Table 4.6 can be analyzed using an "eyeball" approach. Assume that the behavioral or dependent variable of interest is simply going to the beach or not while on vacation. The independent variables are the demographics on the left side of the table. The variables that explain the most variance in going to the beach are those that have the greatest variation in their index numbers.[13] Thus, on a judgmental basis, the three most useful variables appear to be occupation, income, and education. You probably would also want to compare these variables to others, such as psychographics, which would be collected using another method.

- What is the segment size? It is clear that segmenting the market into too many groups results in some that are too small to be economically viable. Thus, one criterion for a particular scheme or level of a variable is whether it is of sufficient size in terms of number of customers, sales revenue, or potential profit to be worth targeting.
- What is the segment's growth rate? A marketing manager might prefer growth, indicating future revenues, over current size. Often, environmental factors such as regulatory, social, cultural, economic, or other exogenous factors affect segment growth rates. For example, targeting health-conscious consumers might make sense if there is a particular health boom in the country to which the product or service is being marketed.
- What is your potential competitive position? You might choose to ignore a lucrative segment if a competitor is well entrenched or if you decide that you cannot offer a product that has a competitive advantage over what is already being offered.

Therefore, the marketing manager's job is not only to develop alternative segmentation schemes, but also to determine which of a large number of alternatives are most appropriate for the product or service.

Application Harley-Davidson

One of the true success stories in American business is the motorcycle manufacturer Harley-Davidson.[14] Until recently, sales of Harley-Davidson motorcycles and parts and accessories have increased 15 percent per year and are constrained by production capacity. Even with cash, the purchaser of a new Harley may have to wait up to two years to take delivery. Although the motorcycles cost about $15,000 new, customers who have their orders in the queue can sell their undelivered motorcycles for $20,000.

This was not always the case. The company was very successful from its beginnings in 1903 as a manufacturer of large, heavy motorcycles until the late 1950s. When Honda introduced its small motorcycles into the United States in 1959, all other manufacturers, including Harley, were caught napping because they believed that the fad for such small motorcycles would be short-lived. Harley was acquired by several firms that sought to increase its share by expanding production. However, it had significant quality control problems, and its share of the heavyweight bike segment declined from 80 percent in 1973 to around 30 percent in 1980. The company was able to right itself after senior management purchased it from its last owner, AMF.

Harley's success resulted from a confluence of environmental changes in the United States and around the world. Harleys are seen as more than just motorcycles. They represent America,

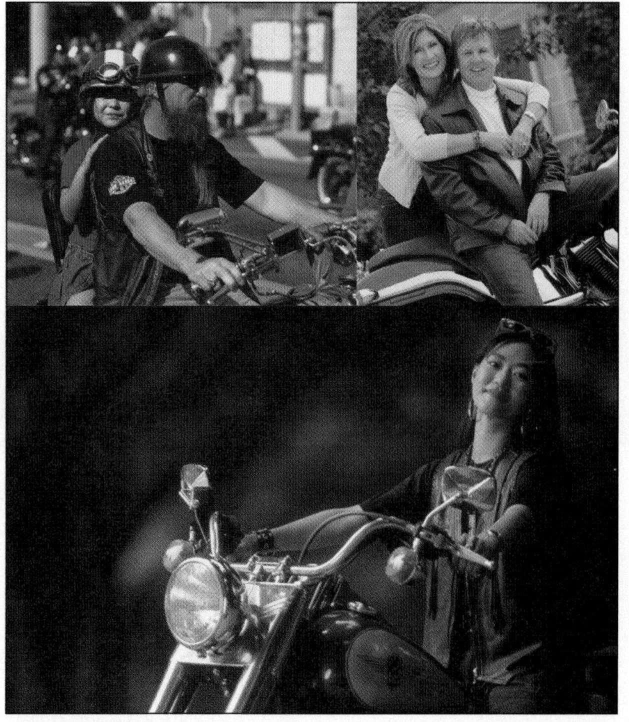

Harley-Davidson owners are a varied lot.

Source: Chris Wilson/Alamy Images (top, left); Don Hammond/Corbis RF (top, right); Michael S. Yamashita/CORBIS–NY (bottom)

Hollywood, masculinity, and a number of other icons. In addition, with the increased number of affluent baby boomers, there are more than enough customers for the product. The company has successfully created brand loyalty through its image and its Harley Owners' Groups (HOGS).

Because of the current excess demand for its products, Harley's problem is not identifying new market segments to pursue for further growth. The company has done an excellent job of focusing its products at the heavyweight end of the market. However, the company, like many, is interested in understanding its existing customer base in order to develop new services such as membership programs and ancillary merchandise. The image of the typical Harley owner is a hard-core gang biker. If the customer base is more diverse, then certain programs tailored to such a group would not appeal to all owners. Increased competition has also made maintaining and building the Harley image more important.

In 1994, a survey was administered to a national U.S. sample of registered owners. Of 2,500 questionnaires mailed, 761 responses were obtained, for a return rate of 30.4 percent. This is a fairly high response rate for a mail survey, indicating that nonresponse bias is likely to be low. The questionnaire included:

- 72 motorcycle lifestyle statements (a 1 to 5 scale, from not at all descriptive to extremely descriptive).
- 78 general lifestyle statements (same scale).
- 33 behavioral questions measuring frequency of participating in various activities as well as magazine readership and television viewing (1 to 5 scale, from not at all to extremely often).
- Demographics.

factor analysis
a multivariate statistical procedure to reduce a set of variable to a smaller set called factors that retain most of the information of the original set

The responses to the lifestyle questions were subjected to a multivariate statistical approach called **factor analysis**, which reduces the 72 questions (in the case of the motorcycle lifestyle questions) to a few underlying factors based on the correlations of the responses to the questions. For example, two of the questions were:

- "I would like to do 'gang' biker things."
- "Sometimes I feel like an outlaw."

One would expect that the responses to these two questions on the 1 to 5 scale would be similar across respondents. Thus, they do not measure different, independent underlying traits, but really just one. The analysis of the 72 questions revealed 11 different underlying lifestyle dimensions, as shown in Table 4.7.

A score was created for each respondent based on his or her answers to the questions in the 11 dimensions. Using another statistical method, **cluster analysis**, and the scores on the 11 dimensions, the respondents were grouped into six owner segments based on similarities of their scores on the dimensions. These are shown in Table 4.8. The averages of the demographic variables for each segment are shown in Table 4.9.

Table 4.7

Harley-Davidson Segmentation Study/Lifestyle Factors	
At-One-Ness	Passenger Preference
Hard Core	In the Dirt
Always in the Saddle	Wear Leathers
Trick Bike Modifications	Solitary Rider
Harley Zeal	Time Poor Rider
Ride Fast and Hard	

Source: William R. Swinyard (1996), "The Hard Core and Zen Riders of Harley Davidson: A Market-Driven Segmentation Analysis," *Journal of Targeting, Measurement and Analysis for Marketing*, 4 (June), pp. 337–362.

Table 4.8

Harley-Davidson Segmentation Scheme

Psychographic Segments

Tour Gliders
- I like long-distance touring bikes.
- I use my bike for touring.
- My bike is made more for comfort than for speed.
- I love to ride long distances. To me, 500 miles is a short trip.
- I like bikes with plastic farings and engine covers

Dream Riders
- Most of the time, my motorcycle is just parked.
- I like wearing a helmet when I ride.
- I don't know many other people who ride motorcycles.
- My bike is pretty much stock.
- I use my bike mainly for short trips around town.

Hard Core
- Some people would call me and my friends "outlaws."
- I have spent lots on speed modifications for my bike.
- Sometimes I feel like an "outlaw."
- Some people would call me a "dirty biker."
- I think it's true that "real men" wear black.

Hog Heaven
- When I'm on my bike, people seem to be admiring me.
- I really believe that cars are confining, like a cage.
- Women admire my motorcycle.
- When I ride I feel like an Old Wild West cowboy.
- I feel close to other motorcyclists I see on the road.

Zen Riders
- I like dirt bikes.
- When I'm on my bike, people seem to be admiring me.
- I like the attention I get when I'm on my bike.
- Most of the time, my motorcycle is just parked.
- I get excited about motocross or scrambling.

Live to Ride
- I love to ride long distances. To me, 500 miles is a short trip.
- Motorcycles are a total lifestyle to me.
- Riding, to me, is often a magical experience.
- It's true that I live to ride and ride to live.
- My bike is everything to me.

As can be seen, the six segments are quite different from each other, both psychographically and demographically. For example:

- **Tour Gliders,** Comprising 14 percent of the sample, they like to use their bikes for long trips. Compared with the other segments, they are somewhat older, more likely to be married, upper income, more professional, and veteran motorcycle owners, particularly Harleys.
- **Hard Core,** These are the archetypal Harley owners. Perhaps surprisingly, they are only 9.7 percent of the sample. Compared with the others, they are younger, less likely to be married, less educated, lower income, and own an older motorcycle. These are the outlaws (or people who would like to feel that way).
- **Zen Riders**, To these 20 percent, riding a motorcycle is a spiritual experience. They are young, most likely to be married, educated, upper income, and tend to use their bikes less than others.

From the company's standpoint, the behavioral data in Table 4.9 are particularly interesting. Note the differences in the money spent on parts and accessories, the model of bike owned, and the percentage who bought their motorcycles new. The survey gives the company a good idea about which group to target for different kinds of products and services. For example, the Hard Core and Zen Riders are the poorest targets for upgrading to new motorcycles because they have the lowest incidence of new purchases. The best target for new bikes is the Dream Rider segment because it has a high incidence of buying new models and is the largest segment (40 percent of the sample). However, the Hard Core segment spends by far the most on accessories and parts (although it is a small group).

Table 4.9

Harley-Davidson Segmentation Scheme

Segment Descriptor and Behavioral Variables

Characteristic	Tour Gliders	Dream Riders	Hard Core	Hog Heaven	Zen Riders	Live to Ride
Relative size of segment	13.8%	39.8%	9.7%	8.7%	20.3%	7.6%
Summary of demographics						
Average owner age	42.6	42.9	36.2	39.2	36.9	36.6
Sex male	93.8%	95.1%	93.5%	85.4%	94.7%	91.7%
Married	60.0%	68.5%	51.1%	56.1%	75.0%	58.3%
Number of children at home	1.3	1.2	1.0	1.2	1.2	1.2
Education: college graduate	15.4%	24.7%	8.7%	7.3%	19.8%	25.0%
Income of $50,000 and over						
Personal	29.7%	30.2%	4.4%	31.7%	26.3%	25.0%
Household	50.8%	52.0%	26.6%	41.0%	55.4%	55.5%
Average income						
Personal	$40,438	$40,087	$27,389	$34,744	$38,816	$33,667
Household	$46,563	$46,500	$34,944	$40,397	$47,435	$44,222
Occupation: professional/managerial	21.5%	30.1%	0.0%	26.8%	19.8%	29.4%
Summary of motorcycle ownership						
Motorcycle is 1991 or newer	24.6%	30.7%	7.3%	22.0%	28.7%	15.2%
Owned motorcycle under 2 years	16.7%	22.7%	10.3%	35.5%	30.4%	30.3%
Bought motorcycle new	40.0%	50.0%	15.2%	45.0%	33.0%	55.9%
Model year of principal Harley	1985.9	1985.8	1980.5	1986.2	1983.6	1985.7
This is their first motorcycle	1.5%	9.0%	15.9%	19.5%	9.4%	2.8%
Number of motorcycles owned	9.06	5.34	6.3	6.82	5.7	9.77
Number of Harleys owned	4.74	1.63	2.85	2.13	1.44	2.12
Money spent on motorcycle for						
Purchase of motorcycle	$9,048	$7,460	$5,082	$6,631	$6,966	$8,976
Parts/accessories this year	$690	$322	$1,260	$321	$767	$860
Parts/accessories in total	$1,571	$1,426	$3,233	$2,419	$1,734	$2,483
Estimated value of motorcycle today	$10,066	$8,414	$8,062	$8,591	$8,827	$10,342
Riding per year						
Number of miles	7,351	3,675	7,099	5,051	4,169	9,662
Number of days	188	109	187	148	112	214
Number riding years	24.1	20.2	16.5	16.9	18	17.7
Type of motorcycle they ride						
Touring	39.0%	16.4%	0.0%	7.9%	12.6%	31.3%
Full dress	18.6%	18.6%	11.4%	10.5%	14.9%	18.9%
Cruiser	23.8%	26.0%	36.4%	29.0%	28.7%	31.3%
Sportster	5.1%	30.5%	29.5%	52.6%	35.6%	0.0%
Other type	13.6%	8.5%	22.7%	0.0%	8.0%	18.8%

Thus, as we discussed in the section on developing target markets, this illustration highlights the need to consider a variety of factors in determining which segments to target for various products. Although we briefly discussed the trade-off between the size of the segment and the potential purchasing power, measured by the different segments' past behavior, characteristics such as segment growth and degree of competition must also be taken into consideration. In addition, it has been assumed that the psychographic approach shown is the best way to segment the market. As we noted earlier, it is important to consider a variety of segmentation schemes and compare them on their differential abilities to explain past behavior and to satisfy the other criteria for a good target segment.

Why Do Consumers Buy?

As we noted at the beginning of this chapter, a customer analysis also must address the question, "Why do customers buy the product or service?" A simplified model of the steps in the purchase process for any kind of product or service is shown in Figure 4.6.[15] The first step in any kind of purchasing behavior is need recognition, or reasons why people make purchases. A consumer realizes that her car is old and worn out and feels that it is more economical to purchase a new one than to continue to repair the old one. Needs can be recognized by the potential customer or someone else—a friend, a salesperson—can make the customer more aware of the need.[16]

Consider the famous hierarchy of needs posited by Abraham Maslow.[17] He theorized five ordered levels of human needs:

1. **Physiological:** basic human needs such as food, sleep, and water.
2. **Safety:** physical safety from injury, job security, and financial security.
3. **Social:** friendship, affection, acceptance by reference groups.
4. **Ego:** success, self-esteem, prestige.
5. **Self-actualization:** achieving one's potential, self-fulfillment.

These are obviously most relevant to consumer products and services. A product could be marketed to satisfy several of the needs simultaneously. For example, in the automobile illustration, the consumer may seek a sporty car that satisfies both transportation and self-expressive needs.

A better way to think about what motivates people to purchase products and services is to think of them as offering not physical attributes but benefits, as we discussed in Chapter 1. That is, the sole reason for a consumer to purchase is to obtain the benefits the purchase delivers.

Thus, one of the jobs of the marketing manager is to translate characteristics into product benefits. This can be done using managerial judgment or marketing research. In

Figure 4.6

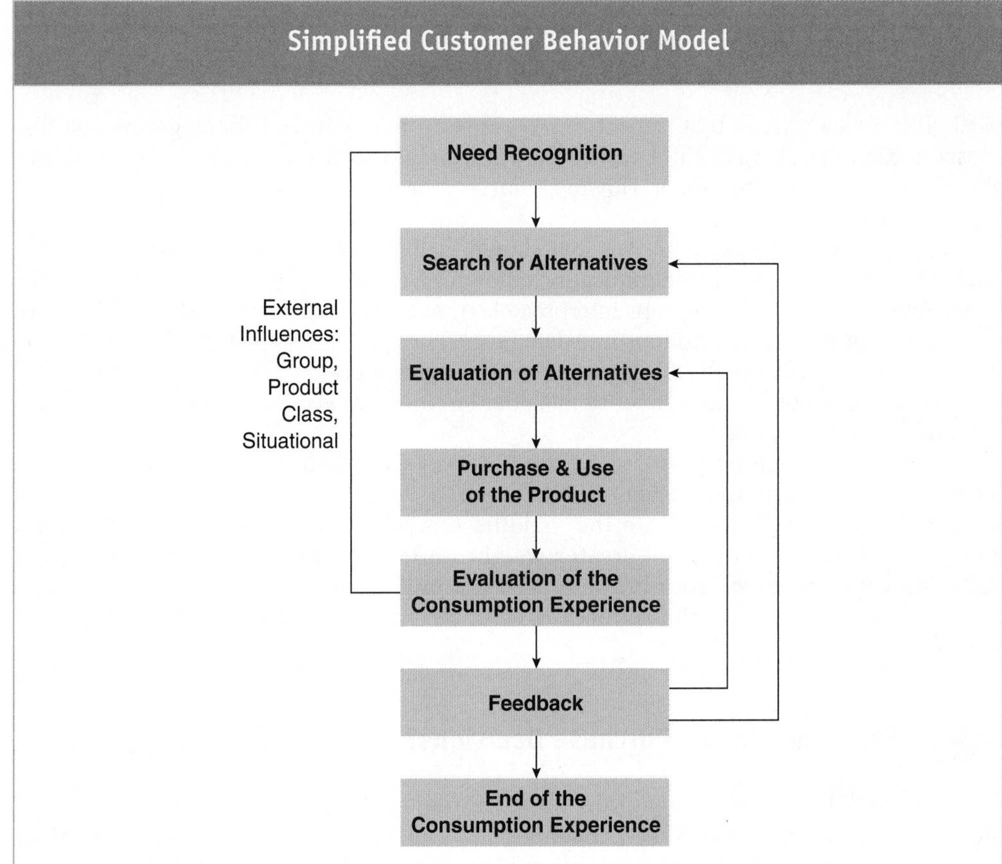

Source: William D. Wells and David Prensky (1996), *Consumer Behavior* (New York: Wiley).

Figure 4.7

Goodyear Tires Web Page

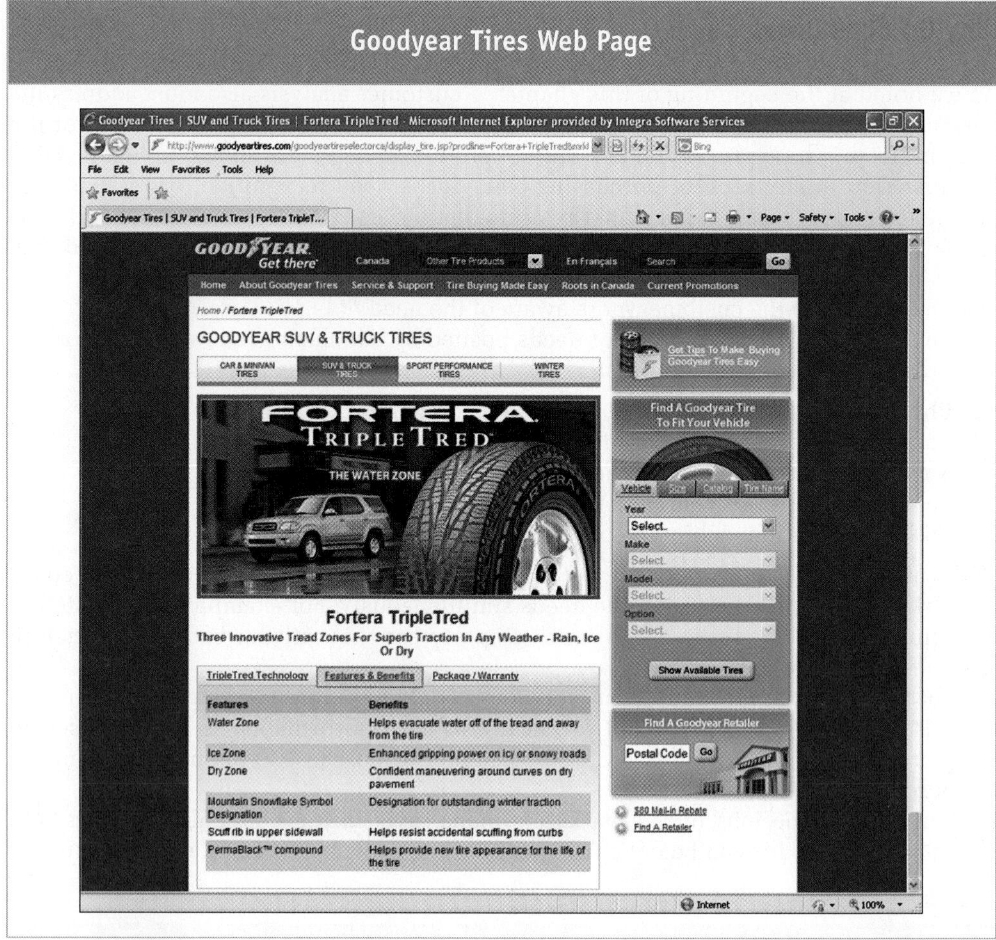

Source: Used by permission, courtesy of The Goodyear Tire and Rubber Company.

particular, focus groups that permit depth research (e.g., clinical focus groups, as discussed in Chapter 3) are useful because they encourage customers to develop lists of benefits they obtain from products. However, surveys or other marketing research methods can also be used.

The page from the Goodyear Web site shown in Figure 4.7 for the Fortera Triple Tred model is a good example of communications drawing a distinction between product benefits and features. The latter are perhaps interpretable by experts. Most of us need to have technical language or feature descriptions translated into how they can help. Thus the "Dry Zone" feature results in the benefit of "Confident maneuvering around curves on dry pavement." Consumers cannot only relate better to the latter but they can also understand what effect it will have on their driving.

It is particularly important to develop an analysis of benefits by market segment. Segments will value product benefits differently. Thus, consumers in rainy climates such as England will appreciate the benefits related to "wet traction," while those who are enthusiasts will put a greater weight on the handling characteristics of the tires. Marketing research should, therefore, not only attempt to uncover the benefits that consumers attach to the product features, but to also match them with the target segments.

How Do Consumers Make Purchase Decisions?

Referring back to the beginning of this chapter, the third key question that a marketing manager must ask in performing a customer analysis is, "How do customers make their purchase decisions?" In this section, we explore some of the ways in which purchasing decisions are made.

Search for Alternatives

As Figure 4.6 shows, following the need recognition stage of the buying process, the customer is hypothesized to search for alternative products that deliver the desired benefits. In general customers use two sources of information: internal and external.

Internal sources of information are those that are retrieved from memory. Examples are:

- Past experiences with products.
- Past conversations with experts.
- Old magazine articles such as those in *Consumer Reports.*

Any source of information that has already been obtained and is recalled is an internal source.

New sources of information that the customer obtains from the environment after establishing the need are considered external sources of information. For example, after establishing the need to take a vacation, a consumer will not only retrieve information from memory, such as the level of satisfaction with other places she has visited, but may also seek out or be exposed to:

- Advice from a travel agent.
- Articles in travel magazines.
- Recommendations from friends and relatives.
- Advertisements.
- Information from Web sites.

Thus, there is overlap between internal and external sources, the difference being in the timing of the receipt of information.

Although it is clear that many external sources of information are provided by the marketing manager, interpersonal communication, or word-of-mouth (WOM), is considered to be the most credible. Managers are interested in WOM because it is often one of the most important drivers of consumer behavior such as the adoption of a new technology, the decision to watch a TV show, or the choice of which laptop to purchase.[18] Word-of-mouth recommendations can also be stimulated both personally (by giving incentives to old customers to recommend and sign up new customers) and electronically (through user groups or other Internet-based discussions).

It is difficult to predict how much information search will occur. Economic theory predicts that rational customers will collect information only to the point at which the marginal benefit of obtaining the information in terms of incremental value to making a choice equals the marginal cost. However, because much of the information in the environment can be collected at low cost (e.g., the passive viewing of a television commercial), economic theory is not predictive in this case. The Web has become a critical source of information for external search. Some estimates indicate that more than 50 percent of purchases of mortgages, insurance, real estate, and new cars are preceded by some kind of online search.

The amount of information collected will vary by some variables that you would expect:

- Expertise in a product category.
- How recently a purchase was made.
- The importance of the purchase to the customer.

Thus, the information search will be more extensive for expensive products and services that are purchased infrequently, such as durables (TVs, video cameras, automobiles) and significant long-term investments (stocks, houses).

What Happens Next?

As a result of the search for alternatives through internal and external information sources, customers form three different sets of options:

1. The **evoked or consideration set**. This is the set of products from which the customer will choose to purchase. Although the brands in the set may have different underlying probabilities of being chosen, all of the brands have at least a nonzero probability.
2. The **purchase set**. This is the set of products the customer has actually chosen within a specified period of time.

evoked or consideration set
in consumer behavior, the set of products from which the customer will choose to purchase

purchase set
in consumer behavior, the set of products that the customer has actually chosen within a specified period of time

Clearly, although being in many purchase sets is the best situation of all, before purchase can even occur, the marketing manager must get the product into as many evoked or consideration sets as possible (i.e., move the product from the evoked set to active consideration). For example, Club Med's marketing managers must ensure that when people are thinking of taking a vacation, they include Club Med in the set of options they are considering. For new products and those with low awareness (i.e., those in most consumers' inert sets), the manager must devote a large portion of the marketing budget to making customers aware that the product exists. When awareness is not low, the problem is probably related to performance, quality, or image.

Primary data collection will inform you about the status of your product in these sets. One approach is to do pure awareness research. This can be done using aided or unaided recall. In the latter case, the researcher simply asks the respondent to list any brands he or she has heard of in the target product category. With aided recall, the respondent is given a list from which to choose brands. However, this kind of research may not always be a good guide to how many evoked sets contain your brand because the feeling about the brand could be negative rather than positive. As a result, the questionnaire may contain more direct questions about whether the respondent would consider buying the brand or the company's product on a subsequent purchase occasion.

It is interesting to note that information collected about the purchase set is only partial information because it does not contain any indication about other brands or options considered. For frequently purchased products, scanner panel data provide information about the purchase set but not the evoked/consideration set. It is useful to have both kinds of information because the evoked set is a better indication of potential competition than the purchase set, particularly if the latter demonstrates considerable brand loyalty.

Evaluating Options in the Consideration Set

Following the purchase process shown in Figure 4.6 and logic, the next task facing the customer is to make a choice from the evoked set.[19] A way to conceptualize this part of the decision-making process is to consider that all products and services can be decomposed into their attributes or benefits (hereafter simply called attributes) that customers want to obtain by purchasing the product. For example, the attribute list for tires would include:

- Quality.
- Brand name.
- Safety.
- Tread type.
- Price.
- Tread pattern.

multiattribute model
a popular model of decision making that requires information about how useful or important each attribute is to the customer making a brand choice (which involves assigning importance weights) and how customers perceive the brands in the evoked set in terms of their attributes

This list forms the basis for a popular model of decision making, called the **multiattribute model**.

In order to understand how customers develop choices from the evoked set using this model, two kinds of information are required. First, we require information about how useful or important each attribute is to the customer in making a brand choice, or how important each attribute is relative to the others. These are called importance weights or importance rankings. The second kind of information required is how customers perceive the brands in the evoked set in terms of their attributes.

Application Hyundai

Despite receiving high marks for quality, the carmaker Hyundai has sometimes struggled with stalled sales.[20] If Steve Wilhite seemed more pensive than enthusiastic, it was because his briefcase held a binder of consumer data spelling out just how tough it was going to be to sell the Genesis. Wilhite, 54, was well aware of Hyundai's challenge before taking on the top job at Hyundai Motor America last August. As senior vice president for global marketing at Nissan in Tokyo and vice president for marketing at Nissan's North American operation before that, he was used to looking at Hyundai as a competitor. He'd seen its quality improve "to scary levels," he says—and sales stall. The South Korean auto maker is desperate to convince consumers that its cars and sport utility vehicles (SUVs) are worth premium prices. Its impatience to see results is understandable. Hyundai's quality is actually ahead of Toyota's in J.D. Power's (MHP) Initial Quality Study, and behind only Lexus and Porsche. *Consumer Reports* just tapped two of Hyundai's new vehicles as "Most Impressive" among five 2007 models it recently singled out. But only 23 percent of all new-car buyers last year even bothered to consider a Hyundai. That compares with 65 percent for Toyota Motor Co. (TM) and more than 50 percent for Honda Motor Co. (HMC). One Hyundai dealer calls its image problem "the Yugo factor." Hyundai entered the U.S. market in the late 1980s at about the same time as the much-joked-about Yugoslavian cars and went on to have quality problems that almost sank the brand.

The model raises four key questions:

1. Which attributes do customers use to evaluate a product?
2. How do we determine how much of each attribute a brand possesses?
3. How are the importance weights determined?
4. How do customers combine the information from the previous two questions to make choices?

The marketing manager must first determine the set of attributes customers use in making purchase decisions. This can be done using managerial judgment (not recommended because of the bias introduced), focus groups, or more systematic survey research. In this stage of the research, the questions asked are usually open-ended to elicit from the customers or potential customers the attributes they consider for purchasing brands in the category.

Assuming that the manager has collected the set of attributes used, the second question to be addressed is how customers perceive the different brands on these attributes. It is critical that to understand how customers make purchasing decisions, you must appreciate the differences between their perceptions and reality (i.e., the "true" values of the attributes for each brand): *the former drive purchasing behavior, not the latter.* As we discussed in Chapter 2, often, these perceptual differences form the core of the value proposition. For example, perhaps Consumer's Union or some government agency has determined that Goodyear tires are the safest on the market. Although this may be the reality, consumers in the market for a replacement tire may believe that Michelins are the safest, based on information from advertising, friends, or other external or internal sources (witness their long-running advertising campaign focusing on the Michelin baby and safety with the tag line, "Because so much is riding on your tires").

How do you measure these perceptions? The most common way is to ask a sample of customers questions of the following type:[21] "Please rate the described brands on the following set of characteristics on a 1 to 10 scale, where 1 is poor and 10 is excellent." The importance weights are determined in a similar fashion. For example, using a survey approach, we can ask the following question: "Please rate the following attributes on a 1 to 7 scale, where 1 is very unimportant and 7 is very important in terms of how important each attribute is to you in making a decision about which sport utility vehicle to purchase." Alternatively, respondents could be asked to simply rank order the nine attributes from most to least important.

Table 4.10 provides an illustration of the kind of data collected using these methods.[22] The entries above the line are average perceptions from a sample of consumers

Table 4.10

Sample Multiattribute Model Data

	Attributes				
Brand	Quality	Brand Name	Safety	Price	Overall Score*
Goodyear	7.8**	8.3	8.0	7.1	247.6
Firestone	5.7	4.1	3.0	6.3	148.6
Michelin	8.1	8.5	7.5	5.2	235.7
Dunlop	6.3	6.7	7.4	7.9	221.6
Bridgestone	6.9	7.1	7.3	8.5	233.1
Importance***	9.1	7.7	8.5	6.3	

*Obtained by multiplying each attribute score by its importance weight and summing across all attributes.

**Entries are average scores from a sample of respondents on a 1–10 "poor" to "excellent" scale.

***Entries are average scores on a 1–10 "very unimportant" to "very important" scale.

who buy tires. In this (fictitious) sample, consumers rated Michelin the best in quality and brand name, Goodyear the best in safety, and Bridgestone as having the best prices. The entries below the line are the importance weights of the attributes. In this sample, consumers gave the greatest weight to quality and safety.

There are many other approaches to obtaining attribute perceptions and importance weight information. No matter how it is obtained, information on perceptions and attribute importance is critical to understanding how your customers are making decisions.

Looking back at the four questions of the multiattribute model, the final question concerns how customers combine the attribute perceptions and importance weights to make purchasing decisions. Perhaps the most obvious way to combine the information is to simply create a score for each brand based on a sum of the perceptions of the attributes weighted by the importance weights. This is called a **compensatory model** because a low score on one attribute can be compensated for by a higher score on another. Using the data from Table 4.10, the weighted scores for the five brands show that the order of preference is Goodyear, Michelin, Bridgestone, Dunlop, and Firestone. By performing the calculations for each brand in this manner, this kind of approach can be used to forecast sales and market shares.[23]

compensatory model
any model in which a low score on one attribute can be compensated for by a higher score on another

However, the process may not always be as systematic as this. For example, the kind of product being considered affects the purchasing decision process. As we will see in Chapter 15, services are unique in the fact that they cannot be touched and, therefore, cannot be easily sampled before purchasing. Durable goods like autos need more extensive information search than, say, chewing gum.

Postpurchase Behavior

After the purchase is made, the buyer "consumes" the product or the service. It is important to note that, from Figure 4.6, the buyer's purchase experiences or evaluation of the consumption of the product become part of the internal memory search. Good experiences create favorable memories and enhance the likelihood of future purchases. For frequently purchased products, repeat buying is critical to success because there are not enough new, untapped buyers to sustain a low-priced product for long. For high-priced, infrequently purchased products, good experiences lead to favorable word-of-mouth and increased chances of buying the same product again (or other products that the company markets). Bad experiences increase the probability that the product will not be repurchased and that the customer will not speak kindly of it to other potential buyers.

How does this evaluation process work? A central concept is that before consumption, customers form **expectations** about the product's performance and the benefits that it will provide. These expectations are developed based on the information the customer has collected from the prior search activities. During and after consumption, customers evaluate the product or service relative to these expectations. Products that meet or exceed expectations receive a favorable postpurchase evaluation and the opposite reaction results for those that do not achieve the expected levels.[24] An herbicide sold to farmers based on its ability to kill insects without significant environmental damage creates those performance expectations. The farmer will analyze the results of applying the herbicide and mentally compare these results to the promises made by the salesperson or the distributor. Future purchases are highly dependent on this postpurchase evaluation.

expectations
are developed based on the information the customer has collected from the prior search activities

Purchase Influences

External to the basic consumer purchasing process shown in Figure 4.6 is a set of external influences. These include a variety of interpersonal and social interactions that shape the way consumers make purchasing decisions.

Group Influences

These include:

Family and friends Family and friends also affect purchasing behavior. An example is the classic typology of the **family life cycle**, where each stage brings with it a different set of values and attitudes. Although there are some variations (Table 4.4), the typical stages of the family life cycle are the following:

family life cycle
the stages of life individuals pass through

1. **Bachelor stage:** young, single people not living at home.
2. **Newly married couples:** young, no children.

3. **Full nest I:** young married couples with younger child under age 6.
4. **Full nest II:** young married couples with youngest child age 6 or over.
5. **Full nest III:** older married couples with dependent children.
6. **Empty nest I:** older married couples, no children living with them, household head(s) in the labor force.
7. **Empty nest II:** older married couples, no children living with them, household head(s) retired.
8. **Solitary survivor:** in labor force.
9. **Solitary survivor:** retired.

Like many of the frameworks used in business and elsewhere, there are plenty of violations of the linear form of the life cycle. For example, today it is not uncommon for Empty nester Is to become Full nest IIIs when a suddenly unemployed child comes home to live. However, as you can see from the stages of the life cycle, it is easy to imagine products and services targeting one or more of the groups.

Social class A popular variable for segmentation is social class (Table 4.1). Sometimes referred to as socioeconomic status (SES), it is often highly correlated with occupation. Social class is often divided into four groups: upper, middle, working, and lower class. Sociologists have found that the different classes have values as a group, and can therefore impact the kinds of products and services you buy.

Culture Cultural values are transmitted through religious organizations, educational institutions, and the family. Various subcultures in the United States (such as Hispanic, Asian, Jewish, and others) have their unique traditions and tastes and, as a result, marketers offer products and services that account for these traditions and tastes.

Cultural differences are particularly important in a global marketing context. The largest issue facing companies wanting to market products in other countries is the fact that significant differences in culture can affect the way customers respond to the product and the marketing strategy. The sociocultural environment is composed of the factors shown in Figure 4.8. Demographic factors include the population size, growth rate, age distribution, and geographic density. These data normally are readily available.

More difficult to obtain and idiosyncratic to the product category are the behavioral attributes—values and attitudes. These are usually determined by a country or

Figure 4.8

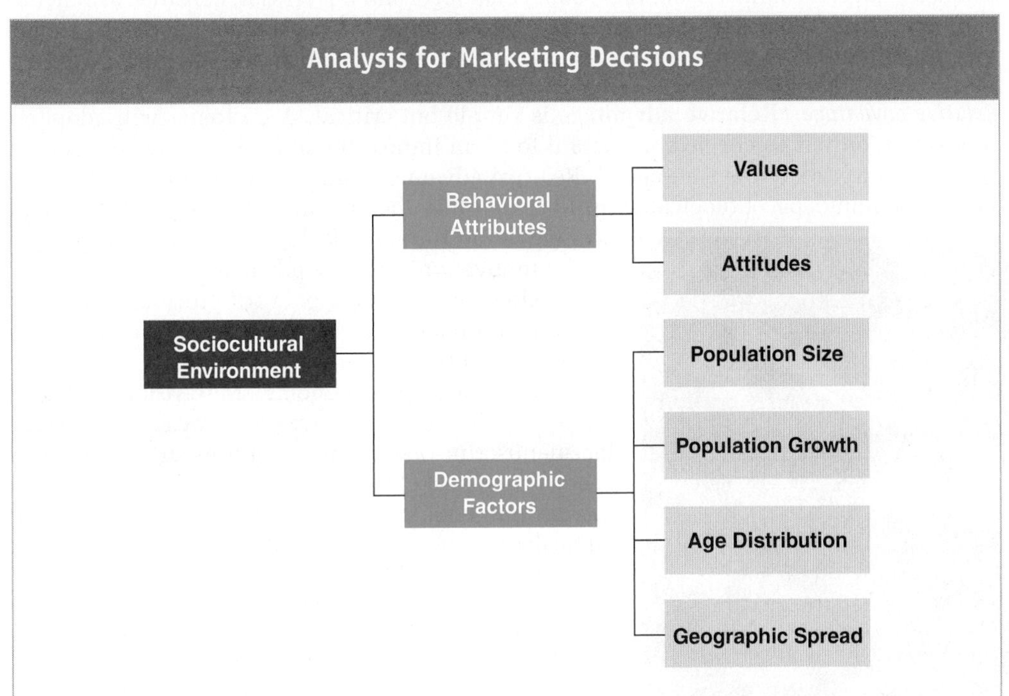

Source: Frank Bradley (1991), *International Marketing Strategy* (New York: Prentice Hall), p. 11. Produced by permission from Pearson Education Ltd.

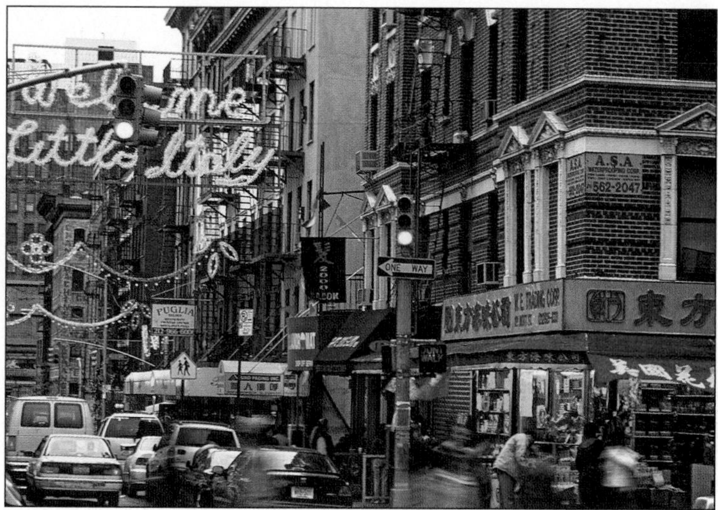

Cultural differences are often exhibited in the same neighborhood such as New York's Little Italy.
Source: Rudi Von Briel/PhotoEdit Inc.

region's culture, the ways of living built up by a group of people and transmitted through generations. The main elements of culture are:[25]

- Language.
- Religion.
- Values and attitudes.
- Social organization.
- Education.
- Technology and material culture.

Obviously, countries differ on these dimensions. Japan and Korea are more homogeneous than India and the United States. Thus, it may be possible to treat the first two as a segment, but the latter two cannot be treated that way.

Sensitivity to cultural differences is necessary for successful marketing of a product into a foreign country. It is not only important in understanding the end customer for consumer products, it is also essential in marketing industrial products and services, where there is considerable face-to-face interaction. There are many guides that can help you to keep from embarrassing yourself and your company when abroad, and they are well worth studying.[26]

Product Class Influences

Technology-based products bring their own unique purchase influences. From the customer's perspective, the unique problems associated with the marketing of technology-based products are concentrated largely in the earliest stages of the product life cycle. After the product category is established, in the late growth or maturity stage of the product life cycle, most products, whether high-tech or low-tech, become well known. They are marketed in much the same way as other kinds of products and services. For example, when DVD players were first marketed in the 1990s, customers had little idea about how to use them and why they would be worth buying. Today, it is a commodity business, with strong price competition and multiple units in many households.

relative advantage
the concept that a customer will adopt an innovation only if he or she considers it to be an improvement over the current product being used to satisfy the same need

What factors affect the success rate of technology-based innovations? The most extensive analysis of how customers, both consumers and businesses, consider whether to adopt new technologies was conducted by Everett Rogers.[27] Rogers identified five key factors or attributes to explain why customers adopt new technologies or why they do not.

Relative advantage **Relative advantage** is simple but critical. A customer will adopt an innovation only if she or he considers it to be an improvement over the current product being used to satisfy the same need. Relative advantage can be stated in many different terms: economic, psychological, or utilitarian. Thus, the rate of acceptance or diffusion of an innovation throughout the population is increased by the innovation's relative advantage.

A number of factors affect the adoption of new technologies like this pen-based video camera.
Source: Michael Probst/AP Wide World Photos

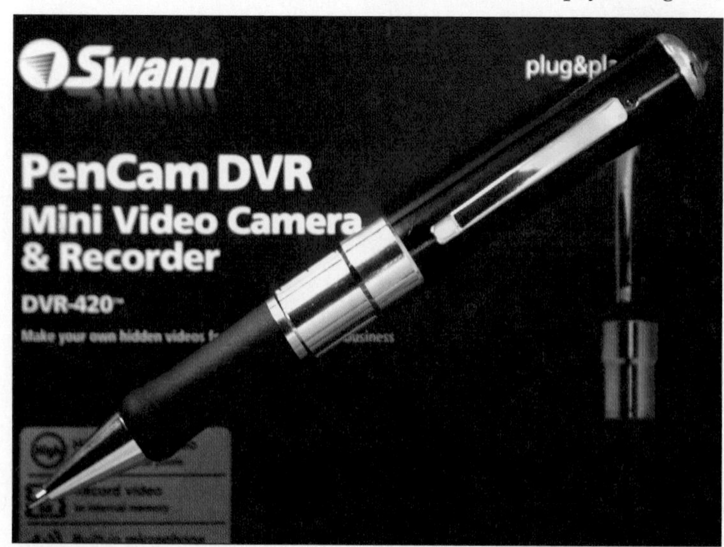

Consider the adoption of word-processing systems (such as those sold by Wang in the 1970s) and word-processing software. Clearly, a key relative advantage of this innovation was economic. Most readers will not remember the error-correcting and revision processes for manuscripts before word processing. Secretaries spent a great deal of time manually cutting and pasting. In addition, book production costs have dropped dramatically because most publishers can produce a book directly from the author's computer files. The benefits of new seed strains developed through biotechnological advances include increased yields of many crops and thus greater profits for farmers. Again it can be seen that relative advantage is often economic.

Particularly for consumer products, relative advantage can be obtained from psychological benefits or status. Although the initial targets for cellular phones were businesspeople, many people with economic justification for the product bought them for the status conferred by the antennas on their cars. The initial purchasers of MP3 players purchased not only the new technology itself but the ability to say that they are among the first in their neighborhoods to own one.

Relative advantage is also obtained from noneconomic, utilitarian benefits of new technologies. Although some consumers may have purchased cellular phones for their status, many others purchased them for the increased ability to stay in touch with children and baby-sitters. DVD players provide economic benefits by enabling people to watch movies at home at a lower price. Digital video recorders allow consumers to time-shift TV viewing by taping programs and replaying them at more convenient times.

Compatibility A second attribute of innovations that is evaluated by customers of new technologies is the **compatibility** of the innovation with existing systems, values and beliefs, or previously introduced ideas. Higher compatibility leads to faster adoption of innovation.

compatibility
an attribute evaluated by customers of new technologically-based innovations that refers to the compatibility of the innovation with existing systems, values, and beliefs or previously introduced ideas

For example, the initial penetration rate of satellite TV dishes was very slow. The earliest dishes were large structures that occupied a large amount of outdoor space. Early adopters were people living on farms or in other rural areas where there was plenty of land, the dishes being incompatible with apartments and houses in urban areas. The sales of these systems increased rapidly in the late 1990s as technological improvements greatly reduced their size and thus made them compatible with more consumers' living conditions.

Other products have succeeded by being compatible with customer knowledge or systems. The rapid penetration rate of cellular phones is at least partially related to the fact that although the technology was new, they were basically still telephones, a product with which customers were familiar. The great success of Iomega's Zip and Jaz drives (computer disk drives holding large amounts of data) was influenced by the fact that the company made them compatible with existing personal computers.

Complexity The perceived **complexity** of the innovation is negatively related to the success of an innovation. Simple innovations are clearly more likely to be adopted than those that require a significant amount of explanation about their use and benefits. One of the problems with the Apple Newton personal digital assistant was that it had too many features for most users. In addition, the handwriting recognition feature of the product was difficult to train to recognize the user's particular style. Sometimes, simplicity is what consumers want. The French automaker Renault has been successful with the no-frills Logan that sells for as little as 5,000 euros in emerging markets like Poland.[28]

complexity
one factor of an innovation that is negatively related to its success

Trialability **Trialability** is the ability of potential users to try a product on a limited basis before adopting. Obviously this is a particular problem for new technologies, where uncertainty about the product is high. It is also a problem for services, as we will discuss in Chapter 15. Their inherent intangibility and experience attributes make prepurchase evaluation difficult.

trialability
the ability of potential users of an innovative or new product to try it on a limited basis before adoption

Many high-tech companies handle this problem by establishing beta test sites for early versions of a product. Particularly large and influential customers are given prototypes to use in their organizations and generate feedback for the company. New services are tested by customers in realistic settings. For example, the cable modem network developed by the now defunct @home was first tested in Fremont, California, in residents' homes.

Observability **Observability** is the degree to which an innovation and its results are visible to others. The cellular phone antenna makes the adoption of the phone observable to others and reinforces the idea that it is a useful innovation (in addition to the status aspect mentioned previously). German software firm SAP is the leader in enterprise application software, programs that manage a company's vital operations, from order-taking to manufacturing to accounting. The category has expanded dramatically as stories about the tremendous cost savings and efficiencies obtainable from such software have been published in most leading business publications and mentioned in numerous speeches around the world. In other words, the economic relative advantage has been enhanced because the innovation is more observable.

observability
the degree to which an innovation or its results are visible to others

network externalities
the concept that, for many products and services, the value of owning them increases as the number of owners increases

Potential for network externalities The previous five aspects of innovations were promulgated by Rogers's work. Another factor that has been found to have a significant impact on the adoption of new technologies is the potential for **network externalities**. The concept behind network externalities is simple. For many products and services, the value of owning them increases as the number of owners increases. The original concept was developed for telephone-like networks as clearly the benefits from owning a phone increase as the number of owners increases. Thus, the attractiveness of many products is driven by how many others are "on the network." Examples include the telephone, online services such as America Online, video game systems (kids like to share games and bring them to friends' houses), and computer software. The importance of network externalities limits a company's ability to develop the market for a product or service because the markets for stand-alone products (i.e., those not subject to network externalities) normally develop more quickly. A relatively new technology, ip telephony (computer-based telephone service), will grow depending on the number of users that companies like Vonage and Skype can enroll.

Application Fax Machines

Perhaps the classic example of a product affected by network externalities is the fax machine. The first transmission of an image over a wire was performed by a Scot, Alexander Bain, in 1842.[29] However, the first commercial applications of facsimile transmissions did not occur until 1910, when news photos were transmitted over long distances. By the 1940s and 1950s, the main uses of fax technology were for transmitting weather maps, newspaper proofs, news photographs, and fingerprints. However, transmission speeds of about 10 minutes per page were too slow for commercial applications. In addition, there were no standards for the machines, so different manufacturers' devices could not communicate.

Although the machines continued to improve, the industry did not really take off until the Consultative Committee on Telegraph and Telephone (CCITT), an international standard-setting group, developed standards for fax machines in 1976. The CCITT developed the retroactive G1 standard to be compatible with the Xerox Telecopier launched in 1967. This machine could transmit documents at a rate of a page every 4 to 6 minutes. The G2 standard, popularized by Matsushita around 1973, halved the transmission time of the G1. However, the G3 standard adopted in 1980, characterized by transmission speeds of 10 to 20 seconds per page, really created the market. In Japan, which was the first market to adopt fax machines in large quantities, the installed base went from 140,000 in 1980 to 1.1 million in 1985 and to 3 million in 1988. This growth resulted from several factors, including product improvements such as smaller machines that could sit easily on desks. However, it was also clearly related to the network aspect of the product—the more that were sold, the more valuable having one became.

The importance of network externalities is made even clearer by the failure of FedEx's ZapMail facsimile service. Launched in 1983, ZapMail promised document-quality transmission, a big improvement over the chemically coated paper that was the standard of the time. However, the machines were proprietary and had to be leased from FedEx. Because they could not communicate with existing fax machines, the success of the product depended entirely on how many were adopted. When few were, there was no incentive for users to adopt more. The company pulled the plug on ZapMail in 1986.[30]

perceived risk
in regard to their adoption of new technologies, the extent to which customers are uncertain about the consequences of an action

An important concept related to these factors affecting the adoption of new technologies is **perceived risk**, which is the uncertainty involved with relative advantage, compatibility, complexity, trialability, observability, and potential for network externalities. It is defined as the extent to which the customer is uncertain about the consequences of an action. Although it may be high in many different purchase situations, the high-tech environment is particularly susceptible to it. There are two components of perceived risk: uncertainty (the likelihood that certain outcomes might occur) and consequences (whether these outcomes will be positive or negative and how severe they might be).

Thus, the challenge for high-tech marketing managers is to reduce either the uncertainty or severity of possible negative consequences. The former can be done using the beta test sites described earlier. In addition, high-tech firms often employ application engineers, who work closely with customers to ensure that the product or service works in their environments. Offering extensive employee training is also a common strategy. Minimizing negative consequences can be accomplished through generous warranty and return policies or discounts on upgrades.

Situational Influences

The final set of purchases influences are situational or those that are unique to a particular time or place. These include:

1. **Physical surroundings:** the weather, the décor of a store, sounds.
2. **Social surroundings:** the people with you when you shop (e.g., children in a supermarket).
3. **Temporal factors:** time pressure.
4. **Task definition factors:** buying a product as a gift for a birthday (versus buying it for yourself).
5. **Antecedent states:** mood or current financial situation.

Situational influences are often called *context effects.* Research has uncovered a large number of different such effects and shown how they affect consumer behavior. One such context effect is called the *compromise* effect.[31] The idea is that a manager can increase the sales of a brand by making it the intermediate rather than extreme option in terms of price. This intermediate option thus becomes a compromise to the customer. The classic example of this is wine. A restaurant can increase the profit on a new bottle of wine by making its price difference compared with a lower-quality bottle greater than the cost difference. As we all know, customers shy away from buying the cheapest bottle on the list and generally cannot afford the most expensive bottle. In this case, the purchasing context has changed due to the addition of a new brand into the choice set. Likewise, the addition of super-premium gasoline has significantly helped the sales of the mid-priced version.

Buying Roles

Although purchasing decisions involving multiple people are more common for business-to-business situations, the purchasing decisions for many consumer products and services involve multiple people in the household. For example, when families are considering purchasing a vacation such as a trip to a Club Med, often the husband, wife, and maybe even the children will be involved.

The different buying roles in such a group buying decision are:

- **The initiator.** This is the person who first recognizes the need for the product or service.
- **The influencers.** These are people who influence the decision about which product is chosen.
- **The decider.** This is the person in the group who has the ultimate authority for a "go/no-go" decision.
- **The purchaser.** This person actually authorizes payment for the product.
- **The users.** These people actually use the product.

Pet food is a good example of a product category where the purchaser is different from the user.

Application Nestlé Purina

Nestlé Purina's ad campaign for Alpo carries some risks, considering humanization and pampering comprise the top trend driving the pet food market.[32] The trend toward pet humanization and pampering supports product premiumization and is the number-one driver in the U.S. pet food market. So when Nestlé Purina decided to poke fun at pampered pets in a high-profile ad campaign, it was not without risks.

Launched in spring 2009, the "Quick, get that dog some Alpo" program features pooches pampered to the extreme, including a dog in a tub with cucumber slices soothing its eyes and an undignified-looking Afghan with rollers in its fur. "Lost!" cry out posters referring to dogs like Spike, who was last seen sporting flashy duds and a sequined collar.

Indeed, Packaged Facts believes Fallon may very well have (inadvertently?) touched on one of the next big things in pet ownership and product marketing: a swing away from the fashion of treating pets like people in ways that are not the healthiest for either the pet owner or the pet.

As Martin Deeley, veteran dog trainer and president of the International Association of Canine Professionals, notes in his introduction to celebrity dog trainer Cesar Millan's bestselling

Cesar's Way: "Dogs are not small humans. Dogs are dogs, and we need to respect them as dogs. We do them a huge disservice by treating them like humans and thus create many of the bad behaviors we see today" (an assessment with which, by the way, Millan agrees).

So then, will we be seeing a shift away from anthropomorphism, toward encouraging our dogs to be dogs and our cats to be cats? Absolutely, Packaged Facts predicts, based in part on the fact that, in the area of pet nutrition, we already are.

This framework has many important implications. Like the market segments described earlier in this chapter, these microsegments, or different entities involved in the buying process, have different needs and seek different benefits. Thus, in the vacation purchase decision, the husband may be the initiator of the decision and value the relaxation aspect but also be concerned about the price. Both parents value good activities for the children. The children are most concerned about having fun. While not the deciders or the payers, they are definitely influencers, as all parents know.

Application Pharmaceuticals

The drug industry has witnessed a significant change in the buying process.[33] Americans spent $220 billion on prescription drugs in 2006, more than five times the amount spent in 1990. Are we much sicker? Some point to the fact that since the Food and Drug Administration loosened regulations in 1997, more companies are advertising prescription drugs directly to consumers (DTC advertising). Drug companies spent $4.7 billion on DTC advertising in 2008. Merck spent more than $135 million on Vioxx, which helps to treat osteoarthritis. Despite Merck's withdrawal of Vioxx in 2005, due to concerns about its possible side effects of strokes and heart attacks, companies continue to spend heavily. For example, Astra Zeneca spent nearly $220 million in 2004 advertising its purple pill, Nexium. The idea, of course, is to persuade consumers to request particular brands of drugs from their physicians. This has dramatically changed the way purchases are made. Before 1997, the doctor was usually the initiator, the influencer, and the decider. Now, while the doctor is still the decider because only he or she can actually write the prescription, the patient has become the initiator and possibly the influencer. Advocates for DTC advertising say that it can be credited with driving patient inquiries, encouraging better doctor–patient dialogues, and increasing consumer health awareness. Critics say that the increased money spent on such advertising drives up drug prices.

Where Do Consumers Buy?

It is important for you to understand where customers are buying your product or service, that is, what channels of distribution are the most popular and what the trends are. These data can be obtained from secondary sources, usually industry trade publications or, if the former are unavailable, surveys.

Table 4.11 shows the changes in shares of sales of consumer electronics in the leading retail channels from 2001 to 2008 (the numbers do not add to 100 percent due to the

Table 4.11

Share of Major Consumer Electronics Sales by Type of Outlet

Channel	2001	2008	Change
Electronics/appliance stores	27.3%	28.4%	4.0%
Mass merchants	25.2	22.5	-10.7
Computer stores	10.4	5.1	-51.0
Electronics only stores	8.9	17.2	93.3
Consumer direct	8.2	12.8	56.1
Home office	8.2	2.8	-65.9

Source: Twice, March 21, 2003, and May 18, 2009.

Table 4.12

Purchase Frequency and Size Trends Among U.S. Channels			
Channel	Penetration	Trips/Year	$/Trip
Mass merchants	95%	31 trips	$50
Apparel stores	45%	4.4 trips	$61
Home improvement	75%	7.3 trips	$45
Grocery	99%	59 trips	$30
Electronics stores	47%	3.1 trips	$101
Military stores	4%	20.7 trips	$62
Home furnishings	32%	2.7 trips	$49
Warehouse clubs	51%	11 trips	$86

omission of smaller channels). This is a broad category covering audio, communications, and video products as well as information technology (PCs) and car electronics. The two largest outlets for these products are electronics/appliance stores (e.g., Best Buy) and mass merchants (e.g., Walmart, Target, Sears). The biggest winners have been electronics-only stores (e.g., Radio Shack [now called The Shack], GameStop) and consumer direct (e.g., Amazon, other Internet retailers). The biggest losers have been computer stores (e.g., CompUSA, which went out of business) and home office stores (e.g., Office Depot, Staples). Clearly, consumers are shifting their buying patterns for consumer electronics due to the growth of the Internet and the wide variety of outlets for many products. For example, cellular service companies such as Verizon and AT&T sell many phones to match with their services.

Table 4.12 compares purchase frequency and purchase size across a variety of U.S. shopping channels for 2007 to give some idea about how consumers vary their shopping habits.

Application Netflix

Netflix introduced its Internet-only DVD rental subscription service in 1999. For $23.99 per month, subscribers can order as many movies as they want, up to four at a time, and keep them as long as they wish (there are less expensive plans if you want to be able to hold fewer than four DVDs at one time). There are no due dates, no late fees, rare out-of-stock problems, and reliable delivery. The service has been so successful that the number of subscribers is now more than 11 million. In addition, giant Walmart entered and then dropped out of the competition, providing an additional demonstration of Neflix's success.

The key to its success has been to change consumer behavior. When people used to think of movie rentals, they did not think of mail, they thought of bricks-and-mortar stores like Blockbuster. Thus, Netflix's communications stress how the "product" works, that is, all the details necessary to understand Netflix. In addition, its communications budget is oriented toward events and activities that will create additional word-of-mouth because their customers can explain how it works just as well as the company can. "Where" consumers are renting videos has changed due to Netflix.[34]

When Do Consumers Buy?

The final question to address is that of purchase timing. For each market segment, it is important to understand when they purchase your product or service in terms of:

- **Time of day:** fast food, utilities, long-distance telephone service.
- **Day of week:** retail shopping, movies.

- **Month or season:** products purchased from firm capital budgets; seasonal products such as ice cream, soft drinks, and cold remedies.
- **Cycles defined in years:** durable good replacement cycles, products tied to economic conditions.

Timing issues affect both marketing and operations personnel. Because communications in media such as radio, television, the Internet, and print can be timed precisely, demand can be generated by placing the communications near the appropriate time of demand. For example, it is common to see advertisements for cold remedies before winter arrives in order to get consumers to stock up before they actually need the product. Channels of distribution must have sufficient stocks of products when demand occurs. Seasonal patterns in demand can wreak havoc with product schedules and personnel management. Thus, some products attempt to smooth out seasonal fluctuations or other timing patterns by trying to build demand in what have traditionally been off-peak periods. For example, the antacid Tums was repositioned to be perceived as a calcium additive as well. This changed the timing of consumption from primarily nighttime to any time of the day.

Executive Summary

Key learning points in this chapter include the following:

- The main elements of understanding customers include *who* they are, *why* they buy, *how* they make purchase decisions, *where* they purchase, and *when* they buy.
- In understanding who customers are, you need to collect descriptive information about them and their buying behavior. It is important to develop links between the two to identify the best market segments to pursue.
- The basis of understanding why customers buy is knowing what benefits customers are seeking. This analysis should be conducted at the market segment level because benefits sought can vary between segments.
- The buying process (how?) for consumers is complex. A simplified model of the process is that consumers search for alternatives that satisfy the motivation for buying, develop a consideration or evoked set of acceptable brands from which the purchase will be made, evaluate the options in the consideration set, and exhibit postpurchase behavior in terms of satisfaction that feeds back into the customer's information set. A set of external influences affect this process.
- To determine where customers buy, you need to understand which channels of distribution are being used by the target customers and how they are changing.
- When customers are buying is defined by time of day, month/season, or buying cycle.

Chapter Questions

1. Think of a product or service that is mass marketed and one that focuses on one or more particular segments. How does the development of marketing strategy differ in the two cases?
2. For a product of your own choosing, pick one logical variable (e.g., age) that can be used to segment the market. Now add a second variable (e.g., gender) so that customers have to satisfy the categories of both variables simultaneously (e.g., 18- to 24-year-old women). Now add a third variable. How many possible segments can you identify from a combination of the three variables? What implications does this have for the marketing manager?

3. Visit the VALS Web site and find out in which psychographic group you fall. Apply the questions to a couple of acquaintances in different age groups (mother, uncle, younger sister, etc.) and classify then as well. Would you have guessed that they would be in those groups?
4. Write a list of physical characteristics for a product. Take each characteristic and indicate what benefits it provides to a customer. How would an advertisement reflect this information?
5. What are the challenges in marketing products that are highly seasonal? Pick some examples to illustrate.
6. Pick a high-tech product that was successful (e.g., digital camera) and one that was not (e.g., the Sony Aibo, the Segway). Using Everett Rogers's five factors facilitating the adoption of new technological products (relative advantage, etc.), explain the difference in the products' success.

Key Learning Points

The purpose of this chapter is to compare organizational or industrial buying behavior with the consumer behavior studied in Chapter 4. Purchasers in companies or other organizations use different criteria to make buying decisions than do individuals and families. Key learning points include:

- The key differences between consumer and industrial marketing
- Market segmentation for marketing to organizations
- Understanding why organizational buyers make decisions
- Understanding the mechanism used by organizations to make purchasing decisions, or how such decisions are made
- The importance of knowing where and when such purchases are made

"netCustomer offers outsourced real-time service to its customers."
Source: Fredrik Renander/AP Wide World Photos

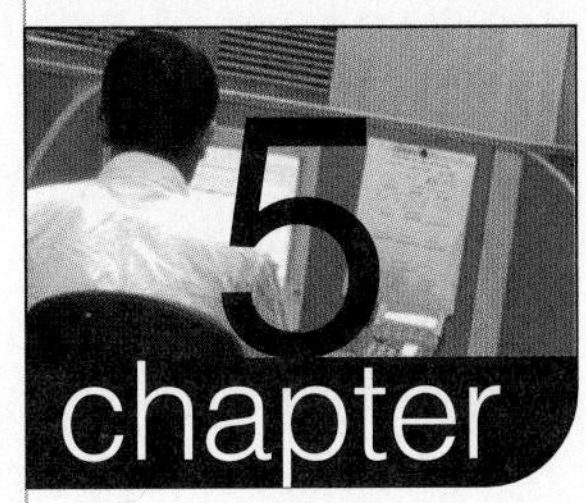

Organizational Buying Behavior

Chapter Brief

netCustomer is a Silicon Valley company that began operations in 1999.[1] The company offers advanced customer support and related business process outsourcing services to global companies. netCustomer services are delivered by leveraging an Internet infrastructure backbone and through multiple contact channels such as the Web, e-mail, phone, and fax. The company's around-the-clock support operations are based in India and client services and business development in San Jose, California.

netCustomer provides sophisticated and cost-effective support outsourcing capabilities to its clients. By basing the majority of its operations in India, it offers prompt, quality, and efficient support on a 24/7 basis. The company's early client implementations included leading companies such as Sony, Dell, and IBM. These relationships were implemented in partnership with iLogistix, a leading supply chain management and outsourcing firm. netCustomer enabled 24/7 Web-based support in conjunction with iLogistix Web-based fulfillment services. The customer inquiries were enabled through a button on the Web site. If customers had questions, they could receive instant help from the Web site (via text chat) or send an e-mail. Queries were seamlessly routed to netCustomer servers in the United States and then to its staff in India. This was a very successful launch and the first of its kind in the industry at that time.

Subsequently, netCustomer evolved to apply its 24/7 U.S.-India service delivery model to more advanced product support on behalf of leading technology companies such as PeopleSoft (acquired by Oracle) and NetScreen (acquired by Juniper). In addition, the enterprise applications marketplace had started showing signs of maturity. With increasing consolidation in the marketplace, vendor alternatives were becoming fewer and buyers were not fully satisfied with the cost structure and level of support from leading vendors. At the same time, in-house support was becoming expensive to maintain and was a distraction from other strategic information technology (IT) initiatives. As a result, many companies were revisiting their IT spending as they looked to invest in innovation as opposed to day-to-day operating costs of stable applications. They were questioning both the vendor support costs as well as their in-house cost of supporting major enterprise applications.

In addition, Vendors had traditionally charged 15 to 22 percent of the net license fee for ongoing support and maintenance. Systems integrators and IT services companies had traditionally charged by the hour for servicing most enterprise applications. Despite the maturity of the enterprise applications market, it was still uncommon to find true pay-for-performance service models that provided immediate return on investment (ROI). The old models of servicing enterprise applications were under tremendous pressure.

NetCustomer decided to address this change in dynamics of the enterprise applications market by adapting its unique delivery model to offer "on-demand" support services to the larger enterprise applications user community beyond product vendors. netCustomer's on-demand enterprise services were designed to provide a true pay-for-performance model, eliminating costly services and other headaches for enterprise users. netCustomer garnered support for its unique service model from leading industry experts and analysts. It strengthened its team and corporate board to become a leader of the next generation of enterprise applications support and services market.

Going forward, netCustomer needs to continue to increase its client base and further build on its service differentiation if it wants to avoid the me-too companies leveraging the India-based support delivery model. The following are among the many questions netCustomer needs to address:

- Which industries are the best targets for advanced support services, and within those industries, which companies?
- Within the targeted companies, what purchasing process is used; that is, how are decisions made? Who are the decision makers? Are decisions made in the IT department, the support department, or some other part of the firm? If it is a multinational client, is decision making centralized at global headquarters or decentralized into the regional operations?
- How do these decision makers vary in terms of the attributes and benefits they are seeking in Web-based advanced customer support?
- Are particular times of year better than others for attempting to sell netCustomer services?

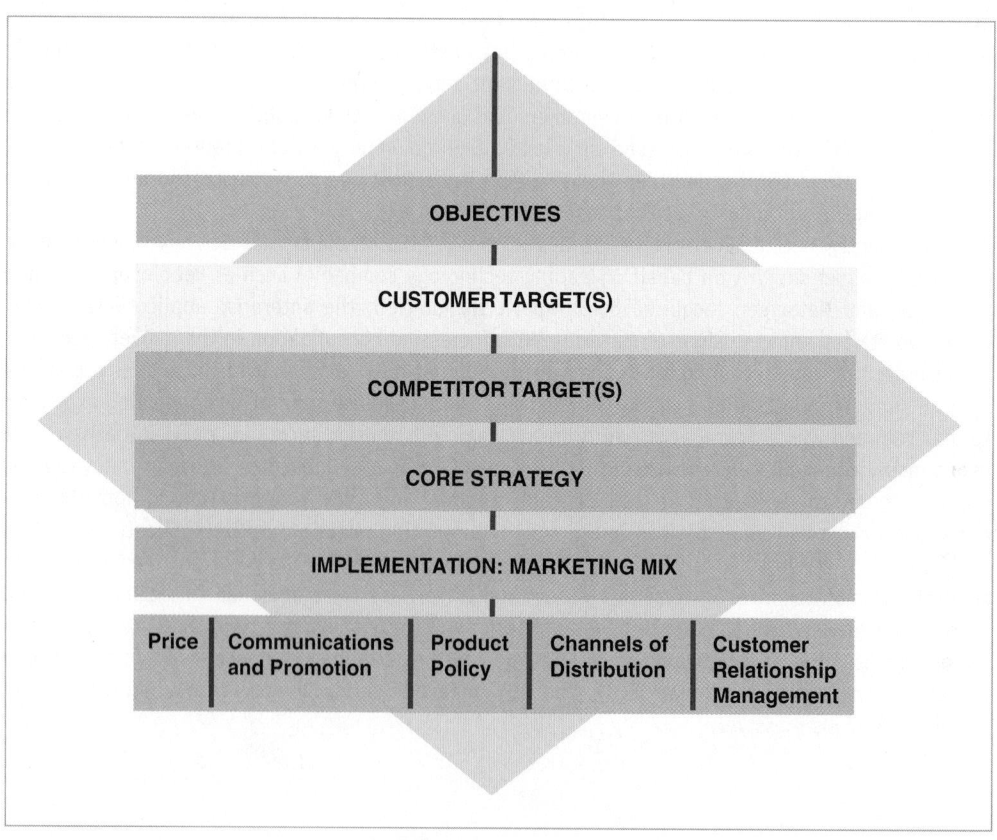

The questions facing the netCustomer managers are the same as those facing the Club Med manager described in the previous chapter:

- *Who* are the customers?
- *Why* do they buy?
- *How* do they make purchasing decisions?
- *Where* do they purchase the product?
- *When* do they buy?

Answers to these questions are critical to the development of a marketing strategy (see the marketing strategy diagram). There are two major differences, however. First, the netCustomer customer base is composed of companies, not individuals purchasing the product for their own use. When a firm markets a product or service to another organization, it is called **organizational marketing**, **industrial marketing**, and since the Internet boom of the late 1990s, **B-to-B (business-to-business) marketing**. Industrial marketing normally targets a group of individuals collectively involved in the purchase decision rather than an individual consumer. This group is usually called a **buying center**. This is an important distinction between industrial and consumer marketing because the dynamics of group decision making are different from an individual consumer's decision-making process, as the different people in a buying center often have different needs. Although we saw a similar phenomenon in the previous chapter, with respect to consumer buying, it is much more prevalent in industrial marketing situations.

In this chapter, we cover organizational buying behavior and show how the general questions addressed in Chapter 4 apply to industrial markets.

organizational marketing
marketing a product or service to another organization, also called industrial marketing

industrial marketing
marketing of a product or service to another organization, also called organizational marketing

B-to-B (business-to-business) marketing
when a product or service is sold to an organization

buying center
a group of individuals collectively involved in a purchase decision

Industrial versus Consumer Marketing

Although the basic marketing strategy framework holds for both consumer and industrial products, there are several differences between industrial or organizational buying and consumer purchasing behavior.[2]

Derived Demand

In many cases, the demand for an industrial product is derived from underlying consumer demand. A marketing manager for an adhesive manufacturer sells her product to companies making toys, computers, televisions, and other products earmarked for consumer use. The demand for netCustomer's customer service products is derived from the demand in the personal computer, software, and many other industries that view the Web as a potential source of revenue. Applied Materials, which makes semiconductor manufacturing equipment, depends on demand from industries using semiconductors, which depend on demand for their products. Thus, industrial customers usually base their purchasing decisions on expectations or forecasts of the demand for their products. This means that the forward-looking company selling to industrial markets is concerned about both possible changes in buying behavior for its product and changes in the underlying consumer markets. In other words, as we noted in Chapter 4, even industrial marketers must be concerned about consumer behavior.

In some cases, the notion of derived demand is more subtle. The networking hardware made by Cisco Systems is not used as a component of a product that is sold to consumers. However, Cisco may sell its products to Hasbro, the toy manufacturer, as part of Hasbro's attempt to improve its information technology. Despite the fact that Cisco's routers and hubs are not toy parts, the company's success selling to Hasbro and other toy manufacturers is still driven by the underlying demand for toys. That is, if the toy business is poor, toy companies are unlikely to make big investments in information technology. Business services usually fall into this category. Waste Management's disposal services obviously are not used by their customers as factors of production, but the demand for such services may be affected by the health of their customers' businesses.

Source: Mark Lennihan/AP Wide World Photos

Application ATX Group

ATX Group is one of the leading competitors in the telematics industry.[3] Companies in this industry develop products and services for wireless communications and navigation systems for autos. The best-known company in the industry is General Motors with its OnStar service. The most visible telematics product is the global positioning satellite (GPS) system that offers satellite-based directions to drivers. ATX offers GPS services; emergency services such as remote door lock/unlock and automatic collision notification; and navigation and information services such as voice traffic information and news, sports, and stock quotes. Unlike OnStar, ATX is an independent company selling its services to companies including BMW, Mercedes-Benz, PSA Peugeot Citroën Maybach, and Rolls-Royce. In addition, ATX has developed a speech-enabled hands-free system that enables drivers to text message while driving, thus greatly enhancing safety.

There are two ways ATX is affected by its derived demand status. First, the demand for telematics services is dependent on the sales of new cars. Therefore, ATX's success is affected by the quality of the marketing programs of its customers. Given the global economic slowdown in 2009, this is a potentially serious liability. Second, although its customers are the automobile companies, the users are consumers who buy and drive the cars. Thus, ATX is successful only if the consumers use and like its services. Importantly, because telematics are options, part of the job of ATX's product managers is to develop marketing programs to help the companies and their dealers market the services to the end-customer. These programs include incentives for the salespeople to sell telematics and information in order to both spur demand for the services and explain how they are used once purchased.

Product Complexity

Industrial products are normally more complex than consumer products. This has several implications for relationships with customers. First, it often means that industrial companies are more likely to be product focused rather than customer or market focused (recall our discussion in Chapter 1 about the differences). For example, biotechnology companies like Celera, working in the genomics area, developed the basic gene sequencing science before identifying specific markets to which it could be applied. Engineers and manufacturing personnel often have greater importance in industrial companies, because such companies have to work harder to focus on customers rather than products. Second, increased product complexity means that product benefits and features are communicated differently. Few industrial marketers advertise on television because it does not enable them to explain complex products that are being purchased on the basis of how they work rather than how they look. Because of the need for more detailed communications, industrial marketers are heavy users of print media (e.g., trade magazines), trade shows, personal selling, and the Internet.

Buyer–Seller Interdependence

With many consumer products, particularly low-cost supermarket or discount store items, the customer purchases the product but has little interaction with the company.[4] However, with industrial products, the customer depends on its suppliers for its operation and ultimately its success in terms of profitability. The seller is part of the buyer's **supply chain** and must provide timely inventory replenishment, service and maintenance, spare parts, and efficient order handling. In other words, the economic success of the business-to-business marketer depends on the economic success of its customers.

supply chain
the organizations involved in the movement of raw materials and components that are part of a product's production process

Buying Process Complexity

As noted in the introduction to this chapter, industrial companies such as netCustomer sell to customers' buying centers. In this case, a variety of people with different backgrounds, valuations of product benefits and attributes, and attitudes toward the seller are all involved in the buying process. Many other factors also contribute to this complexity. Different kinds of organizations purchase in different ways. For example, some companies have centralized purchasing functions, in which all suppliers must work with one office; others decentralize purchasing to divisions or product management.

Some products are very technical so that both parties must work together to finalize the product specifications to meet the buyer's specific needs. Many industrial purchases involve huge sums of money, so the purchasing cycle, or the length of time it takes to make a decision, can last for several years.

Who Are the Customers?

Market segmentation is as important in industrial marketing as it is in the marketing of consumer goods and services. Although most industrial markets are not mass markets because of the more specialized nature of their products, the basic customer characteristics that make segmentation useful—different buying behavior and thus a different marketing mix for different groups of customers—are the same. For example, a marketing manager for an adhesive manufacturer may discover that some of the potential customers find price to be the most important, and others need fast delivery. In this case, segmenting the market may enable the sales force to emphasize the different factors when calling on customers in the two segments, and the company can tailor its operations and marketing mix to suit each one. Alternatively, the manager may decide that because of cost considerations, there is no way to serve the price-sensitive segment. As in consumer markets, market segmentation is more effective and efficient for industrial marketers than simply trying to market the product in the same way to all customers.

Given a particular segmentation scheme, industrial companies often develop different products for the segments. For example, the package delivery company UPS segments its market by how fast the customer needs to receive the package and tailors delivery options to that need, with higher prices being charged for quicker delivery. The company offers five options to meet these needs: UPS Next Day Air®, UPS 2nd Day Air®, UPS 3-Day Select®, UPS Ground, and International.

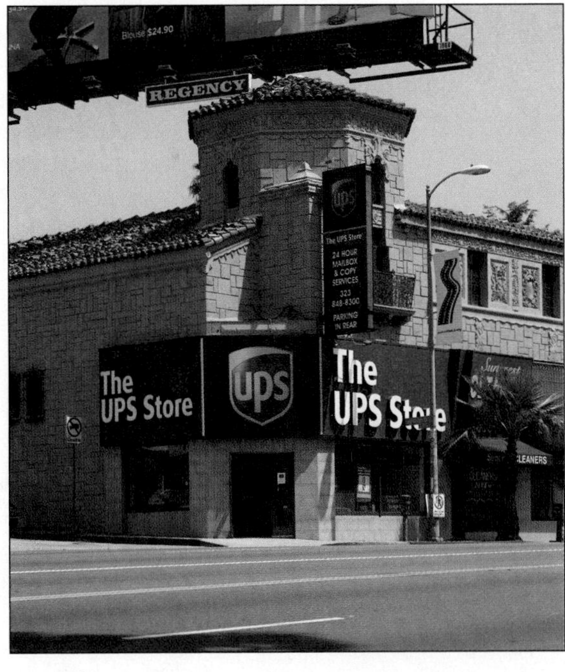

UPS segments its markets in many ways including catering to those who wish to visit their retail stores.

Source: David Young-Wolff/ PhotoEdit Inc.

Segmentation Variables

As with consumer products, the organizational marketing manager must determine the variables that describe the customers in terms of their characteristics (called descriptors) and some kind of link between those variables and customer behavior toward the product or service.

Industrial marketers can use most of the same behavioral variables as consumer marketers. Table 4.2 presented a list of some of the most frequently used behavioral variables. Segments can be created based on benefits (e.g., service, speed of delivery), user status (e.g., past buyer vs. new buyer), different levels of purchasing (e.g., heavy, medium, light), and even attitudes.

One set of descriptor variables for industrial marketing segmentation is shown in Table 5.1. These variables are divided into five categories:

1. **Demographics.** Buyers of industrial products can be segmented by basic descriptors such as company size, industry type, geographic location, and number of employees.
2. **Operating variables.** A second group of potential segmenting variables includes dimensions of the customer's operations, such as what technologies the customer is currently using and how many of your services or products he or she needs.
3. **Purchasing approaches.** You can also segment the market by variables related to the purchasing process and your existing relationship to the company. For example, a segment could be defined based on customers who use a bidding process versus those who do not or those who have centralized purchasing versus those who delegate purchasing authority throughout the organization.

Table 5.1

Market Segmentation Variables for Business Markets
Demographic
Industry: Which industries should we focus on?
Company size: What size companies should we focus on?
Location: What geographic areas should we focus on?
Operating Variables
Technology: What customer technologies should we focus on?
User/nonuser status: Should we focus on heavy, medium, or light users or nonusers?
Customer capabilities: Should we focus on customers needing many or few services?
Purchasing Approaches
Purchasing function organization: Should we focus on companies with highly centralized or decentralized purchasing organizations?
Power structure: Should we focus on companies that are engineering dominated? Financially dominated?
Nature of existing relationships: Should we focus on companies with which we have strong relationships or simply go after the most desirable companies?
General purchase policies: Should we focus on companies that prefer leasing? Service contracts? Systems purchases? Sealed bidding?
Purchasing criteria: Should we focus on companies that are seeking quality? Service? Price?
Situational Factors
Urgency: Should we focus on companies that need quick delivery or service?
Specific application: Should we focus on certain applications of our product rather than all applications?
Size of order: Should we focus on large or small orders?
Personal Characteristics
Buyer–seller similarity: Should we focus on companies whose people and values are similar to ours?
Attitudes toward risk: Should we focus on risk-taking or risk-avoiding customers?
Loyalty: Should we focus on companies that show high loyalty to their suppliers?

Source: Philip Kotler and Kevin Lane Keller (2009), *Marketing Management,* 13th ed. (Upper Saddle River, NJ: Prentice Hall), p. 227. Electronically reproduced by permission of Pearson Education, Inc.

4. **Situational factors.** These include the customer's delivery speed needs, order size needs, and particular uses of the product.
5. **Personal characteristics.** Although you are marketing your products to a business, the personal characteristics of the buyers can be used as segmentation criteria. For example, an organization's attitudes toward risk might help you determine whether it is likely to be an early purchaser of a new technology.

One use of such variables is shown in Table 5.2. This segmentation scheme is used by a company manufacturing medical diagnostic equipment that is used by research labs in universities, pharmaceutical companies, and research institutes. Clearly, industry descriptors could be used to break the market up into segments. However, an alternative approach shown in the table is to classify current and potential customers by the number of researchers using the equipment and the number of samples processed by

Table 5.2

Market Segmentation Scheme

Medical Equipment Manufacturer

	Number of Samples Processed	
Number of Researchers	Many researchers each with a few samples to process	Many researchers each with many samples
	Few researchers each with a few samples to process	Few researchers each with many samples

Table 5.3

Kevlar Segmentation Scheme								
	User Identity							
	Tires		Armament		Gaskets		Marine	
Present Material Applications	Manufacturer	End-User	Manufacturer	End-User	Manufacturer	End-User	Manufacturer	End-User
Asbestos								
Plastic								
Fiberglass								
Steel								
Lead								
Polyester								
Nylon								

the researchers. This results in a four-box separation of customers into different groups characterized by demographic and operating variables. The assumption that must be verified is that the four groups actually behave differently, seek different benefits, and therefore need different products and information.

A second example, drawn from the DuPont product Kevlar, is shown in Table 5.3. This segmentation scheme is a combination of demographic (industry type and manufacturer versus end-user) and a situational factor (current material used that would be replaced by Kevlar). Although it may look as if the scheme results in a large number of segments (56), not all combinations of the variables exist, and the company would not choose to focus on many segments at once. DuPont could also segment the market by other variables, including product benefits.[5] For fishing boat owners, Kevlar's lightness could lower fuel consumption and increase speed. For aircraft designers, Kevlar has a high strength-to-weight ratio. In industrial plant applications, Kevlar could replace asbestos used for packing pumps.

In segmenting markets for organizational buyers, two terms that are often used are **vertical** and **horizontal** segments. A vertical segmenting scheme is when a company focuses on a particular industry, often creating a separate set of channels of distribution (e.g., sales force) for that industry. In Table 5.3, the tire industry would be an example of a vertical segment. Because of the differences in buying needs between the tire and armament industries, DuPont might consider them to be strategically separate. Horizontal marketing would occur across industries, particularly where the needs and uses are similar.

A second set of descriptor variables is based on the different kinds of purchases made by organizations, sometimes called **buy classes**. These are shown in Table 5.4. **Straight rebuys**

vertical marketing
marketing to specific industries with products and services tailored to those industries

horizontal marketing
marketing to different industries with the same product or service

buy classes
a set of descriptor variables used in industrial marketing segmentation that is based on the newness of the purchasing situation

straight rebuys
routine purchases made by an organization from the same supplier used in the past

Table 5.4

Different Types of Organizational Purchases				
Purchase Type	Complexity	Time Frame	Number of Suppliers	Applications
Straight rebuy	Simple	Short	One	Frequently purchased routine purchases such as printer toner
Modified rebuy	Moderate	Medium	Few	Routine purchases that have changed in some way such as air travel (new fares, flights, channels)
New-task purchase	Complex	Long	Many	Expensive, seldom-purchased products

Source: J. Paul Peter and James H. Donnelly Jr. (2010), *A Preface to Marketing Management,* 11th ed., p. 74. (Burr Ridge, IL: McGraw-Hill). Reproduced with permission of the McGraw-Hill Companies.

modified rebuys
a kind of purchasing situation faced by an organization in which something has changed since the last purchase (e.g., a new potential supplier or a large change in price levels)

new-task purchase
a purchasing situation that is unusual or occurs infrequently in a given organization

solutions buy
a purchase situation in which the organization is buying a system that solves a specific problem

are routine purchases from the same suppliers used in the past. **Modified rebuys** characterize purchasing situations in which something has changed since the last purchase, such as a new potential supplier or a large change in the price levels. A **new-task purchase** is made when the purchasing situation is unusual or occurs infrequently. A combination of these three buy classes which is common in technology purchases (not shown in Table 5.4) is called a **solutions buy**. Solutions buys are purchase situations in which the organization is buying a system that solves a specific problem. The solution is usually a system that includes many different parts. For example, many offerings from IBM require an integration of hardware e.g., servers), software, and its services group to create a customized solution to client specific needs.

The marketing tasks differ among the purchasing situations. In the straight rebuy case, the current supplier is in an advantageous position because the buying process is likely to be automatic. The supplier's task is to maintain a good relationship with the customer and focus on timely deliveries at the expected quality levels. The job of the potential supplier who would like to break the straight rebuy is difficult, so strong reasons to switch must be presented. If the purchasing situation has changed in some way, as in the modified rebuy case, new suppliers have more opportunity to present their cases. Some information will be collected by the customer about alternatives, so the current suppliers must realize that the repurchase situation is not automatic. In new-task purchase situations, the purchasing process is a new one. For example, if Air France is in the market for new jet aircraft, it will open the bidding to the major worldwide vendors, Airbus and Boeing. The selling process is long and complex, and Air France will seek extensive information.

Application Panasonic

Panasonic's computer division is one of the most profitable computer companies in the world, on a per-unit basis, with gross margins approaching 30 percent.[6] One of the key parts of the company's strategy has been to focus on the notebook computer market—a part of the overall PC market that is less price-sensitive than the extremely competitive desktop market. More importantly, the company focuses on a particular market segment within the notebook market: those customers needing "ruggedized" laptops—that is, those that can withstand extreme conditions and serious damage. The Toughbook line features a shock-resistant, magnesium case; a moisture-resistant touchpad and keyboard; and a hard disk drive encased in shock-absorbing gel. It has been called the "Rambo" of notebook computers, and it has been supported by an aggressive advertising campaign focusing on industries where ruggedness is important, featuring such tag lines as, "How Did Your Computer Die?" and, as can be seen in the advertisement, "Toughbook, for a Tough World." Not surprisingly, Toughbooks command a premium price—around $4,000 each. Despite the price, they command 60 percent of the market for ruggedized laptops. For example, SBC Corporation purchased 30,000 Toughbook CF-27s for its telephone-climbing repair personnel. The U.S. military forces are also interested in the Toughbook. The U.S. Air Force, Army, Navy, and Marine Corps are among is largest customers, and Panasonic has set up a separate vertical sales organization to sell to these military segments.

Therefore, Panasonic has utilized two different types of segmentation variables: the situational factors/benefits of ruggedness and durability and demographic factors identifying industries where the Toughbook would be a particularly good fit.

Application HSBC Bank

Another example of successful B-to-B segmentation is HSBC. HSBC is the biggest bank in the UK (and one of the largest in the world); it has an award-winning business banking division providing a good product range and service. That said, increasing competition from the rest of the 'big four'—Barclays, RBS and Lloyds TSB—was causing HSBC to lose its leading position in the commercial segment among the 28,000 businesses with sales of £0.5 million to £25 million.

Businesses change their banking arrangements either because they are unhappy with their current bank, normally because of poor service, because other banks offer a better alternative or imply because it is easy to switch. HSBC needed to talk directly with managing directors and financial directors currently banking with a competitor and emphasise why they should bank with HSBC, and how easy it was to switch.

To maximize accuracy, a minimum of ten different data sources were used to compile the target audience. A comprehensive profile of each business was compiled including industry, age, turnover and growth. Certain industries which were against standard HSBC criteria were suppressed as were businesses which traded tobacco or armaments for example. Once the target businesses had been selected, HSBC divided them into three: those with an approximate sales of £0.5 million to £1 million; those with an approximate sales of £1 million to £10 million; and those with an approximate sales of £10 million to £25 million.

The bank planned to address the whole of the prospect pool, but rather than take on too much at once decided to concentrate on following up the higher value prospects first. All prospects were contacted within a maximum of 48 hours and the primary ones within 24 hours.

Managing directors and financial directors have little time and are used to dry, dull mailings from banks. HSBC therefore decided to illustrate that it was the bank that values the difference in business by targeting them with something unusual and unexpected. Jelly beans were selected as colorful and graphic. They illustrated that everyone has different tastes and preferences in the same way that every business has different needs and aspirations. The complimentary jelly beans created a positive association with HSBC and also provided something to share with a team acknowledging the fact that switching banks is a decision made by more than one person. The aim was to show that HSBC takes the time to understand what makes each business different and therefore understands and meets their specific needs. The communications plan proceeded as follow:

Phase 1 - Beans, beans, beans—targeted 28,000 prospects. Each box included personalized mail, four response options (phone, fax, online, email) and pack of jelly beans. Also included was a key explaining that different beans represented different business decisions such as expansion and consolidation.

Phase 2 - Bean Story—was sent to 16,000 prospects. The tone was more familiar as the prospect had already been contacted. The pack contained a personalized letter, a hardback book and a large red inedible jelly bean. The single red bean fitted into each page of the hardback book and was used to illustrate the six key benefits of banking with HSBC; each page told a story. Paul Debney, relationship manager for the Muswell Hill branch of HSBC, was enthusiastic. "In all my time at the bank, I have never seen us do anything so bold. If this doesn't get us noticed nothing will!"

Responses were encouraged in any of four ways:

1. Phone. A dedicated campaign line was set up which went straight to Customer Telephone Service and flashed up when it was a 'beans' lead.
2. Fax. A faxback form was included in the mailer to make a response easy for prospect and underlining that switching was easy. Research had shown that fax responses tended to be few, but of high quality.
3. Online. A campaign microsite was created (www.hsbc.co.uk/unique) and each prospect was provided with a unique code in their DM.
4. Email. A dedicated email address was created.

All incoming responses were passed on to relevant commercial center within 24 hours.

The results of the campaign were all available to the judges of the B2B Marketing Awards and the campaign was assessed accordingly. Client confidentiality, however, restricts publication in their entirety. What can be revealed is that the beans campaign achieved an unprecedented 25.4 per cent response rate overall and a predicted ROI of 42:1, vastly exceeding the target ROI of 3:1. As Mike Durkin from the network leadership team says, "This is the best commercial campaign we have ever done.[7]"

Segmenting in Technology-Based Markets: The Chasm Model

In Chapter 4, it was shown that consumers can be segmented by their stage in the diffusion of innovations process: innovators, early adopters, early majority, late majority, or laggards. Although some of the terms can be adapted to industrial settings (e.g., innovators are often referred to as **lead users**), organizational buyers fall into similar categories. Like consumers, some companies will be earlier adopters of new technologies than others. High-tech companies treasure the innovators. They are often used as beta test sites, where new products are tested and debugged. As with consumer innovators, they spread word-of-mouth and act as industry leaders that are followed by smaller, less innovative firms. For example, when Siebel (now owned by Oracle) released its Siebel 7 customer

lead users
the first buyers of an innovation in industrial marketing situations; also called innovators

relationship management software system, advertisements were developed with recommendations from three large companies, IBM, Bayer, and Avaya (a Lucent Technologies spinoff), all in different industries, to prod the more recalcitrant followers.

The diffusion of innovations model assumes a smooth transition from one stage to the next.[8] A naïve view would be that all you have to do is to get some innovators to try your new product or service and, assuming you do not make any major mistakes and that you support the product with the normal amount of marketing, the momentum of the diffusion curve will lead you to success.

More specifically, you might assume that the following strategy would work:

- Use the technologists (innovators) to educate the visionaries (early adopters).
- Create satisfied visionaries so they can positively influence the pragmatists (early majority).
- Become profitable by serving the early majority well through high-quality products and excellent customer service.
- Gain some of the late majority by reducing costs and prices.
- Forget the laggards.

Of course, this is not true in general and less true in high-tech markets. A revised version of the diffusion curve is shown in Figure 5.1. The gaps between the diffusion groups indicate the potential to lose momentum. The large gap between the early adopters and early majority is called the **chasm**.

chasm
the large gap that can exist between the early adopters of an innovation and the early majority

The first small crack is between the innovators and the early adopters (between Technology Enthusiasts and Visionaries in Figure 5.1). Recall that the innovators are venturesome and interested in technology. The main concern of early adopters is how the new technology will solve their problems. So this crack in a high-tech market occurs when the innovating firms do not do a thorough job of showing how the technology can be put to best use.

There are a number of good examples of this problem. Home banking has been around for many years, with nearly 50 U.S. banks experimenting with it in 1983. In 1989, AT&T and Chemical Bank closed down their joint venture called Pronto after spending $100 million on it. Although home banking has been picking up because of increased use of the Internet, it still accounts for a miniscule proportion of banking transactions. The technology for videophones has existed for more than 60 years. However, there is still no real commercial market for them, although the PC-based videoconferencing market is being adopted by more companies today. The development of laser disk players was a $500 million calamity for RCA because it could not sell the nonrecordable devices to more

Figure 5.1

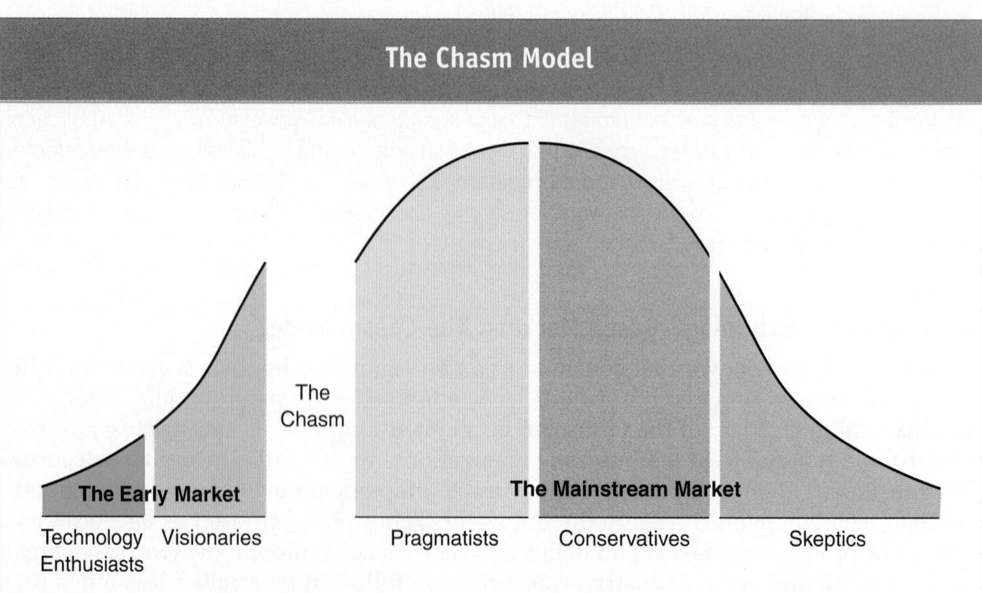

Source: Geoffrey A. Moore (1995), *Inside the Tornado* (New York: HarperBusiness), p. 19.

than a few risk-taking customers. The Segway illustration in Chapter 1 of this book also shows the difficulty of moving beyond innovators.

The second small crack in the diffusion curve occurs between the early and late majority (between Pragmatists and Conservatives in Figure 5.1). In this case, the marketing task is to make sure that the technology can be understood easily by people who are inherently not technologists. This is the problem that faces non-Apple PC makers. Although about 76 percent of U.S. households own PCs, getting the late majority to adopt involves making the computers very easy to set up and use, as well as selling benefits of relevant services such as e-mail. Thus, many companies ship their computers with CD-ROM disks that walk the buyer through the setup process. In addition, Microsoft's upgrades to its ubiquitous operating system make it much easier than it used to be to add peripheral devices such as modems.

The third small crack, between the Conservatives and the Skeptics, is the problem of getting laggards to buy a product. In this case, the laggards simply do not see the advantage of buying the technology. Although about 84 percent of U.S. households have at least one cellular phone, obviously, many still do not. Those 16 percent have not been convinced yet to buy one or cannot afford one. The latter reason is why the companies are attempting to innovate by marketing prepaid plans that are more affordable.

The major crack, between early adopters and the early majority, is called the *chasm.* The early majority wants the products to work and to enhance their lives or their profit margins. The challenge is how to move a high-tech product from the early market, made up of technology enthusiasts and visionaries (early adopters), to pragmatists in the mainstream market. This is not as easy as it sounds. Table 5.5 shows some of the differences between the two groups. Products and services that cannot make the transition fall into the chasm. Successful high-tech marketing management involves figuring out how to move from the more technology-focused early market to the pragmatic needs of the early majority, where sufficient sales volume can occur to sustain the product.

To successfully cross the chasm, we can fall back on the basic strategic principles we discussed in Chapter 2. In that chapter, it was noted that a successful marketing strategy involves targeting specific segments of customers and developing a value proposition for those segments. These concepts can be applied in a high-tech context: to appeal to the pragmatists, you must develop a specific application or general strategic approach (theme) that solves the needs of a sizable segment of the early majority. Preferably, this application or theme provides an entrée into other segments of the early majority that are not initially penetrated.

Some examples of the applications approach are:

- Apple Computer used desktop publishing to cross the chasm. Not only did it have its successful Macintosh and Laserwriter (printer) products; it had the right partners in Adobe (PostScript) and Aldus (Pagemaker).
- Tandem Computers (now the NonStop product line of Hewlett-Packard) was founded to deliver fault-tolerant computing (i.e., computing capabilities that do

Table 5.5

Visionaries versus Pragmatists

Visionaries	Pragmatists
Intuitive	Analytic
Support revolution	Support evolution
Contrarian	Conformist
Break away from the pack	Stay with the herd
Follow their own dictates	Consult with their colleagues
Take risks	Manage risks
Motivated by future opportunities	Motivated by present problems
Seek what is possible	Pursue what is probable

Source: "Visionaires vs. Pragmastists" from Geoffrey A. Moore, *Inside the Tornado,* 1995, New York: HarperBusiness, p. 19.

not fail). Although there were a number of possible segments on which they could focus, the company decided to focus on automatic teller machine networks and online banking applications.

- Silicon Graphics International (SGI) makes computer workstations and high-end servers and competes with Sun, IBM, and a variety of other companies. SGI crossed the chasm by focusing on high-end computer graphic applications, including special effects for movies and animation.[9]

These are all examples of application segments or niches. An alternative approach is to try to pursue a thematic niche. For example, Oracle, the company that dominates the worldwide database market, chose to develop database software that would be portable across incompatible hardware platforms. Another example is Palm Inc.'s enormously successful Palm Pilot, the handheld personal digital assistant (PDA). The themes of the Palm Pilot were ease of use and functionality. Although other PDAs (e.g., the Apple Newton) preceded it to market, none was successful in crossing the chasm because of a lack of understanding of what customers really wanted.

You should note that the application and thematic approaches to crossing the chasm are not the same as simply repositioning the product, something that can be done for any kind of product or service. The difference in the high-tech context is that the products had an initial market success based on the technology alone. As the products gained initial footholds in the market, the challenge became how to change the marketing from a technology sell to a benefits approach. This shift in emphasis is what makes high-tech marketing different.

Application Baan Co.

Before being acquired by Infor Global Solutions in 2006, Baan Co. was an enterprise application software company located in Menlo Park, California, and Putten, The Netherlands.[10] This kind of software integrates all of a company's operations, from raw material acquisition to accounts payable. With annual sales of just over $600 million in 2000, it was dwarfed by larger competitors such as SAP, PeopleSoft, and Oracle.

However, earlier in its history, Baan was successful in jumping over the chasm. A sign that Baan Co. has moved its products from the early adopter, visionary market segment to the more mainstream, early majority market occurred when it signed a contract with Boeing in 1994. A customer of that size and with so much at stake in terms of product quality does not make such vendor decisions without believing that the company's product provides substantial benefits and that these benefits have been well established.

How did Baan cross the chasm to reach mainstream customers such as Boeing? The product sold at the time by its main competitor, SAP's R/3 software, required expensive consultants to implement. In addition, users of R/3 needed to forecast their needs years in advance because the program was difficult to change after it had been installed. Baan chose a thematic approach to crossing the chasm by making its product easier to install and modify, thus reducing a customer's dependency on consultants.

Application PayPal

An example of a company and industry seeking ways to jump the chasm is PayPal and other online payment service companies.[11] PayPal was started in 1998 as a company specializing in safeguards for transferring money through wireless devices. Although there was little interest in that product, the founders of the company noticed that with the growth of the Internet, customers might want a way to transfer money in a safer way than credit cards, money orders, and checks. In late 1999, the company changed the way that money moved through cyberspace. All a user needed was the recipient's e-mail address, a credit card or bank account number (a one-time activity), and an Internet connection. The recipient received the money in his or her PayPal account and PayPal debited the sender's credit card or bank account. At the end of 1999, there were only 10,000 users. By early February 2000, the number of users had increased to 100,000, and by November 2001, PayPal had 10 million users. Today, PayPal operates in 190 markets, and it manages over 184 million accounts, more than 73 million of them active. PayPal allows customers to send, receive, and hold funds in 19 currencies worldwide. Most of this business is from contracts with companies that have or plan to have substantial online revenues. For example, Research in Motion (the maker of the Blackberry smart phone) has announced that PayPal will be the only payment mechanism for its Blackberry App World, which launched on April 1, 2009.

How did PayPal move from attracting innovators and early adopters to the much larger early majority group, such as the pragmatists? The company did a number of things that made the product attractive to its customers, who are the online businesses who pay PayPal 2.9 percent of each transaction plus a fixed fee of $30. Not only is it secure and simple; the company hitched a ride on the success of eBay, its largest customer. Many of eBay's transactions involve small merchants who use eBay as their storefront. Using PayPal means they do not have to worry about setting up expensive banking arrangements, nor do they have to be concerned about the costs and security problems of accepting credit cards online. The eBay–small merchant niche became the company's strategy. Now, PayPal is trying to become a more general online bill-paying agent.

Marketing Research Implications: Data Collection

As in consumer behavior analysis, data useful for developing market segments can be collected either via primary or secondary methods. Industrial product companies can either do their own in-house surveys or commission a marketing research firm to study the customers in a market. Because marketing research budgets in industrial companies are usually lower than in consumer product companies, such research is often done on a shoestring, with judgment often replacing hard data. This is unfortunate because primary data are proprietary to the company and can give it an edge in the marketplace; secondary data are generally available to any company.

Because industrial product companies do not spend much money on primary research, they tend to use syndicated studies or other secondary studies more often. Government studies segmenting industries by industrial codes (e.g., the NAIC described in Chapter 3) are popular around the world, although they are not useful at a particular industry level. Sometimes studies are conducted by trade associations, which distribute the data to all firms in the industry. Alternatively, consulting firms specializing in different industries conduct analyses that can be used for segmentation purposes. Examples are Gartner Dataquest and Millward Brown's IntelliQuest, which specialize in the computer industry.

Many other analyses besides segmentation studies are conducted for B-to-B companies as they are for B-to-C (business-to-consumer) companies. For example, customer satisfaction data are collected from the American Customer Satisfaction Index, the ACSI (www.theacsi.org). Recent ACSI data from the personal computer industry shows that Apple dominates the category with an ACSI index of 85 (the maximum is 100). In addition, the company's satisfaction trend is positive. Hewlett-Packard's performance is below the industry average. These data allow the manager to track how customers feel about their experiences with the company. It would, of course, be useful to start with overall ACSI results and then see how they vary over market segments of buyers.

Application | Cardboard Boxes and Containers

An example of the kind of segmentation data available through secondary sources is shown in Table 5.6. Paperboard boxes and containers (NAICS 32221) are used throughout the United States and global economies to package and ship goods, serve food, provide retail advertising displays, and in other applications. The estimated size of the market in 2008 was more than $50 billion. Although the raw data are compiled by the U.S. Department of Commerce, those data are repackaged by companies specializing in business information and then sold to companies in the relevant industry. In this case, the data are provided in a report compiled by IBIS*World*.[12] As can be seen, the largest customer segment for the industry are the food, beverage, and tobacco companies who account for nearly half of cardboard box and container demand. While the data are not company specific, they provide a starting point for further segmentation research.

Table 5.6

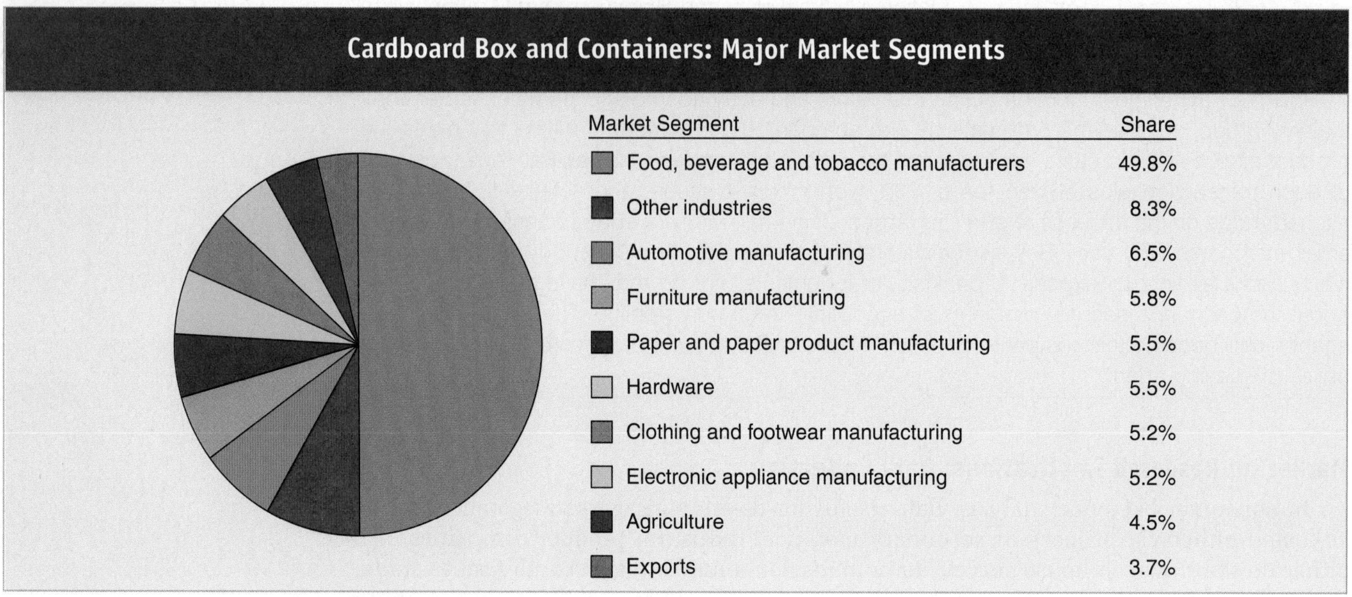

Cardboard Box and Containers: Major Market Segments

Market Segment	Share
Food, beverage and tobacco manufacturers	49.8%
Other industries	8.3%
Automotive manufacturing	6.5%
Furniture manufacturing	5.8%
Paper and paper product manufacturing	5.5%
Hardware	5.5%
Clothing and footwear manufacturing	5.2%
Electronic appliance manufacturing	5.2%
Agriculture	4.5%
Exports	3.7%

Source: IBISWord Inc., March 25, 2009. Reprinted with permission of IbisWorld, Inc.

Marketing Research Implications: Developing Target Markets

As is the case for consumer markets, the challenge facing the marketing manager of industrial products and services is to move beyond the profiling of alternative segments to actively pursuing one or more segments as part of the marketing strategy (see the marketing strategy diagram repeated earlier in this chapter). Even if there were customers in each of the 56 alternative segments shown in the DuPont illustration (Table 5.3), it would not be feasible to focus on each one, except in the cases where the number of customers in each cell was very small. Thus, parsimony is also important in industrial marketing because it is inefficient to pursue too many segments. It may be worthwhile only to pursue a few vertical segments intensively than to attempt a horizontal marketing approach, which can be expensive and leave the company exposed to competitors who do focus on particular verticals.

Again, the criteria used to determine whether a particular segmentation scheme is useful are:

- Does the segmentation scheme explain differences in the behavioral variable of interest (e.g., purchase quantity)? For example, does industry classification explain differences in behavior better than the customer purchasing approach used?
- How many customers are there in the segment?
- What is the segment's forecasted growth rate?
- Are there particular environmental factors associated with the segment (e.g., regulatory, social) that make the segment more or less attractive?
- What is your potential competitive position in the segment?

Why Do Customers Buy?

As we noted at the beginning of this chapter, a customer analysis also must address the question, "Why do customers buy the product or service?" A simplified model of how business-to-business customers make purchase decisions is shown in Table 5.7. The first step is need recognition, or understanding why customers make purchase decisions.

The event that sets the purchasing or procurement process in motion within organizations can be internal or external. In the latter case, a supplier company attempts to anticipate the company's need through targeted communications, often made by a salesperson. There are two points in the first phase in the buying process at which these internal and

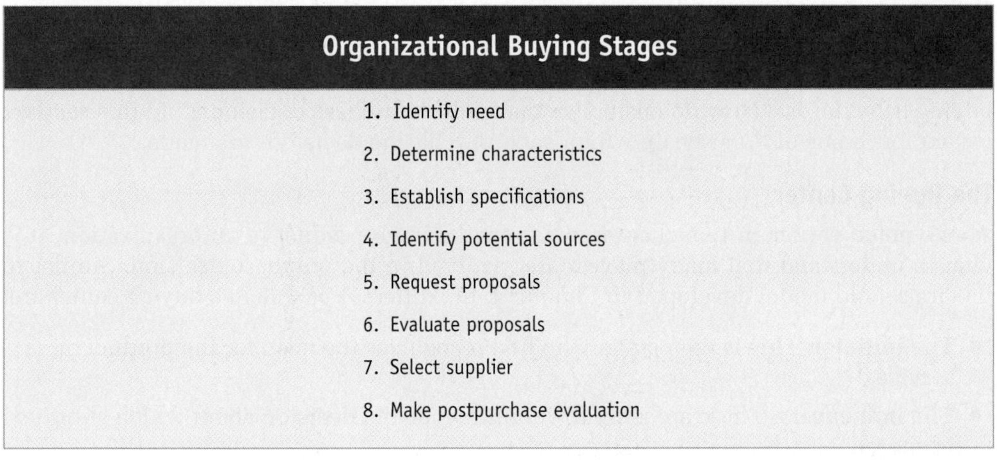

Table 5.7

Organizational Buying Stages
1. Identify need
2. Determine characteristics
3. Establish specifications
4. Identify potential sources
5. Request proposals
6. Evaluate proposals
7. Select supplier
8. Make postpurchase evaluation

external motivators have impact. The first is the recognition that a problem exists. This recognition could be stimulated by something as simple as a low supply of a part or need for replenishment. Alternatively, a salesperson or an advertisement from a potential supplier could alert the buyer to the possibility that the product being currently used is technologically inferior to the new one being offered. This need must be stimulated by or communicated to someone in the buying organization who can influence whether a purchase is made. Otherwise, the problem recognized simply dies. The second part to this phase is that once a problem has been recognized, the buying organization must become aware that the solution to the problem lies with a purchase. Only then does the need become activated, resulting ultimately in a purchase from a supplier. It is possible that the part low in inventory can be supplied by another division's inventory, or the company may not be able to afford the new product or service.

This need recognition phase varies somewhat among the different buy classes introduced earlier in the chapter. In the new-task situation, the purchasing organization realizes that the problem cannot be solved without buying something new. For example, a company may decide that it needs to upgrade its document-copying capabilities. The company could purchase a new version of its existing copier, buy new copying technology, or decide to outsource its copying to a service firm. In the last case, this is a new task. For this need to arise, a senior manager must be aware that such outsourcing options exist and that the company can save money through that option. This manager would need to be exposed to this idea through a service company salesperson, an advertisement, or perhaps an informal source such as another business acquaintance. In other words, more effort by both external and internal parties is necessary for need recognition in a new-task situation.

Straight rebuy situations are straightforward because they are mainly a matter of reordering something that is purchased routinely (e.g., paper clips) and the need occurs when inventory is low. An example of a modified rebuy situation would be upgrading the existing copier to take advantage of new technology. In this case, the need for such an upgrade would not be as straightforward as the straight rebuy situation, but it would not be as complex as the new task. The manager in charge would be generally aware that new technology is available but would have to research alternatives to determine what decision to make.

Like consumer purchases, industrial customers' purchasing decisions are benefit driven. Although industrial product purchases are more likely to be based on features rather than benefits because of the technical nature of the products, industrial buyers are very bottom-line oriented. Even industrial products must be sold on the basis of benefits; the key benefit is usually how much more money the customer can make with your product than with a competitor's.

Most advertisements in trade magazines are very feature or specs (product specifications) oriented. Matrices comparing one product's specs to those of a set of competitors are common. This is usually done because the targets for the trade ads are the technical people involved with the sale. However, the smart industrial marketer understands that somewhere in the buying center is a manager who is interested in the profitability of the purchase.

How Do Customers Make Purchase Decisions?

The third key question a marketing manager must ask in order to understand industrial buying behavior is, "How do customers make their purchase decisions?" In this section, we explore some of the ways in which such purchasing decisions are made.

The Buying Center

As we noted earlier in this chapter, when marketing a product to an organization, it is vital to understand that many players are involved in the purchase decision. Similar to the household model developed in Chapter 4, the different people in a buying center are:

- **The initiator.** This is the person who first recognizes the need for the product or service.
- **The influencers.** These are people who influence the decision about which supplier is chosen.
- **The decider.** This is the person in the organization who has the ultimate authority for a "go/no-go" decision.
- **The purchaser.** This person actually authorizes payment for the product.
- **The users.** These people actually use the product.

This framework has many important implications. Like the market segments described earlier in this chapter, these microsegments, or different entities involved in the buying process, have different needs and seek different benefits. Thus, in the selling process, whether by direct sales or other channels, you must know not only that the particular organization is different from others in different segments, but that the different individuals must be the focus of different marketing approaches, perhaps even different value propositions.

For example, let us return to the netCustomer illustration at the beginning of this chapter. Because of the wide variety of people involved with customer service, different people occupy several of the buying roles:

- The initiator could be the marketing or customer service manager who is interested in delivering a higher level of service than the company has in the past. This manager notes that an increasing number of customers are doing business with the company on the Web and that the response times to customer inquiries are unsatisfactory and below the level of the competition.
- The influencers could include the information system and operations managers. The former would be interested in compatibility issues with current hardware platforms used in the company; the latter would be concerned if the new system affected product returns, for example.
- The decider would be a more senior manager in the company. This person would be concerned with price, expected performance improvements, and perhaps most importantly, the ROI.
- The purchaser might be a purchasing agent whose main concerns are terms of sale, installation timing, and after-sale support.
- The users would be the end-customers of netCustomer's clients, that is, the people who purchased a Sony laptop and obtained a rebate. Thus, it would be important to test the new system on consumers and demonstrate its improvement to customers like Sony. Consumers desire rapid responses to their inquiries. Sony wants higher levels of customer satisfaction.

As shown, each person occupying the different buying roles can have very different needs and seek different benefits, which dictate how your company markets to the particular organization.

Therefore, it is critical for a company marketing to organizations to understand the patterns of influence in each customer organization. A good salesperson understands this and seeks to identify the key decision makers and influencers and tailor his or her message to them. However, a second implication of the buying roles framework is that it may not be possible for a single salesperson or channel to be used to reach a customer, particularly a large one. Often, several approaches to communicating with customers are used at the different levels of the customer organization. For example, a junior salesperson is more likely to be focused on the user and influencers, whereas a more senior salesperson would focus on the decision maker, who is likely to be at a parallel level of authority.

Semiconductor manufacturers selling microprocessors to companies making products such as PCs, cellular phones, toys, and defense-related products must tailor the specifications (specs) of their chips to their customers' products. For example, a talking doll needs a chip with a particular processing capability (not very high in this case), power consumption, and size. Nearly every product using a microprocessor has different requirements.

Although this may be a straightforward observation, it is not always so clear who decides which processor to use in a particular product, with many people being involved in the purchase decision. In this particular case, testing engineers evaluate different semiconductors for a variety of technical factors such as cycle rate (the speed with which a device can form a complete cycle or operation such as reading or writing information).

Of particular importance in many purchasing situations are design engineers. The job of the design engineer is to find products that fit the basic product's specifications. Thus, the design engineer for a cell phone is not as concerned about the technical aspects of the microprocessor (she can ask the testing engineer for a list of suppliers that have products meeting that need), as she is about whether the supplier's semiconductor meets the design specifications of the product.

Recognizing that the design engineer was the key decision maker for many of its customers, National Semiconductor designed its Web site to meet this need. Focus group research determined that design engineers did not want fancy graphics at this web site. Instead, they wanted to search for products whose performance parameters met their criteria, scan abstracts of data sheets, download the ones in which they were interested, and order samples. This should also be done quickly and easily.

An interesting feature of the National Semiconductor Web site is the parametric table shown in Figure 5.2. In this table, the customer can sort through National's products by arranging them in ascending or descending order by attribute (this is done by clicking on

Figure 5.2

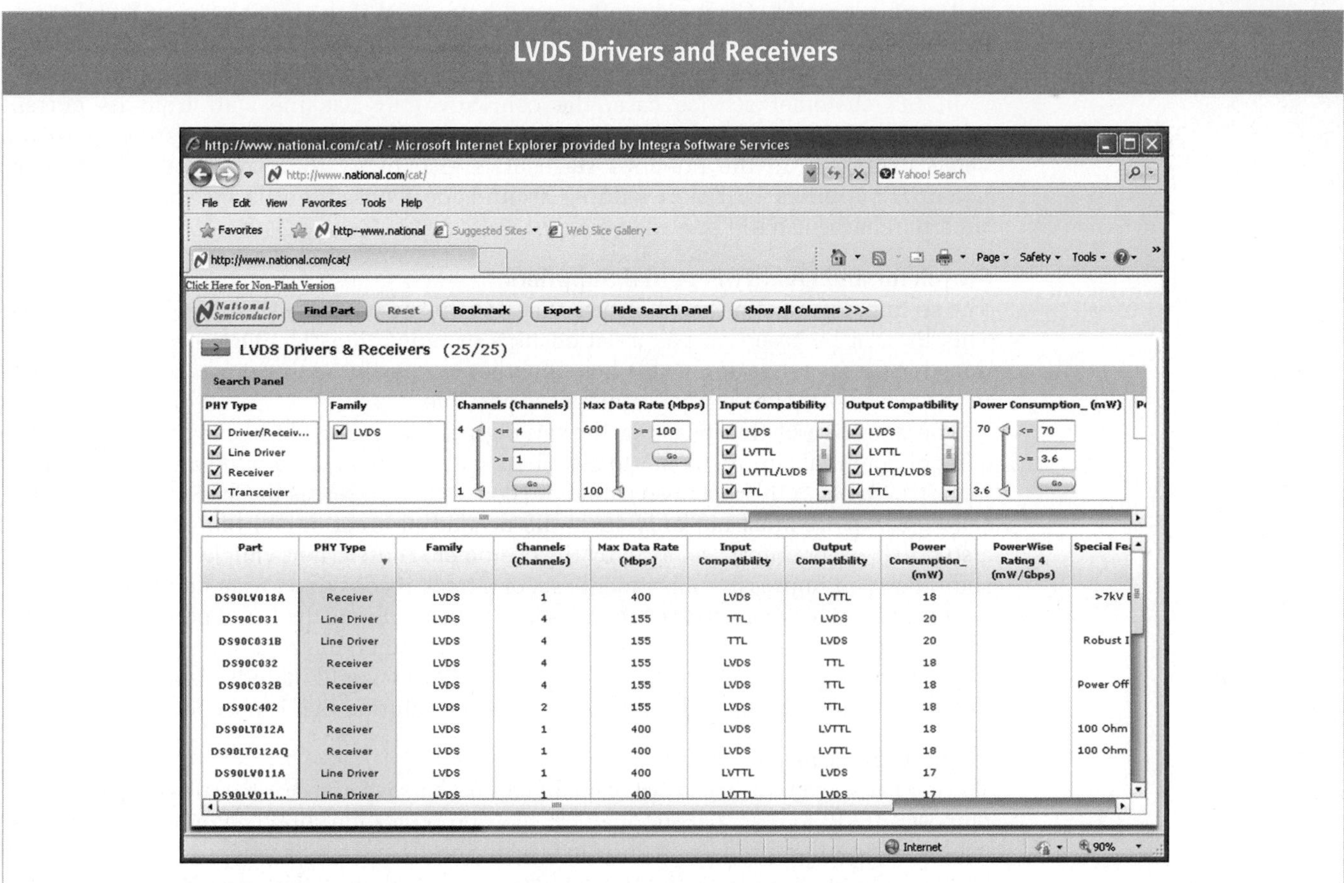

Part	PHY Type	Family	Channels (Channels)	Max Data Rate (Mbps)	Input Compatibility	Output Compatibility	Power Consumption_ (mW)	PowerWise Rating 4 (mW/Gbps)	Special Fe
DS90LV018A	Receiver	LVDS	1	400	LVDS	LVTTL	18		>7kV
DS90C031	Line Driver	LVDS	4	155	TTL	LVDS	20		
DS90C031B	Line Driver	LVDS	4	155	TTL	LVDS	20		Robust I
DS90C032	Receiver	LVDS	4	155	LVDS	TTL	18		
DS90C032B	Receiver	LVDS	4	155	LVDS	TTL	18		Power Off
DS90C402	Receiver	LVDS	2	155	LVDS	TTL	18		
DS90LT012A	Receiver	LVDS	1	400	LVDS	LVTTL	18		100 Ohm
DS90LT012AQ	Receiver	LVDS	1	400	LVDS	LVTTL	18		100 Ohm
DS90LV011A	Line Driver	LVDS	1	400	LVTTL	LVDS	17		
DS90LV011...	Line Driver	LVDS	1	400	LVTTL	LVDS	17		

Source:

up or down arrows at the top of each column). For the price-sensitive customer, the products can be ordered by that attribute. If the customer's needs are more complicated, multiple-attribute sorting can be performed.

The Buying Process

As Table 5.7 shows, following need recognition, there are seven stages in the buying process that ultimately lead to a purchase.

Determine the Characteristics

After the need has been ascertained, the next step in the buying sequence is to determine the characteristics of the product or service needed as specifically as possible (i.e., "How should the problem be solved?"). Usually, this stage is stated in terms of benefits rather than specific characteristics. Typical questions asked are, "What application requirements must be met?" and "What types of goods or services should be considered?" In some cases, this analysis can be done internally, particularly for straight rebuy situations. However, for new-task purchases, it may be difficult for the customer to know what options are available for consideration. In this case, it is critical for the company to make contact with the buyer as early as possible to deliver information about the different options.

Continuing the customer service illustration, at this stage of the buying process, the buying center would consider what benefits they would like to have from a new system. Candidates include a full set of accurate responses to possible customer questions, quick response time, online "chat" format, and easy integration with existing systems.

Establish Specifications

This stage entails the translation of the needs into specific product features and characteristics. The result of this stage is a particular option or set of options from which price, delivery, system compatibility, and other characteristics can be determined. Again, with a straight or modified rebuy situation, this can usually be done in-house, depending on the size of the buying organization. However, with a new task, it is the responsibility of the selling organization to help customers determine what characteristics will satisfy the general need expressed. Companies often need help, even if the buying center members do not ask for it openly. At this stage, the sale can be made or lost, and it is crucial to understand the needs of the different people involved with making the decision.

In the customer service case, the company may use the staff from its current customer service operation to help draw up specifications for products that meet the needs expressed in the previous stage. It is also likely that salespeople from other potential suppliers will start sniffing around for a possible sale because word about such purchases usually spreads quickly.

Search for and Qualify Potential Suppliers

The selling organization must ensure that it is on the buyer's list of potential suppliers. This list can be based on past relationships or reputation. The term *evoked set,* introduced in Chapter 4, is applicable here. In other words, the selling organization tries to be in the evoked set of as many customers as possible.

The objective of this phase of the buying process is for the buyer not only to have a list of potential suppliers, but to also identify those who are *qualified*—a subset of the total list. To be on this list (also called the consideration set, as in Chapter 4), a potential selling company must not only carry the needed product or sell the service, but must also satisfy other criteria set forth by the customer. These criteria might include financial soundness, an impressive customer base, or a track record of on-time delivery.

A company seeking a new customer service system forms the list of potential suppliers from a list of companies including not only netCustomer, but also other small and major global firms (e.g., Hewlett-Packard). Screening criteria would include size, dependability, projected longevity, and the ability to provide the solution that is needed.

Request Proposals

The normal procedure, once a list of qualified suppliers is formed, is to send out a request for proposals (RFP) to potential suppliers. In their proposals the suppliers indicate what products or services they propose, in order to meet the needs and specifications of the buyer. Other terms of the proposal include price, delivery date, and any other aspects of the potential contract that are relevant. Thus, the company seeking a new customer service system would send RFPs to all of the companies on its qualified list, seeking bids for the sale. However, in many cases, the RFP process is not so formal and the customer simply gives a number of companies a general idea of what it wants. RFPs usually are unnecessary for straight repurchase situations. In those cases, customers simply reorder from their current supplier.

Evaluate Proposals and Select a Supplier

After the customer receives the proposals, the buying center deliberates over the alternatives and makes a choice. Although not every member of the center has decision-making authority, all members normally have input into the final decision.

The multiattribute model described in Chapter 4 for evaluating options in a consideration set can be applied to this stage of the buying process. Three parts of the multiattribute model are used to determine which option to choose:

1. The relevant attributes of the product being considered.
2. Perceptions or evaluations by each member of the buying center concerning how much each attribute is present in the products or services being considered.
3. How important each attribute is to the members of the buying center.

These data can be assembled in a matrix like that shown in Table 5.8. Each member of the buying center has a set of importance weights (W) for each attribute (A). In addition, the buying center member has a set of evaluations or perceptions (P) of each product in the qualified list on each attribute. Using the approach described in Chapter 4, each center member forms a score for each product by multiplying the weight of the attribute by the perception or evaluation of the product's attribute and adding up the scores over all of the attributes. The product with the highest score on this index should be most preferred by that center member. Each center member bases his or her preference for a supplier on this combination of perceptions, evaluations, and importance weights. The final choice is the outcome of discussion and negotiation.

Table 5.9 applies the conceptual framework shown in Table 5.8 to the customer service decision in a simplified form. We assume that there are only four key attributes: response accuracy (expertise), overall cost, product (software) quality, and company reputation. As can be seen, the overall evaluations between the two brands, netCustomer and Siebel, differ by center member. The customer service manager gives greater weight to netCustomer's particular expertise in handling online customer service and customizing the responses to the client through extensive background research. The purchasing agent likes Siebel's greater financial stability (especially that it is now owned by Oracle) and reputation, although she or he marks it down for being more expensive. Even if these calculations are not done explicitly in this manner, buying center members implicitly consider these factors in reaching their recommended purchase.

Perform Postpurchase Evaluation

Because of the strong relationship between a supplier and a customer in industrial marketing contexts, information normally flows readily between the parties. Whether

Table 5.8

Buying Center Decision Making

	Buying Center Member 1		Buying Center Member 2		...
Attribute	Weight	P_1, P_2,...	Weight	P_1, P_2,...	
A_1					
A_2					
A_3					
.					
.					
.					

Note: Ps represent perception of each center member on each attribute for brands 1, 2,...

Table 5.9

Buying Center Decision-Making
Online Customer Service Illustration

	Customer Service Manager			Purchasing Manager		
Attribute	Weight	netCustomer	Siebel	Weight	netCustomer	Siebel
Expertise	0.4	6	7	0	5	7
Cost	0.1	6	3	0.5	6	3
Product quality	0.4	6	3	0.1	4	5
Reputation	0.1	4	7	0.4	1	7
		5.8	5.0		3.8	4.8

the information is transmitted to a supplier's salesperson or senior manager, the selling company is constantly informed about how its product is performing. If there is no such information flow, the seller should initiate such contact and demand feedback because the goal is to establish a long-term relationship. Obviously, the buyer will evaluate this relationship with the supplier when the time comes to make another purchase or give a recommendation about the supplier to another company.

External and Internal Influences on Purchasing Behavior

In addition to the steps listed in Table 5.7, a number of external and internal factors influence the decision-making process made by buying centers:

- **Environmental factors.** Legal, cultural, political, economic, competitive, and other factors affect purchasing decisions.
- **Organizational characteristics.** The size of the company making the purchase decision, its level of technology, and the internal reward system are examples of these characteristics.
- **Characteristics of the individuals in the group.** Participants in the decision-making process can differ in terms of education, motivation, personality, experience, and degree of risk taking.
- **Characteristics of the group as a whole.** Size, authority, leadership, and group structure can influence the choice as well.

The Effects of Culture

As was the case with consumer buying behavior described in Chapter 4, culture can have a major impact on organizational buyer behavior. This can happen in two ways. First, every organization has its own unique culture, usually based on the values of its top managers. Second, there is also the fact that global cultural diversity exists. Both kinds of culture can affect on how the organizations make buying decisions.

Corporate cultures can be quite diverse. General Electric's culture is based on its history of being devoted to strategic planning. Its leaders, like former CEO Jack Welch, focus relentlessly on financial performance, leadership in the markets in which it competes, and teamwork.[13] Hewlett-Packard's well-known culture (the HP Way) is based on:

1. Respect for others.
2. A sense of community.
3. Hard work.

Southwest Airlines focuses on hiring the right people, those with a sense of humor, team players, and positive attitudes. When selling into these companies, it is important to understand the basic forces that drive them.

Similarly, when developing marketing strategies into global markets, cultural differences can play a key role in your ability to be successful. For example, it is well known that the Japanese style of decision making is much different than that in the United States, involving more consensus, longer-term selling cycles with extensive relationship building, and a more indirect negotiating style.

To help explain these cultural differences, a classification system for global organizational culture was developed by Hofstede.[14] His original work was based on two surveys conducted in 1968 and 1972, on 50,000 IBM employees in 40 countries. Hofstede's work was based on the notion that attitudes, orientations, emotions, and expressions differ strongly among people from one country to another and that these differences are fundamentally cultural. Based on his research, he found that cultural differences are based on the following five dimensions:

1. **Power distance:** the extent to which less powerful parties accept the existing distribution of power and the degree to which adherence to formal channels is maintained. High power-distance societies tend to be less egalitarian.
2. **Individualism vs. collectivisim:** the degree of integration of individuals within groups. Individual achievement is valued more in the former.
3. **Femininity versus masculinity.** the division of social roles between men and women.
4. **Uncertainty avoidance:** the degree to which employees are threatened by ambiguity.
5. **Long-term orientation:** the time frame used: short-term involving more inclination toward consumption versus long-term with its interest in preserving status-based relationships and deferred gratification.

Figure 5.3 shows a plot of the 40 countries on the power distance and individualism scales.[15] As you can see, Venezuela and Australia are at opposite corners. Venezuela is

Figure 5.3

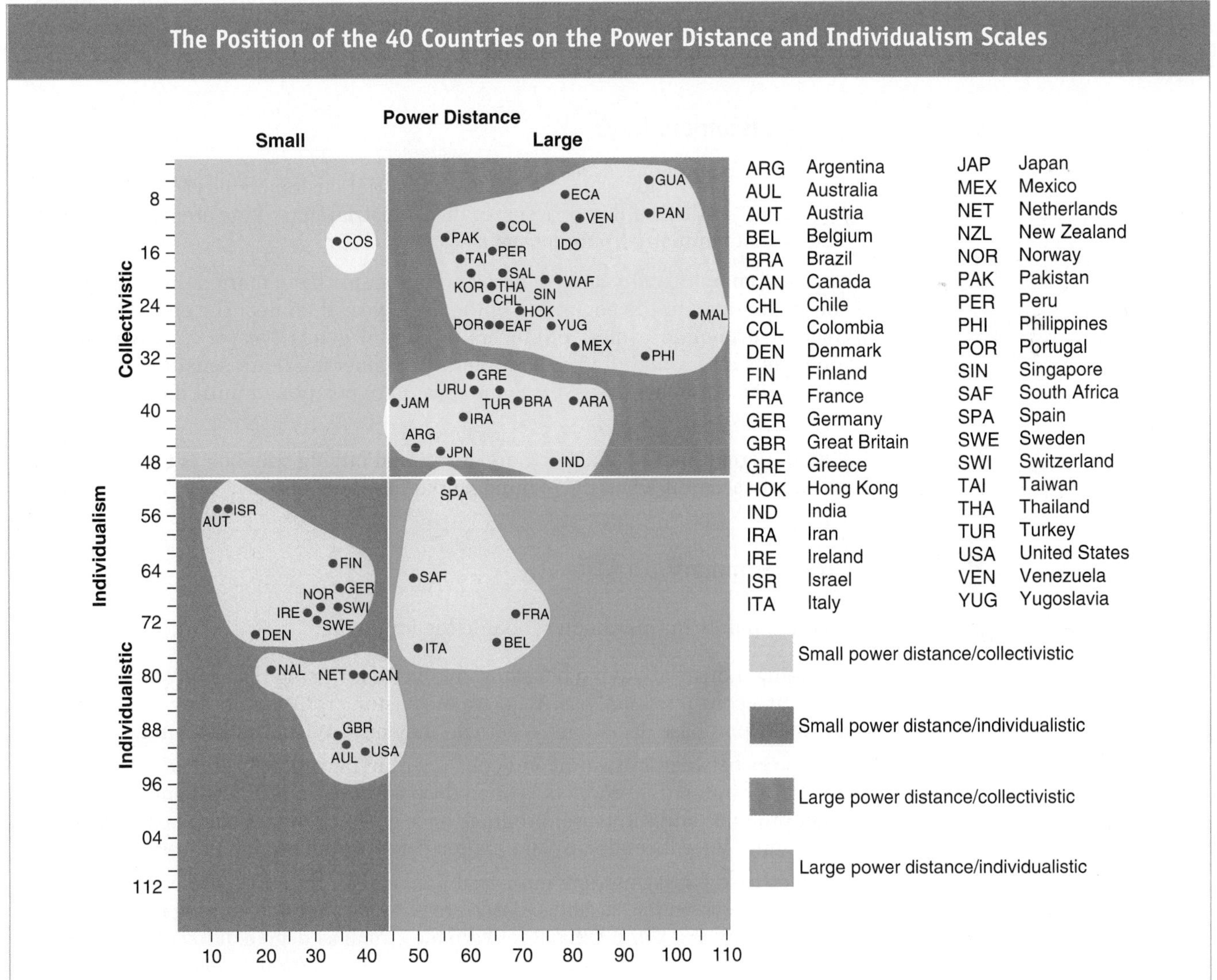

Source: Reprinted by permission of the author from *Culture's Consequences,* published by Sage Publications, © 1990 by Geert Hofstede.

characterized by a large authoritarian-collectivist culture, while Australia is democratic and individualistic. This kind of analysis would be helpful in assessing how easy/difficult it would be to expand to another country. Australian managers, for example, might find it difficult to adapt to the Venezuelan culture if they had to manage a local sales force.

Where Do Customers Buy?

As is the case for consumer products, it is important for you to understand where customers are buying your industrial product or service. Of particular importance are changes in buying patterns that could signal new channels of distribution in which you have to invest.

Traditionally, the sales force and industrial distributors have been the most popular distribution channels for industrial products.[16] However, as we will see later in Chapters 12 and 13, there has been considerable growth in direct marketing (direct mail, telemarketing) and the Internet as channels of distribution. For example, Grainger, the world's largest distributor of industrial and commercial equipment and supplies, has an online catalog providing access to more than 300,000 items. Grainger.com was the first transaction-capable Web site in the industry and achieved $1.5 billion in e-commerce annual sales in 2008 out of $6.9 billion total.[17] It is estimated that nearly 90 percent of the value of Internet commerce involves business-to-business transactions, with a total volume of more than $1 trillion in 2008 and rising every year. There is a general trend toward *disintermediation,* or the elimination of intermediate buyers in the channels of distribution, as improvements in information technology directly link manufacturers and service providers with their customers.

When Do Customers Buy?

The final question to address is, "When do industrial customers buy?" Generally, there is little interest in time of day or week in the industrial marketing arena. However, two key factors affect industrial purchasing:

1. **The customers' fiscal years.** Generally, companies have more money in their purchasing budgets at the beginning of the fiscal year than near the end.
2. **General economic cycles.** Producers of capital goods (very expensive industrial products such as mainframe computers and generators) are sensitive to economic fluctuations. In many cases, these purchases are postponed until the relevant economy improves.

Thus, an important part of analyzing organizational buying behavior is taking these timing issues into account when developing marketing strategies.

Executive Summary

Key learning points in this chapter include the following:

- Analyzing industrial buying behavior involves addressing the same questions as you would in a consumer analysis: Who are the customers? Why do they buy? How do they make purchase decisions? Where do they buy? When do they buy?
- Differences between industrial and consumer buying behavior include the fact that demand for industrial products is often derived from underlying demand for consumer products and industrial products have greater product complexity, greater buyer–seller interdependence, and a more complicated buying process.
- Variables used for segmenting industrial markets fall into the same basic two categories as for consumer variables: descriptors, or variables describing the customer (e.g., company size), and behavioral variables, such as degree of loyalty or purchase quantity.

- To understand why customers buy, you need to know how industrial buyers recognize that they have a need for a new product or service. This need is generated either internally (e.g., company personnel) or externally (e.g., a supplier's salesperson).
- To understand how customers buy, it is critical to recognize that industrial purchases are made by a buying center, or a group of individuals composed of the purchase initiator, influencer, decider, purchaser, and user.
- The buying process is composed of eight steps: determining the product need, identifying product characteristics, establishing specifications, identifying qualified suppliers, requesting proposals from potential suppliers, evaluating the proposals, choosing the supplier, and providing postpurchase feedback to the supplier.
- Where industrial purchases are made is changing to include greater use of the Internet and direct marketing.
- When purchases are made depends on corporate budgeting and business cycles.

Chapter Questions

1. Why is the notion of derived demand so important for companies selling products and services to other organizations? Can you think of an example in which an industrial company has benefited from changes in end-consumer demand? Or suffered?
2. Go to the library and look at government documents that provide sales information by Standard Industrial Classification (SIC) or NAICS code. Become familiar with the different levels of specificity of the codes. How useful are the data for a marketing manager? What are their limitations?
3. Choose an industrial product and try to determine the buying center for customers of that product. What is the customer behavior for a typical member in each group, expressed in terms of the basic customer behavior questions (why? how? etc.)?
4. Suppose that you are hired as a salesperson for a company that sells the product in question 3. How do you find out who occupies each buying role in the center? How do you use the information from question 3 to do your job?
5. Go to a Web site for a company selling business-to-business products or services. Compare this site with one selling consumer products or services. What are the differences? To whom is each targeted?
6. As noted in an illustration in this chapter, an industry that is in the early stage of the product life cycle is telematics, which, among other things, provides information services to autos via wireless technology. The penetration of such services is limited. Other than lowering the price, how would you "cross the chasm" to increase the penetration rate of such services?

Key Learning Points

The purpose of this chapter is to introduce the notion of competitor orientation. Although customer focus has received considerable attention in the marketing literature, recent years have seen an increased emphasis on understanding competitors and predicting their moves. The main learning points in this chapter are:

- Performing a market structure analysis, which identifies your major competitors
- Performing a competitor analysis
- Alternative sources of information for analyzing competitors
- Using game theory in the development of competitive strategy

Coke and Pepsi compete intensely around the world.
Source: Richard Levine/Alamy Images

Market Structure and Competitor Analysis

Chapter Brief

Coca-Cola and Pepsi-Cola are two brands competing against each other in nearly every part of the world.[1] Coke was formulated in 1886 by Dr. John Pemberton, a pharmacist in Atlanta, Georgia, and quickly grew to be one of the best-known brands in the world. Pepsi was developed in 1893 in Bern, North Carolina, by Caleb Bradham, also a pharmacist. Unlike Coke, Pepsi struggled in its early days, nearly going bankrupt several times. Its first major inroad against Coke was in the early 1930s, when it offered its 12-ounce bottle for 5 cents, whereas Coke was selling its famous 6.5-ounce bottle for the same price. Pepsi's radio advertising theme, "Twice as much for a nickel, too. Pepsi-Cola is the one for you," was rated in 1940 as the second best-known song in the United States behind the national anthem.

This was the beginning of what has come to be known as the cola wars, although Pepsi has consistently been the underdog. This has resulted in Pepsi usually being the leader in terms of new concepts and marketing programs. In the 1950s, 1960s, and 1970s, Pepsi innovated in the following ways:

- The company stressed the growing phenomenon of supermarket sales, while Coke continued to emphasize its traditional strongholds of fountain sales (e.g., restaurants, bars, movie theaters), vending machines, and small retail stores.
- Pepsi was the first to introduce a large bottle size, 24 ounces, to capture family consumption.
- The company expanded its product line to include Diet Pepsi, Mountain Dew (a lemon-lime drink), and Pepsi Light.

Coke fought back through advertising, matching Pepsi's use of larger bottle sizes, using cans, and introducing new products such as Sprite (a lemon-lime drink); diet drinks Tab, Fresca, and diet Sprite; and Mr. Pibb (a drink tasting like Dr. Pepper). However, the company refused to use the Coke name on any product other than the flagship brand.

Two significant events in the 1970s and 1980s continued this emphasis on strong, head-to-head competition. The first was the 1974 Pepsi "Challenge," a nationally advertised blind taste test demonstrating that people preferred the taste of Pepsi over Coke. The Challenge was highlighted in store displays, communications to bottlers and other channel members, and in-store Challenge booths, where supermarket customers could take the challenge while shopping. Coke responded by discounting in selected geographic markets.

The second major event is now part of marketing folklore. Coke discovered in marketing research studies that younger consumers, obviously a key target market, preferred a somewhat sweeter drink, somewhat like Pepsi. Coke's sales were suffering. As a result, in April 1985, Coke announced that it would change the formula of its nearly 100-year-old brand. The announcement created an uproar. Surveys indicated that more than 90 percent of Americans heard about the change within 24 hours and that 70 percent had tried the new formula within the first month of its introduction. Consumers were very upset with this loss of a tradition. Pepsi was delighted and felt that it had won the cola wars. In July 1985, Coke reintroduced the old formula as Coke Classic, while the new formula continued to be sold as Coke. This strategy was short-lived, as in January 1986, Classic became regular Coke again and New Coke disappeared.

In the late 1990s, several factors affected the cola wars. First, many alternative beverages were now competing for the ability to quench a drinker's thirst. These included ready-to-drink teas, shelf-stable juices, sports drinks, bottled waters, all-natural sodas, and a fast-growing category, energy drinks (e.g., Red Bull). Brands such as Snapple, Gatorade, Perrier, Arizona, and others were very popular with consumers. Second, Pepsi's corporate diversification into snack foods (Frito Lay) and particularly restaurants (Pizza Hut, Kentucky Fried Chicken, Taco Bell) diverted management attention and resources away from soft drinks.[2] In addition, fast-food growth slowed and the business became more capital-intensive.[3] Third, untapped markets such as China and Islamic countries, in which alcohol is forbidden, were exploding. Coca-Cola was well positioned to capitalize on these growth opportunities because of its vast network of bottlers and marketing muscle. In 1998, Pepsi, becoming frustrated with its inability to compete with Coke in fountain sales and its widening deficit in market share (44 percent for Coke versus 31 percent for Pepsi), filed an antitrust lawsuit against Coke, claiming the latter froze it out of selling soft drinks in independently owned restaurants and movie theaters.

To give you some idea of the market potential left for Coke, the per-capita consumption of Coke in the United States is 363 servings per person per year; in Mexico it is 332, but in France it is only 74, and in China it is less than 10. Another way to look at this is from the perspective of how much Coca-Cola products (mainly Coke) account for as a percentage of daily fluid intake, including water. In the United States, Coca-Cola products account for 14 percent of *all* daily fluids consumed, in France the number is 3 percent, and in China it is 0 percent.

In 2002, with Coke Classic's market share in the United States at 19.9 percent, Pepsi-Cola's at 13.2 percent, and volume growth rates around 4 percent, the companies expanded their advertising spending and made big bets on product tie-ins and spokespersons. With the share of cola drinks in the carbonated soft-drink category declining from 71.3 percent in 1990 to 60.5 percent in 2000, both brands were seeking the same market segment. This included 12- to 24-year-olds, who are the largest consumers of soft drinks and many of whom are still forming brand loyalties. However, industry pundits gave Pepsi high marks for its advertising campaigns, while Coke was struggling to revitalize its marketing. In addition, the cola wars expanded to global locations such as India and China where Pepsi and Coke responded to each other's new ads in 24 hours. Both companies have expanded their efforts in other beverage categories, most notably, bottled water (Pepsi's Aquafina and Coke's Dasani brands) and "new age" sports beverages (Pepsi's Gatorade and Coke's Powerade brands).

By 2009–10, the companies were continuing to face marketing challenges. Carbonated soft drink sales fell 2.3 percent in the United States in 2007; Coke held 43 percent of the market while Pepsi held 31 percent. The decline was attributed to higher prices and more consumer interest in alternative drinks. In order to boost demand, in 2008, Pepsi replaced the ad agency that had held the account for Pepsi-Cola since 1960, BBDO Worldwide, in order to "refresh Pepsi's communications." Pepsico was widely criticized for the new confusing packaging for Gatorade that replaced the brand name on the label with a big "G" and shrunk the signature lightning bolt. As a result, Pepsi's market capitalization, which had been greater than Coke's in 2005, was only 76 percent of Coke's in late 2009. In addition, both Pepsico and Coke announced the purchase of its largest independent bottlers in the United States, marking a major change in strategy. Analysts predicted Coke and Pepsi's deals will strengthen the beverage industry in North America by streamlining costs and spurring innovation and more flexible distribution of new drinks, potentially spelling lower prices and more choice for consumers. Coke and Pepsi can decide whether to distribute a product through the bottling system, which delivers products directly to stores and gives the company greater control over how its products are displayed, or through warehouses—cheaper and preferable for products too small or not profitable enough to distribute directly.

This illustration shows the importance of several analyses critical to development of the marketing plan (see Table 1.3), the marketing strategy (see the marketing strategy diagram), and the marketing manager's job:

- Performing a market structure analysis which identifies your main competitors who are often outside of the obvious set (e.g., soft drinks versus bottled waters, colas versus other flavored soft drinks like Mountain Dew).
- Gathering and analyzing alternative sources of information to understand competitor strategies. Coke must understand Pepsi's corporate and brand strategies to calculate how to react.
- Using game theory to understand the interdependence between your firm and its competitors.

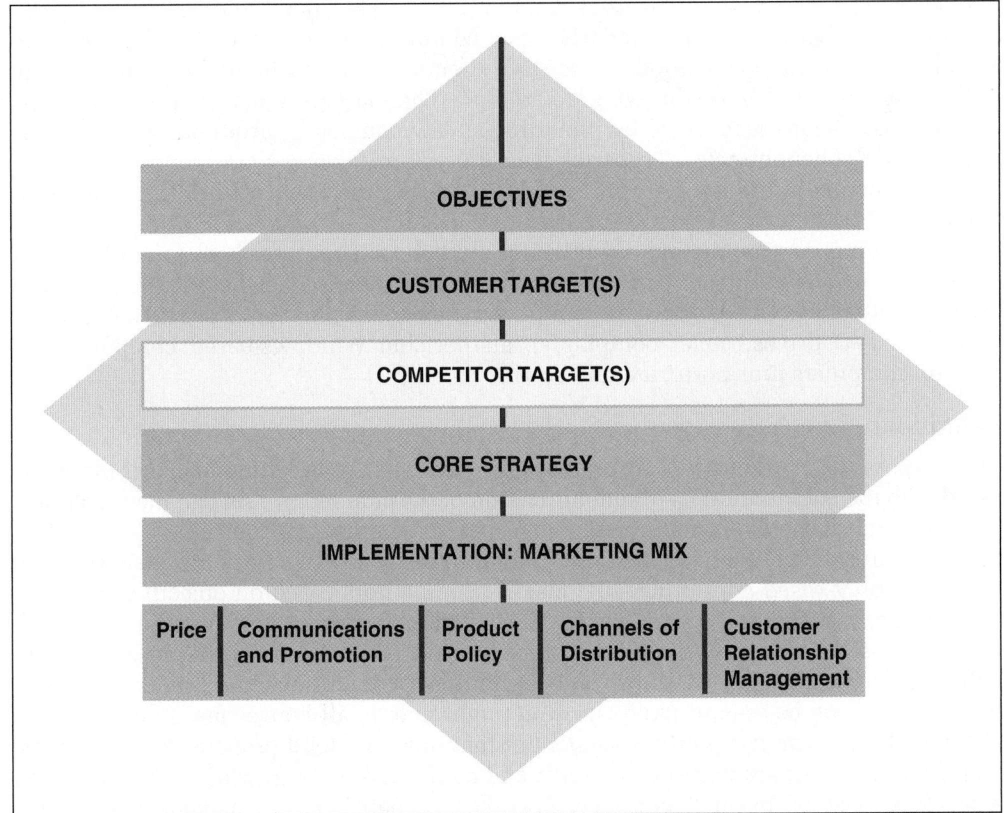

As we saw in Chapter 1, the marketing manager's job is difficult because of the large number of changes in the external environment that must be considered and anticipated. In Chapters 4 and 5, methods for analyzing one element of the external environment—customers—were discussed. In this chapter, we focus on the competition. Note that this is an integral part of the marketing strategy shown in the marketing strategy diagram. The major topics discussed in this chapter include:

- **Market structure.** It is important to understand the nature of competition in the market in which you compete. A **market structure analysis** will identify the competitors for your product or service.
- The strengths and weaknesses of the competitors and their current and likely future strategies. This is usually called **competitor analysis**.
- The development of competitive strategy today rests heavily on notions of game theory, a way of structuring likely competitor moves, anticipating them, and developing preemptive moves. Some basic aspects of game theory are described at the end of this chapter.

market structure analysis an analysis in which the marketing manager seeks to better understand who the competition is and thus define the market

competitor analysis an analysis in which the strengths and weaknesses of competitors and their current and likely future strategies are examined

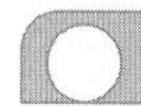

Market Structure Analysis

Overlooking an important competitive threat can be disastrous. For example, for many years the Swiss controlled the market for premium watches and Timex dominated the market for inexpensive watches. When Japanese firms such as Casio developed electronic watches in the 1970s, they were not viewed as a threat or serious competition in either business. Today, both Timex and Swiss firms offer electronic models, and only the strong success of the Swatch brand of inexpensive fashion watches has saved the Swiss watch industry in the lower-priced segment. For many years, Coke and Pepsi consistently underestimated the strength of their competitors in non-soft-drink categories, such as the rapidly growing sports drink category. PepsiCo finally realized this oversight and purchased Quaker Oats in 2000, whose "crown jewel" was the Gatorade brand.

industry
a group of products that are close substitutes to buyers, are available to a common group of buyers, and are distant substitutes for all products not included in the industry

product class/category
one particular product segment of a particular industry

product types
group of products that are functional substitutes

product variants
also called product brands, different specific combinations of features within a specific product type

brands
a name, term, sign, symbol, or design (or a combination thereof) intended to identify the goods and services of a seller and differentiate them from the competition

Ambiguous definition of the competition also creates uncertainty and ambiguity in market-related statistics such as market share. This leaves open the possible manipulation of market boundaries, particularly when compensation or allocation decisions are at stake. Market share is defined as "us/(us + them)." We can undoubtedly measure the dollar sales for "us"; however, who are "them"? The marketing manager can make his or her market share seem large by including as few competing products or services as possible in the denominator. This trick is useful when it comes to the time to be evaluated for a bonus but is not helpful for understanding the market from the customer's perspective.

For example, assume that an objective for a notebook computer is to gain 10 percent market share. The ability to achieve this objective depends on whether the market is defined as all notebooks, all portable computers (notebooks plus laptops with big screens, writeable DVD drives, tablet computers), all portable Windows-based computers, all desktop computers plus portables, and so on.

Definitions

The purpose of a market structure analysis is to enable the marketing manager to understand who the competition is. Misidentification of the competitive set can have a serious impact on the success of a marketing plan, especially in the long run.

One approach to classifying methods of identifying competitors divides them into two classes: *supply-based* approaches that classify competitors based on objective attributes of the firms, and *demand-based* approaches that classify competitors based on customer attitudes and behaviors.[4] Whichever method is used, several different terms are used in defining a market. Figure 6.1 shows one possible set of definitions in a product–industry hierarchy. As can be seen in the figure, you might refer to all houseware products as the **industry**. One particular product segment of that industry, food preparation appliances, defines the set of products more narrowly, and coffee makers form what is usually called a **product class** or **product category**. Specific alternative coffee makers, percolators, drip coffee makers, espresso machines, and so on are **product types**. Different specific combinations of features within each product type are **product variants** and **brands**.

Orange juice competes against many other beverages with similar benefits.
Source: Chris Rank/Getty Images, Inc—Liaison

Demand-Based Methods for Defining Competition

Competition can be defined at every level of the hierarchy (Figure 6.1). The number of competitors grows as you go up the hierarchy. However, the terms *industry* and *product class* do not get at the heart of competition or market definition. A good definition of an industry is the following:[5]

> *An industry should be recognizable as a group of products that are close substitutes to buyers, are available to a common group of buyers, and are distant substitutes for all products not included in the industry.*

Figure 6.1

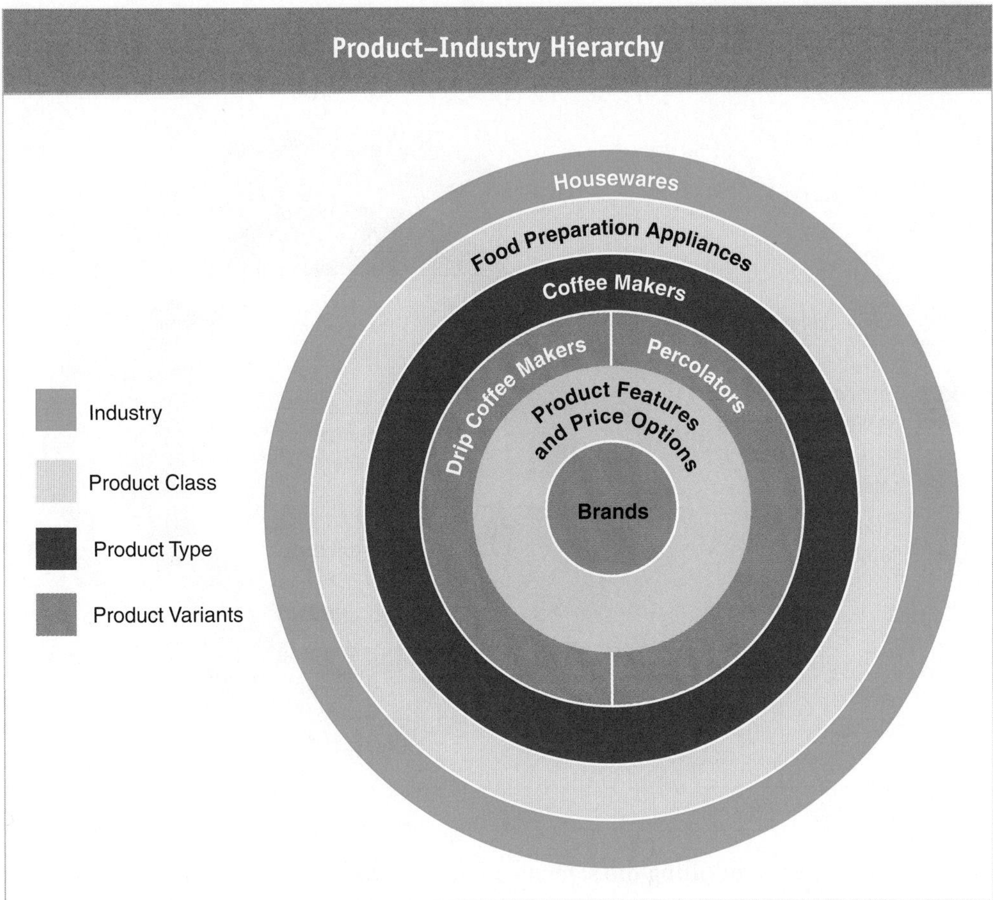

Source: George S. Day (1990), *Market Driven Strategy* (New York: Free Press), p. 97. Reprinted with the permission of The Free Press, A Division of Simon & Schuster Adult Publishing Group, from Market Driven Strategy by George S. Day.

The key part of this definition is the fact that competition is defined by the customer, not by the marketing manager. After all, it is the customer who determines whether two products or services compete against each other.

An alternative way to define the competition that better incorporates the customer's perspective is shown in Figure 6.2. The narrowest definition of competition that results in the fewest competitors would include only products or services of the same product type. This is called **product form competition**. For a drip coffee machine brand, the narrowest way to define competition would be to include only the other brands of drip coffee makers. Although there may be some product variations such as capacity, the most direct competitors are the brands that look like yours. Another example of product form competition is Diet Coke versus Diet Pepsi, because both are diet colas.

product form competition
a level of competition in which only products or services of the same product type are considered

This narrow definition might be useful in the short run because these brands are your most serious competitors on a day-to-day basis. It is also a convenient definition of competition because it mimics the way commercial data services (e.g., A.C. Nielsen) often measure market shares. However, this narrow definition may set an industry standard for looking at competition and market shares in a way that does not represent the true underlying competitive dynamics. Thus, the product form view, though perhaps providing the set of the closest competitors, is too narrow for a longer-run view of competition.

The second level of competition shown in Figure 6.2 is based on products that have similar features and provide the same basic function. This type of competition, called **product class** or **product category competition**, is more inclusive because more brands are considered to be competitors. In the current example, this means that the drip coffee machine would face competition not only from other drip machines (product form competition) but also from percolators, espresso machines, and cappuccino makers.

product class or product category competition
a level of competition in which products or services that have similar features and provide the same function are considered

The third level of competition shown in Figure 6.2 incorporates the customer's notions of substitutability. At this level, competition is defined as the products or services that

Figure 6.2

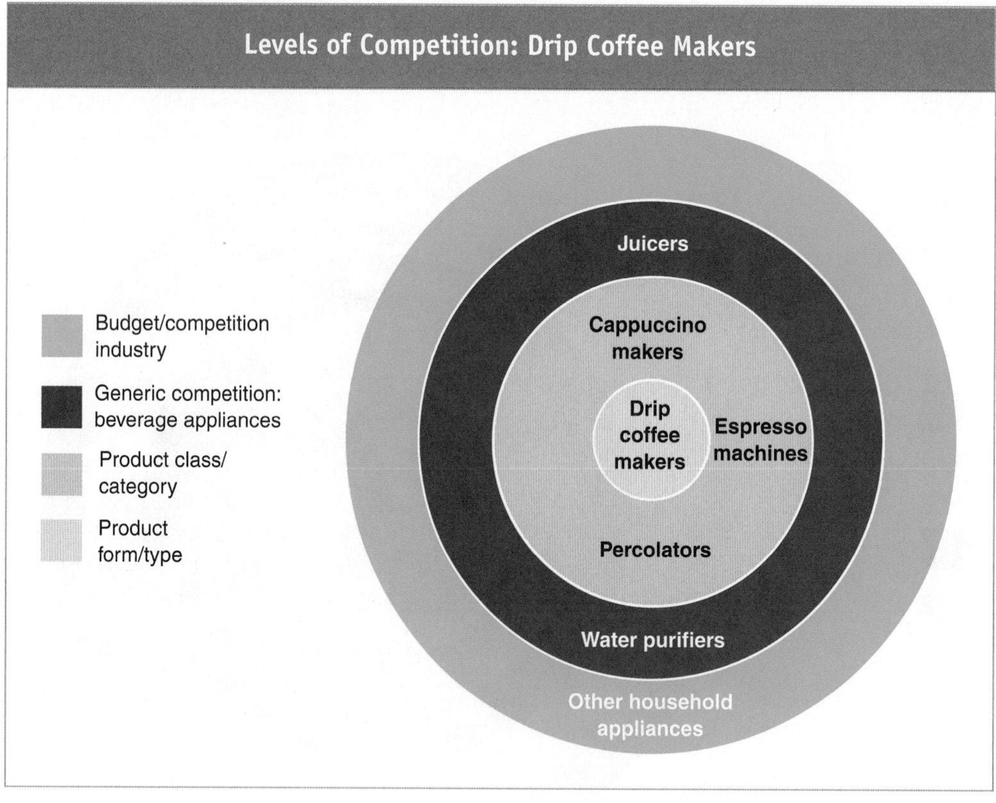

generic competition a level of competition that includes all products or services that the customer views as fulfilling the need requiring satisfaction on a particular purchase or use occasion

the customer views as fulfilling the same need. In the present example, the need, broadly defined, could be for a machine that makes beverages at home. This implies that other brands of machines creating beverages, such as juicers and water purifiers, would be competition. This level of competition is called **generic competition.**

This is a critical way to think about competition. Many products and services compete generically because they satisfy the same need. For example, think of business communications. There are many ways for two managers to communicate with each other: in person (requiring air or some other mode of travel), phone, e-mail, fax, teleconferencing, overnight mail, and regular mail.

Do brands of orange juice compete against soft-drink brands? When a person is thirsty, there are many ways to satisfy that need. The Coca-Cola Company figured that the average person requires 64 ounces of liquid per day. They also calculated that around the world, Coca-Cola supplies less than 2 ounces per person per day. Former chairman Roberto Goizueta responded, "We remain resolutely focused on going after the other 62."[6] More fast-food chains like Burger King and McDonald's are offering hamburgers at breakfast time to compete with more normal breakfast offerings. Victoria's Secret, the purveyor of sexy "special event" lingerie, is interested in increasing its "share of drawer" by offering more daily-use bras and underwear, which will broaden its competitor set to include Sara Lee Corporation (Hanes and Bali brands), VF Corporation (Vanity Fair and Lily of France brands), and retailers such as the Gap and J. Crew.[7]

The point is that there is a critical difference between generically defined competitors and product form or product category competition. The latter two are inward oriented, whereas generic competition is outward oriented. Product form and product category competitors are defined by products that look like yours. Generic competitors are defined by looking outside the firm to the customers. After all, the customer determines what products and services solve the problem at hand. Although in some cases there may be a limited number of ways to solve the same problem or provide the same benefit, in most instances focusing on the physical product alone ignores viable competitors.

The final level of competition shown in Figure 6.2 is the most general, but important for products such as drip coffee makers. Many products and services are discretionary items purchased from the same general budget. Assuming that drip coffee makers cost around $50, there are many other discretionary items a person may want to purchase with that money. Referring again to Figure 6.1, many of these items may come from the same industry (in this case, housewares). A person shopping in a department store in the housewares area faces many other discretionary items for the home that are unrelated to making coffee or quenching a thirst. Products such as pots and pans and knives may find their way into the shopping basket and could be viewed as substitutable in the budget. This kind of competition is called **budget competition**.

budget competition
a level of competition that includes any product, related or unrelated, that could be viewed as substitutable in a budget

This four-level model of competition has significant implications for developing product strategy because a different set of tasks must be accomplished at each level of competition for a product or service to be successful in the market. At each level, part of the marketing manager's job is fairly clear: convince the customer that your company's version of the product, your brand, is better than the others. In other words, your most direct competitors are other brands of a similar product form. What differs at each level is how much additional marketing has to be done beyond touting your own brand's advantages. At the product form level, when the competition is viewed as consisting only of other products with similar features, marketing activities directly aimed at the similar competitors are all that is required. However, the problem becomes more complex as the competitor set grows. At the product category level, you must also convince customers that the product form is the best in the product category (i.e., a drip coffee maker is better than a percolator or espresso machine). At the generic competition level, you must also convince customers that the product category solution to the customer's problem (the benefit derived from the product category) is superior to the solution provided by other product categories (i.e., a coffee maker is better than a juicer). This is the same problem you face at the budget level (i.e., a coffee maker is better than a new set of knives).

It is also important to note that as you move from product form toward budget competition, customer targets also begin to change. Product form competition involves battling for exactly the same customers in terms of who they are and why they buy. As the focus moves outward in the concentric circle model of Figure 6.2, both who your customers are and why they buy begin to differ as the need to be satisfied becomes more general. Because the key to success in business is obtaining and keeping customers, the most crucial form of competition is generally product form competition, in which competition occurs for the same customers. On the other hand, generic competition can destroy entire product categories when a major innovation occurs, so it also requires attention, especially for long-run planning.

Application Telepresence

A new competitor has entered the "travel industry."[8] Cisco Systems and Hewlett-Packard (HP) are the two key players in what is called the *telepresence market,* the high-end videoconferencing technology that some companies are buying to reduce travel costs. Under product category definitions, airlines would compete against other airlines, car rental firms against other similar firms, etc. However, in an era where companies are managing their travel costs very carefully, videoconferencing is becoming a generic competitor to other forms of travel. While companies have used videoconferencing for a number of years, the newest technologies sold by Cisco and HP use high-tech cameras and high-definition televisions to replicate meeting rooms and simulate eye contact. They are obviously expensive at about $300,000 a pop. Although the market for these systems is relatively small at $500 million, it has been growing at 30 percent per year as companies are seeking to save money on travel. Cisco is heavily marketing its TelePresence brand (HP's is Halo), including product placement in the *Transformers* movie released in 2009.

Application Halitosis

The breath-freshening business has become a $3 billion industry in the United States and grew by more than 15 percent from 2000 to 2001.[9] It is an excellent example of generic competition (breath freshening), composed of competition across a number of product categories to solve a common problem. The traditional solutions for the problem have been toothpaste, chewing gum, breath mints, breath sprays, and mouthwashes, each its own product category. The major companies marketing products in these categories—Kraft, Pfizer, Wrigley, Hershey, and Playtex Products—are trying to develop new products and refashion old ones to compete in this exploding industry. The category was stimulated by the clever packaging and marketing of the British-made product,

Figure 6.3

Altoids Advertisement

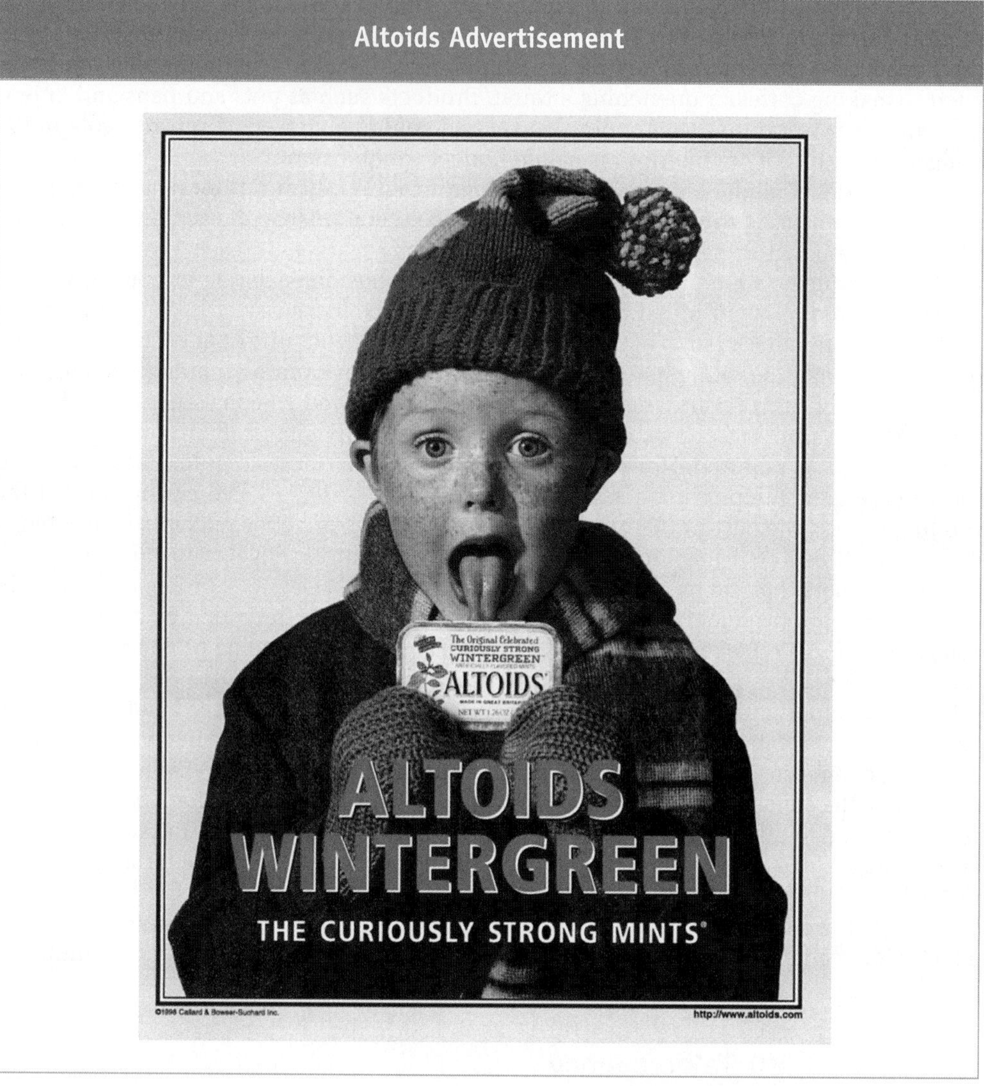

Altoids (see the advertisement in Figure 6.3). Altoids (now owned by M&M Mars) created a desire for stronger or "nasal flaring" products resulting in 2004 sales of $117 million. Pfizer's Listerine PocketPaks, dispensers of small green strips that dissolve on the tongue, has also been a big hit in the market. Thus, the breath-freshening "industry" is motivated by a generic need (bad breath), which can be solved by a combination of a variety of product categories and forms.

cross-elasticity of demand the percentage of change in one product's sales caused by a percentage change in a marketing variable for another product

Economists often use **cross-elasticity of demand** as an indicator of substitutability. Cross-elasticity is the percentage change in one product's sales due to a percentage change in a marketing variable for another product, such as price. If a cross-elasticity with respect to price is positive (a product's sales decline when another product's price drops), the two products in question are considered to be competitive. The major problem with this approach is interpreting the cross-elasticities. For example, a cross-price elasticity of 2.0 implies that a 1 percent drop in a competitor's price causes your sales to drop by 2 percent. However, this assumes that you do not react to the price cut. The interpretation also assumes that the market is not changing in any way (e.g., no new brands or changes in product design). In addition, a positive cross-elasticity does not imply cause and effect. Thus, you cannot be certain that the price decline (increase) of a product actually caused the other product's sales to decline (increase).

Many approaches for customer-based assessments of competition are available.[10] An example of such an approach is substitution in use.[11] This method estimates the degree of competitiveness through judged similarity of products in usage contexts. The typical data collection approach is to use focus groups. First, customers list all possible uses and contexts for a target product or brand. Next, either the original sample or a fresh sample of respondents list other products or brands that provide the same benefits or uses and rate their appropriateness for the different contexts or use occasions. This method can produce a large number of generic competitors or even budget competitors. However, its strength is that the method uses direct input from customers about what products and services they view as substitutes for different purchase or usage contexts.

Supply-Based Methods for Defining Competition

Product form and product category competitors can be determined from observation (managerial judgment) and external data sources. In particular, government documents provide valuable information about product form and category competitors without disclosing the individual firms involved.

Table 6.1 shows some North American Industrial Classification (NAIC) categories based on 2002 economic census data (the most recent available at the time of this

Table 6.1

Concentration by Largest Firms for the United States: 2002

2002 NAICS Code	Kind of Business and Largest Firms Based on Sales	Establishments (number)	Sales: Amount ($1,000)	Sales: As Percent of Total
445	Food and beverage stores			
	All firms	148,901	456,135,887	100.0
	4 largest firms	7,016	128,498,500	28.2
	8 largest firms	10,710	180,110,436	39.5
	20 largest firms	13,581	225,711,132	49.5
	50 largest firms	17,746	270,385,987	59.3
4451	Grocery stores			
	All firms	95,514	415,189,211	100.0
	4 largest firms	7,012	128,488,497	30.9
	8 largest firms	10,667	180,069,323	43.4
	20 largest firms	13,503	225,609,394	54.3
	50 largest firms	17,660	270,256,808	65.1
44511	Supermarkets and other grocery (except convenience) stores			
	All firms	66,092	394,274,447	100.0
	4 largest firms	6,843	128,302,722	32.5
	8 largest firms	10,498	179,883,548	45.6
	20 largest firms	13,333	225,421,724	57.2
	50 largest firms	16,529	268,964,215	68.2
44512	Convenience stores			
	All firms	29,422	20,914,764	100.0
	4 largest firms	1,624	3,260,307	15.6
	8 largest firms	1,992	3,929,729	18.8
	20 largest firms	2,874	4,668,548	22.3
	50 largest firms	3,266	5,328,674	25.5

Source: U.S. Consus Bureau, 2002 Economic Census.

writing). The numbers of digits in the classification scheme are roughly equivalent to the three outer circles of Figure 6.1. The three-digit category 445, Food and beverage stores, defines the industry. The four-digit categories, such as grocery stores, occupy a higher level of specificity; the five-digit categories, such as supermarkets and convenience stores, provide narrower definitions such as product class or type information. These definitions of different levels of competition are useful, although your own definitions would be tailored to the specific product or service. However, the risk of using what might be an inappropriate classification scheme is offset by the vast amounts of information collected by the government that are categorized by NAIC code.

Consulting firms, trade associations, professional publications, and other organizations may supply their own category or industry definitions, which become the basis for managerial decision making. For example, the online broker industry is divided into groups by commission, "deep discount" (Ameritrade), "middle-cost" (E*Trade, TDWaterhouse), and "high-cost" (Merrill Lynch, Charles Schwab). There is also a category for direct access brokers, that is, those that allow customers to trade directly on the Nasdaq via electronic communications networks (ECNs). These are essentially product form data with competition being defined within commission class. The category would be all of the online brokers or perhaps all brokers including offline companies like Edward Jones. The latter are not included here. No extrapolation to generic competition is possible. Investment vehicles other than stocks (e.g., real estate, jewelry, antique cars) are generic competitors, and there are many other things on which you could spend several thousand dollars rather than stocks (e.g., an MBA degree, a new car, a Club Med vacation). Unfortunately, these definitions by commission class do little to help a marketing manager identify the competition. Even worse, dependence on such data could lead you to focus exclusively on the competitors in your commission tier and ignore the others who could easily move into your product form segment by changing its commission structure.

In general, the most difficult kinds of competition to assess using supply-side methods are generic and budget because they cannot be observed readily and competitors may be numerous. In determining these kinds of competition, customer judgments are essential. This makes sense because both kinds of competition are based on how customers, not managers, view the world.

Competitor Analysis

Training employees to collect and analyze information about competitors is one of the hottest areas of executive education. The Society of Competitive Intelligence Professionals (SCIP) has grown from a few dozen members in 1986 to more than 7,000 today. Companies such as Kellogg, IBM, Microsoft, and Intel have hired ex-CIA (Central Intelligence Agency) officers and other professionals to help them better understand their competitors and predict their likely future strategies. Some academic institutions such as Simmons College and Drexel University offer competitive intelligence (CI) certification programs. Like the market structure analysis just discussed, competitor analysis is a critical part of the situation analysis of the marketing plan. It is estimated that over $2 billion is spent per year worldwide on competitive intelligence activities.[12]

At the same time, competitor analysis has an unsavory reputation due to many interpreting it as corporate spying or "snooping" and associating it with Cold War undercover tactics. These feelings are not unjustified, as several well-publicized incidents of large corporations going to great extents to capture information illegally have hurt the reputation of the legitimate CI field. These include Oracle's hiring of a firm to perform "dumpster diving" (trash stealing) activities on Microsoft, Procter & Gamble's corporate spying on Unilever that spun out of control, and Starwood Hotel's claim that two former executives who jumped to Hilton Hotels stole more than 100,000 documents containing highly-sensitive information about a new luxury hotel chain it was developing.[13]

Application Kraft Foods China

From time to time, Kraft Foods' warehouse and distribution manager in China takes unusual day jobs. He gets in line with groups of laborers and hires himself out as a day worker to local logistics companies. The manager is not looking to make extra money, however. He is going undercover to see how the companies run their warehouses. The manager says that such spying gives him the most accurate picture of competing logistical companies' performance, which is critical for their Chinese business that relies on local companies to handle the movement of its goods between production plants, distribution centers, and wholesalers.[14]

A framework for competitor analysis is shown in Figure 6.4. The bottom line of a competitor analysis is a forecast of their likely future strategies (the center circle in Figure 6.4). In most cases, it is impossible to know what the competitors in your market will do in the future. However, the purpose of this part of the situation analysis is to force you to be proactive in the marketplace, anticipating where competitors are headed and to develop appropriate strategies. Without the forecasting aspect of competitor analysis, you are always reacting to where competitors have been rather than where they are going.

The main parts of a competitor analysis are:

- **Determination of the competitors' major objectives.** It is useful to know whether they are pursuing growth (sales volume, market share) objectives or profit-related objectives.
- **Assessment of their current marketing strategies.** This includes the segments pursued, how they are positioning the products or services, their value propositions, and the marketing mix.
- **Assessment of their strengths and weaknesses.** These can be evaluated on a number of dimensions, particularly the key success factors in the market.
- **Internal analysis of your firm's strengths and weaknesses relative to the competitors.** In other words, how do you match up against them?

Figure 6.4

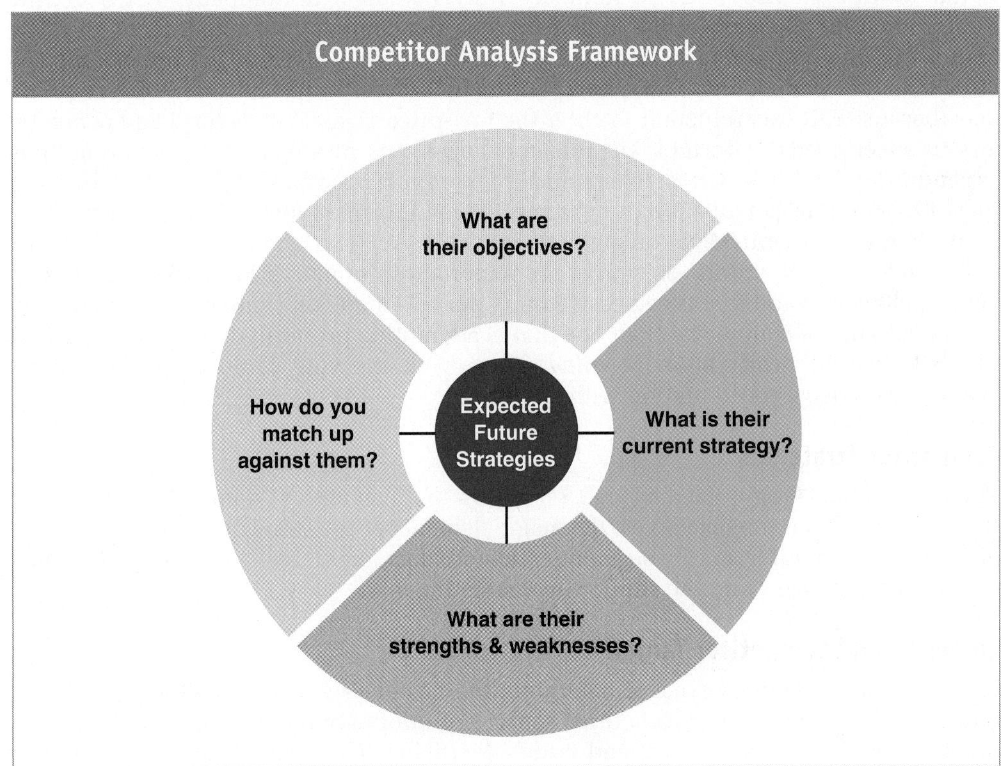

Key Objectives

In Chapter 2, we discussed the importance of the objective as setting the overall direction for the marketing strategy. So determining the competitors' objectives gives us a good idea about their current and perhaps future strategies. It usually does not take much research to uncover the objective. Sensitivity to competitors' actions, through observation, salesperson call reports, and many other resources, is the key.

Suppose you learn that a competitor is going to be aggressively pursuing a market share objective at the expense of short-term profits. This strategy would not be unusual for a new product in the market or a foreign competitor attempting to establish a beachhead in a local market. In this case, a cut in price, increased advertising expenditures, increased promotional activity aimed at end customers and distributors, or increased distribution expenses are likely to occur. In other words, a rival marketing manager who is trying to expand a brand's market share will spend money on market development-related activities or price reductions.

Brands pursuing a profit objective at the expense of some share loss (usually called a "harvest objective" if the ultimate intention is to drop the product) would be marketed in the opposite way. An increase in a competitor's price, decreases in marketing budgets, and so on can be interpreted as a retreat (though perhaps only temporary) from active and aggressive competition in the market.

An important factor in this assessment of competitors' objectives is whether a competitor is publicly owned, privately held, or government controlled or owned. Because privately owned firms do not have to account to stock analysts, long-term profits may be more important than showing consistent positive quarterly returns. A good example of this kind of company is Cargill, the largest privately owned company in the world, which deals in commodities such as grain. Government-controlled firms may have objectives such as maintaining employment, providing service, or facilitating currency exchange. Some of the largest automobile companies in the world, such as Fiat (Italy) and Peugeot (France), have been unprofitable for many years because of high labor costs resulting from their countries' need to keep workers employed.

An interesting variant of the impact of private ownership on objectives occurs if the privatization resulted from a leveraged buyout (LBO). Even though the company is private, it is often more interested in profits and cash flow to pay down debt than it is in plowing money into activities that will help gain market share. An excellent example is the well-publicized LBO by Kohlberg Kravis Roberts & Company (KKR) of RJR Nabisco in 1988. Because of the large debt load the company assumed, many of RJR's brands became vulnerable to competitors, who took advantage of the opportunity to pursue market share gains. These competitors included Philip Morris in tobacco products (because RJR was reluctant to enter the low-price cigarette category) and competitors in snack foods, who took advantage of large cuts in advertising and promotion expenditures for RJR's Ritz crackers and Planters nut products. As of 1995, RJR was free of KKR and began an attempt to regain the market share lost to Philip Morris, particularly for its flagship Winston cigarette brand.[15]

Estimates of competitors' objectives are important information for marketing strategy development. A brand that is aggressive in its pursuit of market share must be viewed as a different kind of competitor than one that is attempting primarily to maximize profits. The latter would clearly be more vulnerable to you, and you would probably want to avoid an expensive confrontation with the former.

Competitor Strategies

The marketing strategy diagram (p. 151) shows the elements of a complete marketing strategy. Other than the objectives, the major elements of the strategy that the marketing manager must monitor are the segments pursued (customer targets), the competitor targets, the core strategy, and the supporting marketing mix.

Customer and Competitor Targets

How can the marketing manager determine the customer and competitor targets? For industrial products and services, three sources of information are useful: product sales literature, your own sales force, and trade advertising. The texts of the sales literature may give information about the kinds of customers for whom the product is best suited and may also mention direct competitors by name. Your sales force should also be able to collect information from informal contacts, trade show discussions, and the like. The media in which the trade advertising is placed can be analyzed for their target markets by obtaining readership information from your advertising agency, information services such as Mediamark Research Inc. (MRI), or the media themselves. For consumer products, media advertising is the best way to track the segmentation strategy and the competitor targets. As with industrial advertising, tracking services can identify the target customers by examining the audiences who view, read, or listen to the medium in which a competitor's ad appears. The copy of the ads themselves can be analyzed for competitor target information.

Product Features

Although we saw earlier in the book that customers buy benefits (i.e., what products and services can do for them), not product attributes, it is still useful to create a matrix of all comparative feature data. You can use this matrix to get a quick visual snapshot of how you compare to the competition, which you can use as part of the marketing strategy or for new-product development purposes. Table 6.2 shows a product feature matrix (2009) for three small sports sedans using data provided by Edmunds.com. For some categories like autos, comparison data are easy to find on the Internet.

Table 6.2

Product Feature Matrix: Small Sports Sedans

PRICING			
Pricing	3 Series	A4	C-Class
MSRP	$33,600	$31,850	$32,900
Invoice	$30,910	$29,620	$30,597
National True Market Value (TMV®) Price	$32,203	$30,099	$30,891
Basic	4 yr./50,000 ml.	4 yr./50,000 ml.	4 yr./50,000 ml.
Drivetrain	4 yr./50,000 ml.	4 yr./50,000 ml.	4 yr./50,000 ml.
Roadside	4 yr./Unlimited ml.	4 yr./Unlimited ml.	Unlimited yr./Unlimited ml.
Rust	12 yr./Unlimited ml.	12 yr./Unlimited ml.	4 yr./50,000 ml.
FEATURES			
Colors			
Interior Color Chips	6 Available	3 Available	3 Available
Exterior Color Chips	12 Available	12 Available	10 Available
Base Engine			
Base Engine Type & Cylinders	inline 6	inline 4	V6
Base Engine Displacement	3.0 liters	2.0 liters	3.0 liters
Valvetrain	24 Valves double overhead cam (DOHC)	16 Valves double overhead cam (DOHC)	24 Valves double overhead cam (DOHC)
Variable Valve Timing	Standard	Standard	Standard
Compressor	Not Available	Turbocharger	Not Available

(continued)

Product Feature Matrix: Small Sports Sedans (*Continued*)			
Horsepower	230 hp @ 6,500 rpm	211 hp @ 5,300 rpm	228 hp @ 6,000 rpm
Torque	200 ft-lbs. @ 2,750 rpm	258 ft-lbs. @ 1,500 rpm	221 ft-lbs. @ 2,700 rpm
Available Engines			
4 Cyl	Not Available	Standard	Not Available
6 Cyl	Standard	Not Available	Standard
Available Transmissions			
6 Speed Manual	Standard	Standard	Standard
6 Speed Shiftable Automatic	Optional	Not Available	Not Available
7 Speed Shiftable Automatic	Not Available	Not Available	Optional
Drivetrain			
Driven Wheels	Rear wheel drive	All wheel drive	Rear wheel drive
Center Differential	Not Available	Mechanical	Not Available
Limited Slip Differential-Center	Not Available	Standard	Not Available
Hill Holder	Brake hill holder	Not Available	Transmission hill holder
Suspension			
Independent Suspension	Four-wheel	Four-wheel	Four-wheel
Stabilizer Bars	Front and rear	Front and rear	Front and rear
Active Suspension	Not Available	Optional	Not Available
Tires and Wheels			
Tires	205/55R16 Run flat	225/50R17 94H All season	245/40R17 All season
Wheels	Alloy 16 × 7.0 in.	Alloy 17 × 7.5 in.	Alloy 17 × 8.5 in.
Spare	Not Available	Temporary steel	Temporary steel

Core Strategies

You can assess competitors' core strategies by studying their marketing communications. What you are looking for is how they are positioning their products in the market, how they are differentiating themselves, and, in total, what is their value proposition.

An example of how this can be done is shown by examining the advertisement for Xerox's ColorQube multifunction printer shown in Figure 6.5. Clearly, the value proposition here focuses on the reduced cost of color printing. There are also secondary emphases on conservation in that the text mentions reduced waste as well as performance. The target market can be discerned by obtaining the demographics for the medium in which the ad is placed, *Wired* magazine. Using SRDS Media Solutions (www.srds.com), the demographics skew male (76 percent), upscale ($83,960 average income), youngish (33 years old), educated (44 percent college grads), and, importantly, professional/managerial (48 percent) with 12 percent in top management. Not much can be gleaned from this ad about the competitor targets. Visiting the Web site (FinallyColorIsLess.com) reinforces the print ad and provides more information about features and benefits.

Figure 6.5

Xerox Advertisement

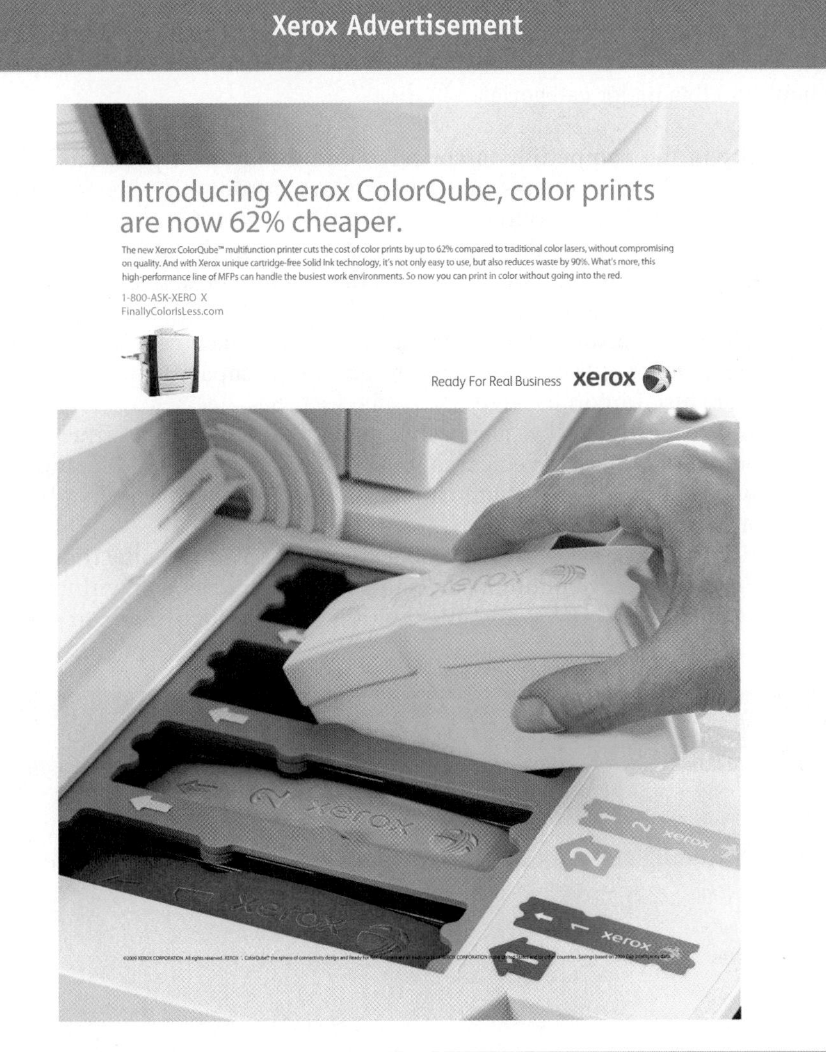

Source: Xerox advertisement, "Ready for Real Business" as seen in *Wired* July 2009, p. 43.

Supporting Marketing Mix

The mix provides insight into the basic strategy of the competitor and specific tactical decisions. These decisions are what customers observe in the marketplace. Customers are not exposed to and do not particularly care about a product's marketing strategy. However, they are exposed to price, advertising, and other marketing-mix elements. The areas to consider are:

- **Price.** Price is a highly visible element of a competitor's marketing mix and so it raises several questions. If a brand's differential advantage is price based, is the list price uniform in all markets? If the strategy is quality based, what is the price differential claimed? Are discounts being offered? If so, to whom? What is the pattern of price changes over time?
- **Communications.** What advertising media are being used? What creative activities? Sales promotion activities such as price promotions, coupons, and other deals are important to track.
- **Distribution.** What kinds of selling approaches are being used? What are the sales commission rates? Have there been any changes in the distribution channels?
- **Product or service capabilities.** Product features have already been discussed; a comparison of customer service operations and capabilities is also useful.

Competitor Strengths and Weaknesses

To assess the strengths and weaknesses of a competitor, a table of the kind shown in Table 6.3 can be used. This table breaks down the information required to perform this assessment into five major categories:

1. **The ability of the competitor to conceive and design new products.** This dimension of the analysis evaluates the new-product introduction record of each competitor as well as their resources devoted to this effort. Clearly a firm with a high ability to develop new products is a serious long-term threat in a market.
2. **The ability of each competitor to produce the product or deliver the service.** A firm operating at capacity to produce a product is not as much of a threat to increasing sales or share in the short term as is a firm that has slack capacity. This assumes a substantial amount of time is required to bring new capacity on-line. Product quality issues are also important here.
3. **The ability to market.** How aggressive and inventive are the firms in marketing their products? Do they have access to distribution channels? A competitor could have strong product development capabilities and slack capacity but be ineffective at marketing.
4. **The ability to finance.** Limited financial resources hamper effective competition. Companies with highly publicized financial problems become vulnerable to competitors. Conversely, large companies with broad product lines can share product

Table 6.3

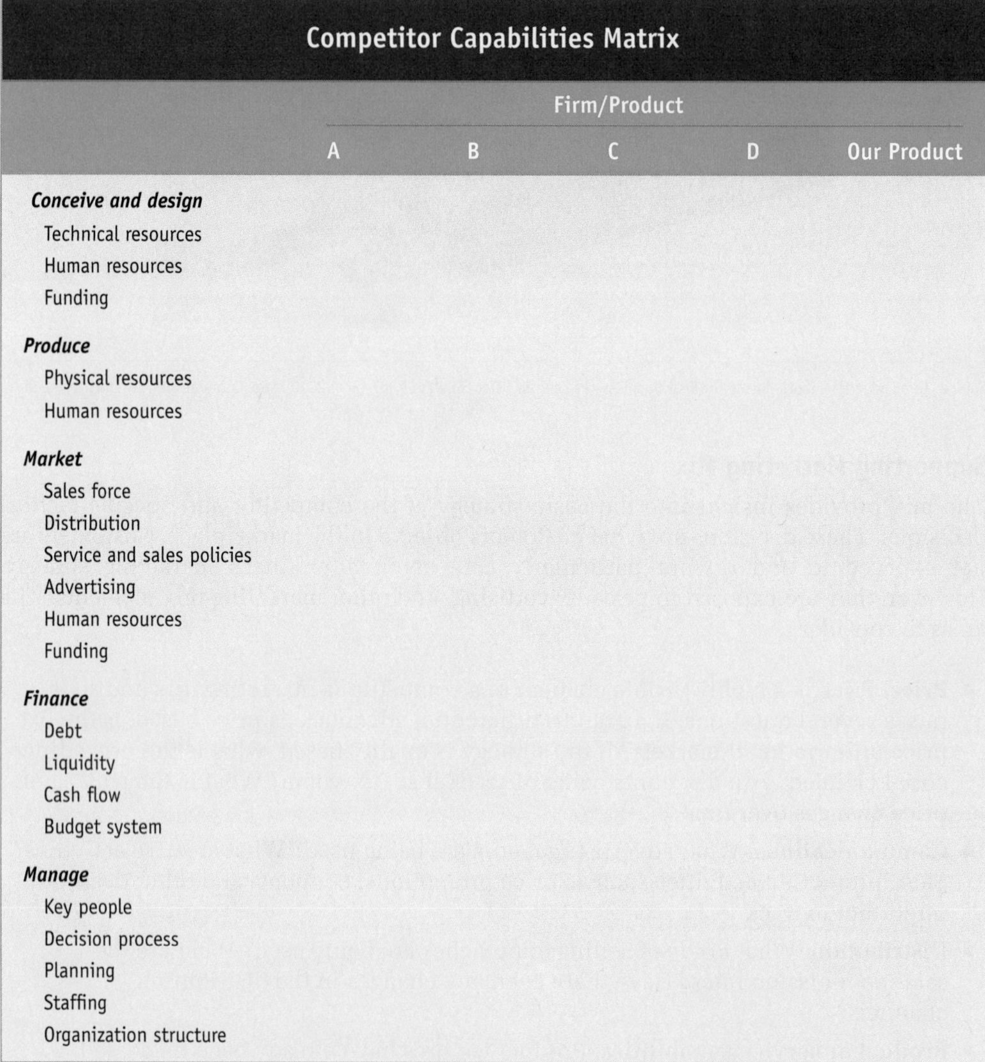

Competitor Capabilities Matrix

	Firm/Product				
	A	B	C	D	Our Product
Conceive and design					
Technical resources					
Human resources					
Funding					
Produce					
Physical resources					
Human resources					
Market					
Sales force					
Distribution					
Service and sales policies					
Advertising					
Human resources					
Funding					
Finance					
Debt					
Liquidity					
Cash flow					
Budget system					
Manage					
Key people					
Decision process					
Planning					
Staffing					
Organization structure					

Source: James Connolly, Kevin Burden, and Amy Malloy (1998), "Direct Hit," *ComputerWorld*, November 16, 1998, pp. 81–88. Reprinted with permission of YGS Group. Copyright © 2005 by *ComputerWorld*, Inc. Framingham, MA 01701. All rights reserved.

development and marketing costs over a large base and thus have a cost advantage in going to market with a new product.

5. **The ability to manage.** You can better understand competitor moves by studying the backgrounds of the competitors' managers. For example, someone just brought in to manage a product or a business, who has a reputation as a cost-conscious, operation-oriented person, is likely to continue that behavior in his or her new job.

Details about the kind of information you might want to collect are shown in Table 6.4.

Note that in Table 6.3 there is a column labeled "Our Product." You also have to do an honest self-analysis of your strengths and weaknesses by assessing your capabilities on the same dimensions as the competition. This is not easy to do because most managers feel that they are stronger than they really are on many of these dimensions. However, the analysis loses considerable value if the assessment is not accurate.

Table 6.4

Examples of Competitor Information to Collect

A. Ability to conceive and design
  1. Technical resources
    a. Concepts
    b. Patents and copyrights
    c. Technological sophistication
    d. Technical integration
  2. Human resources
    a. Key people and skills
    b. Use of external technical groups
  3. R&D funding
    a. Total
    b. Percentage of sales
    c. Consistency over time
    d. Internally generated
    e. Government supplied
  4. Technological strategy
    a. Specialization
    b. Competence
    c. Source of capability
    d. Timing: initiate vs. imitate
  5. Management processes
    a. TQM
    b. House of Quality

B. Ability to produce
  1. Physical resources
    a. Capacity
    b. Plant
      i. Size
      ii. Location
      iii. Age
    c. Equipment
      i. Automation
      ii. Maintenance
      iii. Flexibility
    d. Processes
      i. Uniqueness
      ii. Flexibility
    e. Degree of integration
  2. Human resources
    a. Key people and skills
    b. Work force
      i. Skills mix
      ii. Union
  3. Suppliers
    a. Capacity
    b. Quality
    c. Commitment

C. Ability to market
  1. Sales force
    a. Skills
    b. Size
    c. Type
    d. Location
  2. Distribution network
    a. Skills
    b. Type
  3. Service and sales policies
  4. Advertising
    a. Skills
    b. Type
  5. Human resources
    a. Key people
    b. Turnover
  6. Funding
    a. Total
    b. Consistency over time
    c. Percentage of sales
    d. Reward system

D. Ability to finance
  1. Long term
    a. Debt/equity ratio
    b. Cost of debt
  2. Short term
    a. Cash or equivalent
    b. Line of credit
    c. Type of debt
    d. Cost of debt
  3. Liquidity
  4. Cash flow
    a. Days of receivables
    b. Inventory turnover
    c. Accounting practices
  5. Human resources
    a. Key people
    b. Turnover
  6. System
    a. Budgeting
    b. Forecasting
    c. Controlling

E. Ability to manage
  1. Key people
    a. Objectives and priorities
    b. Values
    c. Reward systems
  2. Decision making
    a. Location
    b. Type
    c. Speed
  3. Planning
    a. Type
    b. Emphasis
    c. Time span
  4. Staffing
    a. Longevity and turnover
    b. Experience
    c. Replacement policies
  5. Organization
    a. Centralization
    b. Functions
    c. Use of staff

Table 6.5

Differential Competitor Advantage Analysis						
	Firm/Product					
Critical Success Factors	A	B	C	D	E	Our Product
1						
2						
3						
4						
5						
Overall rating						

There are two ways to summarize the information from the analysis of strengths and weaknesses. One way is to first determine four to six key success factors for your market (e.g., strong distribution, excellent product quality). The competitors, including your company, can be rated on these factors. The format of the analysis could follow Table 6.5. This method provides an overview of the strongest companies or products in the market and shows what it takes to be successful in a particular market.

A second way to summarize the data is to use a classic format, usually called a strengths, weaknesses, opportunities, and threats (SWOT) analysis. A SWOT analysis focuses only on your business and follows Figure 6.6. Each quadrant of the figure contains a summary of the different components of the analysis, based on the competitive assessment and other information covered in this chapter. It is particularly important to examine the opportunities and threats.

Expected Future Strategies

As we noted earlier in this chapter, the bottom line of the competitor analysis is a forecast of competitors' likely marketing strategies over the next year, the typical marketing planning horizon.

Figure 6.6

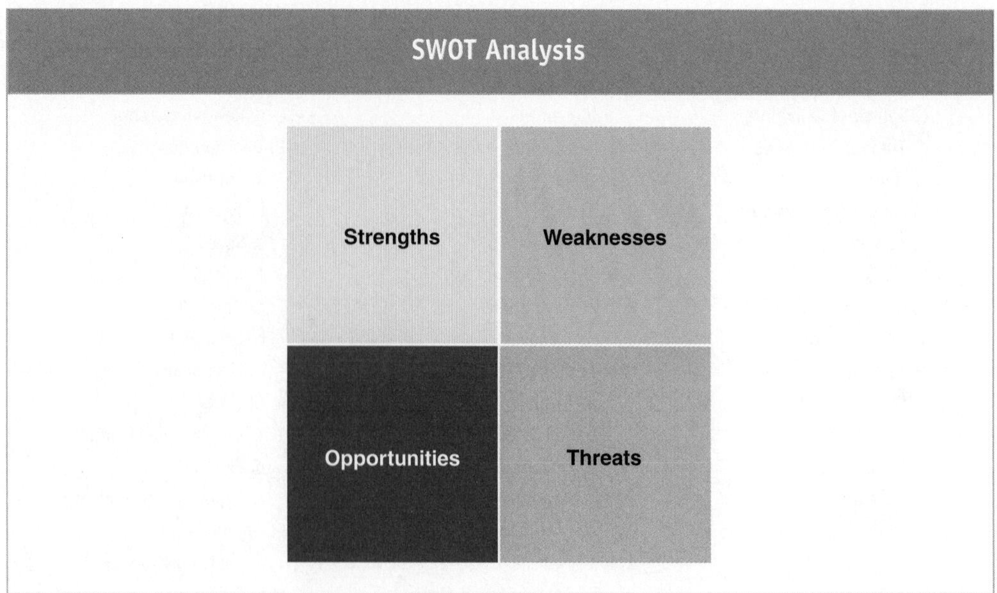

One approach does not involve forecasting at all. Sometimes competitors come right out and tell you what their future strategy will be. For example, the industrial product distributor Grainger described in Chapter 5 publishes a fact book about the company on its web site, www.grainger.com. In the 2009 edition, the company described its future distribution strategy in these terms (p. 13):

> *In 2009, the company plans to expand its distribution center operations in North America ... The company also plans to improve its supply chain capacity in Canada.*

Much of the time, however, you will not be as lucky as Grainger's competitors are. An alternative approach is to use the trend forecasting method described in Chapter 4, in which historical sales data were extrapolated into the future. You can do the same with competitors' marketing strategies by identifying a trend in their past actions and extrapolating it into the future. This requires paying close attention to the competitors' marketplace activities.

A third approach to forecasting competitors' actions is to simulate them. For example, at many companies managers are given data about the competitors in their market. Then they are divided into groups and asked to role-play the competition. In other words, they are asked, "If you were company A, what would your marketing strategy be next year?" Using these simulated strategies, the company can formulate a strategy that accounts for reasonable forecasts of the competitors' actions.[16]

A somewhat more sophisticated, long-term version of this simulation is called **scenario planning.**[17] In this analysis, alternative scenarios of the future are created, based on the structural aspects of the industry and competitor information. They are particularly useful as the basis for planning in uncertain environments, when data are scarce, and when many nonquantifiable factors affect outcomes in the market. Thus fast-moving industries such as technology-based ones are particularly good applications for scenario planning, as are products that are subject to global political and economic forces, such as petroleum. Examples of brief scenarios are shown in Table 6.6. After a considerable discussion, the marketing manager would choose one scenario as the most likely and base his or her marketing plans on it. The analysis is somewhat similar to exploring "what-if" questions by using spreadsheet software.

scenario planning
planning that involves asking "what-if" questions to produce forecasts of alternative outcomes based on different assumptions about advertising spending, price levels, competitor actions, and other variables

Table 6.6

Three Scenarios
Scenario 1: Gradual Adjustment
U.S. dollar remains weak, resulting in limited foreign sourcing. The product undergoes minor technological change without any strong patents or innovations. The U.S. economy grows at moderate pace, averaging about 3 percent per annum in gross national product (GNP) growth. Union power keeps declining without major strikes. Customers remain interested in high service.
Scenario II: High Turbulence
Major customers experience budgetary pressures from declining tax base. A strong U.S. dollar reduces exports and stimulates foreign products to enter the U.S. market. Overseas component sourcing and assembly increase. Product remains simple to manufacture.
Scenario III: Tough Times
Technological changes make the product very simple to produce. The U.S. dollar is very strong, causing stiff competition even at home. Furthermore, customers become increasingly more price sensitive and want less service. Some buy directly from overseas producers, bypassing the dealer network entirely.

Source: Paul J. H. Schoemaker (1991), "When and How to Use Scenario Planning: A Heuristic Approach with Illustration," *Journal of Forecasting*, 10, pp. 549–564.

Application | Rockwell Collins

Rockwell Collins is a leader in the design, production, and support of communication and aviation electronics. In 2002, the company faced a high-stakes bidding situation for a government contract. The company had a one-person "team" in charge of competitive intelligence. He felt that it was critical to develop a forecast of what the major competitor would bid on the project. First, he interviewed his company's salespeople to see what they had heard "on the street" about how the competitor might bid. Then he tapped into his contacts in the engineering department to get their take on how the competitor might act. He set up an internal team and asked its members to role-play the competitor looking for even more insights. Taking all these sources of information into consideration, he concluded that the competitor would be aggressive in its price. To counteract this low-price approach, the Rockwell team assembled a pitch emphasizing its experience and outstanding customer service. Its price was higher but Rockwell won the bid anyway. Had the company not known that the competitor was going to use a low price approach, it might have also bid low and lost to a lower bid that it could not match.[18]

Application | Intuit

On May 10, 2005, Intuit Inc.'s top 40 managers left their Mountain View, California, headquarters for a hotel in nearby Palo Alto. They were divided into two groups, one representing Intuit, the other representing its main competitor, Microsoft. The Microsoft team developed an attack plan against Intuit's small-business accounting software, QuickBooks. Then the team representing Intuit developed a counterattack. This continued throughout the day. The purpose of this simulation was to prepare Intuit's executives for the September 2005 launch of Microsoft Small Business Accounting, a threat to QuickBooks.[19]

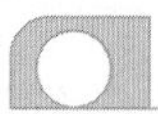

Where Do We Get the Information?

Like the general marketing data sources listed in Table 3.2, information about the market is classified as primary or secondary. Many of the library sources mentioned in Chapter 3 provide the kinds of data that will help you perform the analyses described in this chapter. A complete list of all kinds of sources is beyond the scope of this book. However, some are particularly good for collecting information about competitors.[20]

Secondary Sources

Some of the best secondary sources of information are:

- **Internal sources.** It is convenient to begin the search with internal queries about the existence of old marketing plans, market research studies, sales management call reports, and other documents.
- **Annual reports.** Although these are created only for publicly held companies (Dun & Bradstreet supplies what are called D&Bs on privately held firms) and they tend to be public relations oriented, you can comb through the report and find interesting financial information, plant locations, and general strategic thrusts from a corporate perspective. Public reporting documents at the line-of-business level, known as 10K statements, are more useful.
- **Patent and trademark filings.** These are available from online companies such as CompuServe and from MicroPatent, whose MarkSearch and MarkSearch Pro services contain the text and images from trademarks registered in the United States since 1884.
- **Other government sources.** Although most of the data available through government sources are not at the individual company/brand level, freedom of information laws

can help provide information about competitor's bids, finances, and a variety of strategic documents.[21]

- **General business and trade publications.** As we have noted throughout this chapter, much information can be obtained from publications that are widely distributed (e.g., *Bloomberg Businessweek, The Wall Street Journal*) or from those that are targeted toward specific industries (e.g., *Progressive Grocer, Variety, Twice* [for consumer electronics]).
- **Consultants.** Some organizations specialize in collecting information about particular markets. For example, MarketResearch.com is a broker for research reports in a wide variety of industries.
- **Trade associations.** Most companies are members of trade associations and a list of such associations is available at most business libraries. These associations are usually formed for public relations or lobbying purposes, but they often perform market research for the member firms, which may provide industry data on market shares, price levels, and so on.
- **Help wanted ads.** A casual examination of the want ads in *The Wall Street Journal* or the *Financial Times* shows that companies disclose a good deal of information about their new products, areas of emphasis, job qualifications and standards, new plant or facility locations, and other information. It is useful to scan the Monster Board and similar Internet-based job-posting services.
- **Electronic data services.** The Web has a number of sites that are of particular interest for this kind of analysis. Some of them offer free information and others are subscription based:

  Hoover's Online: Income statement and balance sheet numbers for public companies.

  Dun & Bradstreet's Online Access: Short reports on 10 million U.S. companies, many of them privately held.

  NewsDirectory's 24-Hour Newsstand: Links to the Web sites of more than 14,000 English newspapers, business journals, magazines, and computer publications around the world.

  American Demographics: Provides demographic data as well as a directory of marketing consultants.

  Competitive Intelligence Guide (www.fuld.com): Sleuthing tips along with an "Internet Intelligence Index."

  The largest of all of these services is DIALOG (www.dialog.com), which offers access to such databases as Port Import Export Reporting Service (PIERS), the *Financial Times*, Moody's, press releases by more than 10,000 U.S. corporations, and much more.

A number of specialized web-based services exist that perform a variety of competitive intelligence activities. Here is sample:

- Strategy Software (www.strategysoftware.com) takes the data you have collected about competitors and organizes it into reports.
- AdRelevance (a unit of Nielsen/Net Ratings) offers a Web advertising tracking service that, among a number of services, can help you determine if a competitor is increasing/changing its advertising.
- Keynote (www.keynote.com) offers a service that has a panel of users who are enlisted to test web sites. The company can ask a group of customers in a target market from its panel to go to a competitor's Web site and analyze its strengths and weaknesses.

Trade shows are important for displaying new products but are also good sources of information about competitors.
Source: © Dainis Derics/Shutterstock

Primary Sources

Special studies of the market will always be available from consultants who focus on particular industries. Other primary sources are:

- **Sales force and customers.** Because salespeople interact with customers, including distributors, on a regular basis, they are in an excellent position to find out about competitor sales pitches, pricing, and many other aspects of their activity. Companies on the edge of technology use information from the sales force to make quick updates of their marketing data. With notebook computers and wireless access, salespeople can make their calls, complete call reports electronically, and send the information back to the local office or headquarters. Online databases are immediately updated and ready to be viewed by marketing managers. The Rockwell Collins illustration earlier in this chapter is a good example of how useful the sales force can be.
- **Employees.** Some companies train their employees to be vigilant about collecting market information. Like the salesperson call report, data collected by even nonmarketing employees can be added to a corporate database.
- **Suppliers.** Often suppliers are willing to give information about competitors' shipments to impress potential new customers.
- **Trade shows.** Company representatives often attempt to obtain information at competitors' booths. Peeks at new products and sales literature are always valuable.
- **Reverse engineering or sampling competitors' products.** If the product of interest is manufactured, you can buy the competitor's product and take it apart to study its costs, technology, and other strengths and weaknesses. A medical instruments company tore down its competitors' offerings in one product category and was able to simplify the product's circuitry to reduce its costs by 23 percent.[22] If it is a service such as banking, open a small account and examine the competitor's statements and other information the bank sends. Consultants like Taeus International can provide reverse engineering services for you.
- **Plant tours.** Some companies have recently begun jazzing up their plant tours to attract loyal customers. Although many companies do not allow nonemployees into their manufacturing facilities, it is sometimes possible to obtain competitor information in this manner.[23]
- **Internet newsgroups and blogs.** Online discussion groups have been formed to discuss almost everything, including companies, their products, and their strategies. The search engine Google shows what discussion groups exist in different categories and permits a search of the chat sessions.

Application Palm Inc.

Palm is one the leading manufacturer of personal digital assistants (PDAs) as well as "smartphones" like the Pre introduced in 2009.[24] Jeff Hawkins and Donna Dubinsky founded the company in 1992 and introduced its first product in 1996. By 2000, the product had a 75 percent share of the handheld electronics market, and the company was sufficiently successful to be spun off by its former owner, the networking company 3Com. However, in 1999, the company began to make preparations for the entry of the behemoth Microsoft and its product, the Pocket PC, plus other PDAs using the Pocket PC operating system (OS) Windows CE. Palm's task was to anticipate how Microsoft would enter the market (products, strategy) and develop its own strategies to counter. Not surprisingly, Palm managers felt that

Microsoft's virtually unlimited marketing budgets and vast distribution and software development networks had the potential to do some serious damage to its market share (think Netscape).

To help develop its competitive strategy, Palm hired a consultant, Michael Mace, to test the competing PDA models using Windows CE. He was not impressed, but Microsoft was feverishly working to improve the OS. As a result of his work, Mace was appointed Palm's first chief competitive officer. Besides continuing to analyze competing products, Mace tried to instill fear of Microsoft into Palm's employees in order to sharpen their competitive focus. This was actually not that difficult because many workers were former Apple employees who had seen Microsoft eat significantly into its markets. He analyzed Web sites and chat room discussions and interviewed software developers, and found out that Microsoft intended to include MP3 (digital music) and e-mail capabilities in the new OS. Palm also anticipated Microsoft moves by signing licensing deals with Nokia and Sony to provide them with Palm technology for their phones and handheld devices.

In early March 2000, Palm assembled a team of 20 employees, dubbed the "Tiger Team," with the goal of making the Pocket PC the 21st-century version of Ford's famed Edsel flop. One task of the Tiger Team was to develop aggressive advertising and promotional campaigns. From his constant scanning of the Internet, Mace noticed that Microsoft was demonstrating the Pocket PC to small groups of handheld device enthusiasts. Palm sent an employee as a "mole" to one of the enthusiast meetings, where he picked up more details about the Pocket PC's spreadsheet functions, e-mail, and sophisticated note-taking capabilities. The company then took these data and changed its sales presentations to software developers and other partners. When the Pocket PC was finally introduced in April 2000, at Grand Central Station in New York, Palm had already assigned 25 employees to retail outlets in New York to give demonstrations and divert attention away from the Pocket PC. By May and June of that year, Palm was still dominating the market.

Application | Apple iPad

The Apple iPad, the company's new tablet computer, was announced with considerable hype in January, 2010. It was finally available on April 3, 2010. While lines were filled with eager consumers, early buyers were companies such as iFixit Inc. and UBM TechInsights that tear down technology products to determine who the suppliers are and the approximate cost. By April 5, 2010, it was determined that the most prominent supplier was Samsung. Samsung supplied the flash memory chips and manufactured the main microprocessor for Apple dubbed the A4. Other prominent suppliers included Amperex Technology Ltd. (battery), Broadcom Corp. and Texas Instruments (microprocessors that control the touch screen), and Cirrus Logic Inc. (a chip that manages the audio). Importantly, preliminary figures indicated that the low-end $499 iPad cost Apple about $229 in materials to make.[25]

Competitive Strategy: Some Game Theory Notions

As noted earlier in this chapter, one of the purposes of performing a competitor analysis is to anticipate a competitor's likely future strategies. A way of more formally (i.e., analytically) incorporating this anticipation into your decision making is through the use of a mathematical approach called *game theory*.[26] Game theory was invented by John von Neumann and Oskar Morgenstern to account for the interdependence of economic actors (e.g., marketing managers); interdependence occurs when the outcomes of a firm's actions depend on the actions of a competitor. It is also assumed that conflicts of interest exist in that the competitors differ in what they want to do and they cannot actively collude. Noncooperative game theory seeks to predict the behavior of rational, intelligent firms competing independently.

The simplest form of a game requires three elements:

1. A list of participants or players.
2. For each player, a list of strategies.
3. For each combination of strategies each player can use, a **payoff matrix** indicating the rewards and costs received by each player.

payoff matrix
in game theory, a graphic depiction of the rewards or costs to each player for each possible combination of strategies

Consider the pricing game shown in Figure 6.7. The two players are two managers, A and B. The strategies are to keep the product at the current price of $200 or increase it to $300. The payoffs are in the four boxes. For example, if both managers maintain the current price of $200, each will make $8,000 in profit. It is also assumed that the two managers move simultaneously rather than sequentially.

You should be able to immediately see two general benefits of thinking in game theory terms. First, you are forced to conceptualize the competitor's possible moves. Second, you must consider the financial (or other, such as market share) outcomes under the different scenarios. Thus, without even "solving" the game, there are important benefits to thinking strategically along game theory lines.

Solutions to game theory models require you to determine the game's equilibrium. The most common form of equilibrium is called the **Nash equilibrium.**[27] A Nash equilibrium has the following properties:

Nash equilibrium
in game theory, the most common form of equilibrium, which involves a list of strategies, one for each player, with the property that no manager wants to change its strategy unilaterally

A Nash equilibrium is a list of strategies, one for each player, with the property that no manager wants to unilaterally change his or her strategy. In other words, for each manager, its strategy in the equilibrium is the best response to the others' strategies in the equilibrium.

Let us try to work toward the equilibrium intuitively. Clearly, the best outcome for manager A is to keep the current price of $200 and have B charge $300 (this gives her $13,000 in profit). The best solution for manager B is to keep the price of $200 and have A charge $300. Thus, we have the conflict of interest necessary for a noncooperative game. The best collusive outcome is for both to charge $300, which results in the greatest total profits, $20,000, or $4,000 more than if A and B keep the prices the same. However, this collusive outcome is not an equilibrium because B has a financial incentive of $3,000 to

Figure 6.7

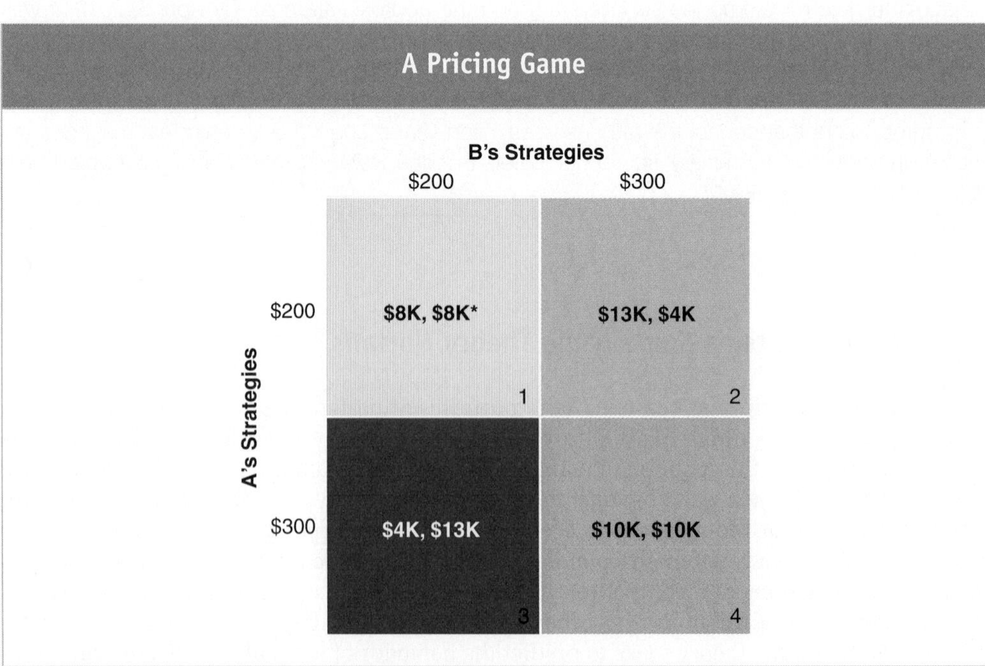

*The first number in each cell is A's payoff; the second number in each cell is B's payoff.

Source: Reprinted with permission from the *Journal of Marketing Research*, published by the American Marketing Association, K. Sridhar Moorthy (1985), "Using Game Theory to Model Competition," *Journal of Marketing Research*, 22 (August), p. 264.

move from box 4 to box 3 (i.e., not change her price). Likewise, boxes 2 and 3 are not in equilibrium. In box 2, B has an incentive to move to lower the price. In box 3, A has an incentive to lower the price. Box 1 is the equilibrium, because neither manager has an incentive to increase the price. Therefore, the prediction is that both firms will keep prices at $200.[28]

This kind of game, in which competition leads to a less-than-optimum outcome for both managers, is called a **prisoner's dilemma game**. It is seen often in highly competitive industries. For example, you might wonder why Coke and bottled water brands continue to run sales promotions and compete so strongly on price. Clearly, the best solution would be for neither to promote (box 4 in Figure 6.7), which would jointly maximize their profits. However, both are worried that if they stop promoting while the other does not (boxes 2 and 3), they will suffer. As a result, the equilibrium is heavy promotion by both (box 1) and lower total profits. A similar situation holds for the airline industry, particularly on certain routes that are served by low-cost airlines such as Southwest. Prisoner's dilemma games also apply to advertising expenditures: Both competitors are afraid to reduce expenditures for fear of falling into box 2 or 3. Thus, the predictions of even this simple form of game theory are consistent with what we see in practice.[29]

prisoner's dilemma game a particular form of competitive game in which neither participant wants to change his or her current strategy because if one does and the competitor matches, both will be worse off

We can extend game theory notions to include the concept of leader–follower. In this case, one manager chooses to make the first move and the other follows. This is often the case in industries in which one company has historically chosen to be the first in changing price or making some other marketing-mix or strategic decision. For example, U.S. Steel used to be the first company in the steel industry to raise prices to the industry's major customers, such as the automobile companies.

An example of this kind of game is shown in Figure 6.8. In this case, we assume that A is typically the leader and B is the follower. In leader–follower games, the decisions are still made at the same time, but the managers consider the market reactions from the perspective of A moving first. Manager A will not choose to raise the price to $300 because she sees that B's optimal move is to price at $200 no matter what she does. B's strategy is to charge $200 no matter what A does (again, A's strategy is not observable at this point). The $200/$200 solution is an equilibrium because if B is going to choose $200 no matter what A does, A will choose $200 because it means $4,000 more in profits. At the same time, if A is going to choose $200, B does best by choosing $200. Although the equilibrium is the same as for the simultaneous game shown in Figure 6.7, there is no guarantee that this will happen in general.

As we noted earlier, the central importance of game theory is the disciplined thinking it imposes on managers. However, other applications beside those already mentioned

Figure 6.8

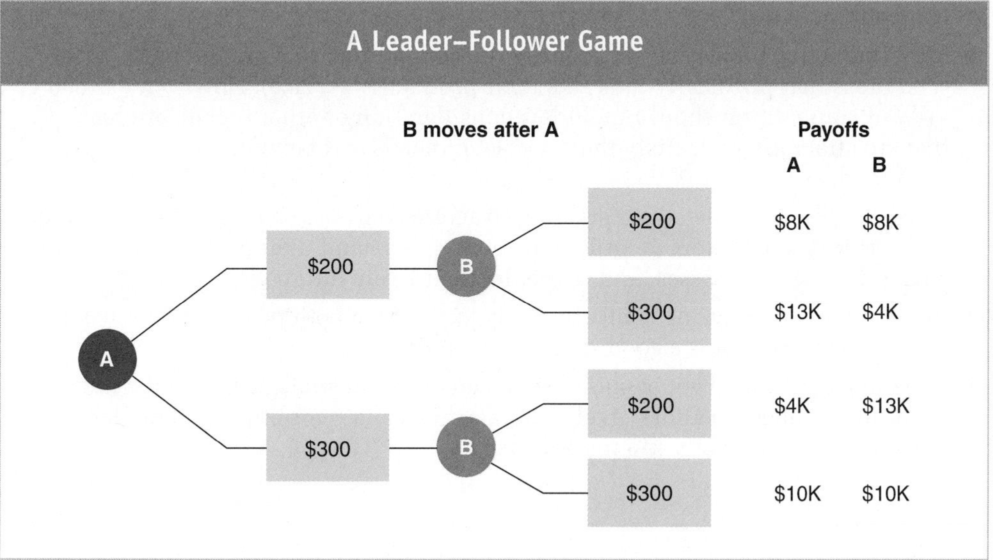

Source: K. Sridhar Moorthy (1985), "Using Game Theory to Model Competition," *Journal of Marketing Research*, 22 (August), p. 264. Published by the American Marketing Association. Reprinted with permission.

can benefit from this kind of thinking. For example, game theory thinking is well suited to decisions about new product entrants. The main issues are:

- Is there a first-mover advantage?
- Can entry be deterred by an incumbent in the market? How?
- What is the incumbent's (entrant's) optimal defensive (entry) strategy?

Game theory has also been applied to model manufacturer–retailer relations in a channel system. Unlike competitors, who have a natural conflict of interest over customers, channel members are supposed to be cooperative. However, by assuming that each party acts independently, one can use game theory to obtain channel coordination rules.

Management consultants have latched on to game theory in their work. One consultant offers the following advice for applying game theory:[30]

- Industries with four or fewer significant competitors offer the best potential for using game theory because, with a small number of competitors, it is easier to envision the possible strategies and payoff matrix. In addition, larger firms have more to gain through its application.
- If there are few purchases but each is large (mainframe computers, jet engines), competition is more intense and there is more value to thinking strategically.
- The same holds in an industry whose costs are largely fixed, such as airlines and financial services.
- Situations involving competitive bidding are excellent applications for game theory because it is crucial to strategize about bidding competitors.

In general, industries subject to strong competition (see the industry structure analysis earlier in this chapter) tend to be fertile application areas for game theory and strategic thinking. However, it also has its limitations: many assumptions that are used to simplify the interactions and outcomes may not accurately reflect the focus and motivations of the different actors.

Executive Summary

Key learning points in this chapter include the following:

- A market structure analysis attempts to assess current and potential competition.
- Most marketing managers can identify the competitors that are the most direct (i.e., those that physically look like their product or service). However, a broad view of competition should include a consideration of other organizations that are attempting to satisfy the same set of needs and benefits as your product does.
- Once you have completed a marketing structure analysis, you should analyze the most critical competitors identified to better understand their objectives, strategies, strengths, and weaknesses, and to predict their likely future strategies.
- Information for analyzing competitors can come from both primary and secondary sources. The Internet is a good secondary source.
- The game theory concept of equilibrium can help you strategically apply your expectations of competitors' likely future actions and their impact on market outcomes such as profits and market share.

Chapter Questions

1. Most marketing managers consider their product form or product category competitors to be the most serious threats. What are the pros and cons of this perspective?
2. Suppose you were the marketing manager for Steinway in charge of its line of grand pianos. How would you design a research study to better understand the generic competitors for this product?
3. In most cases, competitors are viewed as being undesirable, that is, having fewer competitors is better than having many. Can you think of situations in which having competitors can help you?
4. What are the limitations of the game theory approach to understanding competitive strategy?
5. Other than the Coke/Pepsi illustration used in the beginning of this chapter, have you observed any other markets in which the competitors appeared to be acting strategically in the game theory sense?

Key Learning Points

The purpose of this chapter is to focus on areas of product decision making. Although some product-related issues were discussed in Chapter 2 as part of the development of a marketing strategy, in this chapter we expand those discussions and include other relevant topics for marketing managers. The main learning points include:

- The elements of brand equity, building strong brand equity, and leveraging brand equity through brand extensions
- Developing perceptual maps to make positioning and repositioning decisions
- Global and technology-related issues in positioning and branding
- Product line management
- Issues in packaging and product design

Logitech is on the forefront of technology for computer mice.
Source: Ron Harris/AP Wide World Photos

Product Decisions

Chapter Brief

When Sony introduced the PlayStation 2 game "SOCOM: U.S. Navy Seals" in 2002, it featured the ability to bark orders at soldiers by using voice commands.[1] However, you could only do this if you were using a special headset manufactured by a company named Logitech. When the game was released, Sony published two versions: a $50 version with just the software and a $60 package including the Logitech headset. The latter had 40 percent higher sales than the software-only version. Microsoft CEO Bill Gates introduced Windows XP on October 25, 2001, kicking off the company's largest product release since Windows 95. When Gates emphasized XP's video instant messaging capabilities, he did so with a QuickCam, a miniature video camera made by Logitech.

Logitech was founded in 1981 in Switzerland as a software company whose first products were word-processing packages. The company grew after being awarded contracts by Ricoh to develop hardware and software for use with Ricoh's printers and scanners, and by Swiss Timing Ltd. to develop hardware and software for use at the Olympic Games. In 1982, the company bought Depraz, a Swiss watch company that had developed a mouse for interfacing with personal computers. Logitech recognized the superiority of mice over other devices such as cursor keys, light pens, and touch screens and began marketing the mouse in the United States. The company refocused around mice when it obtained a contract from Hewlett-Packard for 25,000 mice. By the end of 1989, the company had reached sales of $100 million and had about 40 percent of the world market.

Since its establishment as the premier supplier of mice to both the industrial and consumer markets, Logitech has continued to grow by adding products and revenue. It has added trackballs, keyboards, videogame controllers, miniature video cameras, PC audio equipment, Internet-based remote controls, and videogame accessories to its list of products. The number of mice variations has expanded to include 32 different types of regular mice with trackballs on the bottom, optical and cordless varieties, mice specially designed for laptop computers, and its latest version, the MX 1000 Laser Cordless. The company's latest hot product is a wireless drum controller for the "Guitar Hero" game run on the PlayStation 3 system. Corporate revenues reached nearly $2.0 billion in 2009.

The company has been successful by taking what many observers feel are commodity products (who thinks about PC peripherals such as the mouse and keyboard?) and developing a strong brand standing for "user-friendly innovation." This has been accomplished by high levels of product quality and strong positioning of its products to the point where 80 percent of the company's sales come at the retail level, where price competition is the most severe. In addition, Logitech has been successful at developing partnerships with some of the top names in the personal computer and home electronics industries: Microsoft, IBM, Dell, HP, and Google. For example, some of its keyboards are co-branded with Google by putting its name on the search key. The company has also been able to differentiate itself at point-of-purchase by its use of product features such as color and packaging, and physically placing itself near its partners.

This illustration highlights a number of the important decisions that Logitech marketing managers have to make with respect to the product:

- How do you address the needs of different segments?
- How do they sustain their successful brand?
- If they continue to expand the product line beyond mice, what do they have to consider when branding them?
- How should they position their products in the marketplace? Is the value proposition being clearly communicated to its customers?
- Other than the branding issue, what else do the marketing managers have to consider when expanding the product line?
- Going forward, how can Logitech continue to differentiate itself at the retail level using color and packaging?

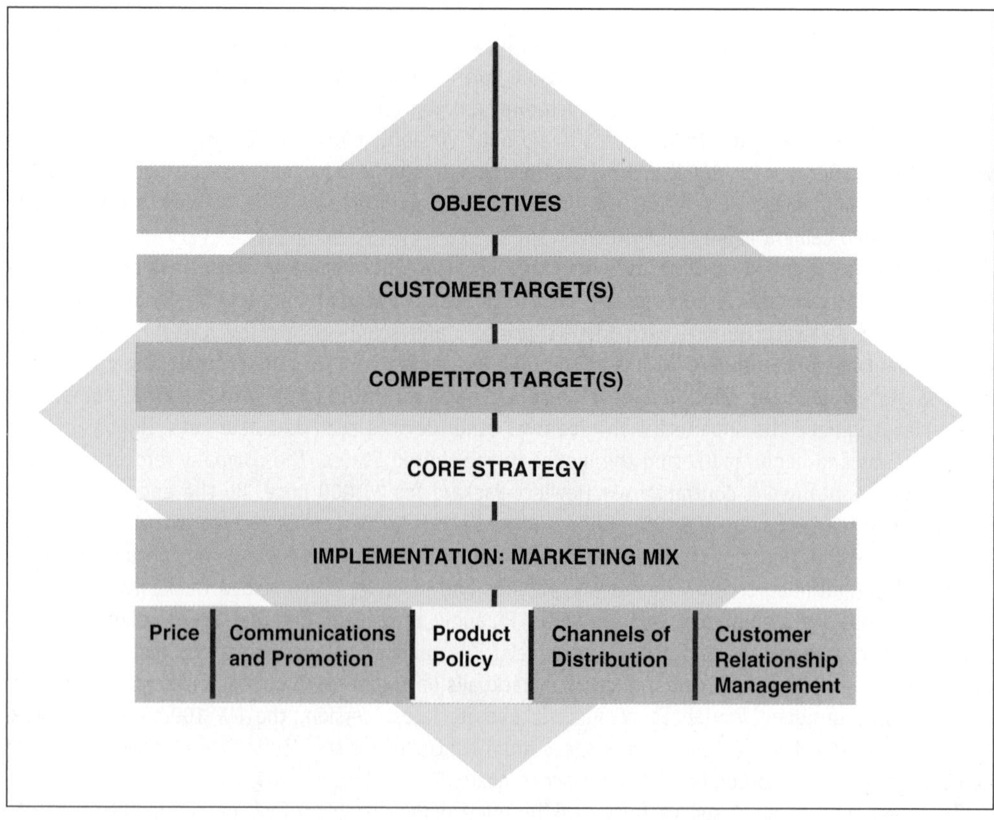

In Chapter 2 we introduced the complete marketing strategy that serves as a framework for this book. An important part of the strategy is the value proposition, the statement summarizing the customer targets, competitor targets, and the core strategy or how you intend to differentiate your product from the competitors' offerings. A key product-related issue is the differential advantage, which today is often heavily based on the brand and what it means to potential customers. In addition, product positioning was introduced as the way that marketing managers put the value proposition to work in terms of communications with customers. Thus, the discussion about these two key aspects of the product is greatly expanded in this chapter to give you a better idea of how to implement them.

We also discuss four other issues related to the product. First, if you are targeting different market segments, you have to consider how to choose which **product features** to include. For example, a cellular phone targeting older consumers would have a different, probably simpler feature set than one targeting 18- to 24 year olds. Second, as the number of products offered by the company expands, also called the **product line**, a number of new issues arise such as the impact on the channel, customer confusion over multiple sizes/flavors, and the efficiency of selling large numbers of SKUs (stock-keeping units). Third, like the Logitech case, **packaging** can be an important differentiator. Witness the huge success of Heinz ketchup's plastic squeeze bottles, for example. Finally, like packaging, exciting **product design** can set your product apart from others. Apple Computer's iPod Nano player is an example.

product features
are the characteristics or attributes of a product or service

product line
a group of closely related products

packaging
the design of the container for the product in which it is displayed in a retail environment

product design
combines art, science and technology to create tangible three-dimensional goods

Branding

Why do customers value brands? Why would a person or an organization purchase one product over another, often spending more in the process, all because of a brand name? Brands provide:

- Reduced information search costs.
- Risk reduction.
- Expectations of quality.
- Prestige and emotional needs.

Thus, when Hormel puts its brand on prepackaged roast beef, it differentiates the product from the plastic-wrapped, unbranded products found in supermarkets in terms of perceived quality and convenience. When Swissair decided to change its corporate brand to Swiss, the company was trying to distance itself from the old brand, which had developed a risky financial reputation. Levi Strauss, once a proud name in the jeans business, is feverishly attempting to understand why its flagship products no longer have a strong fashion image. When Lenovo, a Chinese firm, bought the ThinkPad line of laptop computers from IBM, a key decision was how long to keep the IBM brand (which they could for up to five years by the terms of the deal). The IBM brand would reduce the amount of perceived risk for corporate buyers and consumers but would delay Lenovo building its own brand.

Perhaps a more dramatic example of the power of brands is shown in Table 7.1. This table shows the results of a survey conducted concerning the perceptions of Bayer aspirin versus generic/store brand aspirin and other headache remedies (not shown). Although the product, aspirin, is identical, note the differences in perceptions. More than twice as many people felt that Bayer provided faster relief than the generic version, for example. Perhaps most interestingly, despite the vast difference in price, the generic version of aspirin did not score much better than Bayer in terms of "value for money."

Procter & Gamble uses a "house of brands" branding strategy.
Source: Robert Sullivan/Getty Images, Inc. AFP

The concept of a brand is complex, not only because the components of a brand name are multidimensional, but also because there are a number of different branding concepts. There are at least five different types of brands:

1. **Corporate brands.** For example, GE, JPMorgan Chase, Clorox, Heineken are examples of company names that are simultaneously brands in that they have meaning to customers. This is sometimes referred to as "umbrella" branding or a "branded house" strategy.
2. **Corporate parent brands.** These are brand names where the corporate brand is carried with individual product names. In some cases the company brand is

Table 7.1

Consumer Ratings of Analgesic Brands

Qualities	Bayer (%)	Store/Generic Aspirin (%)
Provides fast relief	53	24
Relieves muscle aches and pains	49	22
Reduces inflammation	42	28
Provides long-lasting relief	41	26
Is good for severe pain	33	5
Relieves arthritis pain	30	17
Relieves menstrual discomfort	9	18
Causes stomach upset	11	14
Is easy to swallow	62	48
Is good value for money	59	68
Is a modern, up-to-date brand	51	31
Prevents heart attacks or strokes	41	19
Is recommended by doctors	37	16

Source: John Quelch (1997), "Bayer AG (A)," Harvard Business School Case #9-598-031. Copyright © 1997 by the President and Fellows of Harvard College. Reprinted by permission.

used with model numbers only. For example, Snap-on Tools's heavy-duty air hammer is the PH2050 and is referred to as the "Snap-on PH2050." In other situations, the parent brand is associated with sub-brands such as the Toyota Corolla and the HP LaserJet series.

3. **Distinct product brands.** These are brand names separate from the corporate brand. Thus, Crest is not marketed with the Procter & Gamble name. This is often referred to as "house of brands" strategy.
4. **Sub-brands:** Sub-brands include the name of the corporate brand along with the distinct product brand. Examples include Sony PlayStation, Nestle KitKat, and Mazda Miata with PlayStation, KitKat, and Miata being the sub-brands.
5. **Co-brands.** Often, two independent companies will cooperate to have both brands highlighted in a product. For example, a flavor of Häagen-Dazs's ice cream has been promoted as having M&Ms.
6. **Ingredient brands:** A special case of co-branding is ingredient branding. This is when a company decides to put the name of an ingredient as part of the product name as in the case of Intel, Dolby, and DuPont's Gore-Tex.

All these types of brands exist in the marketplace and offer strategic options for the marketing manager.

The Dimensions of Brand Equity

Brand equity can be defined as follows:[2]

> *Brand equity is a set of assets (and liabilities) linked to a brand's name and symbol that adds to (or subtracts from) the value provided by a product or service to a firm or that firm's customers.*

The assets and liabilities underlying brand value fall into five categories, as shown in Figure 7.1:[3]

1. **Brand loyalty.** The strongest measure of a brand's value is the loyalty (repeat buying, word of mouth) it engenders in customers.
2. **Brand awareness.** The simplest form of brand equity is familiarity. A familiar brand gives the customer a feeling of confidence, so he or she is more likely to consider and choose it.

Figure 7.1

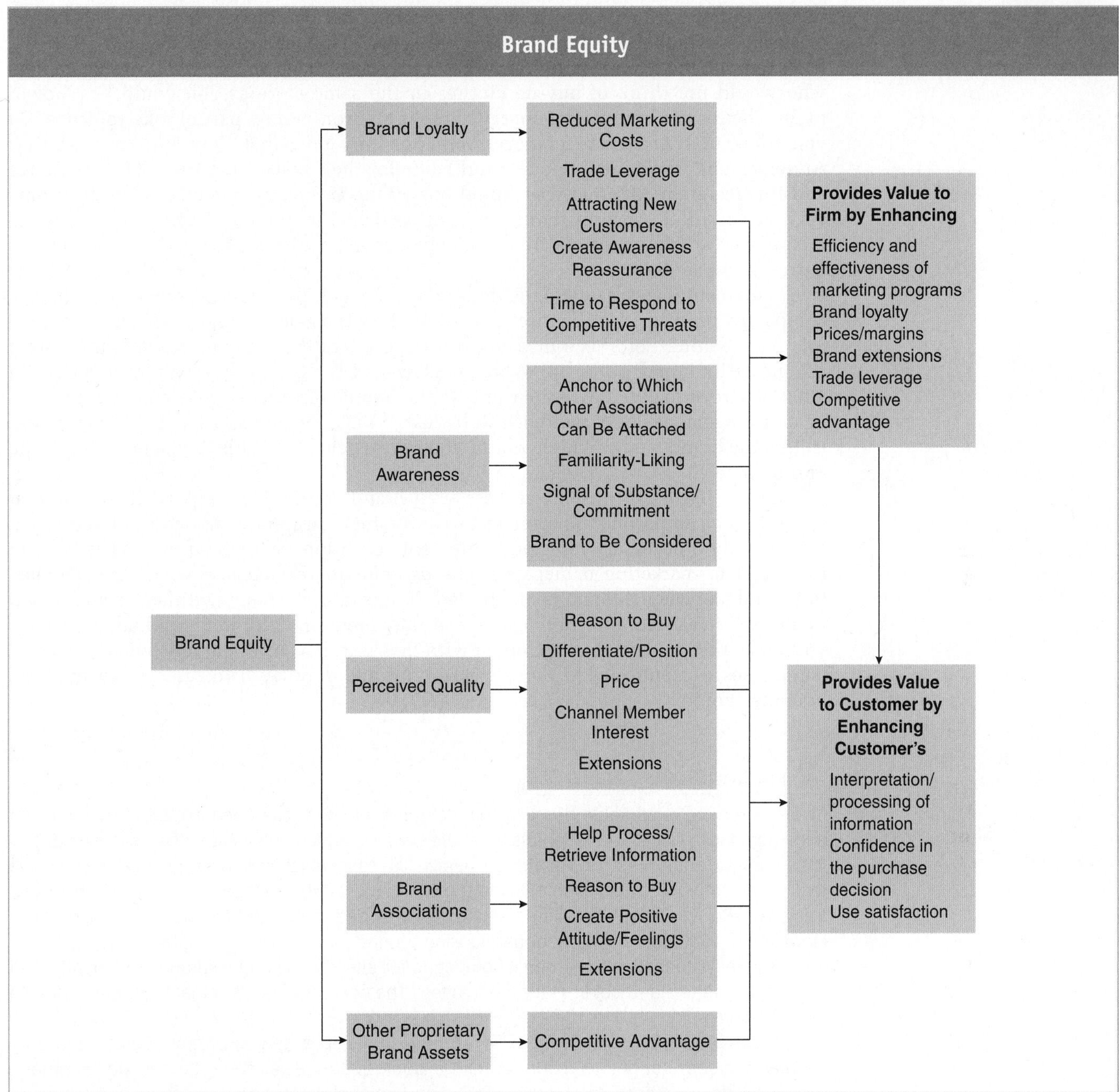

Source: David A. Aaker (1996), *Building Strong Brands* (New York: Free Press), p. 9. Reprinted with the permission of The Free Press, A Division of Simon & Schuster Adult Publishing Group, from Building Strong Brands by David A. Aaker.

3. **Perceived quality.** A known brand often conveys an aura of quality (either good or bad). A quality association can be of the general halo type, such as Hewlett-Packard's outstanding reputation for both its products and as a place to work. It could also be a category-specific association, such as Gillette's reputation in razors and blades.
4. **Brand associations.** Although quality associations are important, more subjective and emotional associations are also important parts of brand value. These could include personal, emotional, and many other kinds of associations. Taken together, these associations form a brand personality that suggests situations for which a brand is (and is not) suitable.
5. **Other brand assets.** Other assets, such as patents and trademarks, are also valuable to products and services.

Thus, marketing managers must be aware that the brand is a product characteristic like any other from which customer perceptions can be drawn. These can be positive or strong, such as those from the preceding list. They can also be negative or weak. For example, the giant retailer Sears has a negative image among wealthier customers who would not think of buying clothes in the same store as you could buy power tools. The former high-flying energy company Enron is now part of joke routines. Do you think that Accenture managers are unhappy now that they split from Arthur Andersen and developed a new brand name for their consulting firm? The insurance and finance giant AIG that was bailed out by the U.S. government in 2008 has some very successful businesses that have been tarnished by the AIG brand. A brand name is thus part of the potential differential advantage (or disadvantage) linked heavily to customer perceptions.

Brands can also create tremendous value for companies. The extent to which a company's market capitalization is greater than the book value of its "hard" assets (plants, machines, etc.) is a measure of the power of the company's intangible assets including its brand portfolio. When Volkswagen bought Rolls Royce Motor Cars in 1999, it agreed to give BMW the rights to the brand starting in 2003. This was due to a prior arrangement BMW had with Rolls Royce PLC, the aerospace company that controlled the brand name. Which would you rather have, the Rolls Royce factories or the brand name?

Many managers confuse awareness with brand equity. It is important to note that while it is an important component of equity, high awareness among the target audience is only a necessary but not a sufficient condition for high equity. What is often important to marketing managers is the *associations dimension*: what do customers think and feel when a brand is mentioned? For example, when "Cadillac" is mentioned to 45- to 54-year-old auto purchasers and they mention "old, my grandfather, cigars," you know that the brand is in trouble with that segment. Alternatively, when "Oakley" (sunglasses) is mentioned to 18- to 24-year-olds and they say "cool, gotta have 'em," the brand is "hot."

Application Aflac Inc.

One of the more remarkable branding efforts in recent years has been executed by the insurance company Aflac.[4] Aflac markets what are called supplemental insurance policies that pay for expenses not covered by standard health, life, and disability coverage that you receive through an employer. Aflac used to follow the standard insurance industry approach in its advertising by showing happy families that are relieved and comforted by having such policies. However, in 1999, the company began looking around for a new way to differentiate itself. The company realized that not only was it competing for attention among insurance companies, but that it also had to stand out from the TV "clutter." The company decided that it needed to take a risk to build a unique brand.

The company hired a consulting firm to help develop a new approach. One of the consultants noticed that "Aflac" sounded like a duck quack. After some time in development, the first ads appeared in January 2000 on national television with the now signature "AFLAAAAAAC" squawk and white duck. Awareness of the brand became very high. But what was more important was that several key associations with the brand became prominent. First, safety is emphasized by having the duck pop up to quack in certain situations, such as when the supplemental insurance is needed. Second, research has shown that the duck is a metaphor for the underdog (underduck?) who can complain mightily but not be heard.

Has the branding campaign helped Aflac? By the end of 2004, sales were up by 20 percent, consumer awareness has risen from 12 percent to 90 percent, and the company's name has been splashed across talk shows and put on lists of great ad campaigns. Because of this "free" advertising, the company can get by with spending only $80 million per year on advertising, a relatively small sum compared to other major brands such as GEICO, which spends $800 million. The company is also expanding its presence on social media sites and has struck co-branding deals with companies such as Disney-Pixar for the movie *Up*. And, according to the new chief marketing officer (CMO) appointed in 2009, the duck will remain an integral part of the Aflac brand going forward.

Application IKEA

The privately held Swedish company IKEA is the world's largest furniture retailer with 285 stores and 140,000 employees in 37 countries on five continents, producing revenues of around $30 billion.[5] Its stores average 186,000 square feet, and a fully stocked IKEA has 9,694 choices, resulting in 80,000 different items after factoring in color and size. The stores feature products that are notable for their low prices and modern styling. College students, singles trying to furnish an apartment, young couples starting out, or anyone on a budget can find stylish, low-priced furnishings at IKEA. To keep costs down, customers serve themselves and assemble the products at home. Young couples with children enjoy the fact that IKEA locations come equipped with play centers, snack bars, and restaurants. In fact, the play centers (called Smaland) have become popular as short-term day care facilities as children are watched by IKEA personnel as their parents (hopefully) shop for IKEA furnishings. This combination of features makes IKEA's parking lot difficult to enter at most times.

The IKEA brand features most of the components of the brand equity model described earlier. Of course awareness is high, as is loyalty, with large numbers of repeat visitors. While certainly not offering products with the highest quality, IKEA's furnishings do offer more than acceptable quality for the price. Finally, the brand associations of price, style, and a friendly, family environment have all combined to make the IKEA brand one of the most powerful in the world.

Building Strong Brands

The preceding section described what characterizes strong brands. How do you actually build these brands over time? One writer describes the process as a series of steps:[6]

1. **Create a brand identity.** This follows from the development of a value proposition. How do you differentiate your brand from the competition? What do you want the brand to mean to your target audience(s)?
2. **Be consistent over time.** Other than a product disaster (e.g., Firestone), there is nothing more damaging to a brand than changing its advertising or selling messages frequently. Customers become confused and do not know what the brand stands for. A good example of consistency is Ol' Lonely, the Maytag repairman created by the Chicago advertising agency Leo Burnett in 1967. Ol' Lonely was depicted as a solitary repairman who took great pride in the Maytag brand, but because of the appliances' outstanding reliability, he never had work to do. It is among the longest-running ad campaigns on network TV.
3. **Track the equity.** This calls for measuring the dimensions of equity over time relative to competitors. What is your awareness? Are customers developing the brand associations you want them to? What are their perceptions of quality?
4. **Assign responsibility for brand development activities.** Often this will be the brand or marketing manager. However, it is critical for someone or a group within the company to have this responsibility.
5. **Invest in the brands.** The brand equity model is clear about where investments need to be made. Strong brand equity will be difficult to maintain if budgets are constantly cut in key areas related to equity.

It has, however, become increasingly difficult to manage brands. As noted at the end of Chapter 1, customers are exerting more influence in the marketplace on brands and their images through user-generated content such as comments, videos on YouTube that satirize brands, blogs, and other sources. The reality is that marketing managers do not fully control their brands any more. For example, in late 2008, Pepsico's Americas Beverages division introduced a redesigned version of its Tropicana Pure Premium orange juice. Consumers complained about the new packaging in thousands of e-mail messages and the old packaging was restored in early 2009.[7] In November 2008, many consumers who used Twitter to criticize an ad for Motrin pain reliever received responses within 48 hours from the brand's manufacturer, which apologized for the ad and told them that it had been withdrawn.

Brand Extensions

After spending millions of dollars on establishing a brand, it is natural for a manager to think of leveraging the brand into new product categories.[8] Many examples of brand extensions exist:

- Montblanc wrist watches (from pens).
- ESPN cellular phone service.
- Nike into clothing and sports products like golf balls.
- IBM into IT consulting.
- Michelin work boots.
- M&M's stereo ear buds.

The attractiveness of brand extensions like these is that the money spent building, say, the Logitech brand name and the associations with the brand, mean that less money is needed to build the extension into videogame peripherals than if it had to be built from scratch.

However, you should not consider the concept of brand extensions to be a "no brainer," no matter how powerful the brand name is. "New" Coke was a flop despite the power of the Coke brand name. Despite this failure, Coke launched Vanilla Coke in 2002 with substantial fanfare, and it had achieved nearly a 3 percent market share by late in the year as well as spawning a line extension, Diet Vanilla Coke. Successful extensions are difficult to predict. Some other notable brand extension failures were:

- Levi Strauss's foray into Tailored Classic suits in the early 1980s.
- Volkswagen's upscale sedan the Phaeton.
- Parfum Bic launched by the company (Bic) known for ballpoint pens, disposable lighters, and razors.
- Web appliances sold by Intel.

In addition to this list, there are doubters about the wisdom of Steinway, the famous maker of the best pianos in the world, expanding into audio equipment, home furnishings, and other "lifestyle" luxury products. Likewise, Tom's of Maine, which makes all-natural care products like toothpaste, is embarking on a foray into the herbal remedy business, which is rife with quack medical claims and pyramid selling schemes. Have you seen anyone wearing M&M's stereo ear phones? Finally, the extension voted the worst of 2008 was Burger King's attempt to market boxer shorts![9]

The main variable that determines the extent to which brand equity can be transferred to the extension is called "fit." The main considerations for the fit of an extension to the parent brand category are:

1. **Transferability of the associations.** The Logitech brand transferred well from mice to trackballs because both are PC input devices. The extensions into the other products like PC audio are broader movements but still within the realm of PC peripherals. The Levi Strauss brand associations of casualness do not transfer well into suits.
2. **Complementarity of the product.** Bill Blass chocolates did not sell well; guess why? Hallmark has had some success selling flowers as complements to its greeting card and other personal communications products.
3. **Similarity of the users.** Intel is used to selling to industrial buyers of semiconductors. The company does not have experience selling retail products like the Web appliances.
4. **Transferability of the symbol.** Brands are supported with logos and symbols. It is difficult to transfer the Cadillac image to a car targeting a young audience.

Another key issue with introducing extensions is whether the new product with the successful brand name can potentially harm the "parent" or incumbent brand if the extension is a flop. Because the extension is not independent of the parent, the problem is not only that the extension might be financially unsuccessful, but that this lack of success could hurt the original source of competitive advantage. Interestingly, on rare occasions, the reverse can happen. The retailer Ann Taylor is concerned that the "fusty" image of its original brand-name stores could hurt the image of the popular and hip Ann Taylor Loft extension.[10]

Virgin has numerous brand extensions including mobile phone service and colas.
Source: PeerPoint/Alamy Images

Application Virgin

The British entrepreneur Richard Branson is one of the richest people in the world.[11] Since founding Virgin Atlantic Airways in 1984, he has put the Virgin brand on many of his ventures: Virgin Records, Virgin Cola, Virgin Mobile (cellular), Virgin Money (online trading), Virgin Trains, Virgin Wines, Virgin Cosmetics, and yes, Virgin Brides. Most critics say that he has developed a conglomerate of unrelated companies and products. How do colas and airlines fit, for example?

While some of his companies have turned out to be failures (Virgin Vodka, Virgin Clothes), the attempt to extend the Virgin brand is based on two premises. First, the well-known Virgin logo is a symbol that has become ubiquitous and seems to travel well. Second, the associations of that symbol, the Virgin name, and Richard Branson himself are a foundation of the brand extensions. Virgin stands for entrepreneurship—a swashbuckling, irreverent, take-on-the-establishment style, and generally low price. However, it is clear that sometimes it works and sometimes it does not.

Application Mountain Dew Code Red

As an example of a line extension, the launch of Pepsi's Code Red, in May 2001, is widely considered to be the beverage world's most successful new product launch since Diet Coke, selling almost 100 million cases by the end of that year.[12] Interestingly, the line extension of the parent Mountain Dew brand had some unexpected help given that 2001 also featured the similarly named global computer virus. This kept the name in the press and resulted in one of the stranger boosts to a brand. The core target market for Code Red, 13- to 19-year-olds, were also the target for Mountain Dew, which had been aggressively advertised to a young audience for several years. The brand associations for the name Code Red were energy and danger, which appeal to this age group. Not surprisingly, its first appearance in public was at the X Games.

Pepsi has continued to use the Mountain Dew brand as a source of experimental extensions aimed at this target audience. It has introduced seasonal extensions such as Mountain Dew LiveWire in the summer, Pitch Black from Labor Day to Halloween, and Holiday Spice for Thanksgiving to Christmas. In a contest started in 2007, consumers generated three ideas for new flavors of Mountain Dew—Mountain Dew Revolution, Supernova, and Voltage—through a Web site that generated 1.6 million visitors. Through a "DEWmocracy" election, Voltage, a brew of raspberry citrus and ginseng, was the winner and went on sale in early 2009.[13]

Global Branding

A discussion of the issues involved with taking a brand from one country to others must begin with the debate surrounding the more general concept of **global marketing**. The term global marketing is used in two ways: as a generic term encompassing any marketing activities outside a company's home market and to refer to a standardization of the marketing strategies used to market a product around the world. Most books titled *Global Marketing* use the term in the first sense. However, the second sense is a distinctly different approach to marketing than that implied by the basics of marketing strategy: that market segments (e.g., countries or parts of countries), if found to require different features, positioning, and marketing-mix elements, should be treated differently.

global marketing
a generic term encompassing any marketing activities outside a company's home market; also a standardization of the strategies used to market a product around the world

The first person to call for a truly global approach to marketing was Theodore Levitt.[14] Levitt's view of the world in the early 1980s was one in which dramatically improved telecommunications enabled people in, say, Africa to witness events occurring around the world. They could see products being consumed, whetting their appetites for such goods. In addition, large global companies were able to produce, distribute, and market on such a massive scale that they could sell for low prices anywhere. Levitt's notions were quickly picked up by the firms most responsible for implementing global marketing strategies: advertising agencies. The agency that most typified Levitt's model of global marketing was London-based Saatchi & Saatchi (S&S), which won the British Airways account in 1982 based on a global branding pitch.[15] S&S's rationale for global marketing was predicated on seven consumer-based factors:

1. **Consumer convergence.** Differences between nations are often less than differences within nations. Upscale consumers in Paris have more in common with their counterparts in New York than with many other French people.
2. **Demographic convergence.** Aging populations, falling birth rates, and increased female employment are common in industrialized countries.
3. **Decline of the nuclear family.** Fewer traditional husband–wife households, fewer children per household, and improvements in the status of women are common occurrences around the world. This has led to more nontraditional meals and increased need for convenience.
4. **The changing role of women.** The major trend here is increasing numbers of women working outside the home. Other related factors are higher divorce rates and lower marriage rates.
5. **Static populations.** Population growth rates have stabilized and the population over age 65 is increasing.
6. **Higher living standards.** This creates a growing demand for consumer durables and more leisure.
7. **Cultural convergence.** As noted earlier, global telecommunication has had an impact on consumer wants and needs worldwide. Teenagers in Tokyo, Hong Kong, London, and San Francisco dress and talk similarly and buy the same kinds of products.

With the world becoming more similar in so many ways, the agency felt that many brands and products could be marketed in a uniform way in all countries.

Almost immediately, Levitt's theory and the S&S approach provoked strong objections to this global marketing perspective.[16] The common complaint was that the concept of global marketing is the opposite of market or customer orientation, being more similar to a product orientation. This is because it ignores a systematic analysis of customer behavior in each market, which may cause the appropriate strategy to be more localized. In fact, there are many intercountry and regional cultural differences that make global marketing difficult to implement (see the sections on culture in Chapters 4 and 5). Not only are there significant differences among countries and regions of the world, but most countries are heterogeneous themselves. Few consumer product companies entering the U.S. market would consider using one positioning strategy for the whole country. Likewise, why should there not be differences within Germany, Japan, or Argentina? In addition, recent arguments have been made that particularly in emerging markets like China, India, and Brazil, the advantage of being a multinational company selling global brands has declined dramatically.[17]

The arguments for or against global branding are consistent with this discussion. A necessary condition for being interested in building a global brand for a company, product, or service is having a concomitant interest in persuading customers around the world to view the equity in a name similarly. Logitech's brand equity in terms of its high-quality, user-friendly PC peripherals becomes a global brand to the extent the company can communicate these brand associations around the world. Due to increased mobility, global brands can help build awareness when customers travel between countries. Brands like Starbucks and MasterCard with its "Priceless" campaign have been successful in establishing a single global positioning. They can also provide country associations when they are an important part of the brand. Examples are Chanel perfume and Mercedes-Benz. People around the world view French perfume and German cars similarly.

However, following the global marketing debate, differences among countries often have to be recognized, and some brands cannot be used everywhere. As many travelers know, Diet Coke is called Coke Light in many countries. In China, Oral-B toothbrushes become "Ora Bee" in Chinese characters.

In addition, local brands can be powerful competitors by emphasizing their home country or ethnic origins. The Thums Up example shown in Chapter 2 is an illustration of how an Indian brand competes successfully against Coke and Pepsi. Another successful regional cola brand is Kola Real in Peru. Mecca Cola and Qibla Cola appeal to Muslims. The Filipino fast-food chain Jollibee is clobbering McDonald's in its home country by emphasizing local flavorings in its hamburgers. One branding consultant predicts brands like Juan Valdez Café, a Colombian coffee chain, Almarai, a Saudi dairy and fruit juice company based in Riyadh, and Patchi, a Lebanese boutique chocolate chain are likely candidates to become global brands.[18] Companies in China are starting to successfully compete with multinationals by creating strong brands. These include Haier in appliances, Geely in cars, Bird in mobile phones, Tsingtao in beer, and Yonghe King in fast food.[19] In general, many industry experts expect the next wave of strong global brands to emerge in regions outside of the United States and Europe, traditional breeding grounds for strong brands.

These differences among consumers imply that marketing managers need to be aware of the different segments of consumers that exist with respect to their attitudes towards global brands. One study found four different segments:[20]

1. **Global citizens (55 percent).** The largest segment relies on the global success of a company to signal its product quality and innovativeness. They are also concerned that companies act responsibly on issues like consumer health and worker rights.
2. **Global dreamers (23 percent).** This is the second largest segment. Consumers in this segment are highly interested in global brands and are less concerned about the companies' social responsibility.
3. **Antiglobals (13 percent).** These consumers are skeptical about global companies. They dislike brands that preach American values and try to avoid buying brands from global firms.
4. **Global agnostics (9 percent).** This is the smallest segment. These consumers judge all products by the same criteria and do not give the global dimension any additional weight beyond other characteristics.

Recall that brand equity has been defined as being composed of loyalty, awareness, perceived quality, favorable brand associations, and other assets (e.g., patents). If you are interested in building global brand equity, you must take steps in each country to focus on these components around a single brand name. Procter & Gamble's definition of a global brand is instructive: to obtain clear and consistent brand equity across geographic markets, a brand should be positioned the same, have the same formulation, provide the same benefits, and have a consistent advertising message. The company does this through the following principles:

- Understand the local consumer.
- Clearly define the brand's equity based on benefits that are common around the world.
- Expand what is successful in one market to other parts of the world.

Table 7.2 shows the top 10 global brands as evaluated by the brand consulting company Interbrand.[21] The rankings are based on an analysis of three financial aspects of the brand: how much of a boost each brand delivers to its parent company, how stable that boost is likely to be in the future, and the present value of those future earnings. For the purposes of this ranking, global brands were defined as selling at least 20 percent outside of their home country.

Although all of these brands are highly successful and visible, the biggest story is, of course, Google, which jumped from number 20 to number 10 in one year with a remarkable 43 percent increase in brand value. Another less visible story is that the list of top global brands has remained fairly stable. Except for Mercedes-Benz, which was bumped from the number-10 spot by Google, the other 9 brands are pretty much in the same order. In fact, this has pretty much been the case for the past ten years.

Table 7.2

Best Global Brands						
2008 Rank	2007 Rank	Brand	Country of Origin	Sector	2008 Brand Value ($m)	Change in Brand Value
1	1	Coca-Cola	United States	Beverages	66,667	2%
2	3	IBM	United States	Computer Services	59,031	3%
3	2	Microsoft	United States	Computer Software	59,007	1%
4	4	GE	United States	Diversified	53,086	3%
5	5	Nokia	Finland	Consumer Electronics	35,942	7%
6	6	Toyota	Japan	Automotive	34,050	6%
7	7	Intel	United States	Computer Hardware	31,261	1%
8	8	McDonald's	United States	Restaurants	31,049	6%
9	9	Disney	United States	Media	29,251	0%
10	20	Google	United States	Internet Services	25,590	43%

Application L'Oréal

The French cosmetics company L'Oréal has very successfully developed a stable of global brands.[22] A good example is its Maybelline line. After acquiring it in 1996, the company decided to position it as cosmetics for the "American urban chic" to promote its U.S. origins. As an example, in 1997, the company rolled out a new makeup line with risky colors such as yellow and green, calling it Miami Chill. Also, the company marketed its quick-drying nail polish under the Express Finish brand and marketed it as a product used by urban women on the go. These products and others in the Maybelline line were exported to more than 70 countries, and sales outside the United States were more than 50 percent of the total. Women in Shanghai are as interested in trendy brands from the United States as are women in New York. The company has clearly recognized that the needs of women are similar around the world and have taken their knowledge of local markets to expand the Maybelline brand into these global markets.

Application Vodafone

This illustration highlights the potential pitfalls of global branding.[23] Vodafone Group PLC of Britain, the world's largest cellular phone operator, acquired control of Japanese cell phone company J-Phone Co. in 2002. Vodafone was acquiring a fast-growing company with a leading-edge image among Japanese youth. The number-three company in Japan, J-phone had just introduced the first phone with a digital camera, which was very popular.

By 2004, now sold under the Vodafone brand, the service's new subscribers had dropped 87 percent from the year before and annual revenues decreased by 8 percent. Even worse, Vodafone's phones are viewed as being dull and unoriginal. This is bad indeed, particularly in a country that values products that are innovative.

What happened? The company faced a typical dilemma faced by global companies: how to implement a global strategy while simultaneously appealing to local demand. By putting too much energy into building a global brand in Japan, the company failed to give Japanese customers what they want—basically, a wide product line with lots of features. As a result, it was late in introducing more advanced services and its phones had a "me-too" look. Using the segmentation scheme described earlier, the Japanese youth buying these phones are "global agnostics." They do not regularly travel abroad and care less about a product having a global brand than new jazzy features on their phones.

Branding for High-Tech Products

As high-tech products mature, the marketing strategies used are very similar to those for any other product in the mature stage of its life cycle. Customer knowledge is high, perceived brand differences are small, and the marketing tactics are heavily priced and distribution oriented. DVD players, microwave ovens, local area networks (LANs) for the home, word-processing software, and other products that at one time were technological innovations are now marketed like consumer packaged goods.

As a result, branding has become important, even for high-tech products. As we noted in both Chapter 2 and this chapter, brand names are often used to develop perceptual-based differential advantages. In many cases what is being stressed is the corporate brand but individual brands or families of brands have also been popular. An example of the latter is Hewlett-Packard's use of the LaserJet, InkJet, and OfficeJet names for their lines of printers.

One of the difficulties in developing brands in the high-tech arena is that there are a number of different entities involved with the production, distribution, and support of many products involving complex technologies. For example, take the IBM BladeCenter HS22 family of bladeservers (stripped down versions of computer servers developed to save space). It contains components manufactured by a number of different companies (e.g., Intel processor, Matrox graphics controller). It can be bundled together with software written by independent companies and then sold by systems integrators, computer resellers, or some other company that establishes and maintains end-customer contact. The problem is how does IBM develop and deliver a brand that promises value to the end-user but with so many entities involved?

A characteristic of high-technology companies is that because they are usually founded and run by engineers, there is an inordinate focus on the technology and product features rather than the customer and the benefits sought. High-tech branding campaigns are attempts to deemphasize the products and their attributes and instead focus on broader goals. Some examples are:

- SAP is the third-largest software company in the world. However, it has a strange name and is regarded as stodgy, unhip, and not terribly innovative. The company therefore decided to spend $100 million on a global branding campaign with a more cutting-edge image and has supported it with Grand Prix Formula One racing sponsorships.[24]
- Cisco Systems spent $150 million in 2005 on a global campaign to put a human face on the networking brand. Prior branding efforts had focused on its products. Now that the company has branched out into services, it wants to show that it is part of everyday life. Although the brand is well known among information technology executives, it wants to be better known among more senior corporate managers or the "c-suite." In addition, with its increasing focus on consumer products (e.g., Scientific Atlanta cable boxes), the company launched its "Human Network" campaign in 2008 to show what its technologies enable consumers to do in their lives.[25]
- Symantec, the computer security software specialist, used the color yellow to launch a branding campaign in 2001. Marketing research showed that customers identified the color yellow with Symantec and its highly successful subsidiary, Norton (think Norton Utilities). The color is meant to express the confidence and trust that comes with Symantec's solutions.[26]

One of the best arguments for developing a brand identity in high-tech marketing is made by companies that sell components or ingredients that are used inside other products and are invisible to the customer. An example is the hard disk drive manufacturer Seagate, whose largest market is selling to PC manufacturers (how many people know the brand of their hard disk drive?). Dolby creates sound-enhancing and filtering technology for stereos and other types of equipment. Branding a component can be valuable in establishing your own credibility as a supplier as well as lending your prestige to the product in which your product is placed, usually called the **original equipment manufacturer (OEM)**. This is an example of co-branding, where two or more brands are represented in a product or service.

original equipment manufacturer (OEM)
a channel of distribution for technology-based products; companies that purchase ingredients or components (e.g., hard disk drives) from manufacturers

Application Intel

The best example of ingredient or co-branding in high-tech markets is the famous "Intel Inside" branding campaign developed by Dennis Carter at Intel Corporation.[27] Since the campaign was adopted in 1991, the company says that more than $3 billion worth of advertisements have carried the "Intel Inside" logo. See Figure 7.2 for an example of the Intel Inside logo used with an in-store display. Interestingly, the motivation for developing the campaign was not co-branding.

Figure 7.2

The "Intel Inside" campaign is one of the most famous examples of co-branding.

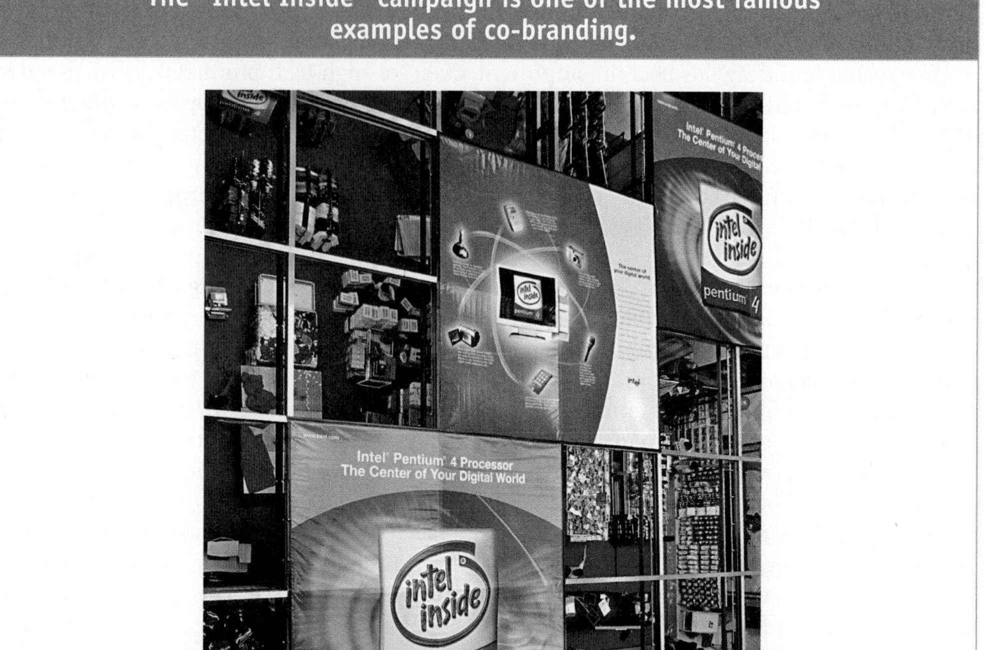

Source: Steve Raymer/CORBIS—NY

Intel was founded in 1968 by computer industry legends Robert Noyce and Gordon Moore to produce memory products based on semiconductor technology. Intel is credited with inventing 16 of the 22 major breakthroughs in microelectronics between 1971 and 1981. Its major coup was IBM's selection of its 16-bit 8086 microprocessor for the IBM PC in 1980. The development and success of the 80286 for the AT, 80386, up through the current Pentium III, have created a company with more than $26 billion in sales. In 1990, an Intel competitor, AMD, copied the 80386 and subsequently, the 80486 microprocessors. This copying is often called *cloning*. Although Intel sued AMD for copying its technology and AMD countersued Intel for antitrust violations, the eventual settlement allowed AMD (and other clone manufacturers such as Cyrix) to develop clones of Intel's chips. Thus, although Intel has always been the first to make technological advances in microprocessor technology, it does not take much time for clones to appear.

Intel's reaction was the development of the "Intel Inside" campaign. The idea has its origins in Japan, where PC manufacturers used the encircled words "Intel in it" to indicate that their computers had the highly valued Intel microprocessor. Because this was the most important part of the computer, the logo reassured buyers that the OEM used high-quality components. This eventually led to the "Intel Inside" logo you see in many ads today.

The campaign is a co-op advertising program. Intel puts aside 6 percent of customers' spending on chips for use in ads containing the logo. Intel reimburses OEMs for half of the cost of TV ads and two-thirds the cost of print ads if they use the "Intel Inside" logo. Has it worked? Intel had 95 percent of the market and $33 billion in sales in 2009, but the competitors are significantly reducing the time it takes to clone Intel chips. In addition, because the clone manufacturers sell at lower prices, the PCs made using non-Intel chips are usually priced lower as well. The key is brand loyalty: because 50 percent of customers coming into a store want a specific processor, developing a brand identity is important to success. In addition, recognition of the Intel brand name is very high (more than 90 percent for business purchasers and 70 to 80 percent for consumers).

Some Branding Issues

A number of other issues related to branding are introduced here to help the reader understand the complexity of developing strong brands.

Brand Personality

In executing advertising to implement a branding strategy, managers will sometimes attempt to ask customers to construct a set of human characteristics that describe the brand. Thus brands can be "cool," "dull," "fun," and "nonconforming," among numerous traits.

Research has identified five different dimensions of brand personality:[28]

1. Sincerity (honest, wholesome).
2. Excitement (daring, spirited).
3. Competence (reliable, successful).
4. Sophistication (upper class).
5. Ruggedness (outdoorsy, tough).

For example, the "Got Milk" ad shown in Figure 7.3 exhibits a combination of personality traits. The basic product, of course, plays to the "wholesome" or "sincerity" dimension—milk is a natural product and is good for you. However, the positioning

Figure 7.3

Got Milk? Ad

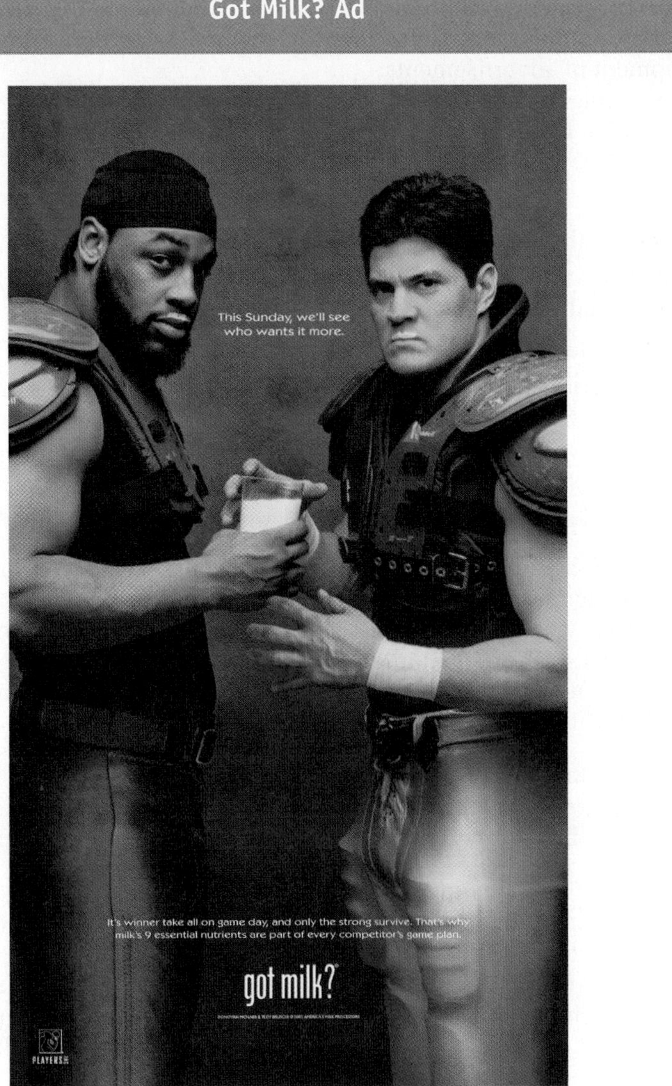

Source: PRNewsFoto/Newscom

clearly attempts to extend the personality to the "ruggedness" dimension as well by showing two football players ready for "battle" who also drink milk. The idea is to give milk a multidimensional rather than unidimensional personality. Given that the ad ran in *People* magazine, the marketing managers behind the campaign are also reaching a very broad audience with the positioning.

Application Audi

Audi was concerned that its main rival, BMW, had superior brand recognition in the United States, not to mention sales, which are twice Audi's.[29] The largest problem that its research has shown is that that the brand lacks a personality. As a result, Audi spent more than $100 million in 2002 to tackle the problem. The campaign, which kicked off during the Salt Lake City Winter Olympics, used the tag line "Never follow." The intention was to create an independent, free-spirited (the Excitement dimension) personality for consumers who can afford a BMW but do not like the status symbol that is attached to the brand.

Brand–Person Relationships

Research has found that similar to human relationships, people find comfort and satisfaction in their relationships with brands to which they are loyal.[30] Depth and ethnographic research (see Chapter 3) provide the foundation for this work. The detailed and rich interviews produced by research on brand–person relationships have helped marketing managers better identify the source of brand loyalty and assist in the development of advertisements.

A strong feeling toward a brand can be manifested in surprising ways. An article in *Fortune* magazine highlighted a number of people who exhibit extreme passion toward different brands:

- The pop music parodist "Weird Al" Yankovic owns about 100 pairs of Vans shoes and describes them as a kind of "comfort food."
- A couple had Mountain Dew tattoos emblazoned on their arms, which helps to keep them emotionally connected.
- A Harley Davidson fanatic put a motorcycle on his tombstone.
- A couple named their daughter Vista after the Microsoft operating system. The husband has been using Microsoft products for more than 25 years.
- A family of Coors beer loyalists have more than 200 lighted Coors signs and many pieces of Coors memorabilia. Of course, they also have a keg and a vending machine with cans of Coors and Coors Light.[31]

Private labels and generics are major competitors to national brands.
Source: Tony Freeman/Photo Edit Inc.

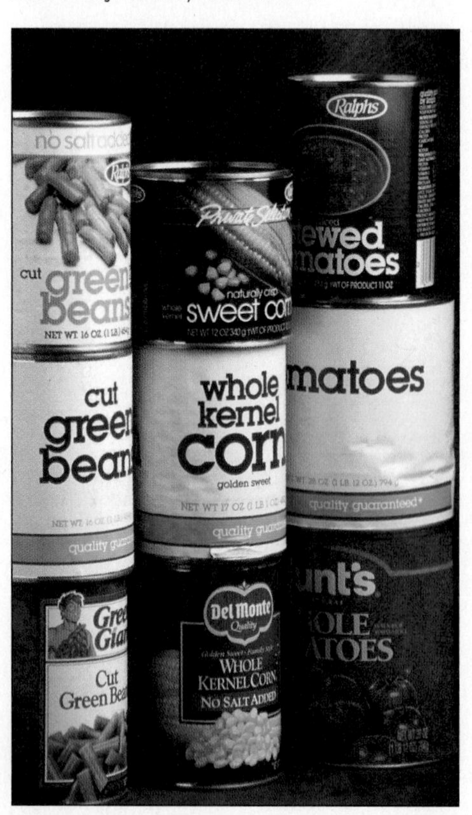

While these appear to be extreme cases, passionate consumers can be useful as a source of marketing research information and can be enlisted to help spread word-of-mouth among other loyal users. For example, Amazon has created a group of Kindle (the e-book) enthusiasts who volunteer to demonstrate the device to prospective owners as part of Amazon's See a Kindle in Your City marketing program.[32]

Retail Branding Issues

Retailers such as supermarkets, grocery stores, and discount stores can choose from five different types of brands to sell:

1. **National brands:** Well-known, heavily supported brands made and distributed by large, often global companies; examples are Coke, Sony, and Budweiser.
2. **Regional brands:** Brands that are only supported on a limited geographical basis. For example, Round Table Pizza, a West Coast pizza retailer, sells some branded products in California in Safeway and Albertson's.
3. **Value brands:** Made to offer a low-price alternative to customers. For example, Apex Digital makes DVD players that are sold through Best Buy, Walmart, and Kmart.

4. **Private labels:** Offer a low-price alternative, like value brands. However, they carry either the retailer's chain name or a brand developed by the retailer.
5. **Generics:** Carry no name at all.

Because of the growth and substantial market share of private labels, they deserve some special attention. As noted earlier, private labels are products that are sold by a company, often a retail chain, under a brand that is created exclusively for that company. Unlike brands made by companies like Clorox and Kimberly-Clark that are sold to any supermarket, drug, or club store, private labels (sometimes called store brands) are only sold in a particular chain. For example, Walmart has started a private label called White Cloud in two categories—laundry detergent and fabric softeners. Sometimes a company puts its own corporate brand on the private-label product. Wells Fargo Bank, for instance, sells a number of financial instruments that are actually managed by another company that is invisible to the Wells customer.

There are a number of reasons a company/retailer uses private-label brands. First, they are usually the low-priced option in the category. Thus, Safeway supermarkets will use a private label as an option for price-sensitive customers. Second, stores often make higher margins on private-label brands despite their lower prices, because they devote little marketing funds to support them and there is no margin lost to distributors. Third, stores can use a good private-label brand to differentiate itself from the competition. Safeway has its Safeway Select private-label brand that no other store can offer. Fourth, stores can use the private label option as a bargaining chip with the national brand manufacturers to get better terms.

Private labels have been very successful in supermarkets. In the United States in 2009, they represented just over 17 percent of total dollar sales (just over 31 percent in volume) with some of the leaders being milk, jams, charcoal, nuts, and frozen orange juice. In addition, 97 percent of all households reported that they consume private label products regularly.[33] The two largest markets for private-label grocery items outside the United States are western Europe and Australia/New Zealand, with shares about 30 and 22 percent, respectively.[34] This growth in share has had a big impact on the number of brands carried by the retailers. Where at one time a retailer might have two or three heavily promoted national brands and a low-priced "fighting" brand, the success of private labels has reduced the number of brands carried in many categories by eliminating the fighting brand.[35]

The growth in private-label sales is a result of two factors. First, the quality of private-labels products has been increasing over time. In fact, in many cases, companies selling major brands also supply private-label goods. For example, Agfa sells both private-label and its own branded photographic film. Heinz makes private-label tomato sauce, soups, baked beans, and relishes and sells its own brand as well. Companies do both for strategic and cost reasons. Selling a high-quality private label may be a good way to attack the leading competing brand. Private-label manufacturing can also keep costs down by increasing capacity utilization. However, the risk of cannibalizing a company's own brands is always there. Sometimes, the private-label products are manufactured by independent companies who do not sell branded versions themselves but they are still of very high quality. For example, the Canadian company Cott Corporation is the largest supplier of private-label soft drinks and does not market its own brand. Loblaw's President's Choice and Kroger's Private Selection soft drinks are routinely given high marks for quality. Sears's Kenmore and Craftsman private labels are similarly highly regarded.

A second reason for the popularity of private labels is that the branded goods companies are having an increasingly difficult time differentiating their products in the marketplace. As noted in Chapter 2, this creates a "commodity" image where consumers cannot tell one brand from another, resulting in price being the determinant buying factor. This has resulted in plummeting prices for some national brands. Some brands like Sony (DVD players), Tide (detergents), and Chicken of the Sea (canned tuna) have seen their prices drop precipitously due to lack of differentiation and strong private label competition.[36]

Logos A readily identifiable part of a brand is the logo. A logo is part of a brand's proprietary assets (see Figure 7.2) and, in some cases, provides a powerful representation of the brand in the customer's mind. The Nike swoosh, Mercedes three-point star, McDonald's golden arches, and other well-known, instantly recognizable logos not only indicate the brand but also elicit all of the brand associations that the consumer has with the brand name. Like product packaging and the product itself, logos are often "refreshed" to represent a change in the brand's positioning or intended communications. Wal-Mart (now Walmart) has changed its logo a number of times since it was founded in 1962 (the history of Walmart's logos can be found at the Web URL walmartstores.com/AboutUs/8412.aspx). The newest version, though, has not been without controversy. More controversial is Pepsi's new logo (www.pepsi.com) which some commentators feel will hurt the brand's equity.

Marketing ROI and Branding

As noted in Chapter 1, a leading current trend in marketing is the evaluation of marketing programs to inform senior managers if the company is obtaining a good return on marketing investment. Even if you cannot obtain a dollar return figure, it is still worthwhile to attempt to follow up on the efficacy of a particular program by measuring relevant metrics.

In the context of branding, there are two approaches to measuring brand equity:[37]

- **Behavioral measures.** These represent how customers have actually responded to the brand.
- **Attitudinal measures.** These are measures of how the brand is represented psychologically in the minds of the customers.

Behavioral measures include sales, market share, brand loyalty, customer churn rates, win–loss rates (a sales force metric), and similar measures. The Interbrand financial analysis of the leading global brands shown in Table 7.2 is also a behavioral measure as it is related to customer activity.[38] An interesting metric is relative price. The difference in price between a brand and its major competitors is a quantitative measure of brand equity.

The various models of brand equity produce a set of intermediate or psychological variables that can be measured to better understand how a brand is performing on the components of brand equity. For example, the model of brand equity shown in Figure 7.1 produces at least three intermediate measures. Besides brand loyalty, which is a behavioral metric, brand awareness, perceived quality, and brand associations can be measured to better understand how a brand is valued. An alternative model has been developed by the advertising agency, Young & Rubicam, called the Brand Asset Valuator (or BAV model). According to the BAV model, the four key dimensions of brand equity are:

1. **Differentiation:** How different or unique is the brand from the competition?
2. **Relevance:** How relevant is the brand to the target customer?
3. **Esteem:** How high is the regard or value for the brand?
4. **Knowledge:** How much information does the customer have about the brand?

These can also be measured and provide information about the value of the brand.

Product Positioning

position
the communication of the value proposition to the customer, which differentiates the product from competition in the mind of the prospect

In Chapter 2, product positioning was described as an activity that takes the value proposition and puts it to work in the marketplace by planting the competitive advantage in the minds of customers. It should be noted that the word **position** is both a noun and a verb. We speak of positioning a product by developing programs that communicate the differential advantage (either actual or perceived). We also speak of the position that your brand occupies in the competitive marketplace that can be used to help you determine what the best positioning and, therefore, value proposition might be.

These differences in the concept of positioning become clearer when thinking about the different steps involved in product positioning:

1. Determine the product's current position.
2. If you are satisfied with the position and brand performance, continue with the current strategy and value proposition. The product is "well positioned."

3. If you are dissatisfied with the current position, the brand needs to be repositioned and the value proposition may need to be modified.
4. If the product is new, step 2 is irrelevant and step 3 becomes the position you are creating for it.

Determining a Product's Position

A variety of methods exist for determining the current position of a brand.

Attribute-based Methods

Because positioning is based on perceptions, the methods described in Chapter 4 to measure perceptions as part of the multiattribute model are a good start. With these methods, customers are asked to rate your brand and the competitors on a number of dimensions. Table 4.8 presented an illustration of this approach in the context of automobile tires. Managers will often take these ratings and plot them in two- or three-dimensional spaces to develop a pictorial representation of the competitive "space."

Figure 7.4 is an example of such a pictorial representation, called a perceptual map (see also Figure 2.5). The researchers asked a set of customers to rate the Discover Card, Visa, MasterCard, and American Express (no specific brand designated) on a series of dimensions: fees and rates, the breadth of acceptance, purchase protection, and value-added tie-ins. The customers also ranked the four attributes in order of importance. The most important attribute was fees and rates, while the breadth of acceptance was second. The brands are plotted on these two dimensions in Figure 7.4. Interestingly, the researchers also asked respondents to rate their "ideal" credit card on these attributes. When an ideal "point" is plotted with the brands, it is called a **joint space**.

joint space
a perceptual map that contains both brand spatial locations as well as consumer perceptions of their ideal brand

Clearly, Visa is positioned most closely to the ideal point. You might wonder why respondents did not consider very low fees to be the ideal (i.e., that the point should be further to the left). It is possible that customers perceive that there is a trade-off between fees and acceptance: if the fees are too low, fewer merchants will accept the card. Notice that American Express is poorly positioned on these dimensions. Although the brand did much better on the value-added tie-ins attribute (not shown), that attribute ranked last in importance.

Figure 7.4

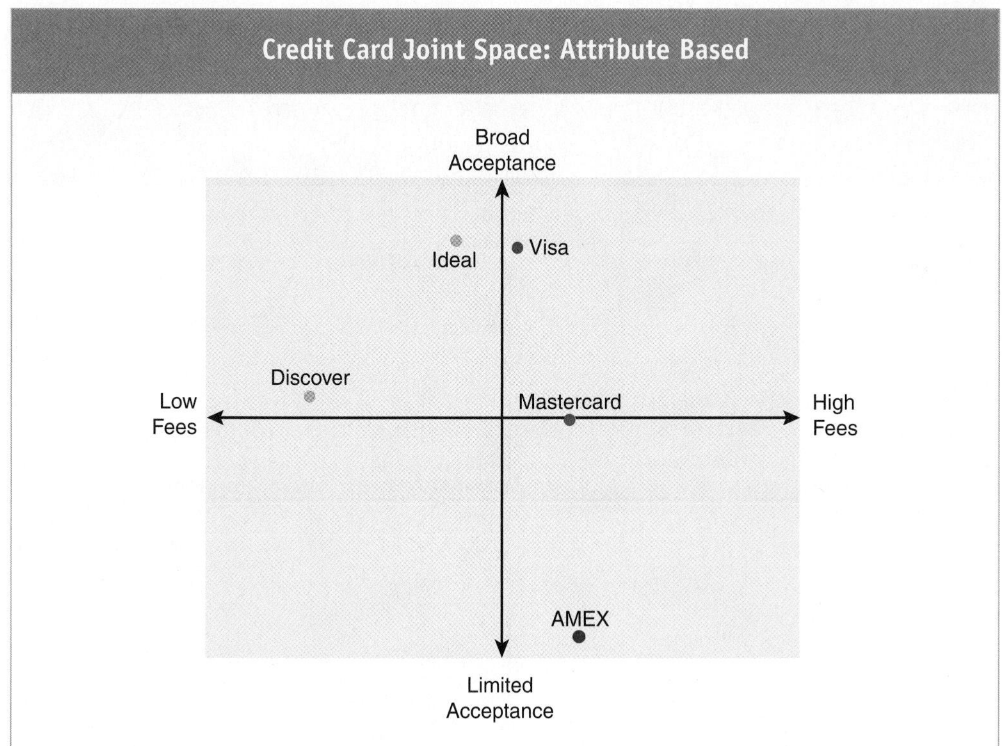

Source: Adapted from "Card-Carrying Members Share Perks, Pet Peeves about Plastic," *Brandweek* February 25, 2002, p. 18.

Methods Based on Similarity Judgments

multidimensional scaling (MDS) develop perceptual maps based only on customer-based judgments of brand similarity

An alternative approach is to develop perceptual maps based only on customer-based judgments of brand similarity. This is what statisticians refer to as **multidimensional scaling (MDS)**. With this method, the respondent gives a rating on, for example, a 1 to 7 scale from very dissimilar to very similar for each pair of brands. Thus, the customer could be presented with the pair Discover Card–Visa and then asked to give a number from 1 to 7 with respect to how similar they feel the brands are with no attributes specified. After doing this for all pairs of brands, including the "ideal," a matrix of numbers from 1 to 7 is analyzed using an MDS computer program to produce a pictorial representation of the brands (like Figure 7.4 but without the attribute labels on the axes). The program locates the brands as points in the space by developing a set of coordinates that best replicates the similarity judgments. The similarities are translated into distances on the map. If it is a joint space, clusters of customers are located on the map based on their individual judgments of similarity of brands to their ideal concept. In addition, the program produces results for $n - 1$ number of dimensions where n is the number of brands. In practice, most managers use maps with two dimensions or three at most.

Figure 7.5 shows a joint space for the credit card example assuming it is estimated using MDS. The brands are in similar locations as Figure 7.4. The numbered circles represent clusters of segment ideal points with the numbers indicating their relative size. Note that the axes are unlabeled. The two brands that appear to be furthest apart are Visa and American Express. If these data had come from similarity judgments, the implication is that, overall, consumers felt that these two brands were the most dissimilar and gave the pair a low score on the 1 to 7 scale. The closest pair is Visa and MasterCard, with these two brands producing a high score on the scale, on average.

How are the attributes determined? One approach is judgmental: managers experienced with the product category examine the plot of the brands and infer the attributes from their locations. Because of the potential for bias, this method is often complemented or replaced with supplementary attribute ratings and importance weights, which upon examination can help explain the relative brand locations.[39] The axes might be labeled "fees" and "acceptance" as in Figure 7.4 but not necessarily so.

Positioning Decisions

Armed with information about how the brands in a market are perceived by customers and your brand's value proposition, you can use perceptual maps to help

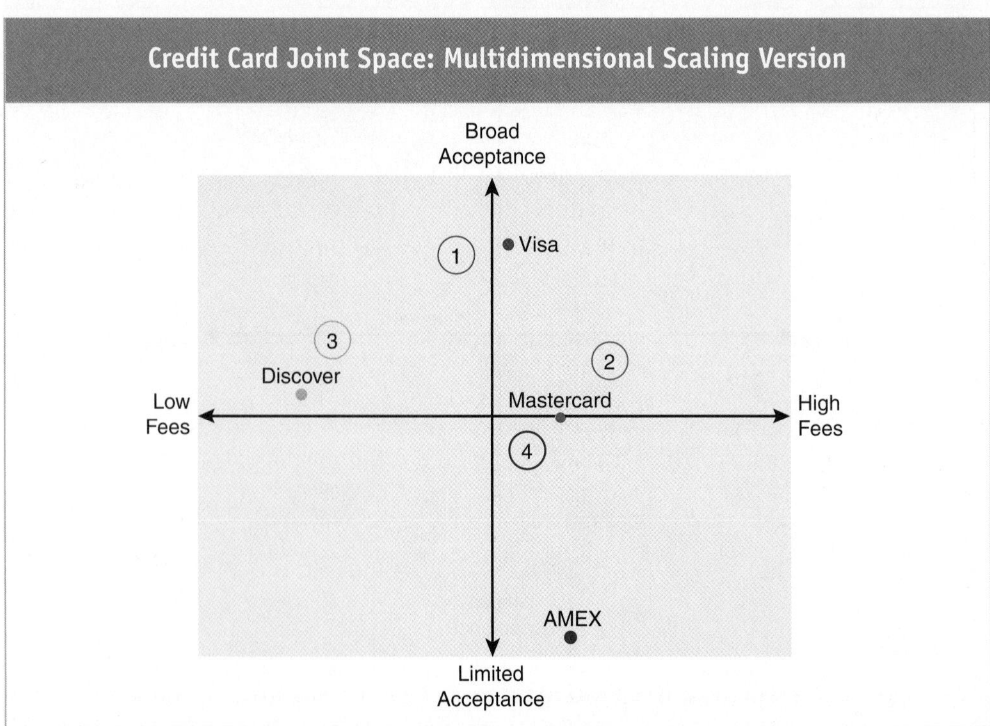

determine if your value proposition has been well implemented. For example, Visa should be well satisfied with its position in Figure 7.5. Based on its highly regarded "It's Everywhere You Want to Be" campaign, the card is perceived as having the broadest acceptance and a fee structure that places it close to the ideal (using the axis labels from Figure 7.4). Alternatively, its rival MasterCard is not positioned badly with respect to the horizontal dimension, fees, but is perceived as being much less accepted relative to Visa. Because it has a large customer base, it is fairly close to the second-largest preference segment, segment 2. If broad acceptance is part of the brand's value proposition, something needs to be done to improve its perception along this attribute.

American Express's position is interesting. Readers might feel that it is lost on the perceptual map by being perceived as somewhat expensive and not widely available. However, you must use caution when interpreting these maps. American Express's target audience is more upscale than the other cards, particularly the Discover Card. Thus, "prestige" could be an important attribute for this segment, but it was not investigated in this study. The lesson is that the map is only useful for a set of brands that are appealing roughly to the same target group. A perceptual map developed on customers with incomes greater than $75,000 might look quite different.

The situation of the Discover Card is also interesting and brings up the issue of repositioning. The card is positioned as a low-fee alternative to the others. This can be a successful positioning/value proposition. However, suppose that the card's marketing managers wish to add "widely accepted" to the value proposition and move it closer to segment 3. This would require a repositioning of the brand, but also some thought about the implications of doing so because moving "north" on the map would bring it closer to Visa.

In general, trade-offs need to be considered between being close to an ideal point, where the competitors are on the map, and the importance of the attributes/axes. Another consideration in repositioning is the awareness level of the old positioning. With respect to repositioning, high awareness may be a constraint on your ability to change perceptions. Finally, it is expensive to change perceptions. While it looks easy to move a brand on a perceptual map, in reality it can be very costly to do so.

Repositioning is a common marketing activity. It often occurs when a brand becomes "tired" and needs a revitalized value proposition. In some cases, it occurs when managers wish to move a product into a new segment. A few examples are:

- The California Prune Board renamed prunes "dried plums" to reposition the product as a vitamin-rich snack for busy people.
- Tropicana has added the health claim that consumption of orange juice can reduce the risk of high blood pressure and stroke.
- GE Plastics repositioned its products as being part of the creative process in the development of new products like the new Volkswagen Beetle.
- The liqueur Kahlua is attempting to reposition its brand away from just a dessert drink to something that has versatility and can be an ingredient in cocktails.
- McDonald's is trying to move towards a healthier positioning by introducing salads, chicken strips, and deli sandwiches.

A number of companies are trying to reposition their products and themselves as "green," that is, socially and environmentally conscious. This was one of the trends noted at the end of Chapter 1. For example, Hewlett-Packard has touted its electronics recycling program, Walmart has emphasized fluorescent light bulbs that use up to 75 percent less electricity than incandescent bulbs, and almost all of the automobile companies are working to improve gas mileage and develop electric or hybrid cars. However, there is concern that this is a fad rather than a fundamental change in the way the companies do business in that complaints about "greenwashing" (misleading consumers about a product's environmental benefits) have risen.[40]

Multiple Positions

When a product is being marketed to multiple target markets, it is normal for the value proposition and, hence the positioning, to be different (see Figure 2.7). For example, a high-quality camera might be targeted to both professionals and high-end consumers. For the former, the positioning would stress the technical capabilities, while the positioning for the consumers would have some technical aspects but also ease-of-use, for example. Apple has used multiple positioning in its advertisements. While you expect that the iPhone largely targets consumer segments, the company has also run some ads positioning the iPhone to small business owners by showing some applications such as FedEx Mobile and others that create billing statements and a mobile credit card terminal for accepting customer payments.

Application Skoda

Skoda is a Volkswagen automobile brand with a Czechoslovakian heritage.[41] Marketing it in Britain is a problem. Although the brand has a 98 percent awareness level, unfortunately the brand was universally known as a worthless, low-end car. In a survey conducted in 2000, 60 percent of respondents said that they would not consider buying one. A famous Skoda joke goes as follows: "How do you double the value of a Skoda? Fill the gas tank." In fact, Skoda means "pity" or "shame" in Czech!

How do you change an entire country's perception of a car? The company's managers figured that to take the usual informational approach would not work, so they decided to use humorous, self-deprecating ads challenging assumptions about the car. Some of the ads featured the Skoda Octavia and Fabia models using characters in situations where they assumed that the cars looked so good, they could not be Skodas. In general, the repositioning took an "underdog," "little guy" approach.

The repositioning, public relations, and direct marketing efforts delivered impressive results. Skoda sold 36,000 cars in Britain in 2001, an increase of 23 percent relative to an overall market increase of 10.5 percent. In addition, the number of people who said they would not consider buying a Skoda declined to 42 percent, creating the potential for a large number of new customers.

Positioning decisions can be linked to the various stages of the product life cycle (PLC) shown in Figure 2.8. At the early stages of the product life cycle, competition is generic (see Chapter 6) and the job of the marketing manager is to convince potential customers that the new product satisfies their needs better than an existing substitute. In this case, products are not positioned against specific competitors because there either are none or very few. For example, when TiVo was introduced, because there was only a very small competitor (ReplayTV), the main job was to position it as allowing people to time-shift their TV watching, show instant replays, pause live TV, etc. There was no mention of ReplayTV in its communications. However, as product categories mature, positioning decisions focus more on competitors and the differentiating benefits and features.

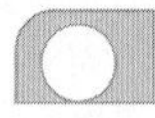

The Product Feature Decision

Once the marketing strategy has been established (target markets, competitor targets, value proposition), a key part of the product decision is what specific features to offer for each target group. These include the intrinsic product features (size, ingredients, color, etc.) as well as packaging and design, the latter of which have received a great deal of attention in the last few years.

The notion of developing different product features for different segments is particularly appealing for services and information goods (e.g., computer software, entertainment, newspapers). For manufactured products, it is expensive to tailor products to segments because of the implications for the manufacturing process. The Jeep division of Chrysler can offer two versions of the Wrangler (the Wrangler and the Wrangler Unlimited) to appeal to different customer interests for number of seats (four versus five) and towing capacity (2,000 pounds versus 3,500 pounds). However, the number of versions is very limited. Logitech offers ladybug and soccer mice for kids with the appropriate coloring and design. However, like the Chrysler example, there are only so many variants Logitech will develop. Alternatively, services and information goods can be very tailored. For example, if you join a health club, there are usually several different membership options: family or single, one-month, six-month, one-year, basic or basic plus swimming, and so on. It does not cost the health club any more to offer these options to customers because the options do not force the club to change its amenities for each segment.

The previous discussion is based on the assumption that the marketing manager takes a product or a service and modifies it to appeal to different market segments. In some cases, an entirely new product or service is developed *ex ante* with the target customers in mind. For example, Marriott has 16 different branded hotel products that service different market segments and that are marketed separately. Among these are Fairfield Inns (low price, low service), Renaissance (high end), Residence Inns (long-term stays), and TownePlace Suites (all-suite hotels).

Product Line Decisions

The examples used in this chapter have been drawn primarily from single products or services. It is often the case that a manager has to develop a **product line strategy** for a group of closely related products. Product variants (such as the Mountain Dew Code Red line extension example provided earlier in the chapter) may be developed to appeal to different segments of the market or to satisfy customers' needs for variety. Alternatively, a line may be developed to compete more directly with major competition. Some analysts have criticized Audi for not having an SUV in its product line in order to better compete with BMW, Porsche, Volvo, and Mercedes.[42] Product lines are also developed in order to gain additional shelf space with distributors. After acquiring Compaq in 2001, Hewlett-Packard decided to use both the HP and Compaq brand names in order to keep competitors from gaining shelf space.

product line strategy
a marketing strategy covering a set of related products

In some cases, the line may share a brand name. For example, Applied Biosystems markets a line of thermal cyclers that perform polymerase chain reaction (PCR) used in DNA analysis. The line consists of the GeneAmp PCR System 2400, the GeneAmp PCR System 2700, and the GeneAmp PCR System 9700. The products are differentiated largely by their production capacity (i.e., how many tests can be run simultaneously), because research labs and pharmaceutical companies differ in their testing needs.

However, in many cases, the brand names in a product line can be confusing. Audi, for example, uses A, Q, R, S, and T designations for its models. Suppose you are shopping for a Sony LCD HDTV with a screen size between 32 and 40 inches. You can choose from a bewildering array of brands including the XBR9, XBR7, L, V, VE5, and others.

Product lines may also include complementary products, which are intended to be used together but also could be marketed separately. In the Applied Biosystems example, the company also markets reagents and enzymes to be used with the DNA samples, as well as disposables such as slides and plastic tubes. Xerox markets its copiers along with toner, paper, and other "consumables," any of which can be purchased separately.

In developing a product line strategy, the marketing manager must address a number of important issues:

- How many products should be in the line?
- How should the products in the line be targeted and differentiated?
- How should resources be allocated across the line to maximize profits or market share?

Number of Products and Differentiation

The answer to the first question looks simple from an economic perspective. Add variants to the line as long as the incremental sales exceed the incremental costs. Often, the direct costs of making the product or delivering the service when it is added to a line are low because there are cost interdependencies. That is, the new product uses machinery or other assets that are already in place. In addition, research has shown that in some circumstances, retailers like adding product variants because it keeps customers in the store.[43] However, there are also hidden costs with product line additions. One such cost is that additional line elements take up additional shelf space or salesperson time. Unsuccessful additions to the line create loss of goodwill from both the retailer and the salesperson, which can have negative long-term consequences for the entire product line. A second such cost is called **cannibalization**, in which the sales for a new element of the line are not entirely incremental—some may come from an existing element of the line. Additional line elements also dissipate the advertising budget and management attention. Thus, the product line manager must fully account for all costs of line additions.

cannibalization
the amount of sales for a new element of a product line that is taken away from an existing element of the line

The number of products and their targeting and differentiation should be determined *before* variants are added to a product line. If the addition to the line does not cover the hidden costs and it is difficult to position relative to existing products in the line, then it is questionable whether such a product should be added unless the other reasons (e.g., combating competition) are particularly compelling.

An issue that many companies are confronting today is the proliferation of brands and products. Obviously, large numbers of brands increase manufacturing and marketing costs. Selective pruning permits marketing managers to do a better job of concentrating resources on the best-selling brands and elements of the product line. Several years ago, Unilever reduced its number of brands and variations from 1,600 to 400. Interestingly, these 400 accounted for 90 percent of the company's annual revenues. Hershey Foods is trying to increase the amount of sales of its top three brands from 35 percent of corporate revenue. Wm. Wrigley Jr. Company gets 53 percent and Mars 67 percent from its top three brands. Nestlé found that 30 percent of its 130,000 product variations were unprofitable and undertook a program to severely cut them back.[44]

Adding new products to a line has implications for branding. For example, a decision might be made to add a high-end product to the line. The key decision for the marketing manager is whether the old brand would be suitable for the new, upscale product. Toyota chose a new brand name, Lexus, for its luxury brand. Likewise, Sony chose the brand, Qualia, for its new line of consumer electronics.

Resource Allocation

Resource allocation decisions depend on the nature of the product line. If the variations in the line are minor, the marketing strategy normally would not single out the individual elements for special advertising or promotion programs. For example, Logitech's PC mice all have pretty much the same functions and look, with minor variations in the technology used (wireless versus attached) (see the Logitech Web page at http://www.logitech.com/index.cfm/mice_pointers/mice/&cl=us,en; note also the confusing brand names!). In such a case, the whole product line is promoted together, except perhaps for particular seasonal or recipe purposes. Sony does not develop different strategies for its different sizes of television sets (within a range).

When the elements of the line appeal to different segments of the market with different characteristics such as growth rates and competition, another approach can be used. The product line can be considered a portfolio of products, with some aspects of one product (e.g., high cash flow) helping with another (e.g., a new product that needs investment). The most popular framework for this kind of analysis of a product line (or even larger groups of products, such as a division or corporation) is the *portfolio approach* introduced by the Boston Consulting Group (BCG) in the 1970s. A key assumption of the BCG approach is that an organization should be balanced in terms of cash flow. Although it is not used any more as a corporate planning tool, it is a useful conceptualization of the product line resource allocation problem. The BCG portfolio, also called the growth share matrix, is shown in Figure 7.6. The two dimensions, relative market share and market growth, incorporate the following definitions:

- **The market is defined as the served market or market segment.** Thus, if we are considering a line of wine, such as the Mondavi line, the served market would

Figure 7.6

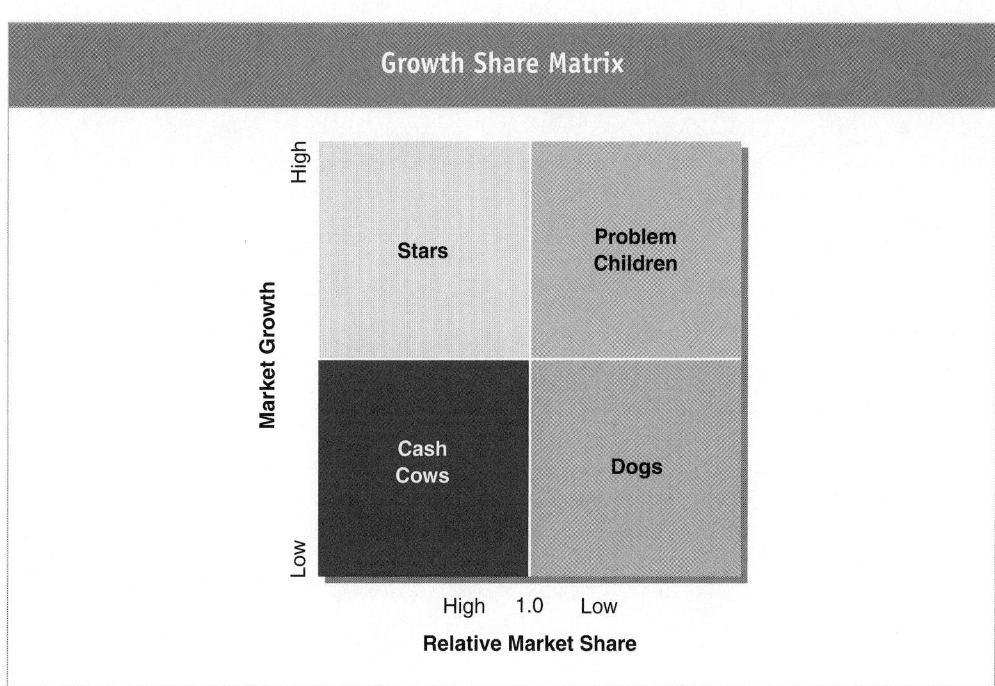

be defined at least on the basis of red versus white but more likely on a varietal (chardonnay, rosé, burgundy, etc.) basis.

- **Market share is defined as relative share.** The ratio of the share of your product in the market segment to the largest competitor. As can be seen in Figure 7.6, high relative market share is greater than 1.0 and low is below 1.0.
- **Market growth is the sales growth rate in the served market.** The dividing line between high and low can be based on gross national product or gross domestic product growth rates, inflation, or more subjective criteria.

The rationale for using growth and share as the criteria for resource allocation decisions is the following. Market growth rate is a proxy for the PLC. In addition, it is easier to gain share when the market is in its early stages (i.e., in the growth stage) than when it is in the maturity stage (when growth rates are stable). As we have seen in Chapter 2, market share (through economies of scale, learning effects, or both) is related to higher rates of profitability, lower costs, and other strengths such as brand awareness and strong channel relationships.

Products in the different quadrants have varying characteristics. The products in the lower right quadrant have low relative share in low-growth markets (usually called "dogs"). Typically, they are eliminated or they can re-segment their markets to gain a better relative market position. The products in the upper right quadrant have low share in high-growth markets (called "problem children" or "question marks"). These products are net users of cash because they need money to make product improvements to compete in the lucrative, high-growth segment. In the upper left quadrant are the "stars," products in the dominant position in a high-growth market. These products also need cash to maintain their market leadership position but they are also generating some because of the high margins they can maintain. "Cash cows" reside in the lower left quadrant. These generate cash because they lead their markets, which are usually large by the maturity phase of the PLC. The cash generated by these products is used to feed R&D and marketing for the problem children and the stars.

Thus, the product portfolio's major use is as a device for managing cash over a diversified product line. One of the implied objectives of this kind of analysis is that the

Table 7.3

Example of a Product Portfolio: Large Southern U.S. Bank, ca. 1986

Product	Growth	Wholesale Product Line Relative Share	Status
Pension management assets:			
Large	High	About 0	Problem child
Small	High	0.13	Problem child
Automation services	Low	0.20	Dog
Indentured trustee	Low	About 0	Dog
Municipal paying agent services	Low	2.0	Cash cow
International services:			
Pacific	High	2.5	Star
Europe	Low	0.50	Problem child
Foreign exchange	High	0.44	Problem child
Brokerage	High	0.20	Problem child
Bond sales	Low	0.33	Dog

manager should strive to have a balanced portfolio. Too many of any kind of product is not good for the long-run health of the line or division. For example, too many cash cows means considerable revenue generation but no future (unless the PLCs are very long). Too many products in the upper quadrants implies significant cash flow requirements that are not being met.

Table 7.3 shows the portfolio for the wholesale (business-to-business) division of a large southern bank. As can be seen, the portfolio is unbalanced, with only one cash cow, one star, five problem children, and three dogs. The obvious problem is that insufficient resources are being generated or allocated to the products on the right side of the matrix, as indicated by their poor market positions.

Mass Customization

As noted earlier, product variants and new line elements are often developed to appeal to new market segments or to customers' desire for variety. However, especially for manufactured products, product lines create problems due to the increase in SKUs, resulting in both manufacturing and distribution inefficiencies.

For some products and services, improvements in information technology have permitted a fundamental change in product line policy—a shift from company-supplied to customer-demanded variations in products called **mass customization** or, alternatively, **customerization**. This is a process whereby a company takes a product or service that is widely marketed, and perhaps offered in many different configurations, and develops a system for customizing (or nearly customizing) it to each customer's specifications. This imparts a feeling that the product was made especially for the customer, an important affective (attitudinal) component of a buyer–seller relationship. Because services can be and often are tailored to each customer, most of the focus of mass customization has been in the manufacturing sector. A combination of information and flexible manufacturing technologies has enabled companies to personalize their products for customers.

mass customization/ customerization
also called one-to-one marketing, a new marketing process whereby a company takes a product or service that is widely marketed and develops a system for customizing it to each customer's specifications

choiceboards
online, interactive systems that allow individual customers to design their own products by choosing from an array of attributes, delivery options and prices

Another perspective is that customers have become product makers rather than product takers through the creation of **choiceboards**.[45] Choiceboards are online, interactive systems that allow individual customers to design their own products by choosing from an array of attributes, delivery options, and prices. Orders through these choiceboards then stimulate a production process at the manufacturer end of the value chain. Witness the product-making activity when you order a personal computer from www.dell.com.

Some other examples of mass customization are:

- Ross Controls is a major manufacturer of pneumatic valves, which force air through machine tools. The company has been turned into a custom manufacturer by training its engineers to be what the company calls "integrators." Integrators are company engineers who work hand-in-hand with customers to get their specifications for the valves and, using computer software, design and build the products in the company's automated machine shop. The custom-designed valves are sometimes delivered the next day.
- Visit www.nikeid.com and custom-create your own pair of running shoes. Similarly, see www.converse.com.
- Stamps.com allows you to print your own U.S. postage stamps with pictures of your choice with its Photostamps service.
- Blank Label allows customers to custom create their own dress shirts.
- Visit www.mymms.com to customize your own M&Ms with a personal message and a variety of colors.

There are four different approaches to mass customization:[46]

1. **Collaborative customizers** talk to individual customers to help determine their needs, identify the exact product meeting those needs, and then make the customized product for them. This is the typical concept of mass customization represented by the examples just cited.
2. **Adaptive customizers** offer one standard but a customizable product that is designed so users can alter it to their own specifications. This would be appropriate when customers want the product to perform differently on different occasions.
3. **Cosmetic customizers** present a standard product differently to each customer. An example would be a company that sells a product to different retail chains, each of which wants its own packaging, sizes, and other features.
4. **Transparent customizers** provide each customer with unique products or services without telling them that the products have been customized for them. This is most useful when customers do not want to restate their needs repeatedly. Internet services such as Amazon.com produce customized recommendations for CDs to customers based on past purchases. These recommendations are sent via e-mail.

The commonality among the four kinds of mass customizers is that they all realize that customers are heterogeneous and want different combinations of product features and benefits. This recognition goes beyond market segmentation because mass customization engenders a feeling among customers that the company cares enough about them to develop products that precisely fit their needs. The desired outcome is a longer-term relationship than would be obtained using conventional marketing and manufacturing approaches.

As the Dell Web site shows, a major application of the Web is for personalization. Every time you visit a Web site, information about you is collected by that site and can be ultimately used to target specific messages. Some of this information is collected by what is called a *cookie*, a small tag of data inserted into your Web browser files that can identify you as a unique entity every time you return to the site that issued it. Other companies that use customization extensively include Amazon.com and BrooksBrothers.com.

However, it is still too early to know if these attempts at customization will be successful. Although there are a number of successful attempts at mass customization, there have been some notable failures. Levi Strauss developed a process for customizing jeans called Original Spin. They pulled the plug on it in 2003. Procter & Gamble launched a Web site, Reflect.com, to create customized beauty products for women. This one died in 2005. Some academic research has hypothesized that while customization sounds appealing, consumers' preferences are notoriously unstable and people may actually prefer products that are made for larger segments than explicitly for themselves.[47]

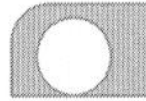

Packaging and Product Design

Packaging decisions have both functional and strategic implications for a product. From the functional perspective, one of the jobs of the package is to protect the contents from damage, spoiling, and theft. The dark color of bottles of many brands of beer keep it fresher so that it can stay on the shelf longer. Today, drugs are sold in tamper-proof packages because of the problems that brands like Tylenol have experienced. Packaging must also be done in the most cost-effective way because it is a large component of the total cost of a product. We are familiar with a brand manager who spent much of his time trying to figure out how to lower the cost of a plastic detergent container. Packaging also contains information on the ingredients, calories, tools needed to assemble, and so on, which is important to consumer choice.

Of more interest is how the package helps the product strategically. Because many decisions are made in the store, the package can have a large influence on which brand is ultimately purchased. Packaging can reinforce a brand—witness the success of L'Eggs hosiery's egg-shaped container. A clever package can differentiate the product. StarKist began selling its tuna in more convenient and easier-to-open pouches in 2000 (see Figure 7.7). Packaging can also aid in product positioning. A popular and expensive brand of vodka, Grey Goose, has an attractive frosted bottle that exudes high quality. For grocery items, packages are frequently updated to keep the image of the product fresh. For example, French's Mustard launched a bright new plastic container in 2002 that, among other things, draws excess mustard back into the bottle to eliminate that annoying mustard-crust gunk often found in squeeze caps.

Like packaging, product design has the potential to differentiate your product from the competition. Apple Computer is famous for its emphasis on design. Its whole product line, from the iBook notebook computer to the iPad tablet, emphasizes not only user-friendliness but attractiveness in form and color as well. Unfortunately, the product with the most radical design, the Cube, was a flop. Black & Decker's SnakeLight (Figure 7.8) is an award-winning portable light with a flexible core that can be bent, coiled, or draped for hands-free convenience. American Express is attempting to create a more exciting image with its cool-looking transparent Blue card with a hologram in the center and a computer chip embedded in the card. The industrial design and consulting company Ideo has been very successful at promoting design as a key component of product differentiation.

Application Heineken DraughtKeg

Beer lovers say that they love draft beer; however, it is difficult to deliver draft-like beer at home, despite a number of tries by companies to do so.[48] In 1997, a new engineer arrived at Heineken's research lab with marching orders to shrink the beer keg to make it small and cheap enough for consumers to take it home and then throw out when it was empty. The Heineken DraughtKeg was introduced in Europe in 2005 and rolled out in the United States in the summer of 2007 (see http://heinekendraughtkeg.com). To say that it has been a hit is an understatement: the company sold about 10 million kegs in 2007 and about 1.5 million in the United States in 2008 at $20 each. Each drum holds about 14 bottles of beer; at about the equivalent of $8.60 for a six-pack, the product is obviously premium-priced to go along with the unique delivery system—further cementing Heineken's upscale positioning in the crowded beer market. The new keg has been so successful that it has been imitated by MillerCoors for its Miller Lite and Coors Lite brands in the form of a Home Draft keg that is being tested in several U.S. cities.

Figure 7.7

StarKist Pouch

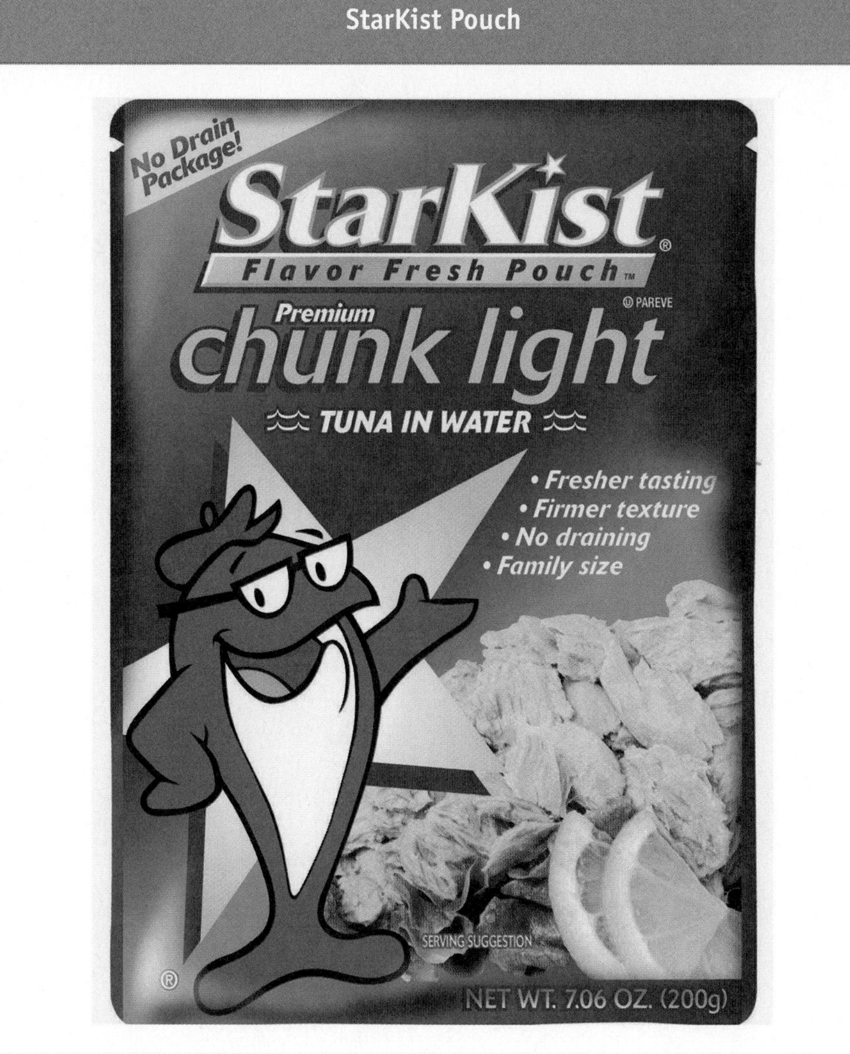

Source: Heinz North America/Del Monte Foods

Executive Summary

Key learning points in this chapter include the following:

- Brand equity is composed of loyalty, awareness, quality, and brand associations.
- Brand extensions can leverage a brand name into other product categories, but success is a function of the transferability of the associations, the complementarity of the new product, the similarity of the users of the new product, and the transferability of the brand symbol.
- A global brand can be useful for providing a unified image around the world.
- Despite their complexity, high-technology products benefit from a strong branding program, like any other product.
- To implement product positioning, you must determine the brand's current position using marketing research methods and, if it is determined that the brand is poorly positioned, develop a repositioning strategy.
- Product features often have to be developed to suit the needs of a particular target market.

Figure 7.8

Black & Decker SnakeLight

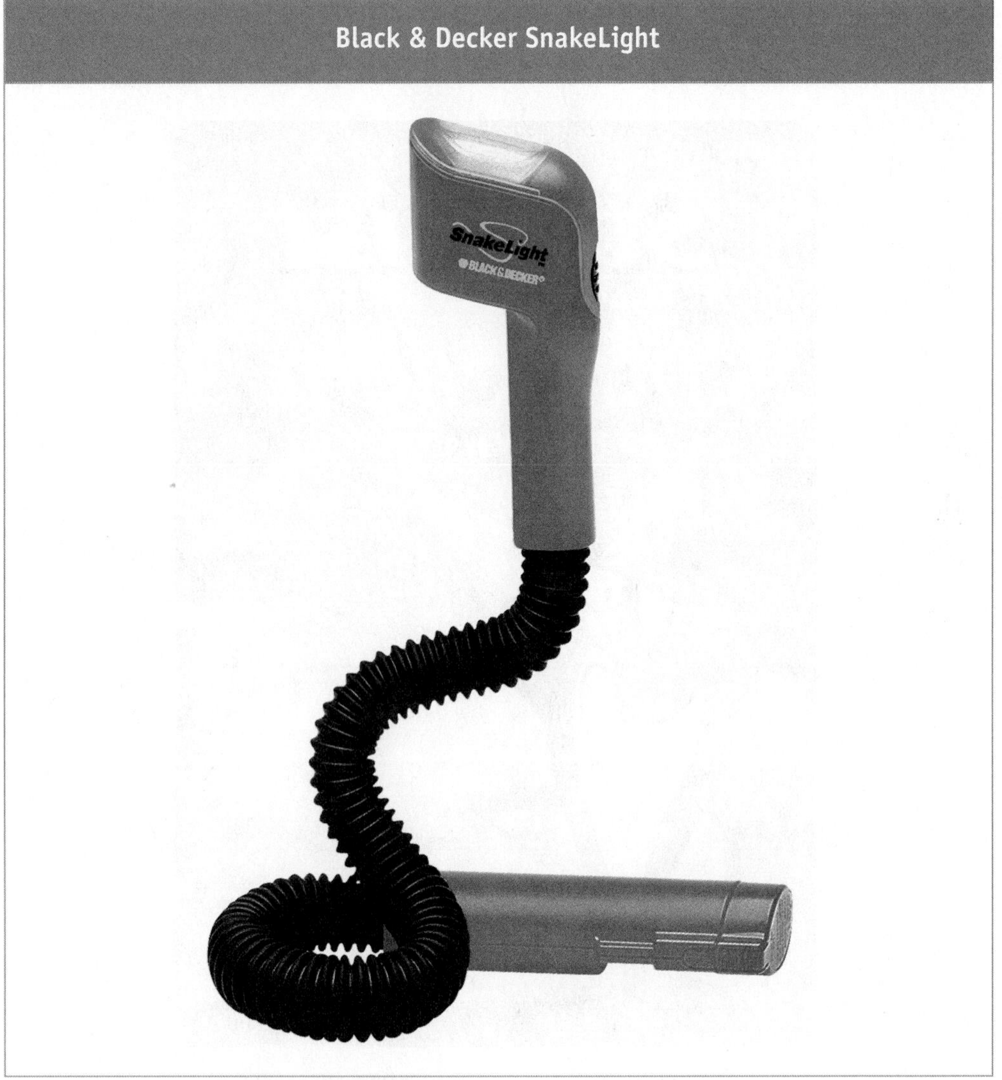

Source: Black & Decker

- Product lines need to be carefully managed by addressing the number in the line, how to differentiate them, and how to allocate resources across the line.
- Packaging and product design can be important parts of a differentiation strategy.

Chapter Questions

1. Pick two companies with different branding strategies (i.e., corporate parent brands versus distinct product brands). Why do you think they are using different branding approaches?
2. Choose a brand that you think is weak in the minds of customers. Using the framework shown in Figure 7.1, what are the elements of brand equity that are deficient for this product?
3. Given the two brand names Nabisco and Mercedes-Benz, choose several brand extensions that you believe make sense and several that do not. Explain why.
4. Are there some product categories that are more amenable to global branding than others? What are the general characteristics of those that work and those that do not?

5. In late 2002, Dell Computer Corporation decided to start selling "white boxes," unbranded PCs, to computer distributors who then put their own or some other private-label brand on them. Do you think this was a good idea? Why or why not? (Hint: Dell killed the idea in 2005).
6. Give several examples of brands that have been recently repositioned. How has this been implemented and for what reason?
7. Are there some kinds of products and services that can be more easily mass customized than others? Are there any negatives to mass customization?

Key Learning Points

The purpose of this chapter is to highlight the importance of new products to firms and to describe alternative new product introduction processes. Key areas of learning include:

- Why new products are important to organizations
- Factors affecting new-product success and failure
- Three major approaches to developing new products: the linear process, the rugby approach, and the target costing method
- The steps in bringing new products to market
- The impact of the Internet on new-product development processes
- Special topics in new-product development, such as the importance of shorter development cycles and better integration of marketing and R&D

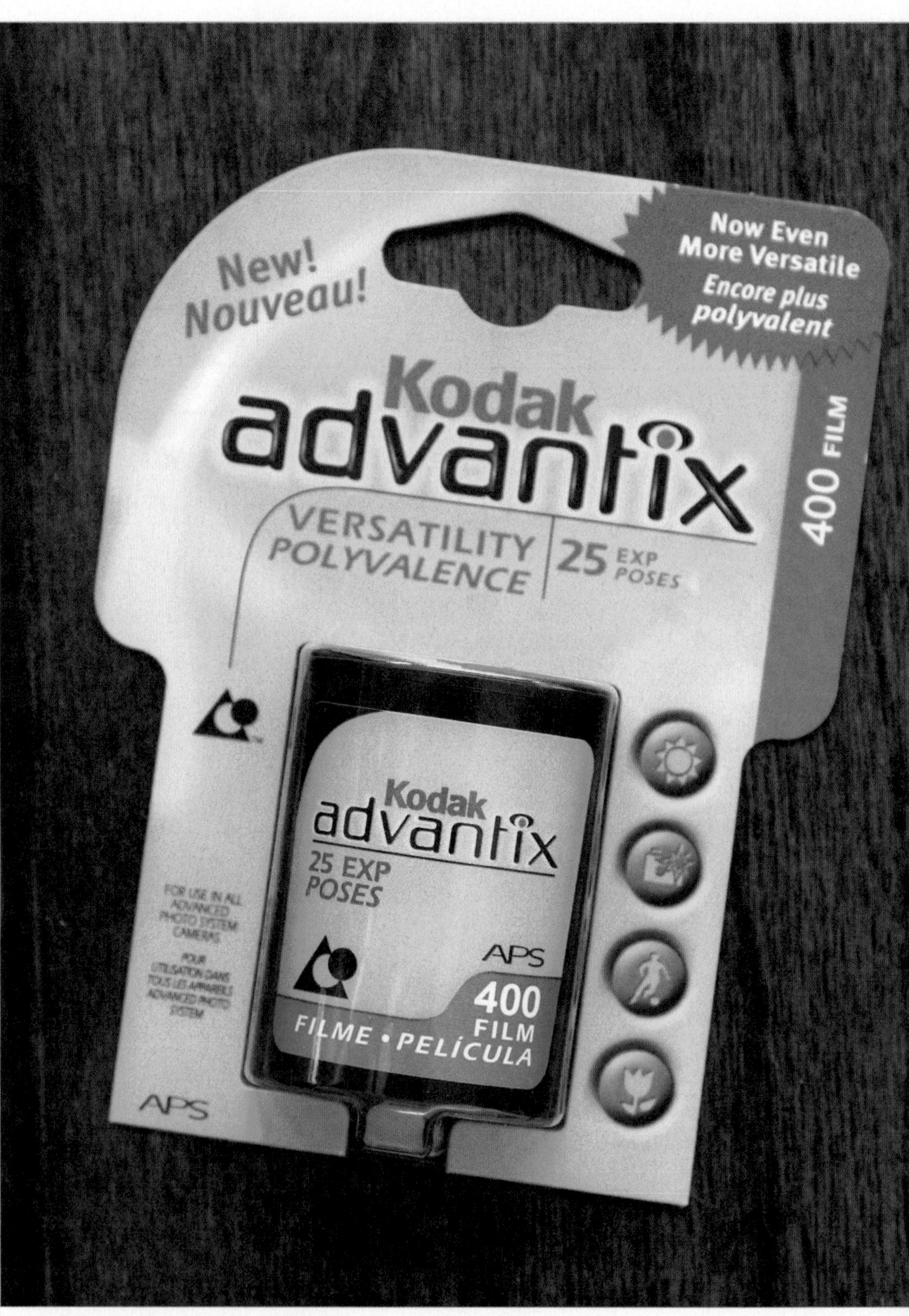

The difficulties of the Advanced Photo System in gaining market acceptance show the risks in developing new products. *Source:* David Young-Wolff/PhotoEdit Inc.

New-Product Development

Chapter Brief

For nearly 10 years, beginning in the mid-1980s, five multinational companies—Kodak, Fuji Photo Film, Minolta, Canon, and Nikon—worked together to develop a new photography system that Kodak called the advanced photo system or (APS).[1] The system is incompatible with existing 35-mm technology (its negatives are 24 mm in size) and is priced about 15 percent higher. However, the cameras are small and light, have easy film loading, and permit photographers to take three sizes of pictures on the same roll of film: classic (4 by 6 inches), group (4 by 7 inches), and panoramic (4 by 10 inches). In addition, some errors in picture taking when a flash is used can be corrected in the development process.

The cameras were introduced in early 1996. However, four months after the product introduction, most retailers did not have the cameras to sell due to production problems and demand-forecasting mistakes. Poor packaging caused some consumers to buy the new film cartridges in the belief that they could be used in their existing 35-mm cameras (they cannot). The companies did not support the retailers well with in-store promotional materials. A multitude of brand names (Kodak called its APS camera the Advantix, Minolta used the brand name Vectis, and Nikon called it Nuvis) also created some confusion among consumers. Finally, when the cameras did arrive on the shelves, the negative publicity surrounding the new product kept consumers from purchasing them. Taking all the problems together, some observers called it the worst new-product launch in the history of the photographic industry. In August 1996, the feeling was that the companies marketing the APS cameras had better recover within the next year or the camera would be history.

In April 1997, Kodak relaunched the Advantix camera with an estimated $60 to $100 million advertising campaign and extensive promotions, including a free camera to any woman who had a baby on Mother's Day. However, when a new photographic technology is introduced, film developers wait to see whether the camera will sell well (and therefore whether the film will sell) before investing in new processing equipment. This, in turn, affects whether consumers will buy the cameras—who will buy a camera with a new type of film if they cannot develop the pictures? Retailers, having been burned by Kodak and the other APS companies the previous year, were reluctant to carry the camera.

By 1999, the camera technology was well established. About 20 percent of all new camera sales used the APS system and advanced products were being launched by the major firms. A large boost to the market was Kodak's launch of one-time-use APS cameras, a very popular product form. Backed by a multimillion-dollar advertising campaign highlighted by a commercial in the popular *Seinfeld* TV series finale in 1998, Fuji's APS models sold well.

However, by 2002, photo industry pundits were proclaiming the APS system was "dead." The increased popularity and decreased prices of digital cameras hurt APS sales as it was caught between the newer technology and the more classic 35-mm format. In addition, disposable instant cameras became very popular. It became a niche product because of its low price and easy film-loading appeal to price-sensitive, nonexpert customers. Minolta, Konica, Olympus, Pentax, and Nikon all dropped APS cameras from their lines, leaving only Canon, Fuji, and Kodak to support it. In 2004, Kodak announced that it was discontinuing the Advantix camera line and only manufacturing APS film. In fact, due to the rising popularity of digital cameras, the company suspended the manufacture of all reloadable (i.e., nondisposable) film cameras. In 2009, the company discontinued making Kodachrome film for slides, which it first introduced in 1935, and was only making 35-mm and APS film.

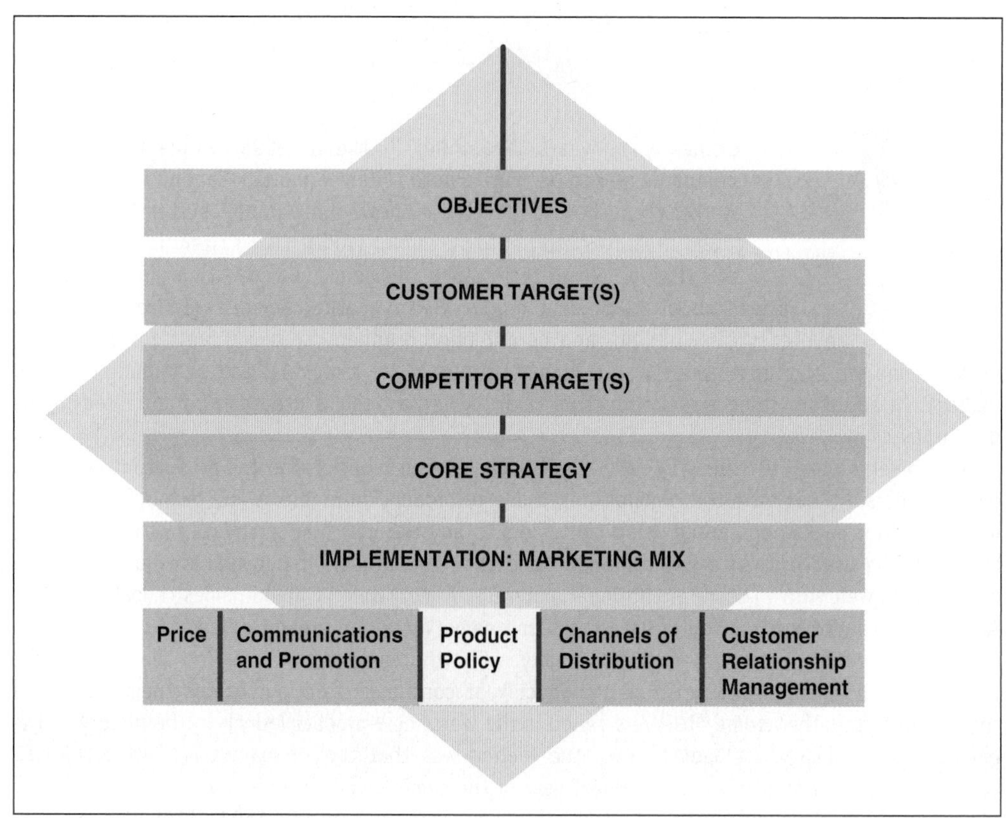

The problems experienced by the companies manufacturing APS cameras are typical of those that occur when new products and services are launched. However, most companies rely on new products for their long-term health. Today, successful companies in a wide variety of industries generate a large percentage of their sales from new products. Figure 8.1 provides some evidence supporting the correlation between this percentage of sales from new products and industry position. As can be seen, the most successful companies generate nearly 50 percent (the "All Firms" line) of their sales from new products, as compared to around 10 percent for the least successful. For firms in high-tech industries, the gap is even larger. Hewlett-Packard, for example, obtains more than 50 percent of its revenues from products introduced within the last two years.

In addition, companies spend a significant amount of money to develop new products. Table 8.1 shows the top 10 companies in 2007 in terms of their spending on research and development (R&D). Table 8.2 shows the leading countries in corporate R&D spending as a percentage of their gross domestic product (GDP). Also, the number of patents issued by the U.S. Patent and Trademark Office (USPTO) is skyrocketing.

Figure 8.1

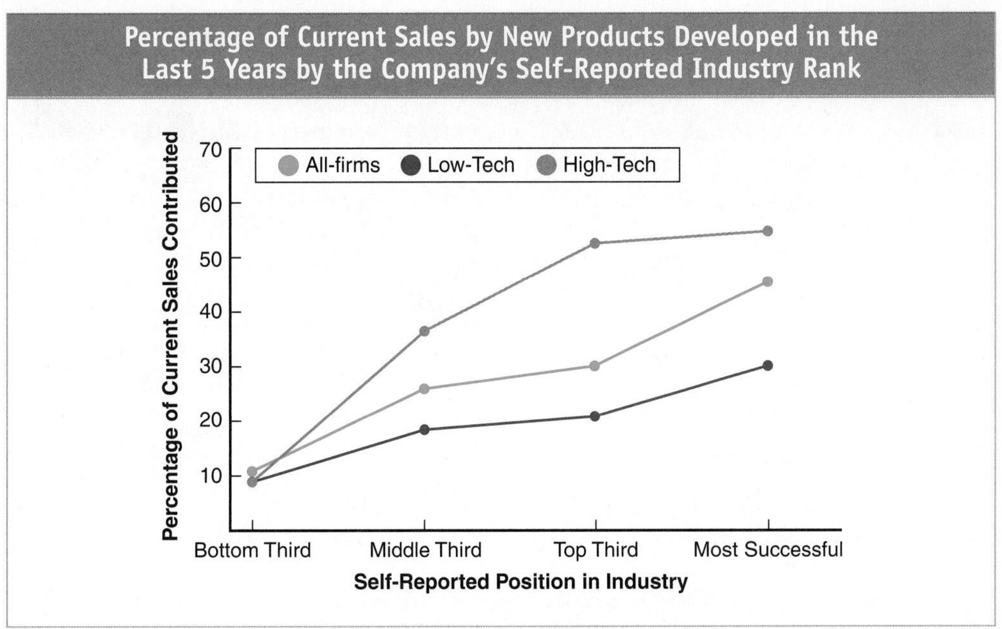

Source: Thomas P. Hustad (1996), "Reviewing Current Practices in Innovation Management and a Summary of Selected Best Practices," in M. D. Rosenau, Jr., A. Griffin, G. A. Castellion, and N. F. Anscheutz, eds., *The PDMA Handbook of New Product Development* (New York: Wiley), p. 490, 1996. Copyright 1996. Reprinted with permission of John Wiley & Sons, Inc.

The top five companies in this patent rush in 2005 were IBM (2,941), Canon (1,828), Hewlett-Packard (1,797), Matsushita (1,688), and Samsung (1,641).[2] Most of these companies are enormous in terms of their revenues and can therefore afford to spend a significant amount of money on R&D.

Interestingly, there is mixed evidence on the relationship between spending on R&D and firm performance.[3] As some evidence supporting this point, *BusinessWeek* published a ranking of the most innovative companies developed by the Boston Consulting Group. The ranking was based on a survey of senior executives around the world who were asked to consider the companies that consistently offer inventive products, customer experiences, business models, or processes. The top 10 were Apple, Google, Toyota, Microsoft, Nintendo, IBM, Hewlett-Packard, Research in Motion (BlackBerry), Nokia, and Walmart. Note that 7 of the 10 are not on the list of top R&D spenders shown in Table 8.1.

Table 8.1

Top 10 Global Companies in R&D Spending (2007)

Company	Amount Spent on R&D (billions of $)
Toyota	8.386
General Motors	8.100
Pfizer	8.089
Nokia	7.727
Johnson & Johnson	7.680
Ford	7.500
Microsoft	7.121
Roche	6.985
Samsung	6.536
GlaxoSmithKline	6.476

Source: Barry Jaruzelski and Kevin Dehoff (2008), "Beyond Borders: The Global Innovation 1000," *Strategy + Business,* issue 53, Winter, p. 10. Reprinted with permission.

Table 8.2

Top 10 R&D Spending Countries (as a percentage of GDP)

Country	R&D as a Percentage of GDP (%)
Israel	4.35
Sweden	4.27
Finland	3.44
Japan	3.12
Iceland	3.10
South Korea	2.64
United States	2.59
Switzerland	2.57
Denmark	2.54
Germany	2.51

Source: The Economist World in Figures (2007) (London: Profile Books), p. 63. Used by permission, courtesy of Profile Books.

Most companies recognize the importance of new products. In the high-tech marketing world described throughout this book, innovation is life. Even in slow-growth markets such as food industries, companies are constantly scrambling for ideas, like Frito-Lay's flavored snack chips (e.g., Cool Ranch), Nabisco's Snackwells, McDonald's Chicken Selects sandwich, and Vanilla Coke, which revitalize product categories and bring significant sales growth. More than 30,000 new products are introduced annually in U.S. supermarkets. The inevitability of the maturity and decline of the product life cycle means that there is constant pressure for companies to find their own "next big thing." Thus, SmithKline Beecham generated $243 million in sales from its new smoking-cessation product Nicoderm CQ. Revenues from this product replace that of older products that are withdrawn or deemphasized.

New products can also form the foundation for a complete turnaround of a company's performance. For many years, Colgate-Palmolive had done a good job selling its toothpaste, deodorants, pet foods, and soaps in markets outside the United States. However, it had been consistently underperforming Procter & Gamble and Unilever within the United States. In early 1998, Colgate introduced a new toothpaste, Total, that was expected to help launch a corporate comeback in the U.S. market. Total contains triclosan, a germ-fighter found in many soaps and other personal care products. It has received approval from the Food and Drug Administration to claim that it helps to prevent gum disease, a claim no other toothpaste can make. Even in large, diversified companies like Colgate, such unique products can have a significant impact on the whole company's competitive performance.

New products are critical to the success of companies like McDonald's.
Source: M. Spencer Green/AP Wide World Photos

The new-product development process is difficult, and most new products fail. The Kodak APS example illustrates only some of issues involved with launching new products. A larger list of such issues is the following:

- What are the sources of ideas for new products?
- How do you take the large list of possible ideas and winnow it down to a more feasible set?
- How do you go from product concept to prototype?
- How do you forecast the demand for a new product?
- What is the ideal organizational form for new-product success?

- Once the new product is finalized, how do you introduce it into the marketplace?
- How can the entire process from idea generation to introduction be done more quickly?

Thus, the new-product development and introduction process is complicated and fraught with difficulties.

One problem in this area is defining exactly what constitutes a new product. New products are commonly divided into three categories:[4]

1. **Classically innovative products.** These are also called **new-to-the-world** products because the firm has created a new-product category. You might separate these into two subcategories: truly new products that are revolutionary (e.g., the disposable diaper, the personal computer) and other new products that create new categories but are based on existing products (e.g., the Kodak Advantix).
2. **New-category entries.** In this case, the product category already exists but the firm is just entering it. These are also commonly called **new-to-the-company** products. For example, Nike's entries into various sporting goods categories (e.g., in-line skates) fit into this classification.
3. **Additions to product lines or line extensions.** These are new versions of existing products already marketed by the firm. Examples are new flavors, colors, or technical variations (see Chapter 7). The Crest Spin Brush is a good example of a line extension.

new-to-the-world
a product that has not been marketed by any company previously

new-to-the-company
a product that has not been marketed by the company but has been marketed by another company

Other, more minor product changes could also result in what are thought of as new products:

- **Product improvements.** Most products on the market are eventually replaced by "new and improved" versions.
- **Repositionings.** Many products are repositioned for a new use or benefit (see Chapter 7).
- **Cost reductions.** In some cases, the only change to the product is a cost reduction through manufacturing, operations, or product cost savings.

Obviously, although many new products are line extensions or the result of more minor changes, we will use the term *new product* to refer only to innovative products and new-category entries. This is because considerably less time (sometimes none) is spent on the new-product development process for line extensions, improvements, and repositionings.

Factors Affecting New-Product Success or Failure

There has been a considerable debate over the success rate of new products. The new-product failure rate mentioned in the popular press and textbooks ranges from 67 to 80 percent. Only 2 percent of new grocery store brands and brand extensions hit $100 million in first-year sales, which is generally considered to be the threshold for success.[5] However, these numbers reflect variations in the definition of what constitutes a new product and how firms measure success, so you should interpret them cautiously. As we have already seen, a new product could be an invention such as the automobile or simply a new flavor of Jell-O. In addition, the notion of success is firm-specific because most companies have their own internal criteria for determining whether a new product should be supported or withdrawn from the market.

Figure 8.2 presents survey data about the success rates of new products introduced in 1990 and 1995 by member firms of the Product Development and Management Association (PDMA). In 1990, for every 100 new product ideas, only about 10 percent were deemed successes by the companies that launched them. By 1995, improvements in the various stages of the new-product development process had increased the success rate to more than 20 percent. In general, the 20 to 33 percent success rule seems to hold, particularly for the first two categories of new products (inventions and new category entries).

What factors lead some products to be successes and others failures? Many studies have attempted to determine the factors that separate success from failure. One

Figure 8.2

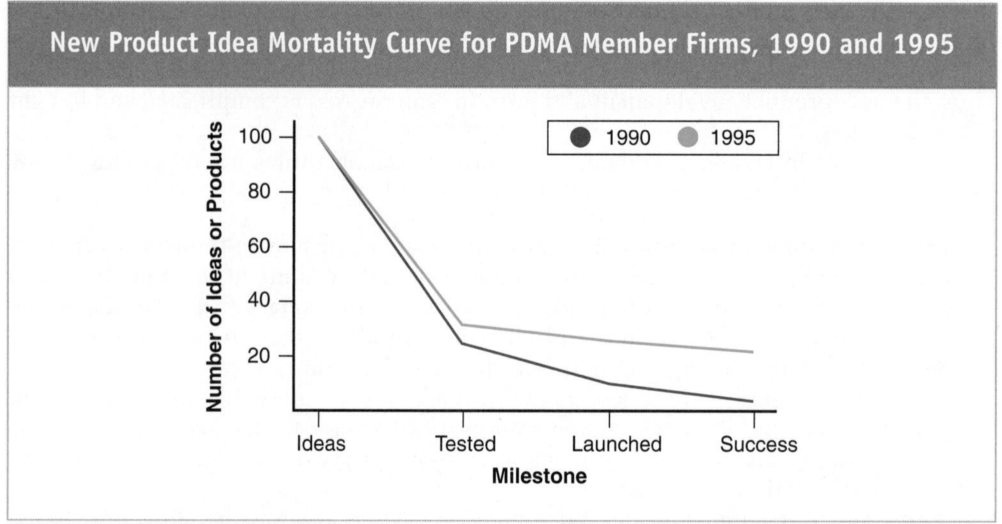

Source: Thomas P. Hustad (1996), "Reviewing Current Practices in Innovation Management and a Summary of Selected Best Practices," in M. D. Rosenau, Jr., A. Griffin, G. A. Castellion, and N. F. Anscheutz, eds., *The PDMA Handbook of New Product Development* (New York: Wiley), p. 491, 1996. Copyright 1996. Reprinted with permission of John Wiley & Sons, Inc.

well-known list of the factors correlated with successful new product introductions is shown in Table 8.3:[6]

- **A superior product with unique product benefits.** This should not be a surprise. No product, whether new or old, can be successful without offering a value proposition that is unique in the marketplace. Note that this does not rule out clones or me-too products that imitate existing product offerings. In such cases, meaningful differentiation can be obtained through a lower price, better service, or some other non-product-based factor.
- **A strong market orientation throughout the new-product development process.** This implies having a thorough understanding of the target customers, likely competitors, and the external environment. A market orientation helps to ensure that the product or service ultimately introduced has a unique value proposition.
- **Sufficient time on up-front activities before the product is launched.** Sometimes this is called the homework part of the new-product development process. It includes casting the net broadly for obtaining ideas for new products and analyzing the opportunities thoroughly.
- **Sharp product definition.** This includes knowing the target market, specifying the benefits to be delivered to the target customers, having a basic idea of how the product will be positioned, and finalizing the features and attributes.
- **High-quality execution of the steps of the process.** Thinking and planning out the process is one thing, actually performing the steps and performing them well are others.
- **The appropriate organizational structure.** As we will see later in this chapter, successful product development involves people from across the organization in interfunctional teams. In addition, companies that are good at launching new products often have an entrepreneurial culture that encourages risk taking and the open exchange of ideas.
- **A good project prioritization process.** Most companies can generate a significant number of ideas or concepts for new products. Because resources are always scarce, it is important to allocate those resources efficiently so that promising projects are not starved for cash. Often, difficult decisions must be made to discard concepts that will not be successful for the company.
- **Careful launch planning.** Earlier in this book, we stressed the importance of the marketing plan. This principle also applies to the launch of new products. The Kodak Advantix may be an excellent camera. However, that does not mean it will be a successful new product. The development and execution of the launch plan (i.e., the marketing) will ultimately determine whether the new product is successful.

- **Strong support by top management.** Goals must be set and articulated to employees, indicating that new products are an important component of the company's business. In addition, the product development process must be given adequate resources.
- **Fast time-to-market.** Due to the quick availability of competitive and market information today, the hallmark of successful new-product introductions is speed, reducing the time it takes from concept generation to launch. However, speed should not come at the expense of the other items in the list.
- **A detailed new-product development process.** As we will see in the next section of this chapter, there are many ways to approach the development and launch of new products. Each company must determine for itself which approach best fits its culture and external environment. However, no matter which approach is chosen, the company should have a well-documented process for new products that employees can follow.

Application FluMist

The product sounds perfect—a vaccine for influenza that is given through a spray in the nose rather than a painful shot in the arm. The product, developed by MedImmune and marketed by Wyeth, was timed for what was predicted to be a significant flu season. The company forecasted sales of 4 to 6 million doses, a small fraction of the 60 to 90 million flu vaccinations each year.

However, despite spending $25 million on a consumer awareness campaign that generated 40 percent awareness in the target market, the company sold only 400,000 doses during 2003, its winter of introduction. In addition, many of the doses sold were returned unused. What happened? FluMist was positioned as a premium product with a price several times higher than a conventional flu shot. Most consumers preferred a little pain to the higher price. Consumers were also concerned about safety because FluMist is a live vaccine that can give people a mild case of the flu. The product also was introduced late to the market after many doctors and pharmacies had already ordered their vaccines for the winter. Finally, the company made what looked to be an attractive promotional guarantee by offering to take back any unsold doses. However, this led to doctors using conventional vaccines first, knowing they could return FluMist without cost. Even as recently as 2009, FluMist accounts for only a few percent of inoculations Americans receive each year.[7]

Thus, comparing the mistakes to the list of success factors in Table 8.3, it is clear that, among a variety of mistakes, FluMist did not offer a superior product to consumers, Wyeth and MedImmune did not have a strong market orientation throughout the new-product introduction process, and the companies did not execute a good marketing strategy.

Table 8.3

New-Product Success Factors
• Developing a superior, differentiated product, with unique benefits and superior value to the customer or user.
• Having a strong market orientation throughout the process.
• Undertaking the redevelopment homework up-front.
• Getting sharp, early product definition before development begins.
• High-quality execution; completeness, consistency, and proficiency of activities in the new-product process.
• Having the correct organization structure: multifunctional, empowered teams.
• Providing for sharp project selection decisions, leading to focus.
• Having a well-planned, well-resourced launch.
• The correct role for top management: specifying new product strategy and providing the needed resources.
• Achieving speed to market, but with quality of execution.
• Having a multistage, disciplined new-product game plan.

Source: Robert G. Cooper (1996), "New Products: What Separates the Winners from the Losers," in M. D. Rosenau Jr., A. Griffin, G. A. Castellion, and N. F. Anschuetz, *The PDMA Handbook of New Product Development* (New York: Wiley), p. 50. Reprinted with permission of John Wiley & Sons, Inc.

Approaches to New-Product Development

Companies have developed a variety of approaches to developing new products in-house. While the most popular is what might be called the "linear" approach, beginning from idea generation and working to test marketing, two other approaches—a "rugby" method and target costing—originate in Japan and have been widely adopted.

The Classic Linear Approach

Figure 8.3 shows a typical linear design of a new-product development process. This process is described as linear because the firm using it goes through a series of processes that occur one after another. After one set is complete, the next in sequence occurs. The process is like a funnel, where the number of concepts diminishes after each step because some will fail the test at each stage. The process shown in Figure 8.3 is also referred to as a "stage gate" process, as each stage has a "gate" that must be passed through to reach the next stage. Although we describe the stages in more detail later in this chapter, a brief overview of each follows.

Opportunity Identification

In the first stage of the new-product development process, the company determines which markets it wants to enter. This requires the integration of new-product

Figure 8.3

New Product and Service Development Process

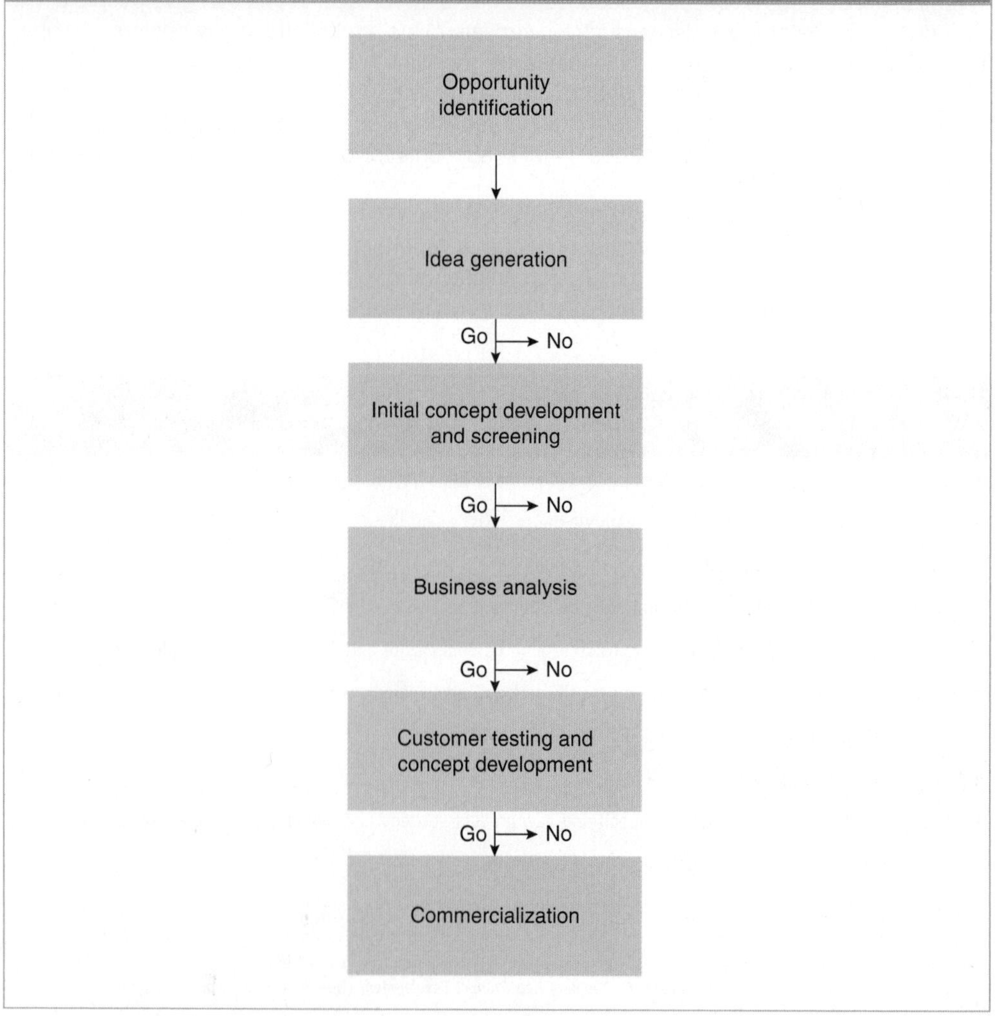

Opportunity identification
↓
Idea generation
Go ↓ → No
Initial concept development and screening
Go ↓ → No
Business analysis
Go ↓ → No
Customer testing and concept development
Go ↓ → No
Commercialization

planning with more traditional marketing or strategic planning. For example, before Colgate developed Total, the germ-fighting toothpaste, the company had to decide that the therapeutic segment was valuable to enter, based on the existing competition, projections of growth, and other information. The company could have decided to enter the benefit customer segment that is more interested in whiter teeth, for example.

Idea Generation

Once the market entry decision has been made, the company searches for new-product ideas. As we will see later in this chapter, there are many possible sources for new-product concepts. Some concepts are easy to develop. For example, a company wanting to enter an existing category with a product similar to a competitor's already has a reference point on which the new product can be based. However, for really new products or inventions, new-product ideas are much sketchier and may not be feasible to produce. Because this is a very difficult and uncertain part of the process given the number of possible concepts, this stage of the process is sometimes referred to as the "fuzzy front end."

Initial Design and Concept Screening

Few new concepts ultimately make it to the marketplace. The initial design phase of the new-product development process includes a step to screen the concepts developed in the first stage. Many of the concepts are not practical to make, require too much investment, or are not as good a fit to the strategic goals as others. Thus, the concepts are matched against customer needs and other requirements of the target segments. Preliminary forecasts are developed and those with lower estimates of potential sales are eliminated.

The concepts that survive are the focus of design efforts. Using information from customer research, prototypes are developed and subjected to further customer testing. These can be physical prototypes (in the case of manufactured products) or specific service concepts.

Business Analysis

Once a new-product concept passes the initial testing phase, it is then subjected to a rigorous business analysis, which accounts for anticipated selling price, manufacturing cost or cost of delivering the service, forecasted demand, and other marketing costs such as advertising and distribution.

Testing and Concept Development

Once the prototype is developed and passes the business analysis hurdle, it is tested with customers from the target segment. Further refinements are made to make progress toward the final product. Advertising concepts are also tested. Based on the customer tests, more sales forecasts are developed and additional product concepts are eliminated. In some cases, the resulting products are test marketed in specific geographic regions. In test marketing, a company simulates the actual introduction of a product or service in a limited number of markets. Different pricing, advertising, packaging, and other features can be tried and evaluated. Unfortunately, test markets also provide an opportunity for competitors to learn about the new product, and some have been known to disrupt test markets using price promotions or other devices to confound the test.

Commercialization

Following product testing (with or without test markets), the product or service is ready to be rolled out nationally or internationally. For all products, the rollout period is critical. For many kinds of products, the two key measures to monitor are trial and repeat. Clearly, for a product to be successful, you must get customers to try it. The greater the number of triers the better, because a product with a low trial rate will probably be withdrawn from the market. However, if customers do not repeat purchase, the product will also die. For consumer durables and other industrial products with long interpurchase cycles, trial or first-time purchasing is the key event.

Life-Cycle Management

Although these are not specifically part of the new-product development process, products and services require continuous updating and refinement. Pressure from customers and competitors forces you to consider whether the price is appropriate, the advertising copy is working as well as it should, the distribution system is appropriate, and so on. In addition—particularly for durables and industrial products—whole product lines often have to be replaced (consider the frequent turnover in automobile models by most major global manufacturers).

The Rugby Approach

As we noted earlier, the classic new-product development process is a linear process in which the new-product concept goes through a number of stages before introduction. It is also a funnel as many new concepts start at the top but few make it out of the bottom. In many companies, new-product development is like a relay race in which different functional specialists carry the "baton" and hand it on to the next group. Often marketing people develop product concepts, R&D engineers do the design work, production personnel make the product, and then it is given to the sales force to sell.

An alternative approach is more like a game of rugby. The product development process results from the constant interaction of a multidisciplinary team whose members work together from the beginning of the project to the product's introduction.[8] Thus, the team moves downfield in a pack from beginning to end. Companies using this method exhibit six characteristics in managing their new product development processes.

Built-in Instability

In this process, top management provides only a general strategic direction for the project team and establishes challenging goals, but provides a great deal of freedom. For example, Fuji Xerox gave a team a goal of producing a copier at half the cost of its most expensive line, but that would perform just as well.

Self-Organizing Project Teams

Project teams are permitted to operate like startup companies within the larger organization by developing their own agendas and taking risks. They are normally given a great deal of autonomy. The result is that the project teams normally increase their goals throughout the new-product development process, thus increasing the probability that they will develop breakthroughs rather than me-too products. The project teams usually consist of members with different functional specializations and personalities. This permits an extraordinary amount of learning within the group, which is translated to the project.

For example, Canon's top management asked an interdisciplinary team to develop a high-quality automatic exposure camera that was small and easy to carry, easy to use, and priced 30 percent below the current prices of single-lens cameras. By the end of the project, the team had achieved several breakthroughs in camera design and manufacturing. These included an electronic brain made with chips from Texas Instruments, modularized production (which made automation and mass production possible), and 30 to 40 percent fewer parts.

Overlapping Development Phases

The members of the project teams often start with different time horizons, which must be synchronized. At some point, the team begins to move forward together, and they adapt to each other's styles and personalities. This movement forward is different from the linear process previously described. In that process, because there is a handing-off of the baton after each phase, there is little integration between phases, and a bottleneck at one phase stops the whole process. Under the rugby process, the phases overlap, enabling the team to continue to work on a later stage in the process even if there is a holdup in an earlier stage.

Multilearning

Members of these teams stay in close touch with external market conditions and continually learn from each other. This learning is transmitted across different levels (individual, group, and company) and functions (hence the term *multilearning*). Marketing people learn from engineers and vice versa.

Subtle Control

The project teams are not left totally alone. Senior management affects the process in a variety of ways, from choosing the people for the team to establishing an evaluation and reward system based on the performance of the group.

Transfer of Learning

An important by-product of this process is the transfer of learning throughout the organization. Some of this is from project team to team. In some cases, the whole company learns from one project team's experiences. As a result of this transfer of learning, many of the companies using this approach have been successful in significantly reducing their cycle time for developing new products.

The Target Costing Approach

With the traditional linear new-product development process, the retail price (or price to the customer) is set near the end of the process. Various price scenarios are used to perform the economic analyses necessary to screen product concepts and prototypes. Final manufacturing costs, a key input into many companies' pricing decisions, are not known until the design specifications are finalized and the size of the production run is known.

An alternative approach starts with the estimated price that the customers in the target segment are willing to pay. Before a company launches a new product, the ideal selling price must be determined, the feasibility of meeting that price assessed, and costs controlled in order to produce the product that can be sold at the target price. This process is called **target costing.**[9] Although a benefit of this approach is a decreased likelihood that low-margin products will be introduced, target costing ensures that market feedback is brought back into the development process right from the beginning.

target costing
in new product development, an alternative approach in which the ideal selling price is determined first, the feasibility of meeting that price is assessed, and costs are controlled in order to produce the product that can be sold at the target price

The steps of the approach are fairly straightforward. The company first researches its markets and segments and determines which it will target. It then calculates what price people are willing to pay in each segment it has chosen in order for the product to be successful. Subsequently, the company determines the levels of quality and functionality that are necessary to meet customer needs, given the target prices. Finally, the company arranges the sourcing of materials and the production and delivery processes that will enable it to achieve the target cost and profit margin at the desired price.

Figure 8.4 illustrates the target costing process. The leftmost circles designate the customer-based research that serves as the foundation for the target costing method. From this research, the quality and functionality targets emerge, as does the price target. Given the price, the organization must determine what its profit margin must be to reach corporate goals (the box labeled "Corporate Financial Requirements"). This then produces the target manufacturing cost. In other words, $C = P - M$, where C (cost) is determined by subtracting the target profit margin per unit (M) from the target price (P). Note the difference from the traditional approach, whereby profit would be determined after a price is set that covers the manufacturing cost (or service delivery cost) at a sufficiently high level to satisfy corporate requirements, or, in symbolic form, ($M = P - C$). Superimposed (top part of the figure) on these target costs are the expected costs from the current manufacturing process. The design challenge then becomes closing of the gap between the target and expected costs.

One of the by-products of the target costing approach is that it forces customers to consider what they are willing to pay for product improvements or design innovations. If the cost of the innovation is greater than the economic value to the customer, it would not be recovered in the price. Here are three examples:[10]

- One of Boeing's customers requested heated floors. Before adopting the target costing approach, Boeing would accept most customers' demands. The company now prices airline options separately. After the customer found out that it would cost more than $1 million to add heated floors, the request was rescinded.
- Chrysler used value analysis to determine which of several lighting options to add. After looking at the cost relative to the price it could charge, the company decided to add new interior control lighting but not lighting under the hood.
- Caterpillar set the target cost for a new product at 94.6 percent of a comparable model given the price it could charge for it. A cost improvement team was then assembled from product design, manufacturing engineering, production, marketing, and purchasing to determine how to close the gap.

Figure 8.4

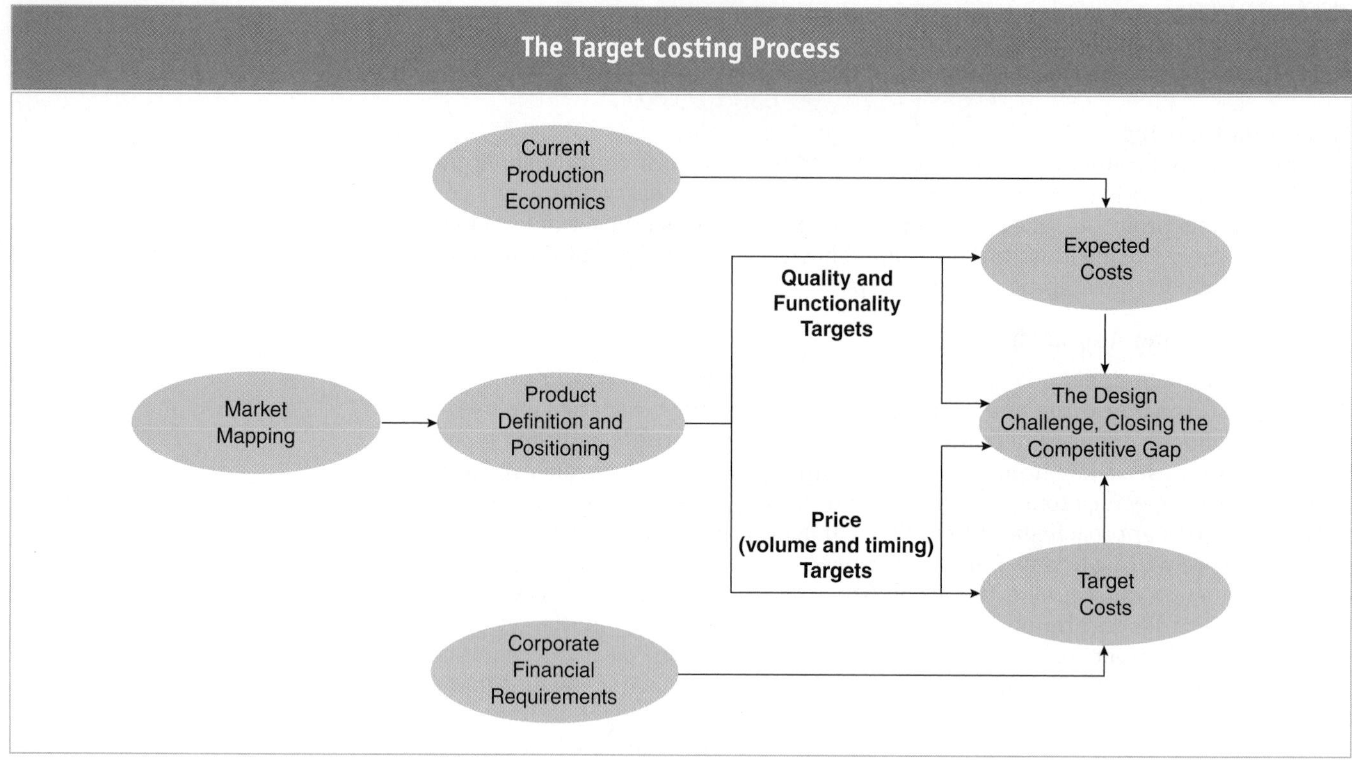

Source: Robin Cooper and W. Bruce Chew (1996), "Control Tomorrow's Costs through Today's Designs," *Harvard Business Review*, January–February, p. 95. Copyright © 1996 by the President and Fellows of Harvard College. Reprinted by permission.

Steps in the New-Product Development Process

Although the three approaches to developing new products are different in concept, they all require the basic steps noted in Figure 8.3. What varies is the sequencing of the activities. Even in the rugby and target costing approaches, new idea concepts must be generated, economic analyses and forecasts of the concepts must be made, products must move from concept to design and prototype stages, and the products launched. Therefore, in this section, we cover some of these major areas in more detail.

New-Product Concept Generation

A distinction can be made between two kinds of new product concepts—those that are provided by others, or ready-made, and those that are generated by some managed creative process.

Sources of Ready-Made Concepts

Figure 8.5 shows the major internal and external sources of new-product ideas in this category.

A variety of employees can be internal sources of new product ideas. Obviously, your own R&D department is an excellent source—that is what they are paid to do. In addition, many employees have customer contact through salespeople, customer service representatives, marketing managers conducting focus groups, and manufacturing personnel. Most companies today encourage suggestions from employees about new products, even if they are not in the job categories mentioned. For many products and services, employees are often customers as well and can therefore spot new product opportunities as well as external customers can.

lead users
the first buyers of an innovation in industrial marketing situations; also called innovators

Customers and other end-users are logical external sources of new-product ideas because they want the benefits that products and services seek to fulfill. Normally, new-product ideas can emanate from focus and user group discussions. However, in some cases, customers will simply contact the company with suggestions. Customers who help companies innovate are called **lead users** (see also Chapter 5 in the context of the

Figure 8.5

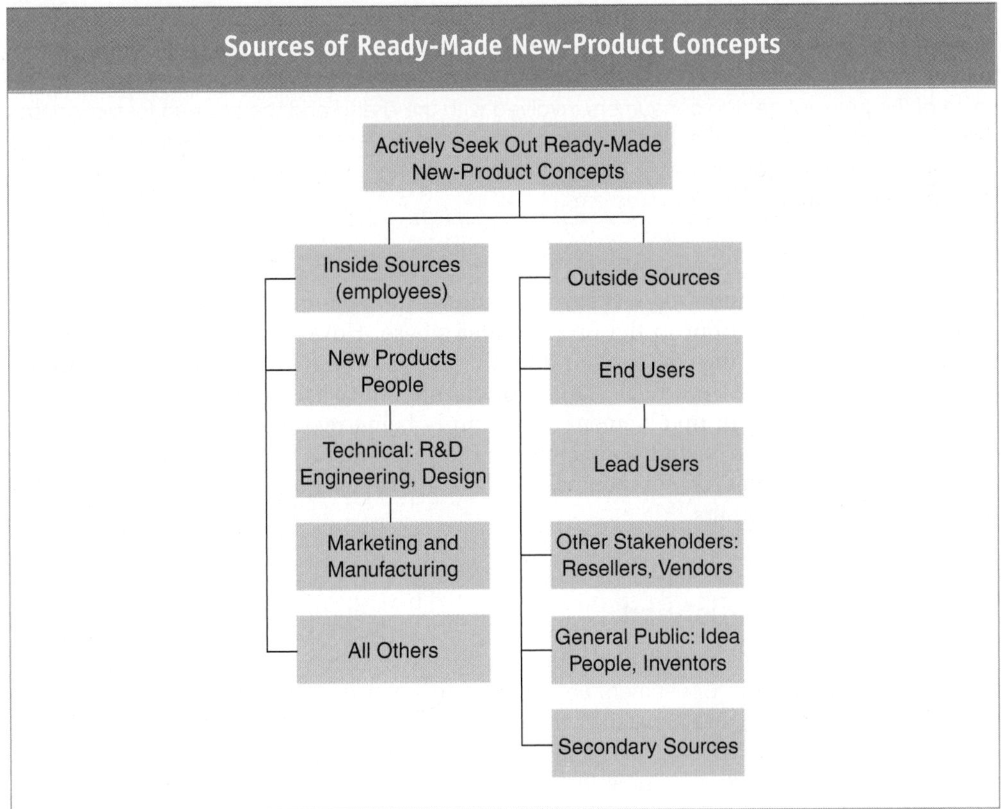

Source: C. Merle Crawford and C. Anthony DiBenedetto (2000), *New Products Management,* 6th ed. (Boston: Irwin/McGraw-Hill), p. 83. Reproduced with permission of the McGraw-Hill Companies.

diffusion of innovations) because they are interested in both helping companies innovate and in being the first to adopt new products. However, companies are discovering more and more that customers are the best source of new-product ideas. This has been called the "democratizing" of innovation.[11]

Application Virgin Mobile

Virgin Mobile has explicitly designed its products and brand of cell phones to appeal to teenagers and young adults.[12] The youth target group has its own challenges due to its constantly changing tastes. However, in the cellular business, an additional challenge is that only 7 percent picked their service without parental involvement. Given that the adult market is saturated, the company decided to take a risk and become the "MTV" of cell phone companies by going around the adults and targeting the youth market.

As a result, the company invited about 2,000 of its customers to serve as "Virgin Insiders," who were asked to help the company design one of its newest phones, the Flasher V7. The company thought a solid white color would complement its iPods. However, the "Insiders" thought that the phones looked plastic with a copycat design. The company thought that Virgin red would be a good color. The young customers thought that blue was better (with a silver "interior" of the clamshell design). The company thought a picture-album feature for the camera's digital photos would be attractive. The customers preferred a system that permitted easier downloads from the camera to blogs and their computers and bypassed the album.

Application Levi's 501

In today's online environment, many companies are employing Internet-based user groups, their home Web sites, social networking sites, blogs, and other technologies to bring their customers into the product development process.

In 2008, Levi's ran a user-submitted design contest called Project 501 through Levi.com.[13] The contest was launched on the TV show *Project Runway* and through an online campaign targeted to women. Word-of-mouth marketing on blogs and social networks were major drivers of awareness of the campaign, resulting in 2,000 design submissions, 134,000 unique visitors to Levi.com, and almost 19,000 new registered users. Interestingly, the company experienced some of the pains of getting consumers involved with the brand and the ensuing loss of control noted in Chapter 7. Once they had chosen a winner, there were some very negative comments from people who did not win. Levi's decided to leave the negative comments on the site and let the brand community police the problem.

co-creation
using people outside of the organization to help develop new product ideas

The Virgin Mobile and Levi's examples indicate how companies can mobilize their consumers to provide input to the product idea phase. However, sometimes customers are either mobilized by the company or do it themselves and then work together with the company to develop new products. This is often referred to as **co-creation**.[14] Co-creation is a much deeper level of involvement than simply being recruited as part of a panel or competition because the customers become active participants in the innovation process. Some notable examples of companies that are active users of co-creation are Nike, Starbucks, and many others.[15]

Application Crushpad

Crushpad is a San Jose–based company that allows customers to make their own wine (www.crushpadwine.com). Consumers can have as much or as little input into the process as they wish—from growing and monitoring the grapes; to picking, crushing, and fermenting the grapes; to aging the wine; and finally, to choosing the packaging. This provides the deep involvement with the company that is the hallmark of co-creation. Crushpad also allows customers to interact with other customers by allowing them to create their own Web sites, enabling community interactions through connecting with wine enthusiasts and blogs, and by sponsoring community events.[16]

Application Lego

Lego's organization for developing new products has five distinct groups:[17]

1. The Executive Innovation Governance Group. This group determines the company's innovation goals and strategies, allocates resources, and evaluates results.
2. Functional Groups. These create business processes from sales to manufacturing and supply chain management to support the innovation efforts.
3. Concept Lab. This part of the organization develops the alternative new-product concepts and play experiences.
4. Product Marketing and Development (PMD). This group performs the actual product development and "go to market" strategy (i.e., the commercialization stage shown in Figure 8.3).
5. Community, Education, and Direct (CED). This group supports customer communities and taps them for new product ideas.

The company extensively used the CED group in developing Lego Games, board games that players construct from classic LEGO bricks. It is planned that the CED will support sales through LEGO stores and online retailers and will form an online community around the product.

Other important external groups are channel members, vendors and suppliers, competitors, and independent inventors. Channel members have many customer contacts and are valuable for collecting information from the marketplace. As we noted in Chapter 6, many companies perform extensive analyses of competitors' products, looking for valuable information such as strengths and weaknesses. The invention industry is large, with many people developing new-product ideas and then selling them to larger companies or obtaining venture capital and building their own companies.

Managing the Creative Process

Although there has been an increase in the number of courses offered in university business curricula on creativity, the creative process is still difficult to understand, predict, and manage. Companies may set up creative thinking groups or pay consultants to manage the process for them. Creative group methods generally involve a process in which group members are encouraged to think and speak freely outside the normal boundaries of their jobs.

One of the most common approaches to group creative thinking is *brainstorming.* In this approach, group members try to generate a large number of diverse ideas without criticism from other members. Variations on brainstorming exist, but all these methods have the following common elements:

- Openness and participation.
- Encouraging many and diverse ideas.
- Building on each other's ideas.
- A problem orientation.
- Using a leader to guide the discussion.

These groups typically do not involve customers. Many experts believe that relying on customers for new products, particularly true innovations, dooms one to failure because of their limited ability to see into the future and conceptualize what could be.[18] Studies are being done to try to better understand what management processes can be applied to the problem of the development of radical rather than incremental innovations.

Application | Using Online Collaboration Tools

The managers at Jim Beam Brands Worldwide were getting burned out on the usual approaches for new-product ideas.[19] The cordials market is very fashion conscious, with apple flavors popular in one year and mocha the next. To keep up with flavor fads, the brand director and a team composed of marketing, sales, and packaging managers, as well as professional bartenders, would get together once or twice each year to try to recreate the huge success of Jim Beam's DeKuyper Sour Apple Pucker.

The managers decided to try Synectics' InSync Web-based creativity tool that stimulates and guides brainstorming and allows this activity to occur at any time, from anywhere. Because participants are anonymous, they do not have to worry about looking stupid for coming up with funny ideas and names. Without that fear factor, innovative ideas can be tossed out and built upon. Once the ideas are out, participants (usually about eight) pick their favorite ideas, again anonymously. InSync tallies and ranks the ideas. In this instance, Jim Beam obtained dozens of new-product ideas.

Screening New-Product Concepts

To reduce the number of concepts to a manageable size and cut it down to those that have good prospects for success, a variety of marketing research methods have been developed to enable you to screen the concepts by attempting to forecast ultimate demand.

Concept Testing

The initial test for most new products involves getting customer reactions to the product concept. The main purposes of a concept test are to choose the most promising from a set of alternatives, get an initial notion of the commercial prospects of a concept, find out who is most interested in the concept, and indicate what direction further development work should take. The subjects used in these tests should be taken from the target segments, if possible.

The most common approach is to present customers with a verbal or written statement of the product idea and then record their reactions. Recently, many researchers have chosen to include physical mockups and advertising statements in the concept test. These are really prototype or prototype/concept tests. The data gathered are both diagnostic ("Why do you like or dislike the product?") and predictive ("Would you buy it if it cost $x?"). Including a concrete "Would you buy?" question is crucial if the results are to be useful from a predictive perspective. The data collection procedures fall into the following three major categories:

1. **Surveys.** Surveys are useful for getting large samples for projection purposes. On the other hand, it is often difficult to effectively convey a concept in a survey, especially one conducted via mail or the Internet.
2. **Focus groups.** The strength of focus groups is their diagnostic power in that they can be used to get detailed discussions of various aspects of the concept. As predictors of actual sales, they are fairly inaccurate because of their small sample sizes.
3. **Demonstrations.** A popular way to present a concept is to gather together a group of customers, present them with a description of the new product, and record their reactions. Questions typically asked are:
   - Do they understand the concept?
   - Do they believe the concept?
   - Is the concept different from other products in an important way?
   - If it is different, is the difference beneficial?
   - Do they like or dislike the concept? Why?
   - What could be done to make the product more acceptable?
   - How would they like to see the product (color, size, other features)?
   - Would they buy it?
   - What price would they expect to pay for it?
   - What would their usage be in terms of volume, purpose, channels for purchasing, and other factors?

The purpose of the concept tests can also vary. The most basic concept test is a screening test that describes several concepts briefly and asks subjects for an overall evaluation. Screening tests are used to reduce the concepts under consideration to a manageable number. Next, concept generation tests (often involving focus groups) are used to refine the concept statements. This is typically followed by concept evaluation tests. These tests are based on larger samples and attempt to quantitatively assess demand for the concept based on samples of 200 to 300. Such tests are typically done competitively in the sense that other new concepts or existing products are evaluated at the same time.[20]

Technology has helped to speed up the concept testing process as well as lower the cost. Web-based concept tests have become popular with marketing research companies like NFO WorldGroup and Merwyn Research Inc. because they offer online concept testing platforms that expose a selected group of target customers to concepts and receive immediate feedback. Two problems with this approach are the representativeness of the sample and the possibility that the concepts can be leaked to competitors. This happened to Procter & Gamble when new concepts for extending its Crest brand were leaked anonymously on the Yahoo! Finance message board.[21] The company now does most of its concept testing online. Companies such as Google, Walmart, and Harrah's perform experiments where they create different versions of Web site layouts, store designs, or gaming promotions and see which one produces the best results.[22] Other sophisticated online approaches have been suggested that use animation and advanced graphics.[23]

Concept Testing Using Conjoint Analysis

Conjoint analysis is a popular marketing research method that enables you to determine how customers value different levels of product attributes (e.g., a 40-gigabyte versus 80-gigabyte hard drive) from theoretical profiles or concepts. The basic idea is that by rank-ordering different product concepts (combinations of attributes), you can infer not only the most popular concept, but also the utility customers derive from specific values of the attributes. This aids management in further refining the concept.

A classic example is from the carpet and upholstery spot remover product category.[24] The following attributes were analyzed as the main part of the concept test:

- Package design (A, B, C).
- Brand names (K2R, Glory, Bissell).

- Price ($1.19, $1.39, $1.59).
- Good Housekeeping seal of approval (yes or no).
- Money-back guarantee (yes or no).

A product concept is one combination of all five attributes (e.g., package design A, brand name K2R, $1.19 price, with a Good Housekeeping seal, and with a money-back guarantee). There are 108 such theoretical concepts if all combinations of attributes and their levels are combined (3 × 3 × 3 × 2 × 2). However, it is unlikely that any potential customer would be able to sensibly rank-order all 108 different concepts. Thus marketing researchers have developed methods for reducing the number of combinations while retaining as much of the original information from the 108 combinations as possible.

Table 8.4 shows the data obtained from one subject. The first five columns of the table represent the different concepts (there are 18 in all). The last column is the respondent's rank-ordering of the concepts. This respondent most preferred the combination C, Bissell, $1.19, Good Housekeeping seal, and money-back guarantee. This by itself is useful information in the new-product development process. However, Table 8.5 is more informative because it shows the utilities for the different levels of the attributes and, by examining the spread of the utilities, the overall importance weights of the attributes. Assuming that this respondent is representative of the market, the concept can be further refined: package design B, the Bissell brand name, a low price, and both the Good Housekeeping seal and money-back guarantee are more highly valued than the other levels of their respective attributes. In addition, by examining the size of the largest utility of a level, you can roughly infer the importance of the attributes. In this case, package design, price, and money-back guarantee appear to be the most important attributes.

Table 8.4

Conjoint Analysis Illustration

Data Collected

Package Design	Brand Name	Price	Good Housekeeping Seal?	Money-Back Guarantee?	Respondent's Evaluation (rank number)
A	K2R	1.19	No	No	13
A	Glory	1.39	No	Yes	11
A	Bissell	1.59	Yes	No	17
B	K2R	1.39	Yes	Yes	2
B	Glory	1.59	No	No	14
B	Bissell	1.19	No	No	3
C	K2R	1.59	No	Yes	12
C	Glory	1.19	Yes	No	7
C	Bissell	1.39	No	No	9
A	K2R	1.59	Yes	No	18
A	Glory	1.19	No	Yes	8
A	Bissell	1.39	No	No	15
B	K2R	1.19	No	No	4
B	Glory	1.39	Yes	No	6
B	Bissell	1.59	No	Yes	5
C	K2R	1.39	No	No	10
C	Glory	1.59	No	No	16
C	Bissell	1.19	Yes	Yes	1

Source: Paul Green and Yoram Wind (1975), "New Way to Measure Consumers' Judgements," *Harvard Business Review,* 53 (July–August), p. 108.

Table 8.5

Conjoint Analysis Illustration Results

Feature	Utility
Package design	
A	0.1
B	1.0
C	0.6
Brand name	
K2R	0.3
Glory	0.2
Bissell	0.5
Price	
1.19	1.0
1.39	0.7
1.59	0.1
Good Housekeeping seal	
Yes	0.3
No	0.2
Money-back guarantee	
Yes	0.7
No	0.2

Source: Paul Green and Yoram Wind (1975), "New Way to Measure Consumers' Judgements," *Harvard Business Review,* 53 (July–August), p. 110.

product definition
a stage in the new product development process in which concepts are translated into actual products for further testing based on interactions with customers

concept development
making further refinements to a new product concept

primary needs
the main strategic benefits that the product or service attempts to deliver

secondary needs
more tactical needs associated with the primary perceptual benefit

tertiary needs
a type of customer need considered in new product development; the operational needs related to the engineering aspect of actually making the product

Product Definition/Concept Development

Through concept testing and conjoint analysis, you now have an idea of what concepts appear to have the potential for success. The next stage in the new-product development process is to translate the concepts into actual products for further testing, based on interactions with customers. This is usually called the **product definition** or **concept development** phase.

The key to successful new-product design is building in quality from the beginning.[25] Historically, quality has meant quality control, that is, minimizing the number of defects in products coming off the production line. However, quality has come to mean incorporating customer feedback into the development process as early as possible in order to make products that meet their expectations. Good design then means not only high levels of functional quality but also not overengineering the product by having more features than the customers really want or need.

Customer needs are divided into three types.

1. **Primary needs** are the main strategic benefits that the product or service attempts to deliver.
2. **Secondary needs** are more tactical needs associated with the primary perceptual benefit.
3. **Tertiary needs** are the operational needs related to the engineering aspect of making the product.

Table 8.6 is an example of this hierarchy of needs in the context of a car door. In this illustration, the primary need "good appearance" has three secondary needs and six tertiary needs. As you can see, the needs get more specific moving from left to right.

Often, new-product designers obtain several hundred tertiary needs from discussions with customers. This voice-of-the-customer (VOC) approach is usually implemented by

Table 8.6

Hierarchy of Needs		
Primary Needs	**Secondary Needs**	**Tertiary Needs**
Good operation and use	Easy to open and close door	Easy to close from outside
		Stays open on a hill
		Easy to open from the outside
		Doesn't kick back
		Easy to close from inside
	Isolation	Doesn't leak in rain
		No road noise
		Doesn't leak in car wash
		No wind noise
		Doesn't drop water when open
		Snow doesn't fall in car
		Doesn't rattle
	Arm rest	Soft, comfortable
		In right position
Good appearance	Interior trim	Material won't fade
		Attractive look
	Clean	Easy to clean
		No grease from door
		Stay clean
	Fit	Uniform gaps between panels

Source: John R. Hauser and Don Clausing (1998), "The House of Quality," *Harvard Business Review,* May–June, p. 65.

asking customers to develop short phrases in their own words about the benefits and needs of, for example, a car door. Table 8.6 lists only 20 of the more than 100 that were obtained for the car door.

Some attributes may conflict in terms of the ultimate design of the product. For example, in a multi-media enabled smartphone, customers may want the keys to be sufficiently large for typing but the device to be small enough to fit into a shirt pocket. The VOC approach involves asking customers to rate the tertiary needs on some scale of importance to permit the design engineers to better understand the trade-offs customers are willing to make. In addition, the customers are asked for their perceptions of the product they currently own and competitors' offerings on these tertiary needs. Figure 8.6 continues the car door example and shows a typical importance weighting and perception measurement. In this case, the customer places a much greater weight on the door being easy to close from the outside than on the lack of road noise. In addition, the customer rated competitors' cars higher than his or her existing car in terms of the most important benefit.

In addition to the customer needs, it is necessary to build into the process the physical characteristics of the product necessary to meet those needs. This is the link between customer needs and engineering characteristics. Continuing the car door illustration, some of the engineering characteristics for the needs shown in Figure 8.6 are given in Table 8.7.

How are the customer needs and engineering characteristics linked together? Figure 8.7 is an example of the **house of quality**. The horizontal customer needs are linked with the vertical engineering characteristics through the use of interfunctional teams, much like those specified in the rugby approach described earlier in this chapter. This use of

house of quality
a matrix used in new product development that illustrates how customer needs and engineering characteristics influence one another

Figure 8.6

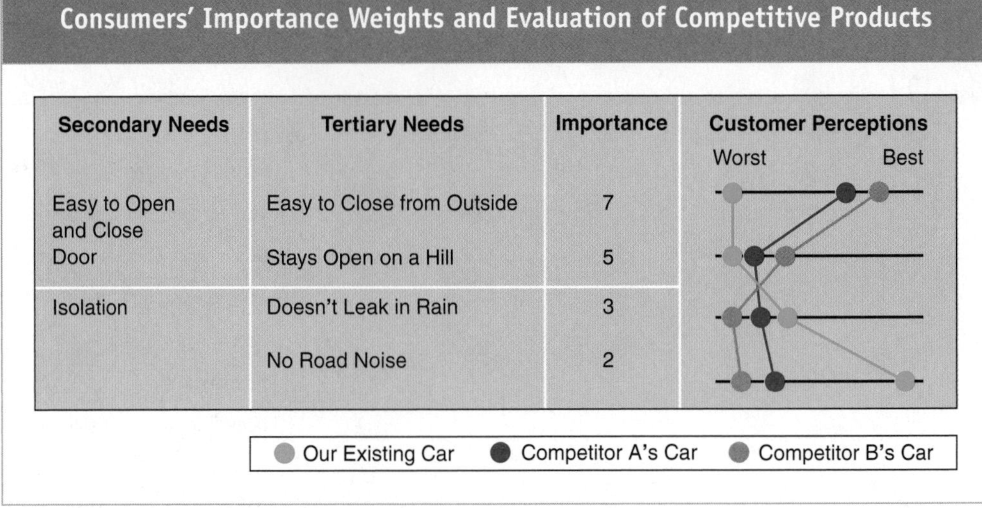

Consumers' Importance Weights and Evaluation of Competitive Products
Secondary Needs
Tertiary Needs
Importance
Customer Perceptions
Worst
Best
Easy to Open and Close Door
Easy to Close from Outside
7
Stays Open on a Hill
5
Isolation
Doesn't Leak in Rain
3
No Road Noise
2
Our Existing Car
Competitor A's Car
Competitor B's Car

Source: John R. Hauser and Glen L. Urban (1993), *Design and Marketing of New Products,* 2nd ed. (Upper Saddle River, NJ: Prentice Hall), p. 38. © 1993. Reproduced by permission of Pearson Education, Inc.

interfunctional teams and VOC is called quality function deployment (QFD) and has been applied successfully in Japan.

The house of quality takes its name from the distinctive shape of the relationships between customer needs and engineering characteristics. In the center of the house, the matrix represents how each engineering characteristic affects each need. For example, decreasing the amount of energy necessary to close the door (the first column) increases the perception that the door is easier to close from the outside (the first row). These assessments are made by the interfunctional design team, possibly based on primary marketing research. The bottom rows are the physical or objective measurements on the engineering characteristics. The attic or roof of the house indicates the interrelationships between the characteristics. For example, the door seal resistance has a strong negative impact on the peak closing force.

To see how the house of quality affects the design, we can take the physical evidence that the doors of the current car are more difficult to close than those of the competitors (11 foot-pounds versus 9 and 9.5). The engineering characteristics affecting customer perceptions of this need are the energy to close the door, the peak closing force, and the door seal resistance (top row of the matrix). Because the first two characteristics have a strong positive relationship to customer perceptions, these are chosen by the engineers for improvement. However, by inspecting the attic, you can see that other characteristics are affected by changing the energy to close the door, such as the door opening energy and the peak closing force. This gives an indication of what other characteristics of the door will be affected by changing the energy to close the door. The team then sets a target of 7.5 foot-pounds (bottom row) for the new door.

Table 8.7

List of Engineering Characteristics for a Car Door

Open-Close Effort	Sealing Insulation
Energy to close door	Door seal resistance
Check force on level ground	Acoustic transmission, window
Check force on 10-degree slope	Road noise reduction
Energy to open door	Water resistance
Peak closing force	

Source: Glen L. Urban and John R. Hauser (1993), *Design and Marketing of New Products,* 2nd ed. (Upper Saddle River, NJ: Prentice Hall), p. 338. © 1993. Reproduced by permission of Pearson Education, Inc.

Figure 8.7

The House of Quality

Relationships
- ✓ Strong Positive
- ✓ Medium Positive
- × Medium Negative
- ✗ Strong Negative

Legend: ● Our Car ● A's Car ● B's Car — Customer Perceptions 1 2 3 4 5

Customer Attributes		Relative Importance	Open-Close Effort: – Energy to close door	+ Check force on level ground	+ Check force on 10° slope	– Energy to open door	– Peak closing force	•••	Sealing and Insulation: + Door seal resistance	+ Acoustic transmission, window	+ Road noise reduction	+ Water resistance	•••
Easy to Open and Close Door	Easy to close from outside	7	✓				✓		×				
	Stays open on a hill	5		✓	✓								
	Easy to open from outside	3				✓			✓				
	Doesn't kick open	3		✓	✓	✓			×				
	⋮												
Isolation	Doesn't leak in rain	3							✓			✓	
	No road noise	2							✓	✓	✓		
	⋮												
Objective Measures	*Measurement units*		*ft-lb*	*lb*	*lb*	*ft-lb*	*lb*	—	*ft-lb*		*db*	*pal*	
	Our car door		11	12	6	10	18		3	.10	9	70	
	A's car door		9	12	6	9	13		2	.10	5	60	
	B's car door		9.5	11	7	11	14		2	.10	6	60	
Technical difficulty			4	5	1	1	3		1	3	3	5	
Imputed importance (%) (all total 100%)			10	6	4	9	1		6	4	2	3	
Estimated cost (%) (all total 100%)			5	2	2	9	5		6	6	9	2	
Targets			7.5 *ft-lb*	9 *lb*	6 *lb*	7.5 *ft-lb*	12 *lb*		3 *ft-lb*	.10	9 *db*	70 *pal*	

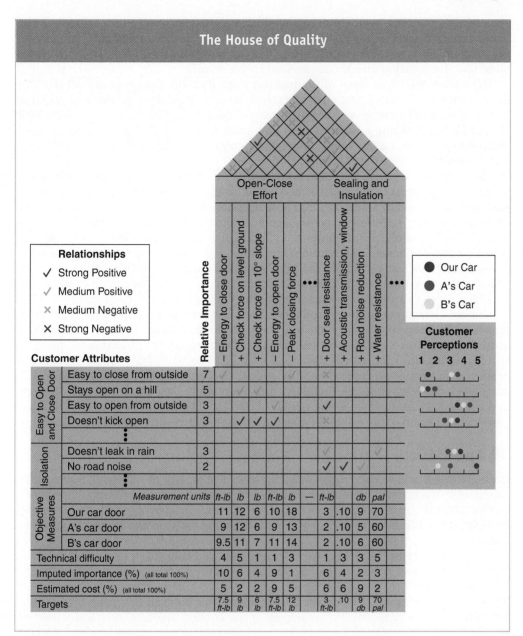

Source: John R. Hauser and Don Clausing (1988), "The House of Quality," *Harvard Business Review*, 66, p. 72.

Some writers have argued that in the case of high-technology products and services, it is important that the product definition not be locked in too soon.[26] This is because customer tastes, competition, or other factors characteristic of such markets could make the definition obsolete by the time the product is ready for launch. Deliberate product definition weighs the costs and benefits of delaying the final specifications closer to product launch. Unfortunately, in such markets, it is difficult to know exactly when the right time comes. Thus, it is not uncommon for new products in high-tech markets to have bugs and other defects, which early adopters of such products often must tolerate.

Business Analysis: Forecasting Demand

Once the product has been designed with the customer in mind, a variety of approaches can be used to forecast demand, a key part of the business analysis.

Product Use Tests

This type of research consists of producing the product and getting potential customers to try it.[27] The purposes of a product test are to uncover product shortcomings, evaluate commercial prospects, evaluate alternative formulations, uncover the appeal of the product to various market segments, and, ideally, gain ideas for other elements of the marketing program. Such tests may be either branded (best for estimating sales) or unbranded or blind (best for focusing directly on physical formulation).

There are three major types of product use tests. Initially, such tests are usually conducted with small samples of customers, sometimes even only with employees. These initial tests are diagnostic and are directed toward eliminating serious problems with the product and getting a rough idea of how good it is compared to competitive products. This phase also allows the company to find out how the product is actually used and to possibly change the value proposition.

The second type of use test includes a limited time horizon trial in which customers are given the product to use and are then asked for their reactions to it. At the end of the trial, the company may simulate a purchase occasion. This may consist of a hypothetical "Would you buy?" question or, better, an actual choice situation in which the customer either chooses one of a set of products, including the new product (usually at a reduced price), or simply chooses to buy or not buy the new product. To get a meaningful result many researchers use a stratified sample. The strata are usually either product category usage rate (heavy, medium, light, none) or brand usually used. This stratification ensures adequate sample size in each segment to predict the popularity of the product.

The most elaborate form of product use test requires placement of the product in homes (or business settings for industrial products) for an extended period. For packaged goods this period is usually about two months. The advantage of this extended period is that the results allow for both the wear-out of initial expectations and the development of problems that manifest themselves only over time (e.g., food that goes stale). Subjects complete before-and-after questionnaires and maintain a diary of actual use of the new and competitive products over the period of the test. The inclusion of an actual choice situation at the end of the test helps give the results a bottom-line orientation.

Application ReplayTV

ReplayTV makes and markets digital video recorders that replace the analog VCR with a hard disk drive.[28] The company competes with TiVo and is marketed through DirectTV, the satellite communications company. When it first entered the market, management decided to use a company called BetaSphere (now VOConline), which organizes early product testing groups via the Internet.

The first group to test the product were "hackers," whose job was to take a detailed look at the machine. They looked for hard-to-find, idiosyncratic bugs in both the unit and the remote control. Next came compatibility testing. BetaSphere obtained a group of geographically dispersed customers with a wide variety of TV models and other electronic devices. This group just wanted to record their favorite programs. Replay wanted to find out how "average" consumers used the product and what they liked and did not like about it. By sending out a survey by e-mail, the company received responses within a day or two. The software automatically tallied the responses and provided managerially useful reports to management online. Thus, ReplayTV was able to quickly receive information about the pluses and minuses of the product before it went to market with a full-scale rollout.

Market Tests

The ultimate in realism is a market test. Despite the problems mentioned earlier in this chapter, test markets are popular for testing all kinds of products and services. The purposes of such a test are to predict sales and profits from the prospective new product launch and for testing, marketing, distribution, and production skills before full-scale operations begin. Projections to national or international levels are typically made for both share and actual sales. The major measures to track are:

- Trial rate.
- Repeat rate (for frequently purchased products).
- Usage rate or number bought per customer.

In addition, awareness, attitudes, and distribution are usually monitored. Given these measures, a sales projection can be made.

In designing a market test, it is important to delineate clearly what information is to be gathered and why before proceeding. Several decisions must be made:

- **Action standards.** Standards for evaluating the results should be set up in advance. These standards should specify when the various possible decisions (e.g., stop the test, continue the test, revamp the product, go national) will be implemented.
- **Where.** The choice of where to test market is a serious problem. For consumer products, most market tests are done in two or three cities. The test is not designed to try out numerous strategies with, at most, two to three alternatives being used. Cities are chosen on the basis of representativeness of the population, the ability of the firm to gain distribution and media exposure in the area, and availability of good research suppliers in the area. Also areas that are self-contained in terms of media (especially TV) are preferred. The result is that certain medium-sized cities are often chosen, such as Syracuse, New York; Fresno, California; and Fort Wayne, Indiana. Finding cities with a good ethnic balance has been a problem for test marketing. In 2004, Acxiom Corporation, a database services company, ranked the top 150 U.S. metropolitan statistical areas (MSAs) for their suitability as test market cities with the top five being Albany, New York; Rochester, New York; Greensboro, North Carolina; Birmingham, Alabama; and Syracuse, New York.[29]
- **What to do?** The best test market designers are careful to make the effort in the geographic area proportional to what would reasonably be expected in a national launch. Note that what is meant by effort is not just budget as the goal is to make distribution, price, and so forth as representative as possible. However, typically the effort afforded to the product is somewhat greater than the comparable national effort.
- **How long?** This question does not have an easy answer. Obviously, a longer run gives more information to the marketing manager, but it also costs more and gives competitors more time to formulate a counterattack. Consumer packaged goods may stay in test markets for 6 to 12 months in order to include several purchase cycles, ensuring that repeat usage as well as trial can be assessed accurately.
- **How much?** For a typical consumer-packaged good, test marketing costs run more than $1 million. Advertising and promotion typically account for 65 to 70 percent of the budget, with the rest of the budget divided between information gathering and analysis and miscellaneous administrative and other expenses.
- **Information gathering.** During a test market, a variety of information is gathered, most of it related to actual sales. In monitoring sales, it is important to recognize that a large percentage of first-year factory sales represent a one-time stocking up by the channels of distribution, not sales to final customers. The three major data sources are actual sales plus distribution and promotion; surveys that measure awareness, attitudes, and similar variables; and panels that report actual purchases and allow monitoring of trial and repeat rates.

Despite its limitations, test marketing new products often provides useful information to marketing managers. For example, in 1997, Unilever, the giant British/Dutch consumer products company, developed a new ice cream snack called the Winner Taco, a taco-shaped wafer filled with ice cream and caramel, covered with chocolate and peanuts.[30] The product was developed at the company's innovation center in Rome and was intended to become a top-selling brand alongside its better-known Cornetto, Magnum, and Solero ice cream brands. As part of the new-product development process, the product was first test marketed in April 1997 in Italy and Holland. After overshooting Unilever sales targets by 50 percent, the product was rolled out in Spain, Germany, and Austria in February 1998 and was launched in the rest of Europe in June.

Sales Forecasting

Forecasting sales for a new product or service before it is launched and while you are going through the new-product development process is always difficult. With no actual sales data at hand, marketing managers must rely on purchase intention surveys or other qualitative methods of forecasting (see Chapter 3).

Many approaches have been developed for frequently purchased products that rely on either test market data or early data after the product is introduced. Most of these methods rely on some or all of the following factors to predict the ultimate success of the product:

- Brand awareness.
- Eventual proportion of consumers who will try the product (trial).
- Proportion of triers who repeat purchase.
- Usage rate of the product category by the eventual users.

Notice that for durable goods, trial is basically first purchase, because this may be the only purchase for several years. For frequently purchased products for which trial is easy to induce, repeat rates are the key to success.

- **Awareness.** The rationale for including awareness in a new-product forecasting model is obvious. Customers cannot purchase a product or service unless they are aware of it. Most models attempting to predict success for new, frequently purchased products either measure awareness directly through survey methods or attempt to predict it from other variables such as advertising spending and gross rating points.
- **Trial.** Like awareness, trial is tracked over time, with the objective of forecasting its ultimate level. Trial is simply the cumulative percentage of households (or companies) that have purchased the product or service at least once. Trial rates usually look like the graph in Figure 8.8, with an increase in trial up to some asymptotic value (in this case, 45 percent). You can estimate the asymptote directly by plotting the points representing trial rates over time and then using some kind of curve-fitting method. The trial rates are obtained from a panel from the test market or early in the introductory phase.
- **Repeat.** The eventual repeat rate can be estimated using the same approach as that used for trial. Of course, unlike trial, which is nondecreasing, repeat rates tend to decrease (Figure 8.9). A product cannot be successful without a high repeat rate. A high trial rate with low repeat means poor product quality, so eventually you will run out of triers. High repeat rates, even among a small number of customers, can result in a profitable product. Figure 8.10 shows the relationship between product success and repeat rates.
- **Usage rate.** This is simply an estimate of the average number of units purchased by customers. Like trial and repeat, it is derived from panels of customers measuring their actual purchasing of the product category.

Parfitt-Collins model
a simple market share forecasting model that uses an estimate of the eventual penetration rate, an estimate of the ultimate repeat rate, and an estimate of the relative product category usage rate of buyers of the new brand to determine eventual market share

An example of a simple market share forecasting model is the **Parfitt-Collins** model.[31] Although it is somewhat old, the basic concepts embodied in the model are

Figure 8.8

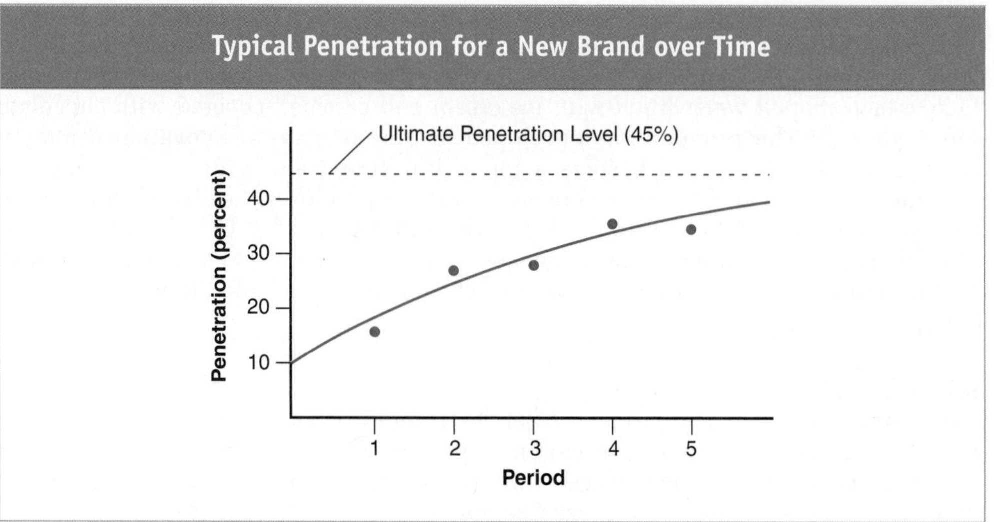

Figure 8.9

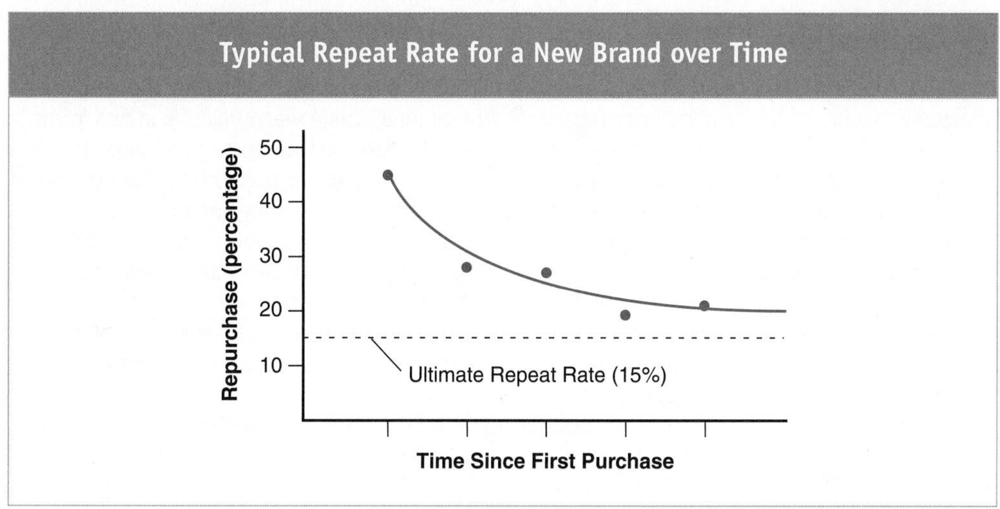

fundamentally sound and are still used today. The three key elements of the model are an estimate of the eventual penetration rate (*P*), an estimate of the ultimate repeat rate (*R*), and an estimate of the relative product category usage rate of buyers of the new brand (*U*). Eventual market share is predicted by simply multiplying the three variables together ($P \times R \times U$). Using the information from Figures 8.8 and 8.9, and assuming that users of the new product consume it at a rate that is 80 percent of the market average, the predicted share is 45 percent × 15 percent × 80 percent = 5.4 percent.

Other forecasting models use pretest market data from laboratory experiments to forecast sales. For example, ASSESSOR, owned by M/A/R/C Research, uses a simulated shopping trip following advertising exposure and an in-home use period to predict how consumers will react to a new product. Evidence has shown that the market share estimates are within one share point of the share observed in the market.[32]

Predicting the success of more radical innovations is more difficult because customers may have difficulty understanding the product and how it will benefit them. One method, called information acceleration, attempts to place potential customers in a future world and familiarize them with a product (using multimedia technology) to improve the usefulness of their responses.[33]

Figure 8.10

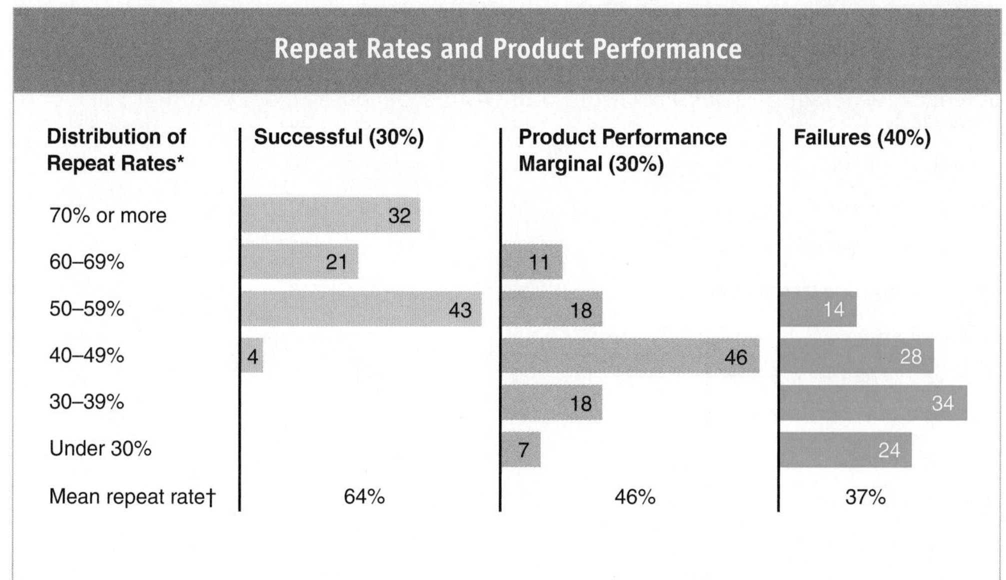

Repeat Rates and Product Performance
Distribution of Repeat Rates*
Successful (30%)
Product Performance Marginal (30%)
Failures (40%)
70% or more
60–69%
50–59%
40–49%
30–39%
Under 30%
Mean repeat rate†
32
21
43
4
64%
11
18
46
18
7
46%
14
28
34
24
37%

*Based upon 120 new products.

†Percentage of triers who repeat.

Source: NPD Research (1982), *We Make the Answers to Your Marketing Questions Perfectly Clear* (New York: NPD Research).

Application Nestlé

In 1987, Nestlé Refrigerated Food Company (NFRC) contemplated entering the market for refrigerated pasta to be sold in supermarkets.[34] At that time, pasta was available in two forms in the United States. Fresh pasta was available in specialty food stores and restaurants, but was not generally sold in supermarkets. Dry pasta was a high-volume staple item for supermarkets. Fresh pasta was considered to be of higher quality and sold at a price premium.

NFRC did not have an entry in the refrigerated food category in the United States. In 1987, the company purchased Lambert's Pasta & Cheese, a small New York–based pasta company known for its fresh pasta and imported cheeses. Lambert had developed a process that extended the shelf life of its pastas from the usual 2 to 3 days to 40 days for sales in supermarket refrigerator cases. NFRC's goal was to introduce a national brand of refrigerated pasta under the Contadina brand name.

Nestlé's new-product development process, established in the late 1980s, had seven steps:

1. Idea generation.
2. Concept screening and idea refinement.
3. Product development.
4. Quantification of volume (forecasting).
5. Test marketing.
6. Commercial evaluation.
7. Introductory tracking.

In 1987, NFRC was at the fourth stage in the development of the refrigerated pasta product. To estimate demand, NFRC used a concept testing and new-product forecasting model called BASES, owned by Nielsen. Among other things, NFRC wanted BASES to estimate first-year trial volume for pasta and sauces and simulate total year-one sales volume.

To do this, BASES completed 301 concept tests (no real product was given to the consumers) in six different cities. All respondents were women, 18 years of age and older. Some of the key findings from the concept tests are shown in Table 8.8. For example, 3 percent of the

Table 8.8

Concept Test Results: Contadina Pasta and Sauce

Item	Total (n = 301) %	Favorable (n = 224) %	Unfavorable (n = 77) %
Likes			
General variety	28	28	28
Filled variety	16	16	16
Natural/not artificial	28	30	23
Quick/fast/saves time	20	22	16
Easy to prepare/already prepared	17	20	11
Packed fresh/packed then refrigerated	6	8	1
Like small size	5	7	1
Clear package/can see what's inside	5	5	4
Like the shapes	5	5	5
Looks appetizing	4	5	1
Good/reasonable price	8	9	4
Fresh/made fresh and dated	26	27	21
Like/eat pasta	13	16	4

(continued)

Concept Test Results: Contadina Pasta and Sauce (*Continued*)

Item	Total (n = 301) %	Favorable (n = 224) %	Unfavorable (n = 77) %
Like Contadina/good name	9	11	4
Good meal/dinner	7	8	4
New/different	7	8	3
Dislikes			
Too expensive	8	3	23
Not like green/spinach color	6	5	11
Not like spinach taste	3	2	5
Not like pasta/rarely buy/eat	2	1	7
Not use this type of pasta	2	—	7
Nothing disliked	61	74	24
Concept Uniqueness			
Extremely new and different	15	17	8
Very new and different	38	41	32
Somewhat new and different	35	32	41
Slightly new and different	8	7	11
Not at all new and different	4	3	8
Mean uniqueness (5-point scale)	3.5	3.6	3.2

Source: V. Kasturi Rangan (1995), "Nestlé Refrigerated Foods: Contadina Pasta & Pizza (A)," Harvard Business School case #9-595-035, p. 20. Copyright © 1995 by the President and Fellows of Harvard College. Reprinted by permission.

women who were favorable towards the concept (224 in total) thought that the proposed price was too high (too expensive) while 23 percent of those who were unfavorable (77 in total) thought it was too expensive. The company forecasted demand based on the analysis shown in Figure 8.11.

Of the 301 women shown the concept, 24 percent indicated they definitely would buy it and 51 percent said that they probably would (see the top box of Figure 8.11). BASES then used industry shrinkage factors: 80 percent of the "definites" actually would buy and only 30 percent of the "probables" would buy. This reduced the interested total from 75 percent to 34.5 percent. It did not expect seasonality to be a factor. The 34.5 percent estimated to be interested was further reduced by the fact that the company planned an advertising expenditure so that 48 percent of the potential consumers would be made aware of the new brand. In addition, it expected distribution in stores representing 70 percent of all-commodity volume (ACV). This reduced the interested and able-to-buy number down to 11.6 percent. Multiplying this figure by the total number of U.S. households provided an estimated number of 9 million households trying and, assuming one unit per trial, 9 million trial units.

BASES then developed three different repeat purchase rates under alternative scenarios of product quality (see the bottom of Figure 8.11). Assuming 2.5 repeat purchases in the first year and a claimed (by the women exposed to the concept) average repeat transaction amount of 1.4 units, the repeat purchase volume ranged from 8.5 million units (mediocre product) to 13.9 million units (excellent product). Given NFRC's hurdle rate of 20 million units for a product to be introduced, BASES recommended that the product be launched because the total units forecasted were greater than 20 million except for the mediocre quality version. For example, for excellent quality, the forecasted amount was 9 million units from trial plus the 13.9 million units from repeat. Contadina Fresh Pasta and Sauces were rolled out nationally in the second half of 1988 and sold 30 million units in only six months; the brand sold 60 million units in 1990.

Figure 8.11

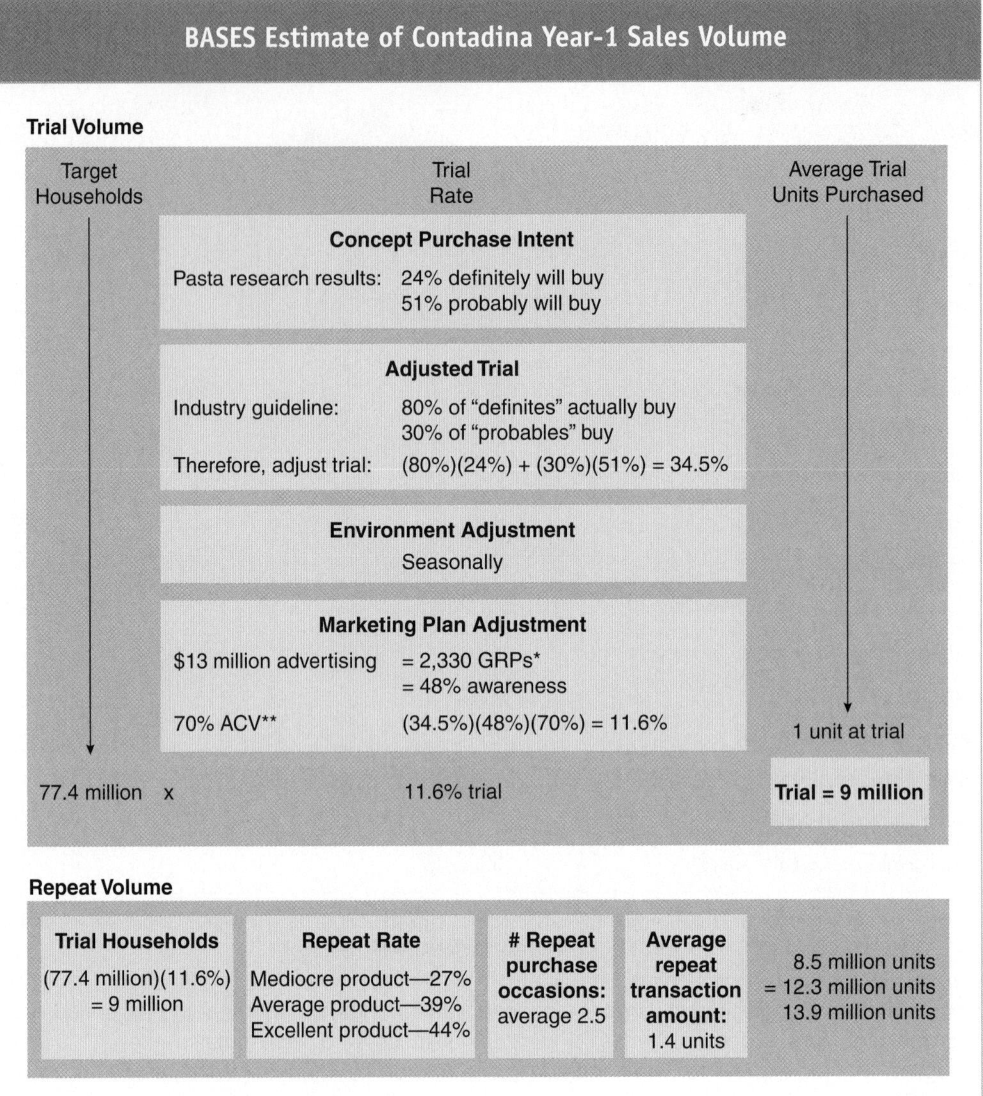

*GRPs: Gross Ratings Points (Reach x Frequency).

**ACV: All Commodity Volume, a measure of distribution coverage.

Source: V. Kasturi Rangan (1995), "Nestlé Refrigerated Foods: Contadina Pasta & Pizza (A)," Harvard Business School case #9-595-035, p. 32. Copyright © 1995 by the President and Fellows of Harvard College. Reprinted by permission.

Launching the New Product

The basics of launching a new product are similar to the description of the complete marketing strategy shown in Chapter 2. That is, you need to set an objective, develop the strategy (target market(s), competitor targets, value proposition, etc.), and plan the implementation (marketing mix).

While products fail for all of the reasons shown in Table 8.3, the implementation part of the launch is particularly important. The product has to be good, the target market has to be appropriate, a good reason to buy (value proposition) has to be established, the price has to be right, the product must be available, and a customer service organization needs to be established. Most importantly, people or organizations will not purchase a new product if they have not heard of it. Thus, many companies spend millions of dollars on the "hoopla" surrounding a new-product introduction with splashy advertising and public relations campaigns, extravaganzas in public arenas, and other programs intended to alert the public that the new product or service is here. The idea is to not only create awareness but excitement, word-of-mouth, and anticipation of owning.

Three illustrations show how significant product launches are done today with a big splash (and big money), product placements in movies, and using the Internet.

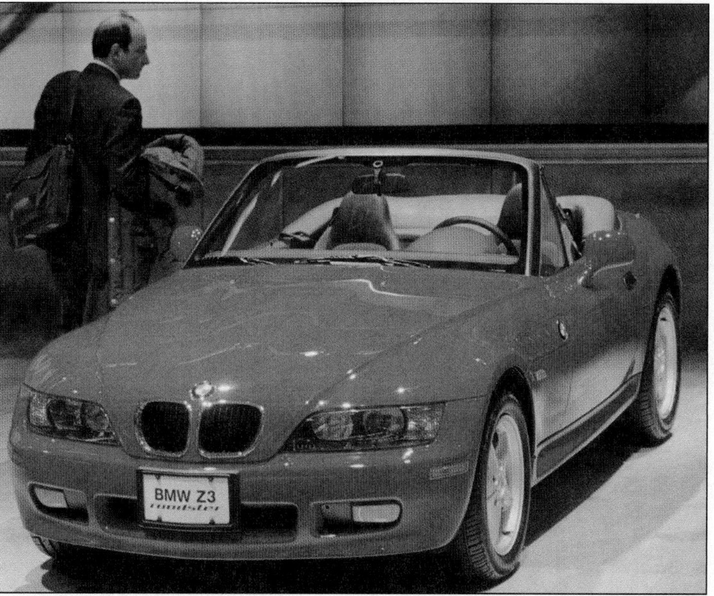

BMW used non-traditional approaches to launch the Z3.
Source: Richard Sheinwald/AP Wide World Photos

Application BMW Z3

A classic early application of online video is BMW's introduction of the Z3 roadster in 1996.[35] When BMW launched the Z3 roadster in 1996, it was the first car to be made by the company outside Germany. The car, manufactured at its new Spartanburg, South Carolina plant, was intended to show that BMW was not just a German auto company but also a global manufacturer. Could the mystique of the BMW brand, so closely related to its Bavarian heritage, survive? The goals of the launch program were to expand the BMW brand by positioning the Z3 squarely in American culture and to establish the car as a cultural icon. To do this, the company wanted to get the Z3 into everyday conversation.

As a result, it decided to use nontraditional programs to promote the launch. The cornerstone of these programs was a tie-in with the new James Bond film *GoldenEye,* starring Pierce Brosnan, which was scheduled to debut in November 1995, a full six months prior to any Z3s being available in dealers. Although the car was in the movie only for 90 seconds, by replacing the venerable Aston Martin, the company obtained a tremendous amount of publicity and awareness.

Additional elements of the launch included:

- A Neiman Marcus Christmas catalog offer of a Special Bond Edition Roadster.
- Featuring the Z3 on BMW's Web site.
- Large-scale public relations event unveiling the car in New York's Central Park.
- Appearance (by both Brosnan and the car) on Jay Leno's *Tonight Show.*
- Radio disc jockey program, where DJs would be encouraged to incorporate the Z3 into their programming.

Of course, the launch was also supported by a multimillion-dollar print and TV advertising campaign, dealer promotional programs, and other more traditional marketing efforts.

This approach has been copied a number of times. For example, Starbucks developed a film about a girl from the Chinese countryside who moves to the big city to discover love and Starbucks. The film, titled "A Sunny Day," was shown on thousands of flat-screen monitors on Shanghai's subway cars and station platforms.

Application Volvo

In October 2000, Volvo took a rather unconventional approach to launching its new S60 sedan.[36] Because more than 80 percent of Volvo brand-loyalists were online, the company introduced the sedan exclusively on America Online (AOL). AOL provided Volvo access to its 26 million (at the time) members via the Welcome screen, banners, and other special "content zones." In return, Volvo offered users a members-only incentive worth $2,100 in free S60 options. The car was also featured on AOL's 6.0 upgrade page, which generated 300,000 requests for more information over a two-month period. The program ran exclusively online through January 2001, when print and TV were added.

Application Pepsi Tava

In 2008, PepsiCo brought out a new line of no-calorie, carbonated beverages named Tava with a campaign that bypassed traditional media like TV and print.[37] Instead, Tava's marketing managers used a Web site (tava.com), Web banner ads, promotions, and "buzz"-oriented programs like the delivery of free samples to the employees of companies such as Apple, Bliss Spa, Google, and MTV. In addition, the company used a free sample program at the Sundance Film Festival and for customers of businesses like Frank's Chop shop, a barbershop on the Lower East Side of Manhattan. At tava.com, you can download songs from emerging musicians like Deccatree, a rock band from California, and Stephanie McKay, a singer from New York. The site also carries information about arts events like the Boston Arts Festival, the Chicago Jazz Festival, and Shakespeare in the Park at Central Park.

Interestingly, Tava's target consumers are not 18- to 24-year-olds, but men and women ages 35 to 49. The idea is to go online to reach this target group that spends a lot of time online—not to IM friends but rather to collect information about art, music, food, and travel. The intention is to create an emotional attachment to Tava that cannot be achieved using traditional media.

Topics in New-Product Development

Several other topics are important to better understand how to develop and launch new products.

The Importance of Shorter Product Development Cycles

Because of shorter product life cycles and faster technological obsolescence, companies are finding that quicker time-to-market with new products has become a competitive advantage. Although there is little empirical evidence that faster cycle times alone are positively correlated with a firm's overall financial performance,[38] speed clearly has become necessary in some industries just to keep pace. In addition, in industries such as semiconductors, where costs and prices fall rapidly over time, faster time-to-market can mean significantly higher prices over the lifetime of a specific product.

Cycle times are particularly important in the struggling automobile market. Consider this quote:

> *The cycle times that were typical and were tolerated in the past are completely uncompetitive today . . . They [the auto companies] can quickly be rendered uncompetitive if they aren't constantly refreshing.*[39]

New technologies are helping to significantly shorten product development cycles.
Source: Dennis Hallinan/Alamy Images

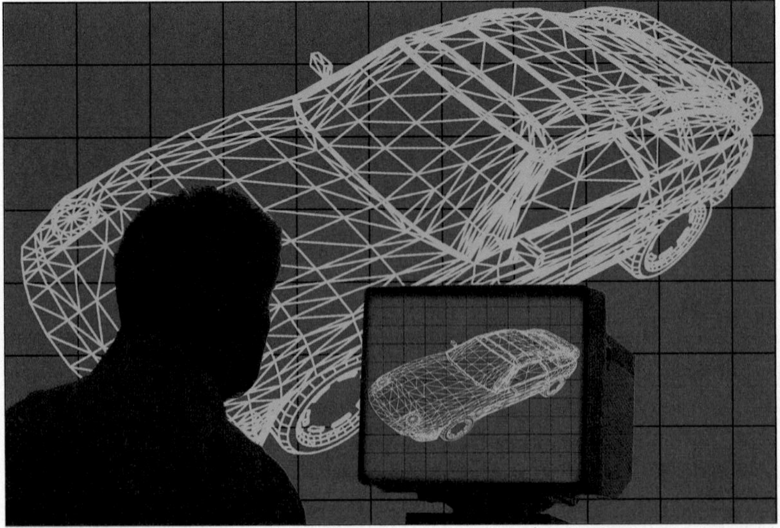

Typically, automakers redesign models every four to five years, sometimes longer. However, in late 2009, Ford announced plans to replace or revamp the models that account for up to 90 percent of its sales in North America and other regions by 2012.

Table 8.9 shows some new-product development cycle time reductions over the period 1988–1992. As can be seen, in many cases companies have reduced the new-product introduction process by more than 50 percent when moving from one generation of a product to the next.

A number of books have focused on time-to-market and how to improve new-product introduction processes. One study has examined the relationship of some project and organizational

Table 8.9

Reported New-Product Introduction Time Reductions			
Product	Company	Cycle Times (months) Previous	Now
Hybrid corn	Pioneer Hi-Bred	96	72
Construction equipment	Deere & Co.	84	50
Jet engine	General Electric	84	48
Helios (medical imaging)	Polaroid	72	36
Viper	Chrysler	60	36
Cars	Honda	60	36
9900 copier	Xerox	60	36
DeskJet printer	Hewlett-Packard	54	22
Personal computer	IBM	48	14
Thermostat	Honeywell	48	10
Checkout terminals	NCR	44	22
Air-powered grinder	Ingersoll Rand	40	15
FX-3500 copier	Fuji-Xerox	38	29
Phone switches	AT&T	36	<18
Electronic pager	Motorola	36	18
Electric clutch break	Warner	36	9
Communication gear	Codex	34	16
Machining center	Cincinnati Milacron	30	12
Pampers Phases	Procter & Gamble	27	12
Leisure lantern	Coleman	24	12
Cordless phone	AT&T	24	12

Source: Abbie Griffin (1997), "The Effect of Project and Process Characteristics on Product Development Cycle Time," *Journal of Marketing Research,* February, p. 25. Used by permission of the American Marketing Association.

characteristics to cycle time.[40] Not surprisingly, factors negatively correlated with shorter cycle times are the newness of the project (the amount of product redesign from the previous version) and the project's complexity (the number of functions performed by the product). Two important factors in shortening the new-product development period are the institution of a formal new-product planning process and the use of inter-functional teams.

The impact of new technologies is also helping to shorten cycle times. A significant improvement in new-product design has occurred through the use of computer-aided design (CAD) software, which enables engineers to simulate complex products that can then be given to manufacturing for production. However, except for some simple metal items, few of these designs can be instantly turned into three-dimensional objects by being fed into computer-controlled machine tools. This capability is necessary to create prototypes for customer testing and further refining. The construction of prototypes can take months. However, a process called rapid prototyping (RP) enables companies to go directly from CAD prototypes on the computer monitor to physical products, using a machine that uses ink jets similar to those in a computer printer. Instead of ink, the machine deposits a liquid binder on layers of powdered ceramics to create different shapes.

In addition, as we have seen earlier in this chapter, the Internet is also helping to shorten development cycles. Besides faster concept and market tests, collaborative software helps companies to work with partners to develop new products more quickly. Web software links companies, suppliers, and contractors together to share designs, track the exchange of documents, and track progress against goals.

Application Microsoft Xbox

To introduce the Xbox in November 2001, Microsoft used Internet-based tools to work with manufacturing contractor Flextronics and cut two months off the original production schedule.[41] In one instance, Microsoft decided to replace a metal bracket, for holding the disk drive, with a lighter and stronger plastic one. The process worked as follows:

1. Microsoft created a 3-D design for the part and, getting into the system, tells Flextronics to make the change. The system sends the alert via e-mail to Flextronics's manufacturing and design teams.
2. Flextronics engineers see the request, discuss it, and decide that the change does not affect manufacturing.
3. Microsoft makes a prototype of the new part and discovers that it is not a perfect fit. It e-mails Flextronics with some proposed changes to the design.
4. Flextronics receives the e-mail and approves the changes. It then sends an e-mail to the division that makes the plastic part.
5. The parts manufacturing personnel see the e-mail, approve the change, modify the tooling machines, and build a new version in two weeks.

The Importance of Product Design

As noted earlier in this chapter, it is difficult to develop successful new products. Enemy number one of any new product is the competition, whether it is inside or outside of the product category (for "really" new products). Developing a compelling, unique value proposition is challenging but necessary for customers to discern that your new product should be considered.

As a result, for manufactured products today, having an innovative design has become a key way to distinguish a new product from the competition. While this was discussed at the end of Chapter 7 along with packaging, it is important to consider design as part of the new-product introduction process. Some companies like Apple, Whirlpool, and the Danish home electronics company Bang & Olufsen consider innovation and design to go hand-in-hand. The Palm Web site, www.Palm.com, shows how important design is for their new Pre and Pixi smart phones.[42]

Perhaps the best-known company in the design industry is IDEO. The company designed Apple's first mouse in 1982 and since then has worked with companies such as Intel, Palm, Polaroid, and Procter & Gamble. IDEO's design process is the following:[43]

1. **Observation.** As described in the marketing research chapter (Chapter 3), the company uses psychologists, anthropologists, and sociologists to first understand the consumer experience with the product.
2. **Brainstorming.** IDEO personnel then brainstorm ideas based upon the customer research.
3. **Rapid prototyping.** The company then quickly develops prototypes for the most promising design ideas.
4. **Refining.** The ideas from step 3 are narrowed down to a few choices. Here, IDEO goes back to the marketing research for validation and works closely with the client company.
5. **Implementation.** IDEO's engineers from all over the world and with a variety of backgrounds (mechanical, aerospace, biomedical, etc.) are then drawn upon to create the new product.

New-Product Development Over the Product Life Cycle

The stages of the product life cycle shown in Figure 2.8 can be a guide to kinds of innovation a company should seek, by stages in the life cycle:[44]

- **Introductory.** Clearly, the company is looking for what might be called a "disruptive" technology or product improvement. This would include new technologies such as laser printing, satellite TV, and so forth.
- **Growth.** In this stage of the PLC, the focus should be on product innovation—that is, making improvements in the product and differentiating from existing competitors on the basis of observed product quality. Thus, video cameras became smaller and lighter and flat-screen TV picture quality improved.
- **Maturity.** While product improvements are still sought, it is important at this stage to invest in marketing differentiation because the products are similar. Thus, new products at this stage can feature design (i.e., the Toyota Scion featured in Chapter 3) or positions that appeal to specific market segments (Coke Zero, no calories for 18- to 34-year-olds). New products could also improve customers' experiences with the existing product category. Line extensions are used heavily at this stage of the life cycle.
- **Decline.** Despite the fact that sales are declining in this stage, the market can still be large (e.g., cigarettes). Product development should focus on product enhancements and line extensions that cater to the segments still purchasing the category.

Improving the Integration of Marketing and R&D

Historically, marketing and R&D do not have a strong record of cooperation. Various reasons have been given. One is that the personalities of the personnel are different (e.g., marketing people have shorter time frames than their R&D counterparts). Other reasons given are language (marketing emphasizes benefits and perceptions, R&D emphasizes specifications and performance), culture (business schools versus engineering departments), and physical barriers (different geographic locations).

Many studies have found that increased levels of cooperation between marketing and R&D result in higher levels of corporate success defined in a number of different ways. This success results from integration in the following areas:

- Analyzing customer needs.
- Generating and screening new ideas.
- Developing new products according to the market's needs.
- Analyzing customer requirements.
- Reviewing test market results.

Some approaches for improving the cooperation between marketing and R&D are:

- **Relocation and physical facility design.** One obvious solution is to relocate one or both groups so they are geographically proximate. However, dramatic improvements in teleconferencing technology and document-sharing software make it easier for people with significant distance between them to communicate easily.
- **Personnel movement.** It is possible to give personnel in both departments temporary assignments to the other. However, barriers of the type mentioned previously make such transfers difficult. Education can help here; executive programs (e.g., "Marketing for Engineers," "Semiconductor Technology for Marketers") for cross-functional purposes are becoming more popular.
- **Informal social systems.** Developing a way for the two groups to interact informally would ultimately lead to better communication and coordination.

- **Organizational structure.** A rigid, departmentalized structure organized along functional groups is not likely to be successful for new-product introductions. For example, as we have noted several times in this chapter, interfunctional teams tend to produce the most successful new products.
- **Incentives and rewards.** R&D and marketing personnel are often rewarded differently. In many companies, particularly consumer products, marketing managers are rewarded on the basis of their brands' market shares. R&D personnel are rewarded for patents, improvements in technology, and the number of new products developed. It has been suggested that more coordination would be achieved if both sets of personnel were rewarded on the basis of ultimate profits derived from new products introduced.

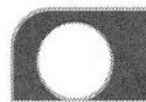

Executive Summary

Key learning points in this chapter include the following:

- New products are the lifeblood of companies and are therefore necessary for their long-term survival.
- Some key factors correlated with success in introducing new products are a superior product meeting customer needs, a customer orientation maintained throughout the new-product development process, collection of the appropriate information, sharp product definition, interfunctional teams, and quick time-to-market.
- There are different approaches to new-product development. The most common is the linear or stage-gate approach, which progresses from idea generation and initial screening to product design to testing to introduction, with fewer product concepts succeeding at each stage.
- New-product concepts come either ready-made from sources such as employees, customers, and channels or from a managed creative process such as brainstorming.
- Product definition comes from combining customer input (voice of the customer) with engineering characteristics to create a house of quality chart.
- Forecasting the demand for new products is accomplished using procedures such as product use tests, test markets, and quantitative models based on market research data.

Chapter Questions

1. Consider the three major categories of new products: classically innovative products (ones that create new categories), new-category entries, and line extensions. How does the job of the marketing manager differ for these three kinds of new products?
2. What are the pros and cons of the three approaches to new-product development discussed in this chapter? Are there some circumstances (e.g., different product categories) in which one approach might be better than another?
3. This chapter explores alternative methods for forecasting the demand for new products before they are launched. Compare these methods with those discussed in Chapter 3, which use existing sales data for products already on the market. How are the forecasting challenges facing marketing managers different in the two cases (beyond the fact that there are no sales data in the prelaunch phase for new products)?

4. For frequently purchased products, successful new products must have high trial and repeat rates. What tools can the marketing manager use to increase trial rates? Repeat rates?
5. How is launching industrial products or consumer products with infrequent purchasing rates (e.g., TVs) different from launching frequently purchased products? What key measures are used to assess trial and repeat rates for frequently purchased products?
6. It is fairly obvious that the success rate of new products would improve if communications between R&D and marketing improved. From a human resources perspective, what are some of the programs and incentives you could put in place to accomplish this?

Key Learning Points

The purpose of this chapter is to introduce the concepts involved with strategic price-setting. Key areas of learning are:

- The need for consistency between price and the marketing strategy
- The concept of perceived value and how it is critical to setting price
- Integrating competition and costs into the pricing decision
- Deciding how much of the strategic pricing gap between cost and perceived value to capture
- Specific pricing tactics such as product line pricing, value pricing, and competing against private labels
- How the Internet is affecting pricing decisions

Apple has used a premium pricing policy for the iPod and a low-price penetration strategy for iTunes (shown on the computer screen).
Source: Paul Sakuma/AP Wide World Photos

Pricing

Chapter Brief

When Apple Computer Inc. launched its pocket-sized music-player, the iPod, in October 2001, there were many skeptics.[1] The critics pointed out that it cost $399, which was far more than its competitors' prices. Some noted that Apple had little experience in the price-driven consumer electronics market because its computers had always been priced higher than those with similar capabilities. Finally, the iPod was launched during the well-publicized technology slump. Jokes were posted on Internet bulletin boards that the name stood for "idiots price our devices."

Who is laughing now? The iPod quickly gained 71 percent of the market for digital music players by 2003. By 2005 its share was 80 percent, with 75 percent of all music downloads occurring through Apple's music site, iTunes. The iPod product line now includes the Touch with video and Wi-Fi capabilities, the "classic" iPod with 120 gigabytes of storage, the iPod Nano (8 and 16 gigabyte sizes), and the iPod Shuffle with 4 gigabytes of storage. In 2008, a whopping 55 million iPods were sold!

The iPod is not the only piece of Apple hardware that can play music. In addition to the iPod, Apple introduced the iPhone in 2007. The iPhone can function like an iPod; in fact, the iPhone 3Gs has up to 32 gigabytes of storage for music, photos, video, etc. Like the iPod, the iPhone has been wildly popular.[2] Since its introduction, Apple has sold more than 21 million iPhones and has 8 percent of the market—dramatically changing the dynamics of the smartphone industry.

What makes the iPod popular, of course, is the content. From its inception in 2001, the price of every individual song on iTunes, Apple's music site, was $0.99 for each song. This basically became the industry standard. However, in 2005 there was a movement by two major companies in the music industry (Sony BMG and Warner) to price songs by their popularity. Thus, for example, a hit song might be sold for $1.49 while a less popular old song would sell for $0.59. The two music companies noted that Apple makes its money from iPods rather than the music, while the latter is all they have to sell and that pricing by popularity allows them to make money as well. Steven Jobs, Apple's CEO, liked the simplicity of the uniform pricing policy. In addition, music industry executives who support Jobs were concerned that higher prices could drive consumers to use illegal but free online music swapping services.

However, in 2009, with the music industry in general in a slump and with a significant decline in the growth rate of song sales, Apple changed its pricing policy. In January 2009, at the Macworld Conference in San Francisco, the company announced a three-tier, or variable, pricing policy with songs priced at $0.69, $0.99, and $1.29, depending on popularity, age, and other factors. In addition, the company eased up on the copyright protection built into each download. This was obviously a significant departure from the flat $0.99 pricing policy that had been in existence from iTune's beginnings and for which Apple's CEO Steve Jobs fought many battles with the music industry.

Apple's pricing policies raises several interesting questions:

- How can Apple consistently price higher than its competitors in computers and digital music devices?
- What was the logic behind the original $0.99 pricing policy?
- Is the variable pricing policy instituted in 2009 a good idea? Is it good for both the companies and consumers?
- How did the initial $0.99 pricing policy affect competitors' ability to price and consumers' subsequent perceptions of what a "fair" price is for paying for music online?

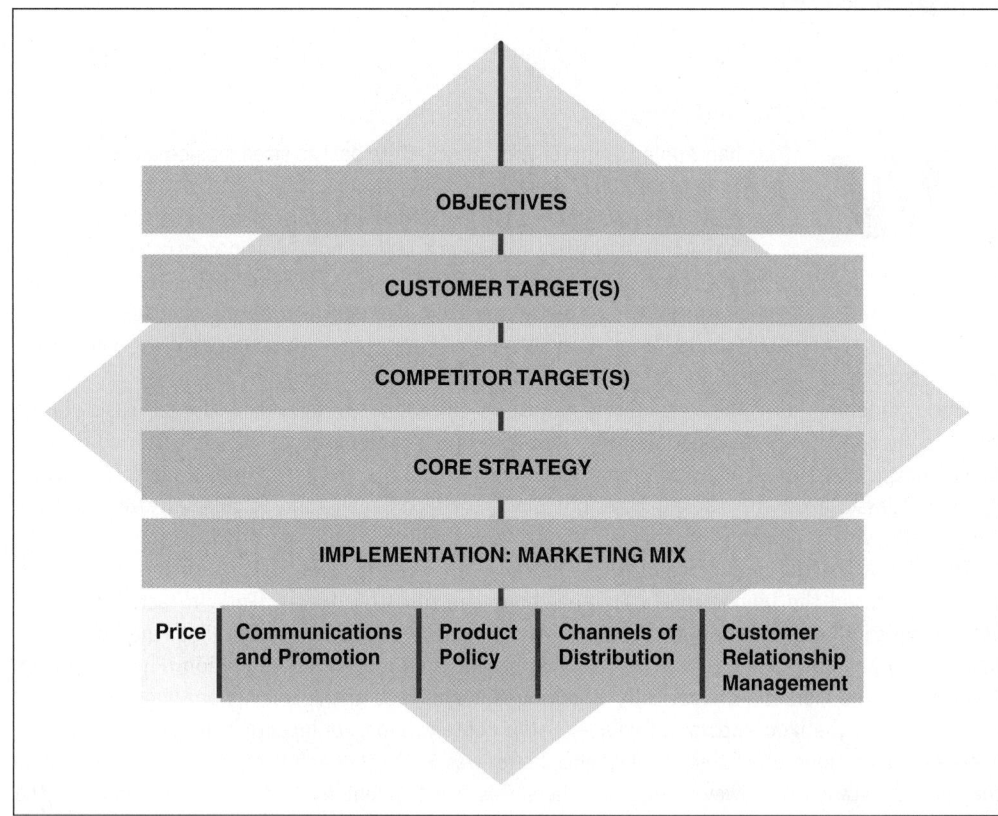

No decision worries a marketing manager more than determining the appropriate price to charge customers because, for most product categories, price is the marketing variable customers react to more than any other. Price is an observable component of the product that results in consumers purchasing or not, and at the same time it directly affects margin per unit sold. Other components of the marketing mix are important, of course, because they must work together to create a unified brand image and produce sales. However, price most often makes or breaks the transaction.

The pricing decision is usually viewed as a way to recover costs. That is, you must determine what price to charge, beyond your costs of making the product or delivering the service, in order to make a profit. For example, many companies try to calculate their costs and then add a standard markup to get a target return on investment. This cost-plus tactic is common in retailing, where the store manager simply marks up the product delivered from the supplier.

However, it is clear that a price developed in this way may not be an optimal price when the customer is taken into consideration.[3] The price could be higher than customers are willing to pay for that product. If the product is priced too low, the company loses potential profits.

As we will see later in this chapter, costs do matter in setting price, because you would not want to price a product below cost, at least for long. However, the customer is also an important consideration, specifically in terms of **customer value**—what a product or service is worth to the customer. As a marketing manager, you must remember that the customer generally does not know or care what your costs are. What is important is whether the product delivers an appropriate amount of value for the price being paid. Thus, the purpose of price is not just to recover costs but to also capture the perceived value of the product in the mind of the customer.[4]

customer value
what a product or service is worth to the customer in monetary terms; also called perceived value

Recent advances in a number of technologies have added interesting additional dimensions to the pricing decision, such as the ability to charge customized prices based on how customers have historically responded to prices, time of day, or season of the year. This has complicated the pricing decision for some products and services. At one time, airlines would have a limited number of prices for a given route, depending on the class of service and number of days booked in advance. Now, with sophisticated "yield management" software, airlines can charge different prices depending on route popularity, number of seats booked on a particular flight, and source of the booking (e.g., Internet versus travel agent). Other technological advances have helped consumers compare prices on the Web, for example.

Therefore, in this chapter we will cover the various aspects of decision making involved with setting price. The major factors affecting price are:

- Your marketing strategy.
- Customer perceived value.
- Competition.
- Your costs.

The latter three factors are sometimes referred to as the "3Cs" of pricing.

A framework for price setting is developed in which the key decision is determining how much of the gap between cost and customer value the firm can keep. In addition, some specific pricing tactics and the impact of the Internet on pricing decisions are described.

The Role of Marketing Strategy in Pricing

As we discussed in Chapter 2, you first design the marketing strategy and *then* the implementation of the strategy, the marketing mix (see the marketing strategy diagram). Thus, a key point is that the price must be consistent with the marketing strategy. The marketing strategy consists primarily of the market segmentation and core strategy, positioning, and value proposition decisions. Strategy decisions do not lead to a specific price-setting rule; rather, they give general guidelines for whether a price should be low or high.

The target market decision affects price because prices can vary widely over segments. Economists call this first-degree **price discrimination**, which is charging different prices to segments according to their price elasticity or sensitivity. It stands to reason that a segment of customers who are attracted to your product are willing to pay more for it than those in a segment who are less interested. Prices can also vary over segments if the products or services vary in quality. For example, a stripped-down version of a car model will be priced lower than a version with many options because each attracts different customers. In business-to-business markets, prices may vary by customer size and ability to obtain quantity discounts from the supplier.

price discrimination
the practice of charging different prices to segments of the market according to their price elasticity or sensitivity

An example of such price variation in a product category is shown in Figure 9.1. Such variations within a category are called **price bands or tiers.**[5] Figure 9.1 shows some of the price variation in the GPS (global positioning system) market. Some of the price variation is within brand; for example, Garmin has five variations ranging in price from $600 down to $120. As the price distributions show, there is a positive relationship between price and quality (as measured by *Consumer Reports*). The idea behind the price–quality variation is to offer a product variant for different consumer target markets depending on their price sensitivity, income, and other segmentation variables. Note that there is even price variability within the highest quality tier (*Consumer Reports* scores greater than or equal to 75) with a price range of $400 to $600.

price bands or tiers
price variations within a product category

Figure 9.1

Price Tiers in GPS Products

Rank	Brand & model	Price	Overall score
	Similar models, in small type, are comparable to tested models.		
1.	**Garmin** Nuvi 885T	$600	78
2.	**TomTom** Go 740 Live	400	75
3.	**Garmin** Nuvi 765T	480	75
4.	**Garmin** Nuvi 760 Garmin Nuvi 770, Garmin Nuvi 780	250	74
5.	**Garmin** Nuvi 265T	200	70
5.	**TomTom** One 140 S	170	70
7.	**TomTom** One 140	140	67
8.	**Magellan** Roadmate 1440	160	67
9	**Magellan** Roadmate 1220	125	63
10	**Garmin** Nuvi 200 Garmin Nuvi 250, Garmin Nuvi 270	120	61

Source: "Price Tiers in GPS Products," *Consumer Reports,* September, 2009, p. 41.

Why does such variation exist within product categories and even within the same tier? For both industrial and consumer products, there seem to be several reasons. First, customers become loyal to certain products or suppliers and so they tend to rate price lower than other factors such as reliability and speed of delivery. This makes them less price-sensitive. Second, in some industries price visibility is low; that is, the price charged is less transparent than it is at supermarkets or other retailers, where the price is marked on the item. For many industrial products, the list price is only the basis from which discounts that vary among customers are given. This method creates more transaction price variability. Third, competitive intensity can vary among segments. The larger the number of suppliers, the narrower the price band because more competition implies greater convergence on a standard price. Finally, some categories have large numbers of product variants because many options are available or because the supplier wants to fill the channel and keep competitors from getting shelf space.

Digital video camera manufacturers use price tiers to capture buyers from different market segments.
Source: Paul Sakuma/AP Wide World Photos

Thus, the marketing manager has to understand the price sensitivity of the different target markets to set the appropriate price. However, as these illustrations show, there may be significant price variations even within a particular segment. In sum, the marketing strategy dictates the pricing policies that can be used at any given time.

Perceived Value

A major factor affecting price is the customer's perceived value. This is a measure of how much a customer is willing to pay for a product or service. Economists call this concept the **reservation price**—the most someone is willing to pay for a product (or the price at which the product is eliminated from the customer's budget). Every customer, whether consumer or business, has a psychological concept of such a price. People receive price information and then assess whether it is good or bad. They compare the price being charged with the perceived value or benefits they would derive from purchasing the product.

reservation price the maximum price someone is willing to pay for a product or the price at which the product is eliminated from the customer's budget

There is no single perceived value in the marketplace. Customer value is unique to the individual customer. Therefore, when we use the term *perceived* or *customer value,* we refer to an average or typical value for a particular market segment or target market.

In addition, perceived value is always relative. Although the absolute level of perceived value of your product is important, in order to use the concept to set a price, it is also important to know how customers value competing options.

Here we explicitly consider three possible relationships among perceived value, price, and cost.[6] While competition is not explicitly considered, you can think of perceived value below in terms of relative to competition. Three key relationships are the following:

1. Perceived value > Price > Cost.
2. Price > Perceived value > Cost.
3. Price > Cost > Perceived value.

Note that in all three situations, we assume that price is greater than cost.

Perceived Value > Price > Cost

In this case, the marketing manager has set a price, either intentionally or mistakenly, below what customers would be willing to pay for the product or service. From the customer's standpoint, the product is a bargain. It is difficult to determine whether the low price is a mistake because customers do not usually write and thank you for pricing your product so low. In some cases, the fact that you have priced it below customer value will result in shortages and present a production and distribution problem.

You may underprice a product intentionally, for strategic reasons discussed later in this chapter. Strategically pricing below customer value is often called *value pricing*, or attempting to provide an exceptionally good value to the customer. This term should be distinguished from *pricing to value*, which means setting a price at the level you have determined to represent the customer's perceived value for your product.

When it was introduced, the BMW Z3 and now the Z4 offer a lot of value for the money.
Source: Carlos Osorio/AP Wide World Photos

A good example of value pricing is the Mazda Miata, introduced in 1990. Mazda's objective was to introduce a two-seat convertible with few power options and luxurious details. This throwback to the 1950s, a simple car with a sporty feel, was introduced at a price of $16,000 to $18,000. However, demand for the Miata was so high during the first few months after it was introduced that prices of $25,000 in the used-car sections of newspapers were common. Customers were buying the cars and quickly reselling them to make a significant profit. Clearly, Mazda could have charged more for the Miata. Perhaps company managers underestimated the demand for the car. However, they probably knew this craze was a short-term aberration and believed that the original price was more consistent with their long-term marketing strategy for the car. Also, high initial prices that are later reduced play havoc with the used-car market. Customers who paid the high price and tried to sell the cars later would find no demand for them because people could buy a new car for less than a used one. The pricing strategy did create a large amount of publicity, which helped create awareness and perhaps some preference for the car. Interestingly, this low-entry-price strategy was copied by BMW and Porsche with their own roadster entries, the Z3 and the Boxster. Also Audi chose to price its European model A3 substantially lower than competing models from BMW and Mercedes, while promoting the fact that the car has similar features.

In most cases, prices are set below customer value simply because the manager does not have enough information. Without information about reservation prices or customer value, pricing is like "shooting in the dark," and when confronted with solid information on costs and competitors' prices, managers often opt for simpler decision rules that are suboptimal.[7] In addition, one study found that prices for bank services such as checking accounts and certificates of deposit (CDs) were surprisingly "sticky" in that few customers would change banks if prices were raised. These customers cited convenience, quality of service, and relationships with bank personnel, which are components of customer or perceived value, as the reason.[8] D'Agostino's, a supermarket chain, experimented with new price optimization software to do a better job of pricing its products. The company's managers were surprised to find that raising the price of vegetable baby food a few cents over the fruit variety did not affect sales. By selectively raising prices, the company boosted profitability by 2.5 percent in the test stores, a significant increase for the notoriously low-margin supermarket business.[9]

In some cases, setting a price below value is not intentional and simple consumer mania takes over. For example, when Nokia introduced its stylish 8810 mobile phone in Hong Kong, it was priced at HK$7,400. However, demand for it was so strong that retailers marked it up as high as HK$12,800, with some buyers indicating willingness to pay as much as HK$20,000.[10]

Price > Perceived Value > Cost

In this unfortunate situation, the manager has set a price that is higher than the target market is willing to pay. The customer looks at this situation as a bad deal and, unless the company has a monopoly or some other kind of market power, does not buy. Customers let you know that there is a problem by not buying. Waiting for customer reaction is an expensive form of marketing research, however, because the customers may have bought another brand and are out of the market for some time. The solution is obvious. Some kind of downward price adjustment or increase in customer value is necessary. However, without knowing the perceived value or willingness to pay, you do not know how much to lower the price. In this case, the competitor often serves as the reference point.

Price reductions in response to lower perceived value are common. Taiwan's Acer, a manufacturer of laptop computers, lowered prices dramatically in 2009, to $300 to $600 for basic machines. This caused the competition such as Dell and Hewlett-Packard to do the same because their perceived value relative to Acer had declined. Many grocery products have reduced their prices because their perceived value has been reduced in the face of strong competition from private labels. Marlboro Friday refers to the event when Philip Morris announced a 20 percent price cut to their Marlboro cigarettes to fight back against generic competitors which were increasingly eating into their market share. Salespeople are constantly offering price reductions to customers when they are nervous about keeping the business.

Price > Cost > Perceived Value

This scenario clearly represents a failure. Usually, such products are weeded out in the new-product development process. If not, they are ultimately withdrawn from the market. For example, the Yugoslavian-made car Yugo was withdrawn from the U.S. market because it received such negative reviews in publications such as *Consumer Reports* that customer value fell even below the manufacturing and marketing costs. One Cadillac dealer even offered to give a free Yugo to new Cadillac buyers.

Application | Online Music

Let us return to the online music category discussed at the beginning of the chapter. Recall that Apple initially charged a flat price of $0.99 per song but then recently moved to a three-tiered pricing schedule of $0.69, $0.99, and $1.29, depending on the song's age, popularity, and other factors. Cost information for new digital music is provided in Figure 9.2.[11] As can be seen, the cost to produce and market a song is estimated to be $0.79. For older songs, the cost is basically the online delivery cost ($0.17) plus the royalties to the publisher and artist ($0.21 per song) because the marketing and production costs are sunk (i.e., spent a long time ago).

Thus, when Apple was charging the flat $0.99 price, it was not taking customer value into account and therefore "leaving money on the table" because they could have charged $1.29 for newer songs and perhaps more. The new pricing policy does a much better job accounting for customer value as newer and/or popular songs are valued more and priced accordingly. Less-valued songs are priced less, consistent with our pricing model.

Figure 9.2

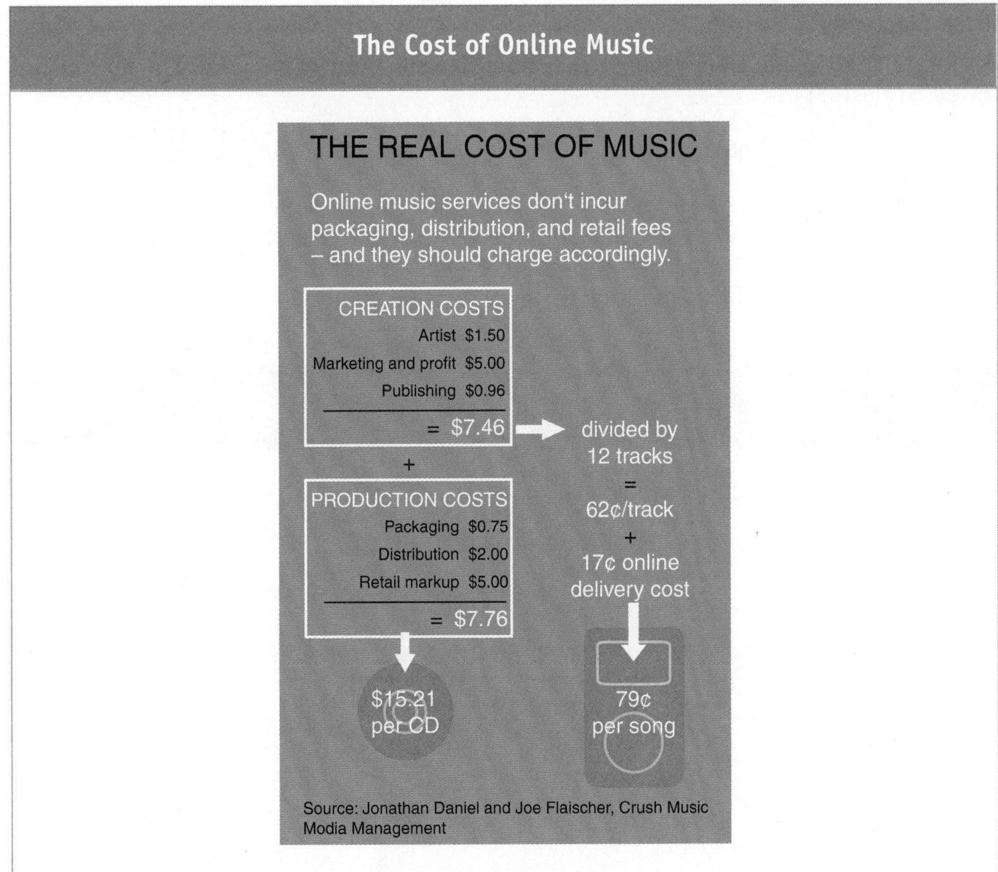

The Cost of Online Music
THE REAL COST OF MUSIC
Online music services don't incur packaging, distribution, and retail fees – and they should charge accordingly.
CREATION COSTS
Artist $1.50
Marketing and profit $5.00
Publishing $0.96
= $7.46
divided by 12 tracks
=
62¢/track
+
17¢ online delivery cost
+
PRODUCTION COSTS
Packaging $0.75
Distribution $2.00
Retail markup $5.00
= $7.76
$15.21 per CD
79¢ per song
Source: Jonathan Daniel and Joe Flaischer, Crush Music Modia Management

Source: Chris Anderson (2004), "The Long Tail," *Wired*, October, p. 176. Originally published in WIRED magazine.

Application | Ethically Produced Goods

As we noted in Chapter 1, many companies are positioning themselves as offering socially responsible products and services. For example, a coffee retailer such as Java Jones may emphasize that it sells only fair-traded coffee or a supermarket chain such as Whole Foods touts its organic produce. An interesting question is whether or not customers are willing to pay more for such products and, if so, how much more.

Researchers recently set out to find out the answers to these questions by running a series of experiments on a number of product categories.[12] They found that consumers are willing to pay a premium but that it is rather small. For example, they found that consumers were willing to pay \$21.21 for 100 percent organic cotton T-shirts ethically produced versus \$20.04 for cotton T-shirts with no information provided about the production process, a difference of only 6 percent. Interestingly, the researchers found that consumers will punish producers of unethically made goods more than they would reward them for being ethical; that is, they will demand a price that is lower than the premium obtained from ethical behavior.

A Framework

The need to understand customer perceived value or willingness to pay is illustrated in Figure 9.3, which shows the creation of a strategic pricing gap. The cost used by the marketing manager as a basis for pricing is the floor of the gap; you would not price below that cost.[13] The target segment's willingness to pay is the ceiling; you cannot price above that because the segment would not buy above that price. Therefore, your task is to figure out how much of the difference between value and cost you want to keep for yourself or structure with a partner. It is important to realize that by understanding customer value, you can make this decision proactively. If you do not understand customer value, the market will help you make the calculation, often at great expense to you.

Price Elasticity

price elasticity of demand the percentage change in a product's demand resulting from a 1% change in its price

An important concept from economics is the **price elasticity of demand.** The formula for the price elasticity is:

$$E = \text{Percent change in demand/Percent change in price}$$

Thus, if price is reduced by 2 percent and demand increases by 3 percent, $E = -1.5$. If price increases by 3 percent and demand decreases by 2 percent, $E = -0.67$. If $|E| < 1.0$, the product category is called price inelastic because the change in demand is less than the change in price.[14] If $|E| > 1.0$, the category is price elastic.

Figure 9.3

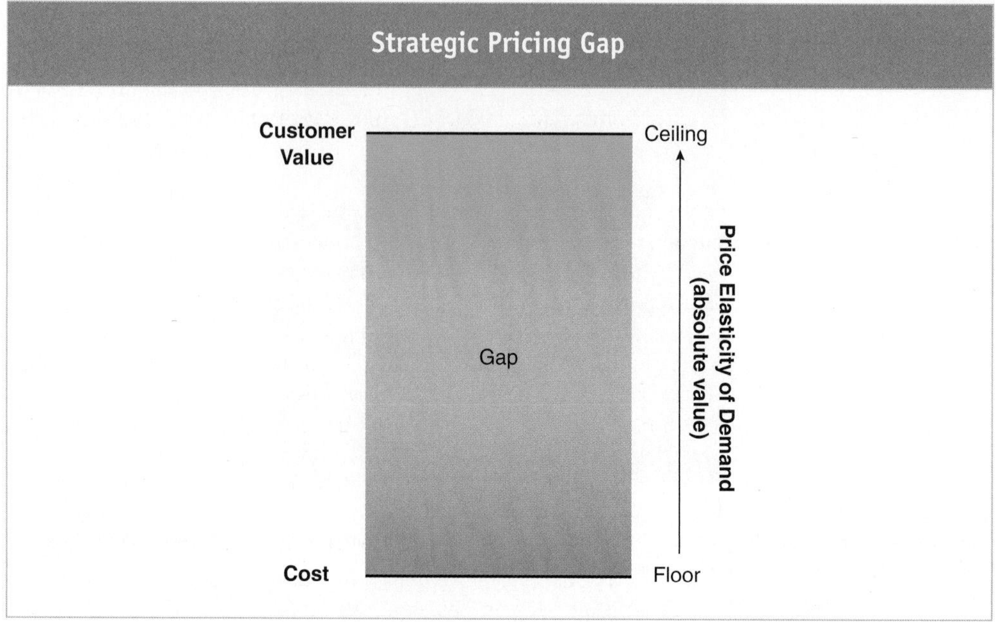

The relationship of price elasticity to customer value is shown in Figure 9.3. If the product's price is low so that there is a considerable amount of value left for the customer (a good deal), a price increase or decrease will not have much impact. However, as the price gets closer to customer value, price elasticity (sensitivity) increases as the point at which the customer will not buy at all draws near. Thus, the vertical arrow on the right side of Figure 9.3 indicates that price elasticity increases as the firm captures more of the value for itself and leaves less for the customer. It is also likely that as price gets closer to the value line, the asymmetry between price increases and decreases grows larger. That is, if customer value is $2.00 and price is $1.98, a $0.01 price increase is likely to decrease sales more than a similar price decrease will increase sales.

Price elasticity is thus an indirect measure of customer value in that a manager can determine how close his or her brand is to the customer value point through planned price experimentation or market reactions to price changes. For example, when General Mills raised its cereal prices by an average of 2.6 percent in 1997, sales dropped 11 percent in the following quarter. This implied price elasticity of –4.23 indicated that the cereal prices were very close to the customer value point. An analysis across a large number of frequently purchased product categories showed the average price elasticity to be –2.5, again reflecting the fact that prices are probably closer to relative customer value than cost.[15] Studies of the retail gasoline market generally show price inelastic demand. However, significant prices in the United States during 2005, due to worldwide increases in crude oil prices and flooding in the Gulf states, led to decreased demand for gas-guzzling SUVs and large shifts to public transportation.

Calculating Customer Value

Although it is clearly an important concept, it is not easy to calculate customers' willingness to pay or customer value. Price elasticities give only a hint at how close to or how far you are from customer value. Some methods used to obtain more precise estimates are described here.

Calculating Value-in-Use

Particularly for industrial products, a useful way to estimate customer value is through a method called **value-in-use**. In this approach, the benefits of the product are put in monetary terms such as time savings, less use of materials, or less downtime. To implement the procedure, you first select a reference product, usually either the product the customer is currently using or a competitor's product. Second, you calculate the incremental monetary benefit to the customer of using the product or brand in question. Assuming it is positive, this incremental monetary benefit describes the range of prices obtainable. In terms of Figure 9.3, pricing to the limit of the incremental benefit gives all the value to you, pricing to capture none of the incremental benefit gives it all to the customer, and in-between prices share the economic benefit.

value-in-use
a method of estimating customer value that puts the benefits of the product in monetary terms, such as time savings, less use of materials, and less downtime

Figure 9.4 shows one approach to the value-in-use calculation.[16] The bar on the far left is the reference product, *Y*. Assume that the reference product cost (i.e., the initial price) is $300. Also assume that the company that purchases it incurs startup costs of $200 (e.g., training) and postpurchase costs of $500 (e.g., maintenance). Together these costs are called life-cycle costs and recognize that the cost of buying a product often goes far beyond the acquisition cost.

Your product, *X*, is represented in the next bar. It is assumed product *X* has $100 less in both startup and postpurchase costs. It is also assumed that the product offers approximately $100 more in value through additional features (e.g., energy savings). Therefore, if the customer is willing to pay $300 for product *Y*, then the customer should be willing to pay up to $300 more ($200 in reduced life-cycle costs plus $100 extra value) for product *X*. The third bar assumes that the variable cost of $300 is the floor. The incremental dollar value to the customer is $600 (this is called the economic value to the customer, or EVC (Figure 9.4). The difference of $300 is the amount the product manager has to play with in setting price. This difference is the supplier's competitive advantage. The last bar shows one hypothetical split of the $300 pricing range. One such split leaves $125 for the customer and $175 for you.

An attractive feature of this approach is that the analysis provides valuable information for the salesperson to use in trying to close the sale. In this case, the salesperson can explicitly quantify the incremental economic benefit to the customer and show that the

Figure 9.4

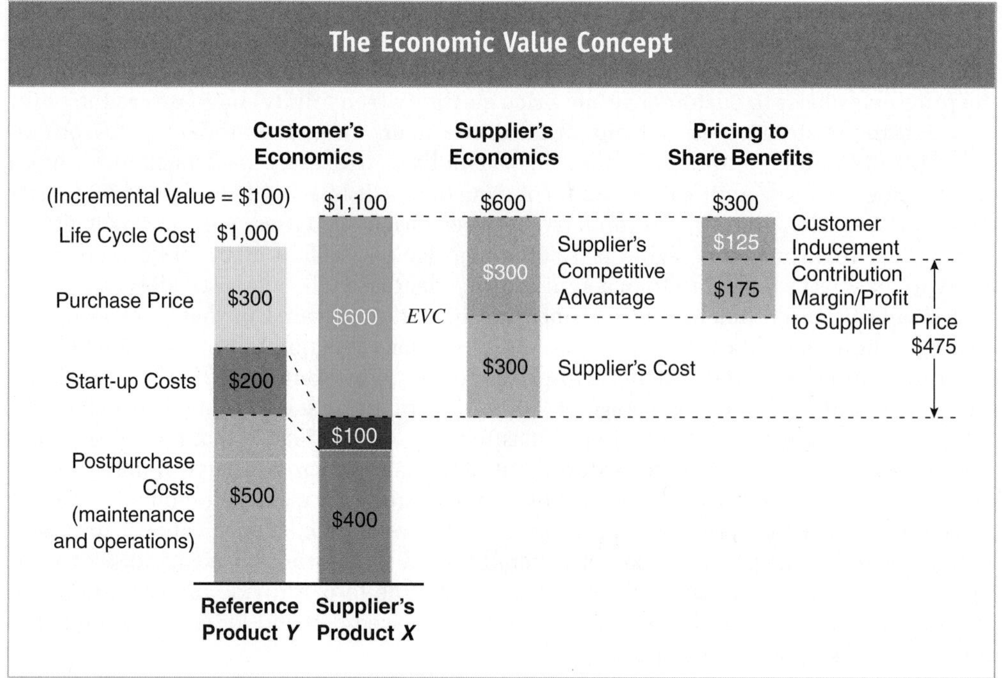

company is willing to give a "discount" of $125 from the true economic value. Because industrial buyers like to be shown how they can make a greater profit by choosing one product over another, this information should be quite persuasive.

The method shown in Figure 9.4 can be applied to both products and services. As we noted in Chapter 1, a trend in business is to purchase a service from an outside vendor to replace the company's operation, a strategy known as *outsourcing.* For example, rather than operating the company cafeteria itself, a company might subcontract the operation to a food service company that specializes in such work. Other examples include General Motors paying PPG Industries to operate its automobile painting facilities and IBM contracting with FedEx to act as a warehousing agent around the world. In these cases, the agents whose services are purchased can use the cost of the company providing the service itself as a reference product. Even if it is more expensive to pay the agent for these services than for the company to provide the service itself, benefits such as better use of employee time and company capital, improved productivity, and better technology can be quantified and shown to produce value to potential customers.

This method works well with products and services for which the economic benefits can be quantified. It is applicable for many consumer products. For example, General Electric can determine how much more to charge for an energy-saving refrigerator than for a competitor's model that is less energy efficient by calculating the average electricity savings over the lifetime of the product. Products such as disposable diapers have some economic benefits over cloth diapers in terms of time, detergent, and electricity savings. For many consumer products though, benefits cannot be stated in economic terms, and this method has limited usefulness.

Survey-Based Methods

When economic-based approaches do not work, an alternative approach is to use survey-based methods to obtain willingness-to-pay information from customers. A variety of such methods have been developed. The problem with these approaches is that it is difficult to get accurate information from pencil-and-paper exercises about what a customer might do in a buying situation. Although this problem is typical of marketing research, it is particularly a problem for pricing research, where people often give inaccurate responses about how much they are willing to pay.

For example, the following question is often used in surveys: "Please check the box next to the price you are willing to pay for this product." There is little incentive for respondents to check anything but the box with the lowest price. Thus, survey-based pricing research must use more subtle approaches for measuring willingness-to-pay.

Despite this problem, a variety of types of open-ended (where alternative responses are not provided) questions have been used to measure customer value:

- "Above what price would you judge (the brand) to be too expensive?"
- "At what price would you consider (the brand) to be so expensive that regardless of its quality it is not worth buying?"
- "What is the highest price you are willing to pay for (the brand)?"
- What is the likelihood you would buy this product at a price of ___?
- How much would you be willing to pay for this product?

The **dollarmetric method** creates a scale that puts responses in monetary terms. Table 9.1 applies and analyzes a dollarmetric scale for soft drinks. This example analyzes five brands—Coke, Pepsi, 7-Up, Dr. Pepper, and Fresca—to determine what should be the relative prices of the brands. Consumers are given the brands in pairs. The respondent first chooses which of the two brands she or he prefers. Next, the respondent indicates how much extra she or he would be willing to pay to get a six-pack of the preferred brand.[17] The marketing manager then analyzes the data by summing the differences, positive and negative, in each brand comparison. As the bottom of Table 9.1 shows, for this customer, a six-pack of Coke is worth 2 cents more than Pepsi, 8 cents more than 7-Up, 5 cents more than Dr. Pepper, and 12 cents more than Fresca. If these results held up over a national sample, they would give some indication of the price difference Coke could maintain over the competing brands.

dollarmetric method
in estimating customer value, a method used in conjunction with survey based methods that creates a scale that puts survey responses in monetary terms

One of the most popular methods for estimating customer value is **conjoint analysis**. This method was described in Chapter 8 in the context of new-product development. Tables 8.4 and 8.5 demonstrate how price is incorporated into conjoint studies. By trying different price levels in the experimental design (Table 8.4), the manager can determine when a potential price is too high for a potential customer to consider buying the brand.

conjoint analysis
a popular marketing research method in new product development that uses theoretical profiles or concepts to determine how customers value different levels of product attributes

Table 9.1

Dollarmetric Example

Pair of Brands (more preferred brand underlined)	Amount Extra Willing to Pay to Get a Six-Pack of the More Preferred Brand (cents)
<u>Coke</u>, Pepsi	2
<u>Coke</u>, 7-Up	8
<u>Coke</u>, Dr. Pepper	5
<u>Coke</u>, Fresca	12
<u>Pepsi</u>, 7-Up	6
<u>Pepsi</u>, Dr. Pepper	3
<u>Pepsi</u>, Fresca	10
7-Up, <u>Dr. Pepper</u>	3
<u>7-Up</u>, Fresca	4
<u>Dr. Pepper</u>, Fresca	7

Analysis

Coke + 2 (vs. Pepsi) + 8 (vs. 7-Up) + 5 (vs. Dr. Pepper) + 12 (vs. Fresca)	= 27
Pepsi − 2 + 6 + 3 + 10	= 17
7-Up − 8 − 6 − 3 + 4	= −13
Dr. Pepper − 5 − 3 + 3 + 7	= 2
Fresca − 12 − 10 − 4 − 7	= −33

Figure 9.5

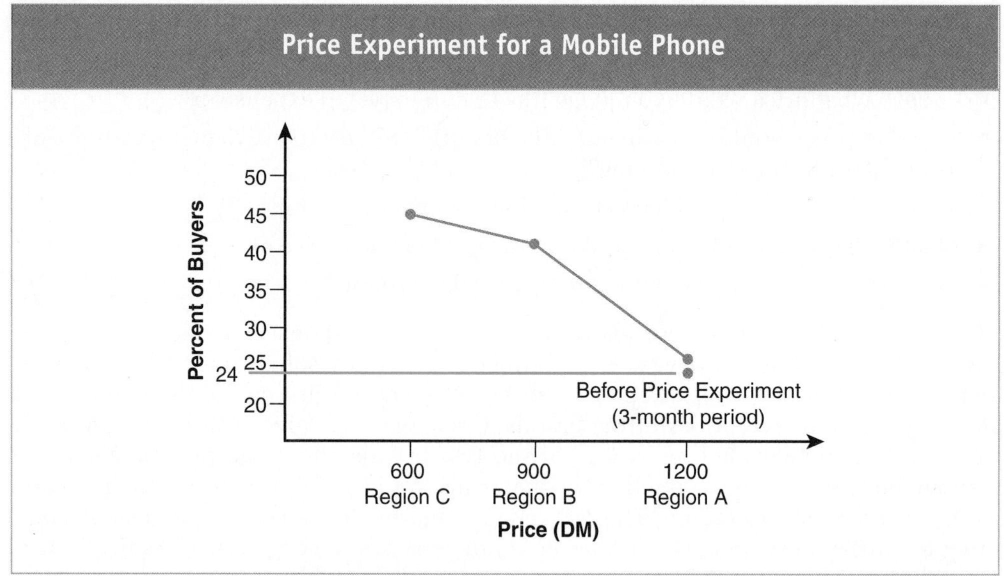

Source: Robert J. Dolan and Herman Simon (1996), *Power Pricing* (New York: Free Press). Reprinted with the permission of The Free Press, A Division of Simon & Schuster Adult Publishing Group, from Power Pricing by Robert J. Dolan and Hermann Simon.

Field Experimental Methods

field experiments
an experiment that takes place in a realistic environment

An alternative to survey-based methods is to try to obtain actual market data after manipulating price in different markets. These are referred to as **field experiments**. Assuming that the markets are comparable on a number of dimensions (sales, demographics, marketing effort), a marketing manager can get a more accurate read on the effects of different prices than can be obtained from pencil-and-paper exercises.

An illustration of this approach is an experiment conducted by Mercedes-Benz in Germany.[18] The company investigated how much people would be willing to pay for a mobile phone installed in their new cars. Before the experiment, the company charged 1,200 DM and 24 percent of the customers opted to have the phone installed. The company set three prices in different regions of Germany: 1,200 DM (control condition) in region A, 900 DM in region B, and 600 DM in region C. The results, shown in Figure 9.5, indicate that a nice downward-sloping demand curve was obtained. About the same percentage of buyers (26 percent) bought the phone at the original price. However, 41 percent bought it at 900 DM and 45 percent bought it at 600 DM. Thus, there was a significant elasticity (2.32) from the price decrease of 1,200 to 900 (58 percent increase in percent purchasing divided by the 25 percent decrease in price), but demand was inelastic from 900 to 600 DM (10 percent increase in percent purchasing divided by the 33 percent decrease in price), indicating that a price decrease to 900 DM but not lower might make sense.

Application Hewlett-Packard

Hewlett-Packard (HP) developed a new test instrument and wanted to find an appropriate pricing level.[19] The company realized that asking direct questions about willingness-to-pay was not likely to produce accurate responses. As a result, it developed a catalog that included competing products and the new product. HP then hired a marketing research firm to conduct the study and disguise who was collecting the data to avoid biasing responses. Potential customers were randomly assigned to different groups, and each group received the same brochure, except that the price for the HP instrument varied. Because all other factors were controlled, the only difference in response had to be due to price. The customers were then asked to indicate which product they would choose, thus simulating the buying experience. Interestingly, HP managers found that as they increased price, demand went up. They priced the instrument thousands of dollars higher than they had planned.

Application | Rolling Rock Beer

The venerable Rolling Rock beer brand, owned by Labatt USA, was considering changing its traditional green bottle with a paper label to a more jazzy-looking bottle with a variety of white painted labels.[20] Although the brand had a long tradition and a stable base of drinkers, its sales were declining because of inroads made by microbrewed and more contemporary brands. An important question that had to be addressed, along with general preferences for the new labels, was how much consumers would be willing to pay for Rolling Rock with the new labels.

The Labatt managers recruited consumers at shopping malls and other venues to view actual shelf sets of beer at every price range. The consumers were given money to spend in the form of chips. They were exposed to the old Rolling Rock bottles (old graphics and paper labels) and the new packages (two new painted graphics) at different prices and asked to allocate their next 10 purchases over Rolling Rock and the other brands in the test. Not only did the new packages gain customer approval, but also consumers consistently indicated that they would be willing to pay more for the brand in the new packages. In three regions, the Northeast, Southeast, and West, purchase intent among Rolling Rock users increased dramatically at prices 20 cents higher per six-pack.

Application | Online Price Experiments

If a business has a significant e-commerce component, it is relatively easy today to get a good idea of customers' willingness-to-pay by running pricing experiments. On the Web, prices can be varied by the day, time of day, or any unit of time desired. In addition, given information obtained from customers who have registered at the site, it is possible to vary prices by buyer versus nonbuyer or any number of demographic variables collected and see how demand changes under the different manipulations.

The National Academies Press was interested in better understanding what price they could charge for electronic (PDF) versus hard-copy publications as well as for a number of product bundles.[21] Researchers for the Press ran an online choice experiment for 500 titles that the publisher was already selling in printed format at their Web site. Two groups of customers were tested: one group that had showed their intent to purchase by having a printed book in their online shopping cart and having clicked on the checkout button, and a second group that was browsing for a book title for which a PDF version existed. PDF prices were set at six levels relative to the printed book prices: 110 percent, 100 percent, 75 percent, 50 percent, 25 percent, and 0 percent (free). The goal was to choose the price that maximized profits for the Press—a combination of the demand at a given price, the price itself, and the cost of the book in either form. The analysis showed that the profit maximizing PDF price was 75 percent of the printed price.

Using the Perceived Value Concept

Marketing managers can use the concept of perceived value by considering a functional relationship among market share, perceived value, and price:

$$\text{Market share} = f\,(\text{Perceived value/Price})$$

As an application of this relationship, consider an observed decline in the market share of a product. How can this trend be reversed? Usually the immediate response is a decrease in the denominator, that is, a price cut (through list price or a price promotion). Cutting the price is certainly one way to bring the relationship between perceived value and price back into balance.

What many managers do not realize, however, is that the cost of cutting price is substantial, particularly if the price cut is met by the competitors—leaving the market the same in terms of sales and share but at a lower price point, implying lost profits for all. To get an idea of what happens to profits with a price cut and no volume or cost change, look at Table 9.2.[22] As you can see, across a variety of industries, the average drop in operating profit from a 1 percent price cut is 8 percent, and it rises to as high as 23.7 percent for food and drug stores. Even if the competitors do not match, there will be a profit loss if the volume does not more than compensate for the price drop (if the absolute value of the price elasticity is less than 1) or if the competitors only partially decrease price.

Table 9.2

Profit Impact of Price Cuts

Industry	Percent Decrease in Operating Profit from a 1% Reduction in Price
Food and drug stores	−23.7%
Airlines	−12.9
Computers, office equipment	−11.0
Average	**−8.0**
Tobacco	−4.9
Semiconductors	−3.9
Diversified financials	−2.4

Source: Janice Revell (2001), "The Price Is Not Always Right," *Fortune,* May 14, p. 240.

However, there is another alternative to cutting price: you can attempt to increase the perceived value of the product. Think of the decrease in profit from a price cut as a pool of money which can be invested in the product. For example, you can:

- Improve the product itself by increasing actual quality or offering better service or longer warranty period.
- Invest in the brand through advertising.
- Institute value-added services such as technical support or financing.
- Improve the sales effort by training the sales force to sell value rather than price.

Note that activities designed to raise perceived value can cost considerably less than the lost profits from cutting price. How much does it cost to improve sales training procedures? How expensive is it to offer improved customer service? Value-enhancing activities are not free, but they are usually fixed costs that can be spread over a large volume, as opposed to per-unit reductions in margins. Companies like Procter & Gamble and BMW do not usually cut their prices but spend money enhancing customer value through product innovation, design, and image-based communications.

Note also that the notion of perceived value does not imply that customers are always looking for the lowest price, even in difficult economic times. In fact, during recessions, customers are particularly looking for products high in perceived value, that is, those that deliver excellent quality for the price. A study during the recession of 2008–2010 showed that consumers relied more on their perceptions of value when deciding which brands warranted their continued loyalty.[23] For example, in the running shoe category, Nike, although it can charge $150 for a pair of shoes, was perceived to be the leading brand in terms of value. Similarly, J. Crew, while not the cheapest, was ranked number one for value, among other attributes.[24]

Also notice that the numerator and denominator of the market share function are not independent; that is, for some product categories, perceived value may be a function of price. In this case, lowering price may not actually produce the increase or stabilization in share desired because the functional relationship will not change: a lower price results in lower perceived quality. In fact, increasing price may raise perceived quality. Even if the increase in perceived quality does not rise proportionately more than the increase in price, it will mean higher profits at the same market share level.

Application Genentech

A good example of this value-adding approach to pricing was provided by biotechnology firm Genentech in 1990.[25] In 1987, the firm introduced a drug called tissue plasminogen activator (TPA) that clears blood clots. At $2,220 per dose, the product is important to the company. In March 1990, a study was released showing that the drug was no more effective than an alternative, streptokinase, that sold for only $220 per dose. However, months later, Genentech was still selling TPA for $2,220 per dose. How? First, it trained its sales force to aggressively point out some of the limitations of the damaging study. Second, it temporarily gave hospital pharmacies a longer period in which to pay for TPA, thus encouraging them to stock up on the drug. Clearly, the costs of these two moves were far less than the cost of dropping the price of the product.

Competition and Pricing

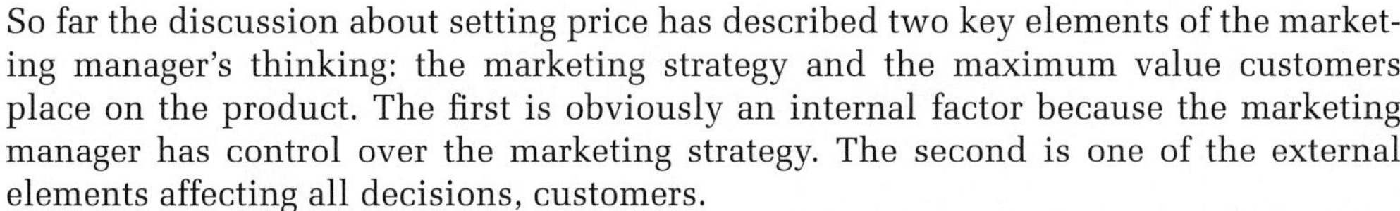

So far the discussion about setting price has described two key elements of the marketing manager's thinking: the marketing strategy and the maximum value customers place on the product. The first is obviously an internal factor because the marketing manager has control over the marketing strategy. The second is one of the external elements affecting all decisions, customers.

A third critical element in pricing decisions is the competition. Competitors' prices act as a reference point, either explicitly (as shown in the value computations earlier in this chapter), or implicitly, as a way to assess the price of the product in question. Competitors' prices do not necessarily represent willingness to pay because the set of possible prices or marketing strategies may have been limited. That is, the competitors may not have an accurate idea of customers' willingness to pay.

Competitors' Costs

Marketing managers cannot make intelligent pricing decisions without having some estimate of the relative cost positions held by competitors. Even better are estimates of the actual costs. An understanding of the cost structure of the market provides at least two types of help. First, assuming that no brand would be priced below variable cost, cost estimates provide you with an idea of how low some competitors can price. This can be very useful in a price battle in which prices are going down. Second, cost estimates give you some idea of the margins in the category or industry. Using data on sales volume, which are usually easy to obtain, and information on marketing program costs, you can then estimate total profits. This can be important information in forecasting the likelihood that a product will stay in the market or estimating the amount of money a competitor has to put behind the brand's marketing strategy.

Costs can be estimated in several ways. A common approach for manufactured products is to use reverse engineering (see Chapter 6) to analyze the cost structure. You should purchase competitors' products and take them apart, studying the costs of the components and packaging. For many products, managers can readily identify components and their costs in the market. If a component is proprietary, such as a custom microprocessor in a computer, the cost can be estimated by engineers or other personnel.

Another way to estimate costs, or at least margins, is to use publicly available data on the competitors. Based on annual reports, 10K statements, and the like, you can ascertain average margins. These can be assumed to apply directly to the cost estimation, especially if the product is a large component of total sales or if, as is often the case, the company tends to use a cost-plus-percent-markup pricing strategy.

Particularly for manufactured products (although it has been found to apply to some services as well), it is possible to understand current costs and forecast future costs through the use of the experience curve. As we described in Chapter 2, the experience curve phenomenon applies to certain products for which repetitive production of larger and larger amounts and concomitant investment in new manufacturing equipment systematically reduce unit costs over time. The conventional functional relationship assumed in experience curve economics is that unit costs (adjusted for inflation) are a decreasing function of accumulated experience, or production volume. Figure 9.6 shows an example of the experience curve phenomenon in the context of pricing. In this case, experience is approximated by market share. Unit costs (and prices) are shown to be correlated with market share: the larger the share, the lower the unit costs. If you can construct a plot like that shown in Figure 9.6 and statistically estimate the implied relationship between share and unit costs, you can forecast future relative cost positions under different assumptions of brand shares.

Figure 9.6

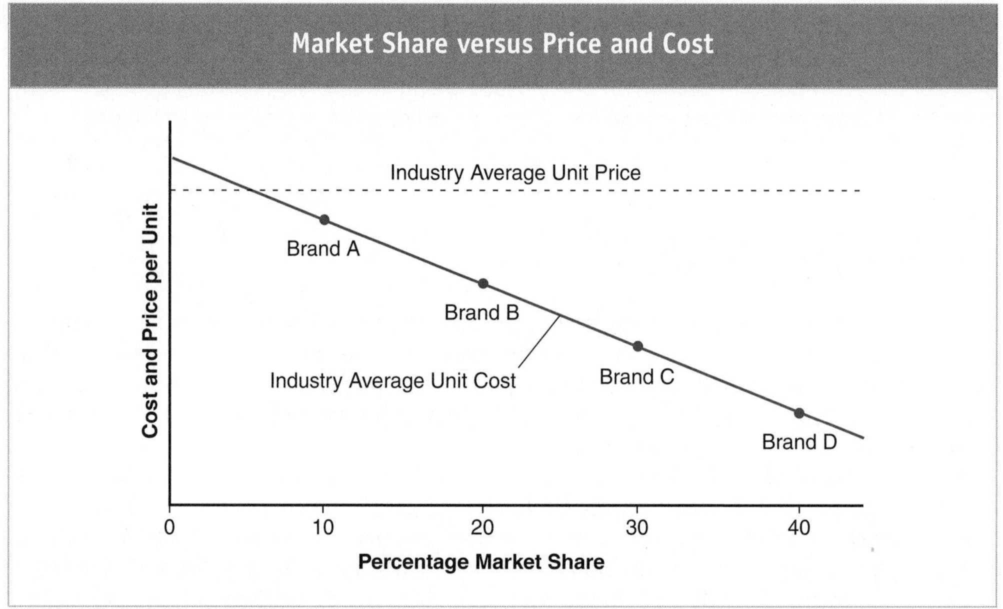

The costs of delivering services are more difficult to estimate. Because the costs associated with service products such as labor and office space are largely fixed, you can estimate relative cost positions by examining the number of employees, looking at efficiency ratios such as sales per employee, and assessing other similar measures. Again, it is particularly useful to understand the cost structure by becoming a customer of a competitor's service.

Application SanDisk

Costs for technology-based products drop for other reasons than experience. SanDisk is a company that manufacturers flash memory chips and cards.[26] Flash memory is a form of rewritable memory that holds its content without the need of a power source. For example, SanDisk CompactFlash memory cards are used to store pictures in digital cameras. Products like flash memory are subject to the famous Moore's Law, which implies that the amount of storage that can be squeezed on to a card doubles almost every 18 months. Thus the price per megabyte drops significantly over time. As a result, SanDisk cuts its prices 30 to 40 percent every year due to the improvements in technology.

The Role of Costs

We suggested earlier in this chapter that costs should have little to do with the pricing decision other than to act as a floor or lower limit for price (see Figure 9.3). In a non-market-driven firm, full cost (variable costs plus some allocation for overhead) plus some target margin are used to set price. This approach totally ignores the customer: the resulting price may be either above or below what the customer is willing to pay for the product.

Other problems exist with using costs to set price. First, there are at least four different kinds of costs to consider. *Development costs* are expenses involved in bringing new products to market. Often these costs are spread out over many years and sometimes different products. Should price be set to recover these costs and, if so, in what time period? In some industries such as pharmaceuticals, patent protection allows companies to set the prices of prescription drugs high initially to recover development costs and then reduce them when the drugs come off patent and the generics enter the category. However, if there is no legal way to keep competitors out of the market, these costs must be viewed as sunk costs that do not affect decision making after the product is introduced into the market. Otherwise, the resulting price may be above customers' perceived value. A second kind of cost is *overhead costs* such as the corporate jet and the president's salary. These costs must ultimately be covered by revenues from individual products, but they are not associated with any one product. Often, the mechanism used to allocate these overhead costs among products is arbitrary and bears no relationship to how individual products use overhead or whether they would change if the product were withdrawn from the market. A third kind of cost is *direct fixed costs*. These costs, such as the marketing manager's salary and product-related advertising and promotion, are associated with individual products but do not vary with sales volume. Finally, there are *variable costs,* the per-unit costs of making the product or delivering the service. Of course, these must be recovered by the price.

Therefore, one problem with using costs to set price is that several kinds of costs are related in different ways to an individual product. When costs are used as the basis for setting price, you should ask, "Which costs?" Are they costs related to marketing the product or product line, or are they costs over which you have no control? Using price as a cost-recovery mechanism can lead to a mismatch between price and customers' perceptions of value for your product or service.

A second problem with using costs to set price, particularly variable or unit costs, is that they may be a function of volume (e.g., the experience curve) and as a result may be difficult to know in advance when developing marketing plans. Even if this is not the case, unit costs may be related to the use of capacity, which is also uncertain.

In most instances, customers do not care what the firm's costs are. As Drucker put it, "Customers do not see it as their job to ensure manufacturers a profit."[27] Using cost increases to justify raising price generates little sympathy from customers, particularly industrial customers, because the price increase has just raised their costs, which they may not be able to pass along to their customers.

Costs do play an important role in pricing. In the new-product development process, the projected costs (however defined) and price determine whether a product is forecasted to be sufficiently profitable to be introduced. This issue was covered more completely in Chapter 8.

Deciding How Much of the Strategic Pricing Gap to Capture

Using Figure 9.3 as the conceptual foundation, the key pricing decision becomes how much of the customer value to keep or give away. The factors involved in this decision are shown in Figure 9.7.

Figure 9.7

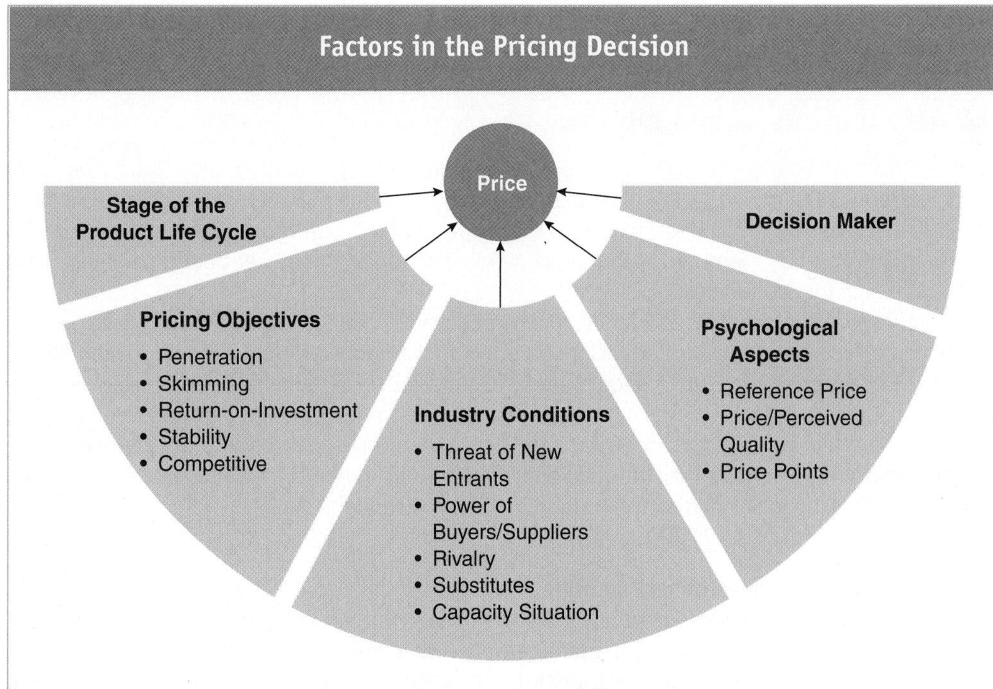

Pricing Objectives

A pricing policy can accomplish many different objectives for a product or service.

Penetration Pricing

penetration/market share pricing
a pricing policy intended to gain as much market share as possible; often used as part of an entry strategy for a new product

Penetration or **market share pricing** entails giving most of the value to the customer and retaining a small margin. The objective is to gain as much market share as possible. It is often used as part of an entry strategy for a new product and is particularly useful for preventing competitive entry. First, there is less of the market for the competition to gain if you have been successful in penetrating the market. Second, the economics of entry look less attractive if the price levels are low. Penetration pricing is also appropriate when experience or scale effects lead to a favorable volume–cost relationship and when a large segment of the potential customer base is price-sensitive.

There are some drawbacks to penetration pricing. It should not be used in a product category when there is a price–perceived quality relationship unless the marketing strategy is at the low end of perceived quality. In addition, if the product has a strong competitive advantage, this advantage is dissipated by pricing at an unusually low level. Another limitation of penetration pricing is that it is always more acceptable to customers to reduce price than to raise it. This limits the flexibility of this pricing approach in some situations. Apple was using penetration pricing when it initially offered music for $0.99 per song. A reason for doing this was to draw customers into the market because it was a new technology that was unfamiliar to many consumers (it was also a simple, straightforward policy). However, there was the risk that when the company eventually raised the price for some songs, consumers would view this as an unjust price increase as they became used to the $0.99 price independent of the popularity or newness of the song.[28]

Skimming

skimming/prestige pricing
a pricing policy used when there is a strong price–perceived quality relationship and the product is positioned at the high end of the market; often used when costs are not related to volume and gaining significant market share is not an objective

The opposite of penetration pricing is **skimming** or **prestige pricing**. Skimming gives more of the cost–value gap to you than to the customer. This strategy is appropriate in a variety of situations. If there is a strong price–perceived quality relationship (e.g., wine) and the value proposition includes a positioning of the product at the high end of the market, this objective makes sense. It is also a reasonable objective when there is little chance of competition in the near future. However, the higher the price, the higher the margins (holding costs constant, of course) and thus the greater the chance that competition will enter because its economic calculations will look better. Skimming is also a good objective when costs are not related to volume and managers are therefore less concerned about building significant market share. Finally, as we noted in Chapter 2, skimming makes sense early in the product life cycle because the early adopters of a new technology are normally price insensitive.

Application Apple iPhone

Apple used a skimming strategy for the iPhone when it was introduced in July 2007. The company charged $599, making it the most expensive phone on the market. However, in September 2007, the company cut the price to $399. The move sparked outrage both by customers who had paid $599 and by members of the press, who were calling the earlier buyers "suckers" and that Apple should give them an "iPology."[29]

While there are a number of ways to interpret Apple's pricing moves, the drop in price is consistent with a skimming strategy. Consumers who wanted bragging rights to be the first to own an iPhone paid more and should have. Unfortunately, it is difficult to know when the number of innovators (see Chapter 4) has been exhausted and when the early adopter stage of the diffusion of innovations has been reached. It is clear, however, from the data presented at the beginning of this chapter that the incident had no long-run impact on the popularity of the iPhone and that the initial skimming strategy has been forgotten.

Return on Sales or Investment Pricing

return on sales/investment pricing
a pricing policy that assumes you can set a price that will deliver the rate of return demanded by senior management; most often used when a product has a monopoly position

Return on sales or **investment pricing** implies that you can set a price that delivers the rate of return demanded by senior management. As a result, investment pricing ignores both customer value and the competition. It is useful only when the product has a monopoly or near monopoly position so that the market will produce the needed sales volume at the price you set. This is typical of the pricing of regulated utilities such as gas and electricity.

Pricing for Stability

Sometimes customers for industrial products are as concerned about price stability as they are about actual price levels. This is because it is difficult to develop profit forecasts and long-range plans when prices for products and services that constitute a substantial portion of the buyer's costs fluctuate dramatically. Telephone rates for large users such as telemarketing firms and banks fall into this category. Such customers expect rates to rise over time. However, significant price hikes at random intervals play havoc with their planning processes. As a result, these firms would rather pay a somewhat higher average rate than be subjected to constant fluctuations. Forward contracts on raw materials play this role in many manufacturing industries.

Competitive Pricing

Competitive pricing describes a situation in which you try to price at the market average or match a particular brand's price. This is appropriate when customers have not been persuaded that significant differences exist among the competitors and that they view the product as a commodity. It may also be necessary in a category with high fixed costs because any loss of sales volume drives down sales and generates less revenue to cover those costs. It could also be used when introducing a new product and you wish to indicate that your product is as good as the leading competitor's by matching its price. For example, when Microsoft introduced the Xbox videogame console in 2001, the company priced it at $299, exactly the same price as Sony's PlayStation 2, the market leader.

competitive pricing
a pricing policy in which the objective is to maintain a competitive price by either pricing at the market average or copying a particular brand

In some industries, competitive pricing is taken to an extreme, resulting in price "wars." A price war exists when two or more competitors are engaged in pricing "interactions" that occur at a quick pace with unsustainable prices spiraling downward. The main industry factors that are characterized when price wars have occurred include new and aggressive entrants into a product category, excess manufacturing capacity, slow sales growth, few but large competitors, high exit barriers, low product differentiation, high customer price sensitivity, and the strategic importance of a product to a company.[30] Airlines, long-distance phone service, electronic brokerage, beer, and soft drinks are industries that have seen price wars in recent years. Almost invariably, competitors end up worse off than they were before the price war. The best solution is to stop the war before it starts. One option is to signal the competition through public statements in various media that you will match any price decrease using all your resources. This indicates that you prefer to compete on nonprice attributes. A second option, if appropriate, is to reveal the fact that you have a cost advantage. For example, it is common knowledge that the consumer–products company Sara Lee has the lowest costs in its industry, though not the lowest prices. The company uses its low costs as an implicit threat to competitors to stay away from a price battle.[31]

Psychological Aspects of Price

Customers actively process price information; that is, they consider the price they observe and make judgments about whether it is fair, whether it is a good deal, or whether it signals information about product quality. They also continually assess prices based on prior purchasing experience, formal communications (e.g., advertising), informal communications (e.g., friends and neighbors), and point-of-purchase lists of prices—using those assessments in the ultimate purchasing decision. This is consistent with price being a communications vehicle as well as a revenue generator. Three key concepts related to the psychological aspects of price are reference prices, the price–perceived quality relationship, and price points.

Reference Prices

Customers assess prices not only absolutely (the price itself) but also relative to some internal standard. A **reference price** is any standard of comparison against which a potential transaction or purchase price is compared. In a retailing setting, the reference

reference price
any standard of comparison against which an observed potential transaction or purchase price is compared

price is often listed on the sales tag as the "original" price from which subsequent markdowns have been made. In this setting, a reference price could also be a competitor's price. These reference prices are external reference prices, and an internal reference price is a mental price used to assess an observed price. Internal reference prices are formed from advertising, past purchasing experience, and so on, and are often called perceived prices because the customer considers them the actual prices of the products in a category.

Reference prices can have a significant impact on brand choice for both durable and nondurable products.[32] In particular, when the observed price is higher than the reference price (the internal concept of reference price), it can decrease sales because the customer perceives this difference as an unpleasant surprise. For example, the large price increases for cars in the 1970s created what became known as "sticker shock" when consumer reference prices for cars were significantly lower than the prices they saw in the showroom. In the online music business, $0.99 has become the reference price for songs. At $1.29 for some songs, sales could suffer. A happier situation occurs when the observed price is below the reference price. This happens when a brand a consumer might buy anyway is being promoted at a lower price. Interestingly, several studies have found that the unpleasant surprises have a greater impact on purchasing probabilities than the pleasant ones.

The concept of reference price has important implications for marketing managers. Consider a brand that has been price promoted for several weeks. The customer will begin to replace the normal price with the promoted price as the reference point. Then when the brand returns to the regular price, the customer may perceive the change as an increase in price and interpret it negatively. This is particularly a problem during a recession when many companies are either cutting prices or running promotions with significant price cuts. When financial conditions improve and prices can return to more normal levels, consumers have already adapted to the lower prices and view the new prices as increases. Instead, the prices could be increased in steps to allow consumers to adapt more slowly to the higher prices. Likewise, steep price cuts from skimming prices could be replaced by gradual reductions so that there is no "punishment" for the firm like that noted earlier for Apple's iPhone pricing strategy.

A second important reference price is expected future price. This is a particularly important concept for any product that experiences significant price changes over time. The airline industry has had protracted fare wars in which the prices of some flights fell rapidly in short periods of time. Some segments of fliers, such as business travelers, are unaffected by changes in fares because they do not have discretion about when they fly. However, fliers who do have discretion, such as people who are traveling for pleasure or have flexible schedules, simply wait for prices to drop further before booking. Price cutting merely exacerbates the airlines' problems because sales are low while discretionary travelers wait for the fares to drop even further. The same situation results from rebate programs in the automobile industry. Why purchase a car while a rebate war is in progress? Why not wait to see whether further price cuts are possible? Finally, new consumer durables are also subject to this phenomenon. Whenever a new Intel microprocessor is introduced and new personal computer models are developed for it, the prices are initially high but drop predictably. Discretionary purchasers can simply wait until the prices decrease further. The problem is predictability, in that if you create a predictable pricing pattern, you should not underestimate customers' abilities to process the information and make decisions based on their personal forecasts of future prices.

Relationship between Price and Perceived Quality

Customers draw inferences about product quality from price. In some situations, contrary to standard microeconomic theory, a higher price can lead to higher rather than lower demand. This occurs when price is used to signal that the product is of high quality. It often occurs under a condition of asymmetric information, that is, when the seller has more information about the true quality of the product or service than the buyer.[33] In addition, a low price could signal low quality. Thus, it is not necessarily the case that continually dropping prices is a good idea. Research has shown that for most products, customers not only have an upper price threshold (customer value) but a lower one as well; that is, a price below the threshold reduces demand.

Many instances of a strong price–perceived quality relationship occur when a product's quality is difficult to assess before purchasing or difficult to assess at all. These products are often called *experience goods* (if you have to try the product before assessing its quality) or *credence goods* (if even after you have purchased and used the product or service, the quality is hard to evaluate). Examples of the former are most services such as haircuts and legal advice. Examples of credence goods are car repairs such as brake servicing (the consumer cannot actually see what happened) and wine (only experts can distinguish between different levels of quality).

Rolex charges high prices for its watches to ensure exclusivity.
Source: Daniel Acker/Getty Images, Inc—Liaison

Marketers often use a high price to signal exclusivity or prestige. A high price means that fewer customers can afford it. Rolex could charge substantially less for its watches and still make a profit. However, because few consumers can afford thousands of dollars for a watch, few will own a Rolex, which is how their owners want it.

The major implication for marketing managers in this situation is that, as we have said earlier in this chapter, the price must be consistent with the marketing strategy. If customer research shows a significant correlation between price and perceived quality, a value proposition stressing quality or value-added features requires a concomitant high price. An exotic vodka supported with a highly creative advertising campaign (e.g., Absolut) cannot be priced at $1.99 per bottle without striking a discordant feeling in the (presumably) upscale consumer.

Psychological Price Points

In some cases, somewhat artificial price levels or price points distinguish between different market segments (see the discussion of the GPS devices earlier in this chapter). In these situations, seemingly minor differences in price that separate price levels defined, say, by the number of digits, can have (or at least are believed to have) a large impact on customer perception of how expensive a product is. For example, in the iTunes example from the beginning of the chapter, the $0.99 level of the initial price may have been a reservation price, but it could also have been a psychological barrier.

An interesting and related phenomenon in pricing is the use of odd prices for many goods. Odd prices are just below an even number. For example, many prices end in $0.99 like the initial iTunes price and many of the applications for the iPhone; many higher-priced items are $499 (e.g., the iPhone) or even $499,999 (e.g., a house). Clearly, many managers feel that the right-most digits of a price have a significant impact on customer decision making.[34]

Stage of the Product Life Cycle

In Chapter 2, the product life cycle was shown to have an important impact on the strategic choices available to the marketing manager. Not surprisingly the method used to set prices can also change over the life cycle. Table 9.3 illustrates how DuPont approaches pricing with the life cycle in mind. The company simplifies the life cycle into three generic stages: sole supplier (introductory phase); competitive penetration (early and late growth); and shared stability, commodity competition, and withdrawal

Table 9.3

DuPont Pricing over the Product Life Cycle		
Competitive Cycle Stage	**Focus of Attention**	**Pricing Method**
Sole supplier	Customers	Value-in-use Perceived value
Competitive penetration	Customers Competitors	Reaction analysis
Shared stability	Competition and costs	Profitability analysis
Commodity competition		
Withdrawal		

(maturity and decline). Particularly interesting is the focus for pricing decisions over the life cycle. When little competition exists, focus is on the customer and value is stressed. Notice that there is no mention of variable or investment costs that must be recovered. When competition enters, focus is on both customers and competitors. Thus customer value is still important, but how competitors will react is also addressed. Finally, in the late stages of the product category, the focus shifts toward competitors and costs to determine whether remaining in the market makes economic sense. There, profitability analysis is the key.

Another way to look at the impact of the product life cycle is through experience curve pricing. Figure 9.8 shows three different pricing scenarios. Increases in industry cumulative volume represent movement along the product life cycle. One possible pricing pattern, A, is strict experience curve pricing, with price declines as costs decline. Sometimes prices drop even in anticipation of the resulting cost decreases with increased volume. This approach is usually an attempt to maintain a low price strategy over the entire life cycle and maximize market share (penetration). In pattern B, the manager keeps margins up for a period of time because there is little competition (segment 1 of the curve is flatter than segment 2) and then drops the price more rapidly as competition enters later in the life cycle. In pattern C, the manager reacts twice: first when competition enters (segment 2 is again steeper than segment 1) and again when competition drops out (segment 3 is flatter than segment 2). Thus, under this last pricing pattern, margins are high in the early phase of the life cycle, then drop due to competition, and then rise again after a category shakeout occurs.

Industry Conditions

Different aspects of the industry situation should also be considered when setting price:

- **Threat of new entrants.** The likelihood of new entrants into a category has an important effect on price. If the likelihood is low (barriers to entry are high), higher price levels can be sustained. If new entrants are possible, either from within the industry or from industries making substitute products, lower prices help protect the market position from potential erosion and make the profit potential of the market look worse for new-product entries.
- **Power of buyers/suppliers.** High buyer power obviously tends to depress prices because it puts more pressure on the product to deliver a good value-to-price ratio. If suppliers have high power, they will often charge higher prices for goods or services supplied, whether raw materials, labor, or anything else. High supplier power thus raises the floor beneath which prices cannot be set.
- **Rivalry.** High industry rivalry clearly tends to be manifested in strong price competition or even price wars. Industries with numerous, equally-balanced competitors leads to higher rivalry than industries with few competitors with a strong leader.
- **Pressure from substitutes.** Like the threat of entry, the more available potential substitute technologies or solutions to customer problems are and the more value they offer, the greater the chance that price competition will exist. For example,

Figure 9.8

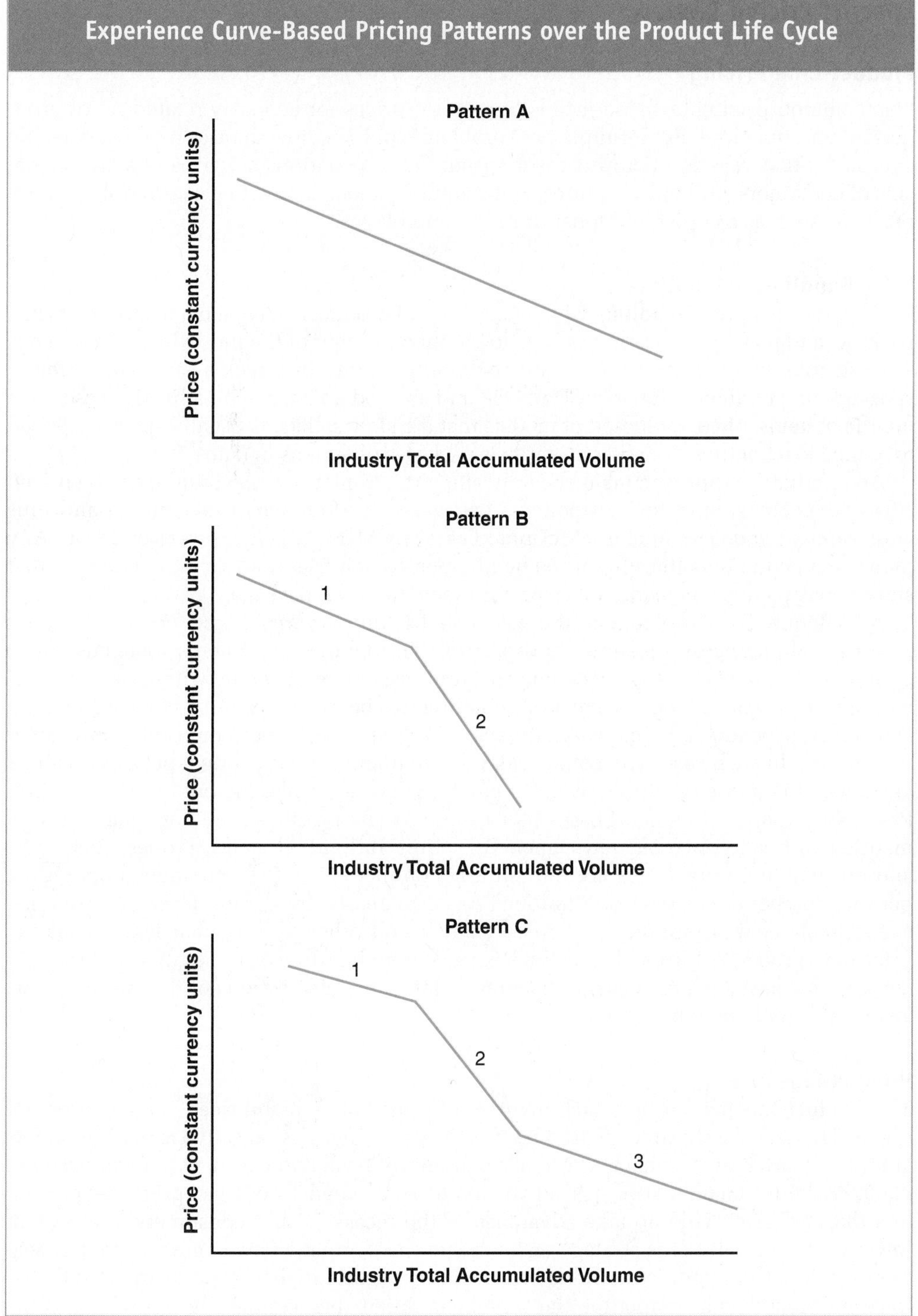

even though the Blu-ray high-definition video standard "won" the war with its rival HD DVD in 2008, prices for Blu-ray players dropped significantly in 2009 and 2010 due to the availability of a number of other technologies for watching HD videos at home, such as direct Internet streaming.

- **Unused capacity.** This concept is particularly important in a high-fixed-cost, high-contribution-margin (price minus variable cost) product category. These markets are characterized by some of the most vicious price battles because there is plenty of margin to give and the products must generate revenues to cover fixed costs. An excellent example of this kind of situation is the airline industry. Where markets are unregulated, price competition between airlines is intense (consider any market in which Southwest Airlines competes).

Specific Pricing Tactics

Product-Line Pricing

One common pricing task you face is how to set prices for a closely related set of products or a product line. For example, one problem would be how to price a line of personal computers that vary in microprocessor speed. Other variations are sizes of a TV screen, size of containers, and other features. A different problem is how to price complementary products such as a copier and toner or razors and blades.

price bundling
an approach to product line pricing in which a set of products is offered to customers in a package, which is usually priced lower than the sum of the individual components

Price Bundling/Unbundling

One approach is **price bundling**, which takes a set of products, offers them to customers in a package, and usually prices the package lower than the sum of the individual components. For example, home stereo systems are commonly offered in a rack system consisting of speakers, an amplifier, a tuner, a CD player, and an iPod adaptor in an attractive case. This bundle of items, often composed of models that are slow sellers, is usually specially priced to eliminate inventory. A similar example is packages of options in autos.

An alternative approach takes the opposite view. Sometimes the bundle can be priced *higher* than the sum of the components because it is attractive or convenient and thus adds value. A good example is a McDonald's Happy Meal, targeted toward children. Any parent who computes the sum of the hamburger, french fries, and drink would find that she or he is paying a considerable sum for the toy and the package.

A different way to look at the issue is by *unbundling*. Some companies offer predesigned packages of features and services that include components some customers do not need. For example, a telecommunications system might come with a standard service contract some customers may not find attractive because they already have considerable on-site technical help. Alternatively, a "value" meal may come with unwanted french fries. In such cases you could seek ways to unbundle the product package to allow customers to choose what they want to pay for.[35] For example, the public relations firm PayPerClip (paperclippr.com) bases its fees on specific results—$750, for example, for a mention in a small-market newspaper. By selling individual songs, iTunes, Rhapsody, and other digital music sites are unbundling complete CDs. Unfortunately, unbundling permits companies to pass on "hidden" price increases by adding fees. For example, some hotels have begun adding house-cleaning and other fees to what looks to be the price of the room. Additionally, airlines have been unbundling services that traditionally come with a seat such as baggage checking, seats in certain sections of the airplane (e.g., aisle seats), and blankets.

product-line pricing
pricing strategy covering a set of related products

Product-Line Pricing

The **product-line pricing** approach involves offering both a high-priced and a low-priced brand. This is a classic strategy used by Procter & Gamble. The objective is to have brands at multiple price tiers, such as Crest at the premium level and Gleem at a lower price. In 2009, P&G introduced a lower-priced version of Tide called Tide Basic, priced 20 percent less than "classic" Tide, to take advantage of the recession and consumers' interests in lower-priced brands. This strategy ensures that the company covers most customer segments. When the intent is to offer a brand that is slightly higher in price and one that is lower in price than a competitor, the strategy is called "bracketing" the competition. The obvious objective is to give customers little reason to buy the competitor.

The pricing of the iPod line is interesting. Apple, like P&G, offers multiple brands in different price tiers. As of 2010, the prices for the iPods were the following:

iPod shuffle: 2GB: $59, 4GB: $79, 4GB stainless steel: $99.

iPod nano: 8GB: $149, 16GB: $179

iPod touch: 8GB: $199, 32GB: $299 , 64GB: $399

iPod classic: 160GB: $249.

For each model, the price per gigabyte declines as the music capacity increases. You would expect this. However, compare the price per gigabyte across models and you will see that size and "coolness" come at a price. Holding capacity constant at 8 gigabytes, the nano costs \$18.63 per GB while the touch, which features video and 3-D graphics, costs \$28.63 per GB. Note also the consistent use of "9" or odd endings.

Complementary Pricing

Complementary pricing applies to products that are used together when one of the products is a consumable that must be replenished continually. Two good examples are razors and blades (the consumable) and printers and paper (the consumable). Gillette prices razors rather modestly but makes huge margins on the blades. Hewlett-Packard makes much larger profit margins (as a percentage of the price) on toner cartridges and other "consumables" than on the printers themselves. Also the replacement market for automobile parts (called the "aftermarket") is huge and composed mainly of companies that do not manufacture cars. Thus premium pricing for parts cannot be used for the do-it-yourself mechanic segment.

complementary pricing an approach to product line pricing that applies to products that are used together when one of the products is a consumable that must be replenished continually

Complementary pricing is also used for services that have fixed and variable components to price. Two examples are private golf clubs and telephone service. Both have a fixed monthly fee and a variable usage fee. Such complementary pricing can be a creative way to keep the marginal costs to customers low ("pennies a day") while retaining a continuous stream of revenue.

Value Pricing

The term **value pricing** was introduced in the 1990s. Although the term has never really been defined, it has been used by airlines, hotels, rental car agencies, supermarkets, and various other companies, usually for consumer products. The originator of the concept may have been Taco Bell. In 1990, Taco Bell developed a value menu that offered several items, such as tacos, for very low prices. The company was successful in making inroads against other fast-food chains, which subsequently caused McDonald's and others to offer value-priced items. The sustained recession of the early 1990s caused other products to pick up the concept.

value pricing giving customers more value than they expect for the price paid

It is important to clarify the distinction between value pricing and pricing to value. As we have already described in this chapter, pricing to value relies on estimates of the dollar value customers place on products and, when coupled with an estimate of the variable costs of producing a product or delivering a service, determines the range of possible prices that can be charged. Value pricing gives the customer most of the value–cost difference, that is, a "good deal." However, the term *value pricing* is not the same as penetration pricing. Penetration pricing implies low price alone. Value pricing is related to customer expectations because it gives customers more value than they expect for the price paid. This does *not* necessarily imply low price. Thus, value pricing is consistent with pricing at less than customer value, but it is accompanied by communications, packaging, and other elements of the marketing mix that indicate a high level of quality.

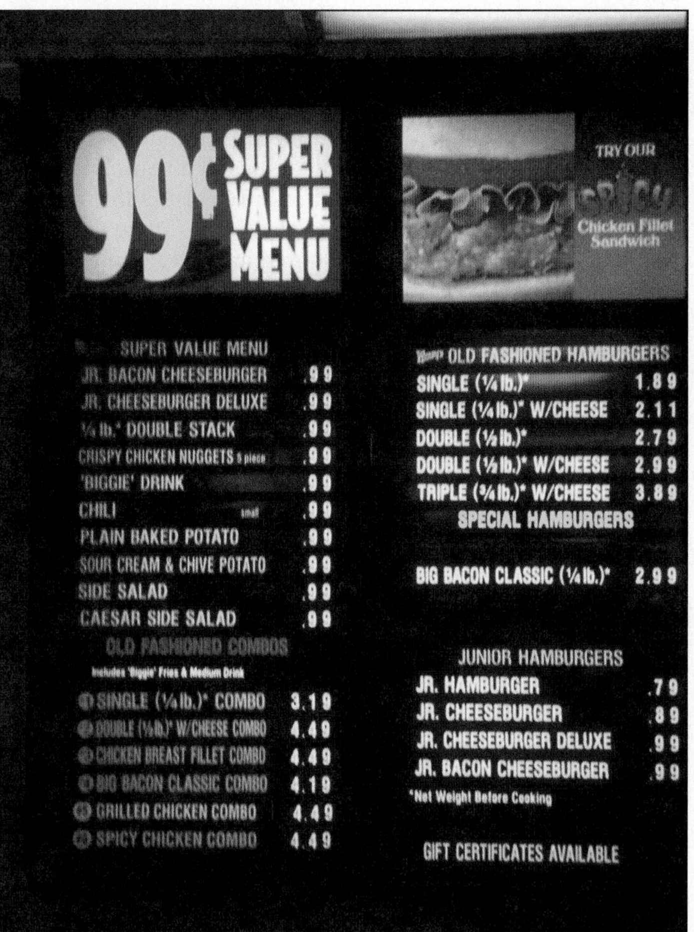

Value-pricing was introduced by fast food companies.
Source: Spencer Grant/PhotoEdit Inc.

Differential Pricing

The key strategic decision of which customers to target recognizes that potential customers' behavior is heterogeneous. This heterogeneity can be reflected in price in various ways.

Direct Price Discrimination

Price discrimination (sometimes referred to as variable pricing) to end-customers, though unpopular with consumer advocacy groups, is not always illegal, and it is done all the time.[36] Witness the senior citizen discounts given at movie theaters or the quantity discounts on personal computers given to large customers. The theory is that price discrimination maximizes products' profits by charging each market segment the price that maximizes profit from that segment because of different price elasticities of demand and customer value. Automobile insurance companies have price discriminated for many years based on age, gender, and driving record. Now companies like Allstate and Progressive are drilling down to smaller segments to offer prices by other demographics, credit history, and other variables.

However, in practice, it is often difficult to implement a price discrimination policy, particularly in consumer product markets, because of the fragmentation of the customer base and the existence of firms that buy at one segment's low prices and resell to others (such as consolidators of airline tickets). One way to implement price discrimination is through target delivery of coupons or other discount mechanisms by direct mail (this is discussed in Chapter 13). Given the quality of databases available today, it is easy to identify households that have the highest probability of buying the product and need a price inducement. Direct-mail companies send coupons from a variety of manufacturers to households, often using a name for the program such as "Carol Wright."

Sometimes the discrimination can be less visible by focusing on more subtle segmentation variables. The authors know of a disposable diaper company that prices its newborn disposable diapers higher than later-stage diapers to take advantage of new parents' concerns and concomitant extreme price insensitivity. Some airlines have begun to charge extra for customers who want aisle seats. London charges to drive in the center city taking advantage of those drivers who either must drive there or those who are price inelastic. This is often referred to as *congestion* pricing.

Price discrimination can also be dynamic where prices are automatically adjusted for different times of the day or seasons of the year. Some sports teams have begun to charge different prices based on a number of parameters. For example, the New York Mets baseball team charges different prices for the same seat depending upon the day of week (weekends are more expensive), the opponent (you pay more to see the Los Angeles Dodgers, a traditional opponent), and time of year (the summer months are higher). The San Francisco Giants experimented with software that weighs ticket sales data, weather forecasts, upcoming pitching matchups, and other variables to help decide whether the team should raise or lower prices right up until game day.[37] An interesting attempt to price discriminate was Coke's announcement in 1999 that it was testing new vending machines that could raise prices in hot weather. The machines could also be adjusted to offer lower prices in times of slack demand. However, while the concept is a perfect example of matching prices to customer value, it was widely derided in the press and talk shows, and the company announced that it never had any intention of introducing it.[38]

Improvements in information technology and the growth of the web have created new opportunities for price discrimination and even more accurate personalization of prices, depending on a customer's historical behavior. Software from companies such as Revionics, Profitlogic (owned by Oracle), and KhiMetrics (owned by SAP) experiment with different pricing schemes, estimate price elasticities, and analyze customer log files. This is all in real time to determine the best price to offer at a given point in time to an individual customer who matches certain criteria. This results in different prices to different customers.

Although this is not a new concept (ask how much the person sitting next to you on the airplane paid for his or her ticket), such individual pricing mechanisms are not accepted for all categories. In late 2000, Amazon was found to be charging different customers different prices for the same DVD during a five-day test. One man ordered a particular DVD at $24.49. The next week, the price was $26.24. As an experiment, he deleted his Amazon cookie containing information identifying him as a frequent Amazon customer and the price fell to $22.74. The ensuing backlash caused the company to apologize to its customers and stop the experiment.[39] Despite Amazon's woes, the trend toward customized prices is not going to stop because technology for tracking customers on the Web is continually improving.

Second-Market Discounting

second-market discounting selling excess production of a product at a discount to a market distinct from the main market

A useful pricing strategy when excess production exists is called **second-market discounting.** With this policy, you sell the extra production at a discount to a market separate from the main market. As long as the product is sold at a price greater than variable cost, the contribution margin produced can help cover corporate overhead. Some examples of secondary markets are generic drugs, private-label brands, and foreign markets.

Periodic Discounting

Periodic discounting varies price over time. It is appropriate when some customers are willing to pay a higher price to have the product or service during a particular time period. For example, utilities such as electricity and telephone service use peak load pricing policies that charge more during the heaviest usage periods, partly to encourage off-peak usage. Clothing retailers mark down items that are slow sellers, with those who want an item when it is first introduced paying a higher price. Theater tickets cost more on weekends.

periodic discounting
a pricing strategy that varies price over time in order to take advantage of particular time periods during which some customers are willing to pay a higher price

Flat-Rate versus Variable-Rate or Per-Use Pricing

An approach to differential pricing that is often used in services is to offer customers a choice between a fixed price, a variable usage fee (with perhaps a low fixed portion), or a per-use charge. The **flat-rate versus variable-rate pricing** concept allows customers to choose the option that best suits their level of usage. This became an important issue for the Internet service provider America Online, which initially priced its service at $9.95 per month plus a usage fee for e-mail and Web access beyond a prescribed limit. In early 1997, the company suddenly switched all its users to a flat rate of $19.95 per month. Although this was a good deal for heavy users (such as small businesses that used AOL as their primary Internet service provider), light users, a large portion of AOL's customer base, were outraged. Ultimately, the company was forced by its subscribers and public opinion to offer customers a choice between the two and allow customers to switch between the programs whenever they want. Research consistently shows that while it may seem illogical, consumers are often better off with per-use pricing when that is an option because they usually overestimate how much they are going to use a service, such as a health or country club.

flat-rate vs. variable-rate pricing
strategy often used in services that offers customers a choice between a fixed price and a variable usage fee

Other Pricing Mechanisms

Depending on the product, some more unusual pricing approaches have been developed. The Web-based customer service company netCustomer (see Chapter 5) charges customers by the number of contacts its service representatives have with its clients' customers. Accrue Software's products analyze Web site traffic. The company used to price based on the number of hits on its clients' sites. However, using that approach, the company depended on the marketing ability of the client to attract visitors. Accrue changed its pricing to be a function of the number of CPUs (central processing units) in the computer servers supporting the site, which is more closely related to the volume of log files processed. In both cases, the pricing policy adopted was intended to capture the value customers obtained from the respective products. Microsoft and many other computer software companies are attempting to change the way they price their software to corporate customers by moving away from fixed prices to a revenue model based on subscriptions that allow for automatic upgrades. This is often called "software as a service." The benefit to these companies is obvious, because a revenue stream is more valuable than a one-time purchase. The companies hope that customers see benefits to them such as reduced information technology costs. A U.S.-based company selling two versions of an industrial product, one made in the United States and the other made in China, set two different prices for the same product, with the U.S.-manufactured product priced higher. Some drug companies are beginning to link what they charge for drugs to how well the drugs improve patients' health. For example, Merck agreed to tie what the insurance company Cigna pays for the diabetes drugs Januvia and Janumet to how well Type 2 diabetes patients are able to control their blood sugar.[40]

An interesting approach to pricing that has not yet been widely adopted is called "name your own price" (NYOP). One version of an NYOP strategy is the well-known Web site Priceline (and its equally famous spokesperson, William Shatner), where an option for a prospective buyer of a vacation is to put in a price request and see if it is accepted by the seller. A variation that has received a lot of publicity is where the seller simply lets buyers decide what they want to pay. The "poster child" for this approach is the experiment by the British music group Radiohead who in October 2007, decided to let their fans decide what to pay for a digital download of their new album, *In Rainbows*. Although there is some disagreement about the precise results, a survey that ran a few weeks after the announcement found that 28.5 percent chose to pay nothing for the download, 56 percent paid between £0.02 and £10.00, 2.5 percent between £10.00 and £39.00, and 13 percent paid £40.00.[41] What is not in disagreement is that the publicity resulted in sales of 3 million copies of the album within a year of its release from downloads from radiohead.com, sales from other Internet retailers, physical CDs, and a box set. The band's best-selling album up to this time sold 990,000 copies.[42] An author of a competitor to this book has offered potential adopters a chance to read it free online for 21 days and then to pay what the reader thinks it is worth (minimum $1).

Some companies play tricks with packages to raise prices. For example, when Wrigley introduced its "Slim Pack" in 2008 to replace its traditional packages of Juicy Fruit and other varieties, it reduced the number of sticks per pack from 17 to 15 but kept the price the same, at $1.09.[43] This stealth approach to price increases has been used by candy bar makers, breakfast cereal companies, and others.

Competing against Private Labels

How should you defend your brands against the incursion of private labels? One obvious way is to reduce the price gap to the point where consumers are willing to pay and therefore value the brand name. However, as we have already said, this is an expensive solution and one to which you should not immediately gravitate. Other ways to battle back are:[44]

- Add value in ways discussed earlier in this chapter.
- Develop new market segments that are less price-sensitive.
- Build stronger relationships with the channels of distribution.
- Prune product lines of sizes or flavors that are not generating profits for the retailer.
- Raise the barriers to entry for private labels by investing in better customer databases and retention programs (information technology).

The key to fighting the price-oriented private labels is not making a knee-jerk reaction to compete on price, but instead exploring other options.

Pricing and the Internet

When e-commerce started on the Internet, many experts believed that the increased ability to offer personalized, interactive products and services conveniently would make price a secondary attribute. However, these experts were quickly proven wrong. For every site that offered unique products, such as eToys, there were more that focused on making transactions at lower prices. Online auto purchasing, stock brokerage, consumer durables, and many other categories were adapted to the Web with an emphasis on price. The success of the travel sites Orbitz and Travelocity is due to their lower prices. This emphasis continues today.

In addition, if you do not think you are getting the lowest prices at a given site, the Web enables you to compare them quickly and easily. A few clicks on the mouse can save considerable time over visits to retail stores or multiple phone calls. Shopping "bots" such as PriceGrabber, mySimon, PriceSCAN, and Shopper.com offer a variety of goods and a comparison of the prices at a number of e-tailers. For example, Figure 9.9 shows a page from PriceGrabber.com for a search for a refrigerator. If you know the brand you prefer, the possible sellers are ordered by price for your convenience. Additionally, reviews from previous buyers help you to trade off price with quality of service. Amazon Price Watch (nukeprice.com) is an Internet Explorer plug-in that alerts you when a prespecified product falls below a preferred price. Price Protectr warns you if the price of a product you recently bought online is reduced so you can claim a partial refund under the store's price guarantee policy.

Companies that have both online and offline businesses often give inducements to customers to purchase online, due to the lower costs of processing the order and the ability to instantly integrate the information into their corporate information system.

Figure 9.9

PriceGrabber.com Web Site

Source: Courtesy PriceGrabber.com Inc., a Delaware corporation.

While this is often done with nonprice inducements, such as Dell offering a free monitor upgrade for online purchases, price is often used as a motivator. Clothing retailers such as Jos. A. Bank offer special discounts to Web shoppers.

Thus, low costs of information search resulting in easy price comparisons, the lack of highly persuasive communications, and the constant attention to price have made it difficult for a company selling on the Web to develop higher customer value and concomitant higher prices and profit margins for Web-based transactions. Despite the fact that many people will pay for convenience, low prices and free goods are what people are looking for when they use the Internet to acquire goods and services. As a result, studies repeatedly show that price is the single most important aspect of the online shopping process.[45] In addition, a study of the life insurance industry provided empirical evidence that the increased use of the Web for selling insurance has reduced term life prices by 8 to 15 percent due to increased competition and lower costs of service delivery.[46]

However, it is also possible that companies are underestimating their abilities to build online brands and charge higher prices. The fact that customers are so price sensitive may be more a creation of current online pricing practice. For example, one study showed that for the equivalent book, buyers were willing to pay $2.49 more to buy it at Amazon.com than from no-name online retailers, and that this edge was still $1.30 over better-known sites like Barnes&Noble.com and Borders.com, which is even hosted by Amazon's site.[47] In addition, a study by McKinsey & Company showed most online buyers actually shop around very little. Eighty-four percent of those buying toys purchase from the first site they visit, as do 81 percent buying music and 76 percent buying electronics.[48] Similarly, another study found that, on average, households visit only 1.2 book sites, 1.3 CD sites, and 1.8 travel sites during an active month surfing in each category.[49]

As a result, many sites have repositioned away from price and toward some other dimension. For example, Priceline used to focus exclusively on its famous NYOP format for airfares and car rentals (you put in a price and the companies bid on your business).

While it competes more directly with Expedia, Travelocity, and Orbitz for the fixed-price, low-price travel customer, the company now also offers city guides, last-minute deals at fixed prices, and a Visa card.[50]

Auctions

One particular market pricing mechanism that has become popular on the Web is the auction. At an auction, bidders indicate their willingness to pay in a continuous fashion, upping their bids until either the price rises to a level greater than their reservation price or they win. In auctions, prices are determined by supply and demand at a particular time. The Internet has spawned a large number of sites on which sellers run electronic auctions to sell merchandise. Market clearing prices reflect underlying customer value more accurately than do normal fixed prices. The main advantage of the Web as an auction site is the size of the audience. People from all over the world converge on these sites to create active markets in all kinds of goods and services. Sun Microsystems uses auction sites as a distribution channel; more than one-third of the customers buying that way are new customers for the company.[51] The biggest and hottest of them all, eBay, has been a phenomenal success as a flea market and garage sale on the Web. The company matches buyers and sellers of anything from Pez dispensers to baseball cards to autos. Although an increasing proportion of eBay's sales are at a fixed price, auction participants bought and sold $60 billion worth of goods in 2008.[52] In the B-to-B space, GoIndustry DoveBid is the world's largest industrial auctioneer and asset appraisal firm. At its Web site, buyers from all over the world conduct online text and Web-casted auctions.

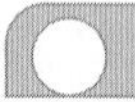

Global Pricing Issues

Because of the impact of "gray" (unauthorized) market channels and other factors, price is difficult to control in international markets. More precisely, a consistent global pricing policy is difficult to implement because of fluctuations in exchange rates, tariffs and other taxes that are added onto imported goods, and the price–quality effects of the country of origin.

Exchange rate fluctuations, unlike tariffs and taxes, are impossible to predict and play havoc with global pricing policies. In late 1997, over a two-month period, the Korean currency, the won, decreased in value by nearly 50 percent, from $0.0011 to $0.00064. A similarly drastic reduction in the value of the Argentine peso (about 65 percent) occurred in 2002. Between 2008 and 2009, the British pound fluctuated between $1.50 and $2.00. As a result, U.S. or other goods purchased in dollar terms increased dramatically in terms of the local currency, assuming the exchange rate decline was passed along to customers. The U.S. dollar declined in value against the euro over the period 2008–2009, making U.S. goods, real estate, and travel inexpensive for people from those countries. Retailers and other channel members usually raise their prices even though they purchased the inventory at a lower exchange rate, because they will have to replace the inventory at the new, higher rates.

Thus, exchange rate changes in unfavorable directions and taxes and tariffs that are simply added to the import costs result in wildly different prices around the world for the same products and a cost-plus pricing environment. In this environment, the final price is based only on costs. Consequently, prices may be considerably higher than the value customers place on the product in the local market, resulting in significantly decreased sales. There is no reason that prices should not vary around the world, because you would expect customer value to be different in different market segments and countries. However, arbitrarily adding costs, even those that are legitimately incurred, only creates a cost-recovery rather than value-recovery approach to pricing.

Interestingly, you do not have to be an exporter to be exposed to exchange rate fluctuations. Consider the situation in which a company that markets only in the United States faces foreign competitors, including some from Korea or Argentina. All of a sudden, the Korean and Argentine companies can significantly reduce their dollar prices in the U.S. market.

Table 9.4 shows different pricing and other policies under different currency conditions. When the domestic currency is weak, full-costing or cost-plus pricing does not hurt

Table 9.4

Export Strategies under Varying Currency Conditions	
When Domestic Currency Is Weak	**When Domestic Currency Is Strong**
Stress price benefits	Engage in nonprice competition by improving quality, delivery, and after-sale service
Expand product line and add more costly features	Improve productivity and engage in vigorous cost reduction
Shift sourcing and manufacturing to domestic market	Shift sourcing and manufacturing overseas
Exploit export opportunities in all markets	Give priority to exports to strong-currency countries
Conduct conventional cash-for-goods trade	Deal in countertrade with weak-currency countries
Use full-costing approach, but use marginal-cost pricing to penetrate new or competitive markets.	Trim profit margins and use marginal-cost pricing
Speed repatriation of foreign-earned income and collections	Keep the foreign-earned income in host country, slow collections
Minimize expenditures in local, host country currency	Maximize expenditures in local, host country currency
Buy needed services (advertising, insurance, transportation, etc.) in domestic market	Buy needed services abroad and pay for them in local currencies
Minimize local borrowing	Borrow money needed for expansion in local market
Bill foreign customers in domestic currency	Bill foreign customers in their own currency

Source: Reprinted from S. Tamur Cavusgil (1988), "Unraveling the Mystique of Export Pricing," *Business Horizons*, May–June, Figure 2, p. 58, with permission from Elsevier.

you so much because the exchange rate keeps the selling price down. However, when your currency is strong, cost-plus pricing would result in prices that are likely to be greater than customer value. As a result, marketing strategies focus on nonprice value propositions.

An additional factor to consider in global pricing is the effect that country of origin has on the price–perceived value relationship. In the United States, Japanese brands have high customer value, whereas Korean brands have lower value and are priced lower. German binoculars and cameras are premium priced to take advantage of that country's reputation in optics. Similar situations hold for French wine, Swiss watches, and U.S. computers. These perceptual differences vary over product categories. Although the French are known throughout the world for their wine, food, fashion, and movies, their reputation for making automobiles is concentrated mainly in Europe.

Ethical Considerations

Other than perhaps advertising, with its potential to mislead consumers, price is the marketing mix variable that is most often the focus of ethical issues. This is probably due to the fact that it is the most visible marketing decision and that price has economic consequences for the buyer. Because the vast majority of global customers, whether consumers or businesses, have budget constraints, purchasing a product usually means making a trade-off between alternatives. In countries with many poor people, purchasing what looks to most of us like a necessity (e.g., toothpaste) can mean forgoing bread for the family.

The implications of such considerations are that firms are often criticized for their pricing policies. Terms like "gouging," "rip off," and "unfairness" have been used to describe companies in particular industries such as petroleum (price of retail gasoline), prescription drugs, and even Nike, which has been criticized for selling shoes for $150 that have resulted in teenagers being assaulted in school. While in all these cases companies feel that their prices are justified, that does not mean that consumers, journalists, and policy makers feel the same way. Thus, the drug company that invests

$500 million in a new drug and feels that it should set a high price to recover its investment is criticized for making that drug unaffordable to consumers who do not have adequate prescription insurance. When a series of hurricanes hit Florida in 2004 and seriously damaged many houses, if you could get a company to fix your roof, you had to pay an amount above what the companies would normally charge. The press accused the companies of price gouging; the companies felt they were pricing to customer value.

Research has examined consumers' attitudes toward this kind of company pricing behavior. What is relevant is the motive for the price increases that is inferred by the consumer beyond purely increasing profit. If consumers feel that the motive for the price increase is negative—that is, to simply take advantage of a short-term situation like a storm—perceived unfairness will be higher than if the motive was positive or justified. What is interesting is that consumers will be more willing to give a firm the benefit of the doubt the better its reputation or brand. Thus, a by-product of having a strong brand is that it can inoculate a firm from these kinds of problems.[53]

The upshot of this discussion is to reinforce the fact that marketing managers have to view price almost as part of the communications mix because, like advertising, customers will mentally process the price not only to determine whether it is greater or less than their value for the product or service but also as part of their overall feelings toward the company. Companies that are perceived to price fairly benefit from favorable consumer reaction such as brand loyalty; those that are perceived to price unfairly suffer in the store.[54]

Executive Summary

Key learning points in this chapter include the following:

- The purpose of price is to recover customer-perceived value for your product or service, not to recover costs.
- The four main components of a price are the marketing strategy, customer value or willingness-to-pay, competitors' prices, and your costs.
- As part of the marketing mix, price must be consistent with the marketing strategy in that it accounts for the target segment's price sensitivity and the value proposition.
- Customer value is the monetary value a customer places on your product. You can measure customer value directly by calculating the monetary benefits of your product or service or by using survey approaches.
- It is important to understand the competitors' cost structures as well as their past pricing practices.
- Price should always be set greater than variable costs. However, cost-based pricing is difficult to implement because there are many kinds of costs (variable, direct fixed, indirect fixed, development).
- The gap between variable costs and customer value is the strategic pricing gap.
- How much of the strategic pricing gap to capture is determined by your pricing objectives, psychological aspects of price, the stage of the product life cycle, industry conditions, and the decision making structure within the buying organization.
- There are a variety of pricing tactics: product-line decisions, value pricing, and differential pricing.
- There is an increased trend toward price discrimination by offering different prices to different segments and, with the Internet, different prices to different individuals, depending on current marketing conditions and past buying patterns.
- The Internet is having an important impact on how customers find price information and use price to make buying decisions, and on how final prices are determined.

Chapter Questions

1. Why is the marketing strategy so important to the pricing decision? Can you think of some examples in which the strategy and the price appear to be inconsistent?
2. Find other illustrations of companies that have set prices lower than customer value. Do you think they were set that way intentionally? If so, why?
3. Suppose your company had just developed a new TV set that had TiVo (the digital video recorder) built into it. What steps would you go through to determine how much more you would charge (if anything) for such a TV over the stand-alone price?
4. What other products and services exhibit a strong correlation between price and perceived quality? Are marketing strategies different for such products than they are for those for which there is no such natural relationship?
5. What are the implications for consumer welfare (i.e., privacy, safety) of the proliferation of auction sites on the Web? Are there any regulatory implications?
6. Develop arguments pro and con with respect to customized pricing. What are the differences in implementing the policy across different product types, for example, B-to-B, consumer durable, consumer frequently purchased, and services?

Key Learning Points

The purpose of this chapter is to introduce the concept of integrated marketing communications (IMC) and explain how to develop advertising strategy within an IMC program. After reading this chapter, the reader should understand:

- The basic model of communication and how technology is changing that model
- The elements of an IMC program
- Setting advertising goals and selecting target audiences
- Developing message strategies
- Key elements of media planning
- How advertising budgets are set
- Alternative approaches for evaluating advertising spending

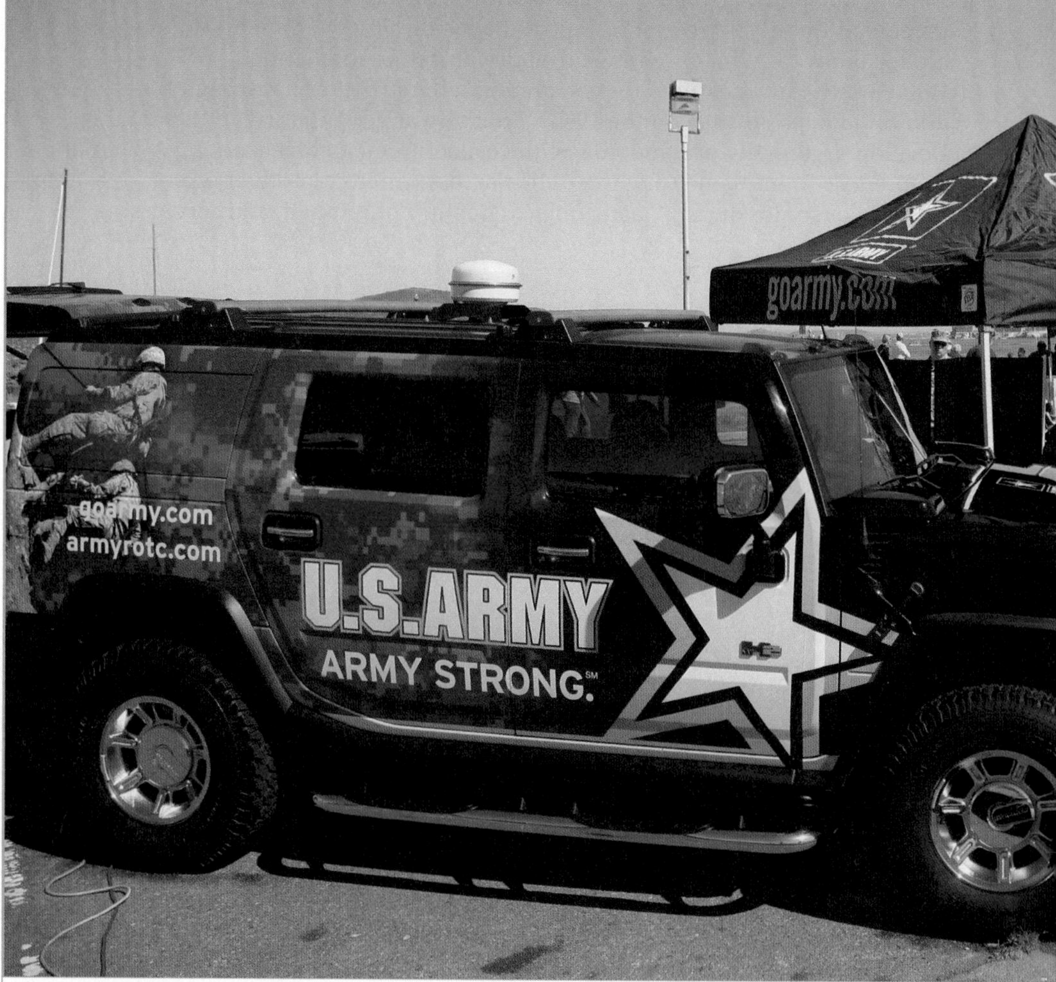

Marketing the U.S. Army is challenging.
Source: Thomas Frey/Alamy Images

Communications and Advertising Strategy

Chapter Brief

Since World War I, the U.S. military has been advertising for young men (and, more recently, women) to join the services.[1] However, the marketing of the military did not begin in earnest until the draft was replaced by the all-volunteer model in 1973. This fulfilled President Richard Nixon's promise made during the Vietnam War. Advertising agencies have worked hard to enlist recruits with themes such as "Today's Army Wants to Join You," "We're Looking for a Few Good Men," "Aim High," and "Be All That You Can Be." In 2004, the U.S. government was the 25th-largest advertising spender with more than $1 billion spent for the four major services—Army, Air Force, Navy, and Marines.

Of these four services, the Army is having the most difficulty attracting recruits. This is most notably due to the war in Iraq and the increase in global terrorism—both of which make the Army a riskier proposition than it was in the 1980s and 1990s. It missed its 2005 recruiting goal by about 12,000 and the pool of those who enlist up to a year in advance is dwindling. This is in spite of spending $290 million on advertising in 2005 using the Chicago agency, Leo Burnett. The next theme was "Army of One" emphasizing personal success, but it did not seem to resonate with either the target audience (typically, high school graduates) or its influencers. The Army intends to continue to spend money on advertising and is looking to sign an advertising agency to a five-year, $1 billion contract. In late 2006, the Army replaced "Army of One" with one it hopes will pack more punch: "Army Strong."

The Army is attempting to court influencers of the young men and women in their target audience. It is trying to reach these influencers (largely parents) through advertising, sponsoring rodeos, all-star high school games, and NASCAR races. In addition, it is trying to reach the target audience directly with its "hip" Web site, www.goarmy.com. As you can see from Figure 10.1, the site shows the benefits of the service as well as digital games that can be downloaded. The Army is also attempting to provide potential recruits with a realistic view of what Army life is like. The Virtual Army Experience is a traveling exhibit providing participants a virtual test drive of the Army. It contains a computer game, rendered with state-of-the-art Army training simulation technology, that creates a life-size, networked virtual world that immerses visitors in the world of soldiering. The Army won a gold "Effie" award for this program in 2009, an award given annually to the most effective communications campaigns.

The marketing of the U.S. Army is arguably one of the most difficult marketing jobs you can undertake. In considering the adoption of an overall communications program for the Army, the marketing managers have to consider:

- Given the dramatic change in the communication environment (recall the discussion in Chapter 1), have all the possible communication activities been considered?
- Are they well integrated; that is, are they sending a consistent message to the potential recruits?

- What is the appropriate advertising strategy for the Army, and how can it break out of the advertising "clutter" for target segments' attention?
- How much money should be allocated for the various communication activities?
- How can we measure if the money is being well spent?

Figure 10.1

Army Web Site

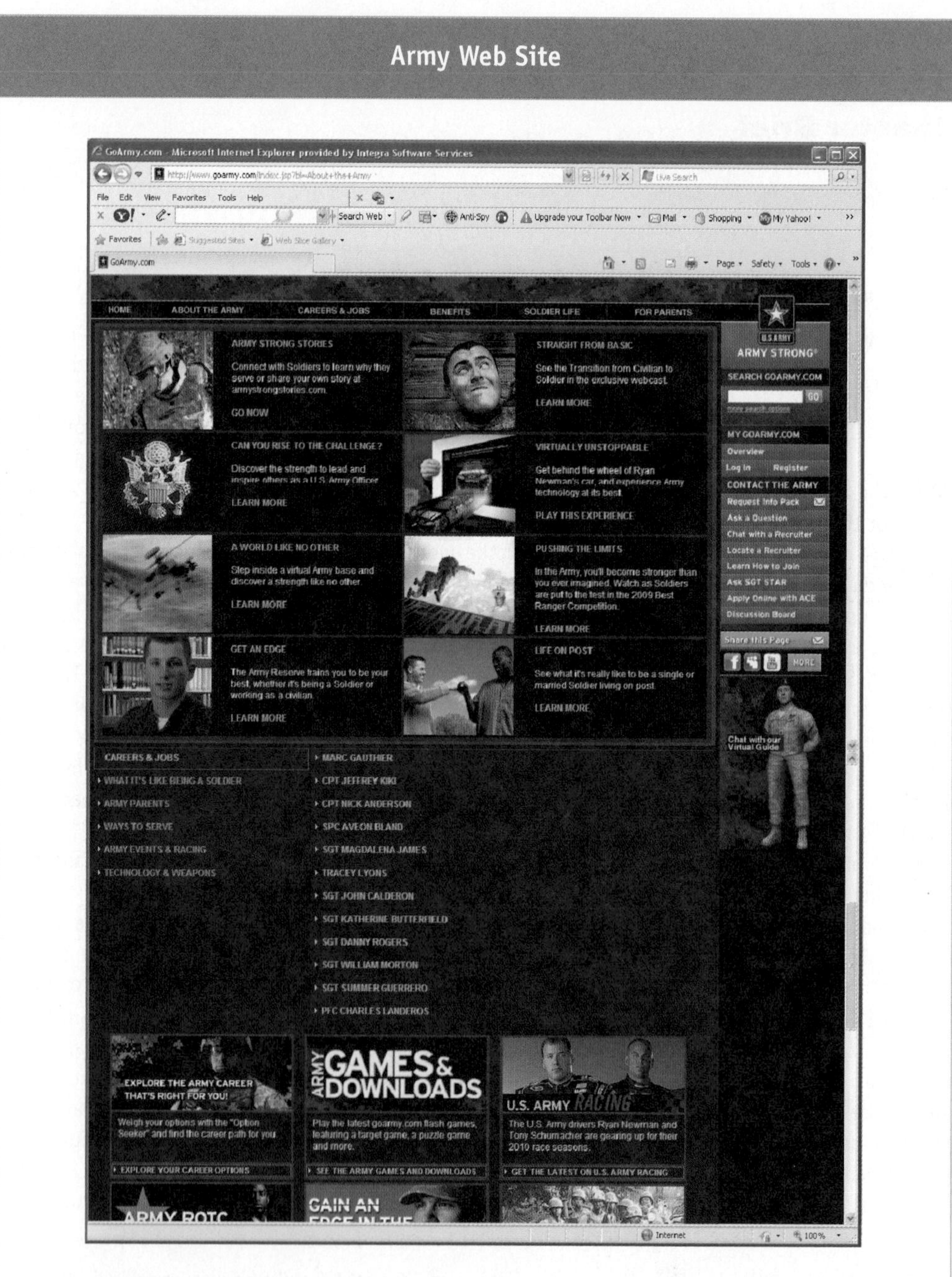

Source: Copyright © 2010 by the U.S. Army. Reprinted with permission.

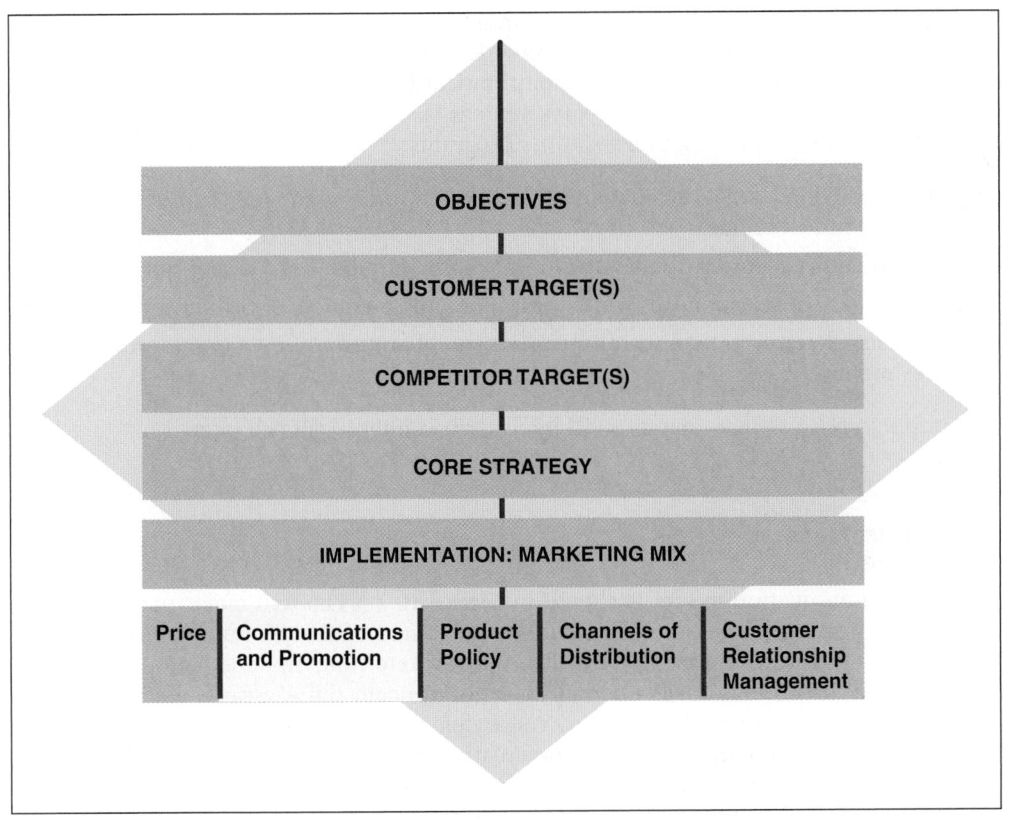

First, in the marketing strategy diagram, it can be seen that a complete marketing strategy involves a strategic part (with a selection of target segments and a core strategy involving the differential advantage and value proposition). Second, it involves a tactical or implementation part involving the marketing mix (price, advertising, channels of distribution, and promotion). In other words, you must first develop the general strategy and then make decisions about how to implement that strategy using devices that are visible to customers.

This chapter is about communications and advertising management. Although most people think only of advertising when we discuss communications, all elements of the marketing mix deliver a message to potential customers. The act of running a sales promotion may indicate to some customers that the list price is too high and so must be lowered. Some customers may interpret a promotion as a sign of lower quality. Price is also a communication tool: a high price relative to competition means something different from a discount price. The product's package delivers messages. The fact that one brand can be purchased only in exclusive outlets can also be interpreted as a sign of quality. For example, Stihl Inc., a German-owned maker of chain saws, emphasizes its aura of exclusivity by running ads for products that it doesn't sell through mass merchants such as Lowe's and Home Depot. Similarly, sponsorship of a professional golf tournament reaches a particular segment and communicates that product's or service's interests in appealing to that segment. The sales force obviously directly communicates with customers.

Therefore, before describing the details of implementing a communications strategy, we provide the reader with some background in communication theory and discuss how the decisions you make affect your target customers. Forward-looking organizations are stressing a concept called **integrated marketing communications (IMC)** in which the marketing manager does not think of all the elements of the communications mix as communicating separate messages. Instead, these messages are coordinated to reinforce what each is saying and to prevent customer confusion from conflicting messages. In other words, the decisions about the marketing mix must be made in concert, which makes developing a strategy before making implementation decisions even more important. This is because the strategy provides the value proposition, which is the basis for all communications to customers.

integrated marketing communications (IMC) the concept that all elements of the marketing mix communicate messages that must be coordinated in order to reinforce what each is saying and to avoid customer confusion

As noted in Chapter 1, the area of communications is perhaps the most dynamic in the marketing field. New approaches to advertising motivated by the difficulty in reaching many customers today have made communications decision making more complex. As a result, besides the traditional issues such as IMC, marketers are asking a number of key questions about their communications programs:

- How can I better target my customers and therefore make my communications spending more efficient?
- How do I choose among the large and increasing number of media options?
- How do I adapt my spending to the new emerging channels of communications?
- How can I determine if I am getting an acceptable return on my communications investments?

The implications of these changes will be described later in this chapter.

Communications

A basic communication model is shown in Figure 10.2.[2] The two major participants in the communication process are the *sender* (the source of the communication) and the *receiver*. In marketing, these are typically the marketer and the customer. The sender uses some kind of medium or channel to communicate the message, which is represented in the middle of the figure. The sender decides how to send the message through an encoding process, which could be the creative part of an advertisement or Web site. The receiver (customer) interprets or decodes the message and decides what an appropriate response is. The receiver may also provide feedback or information to the sender.

Figure 10.2

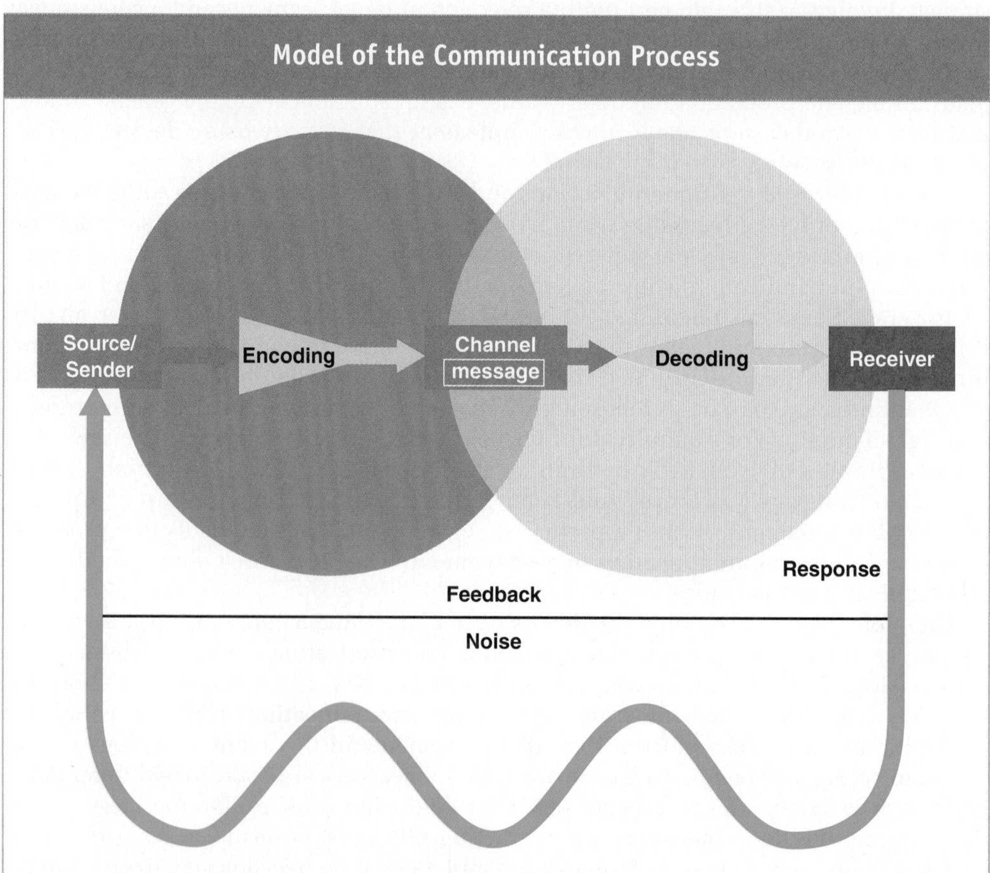

Source: George E. Belch and Michael A. Belch (1993), *Introduction to Advertising and Promotion* (Homewood, IL: Irwin). Reproduced with permission of the McGraw-Hill Companies.

Finally, noise may interrupt or disrupt the communication process. For example, a person watching a television commercial at home may be distracted by a crying baby.

Thus, the communication process starts when the source decides what kind of words, symbols, or pictures to use to encode the message. In some cases, the source could be the company. In others, it may be a spokesperson (e.g., Michael Jordan for Nike). The sender's objective is to encode the message in a way that resonates with the target audience. This obviously requires some marketing research to uncover the types of messages that are appropriate for the audience.

Of particular importance to the marketer are the different channels or media that can be used. A distinction can be drawn between **personal** and **nonpersonal channels of communication.** The former include direct contacts such as a sales force or salespeople in a retail channel. Personal channels also include face-to-face interactions between customers, or what is called word-of-mouth communication. Such communications are critically important for the diffusion of new products and entertainment, such as movies. It is, therefore, important to understand that customers can be attracted by messages directed to them or by an indirect approach in which opinion leaders or other buyers talk to other prospective customers. Nonpersonal channels are often called *mass media* and include television, newspapers, radio, direct mail, billboards, magazines, and the Internet.

personal channels of communication communication channels that involve direct sales as well as face-to-face or word-of-mouth interactions between customers

nonpersonal channels of communication mass-media communication channels, such as television, newspapers, radio, direct mail, and the Internet

A large portion of marketing communication is focused on the mass media. Figure 10.3 shows a modified version of the general communication model shown in Figure 10.2.[3] The basic feature of this model is the one-to-many aspect of mass communication. The marketer is attempting to send persuasive communications to a large group of people. So, in this model, the firm sends content or a message through a medium to a large number of potential customers.

A notable feature of this model is that there is no interaction between customers and firms. This concept of passive customers is erroneous because customers have always participated in personal channels of communication and have given feedback to companies in the form of complaints and responses to surveys. However, these channels have traditionally been slow, making it difficult for companies to be proactive.

In the current electronic environment, with Internet technology, customers can communicate with each other easily and quickly. In addition, customers can provide feedback to companies in real time rather than with a substantial delay. This feedback often comes from user groups who form their own electronic clubs (called listservs), and who can form a collective opinion and quickly supply information about new or developing products. These brand communities can be active and influential. Information can also be disseminated in online forums and social media and blogs. The speed with which

Figure 10.3

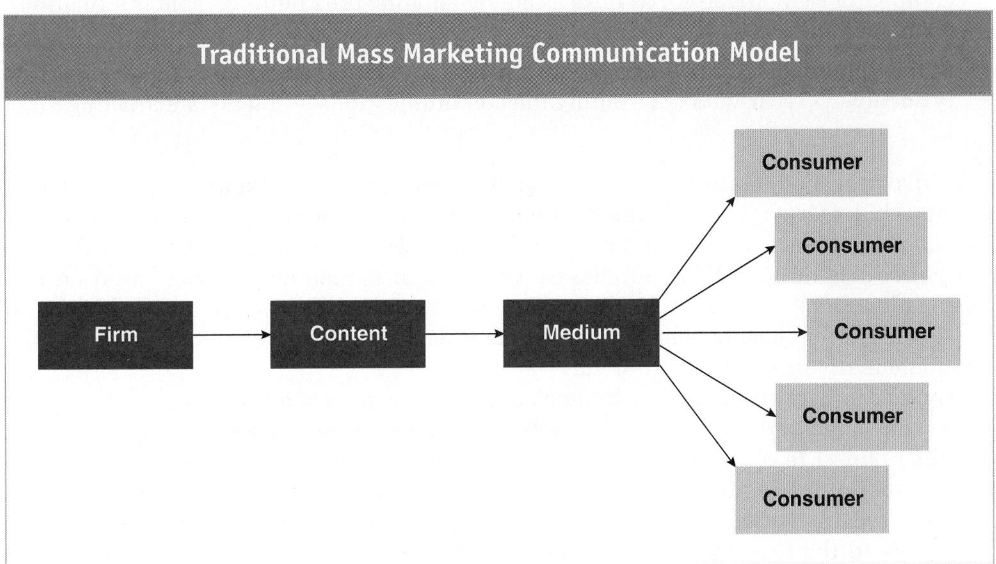

Source: Used with permission from *Journal of Marketing,* published by the American Marketing Association, Donna L. Hoffman and Thomas P. Novak (1996), "Marketing in Hypermedia Computer-mediated Environments: Conceptual Foundations," *Journal of Marketing,* 60 (July), p. 52.

Figure 10.4

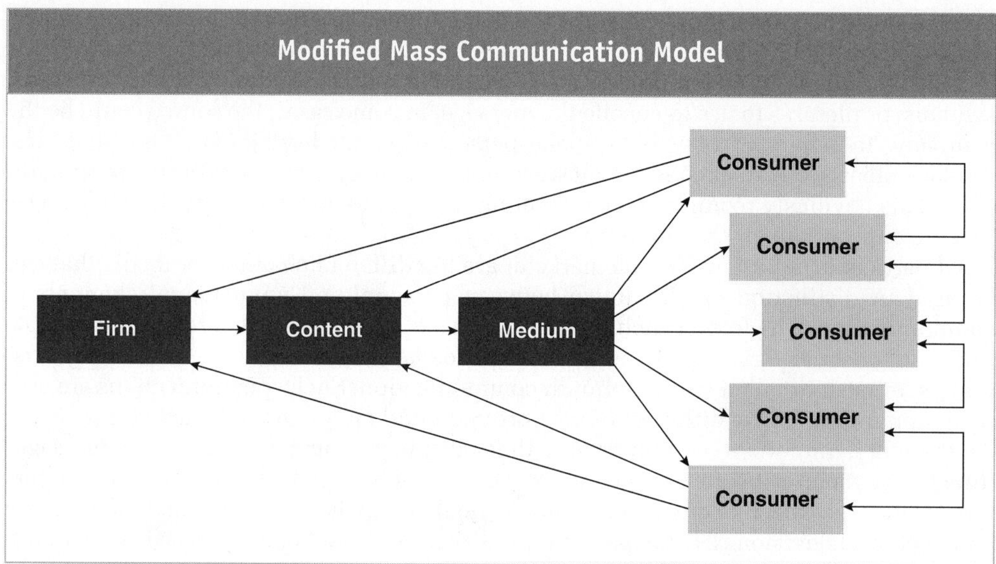

complaints about Tropicana Orange Juice's new packaging reached the public and the company in 2009, as well as the volume of complaints on blogs such as Digg, resulted in the company reverting to the old packaging. Recently, environmental activists have been using social media to criticize Nestlé over its purchases of palm oil for use in KitKat candy bars and other products. Protesters have posted a negative video on YouTube, on Nestlé's Facebook page, and on Twitter with claims that the company is contributing to the destruction of Indonesia's rain forest, potentially exacerbating global warming.

This kind of environment is captured by the model shown in Figure 10.4. In today's environment, marketing managers must be aware of the speed with which communications flow through the system and realize that a considerable amount of word-of-mouth can be generated in special-interest user groups. A number of interesting questions emerge from this conceptualization of marketing communications:

- As the marketing manager, how do you manage these brand communities? If marketing-related communications are being transmitted in these groups, it can be potentially damaging to let negative information go without a response.
- What are the ethical dimensions of these kinds of communications? For example, a competitor's employee could pose as an owner and spread unfavorable information about a brand.
- In this kind of electronic dialog, who really is the sender and who is the receiver? It is not always clear who is initiating the communications and who is marketing ideas to whom.

A final aspect of Figure 10.4 is the interaction between the customers and the content. In this kind of environment, the customer can create the content.[4] For example, at Amazon.com, users provide information about their preferences for books, CDs, and other products through their purchases. The content is then customized based on this information. Books and DVDs (among a number of products) are recommended based on the member's purchasing behavior. Thus, the interaction between the customer and the medium creates user-specific content.

Another impact of the new technological environment is shown in Figure 10.5.[5] This figure shows the traditional trade-off between the reach (the number of people reached) and the richness (e.g., bandwidth or amount of information that can be sent to a receiver, customization, interactivity) of communications. At the upper left of the line would be personal selling, where a very rich, customized message can be sent but with limited reach due to the restrictions on the number of salespeople. TV, magazine, and radio advertising would be at the lower right of the line because a large number of people can be reached but with a limited message. Today, millions of people can be reached with rich messages through customized advertisements on the Web and direct e-mails that

Figure 10.5

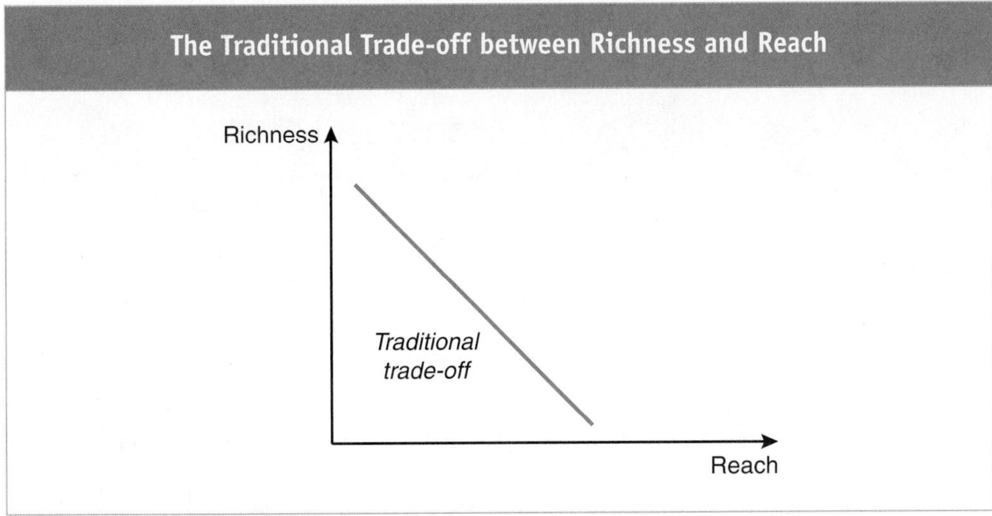

Source: Philip Evans and Thomas S. Wurster (2000), *Blown to Bits* (Boston: Harvard Business School Press). Copyright © 2000 by the President and Fellows of Harvard College. Reprinted by permission.

can send audio, streaming video, and other communications with exciting and colorful graphics. Marketing managers today do not have to be constrained by the traditional trade-off shown in Figure 10.5.

Integrated Marketing Communications

As we noted earlier in this chapter, the objective of an integrated approach to marketing communications is to ensure that all the elements of the communications mix are coordinated with the marketing strategy, delivering the same underlying positioning and value proposition to the target segment. Although different tools are used to accomplish the overall marketing objective, the job of the marketing manager is to aid this coordination by linking the various people and agencies involved.

Elements of the communications mix are shown in Figure 10.6 and a spending breakdown of consumer (2007) versus B-to-B (business-to-business) (2008) advertising is shown in Table 10.1. Although the specific allocations may have changed since the data were collected, it is interesting to note that B-to-B companies spend a higher percentage of their communications money on print advertising and much less on mass media like TV advertising than consumer-products companies. This is logical because the percentage of TV watchers that are B-to-B purchasers is relatively low for many TV shows. Interestingly, B-to-B companies spend a little more on Internet advertising due to its ability to target industrial buyers.

Advertising

Advertising has traditionally been defined as any paid form of nonpersonal communication about an organization, product, service, or idea by an identified sponsor.[6] However,

Figure 10.6

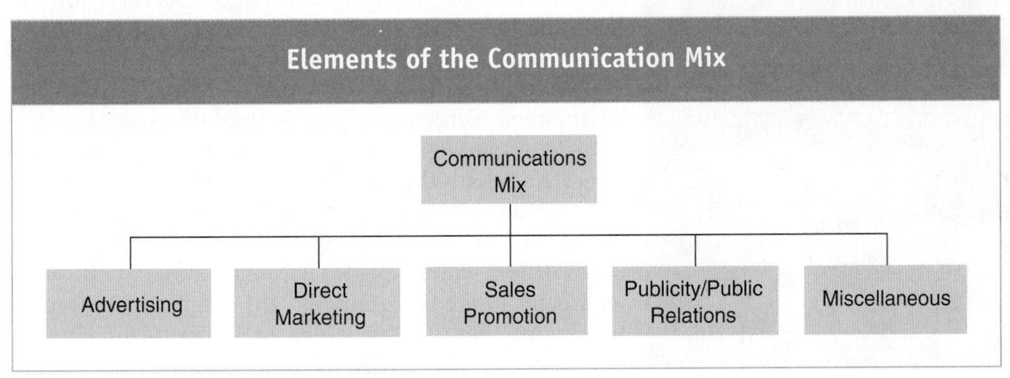

Table 10.1

Advertising Expenditures: Consumer versus Business-to-Business Products		
	Percentage of the Communications Budget	
	Consumer	Business-to-Business
Television	43.3%	28.9%
Print advertising	39.3	50.7
Internet	7.6	9.5
Radio	7.2	8.0
Out-of-home media	2.7	3.5

Source: Advertising Age 100 Leading National Advertisers, June 23, 2008; "2008 B-to-B Ad Spending," *BtoB,* September 14, 2009.

direct marketing
any communication form that sends messages directly to a target market with the anticipation of an immediate or very-short-term response; also, any method of distribution that gives the customer access to the firm's products and services without any other intermediaries

telemarketing
a form of direct marketing that uses the telephone as the mechanism for reaching potential customers

direct-mail marketing
a form of direct marketing that involves sending letters or catalogues to potential customers

direct sales
in the context of direct marketing, an approach that involves the use of friends and neighbors as the sales force in reaching potential customers

as noted earlier in this chapter, advertising is no longer nonpersonal because it can depend greatly on interactions between an individual customer and the organization.

Advertising has several important advantages over other elements of the communications mix. It offers a fair amount of control over what you can say to potential customers. Advertising can also reach a large number of customers efficiently. Although it may cost hundreds of thousands of dollars to put a spot on a national television program, that program is probably reaching millions of potential customers. No other communications program can reach so many customers so quickly and at such a low cost per customer. Advertising is also flexible in that many different kinds of images and symbols can be presented through a wide variety of media. Copy strategies can be humorous, serious, or emotional; show the product in action; and explicitly compare your product to a competitor's.

Advertising also has drawbacks. It is difficult to evaluate the effectiveness of advertising, particularly because it is usually used to build sales in the long term by achieving other intermediate objectives in the short run (e.g., awareness). Because advertising rarely results in a measurable and observable change in sales (except for direct-response advertising such as infomercials, or extended TV commercials), you often wonder what you are getting for your money. In addition, advertising, especially TV advertising, can be expensive and makes it difficult for a small company (or any company with a small budget) to make much of an impact in the market. Much advertising in mass media (e.g., TV and general-audience magazines) is wasted because it is not the best communications element for targeting a specific audience directly. Many people outside the target audience see the ads, which may not be problematic—except when products such as tobacco and alcohol (which are subject to legal age restrictions for purchase) are advertised. Advertising can be ignored or the signal disrupted by noise (Figure 10.2). Finally, customers are bombarded with ads in the United States and other Western countries, which makes it difficult for your message to get through the clutter.

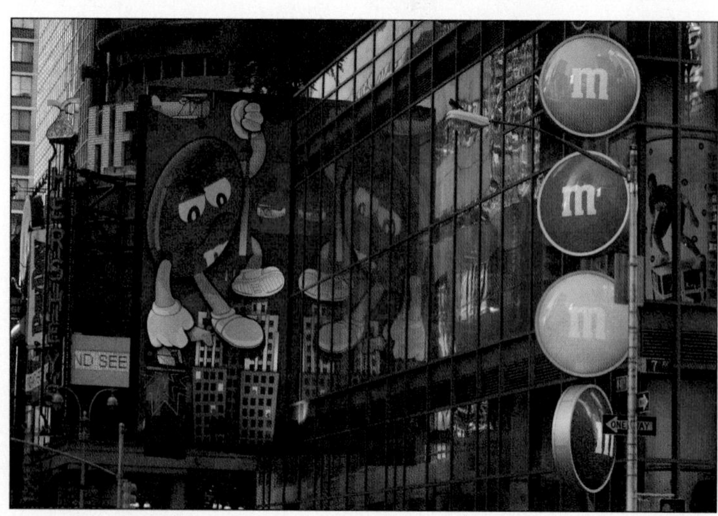

Outdoor advertisements can be effective communications devices.
Source: George Rose/Getty Images, Inc—Liaison

Direct Marketing

Direct marketing is any communication form that sends messages directly to a target market with the anticipation of an immediate or short-term response.[7] There are many ways to implement direct marketing. **Telemarketing** uses the telephone to reach potential customers. **Direct-mail marketing** involves sending letters or catalogs. Some companies such as Amway, Mary Kay, and Tupperware have differentiated themselves from competition using a **direct sales** approach, in which friends and neighbors are used as the sales force. Direct marketing also uses the Internet, with some companies sending e-mails to potential customers indicating that they have a special offer. Many companies rely exclusively on direct marketing as the main form of communication, while others include it as one component of the communications mix. It is used extensively in both consumer and business-to-business marketing contexts.

The main advantage of direct marketing is clear. You can focus on your target and deliver a message intended only for that target. As a result, there is little waste in this customization process. In addition, the effectiveness of a direct-mail campaign is easy to evaluate because the response comes quickly after the date of the promotion, or not at all. In many societies, high levels of disposable income and interest in shopping convenience have made shopping through catalogs very popular.

However, many customers are put off by direct marketing efforts. Too many calls at home make customers wary of telemarketers. In many countries, the activities of such direct marketers are restricted. Since 2003, the **Do Not Call Registry** gives U.S. consumers an opportunity to limit the telemarketing calls they receive. Many people's daily mail is full of direct-mail pieces—what many people call junk mail—thus making it difficult for your message to get through the clutter. Response rates to direct marketing can be extremely low.

do not call registry gives consumers a choice about whether or not they wish to receive phone calls from particular telemarketers

Sales Promotion

Sales promotion involves communication activities that provide extra incentives to customers or the sales force to achieve a short-term objective. **Consumer-oriented promotions** include devices such as coupons, point-of-purchase savings, sweepstakes, rebates, and free samples. Many promotions are oriented toward the channels of distribution, including the sales force; these are called **trade promotions.** The objective of trade promotions—such as sales contests, quantity discounts, and training programs—is to get the channels to carry and promote the product.

The advantage of such promotions is that they can generate a measurable short-term sales response. Sales promotion is much more effective than advertising in this regard. Sampling (free sample) programs are effective for inducing trial of new products. Promotions such as coupons delivered in a magazine can complement an advertising campaign by reinforcing a brand name. They are also effective in getting customers to repeat purchase or buy a larger size. Trade promotions are essential to gaining shelf space in retail outlets.

A disadvantage of sales promotion is that it is almost always focused on price. As a result, customers can be induced to become more price-sensitive and deal-loyal (loyal to the brand that is on some kind of promotion) rather than brand-loyal. In some ways, it actually works against advertising, which is more focused on building brand equity. Customers can also begin to expect sales promotions and delay purchases until a rebate or some other special deal is offered. Finally, most studies of the effects of sales promotions show the results to be short-lived. More details about sales promotion will be covered in Chapter 11.

sales promotion communication activities that provide extra incentives to customers or the sales force to achieve a short-term objective

consumer-oriented promotions a marketing tool such as a coupon that targets consumers and is intended to generate a short-term change in a product's sales or market share

trade promotions sales promotions oriented toward the channels of distribution in an effort to get the channels to carry and promote the product, often including devices such as sales contests, quantity discounts, and training programs

Publicity and Public Relations

Unlike advertising, **public relations (PR)** and publicity are communications for which the sponsoring organization does not pay. PR normally takes the form of an article in a magazine or newspaper or in any other form of nonpersonal news distribution. Often companies employ PR firms or agencies to make sure that articles and other news favorable to the company are placed in media to which a variety of constituents are exposed (e.g., customers, stockholders, legislators).

The main advantage of PR is that it comes from a supposedly unbiased source. Therefore, it has more credibility than advertising, which everyone knows is intended to promote the product or service. In addition, other than the cost of the PR agency, it is inexpensive. PR campaigns are often used by pharmaceutical companies in order to raise public awareness of certain disorders, such as social anxiety disorder (SAD), an extreme form of shyness in social situations.

The problem with PR is that the sponsoring company has little control over it. You cannot control the placement of the item in a publication, what is said about you, or any other aspect of PR. In addition, PR can be negative. If your company is accused of sexual discrimination in hiring and promotion practices, this is likely to damage your reputation. In these cases, PR firms usually attempt to diminish the problem by taking damage control measures, such as releasing favorable information about the company.

public relations communications for which the sponsoring organization does not pay, often in some form of news distributed in a nonpersonal form

Product demonstrations are an important part of the communications mix for many products.
Source: Jeff Greenberg/PhotoEdit Inc.

Personal Selling

personal selling
the use of face-to-face communications between seller and buyer

Personal selling is the use of face-to-face communications between seller and buyer.[8] For companies marketing business-to-business products and services, this is often the largest part of the marketing budget. Salespeople can target their messages to customers, and the personal interaction permits them to respond to customer questions on the spot. In addition, more information can be communicated through a salesperson–customer encounter than would be possible through advertising or other mass-communication approaches. This makes personal selling especially appropriate for very expensive and complex products and services.

The major drawback of personal selling is the expense. Training and compensating salespeople is expensive. In addition, even with the best training programs, it is difficult for the marketing or sales manager to control what happens in the sales encounter. For example, a training program that focuses on marketing the product on a quality basis can fall apart if the sales force sells on price instead.

Miscellaneous Communications Activities

A number of other communications activities are important parts of the communications mix. As noted in Chapter 7, a product's package can deliver a variety of messages to customers, including price, nutrition, ingredients, information about how to use it, and other recipes. In some industries, trade shows (large convocations where sellers, buyers, and suppliers congregate) are important ways to communicate with potential customers and demonstrate new products. Some companies sponsor events such as golf and tennis tournaments, which are intended to target customers who attend and watch them. Companies pay to have their brands placed in movie scenes so that millions of viewers can see them on the big screen. Product demonstrations can also be effective; a trial copy of Checkpoint Software's FireWall-1 installed live at the potential customer's site often stunned audiences as message alerts would pop up indicating that hackers were "pinging" their network.[9]

Application Absolut Vodka

The story of Absolut goes back to 1879, when the Swedish "king of vodka" Lars Olsson Smith started making his "Absolut Rent Brännvin" using a revolutionary new distillation method called Continuous Distillation, which is still used today.[10] At first, the vodka was produced in his distillery on the island of Reimersholme, just outside of Stockholm. Today it is made in Åhus in southern Sweden, where the wheat is taken from nearby fields and the water from their own well.

In the late 1970s, the president of the company made the decision to export the vodka to global markets. The company's marketing team set about trying to develop a new positioning for Absolut Vodka. At first, the ideas centered on the product's Swedish heritage. The team went to New York to get ideas from its advertising agency, TBWA. The first signature concept was the clear bottle with silver text and no label, an idea that was later rejected. The second innovative concept was to link the bottles with art. In 1985 (six years after Absolut was introduced in the United States), Andy Warhol was commissioned to do a painting of the Absolut Vodka bottle. When the painting appeared as an advertisement, it received worldwide attention. This transitioned the brand from a popular product to an icon and a piece of pop art. So far, more than 1,200 ads have been created with the Absolut campaign and its ads remain among the most popular in the world.

The brand has maintained a strong brand equity because of its consistent positioning over time. However, the company also espouses IMC. A visit to the company's Web site, www.absolut.com/us/about/story, reinforces the pop art nature of the product. The company has also distributed knitted Absolut "cozies," like sweaters for the bottles. Not only is the cozy in the shape of the bottle, the packaging reinforces the ad copy by showing the signature bottle in a vertical position.

Application LG Electronics

In 2009, LG Electronics MobileComm U.S.A. Inc. (LG Mobile Phones), in partnership with Twentieth Century Fox and Lightstorm Entertainment, created a multifaceted marketing campaign tied to the epic adventure film, *Avatar,* written and directed by Oscar®-winning filmmaker James Cameron (*Titanic*).[11] LG Mobile Phones created a marketing campaign that appealed to forward-thinking technology enthusiasts. The integrated marketing communications included a TV spot, an interactive micro site, www.lgexpo.com (which includes exclusive movie content), and an exclusive joint-sponsored Facebook page. To promote the film and its involvement, LG Mobile Phones created a 30-second TV spot, which featured the movie trailer for the highly anticipated film. The spot showcased a humorous interchange between co-workers who compete to be in the know about the latest and greatest in technology.

The movie-themed micro site, www.lgexpo.com, gives fans a deep, rich movie-tie in experience. The site, launched on December 3, 2009, contained exclusive content from the film. It also featured two characters—Jim and Dale—who are the ultimate Avatar and LG eXpo fans, and it gave visitors to the site an online video demonstration of LG eXpo and its advanced exclusive features, such as the Mobile Projector. The campaign also included an interactive joint-sponsored Facebook page between FOX, MTV and LG.

Clearly, LG feels that combining media with a similar theme is a powerful way of building the brand in the marketplace.

Advertising Management

Advertising is a major expense for marketing managers worldwide, and a big business. How big? Although estimates vary, about $137 billion was spent on advertising in the United States and $370 billion worldwide in 2008, with these figures expected to be flat in 2009–2010 due to the recession.[12] To give you some idea of the amount of money spent on advertising by companies, Table 10.2 provides the spending levels for the top 10 total advertisers in the United States. Table 10.3 does the same for business-to-business advertising, and Table 10.4 provides the information on the top 10 global spenders.

As these numbers on global advertising expenditures demonstrate (and as you will have noticed), advertising is a widely used communications tool around the world. The discussions earlier in this book about global marketing and positioning noted the difficulty of using the same advertising campaign globally. There are so many differences in language and culture that even a truly global advertising campaign requires some localization. For example, Taco Bell's wildly successful talking Chihuahua, Gidget, could not be used when the company expanded to Singapore, because Muslims consider it taboo to touch

Table 10.2

Top 10 U.S. Total Advertising Spenders in 2006 (millions of dollars)

Advertiser	U.S. Advertising Spending ($)
Procter & Gamble Co.	4,898.0
AT&T	3,344.7
General Motors	3,296.1
Time Warner	3,088.8
Verizon Communications	2,821.8
Ford Motor Co.	2,576.8
GlaxoSmithKline	2,444.2
Walt Disney Co.	2,320.0
Johnson & Johnson	2,290.5
Unilever	2,098.3

Source: Advertising Age (2007), June 25, p. S-10. Copyright 2005 by CRAIN COMMUNICATIONS INC. Reproduced with permission of CRAIN COMMUNICATIONS INC in the format Textbook via Copyright Clearance Center.

Table 10.3

Top B-to-B Advertising Spenders in 2006* (millions of dollars)

Company	U.S. Advertising Spending ($)
AT&T	419.3
Verizon Communications	405.9
Sprint Nextel Corp.	277.0
IBM Corp.	236.3
Hewlett-Packard Co.	219.6
Microsoft Corp.	213.6
Monster Worldwide	155.1
FedEx Corp.	144.0
Citigroup	137.5
JPMorgan Chase & Co.	129.0

* These numbers represent the amount of money spent advertising products and services in B-to-B media.

Source: BtoB (2007), September 12, p. 26. B TO B: THE MAGAZINE FOR MARKETING AND E-COMMERCE STRATEGISTS by BtoB. Copyright 2005 by CRAIN COMMUNICATIONS INC. Reproduced with permission of CRAIN COMMUNICATIONS INC in the format Textbook via Copyright Clearance Center.

a dog.[13] In addition, there are many differences around the world in regulation of advertising and promotion. Most countries regulate advertising content; for example, comparative advertising is widely frowned upon. Muslim countries have strict guidelines about how women can be portrayed in ads. Norway, Sweden, and Switzerland do not allow advertising on TV at all. Other countries have government-owned stations that limit advertising. However, with the global explosion of cable TV, many of these regulations are being relaxed.

The continued march toward the globalization of business mentioned earlier in this book has also affected the advertising agency business. Four large agencies represent more than half of the advertising billings in the world: the Publicis Groupe based in Paris, the Omnicom and Interpublic groups based in New York, and the WPP Group of London. Driving this concentration of billings has been a similar change in their clients, who have also become larger and more global. The growth in the use of other elements of the communications mix beyond TV and print ads to include promotions and public relations, as well as other forms of advertising such as the Internet, has caused the mega-agencies to continue

Table 10.4

Top Global Advertisers in 2008 (millions of dollars)

Company	Global Advertising Spending ($)
Procter & Gamble Co.	9,730
Unilever	5,720
L'Oreal	4,040
General Motors Co.	3,670
Toyota Motor Corp.	3,200
Coca-Cola Co.	2,670
Johnson & Johnson	2,600
Ford Motor Co.	2,450
Reckitt Benckiser	2,370
Nestlé	2,310

Source: Advertising Age (2009), November 30. Copyright 2005 by CRAIN COMMUNICATIONS INC. Reproduced with permission of CRAIN COMMUNICATIONS INC in the format Textbook via Copyright Clearance Center.

to swallow up firms specializing in these areas. It also permits the agencies to handle competing clients as each is assigned to a different agency beneath the corporate umbrella.[14]

Often, for consumer products, marketing managers think of advertising spending in the context of how much to spend on both advertising and sales promotion. For these kinds of products, advertising and promotion (television, print advertising, literature, radio, and out-of-home media) are more than 80 percent of the communications budget. In recent years, the percentage of the advertising and promotion budget spent on advertising has declined because more money has been devoted to promotion—particularly promotion oriented toward trade or distribution channels. In 1993, 52 percent of the advertising and promotion budget went to trade promotion and 28 percent to media advertising (the other 20 percent went to consumer promotions like coupons). By 2001, spending on trade promotion had jumped to 61 percent of the advertising and promotion budget and media advertising declined to 24 percent, with consumer promotions dropping to 15 percent.[15]

Advertising Decision Making

Advertising decision making has six stages often called the *6M model* for communications planning:

1. **Market.** Who is the target audience?
2. **Mission.** What is the goal of advertising?
3. **Message.** What are the specific points of communications?
4. **Media.** Which media vehicles will be used?
5. **Money.** How much is the budget?
6. **Measurement.** How will impact of advertising be measured?

Selecting the Target Audience

In general, this decision follows directly from the marketing strategy. As we showed in Chapter 2, the selection of target markets is a critical step following the statement of marketing objectives and requires an extensive analysis of the various segmentation options. The target audiences for advertising include the segments you have decided are the keys to your marketing strategy.

However, advertising could include noncustomer targets. Some advertising, particularly corporate advertising, is targeted toward potential investors, regulators, channel members, employees, or other relevant constituents. Thus, although customers are the most logical targets and the ones that should receive the most resources, you should consider other relevant audiences as well.

Setting Advertising Goals

Clearly the reason companies advertise is to increase sales and profits, if not in the short run, then in the long run. You may wonder why sales increase would not be the obvious goal of advertising.

The problem is that many factors in the environment affect sales, not just advertising. If a great new advertising campaign is adopted, sales could actually decline if the competitor lowers its price to the point at which many customers respond. Alternatively, the company may not have discovered the appropriate channels, packaging, or other elements of the marketing mix that affect customer response in the marketplace. Changes in customer purchasing habits or other kinds of behavioral shifts can also affect sales of a product. Thus, it is inappropriate to place a sales goal on advertising alone when many things a company and the competition can do (as well as changes in the environment) ultimately affect sales. The exception to this rule is direct-response advertising, in which a toll-free telephone number is given for immediate reaction by the customer. This kind of advertising is actually a hybrid of traditional advertising and direct marketing.

There is a dilemma here that creates tension between the firm and the advertising agency. The firm is interested in getting a measurable return on its investment in advertising, and the agency does not want to be held to sales as a short-term goal. The marketing manager should know that advertising can be mostly effective in building sales, but only to the extent that the complete marketing strategy is appropriate (given the competition and the environment) and that it takes time for advertising to be successful.

Therefore, although some advertising agencies are compensated for achieving sales goals, the majority are evaluated on the basis of more intermediate objectives.

These intermediate goals are based on models of how advertising creates a customer response. A few of the most popular models are shown in Figure 10.7. Although the details of the models vary, they all have three basic stages of movement from a low level to a high level of response:

1. **The lowest level of response is the cognitive stage.** This is the act of thinking about the product; no feelings toward it have been aroused. At this level of response, customers are becoming aware of the product and developing knowledge of the product's attributes and benefits.
2. **A higher level of response is the affective stage.** At this level, the customer has gone beyond mere knowledge of the product and has begun to develop attitudes, preferences, and perhaps interest (although the customer could develop negative rather than positive affect).
3. **The final stage is behavior.** This could be purchase but also other kinds of behavior, such as visiting a retailer to see a product demonstration or returning a reply card in a magazine for more information about the product.

This model is sometimes referred to as the *think–feel–do* or persuasive hierarchy model.[16]

All of the models in Figure 10.7 are hierarchical models in that they posit customers moving up a ladder of interest about the product. They are useful conceptualizations of how customers react to communications because they recognize that customers could be in various states of readiness. The models also imply a set of tasks that persuasive communications such as advertising must perform, from first informing the customers that the product exists to the point of getting the customer to move from favorable attitudes to taking some actions. There is no intended timing of the movement from stage to stage. This could occur over several years in the case of an expensive and complex product to virtually simultaneously in the case of a new product introduced in a supermarket.

Figure 10.7

Models of the Advertising Response Process

	AIDA Model	Hierarchy-of-Effects Model	Innovation Adoption Model	Information Processing Model
Cognitive Stage	Attention	Awareness Knowledge	Awareness	Presentation Attention Comprehension
Affective Stage	Interest Desire	Liking Preference Conviction	Interest Evaluation	Yielding Retention
Behavioral Stage	Action	Purchase	Trial Adoption	Behavior

Source: George E. Belch and Michael A. Belch (1993), *Introduction to Advertising and Promotion* (Homewood, IL: Irwin), p. 199. Reproduced with permission of the McGraw-Hill Companies.

Some researchers and practitioners have found that for products and services where there is relatively little information processing, consumers may move from the cognitive (awareness) stage directly to the behavioral stage and then form attitudes (affective stage) after product usage. In other words, it is cheaper to sample low-cost products and then form opinions about them than it is to process advertising and other information and then make up your mind about what to buy. This is often referred to as the "low-involvement" process. However, the components of the process are the same, as it is only the order that is changed.[17]

The importance of these models is that they provide some valuable objectives for advertising short of sales. An obvious objective can be simple awareness that the product exists. This is clearly a good objective for a new product (creating awareness) or one for which research has determined that the awareness level is too low (increasing awareness). If marketing research finds that awareness is high but few potential customers perceive the product favorably, you can use affective objectives such as building brand preference or positioning in ways consistent with the marketing strategy. Nonsales behavior objectives, such as trial (for new products or those with low trial rates) and repeat purchasing, are also possible.

The choice of objective can be considered in the context of the product life cycle. Figure 10.8 shows how these goals might change over time. When a product category is new, the focus is on educating customers about the features of the product and, if appropriate, its relative advantage over the product it is replacing. For example, when Procter & Gamble launched its Pampers brand of disposable diapers in 1966 (the product had been in test market since 1962), consumers had to be educated about the advantages of the product over cloth diapers and diaper services. In the early and late growth stages of the life cycle, more competition has entered, and there is a concomitant need to stress product differences and brand superiority. Thus, the advertising objectives are more likely to be affective, except for any new brands entering at this stage. Finally, at the maturity stage, competition is intense and the products are fairly similar in terms of their characteristics. At this stage, image (affective) and brand loyalty (behavior) become very important.

Developing the Message Strategy

Marketing managers should always be involved in determining the objectives of advertising. After all, they have developed the marketing strategy and are in the best position to know what communications are required to achieve the overall marketing objectives and persuasively communicate the value proposition to the target markets.

Figure 10.8

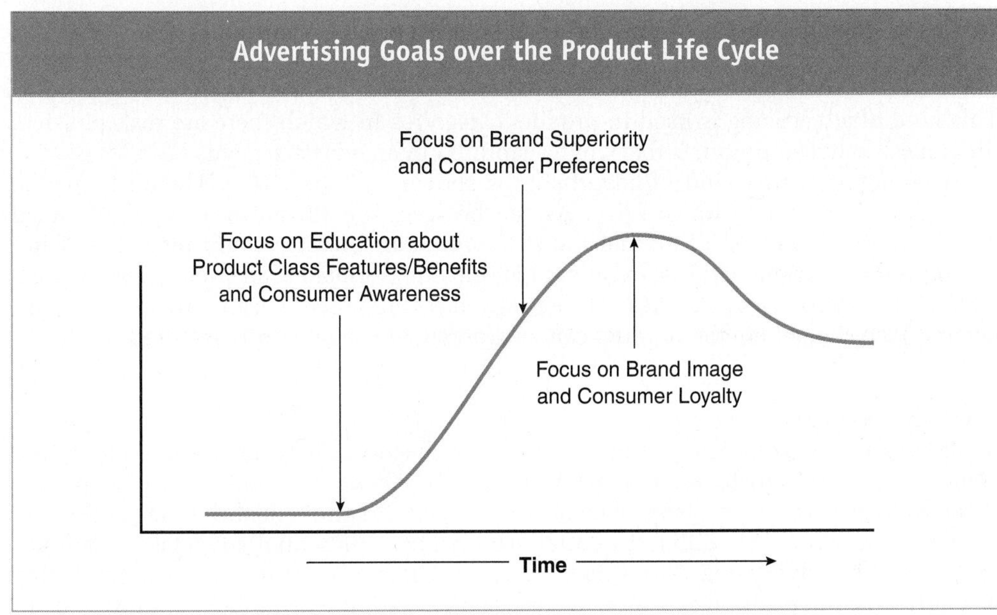

Source: George E. Belch and Michael A. Belch (1993), *Introduction to Advertising and Promotion* (Homewood, IL: Irwin), p. 199. Reproduced with permission of the McGraw-Hill Companies.

However, choosing the best way to attain advertising objectives is the creative part of advertising. This is usually the terrain of the advertising agency, which employs professionals who try to develop the art of advertising, the actual executions that customers see in the media.

Different approaches to creating advertising or appeals can be classified more specifically in the following ways.[18]

Informational or Rational Appeals

informational appeals an approach to developing advertising copy that focuses on the functional or practical aspects of the product

Informational appeals focus on the functional or practical aspects of the product. These messages emphasize facts, learning, and persuasion. The job of this kind of advertising is to persuade the target audience that the brand being advertised satisfies their needs better than the competition. This kind of advertising also may communicate to the audience the value proposition, or what some in the advertising industry call the unique selling proposition.

Informational appeals can be of several general types:

- **Feature/benefit appeals.** These appeals focus on the dominant attributes or characteristics of the product or service, or the benefits provided. These ads tend to implicitly use the multiattribute model of decision making discussed in Chapter 4.
- **Competitive advantage appeals.** This type of ad makes either a direct or indirect claim of superiority against a targeted or general class of competitors.
- **Favorable price appeal.** In these ads, price is the dominant factor. This approach would obviously not be used by the marketer who is trying to differentiate the product on the basis of a dimension other than price because, in that case, the price is likely to be higher than the competition's.
- **News appeals.** These are advertisements in which some kind of announcement about the product dominates the copy.
- **Product or service popularity appeals.** In these ads, the copy touts how popular the product is among the target audience. Because it is popular, the advertisement implies, it must follow that the product is of high quality or has outstanding value.

In some cases, informational appeals focus squarely on product attributes. Product-attribute-focused advertising can try to:

- Influence the attributes used by customers in evaluating the competitive offerings in a product category.
- Increase the awareness and/or change the perceptions of some of your product's attributes.
- Change the perceptions of some of a competitor's product's attributes.
- Increase or decrease the importance weights of the product attributes.

This kind of advertising is used in product categories in which there are real, physical differences between products that can be captured in an advertisement.

An example of this kind of advertising is shown in Figure 10.9. The ad is for the investment company T. Rowe Price. As can be seen, the attributes being emphasized include a wide selection of mutual funds in which an investor could place his or her money, low management costs, excellent historical performance, and specialized investment assistance. This ad also has a direct-response component because the phone number and Web site, where the product can be ordered, are prominently featured.

Emotional Appeals

In other cases, the advertising focuses mainly on imagery and symbols and eschews reference to product attributes. Much television advertising uses this kind of approach because images are more easily remembered in a short commercial than facts. Product categories in which it is difficult to establish tangible differential advantages often use image-oriented advertising. Also this kind of advertising can be used when a marketing manager wants to position a product or service in a certain way in the customer's mind.

Figure 10.9

T. Rowe Price Ad

ROLLOVER IRA

The New T. Rowe Price
FlexChoice Rollover℠
Lets you choose how to make the most of your old 401(k).

Broad selection of funds — We have a wide range of over 60 no-load T. Rowe Price funds to choose from for your *FlexChoice Rollover IRA*. You can also choose from over 1,000 other funds from leading fund families.*

Low cost — T. Rowe Price offers 100% no-load funds with no sales charges or commissions. And our expenses are low—almost all our funds for individual investors have lower expenses than their Lipper averages.**

Proven performance — For each 1-, 5-, and 10-year period ended 6/30/05, over 70% of our funds beat their Lipper average.*** All T. Rowe Price funds are managed in-house by one of the most experienced and respected groups of fund managers in the industry. Results will vary for other periods. All funds are subject to market risk. *Past performance cannot guarantee future results.*

Rollover Specialists to help — Our Rollover Specialists are here to answer any questions you may have about rolling over with T. Rowe Price. If you want, they can help you select the right funds for your *FlexChoice Rollover IRA* based on your long-term goals and tolerance for risk. They can even help take care of the paperwork and open your IRA right over the phone. So call one of our Rollover Specialists today— it's easy to get started.

Request a prospectus or a briefer profile; each includes investment objectives, risks, fees, expenses, and other information that you should read and consider carefully before investing.

TROWEPRICE.COM/ROLLOVER
1-888-789-6510

INVEST WITH CONFIDENCE

*Non-T. Rowe Price mutual funds available through T. Rowe Price Brokerage, a division of T. Rowe Price Investment Services, Inc. Member NASD/SIPC. **114 of 116 funds (excluding institutional and bank institutional funds as defined by Lipper) more than six months old had expense ratios below their Lipper averages based on fiscal year-end data available as of 3/31/05. (Source for data: Lipper Inc.) ***Based on cumulative total return, 97 of 132, 65 of 87, and 44 of 61 T. Rowe Price funds (including all share classes and excluding funds used in insurance products) outperformed their Lipper average for the 1-, 5-, and 10-year periods ended 6/30/05, respectively. Not all funds outperformed for all periods. (Source for data: Lipper Inc.) T. Rowe Price Investment Services, Inc., Distributor. IRARFC072098

emotional appeals
an approach to developing advertising copy that strives to tap an underlying psychological aspect of the purchase decision

Thus, as the name implies, **emotional appeals** are intended to tap an underlying psychological benefit of the purchase decision. Many advertisements for consumer products and even some business-to-business products use humor, fear, and sex to achieve their objectives. Such advertising may stimulate greater memory of the ad (known as recall) and more liking of the brand. Unilever was faced with a huge marketing and advertising challenge when the company decided to introduce its deodorant bodyspray, AXE, into the U.S. market. AXE emphasizes humor and the emotional and social benefits of smelling good that allow the brand's advertising to be among the most admired. The AXE ads on YouTube and their parodies are good examples of the sexually charged social humor that has become synonymous with the AXE brand.

Within the two broad categories of appeals, informational and emotional, are a variety of different tactical or execution approaches. These are specific approaches taken by advertisers to communicate their messages:

- Straight-sell or factual message.
- Scientific/technical evidence.
- Product demonstration.
- Comparisons.
- Testimonials.
- Slice of life, in which a customer's problem is shown and the product is given as the solution.
- Animation.
- Personality symbols.
- Fantasy.
- Dramatization.
- Humor.

Evaluating Message Copy

Normally, marketing managers are not involved with the development of the actual advertising copy. That task is delegated to in-house or agency creative specialists. However, they must be heavily involved with testing the advertising copy (or at least be aware that testing should be done) before committing a substantial amount of money to it. Many variables are usually testable (the spokesperson, the message itself, the execution, media, and other factors).

Laboratory Tests

Figure 10.10 is a classification of the different methods used for pretesting and posttesting advertising.[19] Pretests are measures taken before implementation of the campaign, and a posttest is an evaluation of the advertising after it has been developed but before it has been rolled out nationally or internationally. In laboratory tests, people are brought to a particular location, where they are shown ads and asked to respond to them. The advantage of lab tests is that the researcher can carefully control the environment without distractions to the respondent and manipulate several different aspects of the advertising. The disadvantage is that the situation is not realistic, because the respondent provides answers in an unnatural environment. Field tests provide real-world measures because they are conducted under natural viewing conditions. Their advantages and disadvantages are the mirror image of those of lab tests: the environment is realistic, but the researcher cannot absolutely control other variables that might affect response to the ad, such as a competitor's ad, noise from children, or other distractions.

Consumer jury The most common form of testing for advertising concepts is the use of focus groups. TV advertising concepts are usually presented as storyboards, or rough pictures with captions showing the "story" that will be told in the ad (for radio ads, only words are used). For magazine or other print formats, actual executions are shown. Multimedia technology allows for the use of more realistic ads.

Portfolio tests In this approach, respondents are shown both control and test ads. After viewing the portfolio, respondents are asked what information they recall from the ads

Figure 10.10

Classification of Copy-Testing Methods

	Advertising-related test (reception or response to the message itself and its contents)	**Product-related test** (impact of message on product awareness, liking, intention to buy, or use)
Laboratory measures (respondent aware of testing and measurement process)	Cell I Pretesting procedures 1. Consumer jury 2. Portfolio tests 3. Readability tests 4. Physiological measures Eye camera Galvanic skin response Electrodermal response	Cell II Pretesting procedures 1. Theater tests 2. Trailer tests 3. Laboratory stores
Real-world measures (respondent unaware of testing and measurement process)	Cell III Pretesting procedures 1. Dummy advertising vehicles 2. Inquiry tests 3. On-the-air tests Posttesting procedures 1. Recognition tests 2. Recall tests 3. Association measures 4. Combination measures	Cell IV Pretesting and posttesting procedures 1. Pre- and posttests 2. Sales tests 3. Minimarket tests

Source: George E. Belch and Michael A. Belch (1993), *Introduction to Advertising and Promotion* (Homewood, IL: Irwin). Reproduced with permission of the McGraw-Hill Companies.

and which they liked best. The ads with the highest recall and liking are considered to be the most effective.

Readability tests Readability of the copy of a print ad can be determined by counting the number of syllables per 100 words, the length of sentences, and other structural aspects of the copy. The results provide a sense of the reading skill needed to comprehend it, which should match that of the target audience, and are then compared to norms obtained from successful ads.

Physiological methods A more scientific approach to assessing advertisements involves techniques that measure involuntary physical responses to the ad. These physiological methods include:

physiological methods measured advertising response by taking physical measures, such as pupil dilation or eye tracking

- **Pupil dilation.** Pupilometers measure dilation (an activity related to action or arousal) and constriction (conservation of energy).
- **GSR/EDR (galvanic skin response/electrodermal response).** Response to a stimulus activates sweat glands. This activity can be measured using electrodes attached to the skin.
- **Eye tracking.** Viewers are asked to watch or read an ad while a sensor beams infrared light at their eyes. This can measure how much of an ad is being read, what part of the ad is attracting attention, and the sequence of reading and attention.

Theater tests **Theater testing** is a widely used method for pretesting TV commercials. The service is sold by companies such as Advertising Research Services and Advertising Control for Television. Participants in theater tests are recruited by phone, shopping mall intercepts, and direct mail. A television show or some other entertainment is provided in a movie theater–like facility with commercial breaks ("trailer" tests use smaller, mobile facilities near shopping malls). The show is used so that the respondents do not focus solely on the commercials. A cover story might inform them that the TV

theater tests tests of prospective advertising copy that take place in a theater-like environment

show is a pilot for a new network or cable series. After viewing the ads, the participants are asked questions about recall, attitude, interest, and other behavioral responses.

Laboratory stores In this testing procedure, the researcher attempts to simulate a shopping environment by setting up a supermarket-like shopping shelf with real brands. Respondents are shown advertising copy and make actual brand choices. A popular supplier of this kind of testing is Research Systems Corporation, with its ARS Persuasion copy-testing system.

Real-World Measures

Dummy advertising vehicles Researchers construct dummy magazines with regular editorial matter, regular ads, and a set of test ads. The magazines are distributed to a random sample of homes in a predetermined geographic area. After being asked to read the magazine as they normally would, the consumers in the sample are interviewed on the editorial content as well as the test ads.

inquiry tests
track the number of inquiries received from a print advertisement

Inquiry tests **Inquiry tests** are also used for print ads. The marketing manager or advertising agency can track the number of inquiries generated from an ad that has a direct-response, toll-free phone number or a reader inquiry card attached. In industrial marketing, the use of "bingo" cards, response cards that have numbered holes corresponding to the numbered ads in the magazine, is common.

on-the-air/recall tests
measure advertising effectiveness through follow-up surveys after a TV advertisement is shown

On-the-air/recall tests Information Resources Inc. (IRI), Burke Marketing Research, ASI Market Research, Nielsen, and others sell **on-the-air/recall test** services. A real TV ad (one of perhaps several executions being tested) is inserted into a TV program in one or more test markets. Consumers are then contacted and asked whether they saw the ad. If so, they are asked further questions about recall of copy points, brand, and the like. The services differ somewhat in the questions asked and how the sample is recruited. Gallup & Robinson, for example, recruits subjects who are asked in advance to watch the particular show on which the test ad is being run.

Recognition tests This is the most widely used method for posttesting print ads and is closely associated with Starch INRA Hooper's through-the-book method. With this approach, a researcher interviews respondents at home or at work by first asking whether they have read a particular issue of a magazine. If so, she or he then goes through the issue to obtain information about whether the respondents have seen the ad, how much of it they have read, and how much they recall. The Starch method and the resulting Starch scores are used to track and evaluate complete campaigns.

Sales/minimarket tests In some areas of the United States, IRI has created what it calls BehaviorScan markets, in which a city is wired with two separate TV cables. This split-cable arrangement allows advertisers to manipulate the ad copy by showing one execution on the test cable and keeping the current copy on the control cable. The programming is otherwise identical. A sample of households on both cables is enlisted to have their purchases electronically scanned at supermarkets, drug stores, discount stores, and convenience stores. By comparing the purchase rates between the two samples, an advertiser can determine whether the ad copy on the test cable stimulated more purchases than the ad shown to the control group. The **sales/minimarket test** method is limited to ads for frequently purchased consumer goods with sales objectives.

sales/minimarket tests
advertising tests in controlled geographic areas

Selecting Media

Choosing the media to use for advertising is becoming more difficult with the rapid growth of alternative media beyond the traditional network (national) and spot (local) TV, radio, newspaper, print (magazine), and outdoor (billboards, where legally permitted) media. The emergence of cable television and the Web has created two new major media. Other important media have emerged such as "branded" entertainment (product placement), where brands appear in movies, on TV shows, and in videogames. In addition, numerous minor media (e.g., CD-ROMs, supermarket floors, bathroom stalls, shopping carts, autos, trucks, buses, fruit labels) are also being explored.[20]

Because of changes in marketing strategy, the need for greater efficiency, the development of new media and vehicles (e.g., new magazines and TV shows), and the constant search for better ways to target their segments, managers are shifting their budget allocations between media toward the newer media. For example, in 2005, Ford Motor Co. spent 15 percent of its $1 billion marketing budget on all "digital" forms of advertising.[21]

There are three main aspects to media planning:

1. Selecting the appropriate media for the advertising campaign.
2. Selecting specific vehicles within each medium.
3. Scheduling the advertising.

These decisions are used to create a media plan, which is a detailed document showing the precise scheduling of all the advertising over a planning horizon. Thus, given an available advertising budget, the decision is how to allocate it across media types, then within each medium, and finally, over the appropriate time period.

Media Selection

Media can be divided into "traditional" media and "new" media.

Traditional Media

Television As noted earlier in this chapter, TV can reach many people quickly and efficiently. It is also the best medium for image advertising and movie-like action. However, unless you have a large budget, the production and media costs for TV are enormous, which puts it out of the range of many companies. In addition, it is difficult to narrowly target an audience with TV because of the wide range of people who watch it. Except for extended infomercials, TV is not good for factual (informational) copy because of the speed with which data flash by the screen, combined with a general lack of attentiveness of audiences. Finally, with the increasingly high penetration rate of digital video recorders, it is easy to record a show and then fast-forward through the commercials. The newer digital recorders marketed by TiVo and Replay Networks can automatically delete commercials when recording. However, despite the predictions of TV advertising spending declining due to the lack of targetability and the increased penetration of digital recorders, TV advertising is still popular.

Magazines and newspapers (print) Print is much better for complicated messages. In addition, print has archival value because it can be stored. Consider the old magazines in doctors' offices; the ads in those magazines are still gaining exposure long after the month or week in which they were published. Magazines are better than newspapers for color reproduction. Print is better than TV for targeting specific audiences, and magazines are better than newspaper, which is more limited to specific sections (e.g., sports, entertainment). Print, like spot TV, can also reach geographically defined target segments.

Radio Radio is an excellent medium because of its low cost, attentive audience, and creative flexibility. Of course, product demonstrations are not possible. Radio, like TV, can reach audiences quickly, unlike the lag in publication dates with print (except for daily newspapers). Radio is also excellent for targeting specific audiences, because each radio station has its own marketing strategy aimed at a particular market. Also, you can thus choose to advertise on particular stations fitting your segment profiles.

Cable TV Cable is a nice hybrid of radio and television because it has the best features of both. Like radio, it is inexpensive and reaches targeted audiences. Each cable channel (e.g., MTV; WE, the women's entertainment channel; ESPN) is generally designed around a theme and an audience that can be accessed easily. It has all the creative flexibility of TV. The main drawback is that the number of viewers for many of the channels is very low because of the large number of alternatives.

Outdoor Billboards are a good medium for reminder and image advertising, but the images can be fleeting as you drive by (unless you are stuck in a traffic jam). They are obviously poor for extended messages. Outdoor advertising tends to be used by product categories for which access to other media has been legally denied (e.g., tobacco, alcohol in the United States). Most countries and geographic areas impose legal limits on the use of outdoor advertising, either through banning it entirely, limiting its locations and size, or restricting the products that can use it. For example, Australia has banned cigarette advertising on billboards. However, technology is changing the outdoor business. In 2005, Clear Channel Outdoor launched a trial in Cleveland, Ohio, with seven huge light-emitting-diode (LED) billboards with messages that can be changed dozens of times each day. Billboards are thus being changed from a fixed to a dynamic medium. Table 10.5 displays the U.S. spend on measured media advertising in 2008.

Table 10.5

U.S. Measured Media for All Advertisers in 2008 (billions of dollars)

Media	U.S. Advertising Spending ($)	%
Magazine	28.58	20.1
Network TV	26.71	18.8
Newspaper	25.06	17.7
Cable TV networks	18.83	13.3
Spot TV	15.15	10.7
Internet	9.73	6.9
Radio	9.50	6.7
Syndicated TV	4.44	3.1
Outdoor	3.96	2.8

Source: Advertising Age (2009), June 22. Copyright 2009 by CRAIN COMMUNICATIONS INC. Reproduced with permission of CRAIN COMMUNICATIONS INC in the format Textbook via Copyright Clearance Center.

"New" Media

The Web Advertising expenditures on the Internet continue to grow dramatically, with $23 billion spent in 2009, about 9 percent of all media spending. These are expected to grow high single digits every year over the next few years. In fact, there is concern about the inventory of good Web advertising space to meet the demand.[22] While Web sites themselves act as communications vehicles, the classic Web-based ad is the banner ad, rectangular-shaped ads placed on a site above, below, or on the sides of the sites' main content with a "hot" link to the banner ad sponsor's site. Initial banner ads were static "billboards" with text and graphics. Today, using Flash and other technologies, they can be more exciting, with animated graphics and sound. Although "clickthrough" rates on banner ads are disappointing (less than 1 percent), a considerable body of research is accumulating, which shows that such ads can have significant effects on the other parts of the hierarchical model (Figure 10.7) such as awareness, attitudes, and, ultimately, brand equity.[23] Other Web advertising formats have developed that permit "pop-up" ads to appear almost at any time as well as virtually full-screen ads. These are delivered dynamically as you surf the Web, as well as through direct e-mails and instant messaging. While these ads are annoying, they are extremely effective. Jupiter Media Metrix estimated that in May 2002, the Web site for X10 Wireless Technology Inc., the maker of mini-surveillance cameras, had achieved nearly 33 percent reach, meaning that about one-third of people online that month visited the site.[24] Table 10.6 displays the U.S. online advertising spending by format for 2008 and 2009 and the projected spending for 2010.

Table 10.6

U.S. Online Advertising Spending, by Format, 2008–2010 (in millions)

	2008	2009	2010
Search	$10,546	$10,782	$11,422
Banner ads	4,877	4,765	4,923
Classifieds	3,174	2,215	2,030
Lead generation	1,683	1,521	1,628
Rich media	1,642	1,476	1,558
Video	734	1,029	1,440
Sponsorships	387	313	316
E-mail	405	268	283
Total	23,448	22,370	23,600

Source: eMarketer (2009), December 11. Reprinted with permission from *eMarketer.*

Web advertising offers a level of interactivity that no other medium can. Some innovative uses of Web-based advertising are:

- Swedish dairy products company Fjallfil created the Milko music machine, which permits visitors to create their own videos starring a dancing cow that is the brand symbol for Milko milk. Try it at www.fjallfil.com/index_eng.html.
- BMW has created an advertising campaign using short films directed by some leading directors (Ang Lee, Guy Ritchie) that are available only on the Web (www.bmwfilms.com). Since premiering in April 2001, they have been downloaded millions of times.
- Confectionery giant Mars teamed up with Omnicom's digital shop Agency.com to create "Mix the Rainbow," a Skittles banner ad and Facebook application that allows consumers to create their own musical interpretation of the "Skittles Rainbow." Try it at http://portfolio.ny.agency.com/clients/skittles/mix_the_rainbow/swf/index_01.html.

The hottest area of Internet advertising is what is called *paid* or *keyword search*. Popularized by the search engine Google, the concept is very simple. Google (or the sponsor of the Web site using paid search) gets paid every time a Web surfer clicks on a small text ad posted next to text with particular keywords. Figure 10.11 shows a Google page from the search words "paid search." Ironically, every time a visitor clicks on either of the two ads at the top (GoClick.com and pepperjamsearch.com) or the sponsored links on the right-hand side, most of which are Google competitors, Google gets paid. The amount of payment depends on how much the client is willing to pay Google per click. This business accounts for 99 percent of Google's more than $24 billion in revenues. Of course, clickthroughs do not necessarily produce sales. Thus, some companies are tinkering with a model that rewards the site host only if a product or service is purchased.

Branded entertainment A result of more ad-skipping from digital video recorders and the difficulty of reaching young adults, is a surge of spending on paying to place products and services on TV shows, in movies, and in other media. About $3 billion was spent on this kind of advertising in 2004.[25] Product placement has been around for a long time. Fifty years ago, American TV had shows like *The Colgate Comedy Hour* and *Texaco Star Theater*. However, the number of product placements since then has grown to the point where there were an estimated 100,000 placements on the six major TV networks in the 2004–2005 season. The most placed products on TV shows are shown in Table 10.7. The problems with such placements include the fact that it is difficult to measure their impact and that the quality and popularity of the particular show or movie can affect the brand either positively or negatively.

Influencing word-of-mouth Some companies spend little or nothing on conventional advertising but instead invest in activities that will spread word-of-mouth about the product or service. For example, the Internet-based phone service (known as voice over Internet protocol or VOIP) has become very popular. While one of the major competitors, Vonage, advertises heavily, the other, Skype does not advertise at all. Skype and many other companies rely either exclusively or partially on building word-of-mouth, which spreads among the user population. This kind of marketing is often referred to as *viral* marketing or, more commonly, as *buzz* marketing. While influencing users is not normally thought of as a communications medium, companies that use viral marketing do not just let it happen normally. They spend money attempting to create events and other programs to stimulate positive word-of-mouth or buzz. Skype's viral approach is to make the basic service (Skype user to Skype user, anywhere in the world) free. Note that it is not just the free part that adds customers, but that it is only free if you are talking to another Skype user. This builds additional customers through what we termed network externalities (see Chapter 4). You have to pay for Skype to non-Skype service.

Up-and-comers A number of other media are too new to evaluate in terms of their effectiveness. One of these is the use of cell phones for sending ads to users. While text advertisements have been in use for several years, video is being tested in the United Kingdom. In London's Heathrow airport, transmitters are beaming out video clips of Range Rover's new SUV, the Sport. To reduce customer annoyance and backlash against the brand being advertised, the companies behind the new advertising approach first send a text message asking if the user wants to receive the ad. A second new medium is

Figure 10.11

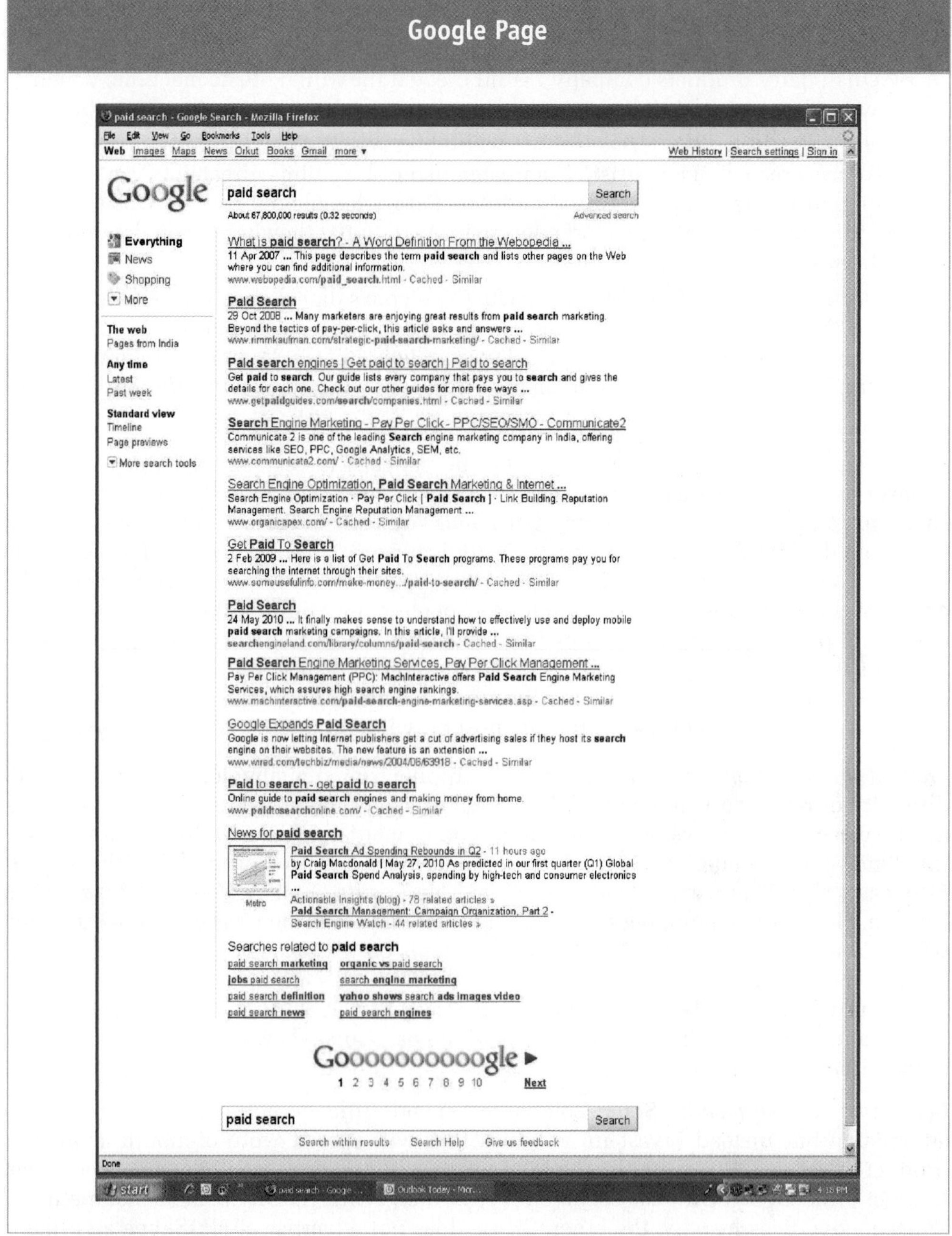

Source: © 2010 Google. Reprinted with permission.

videogames. They are used primarily by 18- to 34-year-old men, and this is a valuable market for many companies. Traditional games played in machines like Sony's PlayStation have product placements embedded in the games. Online games allow advertisers to place all forms of Web ads in the available space. "Advergames" are games that are downloaded from the Web and built around products. For example, in 2002, the U.S. Army created a game called "America's Army," covering basic training and different missions. By 2005, it had more than 5 million registered users. Weblogs or "blogs" are being used to disseminate product information. Social networking sites like Facebook are looking to commercialize their online community. Finally, some advertisers have begun to use MP3 devices like the iPod for "podcasts" touting their products.

Choosing the Specific Vehicles

The budget allocation decision within a specific medium is driven by two major factors: a set of statistics describing each vehicle (e.g., in terms of how many people read or watch, the cost) and the appropriateness of the vehicle for the product being advertised.

Table 10.7

Most Placed Products in TV Shows 20 September 2004–18 September 2005	
Product	Total Occurrences
Coca-Cola Classic	2,900
Everlast (apparel)	1,659
Everlast (sporting equipment)	1,488
Nike (apparel)	1,464
Gatorade drinks	1,222
Chef Revival (apparel)	973
24 Hour Fitness Centers	882
Toyota autos/trucks	846
Home Depot	843
Sierra Mist soft drink	813

Source: The New York Times (2005), October 2, p. BU-6.

Analyzing media Trying to match target audiences to vehicles typically leads to a comparison of efficiency in reaching desirable audiences. An important number is cost-per-thousand (CPM), the ratio of the unit cost to the number of thousands of total audience. CPM is a measure of the efficiency of a vehicle; obviously, lower CPMs are better. Even more importantly, the CPM for the target segment shows the vehicle's efficiency for the important group the advertiser is trying to reach, defined by the demographics the client is targeting.

For television, a popular counting measure is the gross rating point (GRP). The number of GRPs attained by a TV schedule is the product of the reach (the percentage of the potential target audience that are tuned into the commercial) and the frequency (the number of times the commercial is aired). Therefore, a commercial shown four times on a show reaching 20 percent of the target audience would attain 80 GRPs.

Ratings and circulation data (such as Arbitron's radio audience ratings, Nielsen's TV ratings, Standard Rate and Data Services, Audit Bureau of Circulations, and Simmons's magazine audience measurements) are vital inputs to decisions and consequently are hotly contested measures. A.C. Nielsen, in particular, has come under fire by the TV networks for allegedly underestimating its audiences by changing its sampling approach to households. Smaller audience estimates mean lower advertising prices and thus decreased revenues and profits.[26] At all times, your focus should be on cost-per-thousand *relevant* readers, listeners, or viewers (i.e., the cost-per-thousand in the target market).

Despite Nielsen's problems, it is important to recognize that CPM or GRP may also overstate numbers of actual ad readers or viewers. Most people do not read the many pages of ads that fill the fronts of magazines, or study inserts in newspapers, or even stay in the room during TV ads. Hence, adjusting total audience to likely readership or viewership levels is very important. This is why Nielsen has spent millions of dollars improving its TV viewing methodology by introducing "peoplemeters" so subjects can record when they are actually in the room viewing the TV.

One important aspect of targeting spending is product use. A number of services rate media vehicles by product usage. Therefore, for strategies targeting heavy users of a product, CPM can be weighted by such usage.

Another important aspect of choosing media vehicles is regional differentiation. Not only does product usage vary by region and country, but so do features and cultural preferences. Therefore, even though regional vehicles may cost more in a CPM sense, it is often desirable to focus on certain regions (especially if your share or distribution levels vary regionally) and use somewhat different messages and media according to region or country.

Contextual fit It is important to choose vehicles that are a good fit for the product or service being marketed. Contextual fit falls into two subcategories: media fit and program and ad context. The media fit issues are fairly obvious: it is difficult to demonstrate operation of a machine on the radio, incorporate music or other sounds in print media, or provide detailed information that will be recalled in radio or TV ads.

A more subtle level of fit involves the context of the ad, including both the program and other ads. Product fit involves the interaction between the product image and the image of the vehicle. For example, even if professional wrestling delivers upscale viewers at a competitive CPM, does it make sense to advertise upscale products between matches? This issue is magnified if a vehicle airs controversial topics that can lead to a backlash or even a boycott against advertisers.

The interaction of the image of the immediate context is also relevant. For example, a humorous ad may lose its effect if placed in the context of a comedy show or a series of eight other humorous ads. In a serious vehicle, it may be perceived as tasteless. Although it is impossible to control or predict exactly which other commercials will run during a particular TV commercial break, educated guesses are both possible and recommended. Competitive effects are serious when many products in the same category advertise close together, with the result being that many consumers cannot distinguish their claims from one another.

Duplication and wearout Depending on the advertising objective, duplication (multiple exposures to the same ad) may be either desirable or undesirable. Apparently competing vehicles commonly duplicate audiences. For example, a large amount of overlap occurs among readers of *Fortune, Forbes,* and *Bloomberg Businessweek.* Multiple exposures of the same ad are usually necessary for attaining objectives. However, customers might tire of exactly the same message fairly quickly, although evidence seems to suggest that this is less a problem for complex messages than for simple ones. In contrast, some evidence suggests that varying copy slightly, though somewhat expensive, slows down ad wearout.[27] Although the number of possible combinations of vehicles makes thorough analysis difficult (though not impossible, given increased computer power), a reasonable sense can be achieved by estimating the unduplicated audience of each vehicle and, when reach is the objective, concentrating on vehicles with large unduplicated audiences.

Scheduling Advertising

After selecting the appropriate vehicles, the next decision is the actual timing or sequencing of the ads. This decision is based on how your advertising objective responds to the proposed advertising and how much decay is expected when the advertising is not present. Three basic patterns of advertising can be used over a proscribed time period:

1. Flighting, which alternates a burst of advertising with a period of no advertising.
2. A continuous pattern of advertising evenly distributed over the period.
3. Pulsing, or a basic level of advertising combined with regularly scheduled bursts of advertising.

Research has not convincingly demonstrated that one spending pattern is best in meeting all the advertising objectives that can be set. One well-known experimental study found that flighting or pulsing led to a higher temporary peak in recall, whereas a continuous pattern produced higher total recall.[28]

Another factor affecting advertising timing is the seasonality of the sales of the product or service. Timing is affected strongly by the target audience. For example, retail stores make decisions about ski equipment purchases long before consumers do. Likewise, dealers make decisions about purchasing industrial goods long before their customers do. In addition, issues of immediate relevance (which suggests advertising during the buying season) and clutter (which may argue for off-season advertising) have an impact on timing. Alternatively, for seasonal products such as cold remedies, a leading spending pattern is sometimes used that delivers messages before the major usage season (fall and winter) to get consumers to stock up on a brand.

In most cases, specialized media companies use sophisticated computer programs to place ads in the most appropriate medium, within the budget allocated, and that meet the advertiser's objectives. A new approach for TV scheduling called media optimizing takes advantage of the latest Nielsen TV viewing data based on its "peoplemeter" technology, which provides real-time information to companies and their media planners. Peoplemeters attached to TVs are turned on and off when people enter and leave the room and thus provide more accurate measures of actual TV viewing. The meters electronically deliver the viewing data instantly, thus providing the most up-to-date information possible.[29]

Budgeting

Because of the large amounts of money involved and the importance of advertising to marketers, one of the most important jobs of the marketing manager is to determine how much to spend. Setting advertising budgets has an immediate impact on costs and longer-term effects on sales. Consequently, advertising is just as much an investment as R&D and new plants and equipment. Like spending on R&D, spending on advertising has a long history and a weak record for measuring effectiveness precisely.

A crucial distinction exists between viewing advertising spending as an investment and viewing it as an expense. Investments are expected to generate returns over a long period of time. Often, when advertising is viewed as an expense, the budget is cut near the end of a quarter or fiscal year to achieve a profit target. In contrast, marketing-oriented firms view advertising as a long-term investment in the brand.

Figure 10.12 shows examples of successful investments in brands. The two graphs show a positive relationship between advertising investment (measured as cumulative

Figure 10.12

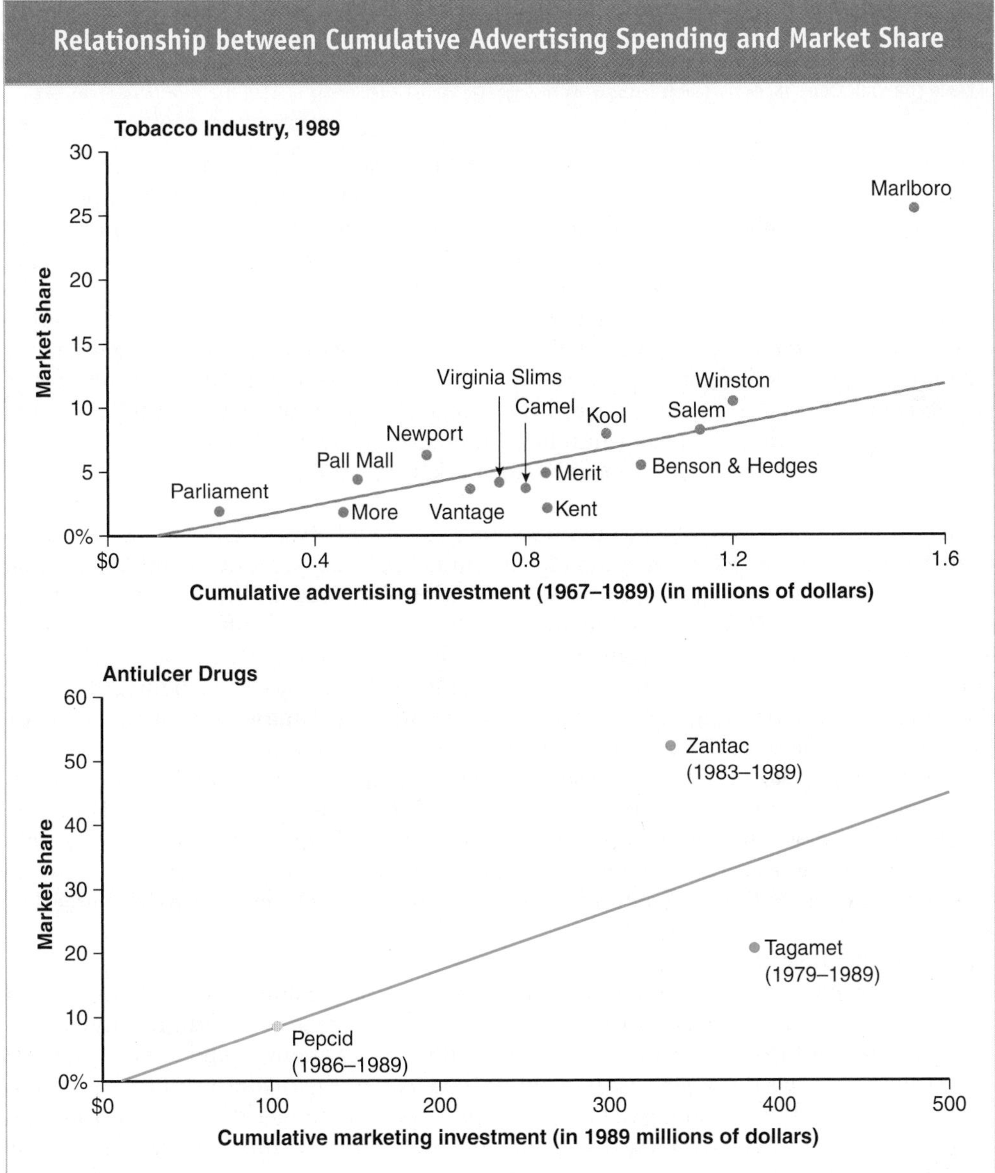

Source: IMS America, Ltd., and CDI estimates.

Table 10.8

Top 5 and Bottom 5 Advertisers in Sales per Dollar of Advertising in 2004

Company	U.S. Revenues per Dollar of Advertising ($)
Best:	
Walmart	236.23
Bank of America	115.83
Kroger Co.	82.25
United Parcel Service	78.67
Albertson's	77.88
Worst:	
Visa International	1.06
Estee Lauder	2.98
MasterCard International	3.38
L'Oreal	3.51
Schering-Plough	3.77

Source: Advertising Age (2005), June 27, p. S-18. Copyright 2005 by CRAIN COMMUNICATIONS INC. Reproduced with permission of CRAIN COMMUNICATIONS INC in the format Textbook via Copyright Clearance Center.

advertising spending) and market share for the tobacco and antiulcer drug categories. Consistent investment in advertising for products can lead to a superior market position.

However, the productivity of advertising can vary widely. One measure of productivity is sales revenues per monetary unit spent on advertising. Table 10.8 shows 2004 data from the highest 100 advertising spenders on the top five and bottom five advertisers in terms of revenues per ad dollar. This ranges from a high of $236.23 for Walmart to a low of $1.06 for Visa International. A number of factors can affect productivity beyond the effectiveness of the advertising—the number of competitors, the degree to which competitors are combative, product factors such as how much and what kind of information is needed to make a purchase, the absolute level of spending which may offer economies of scale, the allocation of marketing funds across different kinds of programs, and others.

In addition, the amount spent on advertising can vary between companies within an industry. For example, in the vacuum cleaner industry, in 2004, Dyson spent $49 million on advertising; Hoover spent $47 million; Bissell spent $22 million; and Electrolux, Oreck, Eureka, and Dirt Devil spent under $10 million each.[30] Interestingly, Dyson' s spending represented a quadrupling of its ad investment from 2003, which enabled it to grab the lead in market share from Hoover. This is further support for Figure 10.12 that there often is a relationship between ad spending and market share. In general, however, intraindustry differences can reflect alternative emphases on advertising vs. promotion, marketing strategies, or financial resources. For example, Apple and Microsoft spent about the same amount of money on advertising in 2008, roughly $300 million. However, Apple spent almost all of its budget on TV while Microsoft split its budget more evenly over TV, print, and a substantial amount on the Internet.[31]

The following are the most commonly used methods for setting advertising budgets.

Objective and Task

Budgeting by advertising objectives and the tasks needed to achieve those objectives is a logically appealing approach in that the marketing manager first determines the advertising objectives to be achieved (e.g., target audience, awareness) and then chooses a media plan to reach those goals. The sum of the costs of the media vehicles needed to achieve the objectives becomes a budget. In practice, the budget that results from this process is usually used as a starting point for negotiating within the organization, as financial constraints and the needs of other products become a part of the overall budgeting process.

Percentage of Sales

The manager using the percentage-of-sales method approaches advertising as a cost to be borne and selects a percentage of sales, either past or expected, to devote to advertising. This method seems to turn normal causal thinking—that advertising causes sales—on its head. Whether based on past or expected sales, it is clear that poorly performing brands will subsequently get lower budgets, lower sales, lower budgets again, and so on if one applies this approach mindlessly, without adjusting the percentage appropriately. By using a percentage, the method views advertising almost as a variable cost, like raw materials or direct labor.

Table 10.9 shows some advertising-to-sales ratios by industry for 2001. Although this table is not meant to imply that all the companies in these industries use some kind of percentage-of-sales method for setting ad budgets, the ratio for a product's industry category or SIC code is a useful starting point for trying to assemble a budget from scratch. The range of the ratios is quite large. The highest advertising-to-sales ratio is for sugar and confectionary products (SIC 2060) at 18.1 percent; the smallest one is wholesale computers and software (SIC 5045) at 0.1 percent.

Competitive Parity

This approach to budgeting attempts to spend at levels proportional to the competition's spending. One argument for the competitive parity method is based on the efficient market hypothesis developed in finance: Firms that survive tend to be those with more optimal budgets, so the survivors' budgets may offer an estimate of the optimal level in a competitive market. In other words, a successful competitor may have a better idea of how much to spend than you do.

A useful way to implement this method is to consider share of advertising dollars spent in the product category, also known as share of voice (SOV), rather than absolute advertising dollars, and compare SOV to market share. Consequently, small-share brands must usually have higher SOVs than market shares in order to rise above the clutter and get their messages out. Conversely, large-share brands gain economies of scale with large advertising budgets, which enable them to purchase large blocks of media time or space. Therefore, they can normally have SOVs lower than their market shares. One study found that the break-even share level, at which SOV can be the same as market share, is between 19 and 21 percent. Above that market share level, you can spend proportionately less on advertising; below that level, you should spend more.[32]

Table 10.9

Top 5 and Bottom 5 Industry Advertising-to-Sales Ratios in 2001 by SIC Code

Industry	SIC*	Ad Dollars as a Percentage of Sales
Sugar and Confectionary Products	2060	18.1%
Special Clean, Polish Preparations	2842	15.7
Wine, Brandy, and Brandy Spirits	2084	15.6
Distilled and Blended Liquor	2085	15.1
Watches, Clocks, and Parts	3873	15.1
Computers and Software Wholesale	5045	0.1
Steel Works and Blast Furnaces	3312	0.2
Electronic Parts	5065	0.2
Help Supply Services	7363	0.3
Auto and Home Supply Stores	5531	0.4

*Complied before the U.S. move to the NAIC system.

Source: *Advertising Age* (2001), September 17, p. 20.

Affordability

The affordability method is the ultimate in "advertising as a cost of doing business" thinking and is similar in spirit to the percentage-of-sales method. If you use this method, you select an advertising budget that, together with projected sales, price, and other costs, results in an acceptable income statement and profit level. Unfortunately, like the percentage-of-sales method, as advertising becomes less affordable because a brand is doing poorly, the role of advertising may become more important. In addition, projected sales should be a function of the level of advertising and should, therefore, vary with different budgets.

Experimentation

With this approach, you try different levels of spending—either in different regions or in more controlled settings—and monitor the results. You then use the results to select among different advertising budgets and plans. Experimentation is increasing in popularity and represents a step toward using a more scientific approach to setting budgets.[33]

The case of the sugar substitute Equal highlights the use of experimentation for setting advertising budgets.[34] Managers for Equal used information from an IRI BehaviorScan split-cable TV market to test alternative advertising budgets rather than testing copy as described earlier in this chapter. When the brand was introduced, the marketing manager tried two levels of media spending: $3.8 million and $5.7 million (extrapolated from the BehaviorScan market to national levels). After a 20-week test, there was no significant difference between Equal purchasing rates by households on the two cables. Thus, the lower spending level was chosen as being more appropriate.

Decision Calculus

Computerized decision support systems (DSSs) such as ADBUDG help structure budget decisions systematically.[35] Managers provide subjective inputs about, for example, the sales or share impact of increasing or decreasing advertising spending by different levels (e.g., 25 percent, 50 percent, and 100 percent). A computer program then estimates likely customer response to various advertising spending levels and calculates the optimal spending amount. Although using subjective data alone produces results that may be hard to sell to others in the organization, DSSs that combine judgment with real data have facilitated decision making and promise to be more useful in the future.

Surveys of companies' advertising budgeting practices have shown varying percentages devoted to the different methods, but the top three methods used are objective and task, affordability, and percentage of anticipated sales.[36]

Measuring Advertising Effects

Given the amount of money spent on advertising, it is surprising how little effort is spent assessing whether it is meeting the stated objectives. Volumes have been written on topics such as copy-testing with focus groups and in theater settings. However, as we discussed earlier in this chapter, these two methods tend to be used for making decisions about different copy strategies rather than for post-implementation assessment.

However, given the ROI-intensive environment described in Chapter 1, companies now are holding their advertising agencies' "feet to the fire" in terms of better evaluation of the return on advertising spending. In the United States, the Association of National Advertisers, the American Association of Advertising Agencies, and the Advertising Research Foundation have joined forces to create an initiative dubbed MI4—Measurement Initiative: Advertising, Agencies, Media, and Researchers—to focus on making advertising (and marketing, more generally) more accountable. The Interpublic Group, one of the largest advertising holding groups in the world, has formed a new business unit, the Marketing Accountability Partnership, that is devoted to helping advertisers figure out the effectiveness of their spending.[37] Some of the popular approaches to doing this are described here.

Tracking Studies

Conventional tracking studies are surveys that ask respondents two kinds of questions. One type is "top of mind," or, more technically, unaided recall, in which the respondent is asked whether he or she can recall seeing an ad for the brand. For example, the respondent might be asked, "Have you seen the advertising campaign that prominently features frogs?" If the answer is *yes,* this technique follows up the question with a request to repeat the main copy points to determine comprehension. If the respondent indicates that the campaign is for Budweiser beer and features the frogs croaking "Bud-weis-er," then the campaign gets high marks. Attitudinal questions might also be asked. The second type of survey uses aided recall: "Have you seen the Budweiser beer campaign featuring frogs croaking 'Bud-weis-er'?" This method detects information not actively in memory that can be important when primed at the point-of-purchase. Not surprisingly, the numbers produced by aided recall are much larger than those produced by unaided recall.

These studies then track the responses over time, often at constant time intervals, using either the same sample of respondents (a panel) or a different, randomly selected group. The manager can then view how awareness, comprehension, or interest builds, plateaus, or never gets off the ground. Often, the percentages obtained from these studies are also compared to norms derived from previous advertising campaigns.

If the advertising objective is more behavioral in nature, tracking studies may also follow sales, inquiries, repeat purchases, or other measures over time. If the manager notes when a new campaign starts, the measures can simply be plotted and inspected for any movement. The major problem with this kind of tracking is similar to the problem with using sales as an advertising goal: it is difficult to attribute movement in sales solely to advertising, given the other aspects of the marketing mix as well as competitors' moves. In addition, except for sales, some of the variables tracked do not necessarily directly link to ROI.

Experimentation

In addition to its use in setting budgets and evaluating potential advertising copy, experimentation as a means of assessing advertising effectiveness has a long tradition in marketing. Unfortunately, field experiments—using real products in an actual setting—are costly and time-consuming because they involve manipulating different levels of marketing variables in different sales territories, in different stores, or to different groups of customers. This has to be over an extended period of time to detect any effects of the manipulated variable. Moreover, field experiments are politically difficult from an organizational perspective, for although it is easy to get a regional manager to accept an increased advertising budget (or price cut), it is hard to obtain acceptance for a decreased budget.

Most experiments focus on sales-related advertising objectives. A comprehensive analysis of 389 split-cable TV experiments found that the average elasticity for new products (26 percent) was higher than for established products (5 percent). The researchers also found that an examination of successful advertising spending tests (as opposed to copy tests) showed that about two-thirds of the original increase persisted in the year after advertising returned to normal levels and one-third persisted into the second year. They also found that most of the increase was caused by greater purchases of the product per household rather than an increase in the percentage of households that buy the product (penetration). This suggested that the advertising reminded or encouraged consumers to do something they were already inclined to do.[38]

Objective Guarantees

Some advertising agencies, in conjunction with media in which they place ads, have begun to give advertisers guarantees on achieving certain objectives. When these guarantees are not met, the advertiser gets additional advertising space for free. An example is the arrangement between the French advertising giant Publicis and the cable channel Court TV. Court TV guarantees not only a certain number of ratings points (viewers) to companies that advertise on its channel but also a minimum number of "engaged" viewers.[39] Although it is unclear what "engaged" actually means and it is not a financial guarantee, such arrangements are closer to ensuring advertisers that they are getting more for their money than just "eyeballs."

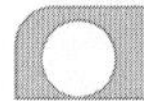

Marketing-Mix Modeling: Linking Past Sales and Advertising

An approach to evaluating advertising effectiveness is to use historical data and statistical methods to estimate the relationship between advertising spending and market response variables such as sales or market share. This is often referred to as *marketing-mix modeling.* The statistical methods used are normally regression or some other advanced econometric technique. For example, given past levels of sales and advertising, you could use the following equation:

$$\text{Sales} = a + b\text{Adv}$$

where a and b are unknown parameters that are estimated from the data. Although this postulates a very simple (and probably incorrect) linear relationship between sales and advertising, the statistical significance of b tells you whether advertising spending levels are importantly related to changes in sales over time. More sophisticated models enable you to incorporate other marketing-mix variables besides advertising, and nonlinear relationships permit the estimation of elasticities, competition, and interactions (e.g., the effects advertising might have on price sensitivity).

A number of studies done in this tradition have yielded some generalizable results.[40] Averaging across 128 studies, it appears that the average elasticity of current advertising on current sales is about 22 percent (i.e., a 100 percent increase in advertising leads to a 22 percent change in sales). The carryover effect (the elasticity of the impact of current advertising on future sales) is about 47 percent, indicating that the long-run impact is more important than its immediate effect.[41]

A number of companies have created real-time systems combining marketing mix modeling and decision calculus models. These systems take data being generated from retail sales information, have statistical model "engines" that continuously update empirical links between the sales and advertising (and other marketing) spending, and provide decision-makers with a computer interface that enables them to tinker with the advertising spending (i.e., perform "what-ifs" in a spreadsheet) to adjust spending according to sales response to advertising. An example is Marketing Management Analytics (www.mma.com).

Technology's Impact on Advertising

New technology is continuously being developed to deliver more creative and better-targeted advertising. While it is impossible to predict what will succeed and what will fail, here are a few examples of new approaches to advertising that are being tested:

- In Tokyo, Northwest Airlines (now merged with Delta Airlines) tested using billboards on the streets and in subway stations with ads containing bar codes that can be read by special readers on cell phones. These codes are unlocked by snapshots taken by the phone's camera, which then direct the phone's Web browser to coupons, games, or further information on the product.[42]
- Time-Warner Cable Inc. tested a system using the digital cable box to target different ads to different households. In fact, if a father and daughter are watching the same TV show but on different TVs, they can see different commercials.[43]
- Some companies are developing new digital technologies for showing images. Pulse (pulse3d.com) has online tools for turning a photo of any person or animal into a lip-synched talking head for ad campaigns. Zebra Imaging (zebraimaging.com) produces large promotional holograms that make images of objects or people three-dimensional, without special glasses.[44]

Executive Summary

Key learning points in this chapter include the following:

- Underlying marketing communications decisions are theories about how communications flow from sender to receiver.
- The concept of integrated marketing communications (IMC) has become central to the communications strategies of companies. The idea is that all communications activities, including advertising, promotion, and personal selling, must be coordinated in order to send a consistent message to customers.
- There are six aspects to managing advertising (6M model of communications): selecting the target audience, choosing the appropriate goals for advertising to achieve, deciding what message strategy is most appropriate for the product or service being marketed, selecting media and developing a media plan, setting the budget, and evaluating or measuring the effectiveness of the advertising.
- New communications technologies have made the decisions about which media to use much more complex.
- Advertisers are using multiple methods to better understand whether they are obtaining a good return on their communications spending.

Chapter Questions

1. Integrated marketing communications (IMC) is an important concept in marketing. What are the barriers to a marketing manager's implementation of IMC? If IMC is not achieved, what is the impact on the marketing strategy?
2. Find two different ads: one with an emotional appeal and one with a rational appeal. How would you design an advertisement for each of the two products with the opposite appeal?
3. Consider two different products: an industrial product and a consumer product. How would the media for these products differ? What would affect the advertising scheduling for these two products?
4. Suppose that a new communications program is being developed for your school. What would be the goals of this program? What information would you collect to measure the effectiveness of the program?
5. As noted in this chapter, although Web advertising spending has increased significantly, low clickthrough rates have discouraged many companies from expanding their Web advertising budgets. Go to several sites with banner ads, and pick some that you think are good and some that are not. Ignoring clickthrough, are they effective at achieving other communications goals? Why or why not?
6. Occasionally, companies will use media contrary to normal industry practice. For example, a B-to-B product might be advertised on network TV and a frequently purchased product would use no TV advertising. Under what conditions might this happen?

Key Learning Points

The purpose of this chapter is to introduce the various aspects of sales promotion decision making. Key areas of learning are:

- How sales promotion differs from advertising and other modes of communication
- The different types of sales promotions available to the marketing manager
- Differences among customer, trade, and retailer-oriented promotions
- Issues in the development of promotional strategy and objective-setting
- Allocating money between advertising and sales promotion

Automobile manufacturers such as Ford are heavy users of promotional incentives like inexpensive financing.
Source: David Zalubowski/AP Wide World Photos

Sales Promotion

Chapter Brief

General Motors made a dramatic turnaround in October 2000, increasing its U.S. market share from 28 percent to 30 percent.[1] Although it should have been a time for celebration, it was not. While sales increased, profits fell due to generous promotional incentives such as five years of 0 percent financing, costing the company about $3,000 for each car sold. GM was not alone; DaimlerChrysler lost $534 million in its third quarter due to similar incentives.

How did promotional incentives become so common in the auto industry? In the 1970s, the industry started offering them as a one-time incentive program as a reaction to consumer "sticker shock" from rising car prices. These continued unabated into the 1990s, where the rationale was to help the industry through the recession. However, by 2000, the industry recognized the hard truth. It is addicted to sales promotional incentives that lower prices. DaimlerChrysler, for example, tried to lead the industry in early 2000 by reducing such promotions, but when competitors did not follow its lead, the company lost market share.

In 2002, the trend toward rebates continued, particularly among the "Big 3" U.S. competitors: GM, DaimlerChrysler, and Ford. GM offered $2,000 cash back on certain models, Ford offered a $1,000 to $1,500 loyalty "bonus" when a lease is renewed, and Chrysler was giving $2,500 cash back on certain models. The incentives drove the companies' marketing costs out of control. Ford's marketing expenses as a percentage of sales rising to 16.7 percent in the final quarter of 2001, lead to a –5.8 percent pretax profit margin. The promotional programs are viewed as a way to keep manufacturing plants running, driving customers into car retailers and maintaining market share, albeit at a cost to the bottom line. While these programs were seen as a necessity after 9/11, when visitors to showrooms became scarce, observers were wondering if they were necessary later in 2002.

In 2005, the U.S. auto companies discovered a new kind of promotional program. Traditionally, the companies have given employees significant discounts on new cars. In 2005, Ford, General Motors, and DaimlerChrysler's Chrysler division instituted a program whereby anyone could get these employee discounts. Although the Big 3 considered eliminating these programs in favor of everyday low pricing with no discounts, the large rise in gasoline prices in late 2005 and the subsequent drop in sales in SUVs possibly meant a return to the cycle of raising sticker prices and offering significant discounts.

Fast forwarding to 2010, the U.S. auto companies are, of course, in terrible shape with Chrysler now a unit of Fiat, GM having just recently paid back its loan from the U.S. government, and Ford gamely continuing to operate independently. This is due to a combination of poor historical marketing decisions and the global recession. The average incentives offered by the major auto manufacturers for July and August 2009 are shown in Table 11.1. As you can see, GM's are in the same range (around

Table 11.1

Automobile Company Average Sales Incentives in 2009		
	August 2009	July 2009
Chrysler Group (Chrysler, Dodge, Jeep)	$ 3,018	$ 4,218
Ford (Ford, Lincoln, Mercury, Volvo)	$ 3,182	$ 3,311
General Motors (Buick, Cadillac, Chevrolet, GMC, Hummer, Pontiac, Saab, Saturn)	$ 3,343	$ 3,647
Honda (Acura, Honda)	$ 947	$ 1,281
Hyundai (Hyundai, Kia)	$ 2,504	$ 3,027
Nissan (Infiniti, Nissan)	$ 2,620	$ 2,608
Toyota (Lexus, Scion, Toyota)	$ 1,543	$ 1,310
Industry Average	$ 2,475	$ 2,706

Source: Reuters.com, September 1, 2009. © 2010 Edmunds.com, Inc. Reprinted with permission.

$3,500) as they were in 2000. However, the desperation level is much greater with the company's survival on the line. In addition, we had the "granddaddy" of all sales incentive programs in August 2009: the government-sponsored "cash-for-clunkers" program that was first tried in Europe. The program was so successful that the government's initial pool of funds was quickly exhausted and had to be replenished.

The marketing communications program most commonly involved with boosting sales in the short term is **sales promotion**, usually just called promotion. Following is a definition of promotion:[2]

sales promotion
Sales promotion is an action-focused marketing event whose purpose is to have a direct impact on the behavior of the firm's customers.
Source: Neslin, Scott A., Sales Promotion. Copyright © 2002 Marketing Science Institute. Reprinted with permission of the author.

> *Sales promotion is an action-focused marketing event whose purpose is to have a direct impact on the behavior of the firm's customers.*

This definition can be broken down to shed some light on specific promotional activities and their purposes:

- **Sales promotions are action focused.** They are intended to get customers to purchase. This is perhaps their most distinguishing feature. In addition, they normally attempt to get customers to purchase within a limited period of time. For example, coupons are intended to encourage customers to purchase the brand by the expiration date.
- **Promotions are marketing events.** More precisely, they are discrete programs with well-defined beginning and ending dates that offer incentives to customers to purchase or use the product. A coupon campaign has a beginning or drop date as well as an expiration date. Contests and sweepstakes also run over a limited period of time. Both are considered events.
- **Sales promotions are intended to have a direct impact on behavior.** As we noted in Chapter 9, advertising usually works through a series of steps, or a hierarchy, from awareness to purchase. Promotions work directly on behavior. As a result, there is no question about how to evaluate the effectiveness of a promotional campaign or event: sales is almost always the measure of effectiveness. Although coupons do affect consumers' psychological processes, the objective is purchase or trial, not attitude change.
- **Sales promotions influence both consumers and customers.** It is important to note that customers include both end consumers and any channel members. Thus, certain promotional devices are appropriate for getting consumers to buy. Others, such as quantity discounts, are targeted toward channel members.

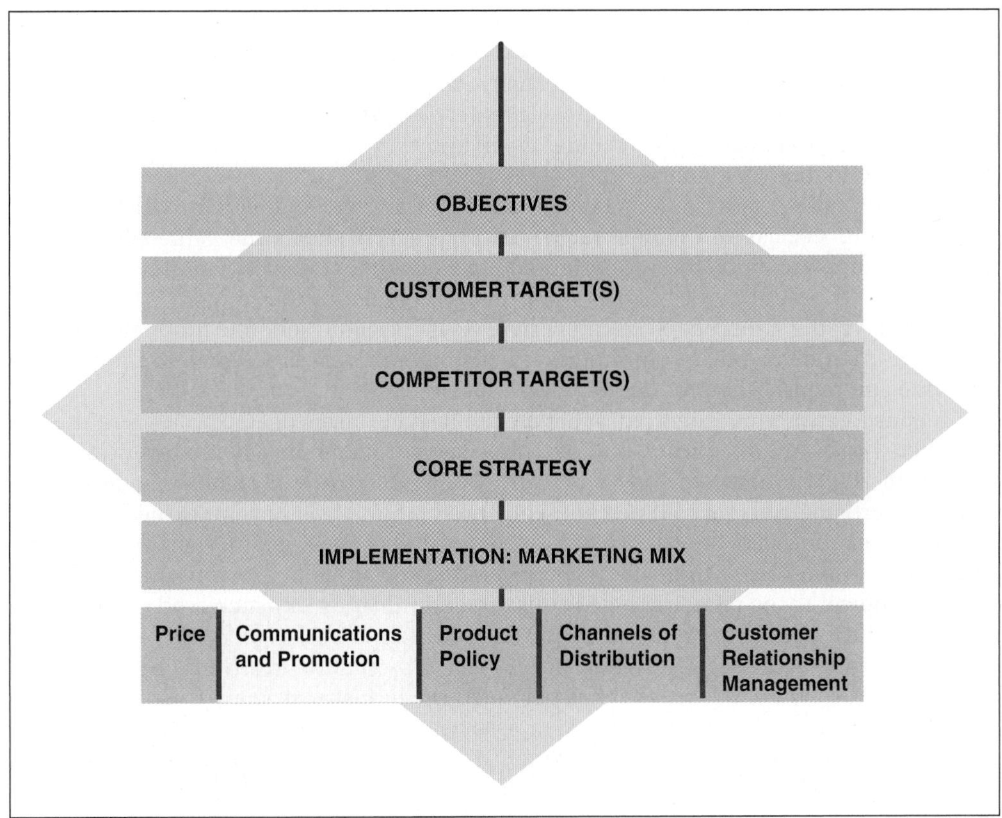

Although promotion is most closely related to price and logically follows the chapter on pricing, it is also part communications and part channels of distribution. We have already seen from the auto industry illustration how it is a pricing mechanism. Coupons, contests and sweepstakes, and other promotional devices not only have a pricing impact but they communicate information about the product as well.

To see how promotions interact with channels of distribution, Figure 11.1 shows a simplified channel structure in which the manufacturer sells to a channel (here a retailer), which in turn sells to the final customer (the consumer). In this situation, promotion falls into three categories:

1. Consumer promotion.
2. Promotion to the channels, or trade promotion.
3. Channel-originated promotion, or retailer promotion.

Figure 11.1

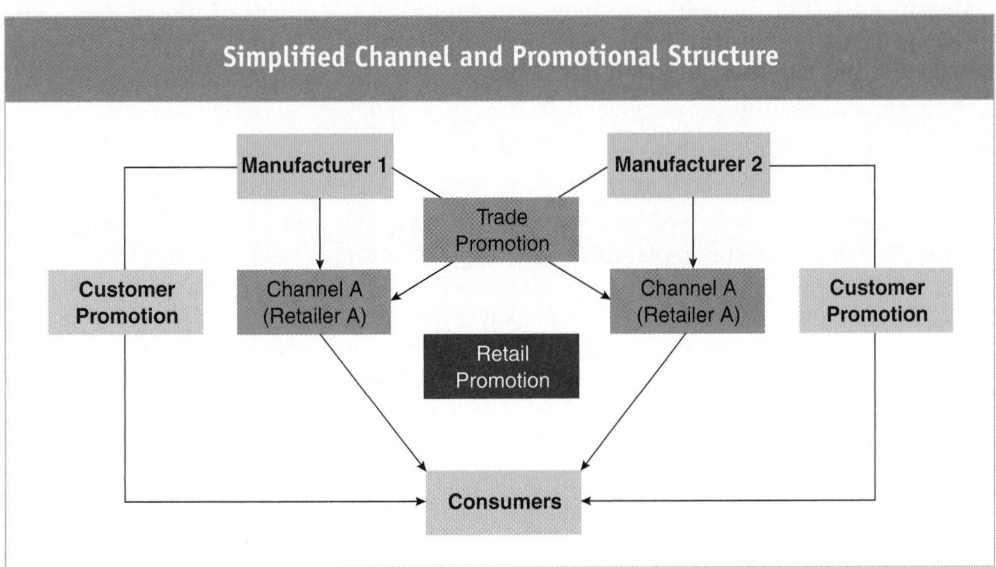

Customer promotion comes directly from the manufacturer. Trade promotion, in contrast, is directed at intermediate channels of distribution in an attempt to get them to stock more of a product and to commit their own efforts (e.g., sales force) to move the product through the next channel and ultimately to the consumer. Channel-originated promotion events are run by the channel itself, either to the next channel in the distribution chain or to final customers.

Therefore, sales promotion is related in an important way to the distribution channel issues we will discuss in Chapter 12, where Figure 12.1 shows the value-added chain used to develop the motivation for establishing a channel system. Promotion is used for both push and pull activities and is the primary vehicle for the former. Trade or push activities give the intermediaries incentives to carry and sell the product, whereas consumer-oriented or pull promotion gives customers a reason to come to the point of purchase and request the product.

For consumer-product companies that are the heaviest users of advertising and promotion, there has been a significant shift over time away from media advertising toward promotion. In 2008, promotion was 61 percent of the advertising/promotion budget while media advertising was only 32 percent, and these proportions have remained relatively constant over time.[3] Of the 61 percent, 24 percent was trade and 37 percent was consumer promotion. This significant proportion allocated to trade promotion is due to the increased power of the retail trade (to be discussed in Chapter 12), increased competition, and the mature state of many of these products (which increases the need for trade promotion to retain shelf space). The almost 2:1 ratio of promotion to advertising reflects the short-term, sales-volume focus that has pervaded the industry for many years.

Although sales promotion is usually associated with consumer products, B-to-B companies also spend a considerable amount of money on sales promotion activities. For example, when Microsoft launched its database software product, SQL Server 7, the company spent hundreds of millions of dollars for short-term promotions. This included a 50 percent discount to any customer that dumped IBM, Oracle, Sybase, or Informix and four months of the services of one of its database experts.[4]

Even though there is heavy spending on sales promotions for both consumer and business-to-business products and services, there is considerable debate about their effectiveness and efficiency. For example, Procter & Gamble is attempting to reduce its use of coupons because of their inefficiency (about 1 percent are redeemed) and costs of printing, distribution, and processing. Similarly, H. J. Heinz is attempting to reduce its dependence on trade-oriented promotion and make greater investments in advertising. Many companies complain about the problems of sales promotion but find it difficult to stop using it because customers have become used to the incentives. For example, when Procter & Gamble announced in January 1996 that, as a test, it would end all coupons in the upstate New York cities of Syracuse, Buffalo, and Rochester, the company encountered boycotts, public hearings, signature drives, and an antitrust suit from the state of New York accusing it of trying to get other companies to stop couponing as well. The test ended in April 1997. In addition, long-term studies of the effects of promotions show that consumers become more sensitive to price and promotions and less responsive to brand-building activities such as advertising.[5]

Types of Sales Promotion

Table 11.2 provides a list of specific retailer, channel, and consumer promotions. Figure 11.2 provides some examples of coupons that have been clipped from magazines or newspaper supplements. The one that is visible is a manufacturer coupon for savings of $1 on a purchase of two packages of the promoted product. Table 11.3 shows the kinds of consumer promotional events run in the major appliance industry. As can be seen, nearly all of the events are price oriented. These promotions are described in further detail here.

Consumer Promotions

The marketing manager can choose from three different types of consumer-oriented promotions. These are those that focus on price such as coupons, those that involve the product such as free samples, and special events such as contests.

Table 11.2

Types of Promotions

Consumer Promotions	Trade Promotions	Retail Promotions
I. Product based A. Additional volume or bonus pack B. Samples 1. Central location (e.g., supermarkets) 2. Direct (e.g., mail) 3. Attachment (in- or on-pack) 4. Media placed (clip-and-send coupons) II. Price based A. Sales price B. Coupons 1. Central location (e.g., in-store) 2. Direct (mail) 3. Attachment (in- or on-pack) 4. In media C. Refunds and rebates D. Financing terms E. Frequent users III. Premiums IV. Place-based promotions (displays) V. Special events	I. Product based A. Free goods B. Consignment and return policy II. Price based A. Buying allowances B. Financial terms III. Place based A. Slotting allowances B. Display allowances C. Warehousing and delivery assistance IV. Advertising and promotion based A. Co-op advertising B. Selling aids C. Co-op selling V. Sales based A. Bonuses and incentives B. Contests and prizes	I. Price cuts II. Displays III. Feature advertising IV. Free goods V. Retailer coupons VI. Contests and premiums

Figure 11.2

Sample Coupons

Source: Jim Barber/Shutterstock

Table 11.3

Typical Promotional Events Held in the Major Appliance Industry

Brand	Program	Products	Dates
Admiral	Buy & Try promotion offers 40-day money-back guarantee with appliance purchases.	Selected washers, dryers, refrigerators, and ranges.	Through December.
Frigidaire	Frigidaire Savings Spectacular offers consumer rebates of up to $100 with selected purchases. Also, Vacation Sweepstakes offers 4-day/3-night vacation getaways to a choice of 80 resorts with purchases.	Savings Spectacular Selected Frigidaire and Frigidaire Gallery appliances. Sweepstakes Precision Wash dishwashers.	Savings Spectacular: October 13–November 9. Sweepstakes: Through December 31.
General Electric	Bring your Kitchen To Life promo offers consumer rebates of $20 to $100 with selected purchases. Also free icemakers and water pitchers with purchases of selected refrigerators. GECAF offers no payments, no finance charges until April 1997 on appliance purchases.	Bring Your Kitchen To Life selected ranges, washers, dryers, microwave ovens, and dishwashers. Free icemakers/water pitchers. 12 refrigerators. Finance offer. Selected GE and GE Profile appliances.	Through December 1.
Kitchenaid	Cash-back offers with laundry appliance purchases, also, 6-month, zero-percent financing on selected purchases.	Cash back. Selected laundry appliances. Finance offer. Selected dishwashers and compactors.	Cash-Back: November 24–December 28. Finance offer: November 3–December 14.
Maytag	Free icemakers offered with purchases of two refrigerator models. Also, consumer rebates of $20–$100 on selected appliances.	Free icemaker. Refrigerator models RTD1900 and RTD2100. Rebate selected dishwashers and refrigerators.	Free icemaker: Through December 15. Rebate: Through September 30.
Whirlpool	Consumer rebates of $20–$30 with appliance purchases. Also, 6-month, zero-percent financing with purchases of selected cooking appliances.	Selected washers, dryers, and dishwashers. Finance offer. Selected freestanding gas and electric ranges and over-the-range microwave ovens.	Rebates: November 24–December 28. Finance offer: November 3–November 14.

Source: Twice (1996), October 7, p. 23. Used by permission, courtesy of TWICE.

couponing
a price-oriented promotion that offers a discount off the price of a product and is accompanied by a physical or electronic document indicating the amount of the discount

Price-Oriented Promotions

The dominant form of price-oriented promotion is **couponing**. The first coupon, an offer for a free glass of Coca-Cola, was distributed in the mid-1890s. In 2007, companies distributed $201 billion worth of coupons in the United States.[6] Unfortunately, as noted earlier, only 1 percent were redeemed. However, their use is widespread because 94 percent of all U.S. households report using a grocery coupon or some other coupon targeted toward supermarket products.[7] This high number has clearly been aided by the economic recession. In addition, most coupon usage is from a small percentage of U.S. households. One report indicates that 81 percent of the units purchased using manufacturer coupons came from just 19 percent of U.S. households over a six-month period in 2009.[8] As shown in Table 11.4, coupons are delivered to households in a variety of ways including mail, in newspaper and magazine advertisements, in the stores at the

Table 11.4

Where Coupons are Distributed	
Method	Percentage
Free-standing inserts	88.1%
Handouts	4.7
Direct mail	2.2
Magazines	2.1
Newspapers	1.2
In/On-pack	1.2
Internet	0.4

Source: Patricia Odell (2008), "Dishing Out Discounts," *Promo Mag*

point-of-purchase, on or in the packages, at the checkout counter, and electronically via the Internet. However, the largest distribution channel for coupons is by far free-standing inserts (FSIs), which accounted for 88 percent of all coupons delivered in 2008. A popular way to deliver FSIs is in Sunday newspapers. Many people just shake them out of the paper, but many others clip them religiously. The coupons shown in Figure 11.2 are from an FSI.

Although not used much yet, new coupon distribution methods are being developed based on new technologies. For example, the widespread diffusion of smartphones such as the BlackBerry and iPhone with wireless and Web capabilities have led to testing of coupon delivery via text messages. Two companies experimenting with this approach are Walmart's Sam's Club chain and JCPenney.[9] One application is to deliver a bar code which can be scanned at point-of-purchase.

With their high cost and a 1 percent redemption rate, why do marketers use coupons so heavily? There are two main reasons. First, coupons are an effective way to target discounts and other incentives to households that are particularly sensitive to price. Depending on how they are delivered, coupons permit marketing managers to price-discriminate, that is, charge different prices to different households. For example, by combining a computer database of purchase histories with a direct-mail program, marketers can target price-sensitive households. As any basic textbook in microeconomics shows, if consumer segments differ in price sensitivity, profits are maximized by charging high (regular retail) prices to price-insensitive customers and lower prices to price-sensitive customers. Second, coupons are flexible in that they can achieve different kinds of goals. Some, like the coupons shown in Figure 11.2, are simply discounts off regular price. Some discounts apply to larger sizes than the consumer normally buys. Some focus on product trial and repeat. More details about the many ways consumers obtain and use coupons are shown in Table 11.5.

E-coupons delivered through the web have become popular. People who surf the Web "clip" (print out) Web coupons from sites such as thecouponclippers.com, coolsavings.com, and coupondispatch.com. Virtual coupons have a much higher redemption rate than those delivered in the old-fashioned way, as high as 13 percent.[10] However, they are less than 1 percent of all coupons delivered. Nearly 57 percent of those who click on them or receive them via e-mail redeem them. Even using more conservative redemption estimates, the resulting promotional costs per product sold are less than half of those using offline distribution methods.[11] The four most popular product categories for e-coupons are groceries, books, health, and music.

There are also several drawbacks to coupons. First, because they are so common, there is no way to gain a competitive advantage using a coupon program. In fact, many product categories are characterized by the prisoner's dilemma described in Chapter 6. No competitor will reduce the amount of couponing for fear of a precipitous drop in market share. Second, the response rates are very low, so the expense per redemption is high. Third, there is considerable potential for fraud, ranging from counterfeiting to misredemption (merchants may intentionally or mistakenly take a coupon for the wrong

Table 11.5

Coupon Distribution and Objectives

Media distributed

Free-standing insert. A leaflet of coupons for various products that can be inserted into a (usually Sunday) newspaper.

Run-of-press (ROP) newspaper. Coupons that appear on the actual pages of newspapers rather than being inserted as a separate page or section. Often these coupons appear in an advertisement for a brand (these are called in-ad coupons).

Sunday supplements. Coupons that appear on the pages of a newspaper Sunday supplement magazine such as *Parade* and *Family Weekly*.

Magazine. Coupons that appear in magazines other than Sunday supplements, such as *Good Housekeeping*. The coupons can be actually on a page, or attached using special tip-in or pop-up cards.

Direct mail. Coupons are mailed directly to consumers using the U.S. Postal Service. One mailing usually includes several coupons from various manufacturers, although much more expensive solo mailings are possible.

Package

On-package. The coupon appears on the outside of the package and can be used for a subsequent purchase.

Instantly redeemable. The coupon is on the outside of the package and can be removed easily and used on the current purchase.

In-package. The coupon is inside the package and can be used for a subsequent purchase.

Cross-ruff. The coupon is for another brand, manufactured by the same or a different firm. The coupon itself can be in- or on-package.

Retailer distributed

Retailer coupons. Coupons distributed by the retailer rather than the manufacturer. The coupons can be distributed by ROP newspaper, included in "Best Food Day" circulars, or handed out in the store.

Coupon-dispensing machines. Manufacturer coupons are distributed by a machine located in the store. The machine displays which coupons are available and the shopper specifies which coupons he or she wants.

Direct Sales Impact	Retail Trade Related	Integrate with Advertising and Other Promotions	Use as a Strategic Tool
Attract new triers	Gain in-store promotional support	Reinforce or enhance print media advertising	Preempt the competition
Attract brand switchers	Increase distribution	Synergize with other marketing instruments	Price discriminate
Increase category consumption	Motivate the sales force		Cushion a price increase
Maintain or enhance repeat purchase rates	More directly control retail price		Reach the appropriate target group
Defend market share			Grain trial for another product

Source: Robert C. Blattberg and Scott A. Neslin (1989), "Sales Promotion: The Long and the Short of It," *Marketing Letters*, 1 (December), pp. 266, 269; with kind permission from Springer Science and Business Media.

brand). For example, the CEO of one coupon clearinghouse (companies that do the coupon redemptions for supermarkets and obtain the money from manufacturers) has been indicted on charges of cheating companies out of $250 million.[12]

Manufacturers run many other price-oriented promotions. These include price, value, or bonus packs, which may offer larger sizes for the same price as a smaller size, or two-for-one kinds of promotions in which the products are shrink-wrapped together. Refunds or money-back offers allow customers to get money back with proof of purchase. Not only automobile manufacturers but consumer durable manufacturers use these kinds of programs extensively. They are called rebates in many cases and offer substantial discounts from the normal retail price. Sometimes, these durable goods companies couch the discount in financing terms such as "no payments for 12 months" or simply lower financing rates. Even financial institutions provide such price-oriented deals to customers through special low-interest loans or reduced customer equity requirements. In-store discounts are also frequent and are promoted in end-of-aisle displays, shelf "talkers" (price signs posted on the shelf), instant pull-off coupons, and a variety of other ways.

Price-oriented promotions are obviously effective ways of motivating customers to buy your brand. However, such promotions may have negative effects on consumer behavior. First, price promotions can dilute brand equity because it is difficult to use advertising or other communications to trumpet the quality of your brand while you are discounting it. Second, product categories with frequent price promotions lead customers to be more price-sensitive. For example, 2009 data show that in the frozen bagel category, nearly 30 percent of all purchases were made using some kind of price promotion.[13] A third problem we have seen with the auto industry illustration is that customers become accustomed to manufacturer deals and time their purchases to coincide with them. The astute car buyer knows that it is only a matter of time before almost any manufacturer starts to offer incentives—instead of buying now, why not wait?

Application | Valassis

One of the largest companies behind the FSI coupon distribution method is Valassis. Its revenues during 2008 were $2.2 billion. The company derives its revenues from selling space in the FSIs to the leading packaged-goods companies (see Figure 11.2 for an example). The company's founder, George Valassis, invented FSIs in 1972, and they quickly became popular because they enabled companies to target customers with coupons by city and, eventually, by neighborhood.

Although this seems like old-fashioned technology, the company uses modern database marketing tools to better target the ads. By capturing detailed coupon redemption and loyalty-card data from supermarkets (whose loyalty programs are managed using Valassis software), the shopping habits of 38 million households can be tracked. This allows the company to identify hot consumption areas for products and then provide manufacturers with that information so highly targeted coupon programs can be developed. Figure 11.2 provides an illustration of a Valassis-distributed FSI. In many geographic markets, Valassis is shifting from newspaper-delivered FSIs to direct mail due to the decline in circulation of many newspapers in major geographic markets like Los Angeles and Detroit.

product-oriented promotions consumer promotions that give away the product itself or a closely related product

sampling a product-oriented promotion in which a product is given away for free

Product-Oriented Promotions

Product-oriented promotions give away either the product itself or a closely related product. Giving away the product free is called **sampling.** Sampling is clearly useful when a new product or brand is being introduced. Free samples are delivered to the home via the mail or delivery, in supermarkets, and on the street. Not only are grocery items sampled, but computer hardware and software companies often give free copies of their products to select customers as beta test sites to eliminate any bugs in the software or other product problems and stimulate early word-of-mouth. For example, Oracle was so interested in getting into the customer relationship management (CRM) business that it offered some of its sales force free contact software. Drug companies spend a substantial amount of money in free samples to physicians. In the cholesterol-reduction category in 2001, Pfizer spent $171.5 million on sampling programs for Lipitor, Merck spent $85.5 million on Zocor, and Bristol-Myers Squibb spent $76 million on Pravachol.[14] Overall, drug companies spent $18 billion on free samples to doctors in 2008. Services use sampling extensively. For example, the Web-based DVD rental company Netflix inserts free trial certificates in new DVD players. Amazon allows potential CD buyers to listen to free samples of songs. Most large consumer food companies like McDonald's, Dunkin' Donuts, Starbucks, and Coca-Cola use sampling programs extensively.

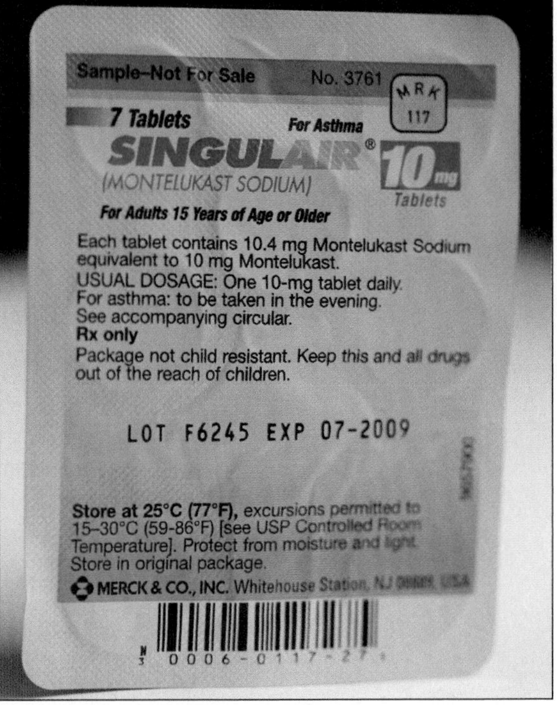

Sampling is particularly effective in gaining recommendations for new prescription drugs.
Source: Chip East/CORBIS-NY

Figure 11.3

TheFreeSite.com

TheFreeSite.com is the best place to find freebies, freeware, free stuff, samples, downloads, e - Microsoft Internet Explorer

http://www.thefreesite.com/

Newest Freebies
Free E-mail
Free Newsletter

Welcome to TheFreeSite.com, Home of the Web's Best Freebies.

Sign up for TheFreeSite.com's free E-mail newsletter and get a weekly roundup of the Web's latest and greatest free stuff.

Anonymous Freebies — Encryption, Security, Web Privacy...
Blog Freebies — Free Stuff for Bloggers...
Business Freebies — Commerce, Marketing, Job Search...
Free Chat Services — Emoticons, ICQ, 3D Chat, VoIP...
E-mail Freebies — E-mail Services, Freeware, Alerts...
Family Freebies — Household Items, Kids' Freebies...
Freebies FAQ
Misc. Freebies — Various Free Stuff Listings...
Newest Freebies — Our Latest Free Stuff Listings...
Other Free Stuff Sites — Freebie Sites Roundup...
Our Freebies Newsletter — Weekly Free E-mail newsletter...
Free Personals Services — Online Dating Services...
Free Postcards — Web Cards, E-Greetings...
Prizes and Contests — Online Giveaways, Sweepstakes...
Free Samples

Search for freebies:
Newest Freebies
FAQ
Link to Us
Submit a Freebie
Our Awards
Join Our Newsletter

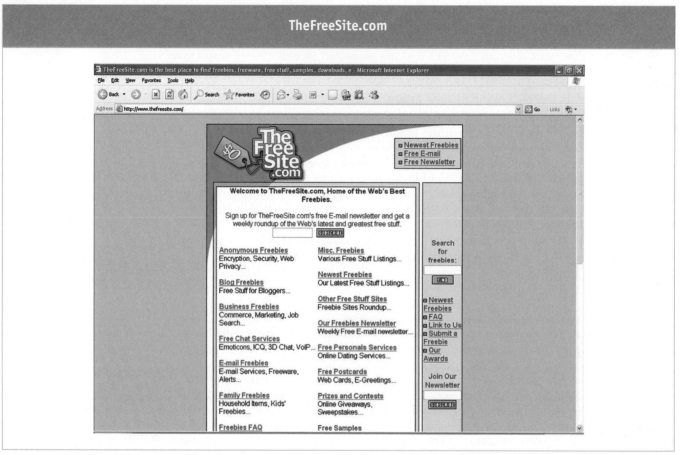

Source: Used by permission, courtesy of www.TheFreeSite.com

Sampling has the obvious benefit of stimulating product trial because it gives the customer the opportunity to try the product free. A survey has shown that sampling is much more effective than coupons, advertising, and games or contests in helping consumers evaluate products.[15] However, it does have some serious shortcomings. First, sampling is obviously very expensive (however, small trial packs may be sold at cost to afford the company some revenue). Second, a sampling program may not target the right potential customers. People who distribute free samples are not discriminating about who receives them. This is particularly a problem for tobacco companies because trial packs could be given illegally to teenagers under 18 years old.

As is the case with coupons, free goods available as samples can be obtained through the web. Some sites that offer samples are:

- TheFreeSite.com (see Figure 11.3).
- Free-samples.com.
- Freecenter.com.

While this is fun for consumers and some paying customers could be created this way, the problems for the companies are that many people who are not in the target market for the samples are obtaining the merchandise and the kind of customer drawn to these sites does not want to pay for the product.

Lcafe

The Lcafe looks like any other fashionable and trendy café in Tokyo's Shibuya district.[16] Although the usual food and drink is served, the café has a side purpose: introducing new products to affluent and influential young Japanese women.

It's called a marketing café; Sample Lab Ltd. opened the café to reach Japanese women in their 20s and 30s with information about and samples of new products. The idea is that once a woman tries and likes a new product, she will spread word-of-mouth and influence other women to buy. The women have to register via mobile phone and provide some personal information such as age and marital status. Once they are registered, the women earn tokens by purchasing food and drink. The tokens can then be redeemed at a "sample bar," where they get free samples of products such as a new vitamin-infused drink, skincare products, or a pretzel stick that comes in different flavors. While men are not prohibited, they are not allowed in the after-midnight hours (it is open until 4:30 a.m.) called "Cinderella Time." The company has plans to expand the Lcafe concept to other major Japanese cities including Yokohama, Nagoya, and Osaka and perhaps even internationally.

A second kind of product-oriented promotion is **premiums**. These might be free merchandise provided with the purchase (e.g., the toy in a Cracker Jack box) or some free or reduced-price item for which the buyer has to send proof-of-purchase, with or without money. Some of these promotions are quite elaborate. The soft-drink brand Mountain Dew sponsored a promotion focused on teenagers that offered a pager and free service for 12 months with a certain number of labels from two-liter bottles. The company then paged the customers with a number they could call for reduced prices on a variety of teen-oriented merchandise sold by other vendors. These kinds of promotional programs are popular but have low response rates and uncertain impact on sales. In addition, in a world increasingly populated by such promotional events, it is becoming more difficult to find unique concepts. Fulfillment can sometimes be a problem. Procter & Gamble ran a repeat-purchase-oriented promotion for its Pampers brand of disposable diapers, where parents obtained points from each purchase redeemable for Fisher-Price toys. Unfortunately, too many parents participated and the company ran out of the toys. This angered many customers, some of whom subsequently switched to Kimberly-Clark's Huggies. The fact that the snafu was widely publicized possibly hurt the brand more than the promotion helped.[17]

premiums
a product-oriented promotion in which free merchandise is provided with a purchase or some free or reduced-price item is made available

Application | McDonald's

In April 2002, McDonald's started a promotion featuring the Madame Alexander doll, the most expensive toy in the history of the Happy Meal.[18] Little girls who ate at McDonald's received the toy, a miniature version of the eight-inch doll that sold for $50 or more at FAO Schwartz and Neiman Marcus. For $1.99, girls received a burger, fries, and a drink, plus a $4^3/_4$-inch doll that was available in eight characters including Little Red Riding Hood, Peter Pan, and others. Boys received a Matchbox class car that retailed for as little as $1.29.

What was interesting about this promotion was that the company offered a better toy in the girls' version of the Happy Meal in order to attract them over the long term. The most loyal and heaviest consuming group of McDonald's customers is young men. However, the company has had problems retaining girls. The data show that 45 percent of 6- to 8-year-old girls say McDonald's is their favorite restaurant, while only 22 percent of 9- to 11-year-olds say that. On the other hand, 47 percent of 6- to 8-year-old boys prefer McDonald's to other hamburger chains; the number drops only to 37 percent in the 9- to 11-year-old group. The doll promotion was part of an overall push by the company to target young females and include changes to the menu.

Special Events

Contests and sweepstakes fall into this category of promotions. Every year, Publishers' Clearing House runs a sweepstakes in which the product being sold is magazine subscriptions but the main enticement is the opportunity to win a million dollars. Contests involve competition among consumers (e.g., the first customer to name a song after hearing a few seconds of it on the radio wins a prize). These activities obviously create excitement and may get some new customers to try your brand. However, the response rate to these promotions is often low and they usually do not attract large numbers of entries. In addition, sweepstakes have a bad image because many consumers are suspicious about the prizes actually being awarded (by law, consumers can obtain a list of the winners) and whether they have a chance to win even if they do not buy the product (by law, they do).

Other special promotions are tie-ins to sports events and movies. Corporate sponsorships of tennis and golf tournaments, car races, and other events provide not only communications opportunities but also merchandise giveaways (i.e., sampling). Blockbuster movies are usually accompanied by merchandising involving toys at fast-food chains. Such promotions stimulate interest in the movies and sales at the retailer or restaurant.

More and more companies are using events and sampling simultaneously to create word-of-mouth or "buzz" about their brands. The companies employ people in the target audience to make contact with other targets and encourage them to talk to their peers. As an example, when Ford introduced the Focus, the company recruited some people it considered to be trendsetters in a few markets and gave them free use of the car for six months. Other than the free use of the Focus, the recruits talked up the car and handed out Focus-themed trinkets to anyone expressing an interest.[19]

Trade Promotions

trade promotions sales promotions oriented toward the channels of distribution in an effort to get the channels to carry and promote the product, often including devices such as sales contests, quantity discounts, and training programs

Like customer-oriented promotions, **trade promotions**, or incentives offered to the members of the channel system, can also be divided into groups based on their characteristics.

Product-based promotions include free goods and generous return policies. Return policies allow the channel to return unsold merchandise for a full or partial refund, reducing the risk of carrying the product.

Price deals include various volume discounts and allowances, as well as financing terms such as a long period of time before payment is due or below-market interest rates. The most commonly used trade promotions are off-invoice allowances. The purpose of an off-invoice allowance is to give the channel member a discount on orders for a fixed period of time. Sometimes there is a performance requirement in which the channel member must sell a certain amount of the product during the promotion. Another variant of the allowance form of promotion is count/recount, which provides an allowance based on sales and is therefore given after the promotion period rather than before.

market development funding any money a company spends to help channel members sell their products

Place-based allowances are especially important for consumer packaged-goods companies. Often, the money a company spends to help the channel members sell its products is called **market development funding**. Display allowances compensate retailers for prominently displaying and promoting goods. An excellent example of a very effective sales tool is the egg-shaped display for L'Eggs hosiery. Another example is the efforts by Zenith to help sell digital video disc (DVD) players. Zenith arranged a countertop merchandising display stocked with two copies of six DVD movies at cost ($199) to demonstrate the video quality of the machines.

Slotting allowances are effective at gaining retail shelf space, particularly for areas like the freezer display in supermarkets, which have limited capacity. *Source:* Martin Diebel/Getty Images, Inc.—Liaison

The largest amount of market development funds is spent on slotting allowances, which are payments to store chains for placing a product on a shelf. These have become increasingly important as power has shifted from manufacturers to retailers. About $60 billion per year is spent on these promotions. Slotting fees, charged to manufacturers, have reduced the number of competitors in many product categories and have been particularly hard on small companies, for which the fees, up to $25,000 per item per chain, can become prohibitive. The retailers claim that the slotting allowances are risk payments for new products: because most new products fail, the payments compensate the retailers for their low sales.[20]

Prior to 2002, it was impossible to know how much money companies were spending on slotting allowances, because the amounts were bundled into other expenses subtracted from gross sales. However, a change in U.S. accounting practices in 2002 provided a one-time opportunity to see how much money companies were spending on slotting allowances, as they had to take a charge on earnings. The results were pretty startling. For example, Kraft spent $4.6 billion or 14 percent of sales, PepsiCo $3.4 billion or 13 percent of sales, and Kellogg $1.3 billion or 15 percent of sales on slotting allowances.[21] Unfortunately, companies have not had to permanently break out slotting fees on their financial statements, which will make it very difficult to get good numbers on how much is being spent on this type of trade promotion in the future.

Companies often provide cooperative advertising money to retailers. In this arrangement, the company and the retailer share the expense of the retailer advertising the company's products in the local market. The retailer sends the company tearsheets of the print ads or the tapes of TV and radio ads to prove that the advertising was actually run, and the company reimburses the retailer for a percentage of the expense. The most common arrangement is a 50–50 sharing and the second most common is the company paying 100 percent of the local expense. These two arrangements account for about 95 percent of all co-op contracts.[22]

Finally, there are sales-based incentives, such as bonuses to the channel for meeting or exceeding a quota. Sales incentives can also take the more controversial (and in some cases, forbidden) form of direct prizes or bonuses (sometimes called "spiffs" or "push money") to the channel's sales force. The problem with spiffs is that the salesperson's financial interests in selling a particular brand or model can outweigh the customer's needs.

Of all of the trade promotions mentioned, price-based ones carry the most risk to the company. In some cases, a company running a price-based promotion gives an incentive to the retailer to carry the product but also would like the retailer to pass some or all of the savings along to the end-customer (the amount a retailer passes along to the customer is called the pass-through). By law, the company cannot force the retailer to do this. Therefore, in many instances price-oriented promotions simply result in the retailer or distributor "forward buying," or stocking up on the product at a discount while the promotion is running and then selling the inventory at the regular price. The company gains sales at the time the promotion is run, but this bump in the sales curve is temporary because the channel must sell the inventory eventually, resulting in lower sales by the company later. Only if the promotion has long-term effects (i.e., if a customer switches because of the promotion and continues to buy the brand) will the company be better off.

Application Clorox

Just as consumers and companies have become addicted to promotions in the automobile industry, retailers and distributors in packaged goods have grown accustomed to receiving trade promotion money and manufacturers to giving it.

The Glad family of products was purchased by Clorox from First Brands in 1998.[23] Under its former management, Glad received little media advertising support but heavy trade promotion and couponing. Clorox managers felt that the brand could be revitalized with an increased emphasis on advertising and a reduction in trade promotion. The company commissioned its advertising agency to create a new campaign that would remind consumers of the classic "Don't Get Mad, Get Glad" campaign that had been developed in the 1970s. Along with new advertising and increased spending, Clorox added new products to the Glad line, including a "Stand-and-Pour" freezer bag and an "Odor Shield" garbage bag.

In 1999 and again in early 2000, Clorox cut trade promotion dollars for Glad to compensate for rising materials costs. However, competitors did not follow its lead. As a result, retailers reacted by withdrawing merchandising support, and Glad sales dropped precipitously. By October 2000, Glad's sales were down 10.3 percent in trash bags, down 10.6 percent in food-storage bags, and down 23.2 percent in lawn and leaf bags. Clorox finally decided to restore the trade promotion and couponing money while keeping the new ad budget.

Retailer Promotions

Through **retailer promotions**, retailers often provide direct incentive to customers to buy. Most of these are simply the retail version of either the customer or channel promotions described previously. For example, a retailer can provide its own coupons or price reductions (see Figure 11.1). In addition, retailers have embraced loyalty or continuity

retailer promotions short-term financial incentives to purchase provided by retail channel members

End of aisle displays or endcaps are a popular form of retail promotion.
Source: David Young-Wolff/ PhotoEdit Inc.

programs designed to get customers to be store loyal. For example, some price reductions are available only to holders of Price Chopper's Diamond Value Card. The customer's card is scanned in after the groceries have been scanned and the customer receives the discounts (in addition to any coupon discounts) on the spot.

Another form of retailer promotion is the special display. There are four general types of displays. End-of-aisle displays, or endcaps, are popular and may feature an accompanying price cut. Displays in the front of the store are seen as the customer enters. Some displays are in the store aisles themselves. A fourth kind is a shelf "talker," a sign hanging on the shelf with information, usually about a special price. These special displays and other company-paid advertisements inside the store (e.g., announcements for contests and sweepstakes, information about recipes, etc.) are called **point-of-purchase (POP) advertising**.

point-of-purchase (POP) advertising
a form of retailer promotion that includes information related displays and other company-paid advertising inside the store

Like the price-oriented promotions run by companies, retailer promotions can be effective in getting customers to increase their purchase quantities, switch brands, and change their purchase timing. Of course, retailers are focused more on their own stores than on the company's brands, and company-distributed coupons can be redeemed at any retailer. However, these promotions have the same drawbacks as any price promotion. Although volume is generally increased, brand names can be diluted, brand loyalty eroded, and price sensitivity increased.

Although retailer promotions are effective, some grocery stores are beginning to reduce them because they are finding that busy consumers are less willing to spend time searching for deals in different stores. As a result, they are resorting to an EDLP (everyday low pricing) strategy. This is also an attempt to be more competitive with Walmart and other stores that reduced prices during the recession.

Promotion Strategy, Objectives, and Evaluation

Promotion decisions involve strategic considerations in terms of when it is and is not appropriate to use them. In addition, marketing managers should set objectives for promotional programs and, based on those objectives, evaluate whether or not the promotional program achieved the stated goals. These considerations hold for both customer and trade promotion.

Customer-Oriented Promotions

Strategic Issues

Because of the short-run nature of customer-oriented promotions and some of their problems (particularly those of price promotions), it may not be in a company's best interest to engage in heavy customer promotion spending. When a new product is being launched, customer-oriented promotions are critical to creating awareness and gaining customer trial, and are thus very valuable. Promotions for existing products have been found to have a large impact on sales and other objectives, but most evidence shows that these effects are temporary and are lost when a competitor retaliates with an in-kind promotion.

The promotion dilemma is similar to the prisoner's dilemma discussed in Chapter 6. If category sales are fixed—that is, if marketing expenditures do not increase primary demand and, in the short run, dropping expenditures does not cause demand to decrease to the benefit of other product categories—and marketing managers are interested in profits and margins rather than market share, all companies are obviously better off at a low level of expenditure. However, short of collusion (which is illegal in the United States), cooperation is risky. As a result, because each participant is wary of losing market share, category promotional expenditures remain high. As a result, managers should approach the use of price promotions with caution and an understanding of the costs as well as the benefits.

Objectives

As we noted earlier, promotion typically takes the short-run view. Even when the marketing manager has longer-term interests such as a sustained increase in market share, the operational objective of most promotions is to generate an immediate increase in sales. Table 11.6 shows some goals that are particularly relevant for promotion.

For example, if awareness is a problem, a company can run a promotion such as a game or sweepstakes designed to increase awareness of a product rather than to increase immediate sales. Similarly, a company can run a tie-in promotion (e.g., with a movie) that may improve brand image in addition to raising current sales. However, such relationship-building motives account for only a small percentage of promotion money spent.

By far the most common objective of a consumer promotion is a short-run transactional goal. The objective is usually stated in specific terms, such as "to increase sales 20 percent in the March–April time period." This statement should be qualified in two ways. First, you need to specify from what level sales should increase. Second, you must select the target customer. You can focus on getting current customers to buy more volume (expanding the market through a market penetration strategy), capturing occasional but not loyal customers (improving share of customer's wallet), or generating sales from current noncustomers (market penetration if customers are diverted from the competition or market development if they are new customers to the category). Many promotions focus on current customers, attempting to get them to buy more through a volume discount, to be more loyal (using coupons or frequent-user programs), or to accelerate their purchases and buy soon (rebate-type promotions).

Attracting occasional customers, typically through temporary price cuts such as coupons and rebates, is effective but also expensive. This expense not only produces lower margins on the sales to occasional customers, but may also lower margins on sales that would have been made in the absence of the promotion to occasional or regular customers. As a result, a major concern is how to target promotions to competitors' customers alone.[24] Promotions to noncustomers are generally used when a product is new (or "new and improved") or when there is a need to induce brand switching, as when the brand of interest has low market share. For example, Pepsi might run a promotion where consumers receive a coupon for its brand when Coke is purchased. Promotions

Table 11.6

Customer Promotion Objectives

I. Short-run (transactional)
   - A. Current customers
     1. Buy more
     2. Buy more often
     3. Buy now
   - B. Occasional customers (brand switchers)
     1. Capture next purchase
   - C. Noncustomers
     1. Trial

II. Long-run (relationship building)
   - A. Awareness enhancement
   - B. Image enhancement

can be effective devices for generating such trial behavior. In a sense, targeting noncustomers implies a long-run, relationship-building objective, not the usual short-term objective. However, most marketing managers will accept a short-term gain in switching and hope that product satisfaction leads to more purchases down the road.

Evaluating Customer Promotions

As we have emphasized earlier in this book, marketing managers are becoming more accountable for their expenditures because senior managers are demanding accountability for this money in terms of return on investment. In the trade promotion area, for example, Nestlé is demanding accountability from retail stores that take $80 billion annually from all companies. The company plans to enforce new minimum-performance requirements that retailers must meet to receive promotional funds that were given away freely in the past. The move by Nestlé is similar to those made by Kraft Foods and Hershey Foods.[25]

The most appropriate way to evaluate promotions is to develop measures consistent with the objectives that they are supposed to attain. A price promotion that increases sales 30 percent but fails to attract a substantial number of new customers may be a failure, because it mainly rewarded existing customers when the goal was to obtain new ones.

The easiest approach to evaluating customer promotions is to look at the incremental results of the variable that has been set as the promotion's goal. This method provides a useful starting point, but may lead to an overestimate of the benefit of promotion as it ignores both where the sales come from and the long-run benefit of promotion.

A standard approach to measuring the impact of a sales promotion is tracking the before-and-after results. Assuming a sales objective for the promotion, Figure 11.4 shows a typical tracking study, with point A on the horizontal axis representing the time when the promotion (e.g., a coupon drop) is given to end-customers. Tracking studies such as these are common because the effects of a sales promotion often show up quickly.

Unfortunately, marketing managers tend to look at the shaded area above point A in Figure 11.4 as the only measure of the impact of the promotion. This kind of simplistic analysis has several problems:

- The gain could be offset by the dip at point B, representing the possibility that consumers have merely increased their home inventories and will not need to buy again soon.
- The gain must be compared to a base amount—the amount of sales that would have been generated had the promotion not run. This baseline is difficult to calculate because it can change depending on time of year, competitive conditions, and other factors.
- The analysis does not account for other factors in the marketplace such as advertising and other promotions run simultaneously, sponsored by both the product in question and the competition.

Figure 11.4

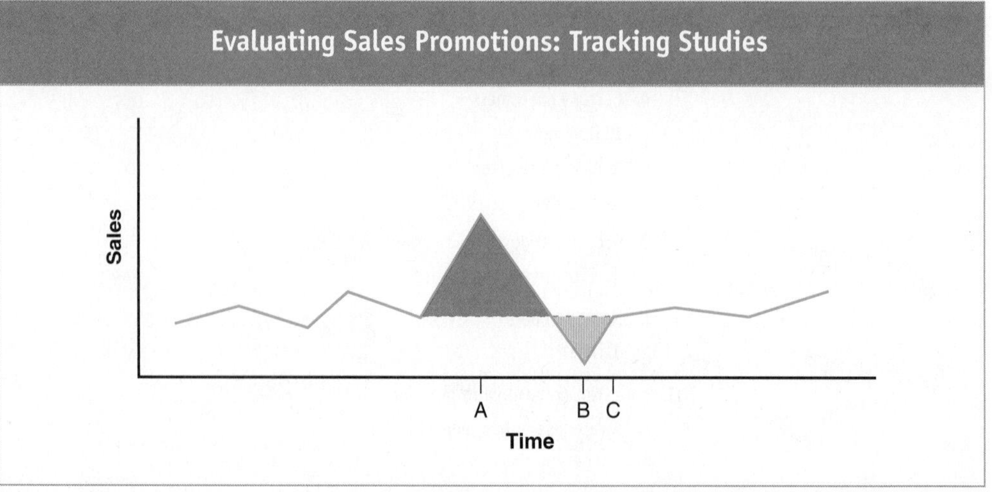

Thus, although the return-on-investment of promotions are easier to analyze than advertising, there are still complicating factors.

Sales increases from customer-oriented promotions may reflect accelerated purchases by loyal buyers (who would have bought the brand anyway) rather than new sales volume from brand switchers. One approach to evaluating coupon promotions, for example, looks at purchase acceleration and brand switching as well as the impact of consumer promotions on regular purchasing.[26] A coupon can have several incremental impacts in the period in which the program is launched:

- **Accelerated regular purchases.** Regular buyers of the brand simply buy sooner.
- **Accelerated captured purchases.** Purchasers who would not have bought at the time or bought the promoted brand are persuaded by the promotion to do both.
- **Unaccelerated regular purchases.** Regular buyers use the coupon as a "bonus" price cut.
- **Unaccelerated captured purchases.** Purchasers of other brands switch to the promoted brand because of the promotion.

Obviously, accelerated and unaccelerated captured purchases are pluses for the marketing manager because they are new business. However, for unaccelerated regular purchases, the amount of the coupon (plus redemption costs) comes out of revenues. Accelerated regular purchases are potentially but not necessarily negative. If subsequent sales are depressed as a result of increased inventory, there is no benefit except for a slight time value of money advantage. If most of the purchases fall in this category, it would explain the post-promotion dip found in Figure 11.4. One possible benefit of promotion is that captured buyers will remain loyal and purchase the promoted brand again later. It is also possible that purchase quantity could increase if the coupon was focused on larger package sizes. In any event, the point is that in evaluating such a program's effectiveness, it is necessary to estimate both the overall magnitude of the impact (i.e., sales) and the source of the additional sales.

Trade Promotion

Strategic Issues

As we noted earlier in this chapter, trade promotion is the largest part of the advertising/promotion budget. Most firms feel that such promotion expense is simply a cost of doing business. However, given its high cost, it is useful to approach trade promotion from a strategic perspective, with some ideas about when it may or may not be useful.

Such a framework is shown in Figure 11.5. The two axes of the figure are the holding costs to the channel member (i.e., how much it costs the channel member to hold inventory) and the promotional elasticity of the end-customers. When holding costs and price elasticity are high, the manager should use trade deals. This is because the channel member will not want to keep a large inventory and the deal gives the member an incentive to stock the product. Given the price elasticity, the channel member will pass the savings on to customers to help clear the inventory. Paper products, soft drinks, and personal computers fit this cell. The lower-right-hand cell is straightforward. There is no incentive to trade deal when the channel member will simply forward buy to build inventory at a low cost and the customers are not interested in price promotions, so there will be no pass-through of the savings. An example of this kind of product is laxatives. Products with high holding costs and low price elasticities also should not have much trade promotion. It is clear that neither the channel member nor the company has an incentive in this cell. Produce items such as cheese, lettuce, and bakery items fit this cell. With low holding costs and high elasticities, the channel will want deals for forward buying. There is also more likely to be pass-through of the deal because price elasticity is high. In addition, even if the company does not want to use trade deals in this situation, competition will probably force it anyway. This describes canned tuna and many other supermarket items that are not bulky and have low economic value.

Figure 11.5

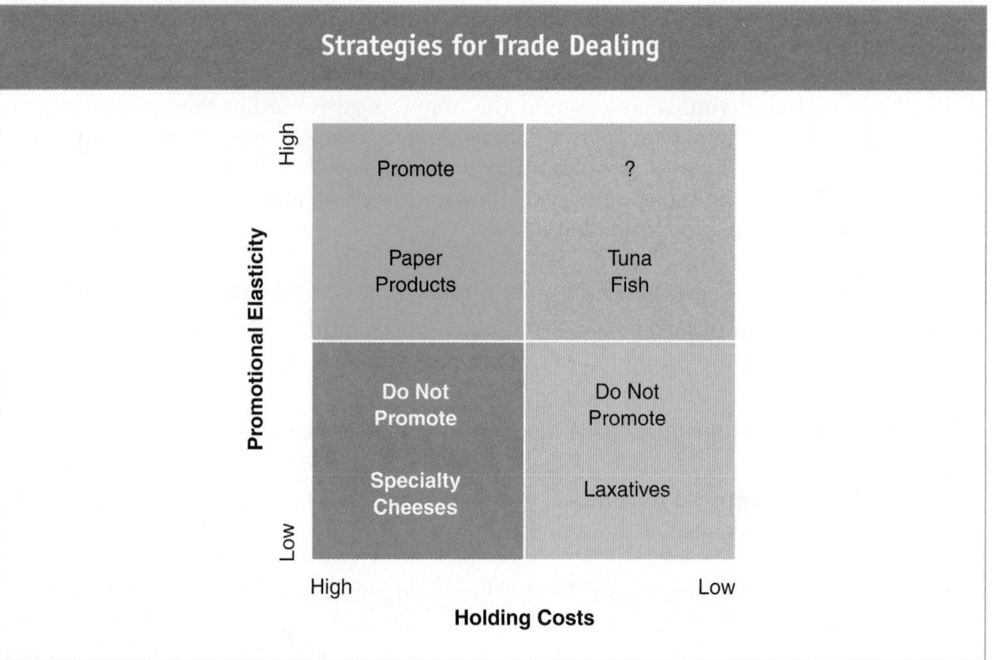

Source: Robert C. Blattberg and Scott A. Neslin (1990), *Sales Promotion* (Englewood Cliffs, NJ: Prentice Hall). Reproduced by permission of Pearson Education, Inc.

Objectives

Common goals for trade promotions are shown in Table 11.7. Perhaps the most important trade promotions are those that motivate the channel member to market your product through advertising, selling, or display. By taking the channel member's perspective (see Chapter 12), you can see that the channel member will be more proactive in promoting the products of companies that are giving more incentives for doing so. Recall that both push and pull activities are necessary for a successful channel system. Promotional incentives are also given to the retailer's sales force. A recommendation by such a salesperson often affects a customer's purchase decision if the customer does not have a brand name in mind when entering the store. Some retail promotions are

Table 11.7

Objectives of Trade Deals
Induce retailers to offer a price discount.
Induce retailers to display the brand.
Induce retailers to advertise the brand.
Offer incentives for the retailer's or dealer's sales force to push the brand to the customer.
Gain or maintain distribution for a model or item within the product line.
Gain or maintain distribution for the brand.
Load the retailer, dealer, or distributor with inventory to avoid out-of-stocks.
Shift inventory from the manufacturer to the channels of distribution and the consumer.
Avoid permanent price reductions.
Defend the brand against competitors.
Induce price fluctuations into the market.
Finance retailer inventories.

Source: Robert C. Blattberg and Scott A. Neslin (1989), "Sales Promotion: The Long and the Short of It," *Marketing Letters,* 1 (December), p. 314; with kind permission from Springer Science and Business Media.

intended to load the retailer or channel member with inventory. This makes out-of-stocks less likely, gives the channel member an incentive to push the product further down the channel system, may account for seasonal surges in demand, and reduces the manufacturer's holding costs.

A particularly important purpose of retail-oriented promotions is to gain or maintain distribution. When a new brand is introduced or when the product category is new, gaining distribution is critical to giving customers access to the product. When a product category is in the decline stage of the life cycle or when a brand's sales are declining, the channel member will begin to consider replacing it with a product that provides greater profit. In order to maintain the profit level of the product to the channel member and keep the product on the shelves, the marketing manager often uses price-oriented promotions to compensate for the decline in sales.

Evaluation

One approach to evaluating trade promotions is tracking before-and-after results. In this case, the baseline sales level is defined as the volume that would have been sold to the channel member in the absence of the promotion. Although it is subject to most of the same limitations of the analysis of customer promotions, one advantage in this context is that few other marketing-mix elements target the channel members, so it is not necessary to separate the effects of different programs. For example, advertising normally targets end customers, not channel members.

An important criterion for evaluating trade promotions is how often a retail promotion is run when the channel members receive some kind of deal. The company's sales force must convince retailers not to load up in inventory and pocket the discount, but to pass it along to end customers. Majers, a subsidiary of A.C. Nielsen, has a service that helps companies track pass-through from trade deals. Majers records all retail promotions in a geographic market for different consumer product categories. Reports indicating the company's share of promotion by retailer and for the total market are generated and used by the sales force to gain cooperation from retailers. These reports evaluate the performance of both the retailers and the sales force.

Application Procter & Gamble

As a result of the strategy and objectives set by the marketing manager, a promotion plan or schedule for a planning period is developed. A template for such a plan is shown in Table 11.8. It is based on a new product introduction by Procter & Gamble and it shows the range and number of kinds of promotions typically considered by a large packaged-goods company. The consumer and trade promotion options for introducing the brand include:

- **Trade allowances.** The sales force advised the brand manager that a $2.70/case trade allowance on all sizes in the first three months was necessary to stimulate initial stocking, in-store displays, and newspaper feature advertising by the channels.
- **Sampling.** P&G considered sampling, particularly through the mail, to be the most effective trial-inducing promotion device.
- **Couponing.** The brand manager could mail them directly to the target audience, deliver them through a co-op program mailed with other product coupons, place them as free-standing newspaper inserts (FSIs), put them in magazine print ads, or offer them through Best Food Day (BFD) editions of local newspapers.
- **Special pack promotions.** Four options considered were trial-size packs (small containers the consumer bought at deep discounts), prepriced packs (trial-size packs of the smallest container), price packs (discounts offered in special displays), and bonus packs (extra detergent for a smaller-package price).
- **Refunds:** The brand manager could develop a program whereby consumers received money back for multiple purchases.
- **Premiums.** These include on- or in-pack (on or in the package), near-pack (displayed on a shelf near the product), free-in-mail (merchandise offered with proofs-of-purchase), and self-liquidators (consumers send in money for a premium, which covers the costs of the promotion).
- **Sweepstakes/contests.**

In addition to the particular promotions that would be run, the brand manager has to be concerned with the timing of the promotions over the introductory year. The sales promotion plan template shown in Table 11.8 can be used to schedule the different promotions in the appropriate months and track their costs.[27]

Table 11.8

Sales Promotion Plan

Event	Timing												Number of Average Weeks of Volume	Cost
	Jan.	Feb.	March	April	May	June	July	Aug.	Sept.	Oct.	Nov.	Dec.		
Stocking allowance														
$/Physical case														
Trade allowance														
$/Statistical case														
Sampling														
6 oz														
3 oz														
1.5 oz														
2 × 0.75 oz														
Couponing														
Mail														
Single														
Co-op														
Extended														
FSI														
Single														
Full page co-op														
2/5 page co-op														
BFD														
Magazine														
Special pack														
Price pack														
Bonus pack														
Trial size														
Refund														
Print														
Point-of-sale														
Direct mail														
In- or on-pack														
Own brand														
Other brand														
Premium														
On- or in-pack														
Near-pack														
Free-in-mail														
Self-liquidator														
Partial liquidator														
Group promotion														

Source: John A. Quelch (1983), "Proctor & Gamble (B)," Harvard Business School case #9-584-048, p. 24.

Table 11.9

Sales Effect of Deal Discount, Feature Advertising, and Displays				
	Discount			
	0%	10%	20%	30%
No merchandising	100	177	313	555
Display	113	201	356	631
Major ad	185	327	580	1028
Display and line ad	254	451	799	1414
Display and major ad	309	548	971	1719

100 = Base sales when no promotions occur.

Source: Robert C. Blattberg and Scott A. Neslin (1989), "Sales Promotion: The Long and the Short of It," *Marketing Letters,* 1 (December), p. 83; with kind permission from Springer Science and Business Media.

Retail Promotion

Because they are mostly intended for end-customers, retail promotions have the same strategic aspects, objectives, and measurement approaches as other end-customer promotions discussed earlier in this chapter. However, the focus of retail promotions is on the retail store or chain rather than a specific brand.

One unique feature of retail promotions is the impact they can have on purchasing decisions right in the store. The Point-of-Purchase Advertising Institute (POPAI) periodically studies the in-store habits of customers in mass-merchandise stores and supermarkets. Its 1995 study found that 70 percent of supermarket shoppers and 74 percent of mass retailer shoppers chose purchases in the store, in what are often called impulse purchases. The categories most sensitive to POP advertising and displays are film/photofinishing, socks and underwear, dishwashing soaps, and cookies and crackers.[28]

A particularly interesting aspect of retail promotions is how they can interact with each other and with consumer promotions to create larger effects than each one would on its own. An example of such interactions between retail promotions is shown in Table 11.9. In this case, the retailer manipulates five retail promotions: a short-term price cut or discount, a special in-store display, a major newspaper ad for the brand, a smaller line ad and a display, and a major ad with a display. As can be seen, the base case is no price cut and no promotional activity for the brand (referred to in the table as merchandising). The sales performance of the brand in this base case is set to an index of 100. Across the top row of Table 11.9, the significant impact of increasingly larger price cuts by themselves (i.e., with no accompanying nonprice promotions) can be found. The table shows that, for this brand, offering a 10 percent discount increases sales 77 percent over the base case. Down the first column (no discounts), the impact of the separate merchandising policies and two pairs can also be seen. A special display with no price cut increases sales by only 13 percent, whereas a major ad increases sales by 85 percent. The inner figures of the table show the interaction effects between price cuts and merchandising. Whereas a major ad increases sales by 85 percent over the base case and a 10 percent price cut increases sales 77 percent when they are run separately, when both are in force together, the increase in sales is a whopping 227 percent.[29]

Promotion Budgeting

Setting a budget for sales promotion generally follows the same approaches discussed for setting advertising budgets (see Chapter 10). Again, the major distinction is between analytical methods (e.g., objective and task, optimization) and convenient guidelines (e.g., percentage of sales, competitive parity). However, two questions must be considered: How much money should be spent on the total advertising and promotion budget? Of this amount, how much should be spent on promotion?

Advertising and Promotion Budget

Seven conditions have been found to affect the total budget for advertising and sales promotion for manufactured products.[30] Companies spend more on advertising and promotion relative to sales under the following conditions:

1. The product is standardized (as opposed to being produced or supplied to order).
2. There are many end-users.
3. The typical purchase amount is small.
4. Sales are made through channel intermediaries rather than directly to end-users.
5. The product is premium priced.
6. The product line has a high contribution margin.
7. The product or service has a small market share.

Note that the first four conditions are typical of consumer products and services. This is consistent with the fact that the marketing managers for these products spend much more money on sales promotion than do their counterparts managing business-to-business products and services.

Allocating Money Between Advertising and Promotion

The second important question is how to allocate money between advertising and sales promotion. In organizations in which the overall marketing budget is set, rather than specific amounts for advertising or promotion (or other expenditures), this may be the most important question.

Several factors affect this allocation decision. First, the total amount of resources available has a major impact. If the marketing budget is small, major media advertising is usually not worthwhile unless the target market is local and can be reached by media such as radio and newspapers. This is because advertising usually needs to meet a minimum or threshold amount to have any impact at all. Beneath the threshold value, the money is wasted. In such cases, spending the money on sales promotion results in a greater market impact than advertising.

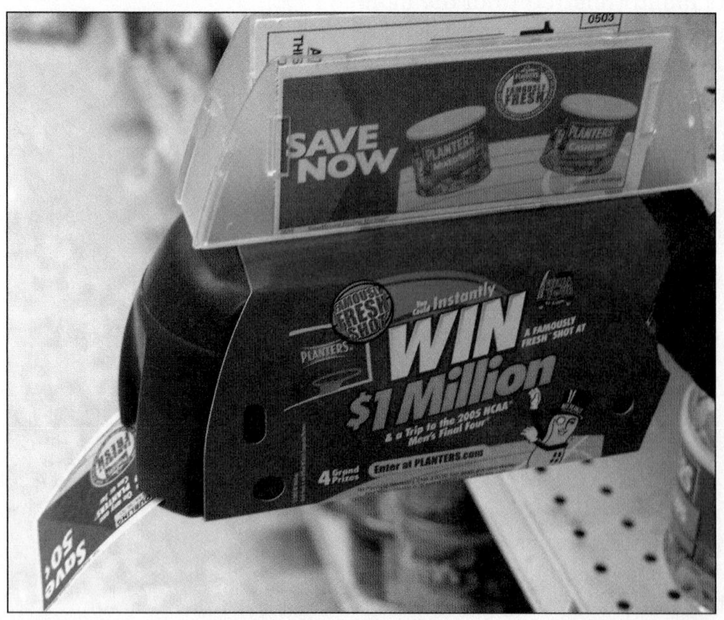

There are a variety of coupon delivery mechanisms.
Source: Susan Van Etten/PhotoEdit Inc.

Second, customer factors affect allocation decisions. Knowing the behavior of customers can help you determine whether advertising or promotion makes more sense. One relevant aspect of customer behavior is the degree of brand loyalty. As noted earlier in this chapter, promotion money spent on a product or service exhibiting high levels of loyalty primarily rewards existing customers. Although this may be what the marketing manager wants to do, it is usually not the best way to spend the money. If customers are not loyal, the marketing manager should try to understand whether their behavior is typical of the category. If so, there may be an opportunity to attract brand switchers with promotions. However, it is also possible that the product manager has created nonloyal customers through frequent price-based promotions, and so all that happens is a temporary swapping of customers.

A second relevant aspect of consumer behavior is the type of decision required of them. If the product is complex and therefore requires a fair amount of information processing, more money should be spent on advertising because it is a better communication device. Alternatively, most sales promotion money is spent on product categories in which decision making is routine and involves little processing of information about the product.

The third factor affecting allocation decisions is whether advertising and promotion dollars highlight the unique aspects of the product, called **consumer franchise building (CFB)**.[31] CFB activities are those that build brand equity, including advertising, sampling, couponing, and product demonstrations. Non-CFB activities focus on price alone and include trade promotions, short-term price deals, and refunds. In this approach, the marketing manager must track the following ratio:

consumer franchise building (CFB)
activities that build brand equity, including advertising, sampling, couponing, and product demonstrations

$$\text{CFB ratio} = \text{CFB\$}/(\text{CFB\$} + \text{non-CFB\$})$$

The CFB ratio should stay above 50 or 55 percent for the brand to remain healthy. The concept behind CFB-based budgeting is obvious. Unless the marketing manager is careful, the funds spent on price-related activities that detract from brand equity and build price sensitivity can dominate the advertising and promotion budget.

Sales Promotion and Information Technology

As with other areas of marketing discussed in this book, the rapid improvements in information technology have had a significant impact on promotion decision making.

In-Store Information Technology

For supermarket and mass-merchandiser shoppers, the combination of universal product codes (UPCs or bar codes) and improvements in information technology has produced a number of ways to deliver promotions directly to shoppers in the store.

The best example is Catalina Marketing Corporation's Marketing Services unit, which produces red-bordered coupons (with UPC codes) right at the cash register after a customer rings up the purchases. These coupons are tied to purchases that have been scanned as part of the customer's order. A company buys time on the coupon delivery system (say, one month) when coupons for its brand are produced and competitors' coupons are not.

For example, suppose you are the marketing manager for the number-two brand of peanut butter. Some steps you might follow to increase share are:

1. For a 12-week period, every scanned purchase of the number-one brand produces a high-value (say, $1) coupon for your brand.
2. When the $1 coupon for your brand is redeemed (scanned), a repeat purchase coupon for a slightly lower value (say, $0.75) is issued. This helps build continuity or repeat purchase.
3. Simultaneously, a medium-value coupon (say, $0.50) is issued whenever a complementary product (e.g., grape jelly) is purchased.
4. A six-month Checkout Direct program is then launched in which customers who use an ATM or check are tracked for their purchase frequency of peanut butter. Customers who purchase peanut butter every six weeks are given a coupon after shopping in the fifth week between purchases (i.e., the week before their forecasted regular purchase).

Application | Vault versus Mountain Dew

Because Coke's Vault brand has only 4 percent of the citrus soft-drink segment compared to Pepsi's Mountain Dew brand, which has 80 percent, Coke launched a promotion where they gave away free samples of Vault to anyone purchasing a Mountain Dew. Coke used Catalina Marketing to distribute point-of-purchase coupons good for a 16-, 20-, or 24-ounce Vault free with any purchase of a 20-ounce Mountain Dew. The offer was billed as the "Vault Taste

Challenge." Coke was taking advantage of the fact that coupon redemption was on an upswing in 2009 as well as the fact that unlike most companies, Coke's marketing budget is sufficiently large to support such an expensive promotion.[32]

The large number of in-store promotions from both manufacturers and retailers have led to a surge in the length of cash register receipts. Store receipts now have coupons, return policies, loyalty points, advertisements, and other information. For example, a consumer shopped at a CVS pharmacy in Atlanta and paid $25.39 for two prescriptions, a beverage, and a roll of toilet paper. These purchases produced a receipt that was almost two feet long![33]

Executive Summary

Key learning points in this chapter include the following:

- Sales promotion is generally focused on the short term, with promotional devices being the main tools marketing that managers use to change customer behavior in the short run.
- There are three kinds of sales promotions: promotions run by companies targeting end-customers; promotions run by companies targeting channel members; and promotions run by channel members, usually retailers, targeting end-customers.
- Customer-focused promotions are most often price related (e.g., coupons), but may also involve the product (e.g., sampling) and special events (e.g., contests and sweepstakes). Customer promotions are incentives to buy the product, but can also increase purchase volume, induce customers to switch brands or use larger sizes, and achieve other purchase-related goals.
- Trade promotions are intended to give incentives to channel members to stock and promote the product. Like customer promotions, the vast majority are price related. However, some also give marketing assistance (e.g., co-op advertising).
- Retailer promotions involve both price and special displays and other forms of point-of-purchase (POP) advertising.
- The most popular way to evaluate the effectiveness of sales promotion is to track the goal of the promotion (e.g., sales volume) and compare the relevant data before and after the promotion is run. This approach does not control for other marketing factors that affect the data and can be confounded if multiple promotions are being run simultaneously.
- Increasing numbers of promotions are being run on the Web and delivered using information systems (e.g., point-of-purchase systems coordinated with bar-coded, scanned purchases).

Chapter Questions

1. How are advertising and sales promotion similar? Different? Which do you think is a more effective communications tool and why?
2. Are particular kinds of customer-oriented sales promotions more likely to have long-term effects on buying behavior than others?
3. Consider Figure 11.5 ("Strategies for Trade Dealing"). What other products or services would fit into the four boxes?

4. Summarize the factors that affect the allocation of money between advertising and promotion. Considering the consumer franchise-building approach, when would you want the CFB ratio to be below the 50 to 55 percent recommended? When might you want it to be much higher?
5. A number of new in-store coupon-delivery systems other than the Catalina system are being developed (e.g., free-standing kiosks). Compared to coupons delivered through the mail or newspapers and magazines, what kind of impact do you expect these coupons to have on consumer behavior other than simply inducing a one-time trial?
6. What are the pros and cons of trade deals from the perspectives of (a) the marketing manager, (b) the distributor, and (c) the retailer?

Key Learning Points

The purpose of this chapter is to introduce methods of distributing products and services to customers. Key learning points include:

- The functions of channels of distribution
- Key factors affecting the choice among alternative channel structures
- Channel options
- Managing channels of distribution, particularly resolving conflicts between channel members
- Special topics in channels of distribution, including the Web, changes in supermarket retailing, and multilevel marketing
- Channel decisions in global and high-tech contexts

Microsoft recently developed its first retail stores to compete with Apple.
Source: Joshua Lott/CORBIS-NY

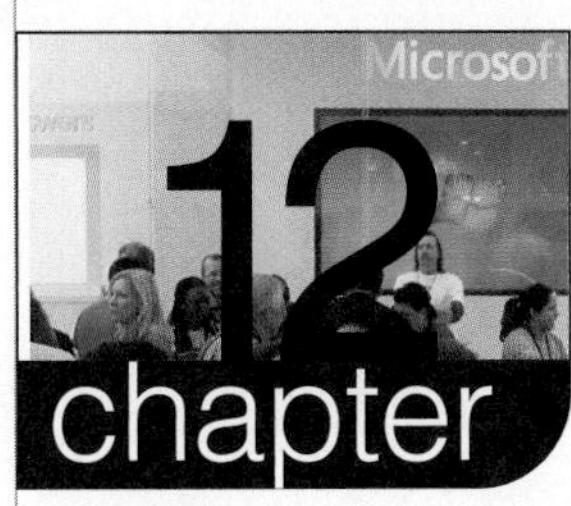

Channels of Distribution

Chapter Brief

he Microsoft Corporation is one of the world's largest companies with more than $50 billion in revenues.[1] While the company is best known for its operating system, Windows, and its suite of office products, Office, it also markets a number of other products and services including:

- The Web browser, Internet Explorer.
- Entertainment and news services such as MSN and MSNBC.
- Hardware such as computer mice, keyboards, and servers.
- The Xbox game device.
- The Zune MP3 player.
- Software developer tools such as its .NET framework and Visual Basic.
- Educational and home software such as Money.

While this list does not fully cover the range of Microsoft offerings, suffice it to say that the company is in many product markets in most countries in the world.

Traditionally, Microsoft has used a wide variety of distribution channels to enable customers to buy its products. These include the company's Web site, Microsoft.com; independent electronics stores such as Best Buy; its own sales force; direct marketing approaches such as telemarketing and direct mail; and others.

However, Microsoft has followed the huge success that Apple has had with its own stores. By 2010, Apple had more than 200 stores that permit customers to purchase iPhones, Mac computers, and iPods in a retail "bricks-and-mortar" environment. These stores have attractive architecture, "genius" bars that give expert technical advice, and a highly trained, enthusiastic staff. Not only do the stores generate sales for Apple, they create an experience for users of Apple's products that cannot be duplicated on a Web site or in a Best Buy.

As a result of Apple's success and the damage to Microsoft's brand from the disappointing performance of its Vista operating system, in 2009, Microsoft decided to open a few stores of its own. The company hired a former executive from Walmart to oversee the operation, which began with only two stores—one in Scottsdale, Arizona, and the other in Mission Viejo, California. The stores will sell almost all Microsoft products, including the Windows software and Xbox with its compatible games. The goal is to deliver an Apple-like experience by allowing customers to touch and feel Microsoft-branded products in a company-controlled environment.

There are, of course, a number of challenges. Unlike Apple, which controls both software and hardware, Microsoft software is used on many different hardware platforms. In addition, the retail environment has become more difficult (e.g., large electronics chain Circuit City shut down in 2009). Other computer companies have failed at this; for example, Gateway closed its 188 stores in 2004 due to weak sales. Finally, how will Best Buy react to a key supplier becoming a competitor?

While the idea of opening company-owned stores presents a unique set of challenges, many of these issues facing Microsoft in managing its channels are typical. As this illustration shows, distribution is a key element of the marketing mix and an important part of the marketing strategy (see the marketing strategy diagram) because they provide customers access to a company's products and services. Key questions that must be addressed when making channel decisions are:

- Given the various functions that channel members can perform, what system of channel members works best for your product or service? Should you sell directly to customers or use intermediaries such as retailers and wholesalers?
- How can you use the channel system to perform important tasks such as physical distribution and marketing research?
- How do you manage channel members that have business and personal goals different from yours?
- How do you motivate the channel members to carry and promote your product?
- How can you use emerging channels such as the Internet and hybrid systems (combining several alternative channel structures) to capture sales when the customers are changing?
- If you use company-owned and independent channels, how do you manage channel "conflict," that is, the problems that can arise from unhappy independent channels with whom you are competing?
- What are the channel issues facing global businesses?

These questions and others are addressed in this chapter.

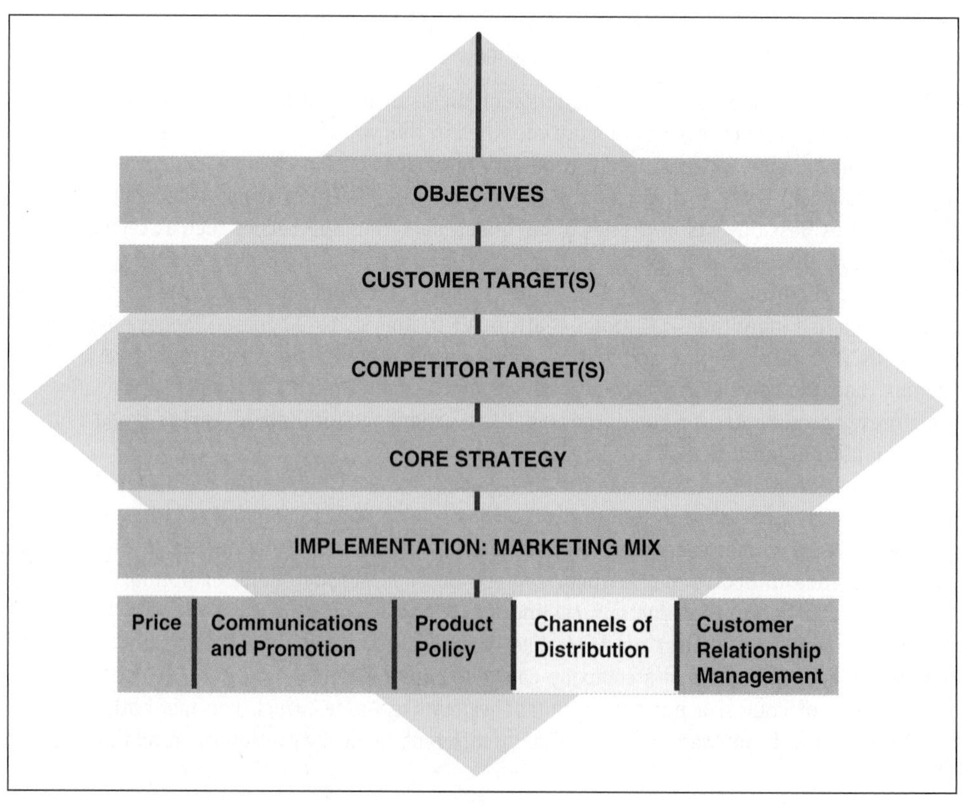

The Importance of Channels of Distribution

The importance of **channels of distribution** in the marketing mix is simple: customers must have access to your product or service to be able to purchase it. The purpose of a system of distribution channels is to provide an efficient means of getting your products to customers and customers to your products. All companies use channels of distribution, whether they sell directly to end customers using a sales force or use a multilevel system made up of many different entities.

channels of distribution
the system by which customers have access to a company's product or service

In many people's minds, channels imply physical distribution, or what is usually called **logistics**. They may, therefore, assume that the concept of channels does not apply to services. However, it is clear that companies that are marketing services must solve the same distribution problems as those that market tangible products. Thus, airlines use company-owned telephone systems or their own Web sites to allow customers to make reservations directly. At one time, travel agents were the most important distribution channel for airlines, but with the elimination of commissions, this will undoubtedly change. Banks have retail branches but also allow customers to bank online.

logistics
physical distribution of goods from one location to another

A useful way to think of channels of distribution is as a value-added chain. This concept is shown in Figure 12.1. The beginning of the chain consists of suppliers that provide raw materials, labor, technology, or other factors of production. The firm then uses channels or intermediaries that enable customers to gain access to the product or service. Importantly, these intermediaries are used only if they add value to the system and are compensated for the added value. In other words, Unilever, Procter & Gamble, and Colgate-Palmolive would not use wholesalers and supermarkets if it did not believe that the value of these two intermediaries' services was worth the cost.[2]

A more subtle point made by Figure 12.1 is that channels of distribution are customers, just like end-customers such as consumers. Indirect channels, those not controlled by the company, must be convinced to carry your products, just as end-customers must be convinced to buy them. The marketing manager attracts indirect channels in two ways. First, as we described in Chapter 11, you must use a variety of promotional devices to induce channels to carry your product and motivate them to sell it. Second, you must realize that channels want to distribute your product only to the extent that their customers want the product. Retailers or other distributors want to be assured that you will spend sufficient money and pay attention to persuading the customers to want your brand. These two activities draw an important distinction between two kinds of basic activities of channel management: **push** (getting channels to carry and sell the product) and **pull** (motivating customers to ask for your brand by name).

push
one of two kinds of basic activities of channel management that requires getting channels to carry and sell the product

pull
one of two kinds of basic activities of channel management that requires motivating customers to ask for your brand by name

A final point made by Figure 12.1 is that channel members are an extension of the firm, but not a substitute. Particularly in the case of independent, indirect channel members, customers may associate problems in the channel with you even if they are not your fault. For example, a customer may buy a Hewlett-Packard personal computer at Best Buy and have problems setting it up or learning to use it. Much of this difficulty may stem from inadequate information provided by Best Buy (the channel). However, the image of the manufacturer, Hewlett-Packard, may be negatively affected by problems created by the retailer.

This issue relates to another common myth about channels: that the channel stops at the loading platform and what happens afterward is the buyer's responsibility. This is clearly false. It is in the best interests of the company to motivate the channels to act in both of their interests. Thus, in the Best Buy example, it is in the best interest of Hewlett-Packard to invest in training programs for Best Buy employees to ensure that end-customers are satisfied with their purchases.

The following two illustrations show how channels are critical to the success of a business and therefore must be treated like customers.

This Subway store in a Walmart demonstrates how many retailers have offered distribution opportunities for other companies.
Source: J. D. Pooley/Getty Images, Inc-Liaison

Figure 12.1

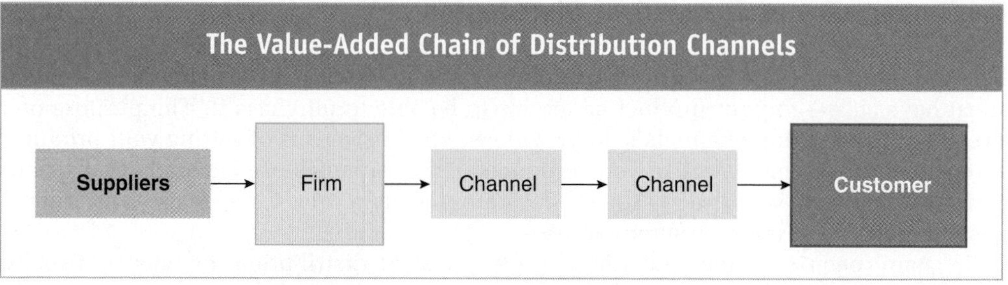

Application Snapple

In 1993, Quaker Oats paid $1.7 billion for the Snapple brand, outbidding Coca-Cola and other interested parties.[3] In 1997, Quaker sold Snapple to Triarc Beverages for $300 million, a drop in value of $1.4 billion in only three years. This disaster is widely credited with costing both the chairman and president of Quaker their jobs, and it helped to end the company's independent existence, as it was later purchased by PepsiCo. Further, in October 2000, Triarc sold Snapple to Cadbury Schweppes for about $1 billion (the brand is now part of Dr Pepper Snapple). What happened during this period to cause the brand's value to diminish so significantly under Quaker's management and then rise dramatically under Triarc's?

While there are a number of reasons advanced, one of them is the problems Quaker created in the channel of distribution system. Snapple grew from a small company in the 1970s through funky promotions (e.g., sponsoring the shock jock Howard Stern) and unconventional distribution channels. The brand started through what is called the "cold" channel. Small distributors served thousands of lunch counters and delicatessens that sold single bottles from refrigerator units, which were consumed on the premises. These many distributors and retail outlets created a large business, and eventually, supermarket accounts were added. By 1994, sales were $674 million, up from just $4 million 10 years earlier.

Quaker's plan was to replicate Snapple's success with Gatorade. The idea was to use Snapple's contacts in the cold channel to help Gatorade and Gatorade's power in the supermarket channel to further help Snapple. Quaker asked Snapple's 300 distributors to give up their supermarket accounts to Quaker in exchange for the right to sell Gatorade to the cold channel. However, the distributors did not want to give up their hard-won supermarket accounts. They were so upset with Quaker that they began to lessen their support of Snapple in favor of other companies' brands. When Triarc took over, its marketing personnel sent a clear message to the distributors that they were crucial to Snapple's success and not an inefficiency to be eliminated. By gaining their trust and through other measures, Triarc resuscitated the brand.

Application New England Confectionary Company

The New England Confectionary Company, better-known as Necco, has been making its trademark Necco Wafers since 1847, which is the oldest continuously manufactured product in unchanged form made in the United States.[4] The company also makes the "conversation hearts"—tiny candies in pastel colors stamped with brief sweet nothings—that have become identified with Valentine's Day since 1867. The company does no consumer marketing and has been privately held since 1963 by UIS Inc., an old-fashioned conglomerate that also markets Champion oil filters. Necco's annual revenues of $100 million are small by today's candy manufacturing standards set by companies like M&M Mars, Hershey's, and Nestlé.

Although old-fashioned in many respects, the company's skills lie in delivering large quantities of custom candy to retailers just the way they want it. A large retailer, Dollar Tree, asked the company to create a 4.5-ounce bag of the company's Clark bars in packages that had holes, to hang on peg boards. The company gave the retailer what it wanted at the necessary price and received an order for 800,000 bags. Another large retailer, Family Dollar Stores, likes all of its products prepriced so that its value-conscious customers know exactly what price they will pay before arriving at the cash register. Necco did that for them as well as, giving Family Dollar the product at a price point it wanted by slightly changing the package size. None of the large candy manufacturers would do that for them. Thus, without spending any money on advertising and promotion, Necco has become successful by treating its channel members—retail stores—in a way that satisfies their needs in the same way it creates products that satisfies its end-customers' needs.

Table 12.1

Major Types of Marketing Intermediaries
Middleman: an independent business concern that operates as a link between producers and ultimate consumers or industrial buyers.
Merchant middleman: a middleman who buys the goods outright and takes title to them.
Agent: a business unit that negotiates purchases or sales but does not take title to the goods in which it deals.
Wholesaler: a merchant establishment operated by a concern that is engaged primarily in buying, taking title to, usually storing and physically handling goods in large quantities, and reselling the goods (usually in smaller quantities) to retail or to industrial or business users.
Retailer: a merchant middleman who is engaged primarily in selling to ultimate consumers.
Broker: a middleman who serves as a go-between for the buyer or seller. The broker assumes no title risks, usually does not have physical custody of products, and is not seen as a permanent representative of the buyer or seller.
Manufacturers' agent: an agent who generally operates on an extended contractual basis, often sells within an exclusive territory, handles noncompeting but related lines of goods, and has limited authority with regard to prices and terms of sale.
Distributor: a wholesale middleman, especially in lines where selective or exclusive distribution is common at the wholesaler level in which the manufacturer expects strong promotional support; often a synonym for *wholesaler*.
Jobber: a middleman who buys from manufacturers and sells to retailers; a wholesaler.
Facilitating agent: a business that assists in the performance of distribution tasks other than buying, selling, and transferring title (e.g., transportation companies, warehouses).

Source: Based on Peter D. Bennett, ed. (1995), *Dictionary of Marketing Terms*, 2nd ed. (Chicago: American Marketing Association).

Technical definitions of marketing intermediaries are provided in Table 12.1 and some general channel structures for industrial and consumer products are shown in Figure 12.2. Note that "retailers" in the top part of Figure 12.2 could include a number of options including bricks-and-mortar retailers, Web sites, and mobile phones. Likewise, in the bottom half of Figure 12.2, the "direct" link between a manufacturer of an industrial product and its customers could also include options like the company's Web site. A more concrete example, from the food service disposable industry (e.g., paper cups, napkins), is shown in Figure 12.3. As can be seen, even without the Web channel, this particular system is complex, involving many kinds of participants:

- A direct sales force.
- Brokers or agents.
- Wholesalers.
- A company-owned distribution center.
- Industrial/institutional buyers.
- Cash-and-carry outlets (small, limited-function wholesalers that may also be open to consumers).
- Small, independent distributors.

Note that we use the term *system* to describe distribution channel networks. The marketing manager must think in terms of maximizing profits for or meeting the goals of the entire system. You become successful only if your channel members are successful. Because the ultimate goal is to get a customer to choose your brand, your job is to design and manage the system to attract customers profitably.

You can look at channel decisions from two perspectives. The natural perspective involves planning how to best design and manage a system for your products and services. Another perspective involves planning how to make money acting as a distributor for another product. Because channel members are compensated for their value-added services,

Figure 12.2

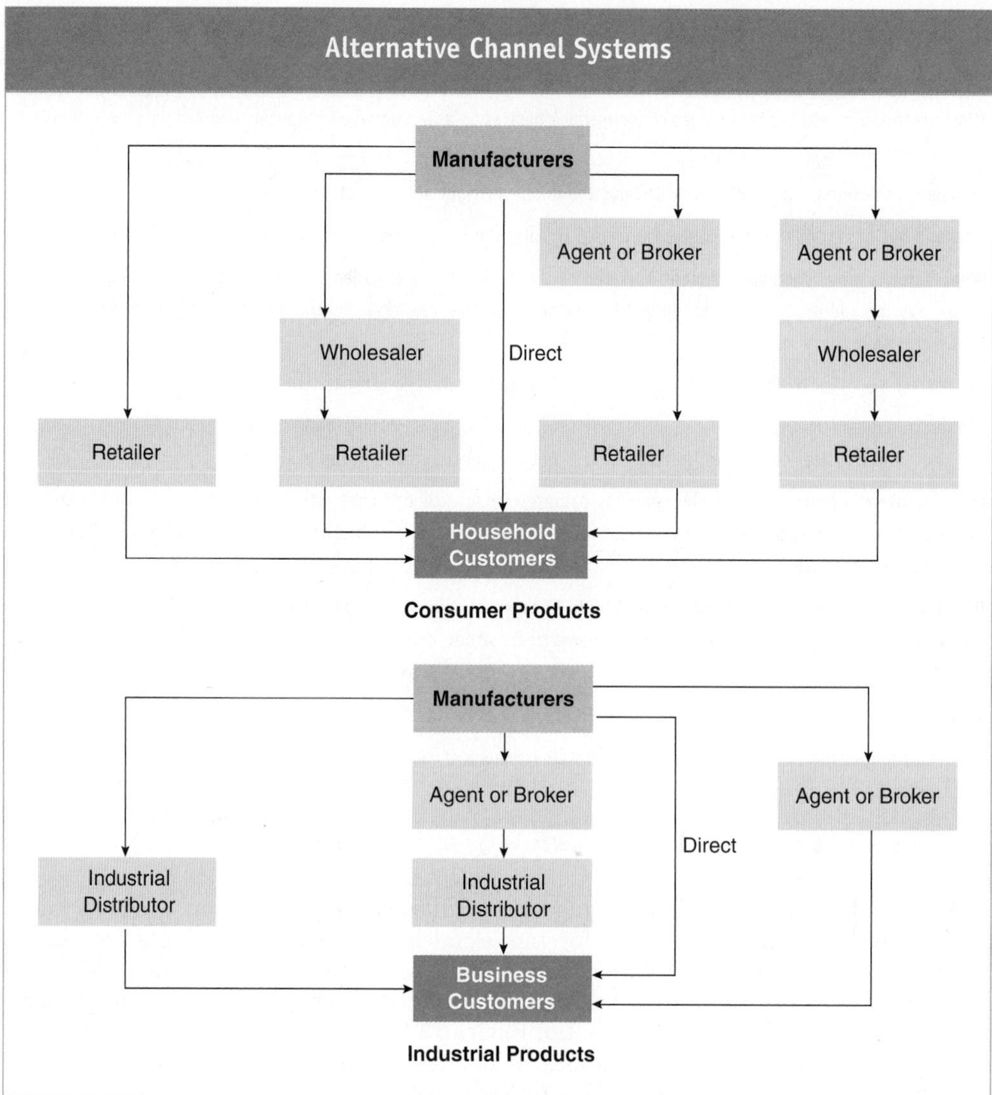

you might take advantage of access to particular market segments or other expertise. Some examples of this are:

- The Safeway supermarket and drug store chain has begun to sell Intuit's TurboTax software.
- Rental car companies like Budget and Avis are putting counters in retail store chains (Walmart and Sears, respectively).
- eBay set up a store for General Motors in 2009 for the company to attempt to sell cars through its enormously popular eBay Motors.

Thus, Safeway, Walmart, Sears, and eBay added products and profit that they would not otherwise have, by using their existing capacity.

Channel Dynamics

Another common myth about channel systems is that once they are designed, the basic structure does not change (of course, individual retailers or wholesalers may). This is simply not true. Channel structures must adapt to changes in the environment. In addition, innovation in distribution can create new marketing opportunities. Microsoft, highlighted at the beginning of this chapter, is a good example of how channels of distribution can change over time, with its addition of retail stores to its set of distributors.

Figure 12.3

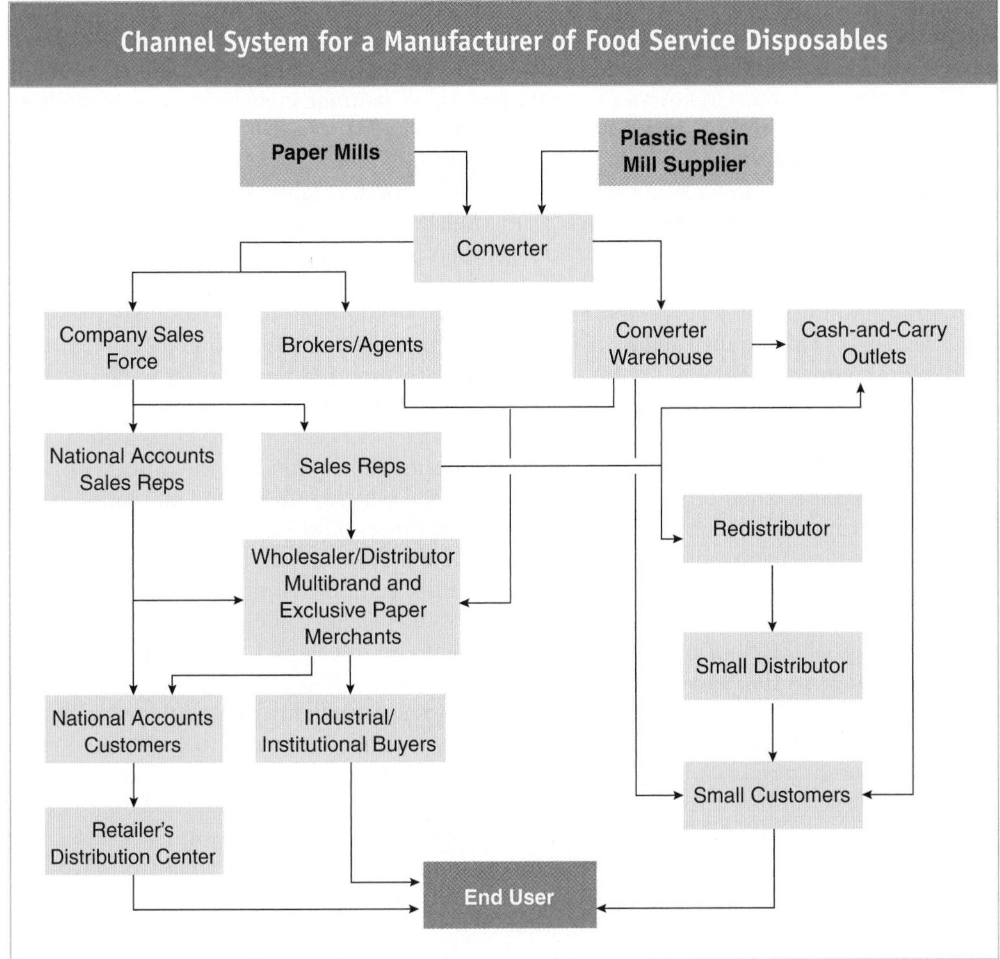

Source: Center for Research and Education in Wholesaling, University of North Florida, 1994.

The online retailer Amazon.com took the reverse path when it launched a hard-copy catalogue. A number of franchisors such as QuickSellIt and OrbitDrop have set up consignment stores for eBay, by extending the company's reach into bricks-and-mortar channels.

Some changes in distribution channels represent structural changes to the industry in question. The personal computer industry is a good example. Traditionally, mainframe and minicomputers have been sold through direct sales forces. These channels were used during the early days of the personal computer industry (the 1970s). However, new distribution channels also developed. Computer retailers became widespread, dominated by companies such as ComputerLand and Businessland. These retailers targeted both households and small businesses, sold hardware as well as software, and gave service and instruction to novice users.

Big box retailers like this Best Buy have grown significantly.
Source: B. O'Kane/Alamy Images

A critical change in the market occurred in the mid-1980s: customer knowledge about PCs grew as the microprocessor and the operating system was standardized, and increased numbers of competitors made price and availability the most highly valued product attributes. The change in the market resulted in three major changes in distribution channels. First, a new channel developed, consisting of mass resellers. These companies purchase large quantities of PCs at a discount and resell them to large corporate purchasers. Second, the Internet has become a very large and important channel for some manufacturers. For example, Dell Computer expanded its highly-successful direct business model using the Internet. All of the other major PC competitors, including Hewlett-Packard, Acer, and Lenovo, also sell large quantities on the Web. Third, PCs have moved so mainstream that dedicated computer stores such as CompUSA have gone out of business and the largest retailers are more general consumer electronics stores such as Best Buy and office supply stores such as Office Depot.

Why has this happened? Although a number of factors underlie the changes in channels in this example, the key reason is that customers' buying habits have changed. In particular, as the products sold through a channel structure mature, customer knowledge of product variants, attributes, and technology also increases. Many computer buyers are now on their second, third, or fourth PC—or more. As customer knowledge increases, their information needs change and often decrease, so the need for personalized service also decreases. This change leads to an increase in sales through outlets (the Web, discount stores, superstores) that do not provide such information but do offer wide product lines and low prices. In sum, channels must evolve as the customers evolve.

An additional change, of course, is due to technology. As every reader knows, the boom period for the Internet from the Netscape initial public offering (IPO) in the middle of 1995 to the crash of early 2000 brought dramatic and permanent changes to the marketing landscape (not to mention some individuals' and venture capitalists' financial conditions). From a marketing perspective, the major uses of the Internet are as a communications medium, including advertising, promotion, and information dissemination (Chapters 10 and 11); as a vehicle for community building (Chapter 14); and, of course, for e-commerce or as a channel of distribution. In particular, as we noted in Chapter 10, the Internet facilitated the change in the tradeoff between message richness and reach by allowing a company to have the richness of a personal sales message sent to many potential customers.

A considerable amount of B-to-C (business-to-consumer) and B-to-B (business-to-business) commerce is conducted on the Web. Online retail sales in the United States were about $134 billion in 2009 or about 3.6 percent of all U.S. retail sales.[5] Much of this total is from four categories: travel, media (books, CDs), electronics, and apparel, but cosmetics, jewelry, and flowers are growing rapidly. E-commerce sales in 2010 are expected to be about $150 billion in the Asia-Pacific countries of Australia, China, India, Japan, and South Korea.[6] The B-to-B market is also strong. W.W. Grainger, one of the top B-to-B distributors of machine maintenance, repair, and operating supplies, had $1.5 billion in sales through its Web site, www.grainger.com, in 2008.[7] More will be said on this topic later in this chapter. As a result, the Internet today is considered by marketing managers to be one of the standard channel options.

Differential advantage can also be obtained through channel structure decisions that deviate from conventional wisdom. Direct-distribution consumer packaged-goods companies such as Avon in cosmetics and Amway in household cleaning products chose to avoid the conventional retail channels—supermarkets and drugstores—used by their competitors. Almost any economic analysis would show how expensive it is to sell detergents door-to-door. However, these companies found that some segments of the population enjoy their personal approach to selling these low-priced products, and they have created very large niches for themselves throughout the world.[8] In the United Kingdom, the Korean company Daewoo Group eschews traditional car dealerships and instead sells from a chain of automotive accessory stores, called Halfords. The company salespeople are in booths inside the stores and cars for test driving are in the stores' lots. Halfords handles service. This arrangement permitted Daewoo to instantly build a retail network with more than 120 outlets. Dreyer's Grand Ice Cream's differential advantage in its industry is its distribution system. It is so efficient that the company derives one-third of its revenues from competitors such as Häagen-Dazs, Ben & Jerry's, and others that use Dreyer's as a wholesaler.[9]

Application Online Groceries

The size of the retail grocery business and the growth of the Internet naturally led companies to view the latter as a new distribution channel.[10] By 2001, online grocery services such as Webvan, Peapod, Streamline, and Homegrocer were suffering huge losses, merging to stay alive, or going bankrupt. The highest-profile failure was, of course, Webvan, which went through more than $1 billion before shutting down in July 2001. While the prevailing model in the United States is to either form a joint venture (Peapod and Stop & Shop) or for the supermarket chain to go it alone (Safeway, Albertson's), given the explosion of the Internet, there are many options today for ordering food online (e.g., see http://mashable.com/2008/06/05/online-grocery-shopping/), including the very successful New York-area company FreshDirect.

There is, however, a major exception. The most successful home grocery venture can be found in the United Kingdom. Britain's largest grocer, Tesco PLC, is profitable and expanding to other international markets. Unlike Webvan, which had its own very expensive distribution system, Tesco started its online business in the mid-1990s with a simple model that relied on its own stores. Because the company did not need to build new warehouses and distribution centers, the initial investment was a modest $56 million. When a customer placed an online order through Tesco.com, the order was forwarded to the store nearest the customer's home. A store employee called a "picker" gathered the items into special trolleys equipped with a computer that guided the trolley through the store to the location of each item ordered. Trolleys could handle up to six orders. Once the order was filled, it was stored in an area behind the store and then loaded on to a van for delivery in two-hour time slots. The company charged £5 per order.

The results have been impressive. In the first six months of 2009, Tesco.com had sales of more than £1 billion and served more than 1 million customers while expanding into e-diets, personal loans, music downloads, and clothing. Interestingly, Tesco reports that one-third of its online shoppers had never set foot in one of the physical stores. Thus, much of the business is incremental, not just cannibalizing existing sales. The total online business in the United States is around $3.5 billion and growing.

Application | Movie Rentals

The movie rental industry changed channels in 1998 with the birth of Netflix.[11] Netflix took advantage of the the new video technology, DVDs, which were just beginning to replace VHS tapes. The company developed its patented ingenious delivery system, which is tailor-made for the U.S. Postal Service. By making it simple for customers to obtain the DVDs they want through the Web-based queuing system and the self-contained postage-paid return envelope, the company has grown to more than 10 million subscribers and has seriously crippled the bricks-and-mortar industry leader, Blockbuster. In 2007, Netflix changed the industry's distribution model again by permitting customers to stream videos to their PCs from the company's Web site. More than 20 percent of the company's customers use that feature of the Web site.

However, today, Netflix is facing its own serious threat from a company named redbox. Founded as a division of McDonald's in 2002, redbox delivers DVDs to customers through its distinctive red (no surprise) kiosks located in supermarkets. Now owned by Coinstar, the company has 15,000 kiosks with plans to grow that to 20,000 by 2010. The kiosks offer fairly limited choice, typically 150 to 200 DVDs, but at a very low price, $1 per night. While the idea seems fairly low-tech, it is quite the opposite. Each machine is connected to the Internet, which permits customers to browse its Web site, redbox.com, to reserve a movie and pick it up later (customers can also rent one on the spot). Each machine has a sophisticated inventory management system that determines how many copies of a movie to carry based on the rentals of similar previous films. The kiosks send the inventory orders to redbox, which then sends representatives out to stock the machines. Revenues for the first six months of 2009 were $344 million, and Coinstar claims that redbox accounts for 13 percent of the movie rental market.

Like the grocery and many other businesses, the movie rental business is dynamic and will certainly change again at some point in the future.

Channel Functions

Channel members provide a wide variety of functions and services for a firm. Although not every member of the system performs each service, the decision about what channel structure to use is based on a matching of company and customer needs, who can satisfy them best, and how much the firm is willing to pay for them.

Marketing Research

Because channel members often have direct contact with customers, it is an ideal situation for collecting information about customer and competitor behavior. Salespeople can include such information on their call report forms. Market research surveys can be distributed at retail outlets. Telemarketing representatives can not only book orders but ask additional questions such as, "Where did you first hear about us?"

Communications

An important role of the channels is to communicate information about the product or service to customers. In supermarkets, for example, end-of-aisle displays can be used to feature a brand. Sales literature and product brochures are distributed through wholesalers and retailers. In some cases, the channel may develop independent marketing programs. For example, a local hardware store may run a print ad in a newspaper featuring a particular manufacturer's lawnmower. In this case, the store would be partially or fully reimbursed for the cost of the ad through cooperative (co-op) advertising.

Contact

Some channel members seek out and interact with customers. Independent agents and wholesalers develop retail accounts for products.

Matching/Customizing

A valuable service provided by the channels is matching or attempting to tailor the product to a customer's needs. For example, automobile dealers try to match customers' desires for particular colors and option packages. Wholesalers try to deliver products to customers in lot sizes that match their needs.

Negotiation

In many cases, the channels also negotiate the final price. This is obviously true for the automobile dealers, although many dealers are moving to a one-price, no-negotiation system. An important job of a salesperson is to work with the customer and his or her superiors on the transaction price.

Physical Distribution

For physical products, channels also provide basic logistical services. For example, Unilever distributes its products through wholesalers, whose job is to supply the supermarket regional warehouses (for large chains, Unilever may ship directly to the warehouses). Ultimately, the products have to get to the supermarkets.

Financing

For durable goods such as TVs and video cameras, an advantage of using a retail system is that the burden of financing falls on the retailers rather than the manufacturers. Thus, Philips, Sony, Matsushita, and other manufacturers do not have to be concerned about how customers pay for their products. Wholesalers may establish credit programs, leasing schedules, or other means of customer financing.

Risk Taking

When the distribution system is characterized by the channel members purchasing and therefore taking title to the products, risk is shifted from the manufacturer to the channel members. This is why both push and pull programs are important. Pull programs such as customer-focused communications help to reduce channel risk. In fact, distributors usually require them before agreeing to carry the product.

Service

Channels can also provide repair service, answer customers' questions about how to use the product, and provide warranty support. Often this service supplements a company's own service operation. For example, Sony has regional service centers throughout the world. However, consumer electronics retailers also service Sony products to make it more convenient for customers and to reach geographic areas that the service centers do not.

Relationship Management

As we noted earlier, the channel is often an extension of the firm, the organization the customer sees when gaining access to the product or service. Thus, the channel member can enhance (or harm) the quality of the relationship between the selling firm and the customer. For example, a retailer can enable a customer to sign up for a loyalty program.

Product Assembly

For some products, the channel may actually be part of the manufacturing process, performing assembly or other "finishing" parts of the process. For example, when IBM was in the personal computer business, it signed a deal with its largest distributor, Inacom. Inacom had traditionally shipped finished IBM PCs to large corporate customers. However, a wholesaler who wanted to answer every customer need would have to stock 2,200 combinations of components and features. Inacom built a new $20-million plant to make PCs from IBM-supplied parts. This cut down total system time (from order to delivery) from two days to four hours and reduced the overall costs by 10 percent.[12]

Framework for Choosing among Channels

A matrix like that shown in Table 12.2 can be used to help determine which alternatives are most attractive at a given time. For example, you can assign a set of weights to the importance of the different functions provided. You then rate each channel option on, say, a 1 to 7 scale, evaluating the ability of the option to provide the function. By multiplying the importance weight of the function by the channel evaluation and adding across all the functions, you can give each channel a score. Although you should not rely solely on a mechanical scoring procedure for making important decisions such as which channels to use, the process of assigning the importance weights and assessing how the different channel options perform the functions shown in Table 12.2 is very useful.

Table 12.2 can also be used to assess the characteristics of a current channel structure. By putting your current channel members across the top of the table and then indicating which channels are doing a good job of performing the functions, you obtain a nice picture of whether the system is performing all the essential services for your product.

Table 12.2

Channel Function Analysis

	Channel			Internal	
	Representative	Wholesaler	Retailer	Sales Force	Direct: Phone, Mail, Internet
Marketing research					
Communications					
Contact					
Matching/customizing					
Negotiation					
Physical distribution					
Financing					
Risk taking					
Service					
Relationship management					
Product assembly					
Overall attractiveness					

Factors Affecting the Channel System

The channel functions noted above impact the channel system as the marketing manager should choose those channels that perform the functions in a superior way compared to competitors as well as satisfy their customers' needs. In addition, your marketing strategy and resources impact the design of the channel system. These factors are summarized in this section.

Customer Behavior

A careful analysis of customer behavior, as described in Chapters 4 and 5, leads to a better understanding of what kind of channel structure is necessary to satisfy the different segments. One question of the customer analysis, "Where do they buy?", helps in understanding current purchasing patterns. However, this does not necessarily help you redesign the channel structure because it does not indicate whether customers are satisfied with current access to your products and whether it could be improved. Electrolux, the Swedish manufacturer of vacuum cleaners, has discovered that people have become more reluctant to buy products from door-to-door salespeople. As a result, the company has introduced specialty retail stores in shopping malls. As we noted earlier in this chapter, channels must be designed with the customer in mind. Thus, understanding the other customer analysis questions (*who, why, how,* and *when*) are vital inputs to the channel structure decision.

A good example of the need to structure channels around customer needs is Coors' and Kirin's distribution systems, designed around customers' perceived need for fresh beer. By starting with a key consumer need, the two companies built their logistics to satisfy that need by relocating plants, using refrigerated delivery trucks, and working with retailers to ensure that the beer remained refrigerated and fresh.

Table 12.3 shows an analysis of primary consumer wants and needs that drove Saturn's original distribution system design (before General Motors divested the division). It is clear from the eventual design of the system that the middle section of the table, "Buying Wants and Needs," had a significant impact. Consumers surveyed wanted a fair price, a fair negotiation process, convenience, honest and courteous treatment, and inventory availability. A key shopping want or need was lack of pressure and a non-threatening environment. Thus, Saturn's No Hassle/No Haggle policy and well-known low-pressure environment fit the needs well.

The rapid growth of automated teller machines (ATMs) reflects a shift in distribution channels by banks, to account for changes in customer behavior. The increased convenience of ATMs took advantage of an increase in the number of dual-career couples and increased technological awareness of the populations around the world, along with an increase in the value of the time that had previously been spent queuing in the banks.

A channel system can also be augmented to reflect the desire to reach a new customer segment. For example, Dell Computer's traditional customers have been businesses that are either reached through the company's direct sales force or that buy through the company's Web site. However, Dell decided that it wanted to make a bigger push to reach the home PC market. As a result, the company has begun selling its PCs on the home-shopping channel QVC as well as in retailers such as Walmart. Who watches QVC? The company claims a broad and varied audience that is interested in jewelry, clothing, and sports memorabilia. Dell is not alone in using home-shopping networks as a channel. The Home Shopping Network (HSN) lists Hewlett-Packard, Acer, Toshiba, and Lenovo among its partners.

Competitors

As we noted earlier in this chapter, a key reason for picking a particular channel system is to differentiate your product or service from the competition. In this sense, the product includes service, packaging, and the place of purchase. Therefore, even though Amway's floor cleaner may not be any better than Procter & Gamble's, the personal selling approach adds a dimension to the product that differentiates it from those purchased in retail outlets.

In other words, in choosing the channel structure it is important to include the competitor's channels in the competitor analysis. These channels are part of the competitor's marketing strategy. The key decision you have to make is whether to emulate it (because that is what customers expect) or try something new and different. If the segment of

Table 12.3

Consumer Wants and Needs Driving the Saturn Distribution System

Shopping wants and needs
- High-quality information
  - Comprehensive, including competitors
  - Accurate, credible, objective
  - Current
  - Easy to understand and compare
- Comfortable, convenient access to information
  - Low pressure, nonthreatening
- Evaluation assistance

Buying wants and needs
- Fair price
- Fair negotiation process
  - Free of pressure
  - Easy to understand, all costs clear
  - Free of deception, dishonesty
- Convenience
- Honest, courteous treatment
- Inventory availability

Service wants and needs
- Quality of work
  - Do right the first time
  - Use high-quality parts
  - Guarantee quality of work
- Convenience
- Timeliness
- Honest, courteous treatment
- Diagnose and recommend needed repairs accurately and honestly
- Fair price

Source: Presentation at Northwestern University by Saturn executives in May 1992.

customers who want the "new and different" channel is too small, then it would be difficult to be profitable by changing your channels in that direction. The only way Calyx & Corolla can be successful selling flowers by mail order is if the convenience segment is large enough. Otherwise, the traditional system of flower distribution and retailing will prevail.

Competitive distribution structures can differ in the same market. In electronics distribution, the two major competitors are Hamilton-Avnet and Arrow. Hamilton believes that customers want local delivery, so it has inventory at more than 50 locations throughout the United States. Arrow takes a different path: it has a few central locations but promises to ship overnight.

The Marketing Strategy

Clearly, as a result of the customer and competitor analysis (and the environmental scan), the marketing strategy developed has a large impact on the channel structure. As we noted in Chapter 2, the value chain can be used to determine various bases for differential advantage:

- Inbound logistics.
- Operations.
- Outbound logistics.
- Marketing and sales.
- Service.

Each of these factors has implications for the channel structure. If you are the marketing manager for Steinway and you differentiate on the materials you use to make the pianos (inbound logistics), you have a high price and a few, exclusive distributors. FedEx differentiated itself by having the most efficient operation in the package delivery industry. Its distribution setup included using its own planes, so that every package stayed in its own system. Walmart sustains low prices by having the most efficient system for providing stock information to its warehouses and replenishing supply (operations and outbound logistics). Companies such as Amway, Tupperware, and Mary Kay Cosmetics differentiate on the basis of door-to-door as opposed to retail sales (outbound logistics, marketing). Lexus differentiates itself from other luxury car brands by its slavish devotion to high levels of customer service, which is manifested by the investment it makes in its retailers' facilities and parts distribution.

Although flexible and dynamic, channel systems cannot be as easily changed as a marketing strategy. Thus, the key to linking the marketing strategy to the distribution channels is through the value proposition, that is, the core or basic way you intend to differentiate your product from the competition. Normally, the value proposition does not change as often as implementation or marketing-mix issues do.

Resources

It is obviously critical for products to have distribution, because no one can buy something that is not available. However, particularly with new products or an existing product being launched in a new market domestically or overseas, the amount budgeted for channels may be lower initially. For example, when the Japanese copier company Savin entered the U.S. market, it used independent agents to sell its products rather than setting up its own direct sales force. Why would the company do this? Because agents are compensated only when they sell, based on a negotiated commission rate, the channel costs become variable costs rather than fixed. This method may be important when demand for the product is uncertain. If the product becomes successful, further investments are made in consolidating the market position. Thus, if resources invested in the product are insufficient to create a captive distribution system, you should look for lower-cost alternatives to give customers access to your products.

Clearly, resources are always a constraint. It makes little sense for every brand to invest in a fully company-owned system down to the retail level. IBM developed its own retail stores in the 1980s. However, the company quickly discovered that it is expensive to develop and market a retail network and that was not the company's strength. Apple, on the other hand, has made its retail stores a key point of difference compared to Windows-based machines due to the way the stores communicate the Apple "experience." As we noted at the beginning of the chapter, Microsoft is attempting to emulate Apple's success. At some point, most companies have to make a hard decision about how much of the channel system to own and how much of it should include indirect or noncompany components.

Changes in Technology

The rapid changes in information technology are adding channel options and broadening the set of channels from which a brand manager can choose. Besides the Internet discussed earlier, emerging technologies such as wireless mobile platforms through "smart" phones (Blackberrys, iPhones, and the like) are opening up new channel possibilities. The iPhone application RedLaser allows users to place the phone near a bar code on any product and then be transported to a variety of Web sites where the product can be purchased. A mobile service called Gifticon (http://www.mobileinkorea.com/tag/Gifticon) developed in South Korea permits users to send gifts via text messages. The receiver saves the text message and shows it to any store in Korea to obtain the gift. Although it has been in development for a number of years, interactive TV shopping is likely to be a reality soon. Someone watching a TV show will be able to highlight a product on the show using a remote device that will then take the consumer to a Web site where it can be purchased. These are only a couple of ways in which technology is rapidly increasing the number of ways companies can reach customers enabling purchasing.

Two channels that are becoming more widespread in use are free-standing kiosks and vending machines. New-generation kiosks are equipped with sophisticated technology that is faster; more reliable; and easier to maintain, administer, and upgrade. Some examples of their uses include the following:

- BestBuy has installed kiosks in a number of U.S. airports. Products include media players, unlocked cell phones, digital cameras, portable gaming devices, many varieties of chargers, flash drives and other storage, cell phone and computer accessories, headphones (important!), and Best Buy gift cards.
- Discovery Channel Stores have kiosks that allow customers to view more than 700 videos and access additional inventory of specialty gifts offered at DiscoveryStore.com.
- In the past, Kmart had in-store kiosks hooked into BlueLight.com, Kmart's e-tail Web site. Customers could order products and specify delivery from the site. The company found that 20 percent of the shoppers at BlueLight.com came from inside Kmart stores.

While there is some potential for cannibalization of sales in these latter two examples, the kiosks introduce customers to the Web sites and offer the possibility of greater sales from a combination of the retail and Web channels. Even the good old-fashioned vending machine is being used to sell some unusual products. While these machines have sold a wide variety of beverages and food items in Japan for many years (including lobsters!), it is possible to buy iPods and even Reebok sneakers now.

Channel Options

Direct and Indirect Channels

There are two broad categories of channels: **direct** and **indirect** channels. A direct channel is one where the product or service remains under the control of the company from production to customer. A company may have independent parties participate in direct channels; for example, you may outsource telemarketing activities. However, these parties are usually transparent to the customer, who perceives that it is the company marketing the product that makes the contact. Indirect channels are independent parties paid by the company to distribute the product. In this case, the channel member and not the company has direct contact with the end-customer. Specific channel institutions such as retail stores, Web sites, and a sales force can be either direct or indirect, depending on whether the company or an independent entity controls it.

direct channel
is one where the product or service remains under the control of the company from production to customer

indirect channel
is an independent party paid by a company to distribute the product; in this case, the channel member and not the company has direct contact with the end organization

Returning to our example of Microsoft, the company uses both direct and indirect channels of distribution. Its own sales force is obviously a direct channel as are the new stores. The use of business partners, such as Toys 'R' Us, Walmart, Best Buy, and other consumer electronics and toy stores (for Xbox), show how indirect channels can be useful to reach customers that the direct channels cannot.

At one time, the trade-off between the two was clear. Direct channels tended to imply a sales force. The main advantage of a sales force is that it is under your control and dedicated to your company's products. You can train the salespeople to deliver a particular message to potential customers and change that message when the marketing strategy changes. The downside to the sales force is that it is expensive to train and maintain and its reach is limited by its size. Indirect channels can reach more customers and perform functions that the sales force cannot (Table 12.2). However, as we discuss later in this chapter, they are not necessarily working exclusively for you. This loss of control is important; when you are not controlling the message given to customers, you must depend on the channel to deliver one that is consistent with your strategy.

Today, the limited reach of the direct sales channel is mitigated by the widespread use of telemarketing, direct mail, and the Internet (recall the discussion in Chapter 10 about the trade-off between richness and reach). All of these methods can reach large numbers of customers efficiently. You can control the messages as well. However, some functions that may be necessary for the product or service you are trying to market cannot be performed by these three methods.

The choice between direct and indirect channels, like any other decision, ultimately rests on the relative profitability of the two methods. How much is it worth to use distributors that give customers access to your products and services? Direct appears to be better than indirect in the following cases:

- Information needs are high because of technical complexity, or for other reasons.
- Product customization is important.
- Quality assurance matters.
- Purchase orders are large.
- Transportation and storage are complex.[13]

In contrast, the following cases tend to lead to the use of indirect channels:

- One-stop shopping for many products is important.
- Availability is important.
- After-sale service is important.

Thus, the automobile, farm equipment, and similar industries have used independent distributors for many years. However, it is also the case that companies have gained differential advantages by violating some of these general guidelines.

Another factor to consider in choosing between direct and indirect channels is the level of commitment you might expect to obtain from potential intermediaries. Channel members must be motivated to sell your product when they have multiple products to sell. Even when a significant amount of pull money has been promised, there is no guarantee about the dedication you can get from indirect channel members. From your perspective, you use multiple channels to get your product or service to customers and the focus is on your company's product alone. However, from the channel member's perspective, she or he has products from multiple companies to sell and is not necessarily focused on yours (unless the channel carries noncompeting product lines).

How do you get higher commitment from an indirect channel other than through promises of money directed at the end-customer? Of course, higher profit margins are important. Giving the channel member exclusive rights to distribute or sell the product in a particular geographic area is another approach. For example, Paul Mitchell hair products were originally sold only through beauty salons, so the company knew it would not have to compete with drug stores or other retail outlets. Providing sales training programs, promotions such as cooperative advertising plans, and sales contests are other ways to gain commitment from indirect, independent channels.

Another factor in the decision between direct and indirect channels is customer loyalty. For some kinds of products, the customer builds loyalty to the channel member rather than to the company. This loyalty can pose a long-term problem if the channel member drops the product. For example, customers are often more loyal to their stockbrokers than to the brokerage firm. As a result, if the broker leaves Merrill Lynch and joins UBS, the customer will often shift his or her business along with the broker. When Microsoft's products are distributed through "third parties" such as Radio Shack (now The Shack) or Staples, the client sees and communicates with the latter, not Microsoft.

Sometimes the choice between direct and indirect channels is based on the likelihood that the channel member will compete with your product. Most channel members are in business solely to act as an intermediary between firms and customers. However, sometimes channel members become competitors. Store brands or private labels are examples of channel–manufacturer competition, and during the early 1990s they gained share at the expense of national brands. The Gap started by selling Levi's jeans and other similar leisure wear. However, it switched to selling its own brand of jeans and eventually dropped Levi Strauss as a supplier.

Finally, advances in information technology are disrupting the channel structure of many industries. Not only are more channels being added to the channel mix as we described above, but in some circumstances, channels are being bypassed. This is referred to as **disintermediation**. A classic example is Walmart, the largest retailer in the world, which used its investments in information technology to create direct links between its own warehouses and manufacturers, thereby eliminating the need for independent wholesalers in its system.

disintermediation
the process by which companies are eliminating intermediate channels of distribution through the use of information technology

Multiple-Channel Systems

Most **multiple-channel systems**, like those shown in Figures 12.2 and 12.3, use a combination of direct and indirect channels. For example, a common approach is to use direct sales for large national or international accounts and a wholesaler for smaller accounts for which direct sales are not cost-effective. Or a company may use a direct sales force to sell to intermediaries such as wholesalers. Thus, multichannel systems take advantage of the strengths of alternatives.

multiple-channel systems a channel of distribution that uses a combination of direct and indirect channels and in which the multiple channel members serve different segments

In today's marketing environment, using multiple channels or **multichannel marketing** has become a necessity, not a choice. As we have noted, different channels have the ability to reach different segments. As we noted in Chapter 10 concerning communications, segments are becoming more difficult to target due to their widely varying behavior with respect to their daily activities (i.e., Web surfing, TV watching, playing videogames, text messaging, and other mobile activities). Thus, designing channel systems with multiple channels is the norm, not the exception. In addition, companies are encouraging customers to use multiple channels. Retailers like Eddie Bauer have stores, catalogues, a Web site, and a phone number to call to encourage customers to shop in different ways (see www.EddieBauer.com). Some research has found, in fact, that multichannel customers spend 20 to 30 percent more money on average than do single-channel customers.[14]

multichannel marketing marketing using multiple channels of distribution simultaneously

The main problems with using a variety of channels are:

- Coordination and management issues become more important. A particular problem is confusion about who should receive a commission on a sale or how it should be divided when several channel members are involved. For example, a distributor may provide a lead on a sale that is then closed by a salesperson.
- Loss of control can be frustrating. The marketing manager can exert control over direct channel members but not independent ones. For example, Microsoft cannot control what its technology partners (PC manufacturers) say about the company or the expertise with which they describe the company's products.

A particular problem occurs when a customer can buy a product at several different channels for different prices. A consumer interested in buying a camera can try out various models at a local camera shop and then purchase it from a mail-order company at a lower price. Although the channels are intended to focus on different segments of the market (service-sensitive versus price-sensitive, as we showed in Chapters 4 and 5), segments are not always so distinctly separated and there is considerable overlap and movement between them.

This problem is illustrated in Figure 12.4. The problem is the area between the price-sensitive and service-sensitive customers, those who wear different hats on different

Figure 12.4

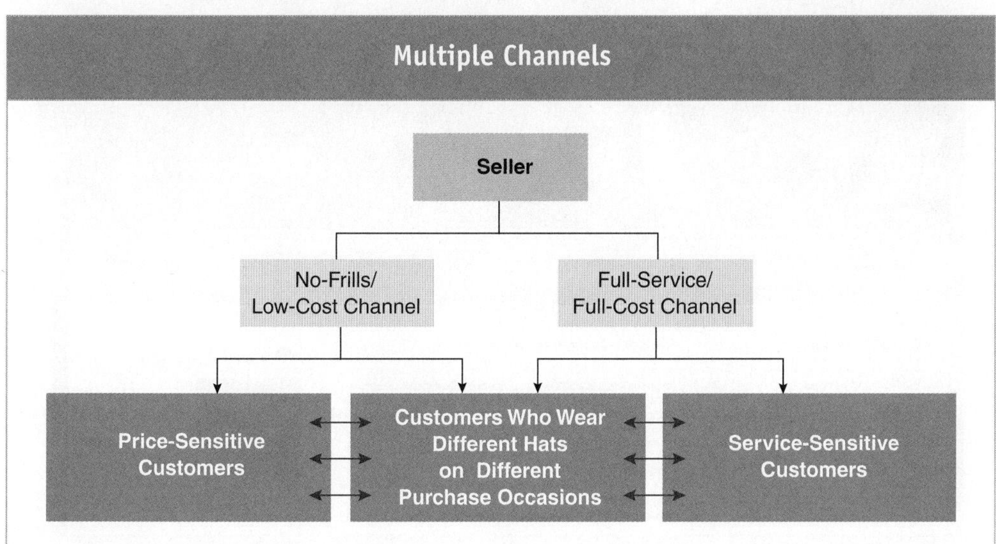

Source: V. Kasturi Rangan (1994), "Reorienting Channels of Distribution," Harvard Business School case #9-594-118, p. 7.

purchase occasions. If the local store offers sufficient service to warrant the price, the customer will still patronize it. For example, the camera store owner may service the cameras bought in his store and provide occasional tutorials on improving photos or other specialized advice that the mail-order firm does not provide.

Application Ingersoll-Rand

Ingersoll-Rand is one of the leading firms in the stationary air compressor industry and owns a number of other well-known industrial brands such as Trane (heating and air conditioning) (see Figure 12.5 for the company's Web site).[15] Compressed air has a wide range of applications, from powering tools and other machinery (plant air), powering and controlling pneumatic systems in certain types of equipment (special machinery), and supplying air for manufacturing processes (process air). The company markets three types of compressors: reciprocating, rotary screw, and centrifugal.

The company uses four different kinds of channels for marketing its products:

- **A direct sales force.** The sales force is responsible for sales to users of all centrifugal compressors, rotary compressors above 450 horsepower, and reciprocating compressors above 250 horsepower. The sales force sells directly to Ingersoll-Rand's largest customers.
- **Independent distributors.** These channel members sell reciprocating compressors below 250 horsepower and rotary compressors below 450 horsepower. These distributors sell mainly to smaller customers. The rationale is that these customers are more numerous and geographically dispersed, so it makes more economic sense to use independent distributors rather than the direct sales force.
- **Company-owned air centers.** These are similar to the independent distributors but have territories that do not overlap. Independent distributors and air centers sell identical Ingersoll-Rand products and accessories at identical prices. However, the former carry other manufacturers' lines, but the air centers carry only Ingersoll-Rand products.

Figure 12.5

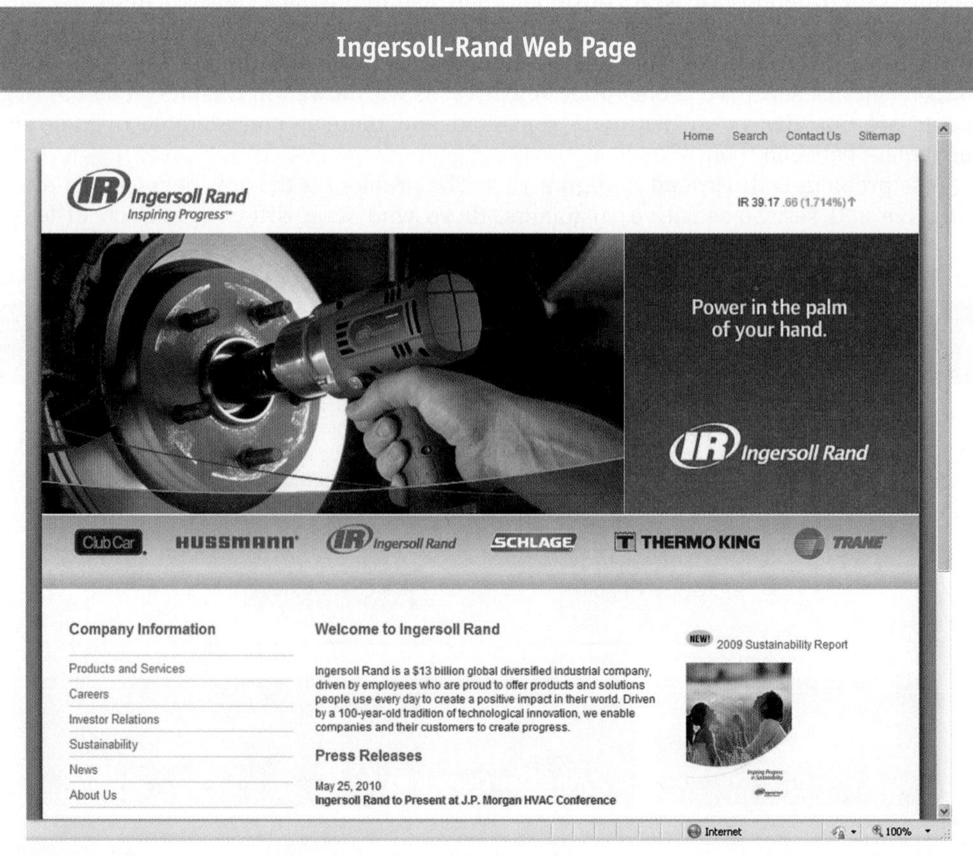

Source: Copyright Ingersoll-Rand.

- **Manufacturers' representatives.** These people are charged with selling the do-it-yourself (DIY) products, mainly reciprocating compressors less than five horsepower. These products are sold through consumer channels such as hardware stores.

Besides the economic advantages of using channels other than direct sales, the multiple-channel design is motivated by underlying differences in segment buying behavior. Large customers such as automobile companies require a great deal of technical sophistication and coordination, and their requests for price quotations contain detailed specifications that have to be met. These customers tend to require the largest machines, have longer selling cycles requiring multiple contacts, and have large buying centers (see Chapter 5), with multiple people involved in the decision process. Customers requiring smaller machines do not require as much technical assistance and have fewer people involved with the decision, but need faster delivery and parts availability that a wider dealer network can provide. Finally, customers using air compressors for filling their tires can satisfy their needs at local retailers.

Thus, this is a good example of a company selling a large product line to multiple segments. Both economics and segment needs drove the design of the channel of distribution system.

Hybrid Systems

A modification of the multiple-channel system is the **hybrid system.**[16] In a hybrid system, rather than serving different segments, the channel members perform complementary functions, often for the same customer. Some channel members may contact the customers, for example, while others perform service functions. The purpose of a hybrid system is to permit specialization and thereby improve levels of performance for the different complementary functions. Figure 12.6 shows this kind of system.

hybrid system
a modification of the multiple-channel system in which members of the channel system perform complementary functions, often for the same customer, thereby allowing for specialization and better levels of performance

As shown in this figure, the key difference between hybrid and more conventional multiple-channel systems is that hybrids are more horizontal; that is, tasks are parceled out among the channel members. In a conventional system, the tasks are often vertical: as each member of the channel gets the product, it performs some function and then gives it to the next member.

A more detailed view of a hybrid system is given in Figure 12.7. The channels vary in the tasks they perform. These tasks include generating the lead, qualifying sales leads, presale marketing, closing the sale, postsale service, and account management (maintaining relations with an existing account). The various methods and channels that can be used to accomplish these tasks are listed down the side of the figure. In this example, direct mail is used to generate leads; telemarketing to qualify leads, for both presale activity and postsale service; and direct sales to close the deal and manage the account once the sale is made. The grid can also be useful for identifying points of overlap and conflict in a channel system.

Figure 12.7 omits the Internet from the channel mix. Companies use their Web sites to complement their other channels in a number of ways, such as customer service, providing timely new product information, and so on. Some companies use the Web site to enhance the customer experience in ways that the off-line presence cannot.

Figure 12.6

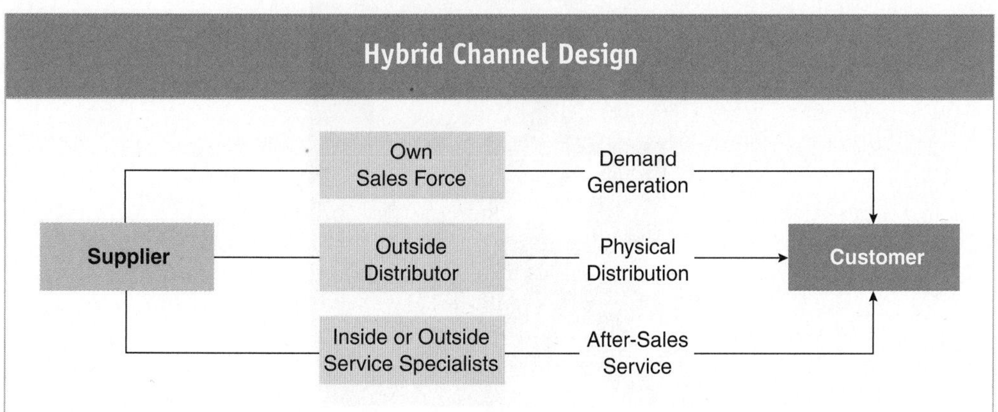

Source: V. Kasturi Rangan (1994), "Reorienting Channels of Distribution," Harvard Business School case #9-594-118. Copyright © 1994 by the President and Fellows of Harvard College. Reprinted by permission.

Figure 12.7

Example of a Hybrid Channel System

Marketing channels and methods — Vendor → Customer

	Demand-Generation Tasks					
	Lead Generation	Qualifying Sales	Presales	Close of Sale	Postsale Service	Account Management
National account management						
Direct sales						
Telemarketing						
Direct mail						
Retail stores						
Distributors						
Dealers and value-added resellers						

Source: Rowland Moriarty and Ursula Moran (1990), "The Hybrid Grid: The Elements of a Hybrid Marketing System," *Harvard Business Review*, November–December. Copyright © 1990 by the President and Fellows of Harvard College. Reprinted by permission.

Application JCPenney

The retailer JCPenney has three main channels of distribution: stores, catalogues, and the Internet. Until recently, the three channels had been run independently without concern for how the three can create important synergies for customers.

Within the last few years, however, management decided to treat the distribution system as one unified channel. This is a different perspective and resulted in several innovations. First, the company developed an innovative service called "Know Before You Go," which permitted customers to check the company's inventory of a particular product on the Web site before they went to a local store. Second, the company developed a service called

Figure 12.8

JCPenney In-Store Kiosk

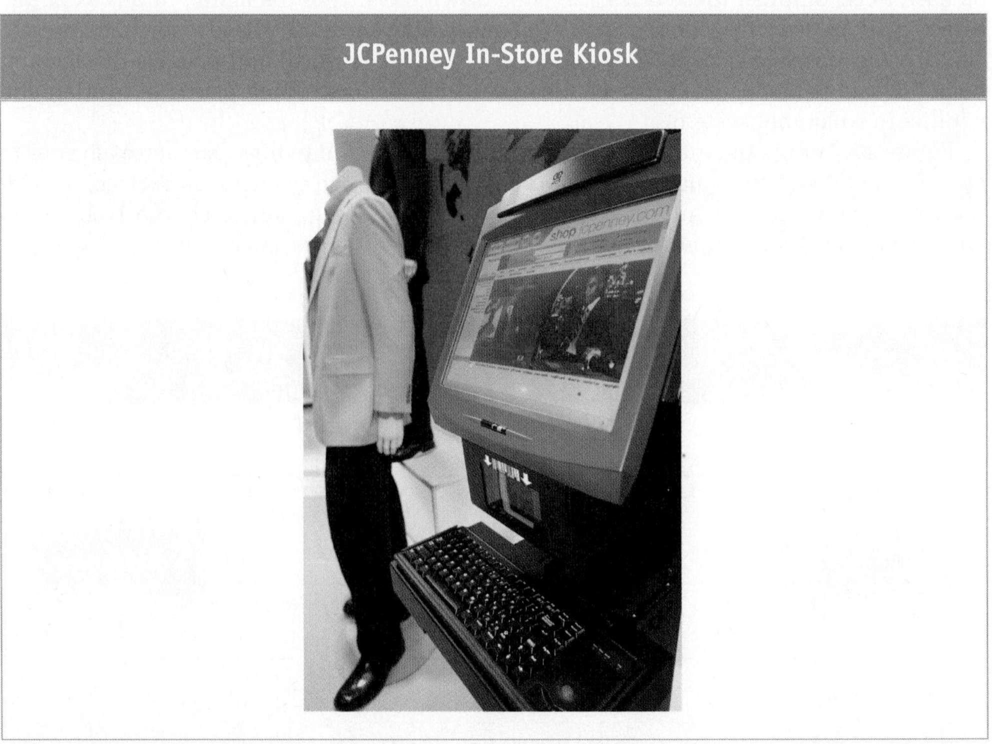

Source: UPI Photo/Monika Graff/Newscom

"Dorm Life" targeting the parents of college students. With this service, parents could order furniture, lamps, and so forth from the JCPenney Web site or catalogue and request availability at a store near the college the student is attending for local pick up. Third, the company expanded its use of instore kiosks where customers could virtually "browse" the entire store (see Figure 12.8). Thus, JCPenney has significantly improved the coordination between its channels to upgrade its customers' experiences and benefits.

Channel Power and Management

In this chapter, we have described a variety of channel arrangements the manager can use to structure a system. However, for every channel system, a different set of problems will be encountered in managing the system and maximizing profits, market share, or whatever objective you have set.

Channel Power

Because of the many goals that exist within channels and because few marketing managers consider channel members as customers, members of a channel system are unlikely to coordinate their activities spontaneously; it usually takes a crisis to bring solutions to channel conflicts. It takes **channel power** to coordinate activities in a system:

> *Power is the ability of one channel member to get another channel member to do what it otherwise would not have done.*[17]

channel power
the ability of one channel member to get another channel member to do what it otherwise would not have done

What factors are in control of who has the power in a channel relationship? Channel members are likely to have significant bargaining power over the marketing manager in the following cases:

- The channel's sales volume is large relative to the product's total sales volume. In this case, channel members with high sales volumes are going to be more effective in extracting terms such as delivery and push promotions.
- The product is not well differentiated from competitors. If the product is perceived to be a commodity by customers, then channel members can play your product against others; that is, they can appear to be (or actually be) indifferent to keeping your brand on the shelf.
- The channel has low switching costs (i.e., it is easy to find an alternative to replace your product).
- The channel poses a credible threat of backward integration or competition with you. A good example is the increase in private labels sold by supermarkets in the United States and Europe. This is one reason supermarkets have increased their power in their relationships with manufacturers.
- The channel has better information than you about market conditions. This can happen when channels are good at collecting market information and using it to their advantage.

This latter point has become very important in channel relationships, particularly with the significant inroads that information technology has made in many industries. This has led to the problem of disintermediation facing many distributors, particularly "middlemen," the wholesalers and distributors "between" the manufacturer and the retailer. Other examples exist besides Walmart (mentioned earlier). If you break the windshield of your car, your insurance company will probably ask you to dial the toll-free phone number of a national network of auto glass installers. The local glass companies that are not connected are bypassed in this application of information technology. Travel, health, music, and many other industries have been dramatically affected by a shift in power between elements of the distribution system as computers and communication networks change long-standing supplier–buyer relationships. The effects have been the elimination of intermediaries, the collapse or shortening of inefficient supply chains, and allowing customers and companies to be linked directly.

Retail marketing in the United States has changed dramatically as Walmart's strategy has spawned a large number of "category killers" or "big box" retailers. These retailers sell products in a particular product category at a discount in huge stores. Examples are Home

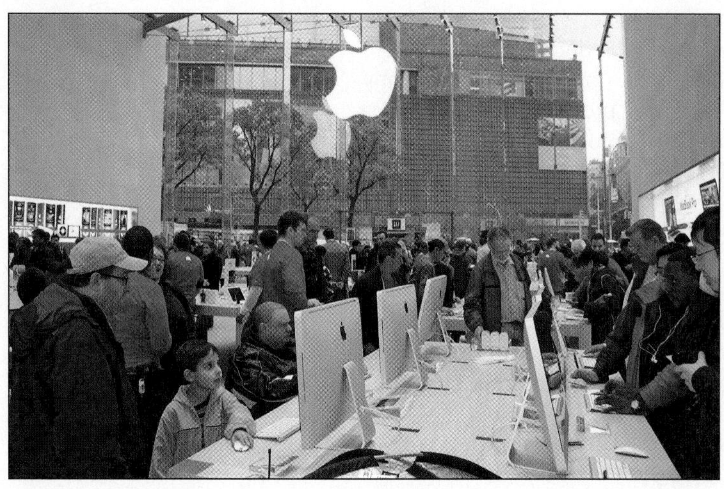

Apple has been very successful with its own retail stores.
Source: Charles Eshelman/Getty Images, Inc-Liaison

Depot (hardware), Toys 'R' Us, Office Depot (office equipment), Best Buy (consumer electronics), PetSmart (pet products and services), and CarMax (used cars). They all rely on information-intensive operations to keep costs down and ensure the lowest prices. They also deal directly with the companies that make the products, to eliminate the intermediaries. Obviously, the category killers pose a significant threat to smaller retailers. Category killers have been so successful in changing the landscape of retailing that in some parts of the country, local retailers have enlisted the help of politicians to keep them out. The largest problem facing these mega-retailers is how to keep from competing against themselves.

On occasion, channel power is manifested in obvious hardball tactics. Dentsply International has more than 70 percent of the market for false teeth. The company demands that distributors give it exclusive coverage and do not sell any competitors' products. If a distributor violates this rule, it can be dropped by the company. The Justice Department claims that this is illegal and has filed suit under antitrust law.[18]

Channel Management

Channels need to be actively managed by the marketing manager. An important problem that can arise without sufficient attention is channel conflict, that is, situations where multiple channel systems (e.g., retailers and a company Web site) are selling your product or service. It is crucial to recognize when such problems can arise and how to resolve them.

Channel Conflict

Managing a channel system usually involves resolving conflicts in which one member of the system believes that another member is impeding its ability to achieve its goals. Such conflict is characterized by the different levels of intensity, frequency, and importance of the disputes that arise. Figure 12.9 illustrates these levels of conflict and divides them into three increasingly fractious intensities.

The four major sources of conflict are:[19]

1. **Goal divergence.** Clearly, your objective and the objectives of channel members can differ. You may be rewarded on the basis of worldwide market share, but the local retailer stocking your product wants to make enough money to send her kids to college and retire comfortably. Often, the sales force is rewarded on a commission basis. It wants to sell quantity and is willing to be flexible on price, whereas your strategy is high quality, high price.
2. **Domain dissensus.** Conflict can arise when the perception of who owns a particular domain differs between channel participants. The domains can be:
   - The population to be served.
   - The territory to be covered.
   - The functions or duties to be performed.
   - The technology to be employed in marketing (e.g., who is responsible for attaching coupons to packages?).
3. **Differing perceptions of reality.** This is a basic human frailty; one side believes it has been wronged and the other believes it has acted in good faith. For example, a retailer may not think that the manufacturer's support in terms of cooperative advertising and training is sufficient while the manufacturer believes that it is offering the same level to that retailer as to others that have been successful.
4. **Misuse of power.** Supermarkets that have gained power now charge fees for stocking products, called slotting allowances. This is a nuisance for large companies, but an even larger problem for small ones trying to break into that channel. In Florida, Disney does not allow tour operators who work with rival Universal to distribute tickets to Disney World.

Figure 12.9

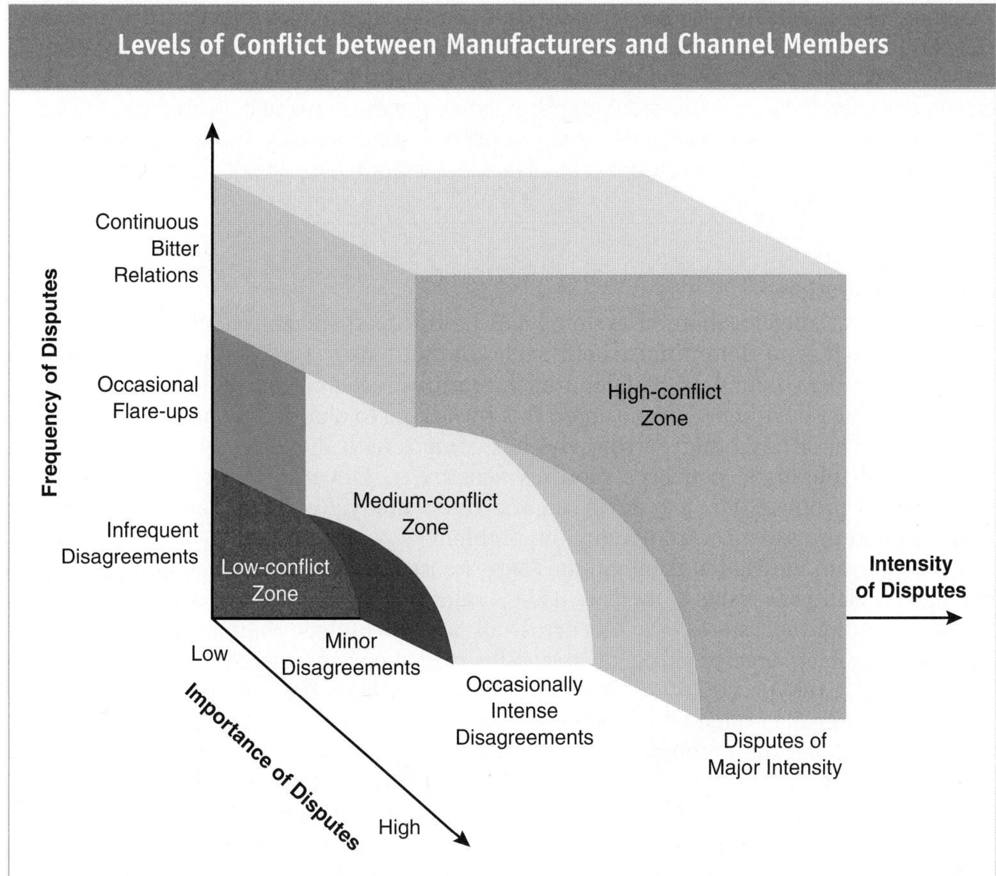

Source: Allen J. Magrath and Kenneth G. Hardy (1988), "A Strategic Framework for Diagnosing Manufacturer—Reseller Conflict," Marketing Science Institute report no. 88-101 (Cambridge, MA: Marketing Science Institute), p. 3.

As noted earlier in this chapter, the domain issue is particularly a problem with multiple channels. The camera retailer is upset that customers can come into his store, try the camera, obtain advice, and purchase the same model at a discount electronics store or by mail order. The retailer feels that the manufacturer is not protecting him. Similarly, Hallmark traditionally distributed its cards through specialty card shops. However, because it has lost market share to competition at discount stores, supermarkets, and drug stores, the company decided in late 1996 to sell Hallmark-branded cards to mass merchandisers such as Walmart, Kmart, and Kroger. This angered many owners of the card shops, who formerly had the exclusive right to sell Hallmark cards and other merchandise. Several years ago, Avon decided to sell its makeup and creams through Sears and JCPenney. The decision obviously made its 500,000 sales reps nervous.

The rise of the Web as a channel has only exacerbated channel conflict as many companies have decided to sell their products on the Web in potential conflict with their channel members. Apple Computer has been notorious for creating channel conflict. Not only does it sell its computers at its Web site; but, as noted at the beginning of the chapter, in 2001 the company decided to open some Apple retail stores. Many companies, however, avoid such conflict either by referring Web site visitors to retail locations or by using the Web to offer increased levels of dealer support.

Application | Goodyear Tires

In 2000, when Firestone recalled 6.5 million tires that were linked to SUV accidents, Goodyear found it relatively easy to convert many Firestone retail dealers to its brand.[20] However, many of these converted dealers switched back to Firestone within one to two years or are pushing other brands. The dealers found Goodyear difficult to deal with and were unimpressed with the quality of its tires.

Importantly, Goodyear also started selling its tires through major retailers such as Sears, Walmart, and Sam's Club. These retailers often undercut the dealers in terms of price. While other tire manufacturers have done the same thing, Goodyear's "fill rate" (the ratio of the number of tires delivered to the number ordered) has been as low as 50 percent. In addition, the larger retailers were getting bulk discounts, which resulted in some smaller dealers paying more for their tires than what Sears was charging at retail. Clearly, Goodyear did not manage this channel conflict situation very well.

Conflict Resolution

The conflict arising in channel systems can be resolved in many different ways. The basic approach is to determine where such conflict exists, then try to understand the channel members' concerns. This approach requires research on the channels (remember that they are customers). You can do this by talking to channel managers, employees, the sales force, or any other person who has contact with the channels. Understanding the channel members' concerns requires sensitivity. Once you know the locus and source of the problem, you can devise an effective remedy. Even then, however, you may make limited progress toward solving the problem.

Let's return to the Hallmark situation. There are two sources of conflict. The first is goal divergence. Hallmark wants to increase its U.S. sales and profits; the card shop owners want the same, but for their stores only, not across all possible outlets. Hallmark's original "solution" to its problem created conflict between the card shops and discounters. The company then devised a two-part solution. The first part was to launch a new product line called Expressions from Hallmark, which is priced lower and sold only in the discount stores. The card shops still get the premium Hallmark brand. The second part of the solution was to launch an expensive advertising campaign promoting its Gold Crown retail stores.

The first part of the solution—demarcating products and product variants or brands by channels—is a common one. Such a strategy makes it more difficult for the camera shopper to use the camera specialist only for information. For example, if Nikon sells its better products only through specialty stores, the information seeker cannot purchase a similar model at a discounter or through mail order. Similarly, golf club lines are usually demarcated between pro shops and sporting goods stores. Although Avon did introduce its products into Sears and JCPenney, it created a new, higher-priced line that did not conflict with what the sales representatives were selling. Goodyear also took this approach by giving a hot new product, the Assurance, only to its dealers.

Let us return to the Ingersoll-Rand illustration discussed earlier. The company uses four channels to distribute its air compressors: direct sales, independent distributors, company-owned air centers, and manufacturers' representatives. Even though the channels appear to be defined clearly, sometimes they compete directly with each other. A salesperson might submit a bid on a 400-horsepower compressor while a distributor would submit a bid to the same customer for two 200-horsepower machines. For smaller compressors, distributors and air centers compete with the manufacturers' representatives for the under-5-horsepower compressors. To reduce interchannel competition, Ingersoll-Rand introduced its Full Partner Program, in which commissions were given for referrals as well as sales. For example, if a direct salesperson refers an inquiry to a distributor or an air center, she or he will get a 1 percent commission if a sale is made and 2 percent if the salesperson actively assisted in the sale.

Finally, in 2000, Mattel began selling a wide range of toys and children's clothing at the Barbie.com Web site. Some of these overlapped with products sold at large retailers like Walmart, Kmart, and Toys 'R' Us. Mattel claimed that the purpose was to increase the visibility of the brands and not to create channel conflict. To emphasize this, the company set prices 15 percent higher than those at the retailers.[21]

Thus, from these illustrations, we have seen different ways to resolve conflict:

1. Demarcating product lines (i.e., separating product offerings by channel to help reduce domain problems).
2. Working with the channel members to develop joint solutions.
3. Putting more money into push and pull activities.
4. Developing financial arrangements such as commissions and higher margins.
5. Charging higher prices in the direct channel.

Channel power can also be used as a conflict resolution tool. If such power exists, the channel member can influence another channel member's behavior. Power sources can be converted into persuasion through:

- Threats.
- Legalistic pleas.
- Promises.
- Requests.
- Recommendations.
- Information exchange.

Of course, not all of these approaches will work; their success depends largely on how the channel member with the power chooses to exercise it.

Channels Issues in High-Tech Marketing

Marketing managers for technology-based products use all of the traditional channels of distribution: retailers, various middlemen, direct sales, telemarketing, and so on. The channel design and management issues discussed earlier in this chapter are therefore relevant to the marketing of these kinds of products and services.

What makes channel issues unique in this context is the use of two different kinds of intermediaries: original equipment manufacturers (OEMs) and value-added resellers (VARs).

OEMs

A company typically uses original equipment manufacturers when an ingredient is used in or as part of another company's products. For example, Canon is the world's largest manufacturer of the engines in laser printers (the part of the printer that produces the copies). Not only does Canon make the engines for its own brand of laser printers, but it also sells them to Hewlett-Packard as an OEM channel for its LaserJet line. Hard disk drive manufacturers such as Quantum and Seagate sell through OEM channels such as Dell, Lenovo, and other PC manufacturers. Software companies also use the PC OEM channel because many PCs come bundled with software. The Logitech illustration at the beginning of Chapter 7 is another example of a company that heavily uses the OEM channel for its computer mice. Microsoft, the subject of the introductory case in this chapter, uses PC manufacturers such as HP and Dell as an OEM for its Windows 7 operation system.

Table 12.4 highlights some of the differences between OEM and branded marketing for products such as hard disk drives. A branded product is sold on a stand-alone basis (rather than as an ingredient) to end customers. For example, as we noted earlier in this chapter, hard disk drives are sold through both OEM and regular retail (both mail order and computer store) channels.

The general characteristic of OEM marketing is that it is a technical sell, with you talking directly to engineers. The customer is interested in how your product fits into its laptop computer, printer, or other device. Thus, knowledge of technical aspects of the product is important. In addition, the sale is usually very price oriented because the customer has a good idea about your cost structure. Because your product is only an ingredient, the brand name is not generally visible ("Intel Inside" notwithstanding) and is therefore not a key selling point for obtaining a higher price. OEM selling is usually more like a traditional sales job versus the branded mass-marketing approach. Terms of supply such as delivery quantities, timing, and quality are of paramount importance to the OEM. As a result, strong negotiation skills are required.

value-added reseller (VAR) organizations that buy products from a variety of vendors, assemble them in packages, and resell the packages to specialized segments; part of the channel of distribution for technology-based products

VARs

A **value-added reseller (VAR)** is an organization that buys products from a variety of vendors, assembles them in a package, and resells the package to specialized segments,

Table 12.4

OEM versus Branded Marketing

OEM	Branded
Customer	
Heavy engineering influence	Not necessarily a technical sell
Cross-functional decision making	Individual decision makers
Multimillion-dollar account size	Thousands of customers
Horizontal market orientation	Vertical market orientation
Promotion	
Executive selling	PR activities: articles, white papers
Key industry analysts and influencers	Advertising
	Events: trade shows and seminars
Word of mouth	Channel programs
Pricing	
Usually cost based	Value based
Negotiated by each OEM	Standard price lists and discount structure
Detailed pricing schedules	Marketing ownership
Senior executive involvement	Periodic pricing adjustments
Frequent pricing action	
Product	
System component	A stand-alone product
Requirements often set by customer	Ease of use very important
Close engineering coordination with customer	Market orientation and product position determine specification
Integration testing a major element of sales cycle	Short evaluation cycle
Place	
Direct sales dominate	Mix of indirect and direct sales channels
Product fulfilled by manufacturer	Channels change with product life cycle
Account teams deliver service and support	Product fulfilled at several levels

OEM	Branded
Competition	
Similar product	Feature set differentiation
Overlapping customer set	Narrow product line
Business won or lost at design	Alliances common
Support and relationship key	Company and product awareness key
Cost	
Many hidden costs	Large non-product-related expenses
Significant engineering effort in cost reduction	Product positioning and feature set drive product costs
Customers often know your costs	Customers care about price, not cost
Communication	
Direct marketing and sales contact	PR and advertising play a major role
Emphases on relationship building	Simple, clear messages
Marketing effort spans several organizations	Marketing control
Ongoing communication	Heavy competition for end-user attention
Summary	
Great general management training	More classic marketing
Technical background a plus	Product knowledge required
Program management role	Convey market requirements internally
Strong interpersonal skills, one-on-one selling	Strong communication skills
Business creativity	Product and program creativity
Know your customer's business	Know the vertical markets for your product
Sharp negotiating skills	Channel knowledge
Execution drives success	Strategy and marketing intelligence

Source: Bill Rossi, Google.

often called vertical markets. For example, a VAR focusing on the law firm segment would purchase personal computers from a company, bundle together special software designed for client management and law firm accounting, and then sell the package as a turnkey (i.e., simply "turn the key" to start) system to customers. Similarly, a telephone company would work with companies selling local area network software (e.g., Novell) and hardware (e.g., Cisco) to design a system to install in large office buildings. This would enable the builder to buy an external and internal data and phone system as a package. In this case, the phone company is a VAR to Novell and Cisco. Cisco, in fact, differentiates its VARs as Silver, Gold, Premier, or Global according to the technical expertise of the VAR's engineering staff.

Differences between OEMs and VARs

One difference between an OEM and a VAR is the number of ingredients: an OEM normally has a much larger number of suppliers, whereas the VAR has a few discrete components to its system. Occasionally, the components of a VAR system are identified to the customer. As a result, the VAR must be particularly sensitive about who is responsible for customer service. A law firm may experience a hardware problem with its customer management and accounting system. Who is responsible: the hardware company or the VAR? This is not usually a problem with an OEM channel. If a Dell computer has a hard disk problem, the customer does not contact Seagate or Toshiba, but Dell.

Another difference between a VAR and OEM is that the former is more like a joint venture. Therefore, selling through a VAR is more like a partnership relationship than a supplier relationship. An OEM sale is usually the end of the transaction until the next supply is needed.[22] With a VAR, there are longer-term issues such as customer service and joint marketing. Companies using VARs as a key channel often spend a considerable amount of money working with the VARs to help them sell systems to customers. For example, Kana Communications works with companies selling telephone call centers to help them better sell the total CRM system to potential customers.

Finally, companies selling through VARs also have well-established markets into which they can also sell by themselves. Thus, marketing managers for products using VARs also have to have significant branded marketing skills. Although some OEM products, such as hard drives, are also sold on a stand-alone basis to end-customers, most are not. As a result, products sold through OEMs are significantly driven by derived demand; that is, their markets expand only to the extent that the markets for OEM products expand.

Global Channels Issues

One of the issues raised in Chapter 7 is the limit to true globalization, the concept that you can market a product or service around the world in the same manner.[23] The same question can be asked about distribution channels. Is it possible to have a global channel strategy? In this chapter, we discussed the fact that channel structures exist to serve the company's customers. Throughout this book, we have noted that not only do customers' habits and tastes vary around the world, but so do economic, regulatory, and other conditions. Thus, cultural and other country differences affect strategic decisions such as positioning and branding, but they also affect tactical decisions such as channels. No matter how you choose to enter a foreign market, whether through a joint venture, independent agents, or a wholly owned subsidiary, you have to consider global vagaries in retail and wholesale customs that restrict your ability to develop a truly global approach to channels.[24] Some of these country and regional differences are the following.

Western Europe

The European retailing scene today looks much like that of the United States. Increased price sensitivity has resulted in the proliferation of private label or "own" brands in the major chains such as Sainsbury, Safeway, Tesco, and Carrefours. Superstores such as Price/Costco have established footholds, as have well-known retailers such as IKEA, Toys 'R' Us, and Staples.

However, local regulations still exist and must be considered. For example, Portugal has limited the establishment of new hypermarkets to protect small retailers. Germany has a large number of retail laws. The number of hours stores can remain open is significantly restricted, although the government is experimenting with relaxing those laws.

Russia and Other Former Soviet Bloc Countries

The lack of a high-quality distribution structure, not to mention a shortfall of disposable income, has hampered the development of retail activity in these countries. In addition, a significant amount of purchasing (up to 25 percent of grocery purchases by some estimates) is done on the black market. Excise taxes can make the prices of consumer durables sold through conventional retailers (such as cars) prohibitively expensive (it is not surprising that the black market thrives). Brand loyalty is notoriously low. At the same time, foreign companies are entering major cities such as St. Petersburg, Moscow, and Warsaw. A first-time visitor to Prague or Budapest will be amazed at how "Western" the cities are (if you consider Pizza Hut and McDonald's representative of Western culture), sometimes to the detriment of their former charm.

Japan

Japan is a difficult country for foreign companies to penetrate because of its maze of importation and operational laws. For example, the Large-Scale Retail Store Law can delay a store's opening, reduce its size, force it to close early, and restrict the number of days it can be open. The retail market is extremely fragmented, with mom-and-pop operations dominating. As a result, there is little price competition. However, these barriers are dropping as discounters in a number of categories, from men's clothing to toys, are springing up.

China and Other Asian Markets

In China, foreign firms are often forbidden to set up their own distribution networks. In fact, the Chinese Army (the People's Liberation Army) has a thriving subsidiary that distributes a variety of goods throughout the country. As in Japan, the retail market is extremely fragmented, with most Chinese living in rural areas. In these areas, personal, door-to-door selling is very common. However, in the cities such as Shanghai and Beijing, the retail scene looks very familiar to Westerners.

Several examples already provided in this chapter indicate that Southeast Asia is undergoing rapid economic development. Shopping malls have sprung up in Manila, Ho Chi Minh City, Singapore, and many other cities. However, frequent currency fluctuations demonstrate how vulnerable these economies can be to short-term economic problems.

Application Procter & Gamble

Procter & Gamble has been successful in entering both Japan and China, although it has been in the former country for a long time.[25] It is instructive to read this example showing how the company used different approaches to distribution in each country by adapting to the local retail structure and consumer needs.

In 1995, P&G sold $450 million worth of shampoo and detergent, becoming the largest daily-use consumer-products company in China. China has a poor infrastructure and is years away from having a national distribution system. How did P&G get its products into the millions of small and large stores throughout the country? The company targeted the 228 Chinese cities with more than 200,000 people and determined the location of every store in those cities. Then they sent in their "ground troops," thousands of trainees whose job was to get P&G products on the shelves of every store, into every kiosk, and even into street stalls. Thus, in a switch from traditional economics, the company substituted labor for capital: the distribution system is based on human beings, not trucks or rail cars shipping vast amounts of products into warehouses. In addition, the company used an old Western distribution strategy of linking its Ariel and Tide brands with washing machine manufacturers, who pass out free products when a customer purchases a machine. Promotions such as free samples have been distributed generously.

Until 1995, P&G did not sell dish detergent in Japan. By the end of 1997, the company had Japan's best-selling brand, Joy. Not only is the market for the product mature, but there are two giant Japanese competitors, Kao and Lion. The success was driven by introducing a new, technologically advanced product (a more concentrated product requiring a smaller amount to be used) and through popular TV commercials.

However, the product was also successful in winning over Japan's notoriously difficult retailers. Not surprisingly, retailers in Japan care about the same thing that retailers everywhere are concerned about: profitability of the category. Simply put, Joy is the most profitable product on the market. The Kao and Lion products were sold in long-necked bottles that wasted space. Joy is sold in a compact cylinder that takes less space in trucks, stores, warehouses, and, importantly, on the shelves. This permits retailers to increase the number of units on the shelves, leading to lower restocking rates. That the product is sold for somewhat higher prices, giving higher margins per unit, does not hurt either.

Gray Markets

The **gray market** is where trademarked goods are sold through channels of distribution that are not authorized by the holder of the trademark. It is common that gray markets develop across country lines. This phenomenon is often called **parallel importing**. Parallel importing is most often found when there are significant currency-exchange-rate or price differences between countries that make it profitable to purchase goods in one country and then import them into another for resale. Most readers are familiar with friends from foreign countries who find some products cheaper to buy in the United States than in their home countries and who load up before returning home. Parallel importing is exactly this behavior, except that institutions are involved in the purchasing and shipping and the products are resold in the home market. For example, an automobile dealer in Europe may find it prohibitively expensive to purchase and resell BMWs by going through normal channels. However, the dealer could purchase some in the United States and ship them back for resale at a lower price than legitimate BMW dealers can. Such gray markets are initiated by intermediaries known as **diverters**. These agents either purchase products or arrange for their purchase and divert the products away from normal channels.

gray market
a market in which trademarked goods are sold through channels of distribution that are not authorized by the holder of the trademark

parallel importing
the development of gray markets across country lines, often as a result of significant currency exchange rate or price differences between countries that make it profitable to purchase goods in one country and import them into another for resale

diverters
in international marketing, middlemen who purchase products or arrange for their purchase and thereby divert the products away from normal channels

It looks like a good deal for both the manufacturer and the customer. The former sells more products and the latter enjoys lower prices. However, legitimate channel members become agitated when a significant amount of gray market goods flood their markets. This leads to decreased goodwill in the channel. In addition, warranty support is not necessarily equivalent to that of goods bought through legitimate channels. Finally, brand image and equity can be diluted by gray marketers focusing on low prices.

Some Special Topics in Channels of Distribution

Some Supermarket Issues

With the increased power retailers have obtained in the distribution channel system, particularly for grocery items, the difference between manufacturers' and retailers' perspectives is magnified. Due to industry consolidation, the five largest retailers' share of the grocery business rose from 26.5 percent in 1980 to 45 percent in 2008.[26] Retailers' scarce resource is their selling space, and they care less about how a particular brand is selling than what is happening to the sales of a product category, department, or store as a whole. Of course, the reverse is true for manufacturers.

This category perspective can be coupled with the data explosion that has given retailers, manufacturers, and data suppliers a microscope with which to analyze the performance of different product categories in different parts of the country, different parts of a state, and different areas within a city. To optimize their product mix, retailers want to offer the appropriate brands in a category, and they want the mix of brands and product varieties to be appropriate for the ethnic and socioeconomic composition of the shopping areas in which particular stores are located. In addition, manufacturers are seeking ways to move some of the channel power back in their direction.

Thus, in the early 1990s, the **category management** concept was introduced and has since been dramatically expanded. In category management, product categories are considered to be the business units that should be customized on a store-by-store basis to satisfy customer needs. Retailers have category managers, who are empowered to operate their categories as separate businesses. The idea is that retailers plan marketing and strategy for an entire group of products rather than brand by brand. The category management system has been found to increase retailers' prices and profit margins.[27]

category management
a process that considers product categories to be the business units that should be customized on a store-by-store basis in a way that satisfies customer needs

Under a category management system, manufacturers must be concerned about meeting not only their objectives but also the retailer's. Within the manufacturer's organization, the product management, sales, and marketing research organizations must work as a team because, typically, a salesperson sells a large number of a company's products, managed by an equivalently large number of product managers. Salespeople work closely with product managers, and marketing research managers and management information specialists provide information to both marketing and sales. Interestingly, in this era of category management, the salesperson is really the key person because she or he is the link between marketing managers interested mainly in their brands and retailers interested mainly in their categories. The job of the salesperson in this environment is to become intimately familiar with the needs of both the retailer and the customer, so that he or she can adapt the company's offerings to the needs of a particular store. For example, Kraft has one customer manager for each major chain in a city or region. Additionally, because grocery chains operate on slim profit margins and consumer tastes change rapidly, the chains have come to rely on manufacturers to help plan category strategies because they spend considerable sums on marketing research and have considerable marketing expertise. In turn, manufacturers and retailers rely on market research firms like A.C. Nielsen and its software Category Business Planner to take market data and make it accessible in real time to managers.

Some companies have developed their own category management systems to aid retailers. Clearly, category leaders such as Anheuser-Busch are very interested in helping the retailers manage their categories, which helps manufacturers consolidate and enhance their own positions.

Application General Mills Yoplait Yogurt

The dairy aisle is one of the top-performing areas of the supermarket.[28] Space is at a premium due to the constraints of the refrigerated displays, and there are many new products introduced almost daily, particularly with the "natural" and "organic" trends exploding. While other areas of the store may receive more attention, the "quiet" dairy department serves 99.6 percent of households and generates 47.4 store trips per year. It is the largest aisle by dollar volume and has the highest growth trends.

General Mills and Yoplait won *Progressive Grocer*'s 2008 Category Captain award based on the work its category advisors did with 24 major retailers to increase yogurt dollar volume by 10.6 percent versus 7.9 percent at retail accounts without the new aisle strategy. The company has worked with grocers to increase the yogurt "footprint" to eight feet and has generated a 9 percent increase in yogurt volume nationwide.

To achieve these results, General Mills tried to answer several questions: (1) How should a grocer allocate space within the aisle? (2) How can grocers maximize dairy sales by placing yogurt near to other complementary dairy products? (3) What customer segments shop the dairy aisle? These are typical questions that category captains have to address. In addition, General Mills has developed virtual store technology linked with store-level sales data to permit grocery store managers to envision the impact on category sales from changing the layout of the aisle on a 30-foot long screen.

Yoplait is the category captain for the yogurt category in many supermarkets.
Source: Jim Mone/AP Wide World Photos

Another development in supermarket retailing is the increased need to control costs and operate efficiently to compete with category killers. This need to be efficient has driven category management and created two concepts initially introduced in the United States in the early 1990s: **efficient consumer response (ECR)** and the **continuous replenishment program (CRP)**. ECR is the process of reducing costs throughout the entire distribution system, resulting in lower prices and increased consumer demand. Part of this process is CRP, in which the members of the supply chain partner with supermarkets.

efficient consumer response (ECR)
a process seeking to reduce costs throughout the entire distribution system, resulting in lower prices and increased consumer demand

continuous replenishment program (CRP)
a program wherein members of a supply chain partner with supermarkets, working together to attempt to accurately forecast demand, which is then used to generate inventory replenishment data electronically

In CRP, retailers, wholesalers, and marketing managers work together to attempt to accurately forecast demand. These forecasts drive the electronic inventory replenishment system. When it works, CRP can reduce inventories at both the retail and warehouse levels by 15 to 60 percent. The difficult part is getting manufacturers and retailers to work together, because both must be open about their strategies and performance. When they do not work together, third-party consultants try to predict sales in particular markets by counting individual stock-keeping units (SKUs).

Strategies for Intermediaries

With the rapid growth of the Internet and other information technologies directly linking manufacturers and other companies with their retailers or the channel reaching the end-customer, many business observers have predicted the ultimate demise of "middlemen" and a trend toward disintermediation. These middlemen compose the vast network of largely invisible (at least to consumers) companies that move products in the channel system.

Despite the dire predictions of their ultimate fate, many of these companies are of significant size. For example, the largest food wholesaler serving supermarkets, SuperValu, had more than $43 billion in sales in 2008.[29] In fact, 6 of the top 50 private companies in the United States are involved with food wholesaling.[30] Ingram Micro, the largest distributor of information technology products, sells more than $30 billion worth every year.

How have some intermediaries remained successful? Here are some examples:

- Auto dealers are focusing on customer service to combat sales through independent Internet sites and manufacturers who use the Web to permit customers to order direct from them. Some dealers permit customers to schedule service appointments, order parts, and check inventory through their own Web sites and use their e-mail lists to send out discount coupons by e-mail.
- Information technology equipment distributors like Ingram Micro and Tech Data not only sell PCs but also offer peripherals, inventory management services, next-day delivery, financing, and technical service support.
- In health care distribution, companies like Cardinal Health offer services to both upstream suppliers and downstream customers by packaging drugs for pharmaceutical producers and offering contract manufacturing services and alternative drug-delivery formulations. It also leases automated drug dispensers to hospitals and nursing homes.

Thus, the key for middlemen is to offer services to suppliers and customers that no one else in the channel system is willing to provide and to take advantage of being in the middle rather than seeing it as a handicap.

Application Arrow Electronics

Arrow Electronics is an $11 billion company that supplies computer chips, capacitors, and many other electronic components to 150,000 customers that make subsystems for personal computers, cell phones, and autos.[31] Its main competitor, Avnet, is about the same size. However, large contract manufacturers such as Flextronics and Solectron are buying more parts directly from manufacturers cutting out both companies.

As a result, the company is extending its business to services beyond matching suppliers with end-customers. These include financing, on-site inventory management, parts-tracking software, and chip programming. In addition, Arrow gets fees for helping parts-makers win customers, a kind of sales operation. For example, Arrow stole the audio and video equipment manufacturer AMX Corp. account from Avnet. This was achieved by offering services such as keeping three material planners on-site at AMX who handle parts flow and look for ways to substitute parts that Arrow can supply for less cost. This is a good example of how channel partners can provide additional services beyond straight distribution and how these can evolve over time.

Executive Summary

Key learning points in this chapter include the following:

- The distribution channel system gives customers access to your products and services and is a value chain in which different members of the system add value and are compensated accordingly.
- There are many different channel structures. No one channel system is appropriate for every industry, product category, or firm.
- The channel structure depends on customer and competitor behavior, the marketing strategy used, and the resources available. Channel systems can evolve over time as these elements change.
- Channel members perform a wide variety of functions for the system.
- A common decision sequence is to first choose between direct and indirect channel systems and then choose particular channel members.
- Hybrid channel systems include a number of different channel types that complement one another and perform different tasks to obtain a sale.
- Channel power enables a channel member to exert some authority to get another member to do something it would not otherwise do on its own.
- Channel management involves maintaining good relationships and resolving conflict between channel members.
- Conflict can be resolved by demarcating products between channel members, helping the channel members to achieve their goals, and offering more push and pull money.
- New channel opportunities are arising from changes in supermarket retailing (category management, efficient consumer response [ECR], and continuous replenishment programs [CRPs]), multilevel or network marketing, and changes in technology.

Chapter Questions

1. Develop two examples of companies that are using other companies as distributors (such as AT&T using Fry's Electronics for Internet service). What benefits are the original companies receiving in these two cases?
2. Besides the illustrations in this chapter, give an example of another industry that has witnessed substantial change in channels of distribution. What are the fundamental reasons (e.g., consumer behavior, competition) for this change?
3. An executive at a large package delivery company has complained that by shifting some of its business to independent channel members, the company has "lost control of the customer." What do you think he means by this statement? Why does he consider this to be bad for the company?

4. Levi Strauss sells the same products, Levi's and Dockers, to multiple channels of distribution, from high-image (Bloomingdale's) to low-image (Sears, Mervyns) outlets. What would you suggest as a distribution strategy so that the company can better differentiate its product by channel and not suffer brand confusion problems?
5. What are the pros and cons of using the Web as a distribution channel? Are there some situations where it should not be a part of the channel mix?
6. There can be considerable variation in how products are sold in different countries. For example, cars are sold door-to-door in Japan and in retail showrooms in most of the rest of the world. Besides institutional differences (e.g., laws), why does culture matter with respect to global channels decisions?

Key Learning Points

The purpose of this chapter is to introduce some of the issues in managing two major direct channels of distribution: personal selling and direct marketing. After reading this chapter, the student will have learned:

- How the sales force fits into the marketing organization
- The major duties of a salesperson
- Managing the sales force in terms of managing sales force performance, designing sales territories, determining sales force size, and assigning salespeople to territories
- Setting sales quotas
- Issues in sales force compensation
- The impact of technology on sales management
- The importance of direct marketing
- The major direct-marketing media

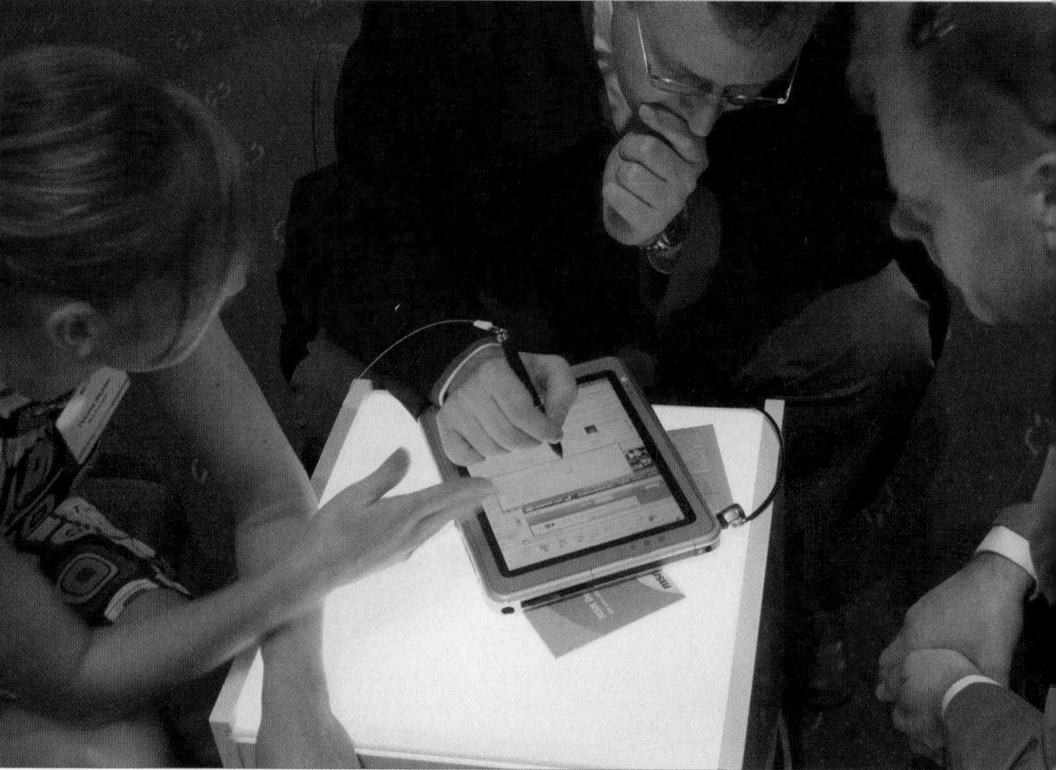

Personal selling today relies heavily on advances in information technology.
Source: kolvenbach/Alamy Images

Direct Channels of Distribution: Personal Selling and Direct Marketing

Chapter Brief

Cisco Systems is the dominant player in the market for computer networking equipment.[1] With sales of $35 billion in its 2009 fiscal year and a market capitalization of just over $138 billion, the company was a leading force in moving the United States into the "new" economy represented by the Internet. The company has spent the past several years positioning itself as more of a home entertainment company through the acquisitions of Linksys in 2003 (home wireless networks), Scientific-Atlanta in 2005 (set-top cable TV boxes), and Pure Digital Technologies in 2009 (the inexpensive Flip video camera).

At Cisco, the sales force has so much clout that its 14,000 members receive perks such as lengthy titles and executive assistants, usually reserved for more senior managers. The philosophy behind this approach is that the salespeople are the ones who have the closest contact with customers and therefore have the greatest potential to either make or break the company. The fact that the company is so successful is proof that the sales force is an excellent one. It was named the co-winner of the title of sales force of the year for 2000 by *Sales & Marketing Management* magazine.

One key to the success of the sales force is its use of information technology. At Cisco, 80 percent of its orders and 80 percent of customer inquiries are handled through the Web. This allows the salespeople to spend more time with customers in order to build long-term relationships through customer satisfaction. The company emphasizes continuing education for its sales force, but not through traditional classrooms—through "virtual" classrooms via text and videos on the Web. In addition, salespeople conduct all of their benefits and travel and entertainment transactions online. Each salesperson has a customized Web page so he or she has all the personal and up-to-date customer information needed to handle the job conveniently while on the road. Cisco's CEO John Chambers is passionate about the Internet and the way it has transformed his company, and this has greatly affected the sales force as well.

The company's Web site is also used to reach customers for direct marketing purposes. When visitors come to Cisco.com, they find video, "click-to-chat," and WebEx (videoconferencing) connections to speak with Cisco sales representatives. In addition, these visitors often turn into leads for the sales force.

At the same time, Cisco faces the same issues confronting any other company that has a sales force:

- Recruiting and selecting the sales force.
- Training, evaluating, and supervising the sales force.
- Motivating the sales force and setting quotas.
- Assigning the appropriate geographic territories and customer accounts to each salesperson.

As mentioned earlier in this book, personal selling and sales force management fulfill several important marketing tasks. First, it was noted in Chapter 10 that the sales force is part of the communications mix. The sales force must be given the tools and training to implement the marketing strategy and integrate its efforts with the rest of the communications programs. In Chapter 12, we discussed the sales force as a channel of distribution, a direct channel to the customer. Clearly, the sales force satisfies the major criterion for a channel: it gives customers access to the firm's products and services. This is such an important function that it is estimated that there are at least 20 million people involved in sales in the U.S. with a conservative estimate of $800 billion spent on sales forces each year.[2]

Another important direct channel in today's mix of channel options is direct marketing. While many consumers have a negative perception of direct marketing, perceiving direct mail as "junk" mail and expressing irritation at telemarketers, the fact is that it is a huge business.

One estimate is that direct marketing accounted for about 10 percent of U.S. gross domestic product (GDP) in 2008.[3] For example, more than $56 billion is spent on both catalogues and direct mail.[4] Although more precise statistics will be reported later in this chapter, it is interesting to note that while most people associate direct marketing with consumer products and services, nearly half of the spending was from B-to-B products and services. What makes the direct marketing field particularly relevant today is the rapid growth of direct e-mails for both communications and sales. Almost two-thirds of all companies reported using e-mail to connect with customers.[5]

Thus, in this chapter we will discuss both sales force management and direct marketing, the two most important direct channels of distribution.

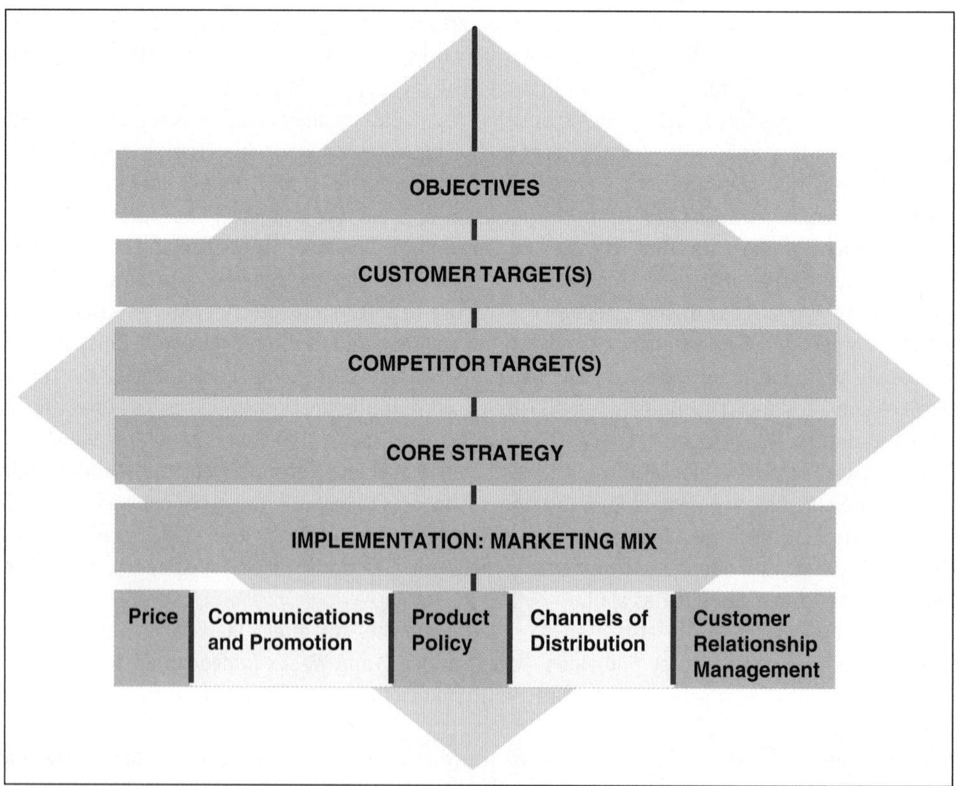

The Sales Force and the Marketing Organization

As part communications and part channel, the sales force has a dual role in the implementation of the marketing strategy (see the marketing strategy diagram). The salesperson not only communicates information about the product or service and delivers the key value proposition to the customer, but also attempts to complete the transaction

Figure 13.1

Sales Force Organization in a Medium-Sized Firm

Number	
1	Vice President of Marketing
1	National Sales Manager
2	Regional Sales Manager
8	District Sales Manager
96	Field Sales Representative

Source: Douglas J. Dalrymple and William L. Cron (1988), *Sales Management*, 6th ed. (New York: Wiley), p. 6. Copyright 1996. Reprinted with permission of John Wiley & Sons, Inc.

with the end customer (a key role of some channels). In addition, many companies spend a significant sum of money on sales force activities. Some sales forces are very large. As noted earlier in this chapter, Cisco has 14,000 salespeople. Even larger are PepsiCo's with 36,000 and Hartford Financial Services with 100,000. Avon is the largest multilevel seller direct to homes with 5.4 million sales representatives. The total number of sales representatives for drug companies has been estimated to be about 90,000.[6] The resources spent on training, motivating, and rewarding these salespeople rival or surpass the money spent on other channels and types of communications. Data indicate that depending on the size of the sales force, the cost of each sales call can range from $158 per call for a company with 20 to 49 sales reps, to $224 per call for a company with 1 to 5 reps.[7]

There are different titles used in sales management, depending on the level of the organization. Figure 13.1 shows the different titles typically used in a mid-sized sales organization. The vice president of marketing or sales heads the sales organization. Most of the other titles describe job responsibilities defined by the size of the geographic territory covered (national, regional, and district sales managers). The largest part of the organization is made up of the field sales representatives, or reps.

Although we will not cover all issues a particular sales manager has to deal with, this chapter should give you a good sense of the diversity of the salesperson's and sales manager's jobs. Because there are many different titles and duties assumed by the people within a sales force and because they vary across companies and industries, we will cover the general area of sales management, rather than focusing on one particular organizational level.

In Chapter 1, the marketing manager's job was defined and some aspects of marketing organizations illustrated (see Figures 1.4, 1.5, and 1.6). The relationship between sales and marketing organizations is unusual. Although you might think that the sales organization would be part of marketing because the sales force helps to implement the marketing strategy, sales organizations are often separate and powerful entities within companies. In such firms, marketing is viewed as providing a support function (advertising, selling materials, trade shows) to sales.

Figure 13.2 shows the organizational structure of Adobe Systems Inc., a computer software company. The product marketing group includes product managers responsible for putting together marketing strategies and programs for products such as Acrobat (text formatting), Photoshop (imaging), and PageMaker (desktop publishing). In this organization, product marketing is different from marketing in that the latter is more tactical in nature. That is, marketing offers support to product managers by planning promotional events, designing trade show displays, and so on. In this case, the sales organization is

Figure 13.2

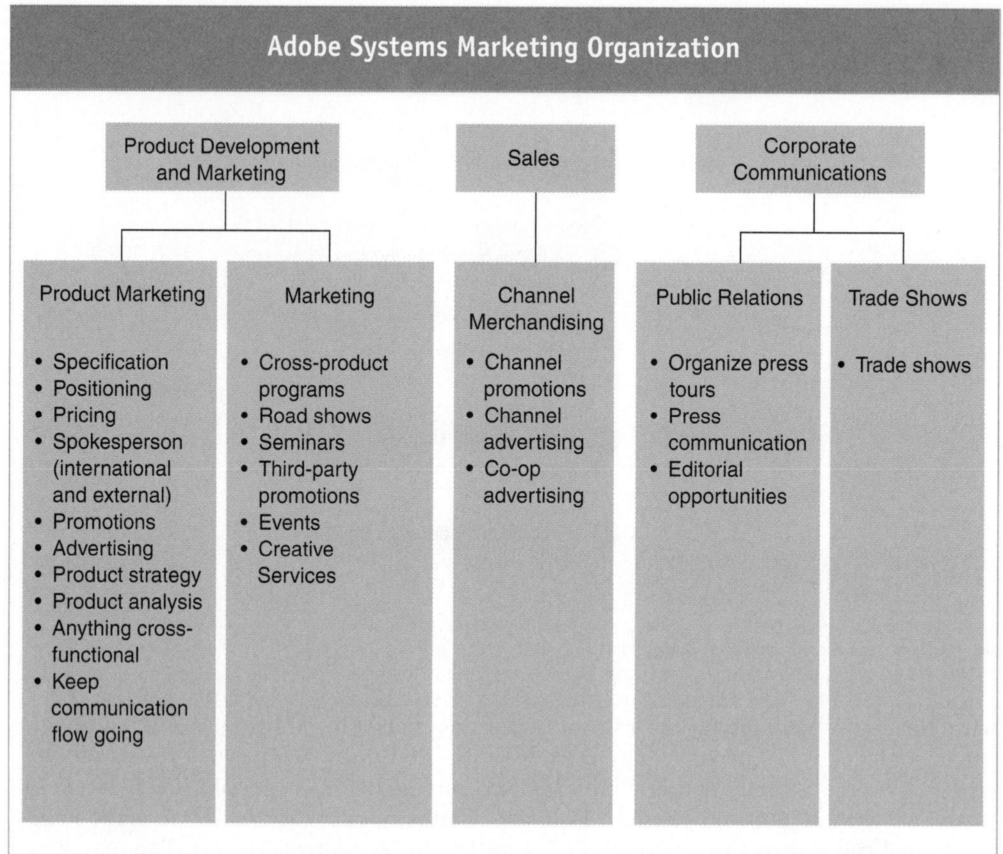

separate from marketing. The sales force is responsible not only for calling on corporate customers but also for channel merchandising (handling relationships and other matters with distributors).

Types of Sales Organizations

There are three kinds of sales organization structures. One structure is organized around product lines. The product/product sales organization sells a product or product line to all markets and often coexists with a product-focused organization. A disadvantage of this structure is that a customer may be called on by several salespeople from the same company.

An example of the product/product structure appears in Figure 13.3, which shows the organizational structure at one time for Hewlett-Packard's Medical Products Group (MPG).[8] MPG sells a variety of products, including patient monitoring systems, operating room systems, perinatal monitoring devices, and clinical information systems. On the right side of the chart is the U.S. Field Operations, with different national sales managers (NSMs) for the different product groups within MPG. The Imaging Systems Division (ISY), which manufactures ultrasound devices for cardiologists and vascular surgeons, has its own sales force and national sales manager, as do the other three product groups. The ISY sales force only sells the products made by that division.

A second type of organization is a market/market system, in which the marketing organization is aligned by market segment, as is the sales force. In this case, the sales force sells the entire product line to customers in the segment. An illustration of this kind of organization is shown in Figure 13.4.[9] MCI's U.S. marketing operations were organized by geographic market segments (the company is now part of Verizon). In each geographic territory, the sales force is responsible for selling all telecommunications services to the customers.

A third organizational form is called product/market. In this case, the company has a product management structure but the sales force sells all products marketed by a division to a single market. An example of this kind of structure is the General Foods dessert division shown in Figure 1.4. In this case, there are individual product managers

Figure 13.3

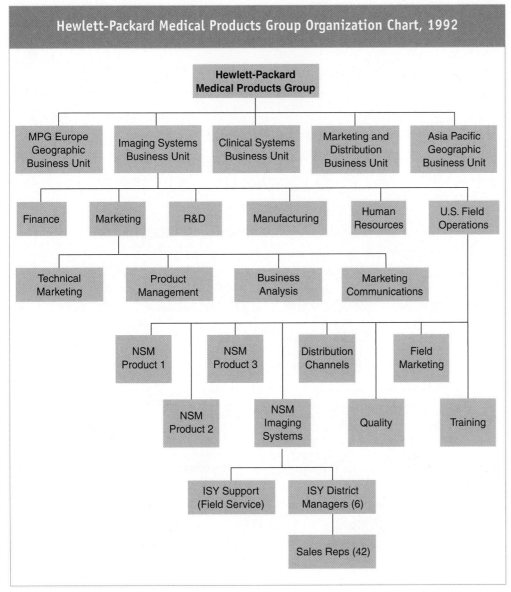

Hewlett-Packard Medical Products Group Organization Chart, 1992

- Hewlett-Packard Medical Products Group
  - MPG Europe Geographic Business Unit
  - Imaging Systems Business Unit
    - Finance
    - Marketing
      - Technical Marketing
      - Product Management
      - Business Analysis
      - Marketing Communications
    - R&D
    - Manufacturing
    - Human Resources
    - U.S. Field Operations
      - NSM Product 1
      - NSM Product 2
      - NSM Product 3
      - NSM Imaging Systems
        - ISY Support (Field Service)
        - ISY District Managers (6)
          - Sales Reps (42)
      - Distribution Channels
      - Quality
      - Field Marketing
      - Training
  - Clinical Systems Business Unit
  - Marketing and Distribution Business Unit
  - Asia Pacific Geographic Business Unit

NSM = National Sales Manager

Source: Frank V. Cespedes (1994), "Hewlett-Packard Imaging Systems Division: Sonos 100 C/F Introduction," Harvard Business School case #9-593-080, p. 18. Copyright © 1992 by the President and Fellows of Harvard College. Reprinted by permission.

for Jell-O Gelatin, Jell-O Pudding Pops, and other products, but the sales force for the desserts division is responsible for selling all of the division's products to the national supermarket chains.

A reorganization of a sales force can have negative effects on the financial performance of a company. Xerox's financial problems in the late 1990s were generally attributed to a sales force reorganization that failed.[10] On the other hand, such organizations have to change as companies grow or customers change, or when there is a significant change in industry structure. For example, as the Internet advertising media placement company DoubleClick (now owned by Google) grew, the sales force was reorganized around six industry segments: automotive, business, entertainment and youth, technology, women and health, and travel.[11]

National/Key Accounts Organizations

Many companies have an additional layer of salespeople who deal with the largest accounts. Because in many companies a few large corporate accounts make up a large percentage of sales, a higher level of attention to their business makes good sense. For example, a national study showed that 50 percent of the sales of the firms surveyed were accounted for by only 10 percent of their customers.[12] National account personnel are

Figure 13.4

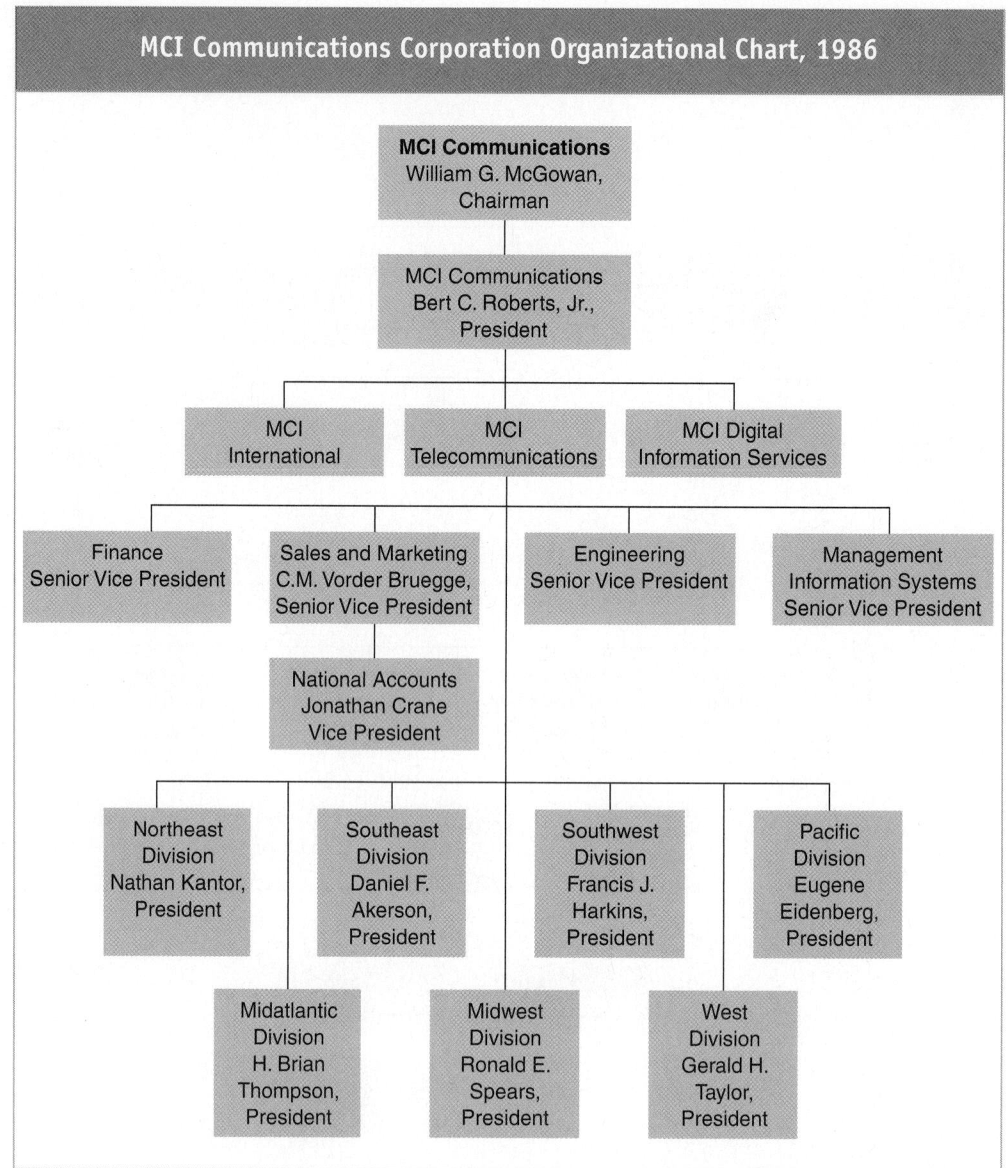

Source: MCI Communications Corporation: National Accounts Program, Harvard Business School case #9-593-044, p. 15.

charged with developing new accounts and maintaining existing ones; the latter is particularly important for long-term relationship building. Key account managers become very familiar with customers' operations and problems and are in an excellent position to satisfy customers' needs by helping them develop a strategy for the product in question. In addition, such positions are considered plums in the company and serve as a career goal for the sales force.

It is common for companies to establish a separate organization to deal with major accounts. As shown in Figure 13.5, there are four common ways to organize the key account sales force. The most common form of organization is for the national key account sales force and the regular sales force to be on the same level organizationally and for both to report to the corporate vice president of sales.

The ways in which the national account and regional sales teams interact can vary. In some cases, the national account team calls on national or international headquarters, whereas the regional salespeople concentrate on the local offices. In others, the national account manager acts as a coordinator for the regional team. With either kind of arrangement, there are often difficulties dividing up the commissions earned from sales as it is often unclear who contributed the most to the sale.

Figure 13.5

Ways to Organize National Account Sales Forces

Functional unit equal to sales and marketing

President/ General Manager
- Vice President Sales and Marketing
- Vice President Major Accounts

Headquarters unit reporting to sales and marketing

President/ General Manager
- Vice President Sales and Marketing
  - Vice President Sales
  - Vice President Major Accounts

Unit of field sales, one level below top sales executive

President/ General Manager
- Vice President Sales
  - Region Manager(s)
  - Major Accounts Sales Representatives

Unit of field sales, two levels below top sales executive

President/ General Manager
- Vice President Sales
  - Region Manager
    - District Manager(s)
    - Major Accounts Sales Representatives

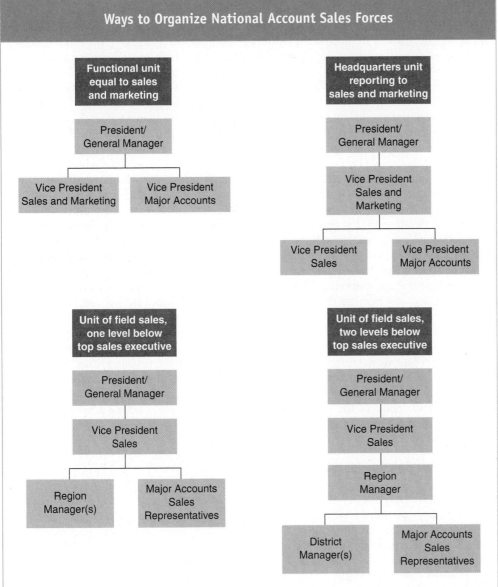

Source: Gilbert A. Churchill, Jr., Neil M. Ford, and Orville C. Walker, Jr. (1993), *Sales Force Management*, 4th ed. (Homewood, IL: Irwin), p. 157. Reproduced with permission of the McGraw-Hill Companies.

Application Marriott Lodging

Marriott Lodging's key account managers (KAMs) handle three to six major accounts.[13] These KAMs report to the vice president of sales, who reports to the senior vice president of sales and marketing. Each KAM is the main contact point between Marriott and the customer (e.g., large corporate clients) and is responsible for developing long-term relationships with the customers assigned to him or her. The KAMs are compensated by a combination of salary (70 percent) plus bonus (30 percent). The bonus is based on a combination of revenue targets and the quality of the relationships established.

The advantage of focusing on individual customers is that the KAM assigned to an account gets to know the customer's business very well. Marriott KAMs are expected to use online newspapers and other resources to research customer financial data, industry trends, and anything related to the customer's business. The objective is to be proactive and recommend money-saving ideas to customers to help them reengineer their travel processes. Of course, these ideas include recommending a mix of Marriott hotels across the spectrum from full-service to economy. The KAM system is working so well that in many accounts, a one-percentage-point increase in Marriott's market share is worth $1 million in incremental revenue.

Multilevel Marketing

Amway, Mary Kay, Tupperware, Avon, and many other product and service lines are sold using multilevel or network marketing distribution systems. These are basically direct sales organizations. Not all products sold this way are cosmetics and plastic goods; Excel Communications (a former division of the now bankrupt VarTec Telecom) used a multilevel approach to sell more than $1 billion worth of telecommunications services. The concept behind the system is simple: people recruit other people, who recruit others, and so on, to sell the products. Part of the commission on each sale is transmitted through the system so that the person at the top of the pyramid can receive substantial income by managing the network.

The use of the term *pyramid* is unfortunate because multilevel selling has been linked to illegal pyramid schemes that have bilked people out of their money. Although legal and very successful, these systems still have image problems. One problem is that some systems force salespeople or distributors to purchase a significant amount of inventory in advance. Another is that the amount of sales that actually occur is far less than that promised (how many relatives do you have?). The riches some people have made rarely accrue to the average distributor. Thus many network marketing systems are plagued by high turnover and shattered dreams.

However, network marketing does offer individuals the opportunity to make extra money and perhaps manage their own businesses. In addition, in the past several years, the industry has tried hard to reverse its negative image. In 1992, the Direct Selling Association adopted a new ethics policy that requires members to buy inventory back from distributors for at least 90 percent of the purchase price. Many managers, displaced through corporate downsizing programs, have joined these organizations, bringing an element of professionalism that was previously missing. Courses are being taught on the subject. Perhaps most importantly, many have been very successful. A look at the *Inc.* 500 shows that many of the fastest-growing small companies in the United States use this kind of distribution system.

What Does a Salesperson Do?

Obviously, a salesperson is rewarded on her or his ability to sell, or to close orders from customers. Less obviously, salespeople are also charged with maintaining and enhancing customer satisfaction with the selling firm and are often rewarded at least partially on that basis. Today, most sales people talk about selling "solutions" to customers or, in other words, solving a customer's problem. The anecdote shown in Figure 13.6 does a good job of illustrating one General Electric (GE) salesperson's approach to solutions selling.

One of the key jobs of a salesperson is maintaining a good relationship with the customer. *Source:* Jeff Greenberg/PhotoEdit Inc.

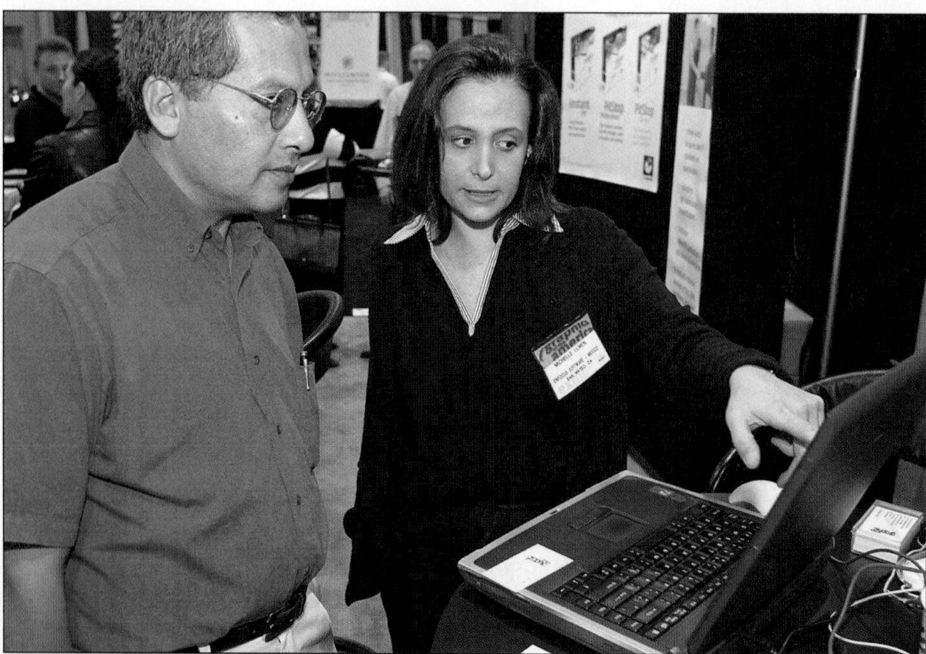

However, this general concept of solutions selling does not adequately describe the different kinds of selling that occur in business. A common way of classifying selling situations is:

- **Response selling.** In this situation, the salesperson is basically an order taker. The customer initiates the sale and gives the order to the salesperson.
- **Trade selling.** This kind of selling includes order taking, but also entails responsibilities such as making sure the stock is adequately displayed on shelves, setting up displays, providing demonstrations, and other activities sometimes called merchandising.

Figure 13.6

Solutions Selling

Lawrence Jackson, president of a major automotive supplier (with over $1 billion in sales) warmed to his topic. He had recently been promoted and loved to talk about the deals he had been working on.

"Let me tell you about three different sales pitches that I experienced over the last two months. The first was from a major chemical company that manufactures a broad line of chemicals we use in our process. This man was smooth, polished, professional. He knew the technical specs and characteristics of his products to a 'T.' He went on and on about why his products were so good.

"He was right, of course. His company makes very good products. But then, so do all of my other suppliers. His pitch was that he could be a one-stop shop. Nice concept, but it doesn't do much for me, because my other chemical suppliers have products just as good, and their delivered costs are low. What's the benefit to *me* of a single supplier of a dozen commodity products?

"The second rep was different. He sold plastics. We use a lot of plastic. He, too, was technically solid. And he was passionate about his product and his company, talking about all the new value-added programs they were developing. That was all great, but what did it mean for me? He said, it would create benefits in the future. I said, then come see me in the future.

"The third rep was from GE. Although his job was to sell plastics, he didn't tell me anything about his product. He just asked questions. How much capital do I have tied up in equipment? What are my yield losses in the plant? What are the biggest operational problems I run into at the plant, using my current materials, and process set-ups? How much capital do I have tied up in my trucks and logistical operations?

"We really got talking. As I described the operational problems we faced, we got into some very interesting issues. There were big numbers involved.

"He come back in two weeks. Showed me how GE Capital can reduce my capital intensity and my financing costs. In both plant equipment and logistics. Showed me how we could save on warehouse space. Described an approach for GE engineers to work with my plant people to make changes that would optimize my materials usage.

"Then he went on to talk about global support. We're growing like crazy internationally. He described how GE could support us in our global expansion.

"When I added it all up, he was saving my operation a lot of money. On capital, on financing, on yield losses. Of course, he got my plastics business. Almost all of it. And he's going to get it on a global basis.

"I'm not the only one who's delighted with this approach to doing business. My plant guys love it. They're used to dealing with product pushers. With GE, they're dealing with a group of people who have taken the time to learn their problems, and to help solve them. When it comes to deciding who's going to get our plastics business, it's not even close.

"Also, getting this support on a global basis makes our lives much easier. And given all the scrambling we have to do to serve our own tough customers, the automakers, that kind of support helps us out a lot."

Source: Adrian Slywotzky (1998), *The Profit Zone* (New York: Times Books), pp. 81–82.

- **Missionary selling.** In this kind of selling, the salesperson attempts to influence the decision maker rather than the user or purchasing agent. The missionary salesperson helps the buyer promote the product to internal or external customers.
- **Technical selling.** In many industries, the salesperson also acts as a technical consultant to the purchaser. For this to be successful, the salesperson must have strong technical training. For example, the Hewlett-Packard salespeople in the Imaging Systems Division must be knowledgeable about the latest developments in ultrasound and other medical imaging technologies.
- **Creative selling.** This method involves developing new customers and maintaining old ones by investing a considerable amount of time in understanding buyers' needs and wants.

A salesperson performs a wide variety of activities, including:

- **Planning the sales call.** The good salesperson spends a considerable amount of time planning the call. This planning includes using information provided by the company and past sales calls about competition (both the salesperson's and the customer's); the economic, technological, political, and social environment; and the product or service. Today, preparation also involves learning how to use the latest technology in giving presentations.
- **Traveling to the customer site and making the call.**
- **Filling out the call report.** This involves a detailed examination of what happened during the call, "win–loss" reports on new business won or customers lost, any information picked up about competition such as their prices, and any other market intelligence.
- **Post-call analysis.** The good salesperson analyzes what happened, talks with his or her supervisor, and collects feedback about the call that can be used in future efforts.
- **Communicating with the customer.** It has been said that after a sale is made, for the seller it is the end of the process, for the buyer it is only the beginning.[14] Thus, the good salesperson knows that establishing and maintaining rapport with the customer is necessary for future business. Even if no sale is made or a sale is lost, communicating with customers or potential customers is vital.

Thus, there are different kinds of sales jobs and different tasks to perform.

Managing the Sales Force Performance

What factors contribute to the success of a salesperson? Like other resources such as advertising and promotion, money spent on the sales force is expected to produce revenues and profits. As a result, companies are always interested in improving the performance of their sales forces. It is important for the marketing manager to develop a better understanding of the factors that contribute to a salesperson's success, in order to help improve one person's performance or the performance of a group of salespeople.

A number of models have been developed to help explain performance.[15] Figure 13.7 shows one such model. As can be seen, performance is a result of both internal or individual factors and external factors. We review these factors in more detail here.

Internal Factors

The salesperson's motivation is a basic force behind how much effort he or she devotes to the job (planning sales calls, following up on customer questions, filling out reports) and how he or she responds to different kinds of incentives. Clearly, the sales force is motivated by financial incentives such as commissions on sales, salary guarantees, and bonuses. However, salespeople can also be motivated by sales meetings and contests, education and training, and information about the company and its plans.

In a way, the marketing manager must understand what motivates his or her salespeople, just as the manager would have to know what motivates his or her customers to buy. Different salespeople are motivated by different factors. For example, a salesperson who has been with a company for many years may be more motivated to sell from company loyalty than is a younger salesperson who is looking to develop a track record for future career moves. Some salespeople (like people in general) are more motivated by money than others. Thus, it is critical to understand what motivates each salesperson on the force.

Salesperson performance is also affected by aptitude for selling, or natural ability to sell. It is generally thought that some people are born salespeople and others are not. However, this implies that selling skills cannot be taught, which is not true. At the same time, some aspects of aptitude, such as empathy and persuasiveness, cannot be taught easily and do give one person an edge over another.

Aptitude is a person's natural ability. Acquired skill is also important for a good salesperson. As we have just noted, good selling skills can be taught. There are many courses available, offered both within companies and by specialized firms. These can teach aspiring and experienced salespeople how to improve their communications, negotiation, closing, and other skills involved with personal selling. In addition, in technical selling

Figure 13.7

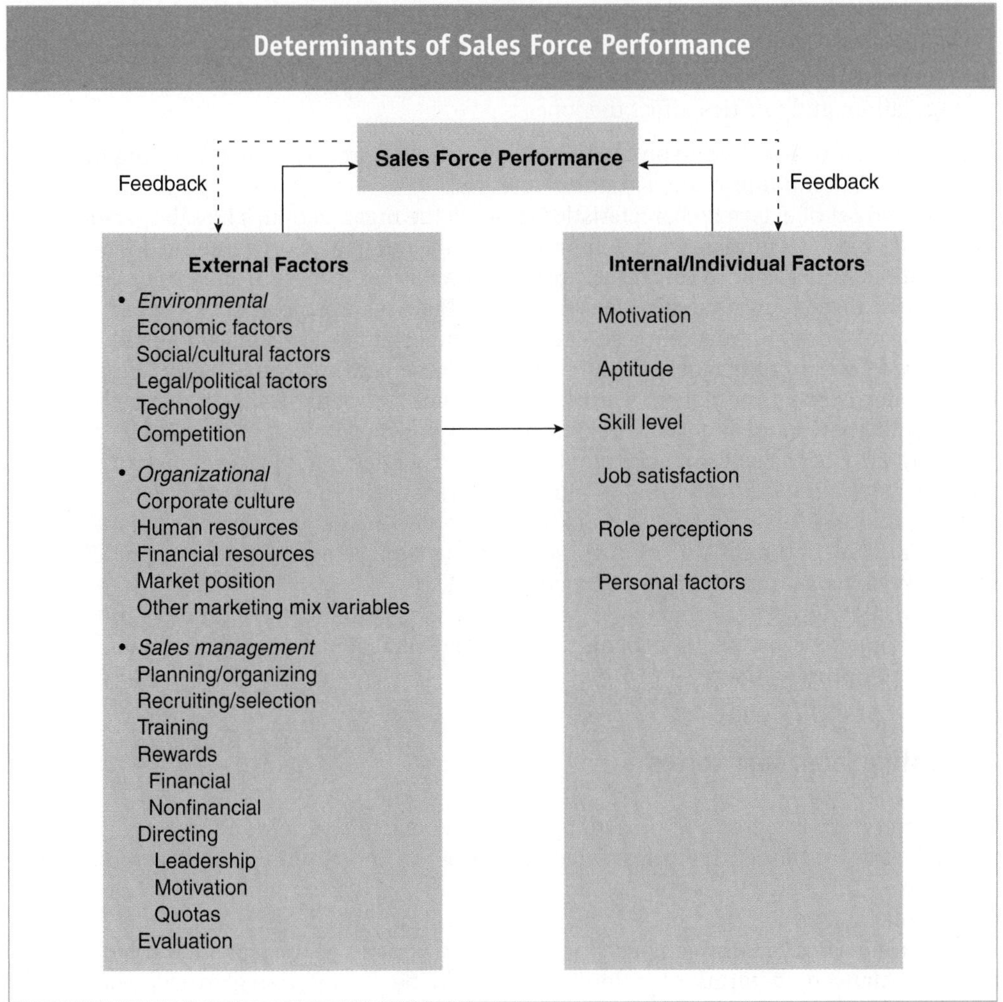

Source: Rolph E. Anderson, Joseph F. Hair, Jr., and Alan Bush (1992), *Professional Sales Management*, 2nd ed. (New York: McGraw-Hill). Reproduced with permission of the McGraw-Hill Companies.

situations, selling skill is enhanced by continuous updating of the scientific knowledge relevant to the product.

Not surprisingly, higher levels of job satisfaction have been found to be positively correlated with salesperson performance. Research has found that satisfaction is related to both intrinsic and extrinsic motivation. Intrinsic motivation comes from within and is related to the satisfaction a salesperson obtains from the different aspects of the job, such as being on the road and meeting people. Extrinsic satisfaction is derived from rewards such as promotions, salary increases, and sales contests.

The salesperson also needs to understand both his or her superior's expectations and the kind of selling that is necessary to be successful. This knowledge is called role perception. For example, if the sales manager expects the salesperson to spend half of his or her time taking care of the stock on the shelves and the salesperson thinks that is a minor part of the job, this mismatch in expectations will lead to lower performance.

Finally, personal attributes such as gender, attractiveness, education level, and other factors are often related to success in particular industries.

External Factors

Environmental factors have a major effect on performance. These are derived from the marketing plan described in Chapter 1. Included are:

- **Customers.** Obviously, changes in customers' tastes, buying behavior, and their own competitive conditions make the salesperson's job more difficult.
- **Competitors.** Tracking the competition is important for successful selling. This involves more than prices (the usual focus of salespeople). It also

involves changes in their strategies, financial condition, product line, and other factors.

- **The industry environment.** Changes in technology, social changes, economic shifts, regulation, and politics affect the job.

In general, the wise salesperson obtains the product or product line marketing plan and absorbs the information in the situation analysis.

A second set of external characteristics relate to the organization. The salesperson's success is affected by a number of factors internal to the company for which he or she works. For example, it is easier to sell if the products are market leaders. Conversely, the market position is affected by the sales force's efforts. Poor market position is not necessarily caused by unsuccessful marketing strategies. An important factor is the amount of financial resources a company puts into sales efforts. Sales force performance is likely to improve as more money is spent on higher salaries, better incentives, better training, and selling aids. High-quality personnel and a culture that supports personal selling efforts also help.

The quality of the sales management also directly affects the performance of the sales force. This quality is affected by the amount of resources the company spends on sales management. It is also affected by the kind of people who occupy key sales management posts. They affect the organization by selecting capable salespeople, designing effective reward systems, and motivating salespeople.

Thus, sales force performance is affected by many elements, including individual, internal, and external factors. Senior marketing management must understand these factors and optimize them.

Designing Sales Territories

sales territory
a group of present and potential customers assigned to a salesperson, often designed on a geographic basis

A **sales territory** is a group of present and potential customers assigned to a salesperson. In most cases, as the term implies, sales territories are geographic areas selected to minimize travel time between accounts and delineate clearly which person is responsible for a particular account.

Designing sales territories is an important part of sales management. Territories that are not balanced in terms of potential sales can be demoralizing to the salespeople assigned to them. An insufficient number of territories means salespeople spend too much time traveling and not enough time selling. Too many territories means lower income and salespeople fighting over the geographic boundaries. This latter problem is particularly important to Cisco Systems, because it increased the size of its sales force as the company grew. Its sales force is very aggressive and used to be rewarded with significant bonuses for exceeding their sales quotas. If territories are shrunk, reps may wonder how they will meet their ever-increasing quotas with fewer potential customers.

There are three major, interrelated decisions concerning sales territories:

1. Deciding how many salespeople to have.
2. Designing the territories.
3. Allocating selling effort to the accounts.

Determining the Size of the Sales Force

Three major methods are used to estimate the sales force needed.

Breakdown Method

breakdown method
a major method used to determine the size of the sales force that is based on the forecasted sales level divided by an assumed average sales per salesperson

The **breakdown method** is a simple method that assumes an average productivity level for each salesperson. The number of salespeople needed can be computed from the following equation:

$$n = s/p$$

where n equals the number of salespeople needed, s equals the forecasted sales, and p equals the average sales per salesperson. Therefore, a company expecting to sell \$100 million worth of goods in 2010 with a sales force currently averaging \$5 million per salesperson needs 20 people.

The major problem with this method is similar to using the percentage of expected sales to set advertising budgets (see Chapter 10). This formula assumes that the number of salespeople is determined by the expected sales level when, in fact, the opposite is also true. That is, in many cases sales could be increased with more salespeople.

Using the "average" salesperson does not account for other factors. These include variations in territory potential, the mix of experienced and inexperienced salespeople if there is turnover, and other factors. In addition, the number is highly dependent on an accurate forecast for sales. As we noted in Chapter 3, forecasting sales accurately is highly problematic in most cases.

Workload Method

The **workload method** is based on the ability to calculate the total amount of work necessary to serve the entire market. The number of salespeople required is the total workload calculated divided by the amount of work the average salesperson is expected to handle. Six steps are required to implement this method:

workload method
a major method used to determine the size of the sales force that is based on the ability to calculate the total amount of work necessary to serve the entire market

1. **Classify all the firm's customers into categories.** It is common to divide the set of customers into three categories, based on the amount of sales for which they account (other criteria could be used as well). For example, you might classify your customers into A, B, and C customers based on an analysis of the distribution of sales. Customers classified as A might be the top 25 percent, B the next 50 percent, and C the bottom 25 percent. Even better, the assignment could be based on sales potential rather than actual sales.
2. **Determine the frequency with which each type of account should be called upon and the necessary length of each call.** For example, based on experience and judgment, the following data might be used:

   Class A: 12 times/year × 120 minutes/call = 1,440 minutes, or 24 hours

   Class B: 6 times/year × 60 minutes/call = 360 minutes, or 6 hours

   Class C: 2 times/year × 30 minutes/call = 60 minutes, or 1 hour
3. **Calculate the workload necessary to cover the entire market.** Let us assume that there are 200 A customers, 400 B customers, and 200 C customers. Then the total workload necessary would be:

   Class A: 200 customers × 24 hours = 4,800 hours

   Class B: 400 customers × 6 hours = 2,400 hours

   Class C: 200 customers × 1 hour = 200 hours

   or a total of 7,400 hours.
4. **Determine the time available for each salesperson.** Assume for this illustration that the typical salesperson works 48 weeks each year (4 weeks of vacation) for 50 hours each week. This gives a total of 2,400 hours per year for selling.
5. **Allocate the salesperson's time by task.** As we noted earlier in this chapter, the salesperson has activities other than selling (planning, writing up call reports) that take time. Supposing that selling is only 50 percent of the salesperson's time, then this implies that 1,200 hours (50 percent × 2,400 hours) can be allocated to selling.
6. **Calculate the number of salespeople needed.** This is simply the workload of 7,400 hours divided by the 1,200 hours available or 6.17 (rounded to 7) salespeople.

This method makes intuitive sense and is more logically appealing than the breakdown method. However, it also makes several assumptions that may not hold. Different accounts within a class may require different amounts of effort. For example, a class A account that has been active for many years may require little time, whereas a new account may require a great deal. Also, different salespeople operate with varying amounts of efficiency and can allocate more or less time for traveling, planning, and other activities.

Marginal Economic Method

Basic microeconomics teaches us that we should allocate a resource up to the point where the marginal revenue obtained from an additional unit of the resource equals the marginal cost. If we recast this method in terms of profit, particularly contribution margin (the amount of revenue that goes to cover fixed costs), it is very appealing. Suppose that it costs $60,000 to hire a salesperson. Based on this approach, salespeople should be hired as long as they can sell enough to generate $60,001 in contribution margin (much more in sales, depending on the variable margin rate). The $1 in contribution generated was previously unavailable and would go toward covering fixed costs.[16]

marginal economic method
a major method used to determine the size of the sales force, based on the microeconomic concept that a resource should be allocated up to the point at which the marginal revenue obtained from an additional unit of the resource equals the marginal cost

Although this **marginal economic method** sounds theoretically appealing, it is more difficult to implement than the other two because it is difficult to know what the "marginal" salesperson can generate in sales. In addition, the marginal sales volume will decrease as additional salespeople are added because the remaining customers are more difficult than those who are already buying your product or service.

Designing Sales Territories

The steps involved in designing sales territories are shown in Figure 13.8.

1. **Select the control unit.** This is the basic geographic unit that will be used to form the territories. The most common units are (in decreasing size) countries, states, counties, cities/standard metropolitan statistical areas (SMSAs), ZIP codes, and blocks. Obviously, the control unit varies by the kind of product or service. For a consumer product sold door-to-door, neighborhood-by-neighborhood, through Mary Kay or other multilevel selling companies, blocks would be appropriate. For nuclear power plants, countries would probably be more relevant. Of course, most products are somewhere in between those two extreme examples.
2. **Estimate the market potential in each basic geographic unit.** The methods described in Chapter 3 can be used.
3. **Form tentative territories.** To do this, contiguous geographic units should be combined so as to make the territories equal in market potential. This is only a first pass at the territory design. The number of territories should be based on calculations of the appropriate number of salespeople (note that this assumes the assignment of one salesperson per territory).
4. **Calculate the workload for each of the tentative territories.** The tentative territories formed in step 3 may be close to each other in market potential but may differ significantly in terms of workload. The first part of the workload analysis is to determine the distribution of accounts by their size (based on actual revenues, potential, or some other measure). However, in this case the analysis must be done at a micro level, that is, account by account. Subsequently, each account must be assessed for the amount of time necessary to serve it. A potential account would be allocated more time because more selling effort is needed to create a new account than to maintain an existing one. An account planning matrix like the one shown in

Figure 13.8

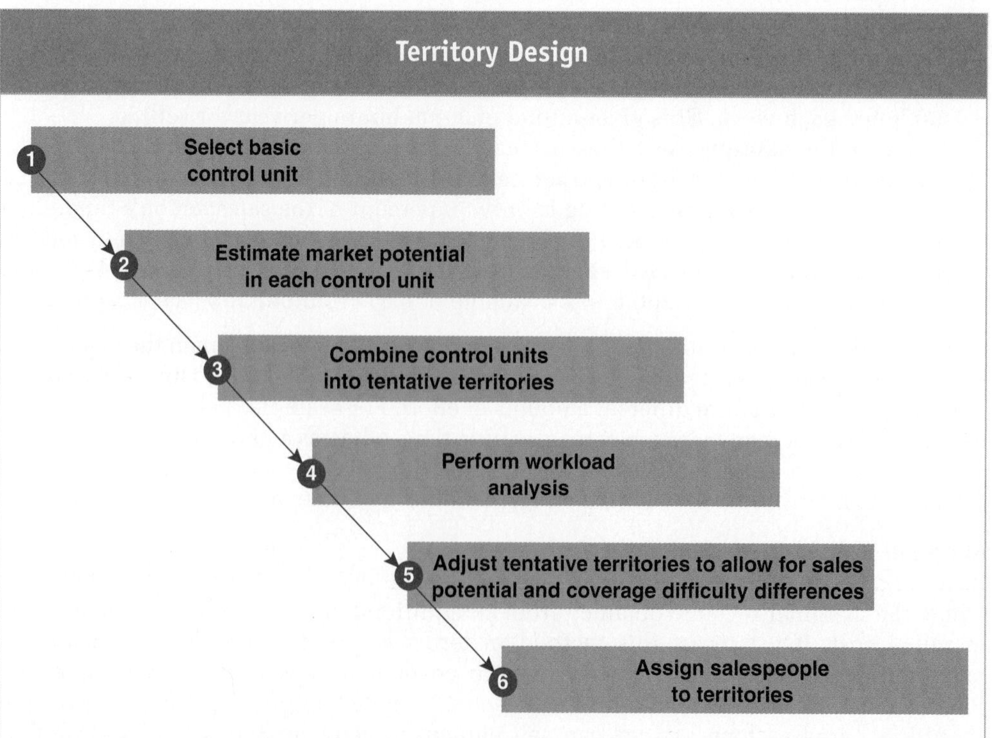
Territory Design
1 Select basic control unit
2 Estimate market potential in each control unit
3 Combine control units into tentative territories
4 Perform workload analysis
5 Adjust tentative territories to allow for sales potential and coverage difficulty differences
6 Assign salespeople to territories

Source: Mark W. Johnston & Greg W. Marshall (2006), *Churchill/Ford/Walker's Sales Force Management*, 8th ed. (Boston: McGraw-Hill/Irwin), p. 160. Reproduced with permission of the Mc Graw-Hill Companies.

Figure 13.9

Account Planning Matrix

Account Potential	Strong	Weak
High	**Opportunity** Account offers good opportunity. It has high potential and sales organization has a differential advantage in serving it. **Strategy** Commit high levels of sales resources to take advantage of the opportunity.	**Opportunity** Account may represent a good opportunity. Sales organization needs to overcome its competitive disadvantage and strengthen its position to capitalize on the opportunity. **Strategy** Either direct a high level of sales resources to improve position and to take advantage of the opportunity or shift resources to other accounts.
Low	**Opportunity** Account offers stable opportunity since sales organization has differential advantage in serving it. **Strategy** Allocate moderate level of sales resources to maintain current advantage.	**Opportunity** Account offers little opportunity. Its potential is small and the sales organization is at a competitive disadvantage in serving it. **Strategy** Devote minimal level of resources to the account or consider abandoning the account altogether.

Competitive Advantage

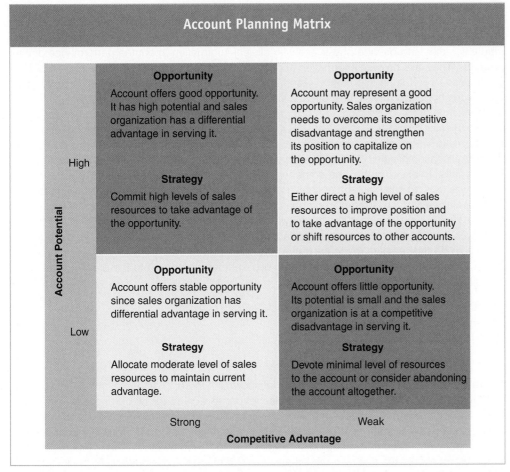

Source: Gilbert A. Church, Neil M. Ford Jr., and Orville C. Walker. *Sales Force Management,* 8th ed., p. 191. Reproduced with permission of the Mc Graw-Hill Companies.

Figure 13.9 could be used to prioritize the accounts and determine the effort needed to service each one. The total workload can then be computed for each territory.

5. **Adjust the tentative territories.** The workload analysis (and any other relevant information) is then used to adjust the initial solution to territory design. Again, adjustments should be contiguous so that salespeople do not waste time traveling through another salesperson's territory.
6. **Assign salespeople to territories.** This step is more difficult than it sounds. Salespeople have varying abilities and fit better with different kinds of accounts. Some are better at developing new accounts, some are better at maintaining relationships, some are better with smaller accounts, and some are better with larger accounts. There are also personal aspects that must be considered. A salesperson who was born and raised on the West Coast may not be interested in moving to the Southeast.

Application | Syntex Corporation

An approach combining management science and managerial judgment called decision calculus can be used to develop sales territories and assign salespeople to them as well as make other sales planning decisions. This approach was applied to Syntex Corporation (now owned by Hoffman-La Roche), an international life sciences company that develops, manufactures, and markets a wide range of health and personal care products.[17] Syntex Laboratories is the U.S. human pharmaceutical sales subsidiary. A main product line is anti-inflammatory drugs to treat arthritis, analgesics for pain, oral contraceptives, a variety of topical products for skin diseases, and other related products.

Syntex's major products include Naprosyn, used to treat arthritis; Anaprox, an analgesic; Lidex and Synalar, topical steroid creams for skin inflammations; Norinyl, an oral contraceptive; and Nasalide, a steroid nasal spray for treating hay fever and other allergies. The success of these drugs propelled the division to account for 46 percent of the total corporate sales.

In ethical or prescription pharmaceutical sales, often called detailing, the target customers are normally physicians who prescribe the drugs for their patients. This is a difficult job because appointments are hard to obtain and the competition is fierce. Pharmaceutical salespeople distribute samples and provide physicians with clinical information about the performance of their products. They also provide information about recommended dosage levels and thus must be a credible source of such information. As in any salesperson's job, the major decisions to make are which physicians to visit, how often to visit them, and what information to present.

At the time of this illustration, the vice president for sales at Syntex oversaw six regional and 47 district sales managers, as well as 433 general sales representatives. The major decisions he had to make were how many salespeople to have, their geographic allocation and call frequency, allocation of sales calls across physician specialties, and which products to feature during the calls. To assist in this, the company used a version of a model called CALLPLAN. The model was used to calculate the optimal amount of sales effort needed for the different products and specialties and the different contribution margin opportunities available for different sizes of the sales force. One version of the model was used to allocate sales calls to specialties, and the other was used to determine the appropriate number of sales presentations for each product.

To help do this, a sales response curve was estimated for each brand. The sales force was asked to estimate the sales level that would be expected compared to the present level under the following levels of sales effort:

- No sales effort.
- One-half of the current sales effort.
- 50 percent more effort than current level.
- A saturation level of effort, a huge increase from current level.

The result was a sales response curve like that shown in Figure 13.10.

Figure 13.10 shows two hypothetical sales response curves for two brands, A and B. The basic idea comes from microeconomics. An additional salesperson should be assigned to pursue the customer that provides the greatest incremental contribution to profit. Suppose that the company has three salespeople assigned to brand A and two to B. Using Figure 13.10, to which brand should the first new rep be assigned? If the rep is assigned to A, the incremental profit is $100; if assigned to B, it is about $75. Thus, the first new rep should be assigned to A. To which brand should a second rep be assigned? The marginal contribution obtained from going from four to five reps is only about $50. Thus, the second new rep should be assigned to B. This process would continue until no incremental profit was obtained from hiring another salesperson for either product.

Figure 13.10

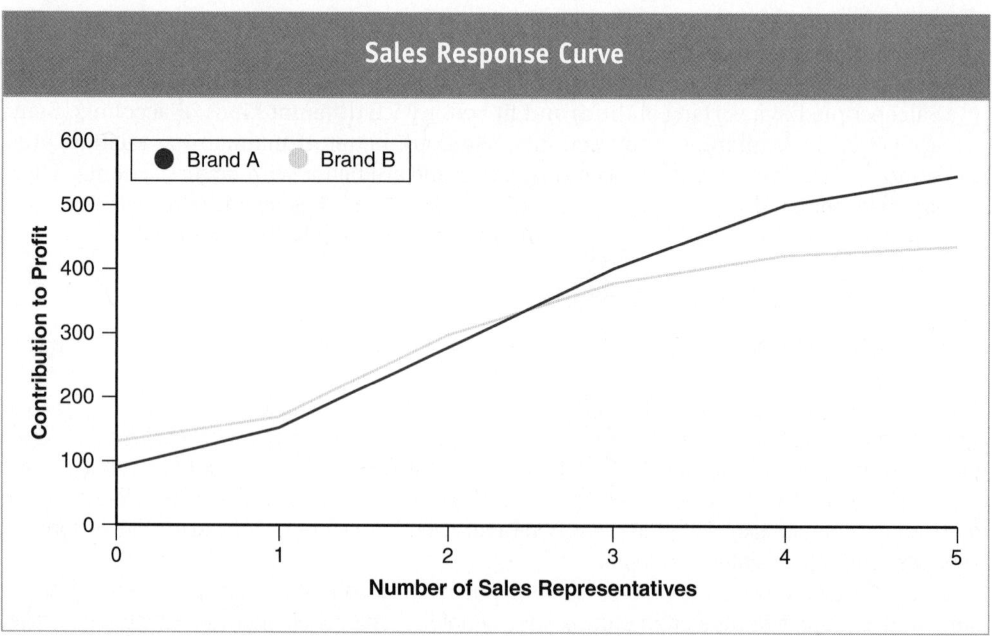

Source: Darral G. Clarke (1983), "Syntex Laboratories (A)," Harvard Business School case #9-584-033, p. 12.

The application of the model to Syntex data showed that the sales force should be increased to more than 700 representatives and that this would produce more than $7 million in additional profits. The analysis is based on a combination of managerial judgment and statistical modeling. However, the company had been previously using very informal, simplified analyses.

Computer analyses for territory design and salesperson assignment are common today. These programs combine sophisticated geographic mapping capabilities with optimization algorithms. Such software is sold by TerrAlign (http://www.terralign.com). TerrAlign:

- Automatically generates optimal calling plans for the field sales force.
- Minimizes distance between calls.
- Calculates call frequency requirements for customers.
- Balances the weekly calls across customers.

Setting Sales Quotas

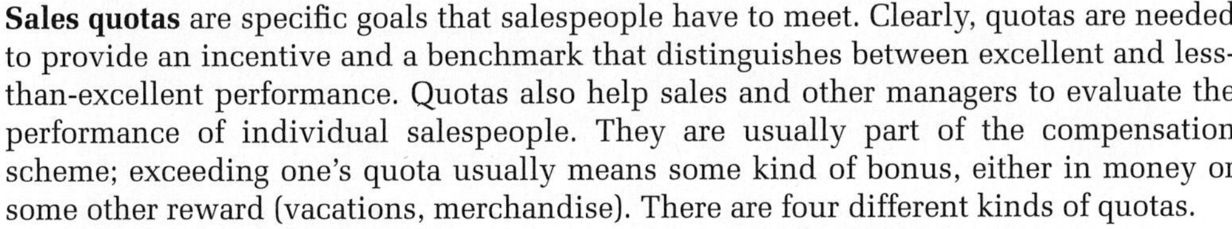

Sales quotas are specific goals that salespeople have to meet. Clearly, quotas are needed to provide an incentive and a benchmark that distinguishes between excellent and less-than-excellent performance. Quotas also help sales and other managers to evaluate the performance of individual salespeople. They are usually part of the compensation scheme; exceeding one's quota usually means some kind of bonus, either in money or some other reward (vacations, merchandise). There are four different kinds of quotas.

sales quotas
specific sales goals that salespeople are required to meet

Sales Volume Based Quotas

The most commonly used quota is based on sales volume, in dollars or units sold. Quotas could be based on total sales volume or on individual product or product line sales. The latter criterion is particularly useful when new products are introduced because salespeople are more inclined to sell proven winners than uncertain products. Monetary quotas are easy to understand but may give extra incentives to sell higher-priced items, which may not necessarily produce the most profits.

Profit Based Quotas

These quotas normally are stated in terms of profit margins (gross or net). Such quotas steer the salespeople toward the products and services that are the most profitable to the company rather than those that are the highest priced or easiest to sell. A problem with this kind of quota is that it is more difficult for the salesperson to know where she or he stands in relation to the quota than when sales volume–based quotas are used. Profit margins can be manipulated by accounting procedures, which are a mystery to most marketing personnel.

Combination Quotas

More and more companies are basing their quotas on combinations of metrics. These quotas are based on the different activities that must be performed by a salesperson as well as sales or profits. Some of these activities include:

- Number of customers called on.
- Number of demonstrations made.
- Number of new accounts established.

Because the job of the salesperson is moving away from strictly selling to developing and managing long-term customer relationships, quotas are also changing to combinations of traditional measures plus information from customer satisfaction surveys. Before being acquired by Oracle, 40 percent of each salesperson's incentive compensation at Siebel Systems was based on customer satisfaction. Other large companies such as Nortel, eBay, and AT&T are changing their incentive schemes in a similar manner.

Compensation

Figure 13.11 shows the different components of potential compensation and their objectives. The basic form of compensation is normally salary plus commission. A **commission** is a payment based directly on a sale or some other activity. For example,

commission
a form of compensation based directly on a sale or some other activity

Figure 13.11

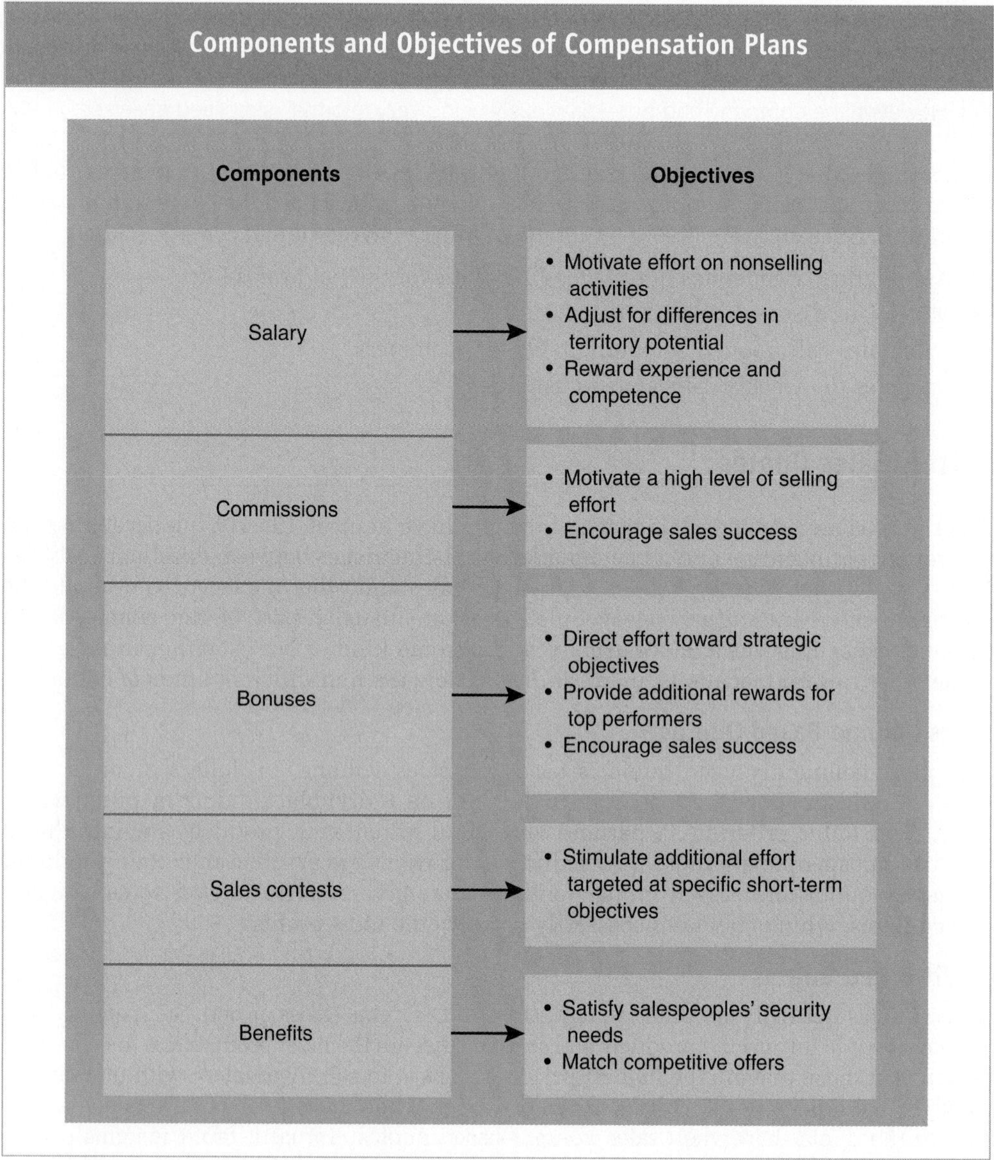

Components and Objectives of Compensation Plans
Components
Objectives
Salary
• Motivate effort on nonselling activities
• Adjust for differences in territory potential
• Reward experience and competence
Commissions
• Motivate a high level of selling effort
• Encourage sales success
Bonuses
• Direct effort toward strategic objectives
• Provide additional rewards for top performers
• Encourage sales success
Sales contests
• Stimulate additional effort targeted at specific short-term objectives
Benefits
• Satisfy salespeoples' security needs
• Match competitive offers

Source: Mark W. Johnston & Greg W. Marshall (2006), *Churchill/Ford/Walker's Sales Force Management*, 8th ed. (Boston: McGraw-Hill/Irwin), p. 336. Reproduced with permission of the Mc Graw-Hill Companies.

the sale of a $10,000 pump might mean a 1 percent or $100 commission to the salesperson. **Salary** is the basic amount of money paid regularly to the salesperson. Other forms of compensation are available to sales managers. **Incentive payments** are monetary awards for special performance. They are usually given in recognition of particularly outstanding sales performance, such as a President's Circle of the top 1 percent of the salespeople in a company. **Sales contests** are competitions to achieve some short-term goal (e.g., the introduction of a new product).

salary
a form of compensation in which a basic amount of money is paid to a worker on a regular basis

incentive payments
monetary awards for special performance

sales contests
sales force competitions to achieve a short-term goal.

The most common decision to be made by a sales or senior marketing manager is what combination of salary and commission to use. A sales force could be paid on straight (100 percent) salary, straight commission, or some combination of both.

Straight Salary

This kind of compensation scheme is useful when management is more interested in long-term goals than simply selling as much volume as possible. For example, as we have noted earlier, because of the increased recognition that long-term customer relationships are more profitable than simple transactions, more time is spent on relationship-building activities than in past years. Much of the time spent in relationship building does not generate immediate revenue. In addition, other activities such as competitor analysis and market research are valuable investments of time that do not generate revenue. If management wants to encourage such activities, straight salary is more logical than commissions. Another instance in which straight salary makes sense is one in which the products and services have long selling cycles. It takes several years for Boeing salespeople to close a deal to sell airplanes to British Airways. Similarly, large construction projects, nuclear power plants, supercomputers, and other products take a long time to sell. In such cases, compensation based largely on commission would not work well. Finally, straight salary is often used for new salespeople, who are unlikely to generate substantial sales in the short run. The challenge with compensation schemes based largely on salary is to tie salary increases to performance.

Straight Commission

Clearly, commissions give salespeople incentives to sell because there is a direct relationship between income and performance. Such a scheme also rewards the best performers. Underperforming salespeople do not receive as much income. Commission schemes are also easy to manage because the payments are tied directly to visible performance. In addition, commission programs can be targeted. New products that are important to the company can be awarded higher commissions than existing products. However, in general, straight commission programs give management little control over what the sales force does because each salesperson will try to maximize his or her income in his or her own way. This usually means that activities that do not result directly in a sale are ignored. Such programs can also be discouraging during a period when the company's products are not selling well. Commission-based compensation schemes can be difficult to implement when a national accounts program overlaps with a local sales force. There are often problems allocating the commissions between the relevant parties when a sale is made. Finally, straight commission schemes produce fluctuating incomes for the sales force. In practice, there are few straight commission selling jobs. Many are found in the multilevel marketing industry (e.g., Amway, Mary Kay).

Commission plans can become complicated in multichannel systems. This is actually a channel conflict issue, which was discussed in the previous chapter. Companies are giving salespeople commissions on products even when they do not make the sale, if that sale is made with one of "their" customers but through another channel. The Ingersoll-Rand illustration from the previous chapter is one example of how this works. Additionally, Amway runs a Web site, Quixtar, where you can input a local Amway IBO's (Independent Business Owner) ID number before you make a purchase. This permits the local rep to get credit for the sale even though he or she did not make a presentation. It does not cost the customer any more money and maintains the personal relationship with the sales rep, who is usually a neighbor or relative.

Combination Plans

Most compensation schemes combine salary and additional financial incentives (commissions or bonuses). These plans provide some incentive to perform nonrevenue activities and a base, secure level of income while still rewarding the best performers above the rest.

Controlling and Evaluating the Sales Force

The sales manager must perform some kind of analysis of sales force performance given our emphasis in this book on understanding the ROI of marketing expenditures. Many objective or quantitative measures can be used in this evaluation. Table 13.1 shows some of the more typical ratios of input and output measures that can be used.

There are two types of output measures:

1. **Orders.** Of importance are the number and size of the orders obtained.
2. **Accounts.** Typically measured are the number of active, new, lost, prospective, and overdue accounts.

Table 13.1

Common Ratios Used to Evaluate Salespeople

Expense ratios		
• Sales expense ratio	=	$\frac{\text{Expenses}}{\text{Sales}}$
• Cost per call ratio	=	$\frac{\text{Total costs}}{\text{Number of calls}}$
Account development and servicing ratios		
• Account penetration ratio	=	$\frac{\text{Accounts sold}}{\text{Total accounts available}}$
• New account conversion ratio	=	$\frac{\text{Number of new accounts}}{\text{Total number of accounts}}$
• Lost account ratio	=	$\frac{\text{Prior accounts not sold}}{\text{Total number of accounts}}$
• Sales per account ratio	=	$\frac{\text{Sales dollar volume}}{\text{Total number of accounts}}$
• Average order size ratio	=	$\frac{\text{Sales dollar volume}}{\text{Total number of orders}}$
• Order cancellation ratio	=	$\frac{\text{Number of cancelled orders}}{\text{Total number of orders}}$
Call activity or productivity		
• Calls per day ratio	=	$\frac{\text{Number of calls}}{\text{Number of days worked}}$
• Calls per account ratio	=	$\frac{\text{Number of calls}}{\text{Number of accounts}}$
• Planned call ratio	=	$\frac{\text{Number of planned calls}}{\text{Total number of calls}}$
• Order per call (hit) ratio	=	$\frac{\text{Number of orders}}{\text{Total number of calls}}$

Source: Mark W. Johnston and Greg W. Marshall (2006), *Churchill/Ford/Walker's Sales Force Management*, 8th ed. (New York: McGraw-Hill), p. 418. Reproduced with permission of the Mc Graw-Hill Companies.

There are several kinds of input measures:

- Sales calls.
- Time efficiency (how many calls per day the salesperson makes).
- Expenses.
- Time spent on nonselling activities.

Numbers are important, but they do not tell the whole story. Without further investigation, the sales or marketing manager sees the results but not the process. Understanding the process is critical to a better understanding of the results, and therefore provides a blueprint for change. As a result, subjective or qualitative measures are also used to evaluate sales force performance. An evaluator uses a rating scale to evaluate each salesperson on the following dimensions:

- **Sales.** This includes not just sales volume, which can be measured using external metrics, but how well the person is doing with different kinds of accounts and the whole product line.
- **Job knowledge.** Does the person understand the role of a salesperson in the company? Does the salesperson understand the company's policies and products?

- **Management of the sales territory.** This rates how well the salesperson manages his or her time, completes call reports, and so on.
- **Customer and company relations.** The salesperson must have good relationships with customers and internal personnel (shipping, product management).
- **Personal characteristics.**

The Changing Nature of the Sales Force: The Impact of Technology

The typical salesperson of today is not the classic Willy Loman from *Death of a Salesman*. The successful salesperson is now highly skilled in using technological tools that enable her or him to work with prospective customers in an efficient way to solve problems. These include computers, information systems, and efficient communication links from the field to the home office. Investments in such technology invariably pay off in increased sales and return on investment.

This reengineering of sales, called **virtual selling**, has occurred for several reasons:[18]

virtual selling
the reengineering of sales in the 1990s, especially the impact of sales force automation and the salesperson's educated use of technological tools in working with prospective customers in a highly efficient way

- The personal selling job has become more complex and it is getting more difficult to make a sale. This is because products in some industries have become more complex (mainly in technology-based industries). The notion of a salesperson trotting around with a product catalogue has virtually disappeared.
- Customers have become more knowledgeable about what they want, but they also need guidance and advice about what products and services would help them the most.
- Corporations are becoming increasingly flat, with fewer middle managers providing product information for more senior managers. Salespeople are thus being called on to provide more information directly to decision makers. This flattening phenomenon is also hitting sales forces.
- Intensifying global competition means more pressure at the point-of-sale as there are more companies competing for the sale.
- Demand for productivity improvements from all parts of the organization, including sales, has increased.

Ideally, the virtual selling organization would have the features shown in Table 13.2. Although these are worthwhile goals, few companies are anywhere near achieving all of them. However, many have made substantial progress toward fully automating their sales forces. Most of the features shown in Table 13.2 are available through software provided by companies such as salesforce.com and Sage Saleslogix for small companies, and Oracle for large firms. Using laptop computers, smartphones, and the Web, salespeople find new sales leads, share information with management and other salespeople, better understand their customers, customize presentations and products for customers, and make the overall selling process more efficient and effective.

Sales force automation (SFA) can also help companies deliver more value to the customer. Today, SFA is generally considered to be a component of an overall customer relationship management (CRM) strategy, which we will cover in the next chapter. For example, the sales force for a truck manufacturer asks each potential customer what kinds of jobs a new truck will do and what kinds of loads they will be hauling. On a laptop computer, a salesperson can examine maps of the truck routes and determine the grades of the hills along the routes. Based on this and other information, the salesperson can recommend the appropriate model and features on the spot and even recommend financing options. The truck company is also planning to phase out preprinted brochures and replace them with materials that can be printed out on the spot when requested.

Special-purpose computer software has also been developed to help salespeople perform standard activities. For example, contact management software tracks different kinds of information, from what happened on the last sales call with a customer to birthdays and other special events. For companies with large product lines, order configuration software keeps track of pricing structures and technical specifications so that the field salespeople are always up to date. This frees the rep from having to carry around volumes of literature or memorize large numbers of facts.

Table 13.2

The Virtual Selling Organization
• Equips salespeople with all of their leads, prospects, and contacts
• Provides the facility to track, record, and communicate all the history of an opportunity or account
• Supports team selling and workgroup collaboration
• Facilitates work flow and routing for approvals
• Provides access to all relevant information on products, price, competitors, and decision issues
• Incorporates support for unique selling methods and processes that support sales cycle tracking and analysis
• Provides salespeople with the ability to create custom presentations and on-demand, customized sales literature
• Enables the salesperson to find the best combination of products and services based on a customer's unique profile
• Empowers the salesperson to make his or her own decisions, develop custom contracts and proposals, and, acting as the customer's advocate, organize ad hoc interdepartmental company teams
• Offers online sales training on sales processes and new products and services
• Automates the administrative tasks of recording, tracking, and reporting salespeople's appointments, activities, correspondence, literature fulfillment, expenses, and forecasts
• Creates closed-loop marketing and sales systems that ensure complete traceability from marketing spending on lead generation through sales closure, product shipment, and customer support

Source: Thomas M. Siebel and Michael S. Malone (1996), *Virtual Selling* (New York: Free Press), pp. 13–14. Adapted with the permission of The Free Press, A Division of Simon & Schuster Adult Publishing Group, from *Virtual Selling: Going Beyond the Automated Sales Forces to Achieve Total Sales Quality* by Thomas Siebel and Michael Malone.

Application Waters NuGenesis Technologies Corp.

Waters NuGenesis Technologies Corporation sells software designed to help pharmaceutical and biotech researchers capture, share, and sift through large quantities of data rapidly.[19] Although the company specialized in products that helped its customers automate its data analysis procedures, it had no sales force automation system of its own. The company's five-person sales force used Excel spreadsheets to keep records and relied on faxes from trade shows to identify potential prospects. To better penetrate multinational companies and coordinate multi–sales representative/multichannel offers to large companies like Merck, company managers knew they had to significantly upgrade their sales force's tools with modern SFA products.

The company used software from SalesLogix to outfit its sales force. Among the standard features noted earlier, the software was customized to add data fields with managers' sales forecasts to enable a comparison to each salesperson's forecast. This was used to reach agreement about which prospects would receive additional sales support from senior managers. The software also enables the sales force to send customized e-mails to 90,000 contacts tailored by industry such as biotech, genomics, or medicinal chemistry. The software also enables Waters NuGenesis to track e-mail response rates and trade-show effectiveness.

The results of adopting the SFA software were impressive. Since 1999, the company's client base grew from a small number of companies to nearly 100 in 2001, including luminaries such as 3M, Pfizer, and Genentech.

Application Lanier Worldwide

Lanier Worldwide, a wholly owned subsidiary of Ricoh Corporation, is one of the world's largest providers of document management systems, services, and support, with revenues of more than $1 billion.[20] In 1995, Lanier managers faced a problem: the cost of getting and placing an order for any of its office equipment was averaging $27 per order, substantially higher than the figure of $3 that came from research conducted in similar firms.

Lanier managers discovered that there were three reasons for this discrepancy:

1. All orders were taken and processed manually.
2. The information on customers was often inaccurate and duplicative.
3. Because the sales force lacked modern sales tools to help generate leads and make sales, the turnover rate among the sales force was 120 percent.

The manual order entry and processing caused a high error rate and delayed the fulfillment of orders because the sales force was quoting inaccurate prices, necessitating manual correction by back-office personnel. Inaccurate records on what customers had purchased led to free service being given to customers who may not have deserved it. High turnover rates of salespeople eroded records of the customer base as they left with the index cards on which they had recorded customer data. Profitability of product lines was impossible to compute.

The new Lanier system was developed in three phases:

1. **Phase one.** The company introduced its Market Encyclopedia System to provide the sales force with the tools needed to make customer presentations. It contains the sales and marketing information Lanier used to distribute in hard copy every week, including technical specifications on all its products and services, price and performance comparisons with competitors' products, and information on trends in the industry. It also provides video clips and slides that sales representatives can use to make different types of presentations.
2. **Phase two.** The company created its Opportunity Management System, a lead qualification process. The system gives the sales force access to a list of more than 10 million names of managers at U.S. companies, with details on the companies and the types of equipment they have purchased in the past. The system also provides a checklist of steps each sales rep should take to move from the lead stage to closing the deal. When a sale is completed, an order form is generated for the customer's signature.
3. **Phase three.** The Zero Defect Order system builds and prices the system that meets the customer's needs, including all required and optional equipment and accessories. The system permits the rep to give discounts, but also indicates at what point a discount will reduce his or her sales commission.

The financial benefits of the new system appeared quickly. Lanier achieved $48 million in cost savings in the first year through higher productivity because sales force turnover fell from 120 percent to 50 percent and free service was given only to customers who warranted it. In addition, the cost per order dropped from $27 to $16 to $15. The system also generated important information for the company. Lanier's managers could now perform a profitability analysis of each national account, which enabled them to tailor compensation and add or subtract resources on an account-by-account basis. In addition, the company can track profits by product segment. For example, Lanier discovered that the profit margins on its analog copier business are increasing when they thought they were decreasing.

Other Innovations

Because of its importance to many companies, sales force management is constantly being scrutinized for new approaches that can increase efficiency and effectiveness. For example, AstraZeneca, a London-based pharmaceutical company, is testing an approach that would entice doctors to initiate the sales call rather than its salespeople. Using products from a company called iPhysicianNet, the company installed computers with Internet access and videoconferencing capabilities in the offices of 7,500 physicians in the United States. In exchange for free use of the computer and Web connections for other purposes, the doctors agreed to use the system to participate in at least one video call each month with one of the eight pharmaceutical companies sharing the service. Because the call takes place at the doctor's convenience, it lasts an average of nine minutes, four times longer than a salesperson usually gets. Although the company's 6,000 salespeople were concerned that the system would replace them, many doctors requested follow-up visits, so it opened the doors to some doctors who refused to meet with any salesperson.[21] Another approach being used is to simply allow doctors to see live medical presentations on the web. Medconference (see Figure 13.12) is a service that brings experts and new findings directly to doctors through the presentation, which also allow the doctors to submit questions by voice or online chats.

Figure 13.12 Medconference website

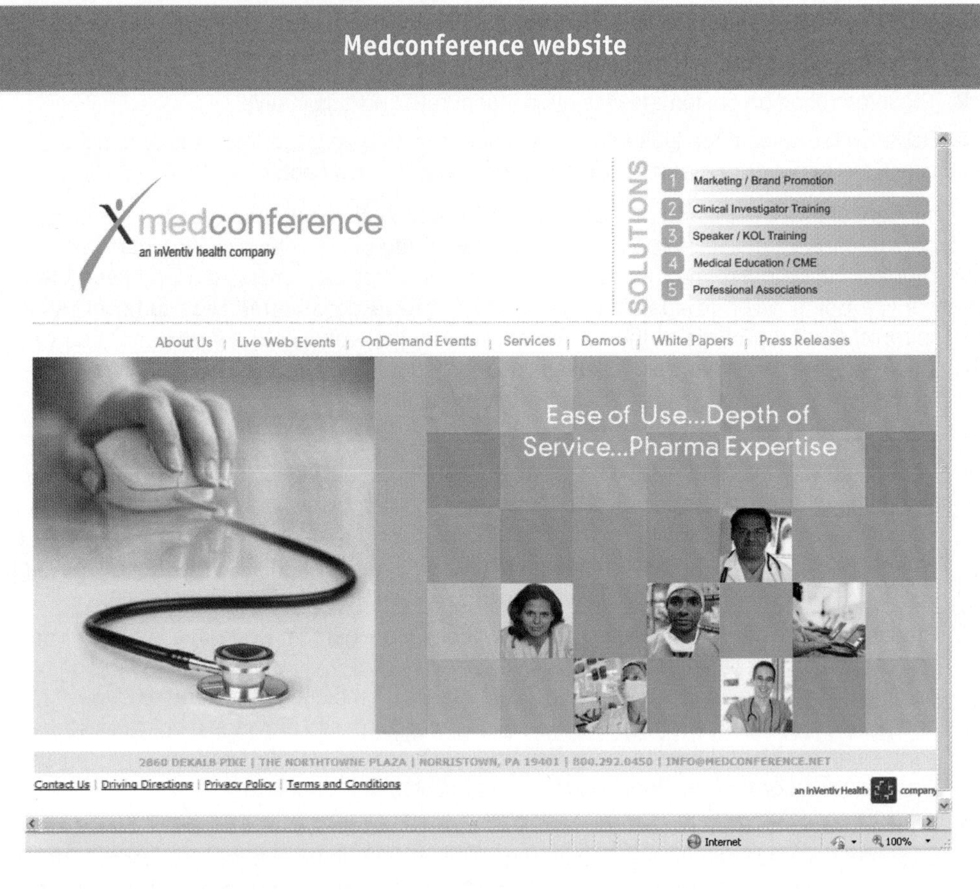

Source: Medconference.com. Copyright © 2010 by MedConference LLC. Reprinted with permission.

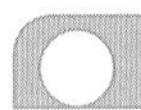

Direct Marketing

direct marketing
an interactive marketing system used to generate incremental sales or revenues for any organization in any industry
Source: www.thedma.org, Power of Direct Marketing, 2009-2010 Edition, p. 59. Used by permission, courtesy of the Direct Marketing Association.

One of the strongest trends in marketing has been toward increasing use of **direct marketing**. Direct marketing is most often associated with traditional methods such as direct mail (often called junk mail) and telemarketing. However, it also includes Internet-based marketing as well as radio, TV (e.g., "infomercials" and home shopping channels), and teleconferencing. In general, direct marketing includes any method of distribution that gives the customer access to the firm's products and services without any other intermediaries (generally, direct marketing excludes the sales force) through some form of communications. Thus, like personal selling, direct marketing is a hybrid of a channel and communication device.

The definition of direct marketing is:[22]

> *Direct marketing is an interactive marketing system that uses one or more advertising media to affect a measurable response and/or transaction at any location.*

measurable response
the estimation of the effects of a marketing program such as direct marketing

Two key parts of this definition are the word **interactive** and the phrase **measurable response**. Direct marketing is a one-to-one activity and targets individual people or organizations. In addition, it is engaged to deliver a short-run response (much like sales promotion) that is easily measurable by the sponsoring organization.

In the introduction to this chapter, some overall numbers on the size of the direct-marketing business were given. Table 13.3 gives more details about the size of the market by medium and by consumer versus business-to-business. Direct marketing-driven sales represents sales within particular industries or geographic areas (nation or state) directly caused by direct marketing advertising activities. Expressed differently, direct marketing-driven sales are incremental sales to the industry or region that would not exist but for the successful use of direct marketing advertising communications. Direct marketing-driven sales excludes those sales caused by factors other than direct marketing. Direct marketing-driven sales grew 5.7 percent per year from 2003 to 2009 and are projected to grow by 5.3 percent from 2009 through 2013.

Why has there been such an increase in the use of direct response methods? Two events, occurring simultaneously, have driven this trend. First, in an era where cost control is of paramount importance, direct marketing can be used to make the channel system more efficient. For example, direct mail can be used to reach prospects that would be too expensive to reach with a sales force because of their disparate geographic locations or low purchase

Table 13.3

DM-Driven Sales by Medium and Market (Billions of Dollars)

	2003	2007	2008	2009	2013	Compound Annual Growth 2003–08	Compound Annual Growth 2003–13
DIRECT MAIL (NON-CATALOGUE)	**$407.2**	**$533.7**	**$547.7**	**$561.7**	**$639.1**	**6.1%**	**3.1%**
Consumer	269.7	347.8	354.9	362.0	410.7	5.6%	3.0%
Business-to-Business	137.5	185.2	192.8	199.8	228.4	7.0%	3.4%
DIRECT MAIL (CATALOGUE)	**117.4**	**149.0**	**154.7**	**158.6**	**182.5**	**5.7%**	**3.4%**
Consumer	78.0	98.4	101.9	104.2	120.5	5.5%	3.4%
Business-to-Business	39.5	50.6	52.8	54.4	62.0	6.0%	3.3%
TELEPHONE MARKETING	**372.8**	**370.7**	**363.8**	**359.4**	**366.1**	**−0.5%**	**0.1%**
Consumer	172.8	166.5	161.7	158.5	159.3	−1.3%	−0.3%
Business-to-Business	199.9	204.1	202.1	200.9	206.8	0.2%	0.5%
INTERNET MKTG(NON-EMAIL)	**197.5**	**415.5**	**481.5**	**559.0**	**903.0**	**19.5%**	**13.4%**
Consumer	93.0	199.0	230.3	270.0	452.6	19.9%	14.5%
Business-to-Business	104.5	216.5	251.2	289.0	450.4	19.2%	12.4%
COMMERCIAL EMAIL	**11.9**	**24.0**	**28.0**	**32.6**	**53.2**	**18.7%**	**13.7%**
Consumer	5.5	11.4	13.3	15.6	26.6	19.2%	14.9%
Business-to-Business	6.3	12.6	14.7	17.0	26.7	18.3%	12.7%
DR NEWSPAPER	**192.1**	**182.0**	**166.1**	**158.7**	**156.3**	**−2.9%**	**−1.2%**
Consumer	133.1	125.1	113.5	108.0	106.5	−3.1%	−1.3%
Business-to-Business	59.0	56.9	52.5	50.7	49.8	−2.3%	−1.1%
DR TELEVISION	**125.8**	**150.3**	**155.3**	**156.7**	**179.3**	**4.3%**	**2.9%**
Consumer	81.5	96.3	98.7	99.2	113.4	3.9%	2.8%
Business-to-Business	44.2	54.0	56.6	57.5	65.9	5.1%	3.1%
DR MAGAZINE	**73.0**	**89.3**	**90.2**	**91.7**	**101.1**	**4.3%**	**2.3%**
Consumer	38.5	45.9	46.1	46.7	51.4	3.7%	2.2%
Business-to-Business	34.5	43.4	44.1	45.0	49.6	5.0%	2.4%
DR RADIO	**39.5**	**40.9**	**39.4**	**39.5**	**44.8**	**−0.1%**	**2.6%**
Consumer	24.6	25.3	24.2	24.2	27.6	−0.3%	2.6%
Business-to-Business	14.9	15.6	15.2	15.3	17.3	0.4%	2.6%
INSERT MEDIA	**8.6**	**10.7**	**10.9**	**11.2**	**13.1**	**4.9%**	**3.7%**
Consumer	5.7	7.0	7.1	7.3	8.5	4.5%	3.5%
Business-to-Business	2.9	3.7	3.8	3.9	4.6	5.8%	4.0%
OHTERS	**16.8**	**19.7**	**20.2**	**20.4**	**23.3**	**3.8%**	**2.9%**
Consumer	11.5	13.4	13.7	13.7	15.6	3.4%	2.7%
Business-to-Business	5.2	6.3	6.5	6.7	7.7	4.5%	3.3%
TOTAL	**$1,562.6**	**$1,985.3**	**$2,057.8**	**$2,149.6**	**$2,662.0**	**5.7%**	**5.3%**
Consumer	914.1	1,136.3	1,165.3	1,209.4	1,492.7	5.0%	5.1%
Business-to-Business	648.5	82.1	85.6	89.0	106.2	6.6%	5.6%

DR: Direct Response

Source: Direct Marketing Association's U.S. Direct Marketing Today: Economic Impact 2010. Used by permission, courtesy of the Direct Marketing Association.

rates. As we showed earlier in Chapter 12, mail or phone also can be used to complement other channel activities in a hybrid channel system. Second, an effective direct marketing operation relies heavily on an excellent database of customer names, addresses, and phone numbers, and companies have been making significant investments in such databases for direct marketing and for building and maintaining customer relationships. Improvements in computer technology and data mining software (programs that sift through vast amounts of customer information) have made it easier to use direct marketing and have resulted in greater efficiency in this channel and higher profits.

Even though both consumers and companies are purchasing more goods through the Internet, the older direct marketing methods of telephone and "snail" mail (catalogues, letters) still work quite well as can be seen in Table 13.3. More detailed information by some demographic segments is shown in Table 13.4. As can be seen, about 30 percent of households earning more than $100,000 bought a product or service using either mail or phone during the period of the data (as of spring 2008).

The Direct Marketing Process

Developing a direct marketing campaign entails a systematic approach with the following steps:

1. **Set an objective.** Because of the measurability of direct marketing campaigns, you need to set a quantitative goal in terms of sales, number of new customers, and so on.
2. **Determine the target market.** Like the marketing strategy described in Chapter 2, a direct marketing campaign requires that you determine which customers are the targets. Most direct marketing methods are too expensive to use a "shotgun" approach.
3. **Choose the medium/media.** As noted above and in Figure 13.3, there are a variety of media from which you can select for the campaign. The pros and cons of the major types will be discussed later in this chapter.
4. **Obtain a list.** Because of the targeted nature of direct marketing, a list of members of the targeted customers is required. There are two basic sources of lists: internal lists from customer records and externally purchased lists. With respect to the latter, lists can be purchased from list brokers or companies (e.g., publishers) that sell their own customer lists. Companies such as Dun & Bradstreet and

Table 13.4

Total Population Ordering by Mail or Phone: Spring 2008

	Total U.S. (000)	Total Buyers: Mail or Phone (000)	% Any product %
Household Income: $100,000–$149,999	30,020	8,997	29.97
Household Income: $150,000–$199,999	11,636	3,456	29.70
Household Income: $200,000+	8,956	2,834	31.64
Household size: 1	31,055	7,416	23.88
Household size: 2	73,053	20,090	27.50
Household size: 3–4	81,739	17,835	21.82
Household size: 5+	36,364	6,659	18.31
No Children in Household	130,810	33,293	25.45
Children under 2 years	18,592	3,265	17.56
2–5 years	32,507	6,343	19.51
6–11 years	42,307	8,802	20.81
12–17 years	44,788	9,411	21.01
Home owned	154,672	41,389	26.76
Rent Home	64,622	10,069	15.58

Source: Spring 2008 from Direct Marketing Association, 2009 Statistical Fact Book, p. 4. Used by permission, courtesy of the Direct Marketing Association.

Donnelley (which compile lists of prospects with particular characteristics), and InfoUSA.com are sources for mail and telephone while Yesmail (a division of InfoUSA) is a source for e-mail lists. Some companies such as Yahoo! have come under fire for selling their lists to companies launching direct marketing programs without the permission of their customers or registered members. The cost of renting a mailing or e-mail list is about $110 to $125 per 1,000 names.

5. **Analyze the list.** For companies that keep sufficiently accurate internal records of customer purchasing behavior, significant effort is made to constantly analyze their lists to see who are the best prospects for the target audience. This is a major priority, particularly for catalogue companies such as Lands' End. A particularly popular model that has been used for many years is called the *R* (recency) *F* (frequency) *M* (monetary value) model. Companies using this model develop a scoring method for each customer on its internal list, with higher scores given for customers who have most recently purchased, who purchase the most often, and who spend the most.[23]
6. **Develop the offer.** The "offer" is the text of the direct marketing message. This is obviously tailored to the particular circumstances.
7. **Test the offer.** A unique characteristic of direct marketing is that it is relatively easy and inexpensive to test alternative offers. Thus, Lands' End will often experiment with different catalogues to test different layouts and product mixes. Testing the offer is particularly easy and cheap with direct e-mails.
8. **Analyze the results.** The "bottom line" is, of course, how the campaign performs relative to the objective. It is also important to measure response rate and cost per customer acquired.

Direct Marketing Methods

The marketing manager can choose from a variety of direct marketing methods that permit customer targeting at the individual level, including telemarketing (telephone), direct mail/fax, and direct e-mail. While other media allow for an immediate response from the customer (e.g., TV infomercials), they do not permit as much individual targeting as those methods previously mentioned.

Telemarketing

As can be seen from Table 13.3, despite what people might think, telemarketing works for many companies. In fact, in a recent survey conducted by the Direct Marketing Association, telemarketing had the highest response rate—4.4 percent for in-house lists and 2.9 percent for purchased lists—of any other direct marketing method.[24] Clearly, the human interaction aspect is a plus in that (at least in principle) the telemarketer can tailor the presentation to the customer. However, it is expensive ($1 to $3 per message) and intrusive. With respect to the latter, telemarketing engenders a considerable amount of negative publicity and bad will toward the direct marketing channel and the industry.

The three keys to successful telemarketing are:

1. **The list.** Demographic targeting, beginning with a good list of prospects, can increase the success rate by as much as 60 percent.
2. **The offer.** There must be a compelling reason for the customer to buy over the phone. The reason can be a significant discount from the normal price or, more often, the offer of a product or service that cannot be purchased elsewhere. This offer must be stated early in the conversation and communicated clearly.
3. **Integrity.** There is considerable perceived risk when buying over the phone. The telemarketer must reduce this risk through devices such as money-back guarantees or a well-known brand name.

Direct Mail

Direct mail is cheaper than telemarketing ($0.75 to $2 per message) and, despite people's complaints about too much "junk" mail, it does not generate the bad will that telemarketing does because it is less intrusive. It is, of course, easy to ignore direct mail by quick disposal and, for B-to-B markets, it is very difficult to get the mail piece to the customer target in an organization. Based on Direct Marketing Association data, the average response rate for a direct mail piece is around 2 percent.

Direct mail can be delivered both the old-fashioned way and through e-mails.

Source: Jerry Arcieri/CORBIS-NY (top); Richard Levine/Alamy Images (bottom)

For a successful direct mail effort, the following guidelines apply beyond the telemarketing guidelines listed earlier:

- **The copy.** In general, longer copy (the text of the direct mail letter) is better because it gives you the opportunity to inform and persuade. The letter should be as long as it takes to communicate your product's benefits. However, you have about four minutes to convince the reader that the offer is worth buying. Words, sentences, and paragraphs should be kept short, with a friendly tone.
- **Layout/design.** Decisions about typeface, colors, graphic elements, personalized addressing, and other visual elements should be considered carefully. Format is important because direct mail is often screened, particularly in a business-to-business context.

Application Caterpillar

In 2007, Caterpillar, one of the world's largest construction equipment companies, designed a new industrial loader built to handle home construction projects in the U.S. Southwest and California.[25] In those areas, houses are normally built on concrete slabs that require heavy equipment designed to level rough ground and prepare it for laying concrete. The market was dominated by two major competitors, Case Construction Equipment and John Deere. The "Cat" 414E industrial loader is a $75,000 piece of equipment that was introduced after a four-year development period.

The company wanted to launch the product with considerable fanfare. The company's marketing managers, in conjunction with an advertising agency, developed the idea that the best way to introduce the 414E was to give prospective buyers a chance to try it out. As a result, they decided to build a racetrack with it, because many of their customers like racing, and to build a special event that would enable prospects to use the 414E in constructing the track.

The company first purchased a list of 1,700 names of people who had purchased an industrial loader over the past five years. They then devised a sweepstakes called "Eat My Dust" that was implemented with a direct mail campaign and allowed contractors to sign up either online or at a local Cat dealership. Winners would get a chance to help build the racetrack and then race dune buggies on the track.

The results? The response rate was 18 percent and more than 300 qualified sales leads that ultimately lead to 28 purchases of the $75,000 machine.

An important subcategory of direct mail is catalogue marketing. More than 15 billion catalogues were mailed in the United States in 2009, about 56 for every American. Catalogues account for 3 percent of the 80 million tons of paper products used in the country. Unfortunately, only 1.3 percent of the catalogues mailed result in a sale (see Figure 13.13). However, no one is predicting the demise of catalogues. Not only do they generate a lot of sales ($155 billion as shown in Table 13.3), they also drive people to Web sites, where the ultimate purchase is made. This is part of a multichannel strategy, as described in Chapter 12.[26]

Figure 13.13

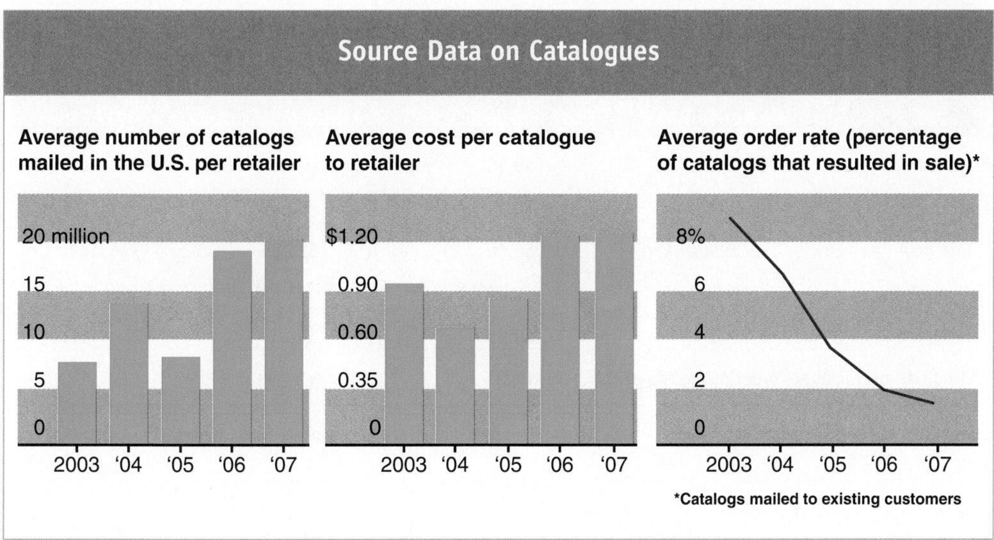

Source: Jeffrey Ball (2009), "In Digital Era, Marketers Still Prefer a Paper Trail," *The Wall Street Journal*, Oct. 16, p. A13. Reprinted by permission of *The Wall Street Journal*, Copyright © 2009 Dow Jones & Company, Inc. All Rights Reserved Worldwide. License number 2365350821298.

Direct E-mail

Much of the excitement in the direct marketing field has come from the explosion in the use of e-mails as a direct marketing medium. This can be readily seen by a simple examination of your e-mail in-box every day. Companies have discovered that e-mails are inexpensive ($0.20 per message, including creative and list generation, but only $0.005 to deliver) and flexible as they can deliver text, HTML, and streaming video and audio. E-mails are also very easy to test; are highly trackable; and, unlike the other media, can be part of an overall customer relationship program due to the high level of interactivity offered by the Web. Companies like Kana Communications, Digital Impact, and others offer services to companies looking to use this direct marketing medium.

The downside of e-mail is that, like telemarketing, unsolicited or "spam" e-mails have proliferated. Various surveys report that consumers receive between 1,000 and 1,500 unwanted e-mails each year. In addition, many large Internet service providers (ISPs) like America Online are including filters with their software to reduce the spam reaching their customers. In addition, response rates are low, although not as low as you may expect. The Direct Marketing Association study reported an average response rate to an e-mail of around 2 to 3 percent, depending on format and degree of personalization.

One analysis has compared direct e-mail to FSIs (free-standing inserts), direct mail, catalogues, and telemarketing in terms of response rates, costs, revenues, and return on investment (ROI) index (the ratio of the revenue per contact to the cost). This is shown in Table 13.5. As can be seen, telemarketing has the highest ROI index because even though it has much higher costs than the others, it has the highest avenue revenue per contact which offsets the costs. However, direct e-mails and direct mail are not far behind. Trailing badly are catalogues and FSIs. Catalogues suffer not so much from the response rate but the high costs and relatively low revenues obtained per mailing.

Application Seiko

Seiko, the well-known watch brand, spends about 20 percent of its advertising budget on digital channels such as e-mail.[27] Seiko uses e-mail to communicate with three target audiences: retailers that sell its products, consumers in its loyalty program (called the Elite Group), and members of the press. The company sends tailored messages to each of these three groups every 2.5 weeks and gets a 6 to 7 percent clickthrough rate. Seiko also sends weekly e-mails to 25,000 of its 72,000 Elite Group members who have agreed to receive updates on products (i.e., they have "opted in," which is discussed in the next section). For retailers, the company provides information on popular training programs and gives product updates.

Table 13.5

The Relative Effectiveness of Direct E-mail				
	Response Rate	Cost per Contact	Revenue per Contact	ROI Index
E-mail	1.12%	$0.10	$1.60	16.0
Inserts	0.45%	$0.14	$0.49	3.5
Direct mail	1.88%	$0.56	$11.36	14.9
Catalogue	2.18%	$0.69	$1.48	6.4
Telemarketing	5.78%	$2.50	$45.37	18.2
(All figures are for direct order marketing across industries)				

Source: "The DMA 2004 Response Rate Report" October, 2004. Used by permission, courtesy of the Direct Marketing Association.

Privacy Issues

Of the three direct marketing channels described in this section, telemarketing and e-mail have received the most attention from regulators, particularly the latter. In the United States, the Federal Trade Commission has established a national "do not call" registry, where consumers can supply their home phone numbers and indicate their wish not to be disturbed (www.donotcall.gov). You can also apply for this service for your cell phones. In some states, telemarketers ignoring this registry can be fined up to $11,000. Although telemarketing does provide a service that many consumers and businesses utilize, it is reasonable to permit those who do not want to receive telephone calls to be able to block them.

An interesting by-product of the do not call registry, however, is that it makes the people left for telemarketers more productive customers. The response rates for telemarketing have been increasing over the past several years, despite a shrinking base, because those left do not mind talking to people from call centers.

A livelier battle is shaping up over Internet privacy in general and, specifically, with respect to the direct e-mail industry. As noted earlier, people dislike junk mail but seem to dislike spam even more. A book titled *Permission Marketing*[28] introduced the notion that marketers would receive greater response rates to direct e-mails if they sent them only to customers who had agreed in advance to receive such contact. These are called "opt-in" programs. Although there is debate about whether permission should be obtained by customers actively checking a box that indicates they are willing to receive e-mails versus "unchecking" a prechecked box indicating such willingness ("opting out"), the current P3P—or Platform for Privacy Preferences—standard on the Internet mandates that Web sites offer either opportunity to customers. Unfortunately, despite these safeguards, most readers undoubtedly still find it much easier to get on an e-mail list than to remove themselves from it.

A potentially larger battle looms over Internet privacy. This goes beyond the e-mail issue to include the way companies assemble lists of e-mail addresses and what other information they are sharing. The largest uproar in this area occurred in February 2000, when the online advertising placement company DoubleClick (now owned by Google) announced that it was going to merge its information on the browsing habits of Internet users with offline purchasing information owned by Abacus Direct, a company in which it had a significant strategic investment. Abacus Direct was the leader in collecting information from catalogue purchases and using that data to target advertising to consumers. The company had five-year buying information on 88 million households, including name, address, phone number, credit card numbers, income, and purchases. DoubleClick realized that the value of targeted online advertising including direct e-mails would be substantially increased if information from online browsing activities was merged with these data.[29] Although DoubleClick quickly abandoned its plans, many consumer advocacy groups are concerned about how online companies are assembling their lists for direct e-mails and how much information they have about consumers. As a result, the United States is moving toward the European Union Directive on Data Protection that was established in 1998, which stipulates that:

1. A company must obtain the permission of the customer to obtain personal information and must explain its purpose.
2. It must promise not to use it for anything other than the stated purpose without consent.

Executive Summary

Key learning points in this chapter include the following:

- The sales force has a dual role in the implementation of the marketing strategy: it is part of both the communication mix and a distribution channel (i.e., a way to give customers access to the product or service).
- The sales force can be organized in a variety of ways, depending on how product or marketing management is organized. A national or key accounts organization is a layer on top of the usual sales organization that deals with the company's largest accounts.
- Both internal (e.g., motivation) and external (e.g., the competitive environment) factors affect a salesperson's performance.
- Three important decisions that must be made by the sales manager are the size of the sales force, the design of sales territories, and the assignment of salespeople to the territories.
- Sales quotas or goals provide key incentives. Quotas are based on sales volume, financial indicators such as profit margins, or activities such as the number of customer calls.
- The most common form of compensation plan for salespeople is a combination of salary and financial incentives such as bonuses or commissions.
- Technology is changing the nature of the salesperson's job, particularly in the use of laptop computers, which enable the representative to make better sales presentations and deliver more value to customers.
- Direct marketing is becoming an increasingly important direct channel of distribution for many companies.
- The two most important direct marketing media are telemarketing and direct mail; direct e-mail is becoming increasingly important.

Chapter Questions

1. It is sometimes said that salespeople should be familiar with their customers' marketing plans (e.g., understanding the customers' competitors and customers). Of what use would this information be to the salesperson?
2. Considering the different tasks a salesperson must perform, how is the job different for an automobile salesperson and a representative selling a computer system?
3. What products or services would be more appropriate for implementing the three different approaches to determining sales force size described in this chapter? Be specific.
4. Besides the criteria for assigning salespeople to territories described in this book, what other factors should be taken into account?
5. How should the increased use of technology in the salesperson's job affect companies' recruiting and hiring practices? What are the benefits of having a sales force that is sophisticated in its use of technology?
6. For what kinds of products and services would direct e-mail be appropriate? Other than sales, what goals can direct e-mail achieve?

Key Learning Points

The purpose of this chapter is to introduce concepts underlying the development and maintenance of long-term customer relationships. After reading this chapter, the student should understand:

- The economics of customer loyalty (i.e., why long-term customer relationships are good business)
- A general framework for customer relationship management
- The importance of a customer database
- Defining, measuring, and building customer satisfaction
- Loyalty or frequency marketing programs
- The growing importance of mass customization
- New metrics for measuring the success of customer relationship management

Harrah's Total Rewards loyalty program is an excellent example of a successful customer relationship management program.
Source: Jae C. Hong/AP Wide World Photos

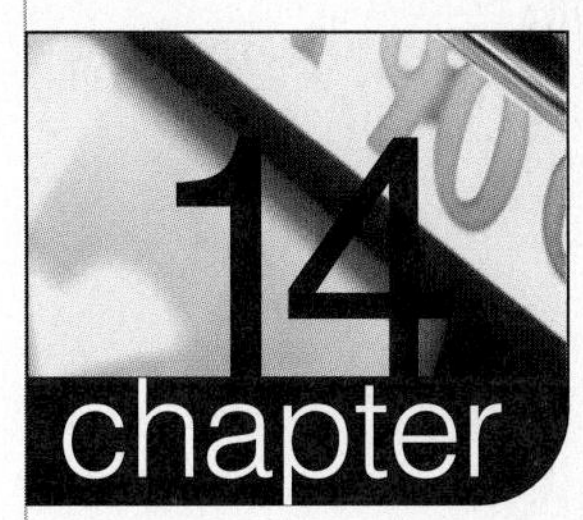

Customer Relationship Management

Chapter Brief

Consider the following saga of a gambler at Harrah Entertainment's Rio Resort in Las Vegas.[1] For 10 minutes, this person fed quarters into Bally's "Deuces Wild" video poker machine until he lost $20. Then he moved on to the "Monopoly" slot game, video blackjack, and other video poker machines. After nearly two hours, he had lost $350. While he was losing, Harrah's was not only winning money but also gaining valuable information about him. Computers in Harrah's Memphis data center noted how many different machines he had played, how many separate bets had been made, his average bet, and the total amount of money that had been wagered. By the time he had left the Rio, Harrah's had enough information about him to construct a detailed profile of his gambling habits, a plan for getting him to come back, and an individual profit-and-loss forecast that would determine how much money the company would invest in trying to get him to return.

All that information comes from a plastic card that Harrah's players insert into the machines at any of its gambling facilities (including Caesar's, which Harrah's purchased in 2005). Harrah's Total Rewards loyalty program is the only such program in the gaming industry. Its 25 million members use these frequent-gambler cards to earn free trips, meals, hotel rooms, and other services while they play. In turn, Harrah's uses the data to refine its customer database and to develop 90 customer segments, each of which receives customized direct-mail incentives. In addition, the company attempts to predict how much a customer will spend and analyze gaps between the predicted and actual spending. Since the Total Rewards program began in 1999, the company calculated that it has received hundreds of millions of dollars in incremental revenue from customers who gambled at more than one Harrah's casino. In addition, half of Harrah's total revenues from its Las Vegas casinos are generated by Total Rewards cardholders. The program has been so successful that the company generated $10.8 billion in sales in fiscal year 2008 and just over $600 million in profits.

Note that the company has not necessarily increased its customers' interests in gambling. The incremental revenues and profits resulting from the Total Rewards program are simply due to the company knowing its customers better than its competitors do and finding some individualized incentives to attract them to Harrah's rather than to rival casinos. Harrah's views its relationship with its customers from a long-term perspective rather than simply as a one-time occurrence.

The company has also developed an interesting set of metrics for evaluating the effects of the program. The board of Harrah's receives regular reports on four metrics: Harrah's share of its customers' gaming dollars, percent of revenues from customers who play at more than one of the company's casinos, percent of loyalty program members advancing to higher status as a result of their higher expenditures, and customer satisfaction across the casinos. Interestingly, this latter metric has an impact on the CEO's annual bonus.

All companies face this problem of how to develop profitable long-term relationships with their customers. Providers of frequently purchased products and services such as retail gasoline, as well as less frequently purchased durable and industrial goods, have attempted to build higher levels of customer satisfaction through the development of better relationships with their customers. Many of these relationships are intended to increase repeat-purchasing rates, which increase long-term sales and profits. Some relationships are not long-term in nature. However, it is still important for a marketing manager to understand what kind of relationship the customer wishes to have with the company and its brands. This chapter discusses the necessary steps to creating programs that achieve higher customer satisfaction through this matching process.

What is the impact of high switching rates between products? The cellular phone industry is an excellent example. Consider the huge expense of getting customers to switch cellular suppliers in the United States. AT&T, Sprint Nextel, and Verizon spend considerable sums of money on direct marketing to attract switchers. Often, the switchers are customers who had been their own customers in the past. Cingular and Sprint lost nearly 3 percent of their customers in each quarter of 2003.[2] It has been estimated that it costs a cellular company $275 to $450 in discounts, promotions, and advertising expenditures to sign up each subscriber. Each percentage point increase in customer "churn" costs enough to reduce the total market value of the cellular companies by $150 million.[3]

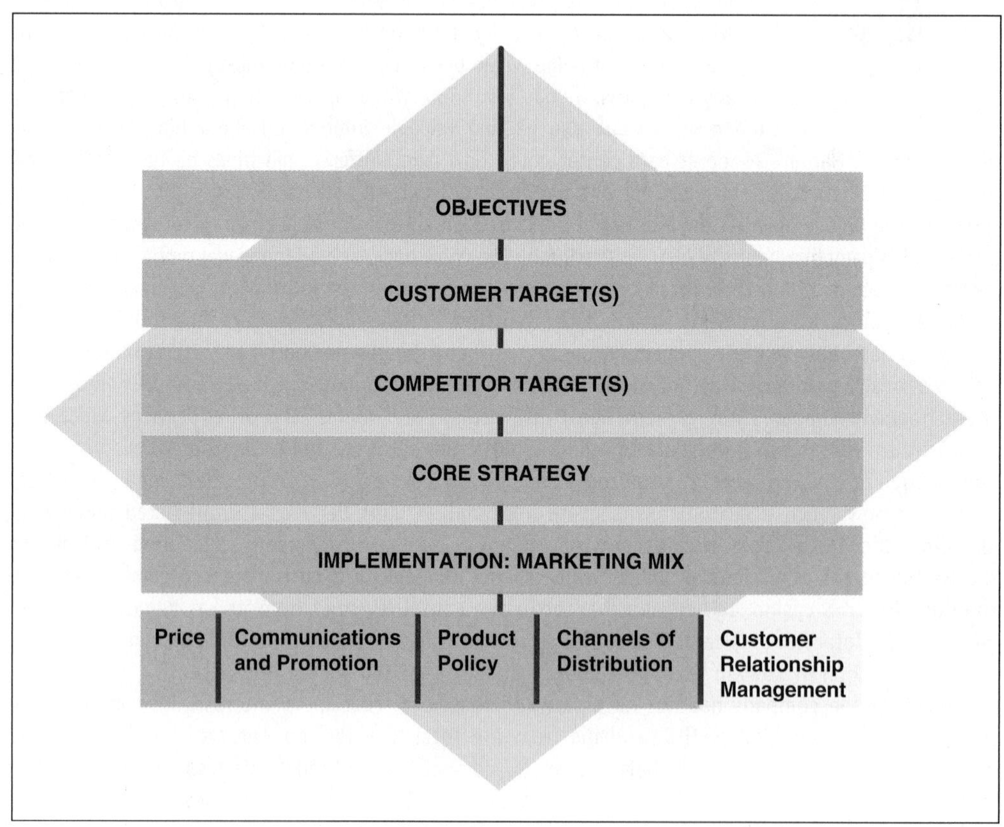

Different perspectives on the buyer–seller relationship are shown in Figure 14.1. Panel A of Figure 14.1 is very much like the sales orientation discussed in Chapter 1. In this situation, the seller figures out a way to make the sale to the buyer. The relationship between the two is at a distance because the seller has done little to try to understand the buyer's motivations and needs. The salesperson has used his or her creativity or personality to make the sale, not an understanding of the customer.

Figure 14.1

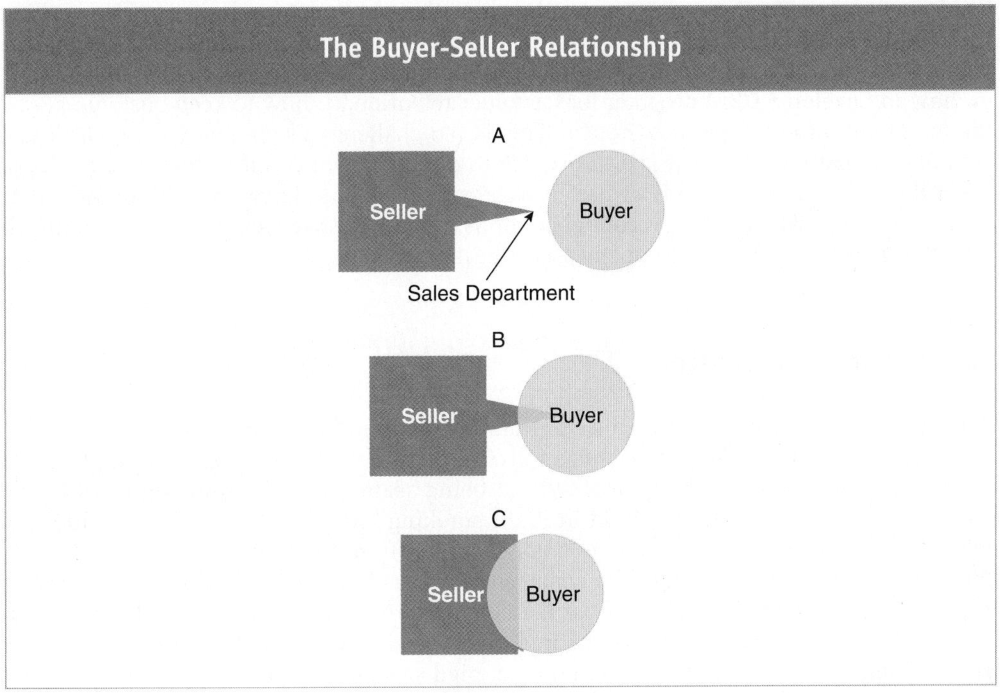

The Buyer-Seller Relationship

Source: Theodore Levitt (1986), *The Marketing Imagination* (New York: Free Press), pp. 113–14. Copyright © 1986 by the President and Fellows of Harvard College. Reprinted by permission.

In panel B, the company selling the product or service has done a better job of understanding the customer by getting "into" the buyer, determining enough about his or her needs to make the sale. This is the more traditional marketing concept or customer orientation. A panel B company spends money on marketing research, segments its markets appropriately, and has developed a marketing strategy on the basis that the value proposition fairly represents what its target segment wants.

However, while both panel A and B relationships are necessary to be successful, neither concept is sufficient in today's globally competitive environment. Both can be characterized by the following:

For the seller, the sale is the end of the process; for the buyer, it's the beginning.[4]

In today's competitive environment, where long-term relationships are critical to marketing and general business success, it takes more than the execution of the marketing concept to satisfy customers over a long period of time. Panel C illustrates the new model of relationship marketing. Here, the buyer and seller have become interdependent. Each party to the relationship depends on the other in some way. The sale cannot be the end of the process for the seller anymore.

A distinction has been made between different kinds of industrial buyer–seller relationships.[5] This distinction is applicable for all kinds of goods and services. **Transaction buyers** are those who are interested only in the purchase at hand. They may not be interested in a long-term relationship at all, or the sellers in the market may not have done a good job of showing the customer the benefits of such a relationship. The former situation exists when a company sees the benefit in sharing the business among a number of suppliers. **Relationship customers** see the benefits of the interdependency shown in panel C of Figure 14.1. Both kinds of customers can be loyal, but the nature of the loyalty is different. For example, transaction buyers may buy from the same supplier each time, but their motivation to do so may be based on price and not the value of maintaining a relationship.

transaction buyers
buyers who are interested only in the particular purchase at hand, rather than a long-term relationship

relationship customers
customers who see the benefits of interdependency between the buyer and the seller

The previous chapters of this book focused on what might be called *customer acquisition*, or the ways marketing is normally used to obtain customers. Companies spend considerable sums acquiring customers; how much does your company, or ones that you know, spend on retaining customers? More and more companies are spending money for computer systems and marketing programs on what is called **customer relationship management**, or **CRM**.

customer relationship management, or **CRM**
develops programs that match the kind of relationship the customer wants with the company, whether it is relational or transactional

CRM is often used in the context of relationships that are long term in nature. However, a true CRM strategy develops programs that match the kind of relationship the customer wants with the company, whether it is relational or transactional. In this chapter, the focus is on how to develop a CRM program for customer retention, or how to keep customers over the long term for any type of customer. This is the challenge facing many companies like Harrah's. In many ways, CRM is a throwback to old-fashioned country store-type retailing. Then the store owner knew his or her customers by name and knew their shopping habits well enough to make product recommendations. Today, we use technology to accomplish the same goal—even when a company serves millions of customers.

The Economics of Loyalty

A simple example demonstrates the economic power and importance of loyalty.

A number of years ago, a passenger flying on a British Airways (BA) flight from London to San Francisco complained about being seated near the smoking rows in the coach section. Although there is no in-flight smoking today, many readers will identify with this traveler's complaint. Being one or two rows from the smoking area on a 10-hour flight was more than annoying. The coach section was full and the dissatisfied customer was (or at least claimed to be) a regular BA customer. A simple solution would have been to move the customer to business class in an unobtrusive way (so other passengers do not get the same idea) because there were unoccupied seats in that section. Our guess is that such a move would have gained a strongly loyal customer at a very low marginal cost (for business-class food). However, the BA personnel declined to move the passenger, who very loudly indicated that he would never fly BA again.

lifetime customer value
the present value of a stream of revenue that can be produced by a customer

This example illustrates a very important concept: **lifetime customer value (LCV)**. Compare the amount of revenue and profits that would be derived from the customer to the small incremental cost of moving him to business class. When you lose a customer for life, you are actually losing the (discounted) stream of income that passenger would have produced over his lifetime. In addition, how many other potential customers will he tell about it?

Compare that illustration to Lexus's approach to customer loyalty. A CEO unexpectedly received a $200 check from Lexus after a few customers had complained that the cars' original tires wore out too soon. This impressed the CEO, who was adamant in saying that he would be a Lexus customer for life—not just because of the money, but because the company did the right thing.[6]

Clearly, no company is going to have a 100 percent loyalty rate. As noted earlier, some business customers have multiple vendors as company policy. Other customers do not want to feel any kind of obligation to purchase from the same vendor. In addition, if many customers are involved, it is impossible to satisfy all of them. However, the economic reasons for increasing the retention rate are compelling. Figure 14.2 shows the impact of a five-percentage-point increase in retention on the net present value of a customer revenue stream for a variety of industries. For example, in the advertising agency industry, increasing its client retention rate from, say, 80 to 85 percent results in an increase of 95 percent in the net present value of the average customer's billings. There are two reasons for this. First, what looks like a small difference in retention rates is greatly magnified over a long period of time. Second, retained customers are much more profitable than switchers.

Figure 14.3 breaks down the difference in profits. Loyal customers are more profitable because they stimulate revenue growth (i.e., loyal customers buy more and buy more often), they are less expensive to serve, they refer new customers to the company, and they are often willing to pay a price premium. Let us look in more detail at the components of Figure 14.3.

Acquisition Cost

acquisition costs
the incremental costs involved in obtaining any new customer

Obviously, obtaining any new customer requires some incremental costs, called **acquisition costs**. For example, American Express must send a number of direct-mail pieces or make telemarketing pitches to obtain new customers. New customers of industrial equipment require more sales calls than existing ones. Thus, acquisition costs represent an initial loss

Figure 14.2

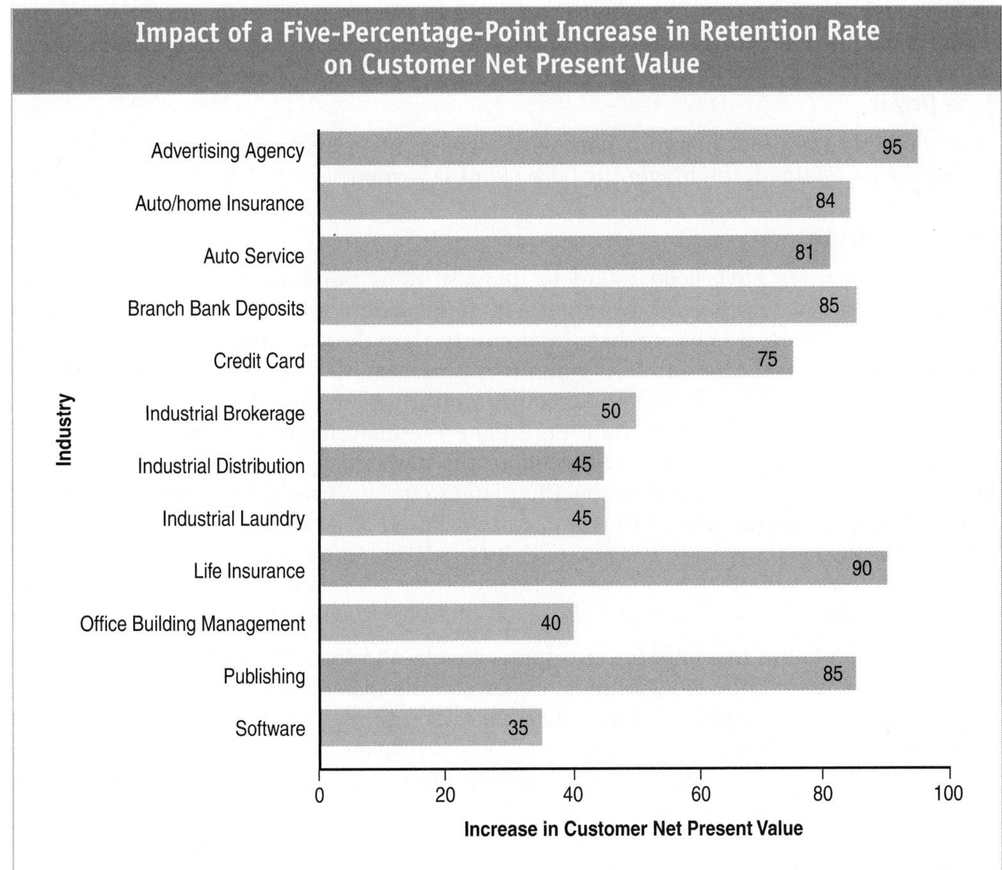

Source: Frederick F. Reichheld (1996), *The Loyalty Effect* (Boston: Harvard Business School Press), p. 37. Copyright © 1996 by the President and Fellows of Harvard College. Reprinted by permission.

Figure 14.3

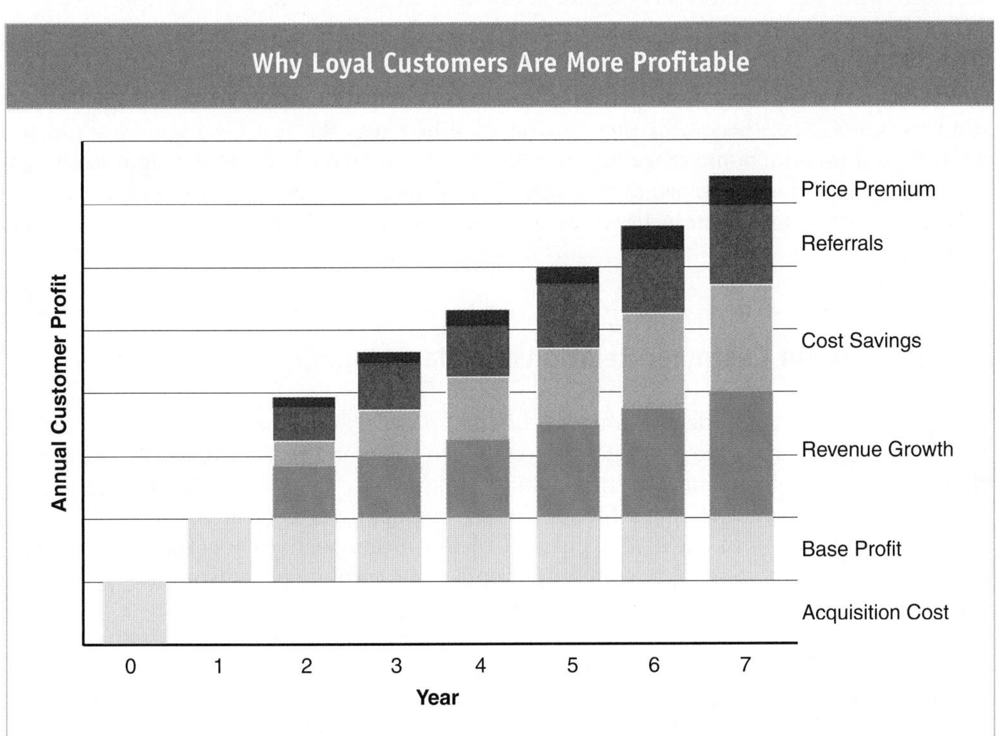

Source: Frederick F. Reichheld (1996), *The Loyalty Effect* (Boston: Harvard Business School Press), p. 39. Copyright © 1996 by the President and Fellows of Harvard College. Reprinted by permission.

on any customer. The cost of customer acquisition can be quite high—in 2009, Vonage reported that the marketing cost for acquiring a new customer averaged $309 per customer.

Base Profit

This is simply the profit margin a company earns from an average customer. The longer a customer is retained, the longer the base profit is earned.

Revenue Growth

Retained customers have been found to increase their purchase quantities over time. This is an intuitive finding. Think about a store to which you have become more loyal over a period of time. It is likely that you not only shop there regularly, but that you also buy more items there. Alternatively, you might purchase life or home insurance from the company from which you purchase auto insurance. It is important to note that, in practice, a customer may often buy from more than one manufacturer; revenue growth can happen by increasing the "share-of-wallet" or the percentage of total spending of a customer in a category that goes to a specific manufacturer. Thus, a loyal customer would provide a high share-of-wallet to a company in relation to its competitors who provide a similar offering.

Operating Costs

It has also been found that existing customers cost less to serve than new customers. The former have a better knowledge of the company's systems and procedures. For example, if you are a good customer of the direct-mail clothing company Lands' End, you undoubtedly know how to fill out the form (fewer mistakes for the company to follow up on) and how to read the product descriptions (less time on the phone for customer service representatives).

Referrals

Good customers also talk to their friends and neighbors about your company. Additional business comes from favorable word-of-mouth by satisfied customers. This is a particularly good source of new business for service companies. As we will see in the next chapter, service quality is more difficult to ascertain before purchasing, so advice from someone who has tried the service and is satisfied with it is particularly important.

Price Premium

Loyal customers are often more price-insensitive than customers who need a price inducement to switch or to become a new customer. When was the last time you checked the price of your favorite brand of toothpaste? Such loyal customers are getting significant customer value from using the product or service and are not concerned about price.

Thus, building and sustaining long-term relationships is both strategically sound and profitable.[7]

A Framework for Customer Relationship Management

CRM has come to mean different things to different people. For some managers, CRM means sales force contact software like salesforce.com (see Chapter 13). For others, it means telephone call centers for contact management. Additionally, many focus their attention on loyalty programs such as Harrah's Total Rewards program described earlier.

A systematic view of CRM that puts all of these perspectives together is shown in Figure 14.4.[8] As can be seen, major components of a complete framework are:

1. Constructing a customer database.
2. Analyzing the database.
3. Based on the analysis, selecting customers to target.
4. Targeting the selected customers.
5. Developing relationship programs with the customers in the target group(s).

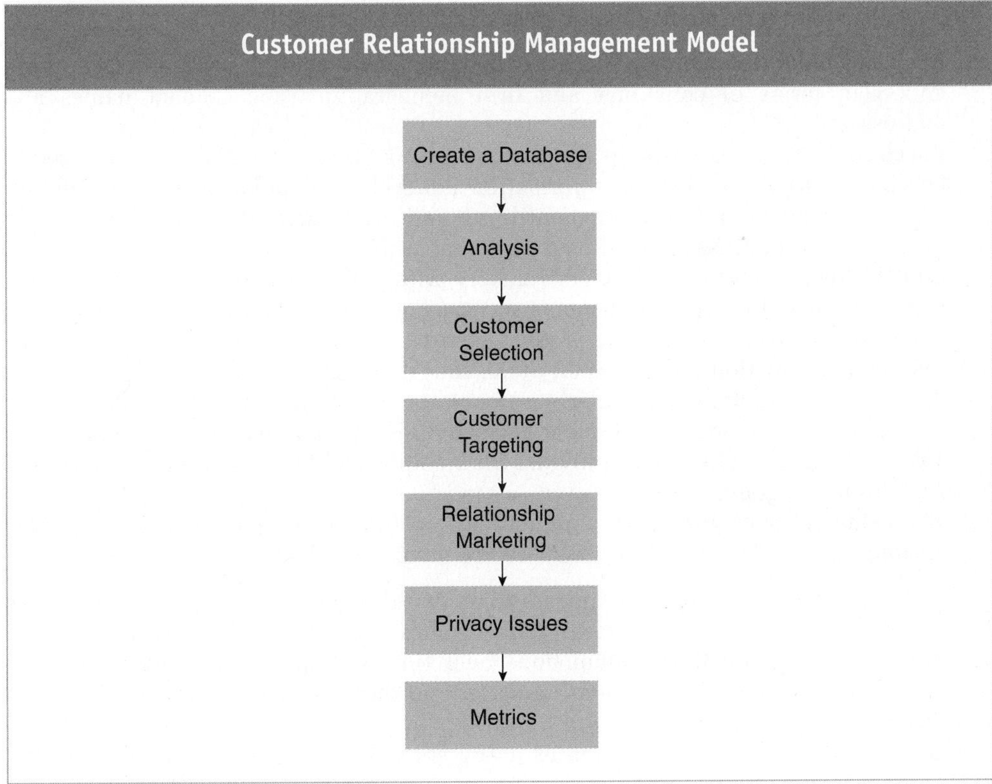

Figure 14.4

6. Considering privacy issues.
7. Measuring the impact of the CRM program.

These steps in the comprehensive approach to CRM will be covered in more detail throughout the rest of this chapter.

Creating the Database

The core of a CRM program is a customer database, sometimes referred to as a **customer information file** or **CIF**.[9] The CIF is the repository of information about the customer and serves as the basis for identifying and targeting both current and potential customers. The basic idea behind a CRM program is to assess the value of each customer in the CIF to the firm and then develop relationship programs that will be customized both in content and intensity, depending on that value. The optimal contents of this CIF are shown in Figure 14.5.

customer information file, or **CIF** a customer database including information on past and current purchasing, contact, response to marketing variables, and monetary value to the company

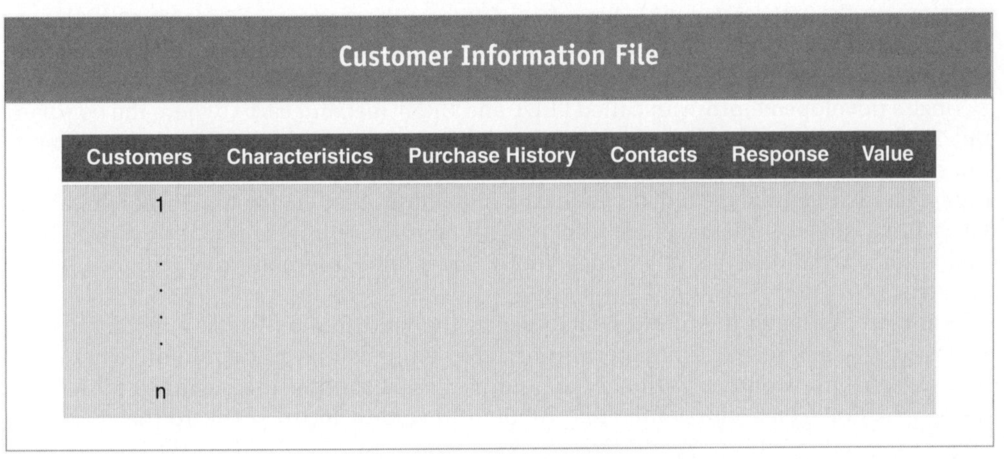

Customer Information File
Customers
Characteristics
Purchase History
Contacts
Response
Value
1
.
.
.
.
n

Figure 14.5

As can be seen, there are five major areas of content in the CIF:

1. **Basic customer descriptors.** These are the kinds of variables described in Chapters 4 and 5 in terms of consumer and firm demographics and contact names and addresses.
2. **Purchase history.** Like descriptors, the customer's purchase history is considered to be a basic part of the CIF. This information should be as detailed as possible, including products bought, the channels utilized, and prices paid. If possible, the margin made on each purchase should be recorded as well.
3. **Contact history.** Part of a customer's history with you is any recordable contact that person has had through, say, customer service. For example, any time a customer calls you with questions about your product or service, this should be noted. Similarly, sales call information would be part of this area of the CIF.
4. **Response information.** Particularly valuable is information about how customers have responded to prior direct-marketing activities, promotional offers, or other traceable marketing activity.[10] This provides information about potential responsiveness to such future programs.
5. **The value of the customer.** This number is an estimate of the monetary value of the customer to the firm. It will be discussed in more detail later.

The CIF shown in Figure 14.5 appears to be two-dimensional. However, there is an important third dimension that is difficult to show—time. It is critical that the CIF contain information on these dimensions over time so that you can spot trends in terms of which customers are becoming better and those whose relationship with the firm is becoming worse.

Many companies view their CIFs as a key source of competitive advantage. For example, UPS does not want to be known as a package shipping company. The company views itself as an information technology company. From all of the information it collects about shipping, it compiles a database that is useful to its customers in terms of the products purchased, geographical locations, addresses, and other parts of the CIF. This is only part of the information UPS collects that is useful to its customers.[11]

The challenge for many companies is to create the kind of CIF shown in Figure 14.5. Figure 14.6 characterizes the ease with which the CIF can be created by conceptualizing the problem as a 2 × 2 matrix defined by the kind of interaction the company has with the customer (direct versus indirect) and the frequency of that interaction (high or often versus low or infrequent).[12] Companies in the upper-left quadrant are able to develop most of a CIF relatively easily. Banks, telecommunications firms, and retailers have direct and frequent contact with customers that results in those types of firms having generally excellent CIFs (at least in terms of customer and purchase information). However, firms with indirect customer contact have to work much harder to collect such information. For example, Clorox and BMW have to rely on their distribution networks to provide customer information back to them. This is not the most reliable way to collect accurate data. Consumer durable companies such as Sony rely mainly on warranty cards; however, their completion rate is only about 30 percent.

As a result, many companies have to create special programs or events to collect as much customer information as they can. Some of this comes through loyalty or frequent-shopper programs. Some of these special programs can be quite creative. For example, Kellogg's developed a program called "EET and ERN" (eat and earn), where the company put 15-digit encrypted codes inside of cereal boxes and a Web site URL. After going to the site, inserting the code, and registering, participants (mainly kids) can receive free toys. The idea is to create a database of the company's best customers. Professional services firms such as management consultants often host free seminars in specialized topic areas, where the goal is to develop a list of and information about prospective clients.

Another challenge to creating databases is the fact that (as we saw in Chapter 12) with the expansion in the number of possible channels or "touchpoints," where customers can have contact with the company, it is becoming increasingly difficult to track behavior. Some companies like Acxiom have developed software that is part of an overall CRM strategy, where preferences and customer purchases from brick-and-mortar stores, catalogues, and the Web are tracked and pulled into one centralized database.

Application Harrah's

Returning to the Harrah's illustration, the company builds its Total Rewards database in two ways. First, customers can sign up in a casino. However, in addition, the company runs three annual promotions, two of which are staged regularly: Millionaire Maker, the largest slot tournament in the United States, and Total Reward Giveaway, a six-month sweepstakes culminating in a big prize awarded in a program simulcast across all of Harrah's properties. Contestants in these promotions must register for the Total Rewards program to participate.

It should be noted that building the database with customer information is only part of the challenge. To fully reap the benefits of CRM, the company must collect all the information shown in Figure 14.5 and be prepared to continually update the database. Thus, it requires a considerable investment of time and money and a strong customer orientation to fully implement this stage of the process.

Application Nestlé in Japan

Because of the difficulty Nestlé has in touching individual customers, the company decided to try something novel in Japan.[13] The company created the Together Nestlé Relationship Center in conjunction with an advertising agency, McCann Worldgroup's MRM Partners Worldwide, and a CRM consulting firm, Bellsystem24. It brings the company into direct contact with 1.4 million consumers, representing 4 percent of all households comprised of two or more people. The idea behind the relationship center is to act as a hub of every communication with consumers. All telephone calls, e-mails, and written letters from consumers are responded to by the relationship center employees. Center "members" have access to a call center hot line, a Web site with a bulletin board, and other interactive mechanisms. They are also sent a magazine and invited to special events. Call center staff attempt to build an emotional bond between the company and its consumers. The insights obtained from the consumers in the database are shared with production, sales, and marketing teams.

Thus, although the relationship center does not "touch" a large percentage of Nestlé consumers, it is a creative approach for a company that would otherwise have difficulty connecting with its customers, that is, those in the "indirect" column of Figure 14.6.

Figure 14.6

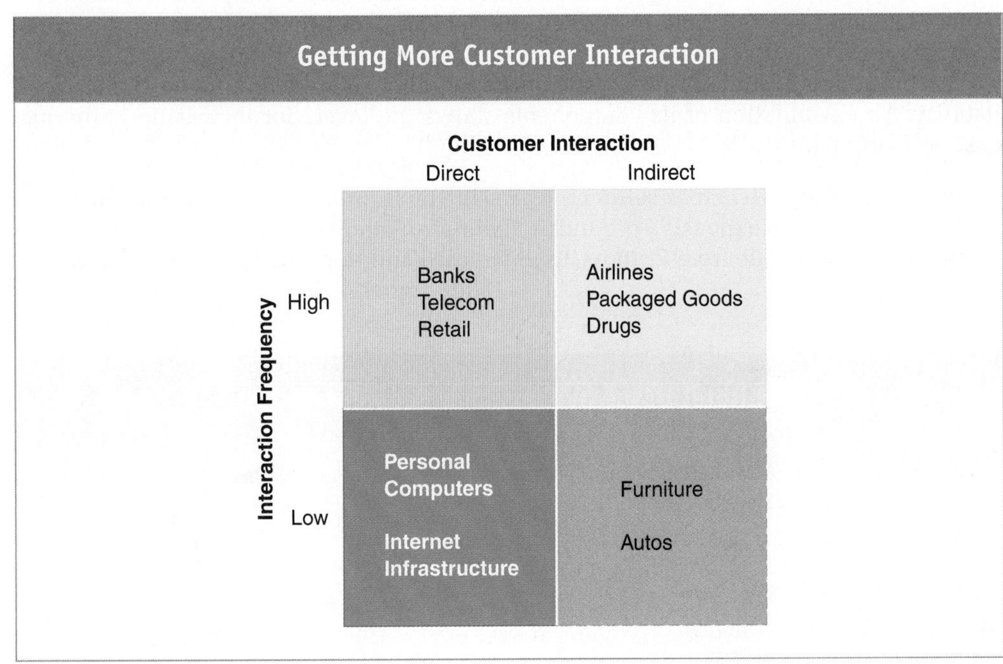

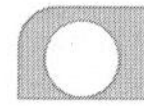

Analyzing the Database

data mining
analyzing a customer information file for the best prospects to target

There are many types of analyses that can be performed on a CIF once it has been assembled. The general name given to such analysis is **data mining**. People with significant statistical skills use computer software and large computer resources to troll through the CIF to find segments, purchasing patterns, trends, and other useful outputs.[14] Large companies such as Oracle, SSA Global, SPSS, and others provide such software to their corporate customers. Several advantages of a CIF include the following: identifying the best customers and providing them with appropriate incentives, tracking purchases made over time in order to make recommendations, and allocating marketing resources across customers in a manner that optimizes revenue growth. As can be seen from Table 14.1, frequent travelers make up only 10 percent of hotel guests but spend 44 percent of the hotel nights.

A particularly important analysis that provides the information in the last column of the CIF shown in Figure 14.5 is estimating lifetime customer value (LCV). This analysis takes the purchase information and, together with information about profit margins on each product purchased, projects the profit implications of each customer or row in the CIF. While not an exact science due to the difficulties of making projections far into the future, the goal is to ultimately place a monetary value on each customer that the firm can use to make resource allocation decisions.

While there are a number of formulas that can be used to estimate LCV,[15] one way to start is with a relatively simple formula that utilizes only the available purchase information in the CIF to calculate each customer's cumulative profitability to the present time:

$$\text{Customer profitability} = \sum_t \sum_j (P_j - C_j) - \sum_k MC_k - AC$$

where

t = the number of past and current time periods measured
j = the number of products purchased in a time period
k = the number of marketing tools used in a time period
P = price
C = cost
MC = cost of marketing tool (e.g., direct mail)
AC = cost of acquisition for the customer

Basically, the formula computes the total profits generated by a customer by taking the total margin generated by the customer ($P - C$) in each time period from all products and services purchased, subtracting off the traceable marketing costs attributable to each customer, summing over all time periods in the database, and then subtracting the initial acquisition costs.

The preceding formula is useful for purposes other than computing customer profitability. An examination of its components shows the levers for increasing individual customer profitability. Profits can be increased by:

- Increasing P and j by cross-selling (purchasing more products) and/or upselling (purchasing more expensive products). *Example:* American Express asking its members to upgrade from Gold to Platinum card and to purchase other services.

Table 14.1

U.S. Hotel Usage by Consumer Segment in 2002[a]

	Individual Guests	Share of Hotel Nights
Frequent travelers (≥23 nights a year)	10%	44%
Moderate travelers (6–22 nights a year)	40	44
Light travelers (1–5 nights a year)	50	12

[a] For U.S. population aged 21 to 74; in 2002 approximately 83 million individual guests accounted for approximately 860 million hotel nights.

Source: Travel Industry Association of America (TIA); TNS; U.S. Census Bureau; McKinsey analysis.

- Reducing the marketing costs *MC* over time as the customer loyalty is better established. *Example:* retail banks shifting their customers from visiting tellers in a bank branch to banking online or through ATM.
- Increasing the number of time periods *t* that the customer purchases. *Example:* hotels like the Four Seasons that delight their customers through excellent customer service.
- Reducing the acquisition cost for each customer. *Example:* identifying new and cheaper ways to acquire customers through new media vehicles (as discussed in Chapter 10).

To compute the LCV, you have to project the customer's generated margins and marketing costs into the future and discount back. This involves a number of heroic assumptions about the nature of a customer's purchasing pattern in the future. A back-of-the-envelope approach to calculating LCV is a margin "multiple," which can be used to multiply the current margin generated by each customer to estimate the LCV.[16] This multiple is

$$\frac{r}{(1 + i - r)}$$

In this formula, r is the retention (loyalty) rate for your product and i is the discount or cost of capital rate used by your company. Some sample multiples are shown in Table 14.2. Thus, for a product whose retention rate is 70 percent and with a discount rate of 12 percent, take the margin generated by each customer and multiply it by 1.67. This approximates the LCV for that customer.[17] If this LCV figure is multiplied by the size of the customer base, an interesting way to value the firm is produced in terms of the total present value of the lifetime stream of income produced by its customers.[18]

A different way to look at LCV is from the perspective of customer acquisition costs. Figure 14.7 is an illustration from the credit-card industry showing the increase in value of an active account over 20 years. For example, the value of a customer who stays for three years is $98 ($178 in profit over the three years minus the $80 acquisition cost); if a credit card issuer can retain a customer for five years, the net profit is $264.

An interesting question is how much you would pay today to acquire a customer, given the kind of information shown in Figure 14.7. Suppose we knew that the average account remained active for five years. You should not be willing to pay $264 for that account today because the cash flows occur in the future and those dollars are worth less today because of the time value of money. The present value of a five-year customer, assuming a 10 percent discount rate, is $\$40/(1 + 0.10) + \$66/(1 + 0.10)^2 + \$72/(1 + 0.10)^3 + \$79/(1 + 0.10)^4 + \$87/(1 + 0.10)^5 - \$80$, or $172.98. In other words, you should not pay more than $173 to acquire an account that you expect to retain for five years. Another way to look at these numbers is from a retention perspective. If a credit card customer in the third year indicates that he or she is thinking about switching, the present value of the incremental profit for years 4 and 5 is $\$79/(1.10) + \$87/(1.10)^2$ (recall that we are in year 3 already) or $143.72. This gives you an idea of how much you would spend to retain that customer (e.g., using a reduction in the interest rate on the card or adding benefits such as life insurance or lost-card protection).[19]

An advantage of the Internet is that customer movements on the Web can be tracked, stored, and analyzed in real time to form the basis of increasingly customizable offerings.

Table 14.2

Margin Multiple

$$\frac{r}{1 + i - r}$$

	Discount Rate			
Retention Rate	10%	12%	14%	16%
60%	1.20	1.15	1.11	1.07
70%	1.75	1.67	1.59	1.52
80%	2.67	2.50	2.35	2.22
90%	4.50	4.09	3.75	3.46

Source: Reprinted from *Journal of Interactive Marketing*, Volume 17, Issue 1, Sunil Gupta and Donald R. Lehmann, Customers as Assets, Pages 9-24., Copyright (2003), with permission from Elsevier.

Figure 14.7

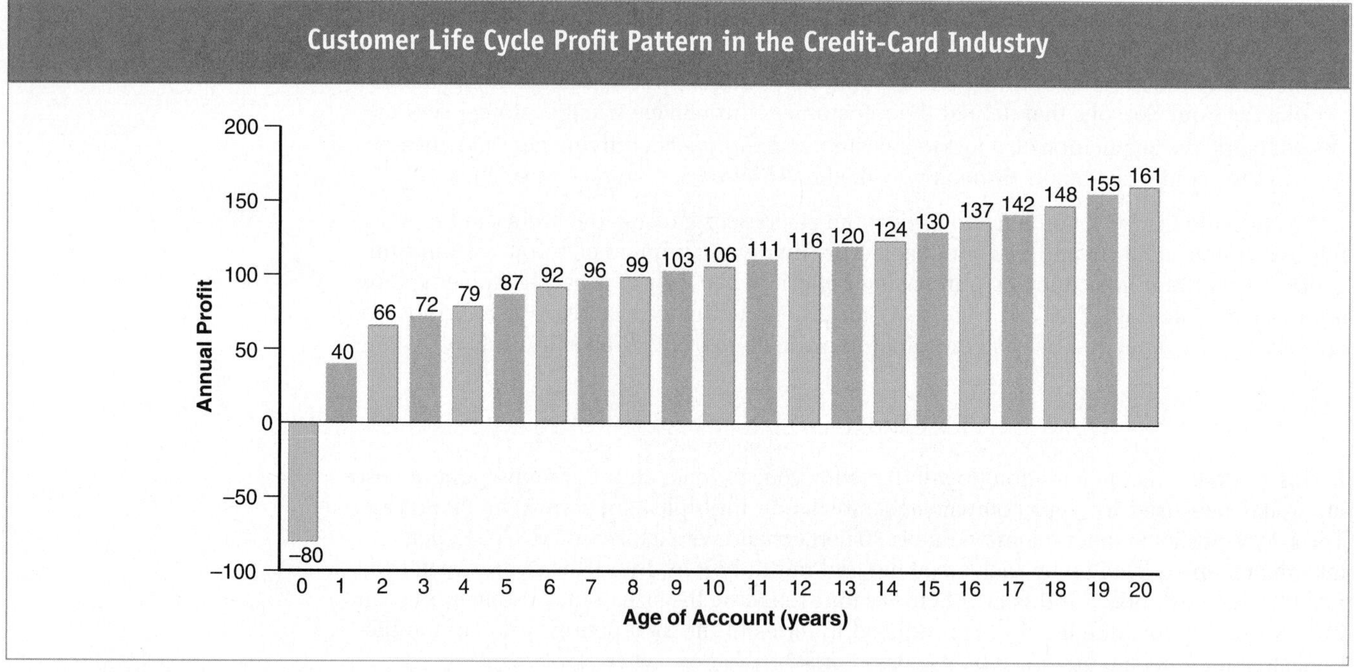

Source: Frederick F. Reichheld (1996), *The Loyalty Effect (Boston: Harvard Business School Press)*, p. 39. Copyright © 1996 by the President and Fellows of Harvard College. Reprinted by permission.

Brooks Brothers, the retailer of classic men's and women's clothing, is testing a new approach to increasing it e-commerce sales. When a visitor comes to www.brooksbrothers.com, software scans the visitor's computer for its Internet (IP) address and the user's list of previously visited sites. It then develops a profile of the visitor based on matching the information with others in its vendor's database of 100 million people. The visitors are then sorted in real time by the site's best guess on gender, marital status, and geography. Subsequently, the visitor is presented with a Web page based on that guess. As a result, a (hypothesized) single male would receive a different page than a woman and an urban male would receive a different product assortment than a rural male.[20]

Customer Selection

The customer profitability analysis just described can be used to separate the customers who will provide long-term value to the firm from those who are likely to be unprofitable. The venerable 80–20 rule in marketing often applies (if only approximately) in that 80 percent of the company's profits are provided by 20 percent of its customers. Thus, a major benefit of the LCV and profitability analyses previously described is to permit the marketing manager to make informed decisions about (1) which customers to keep (or, which to "fire"), and (2) for those kept, how much money to spend on keeping them.

Application | Best Buy

In 2004, the giant electronics retailer Best Buy decided that it wanted to separate its best customers from its worst.[21] The good customers were referred to as "angels" and the worst as "devils." The angels buy HDTVs, portable electronic products, and other goods without waiting for sales or using rebates. The devils buy products, apply for rebates, return the purchases, and then buy them back at returned-merchandise discounts. They buy "loss leaders" and then sell them at a profit on eBay. They find the lowest prices on the Web and demand that Best Buy match the price.

Best Buy estimated that as many as 20 percent of its customers fit into the "devil" category. The question was, How should the company "fire" these customers? The company examined sales records and demographic data to identify members of both groups. While it was difficult given the data available to identify individuals, the company could locate particular stores that tended to be frequented by them. Although Best Buy could not keep "devils" from entering the stores, the company cut back on promotions and enforced a restocking fee of 15 percent of the purchase price on returned merchandise. Using a similar analysis, the company found that its best customers fell into five groups: upper-income men, suburban mothers, small-business owners, young family men, and technology enthusiasts. To attract more of these "angels," the company told each store manager to analyze the demographics of his or her local market, focus on two of the groups, and then stock the appropriate merchandise. Early results from testing the new programs showed that sales gains by the pilot stores were double those of traditional stores.

Application ING Direct

ING Direct USA, a division of the Dutch bank ING Groep, is a direct-to-the-customer operation with no branches or ATMs.[22] It is an Internet-only savings bank. There are no fees, no minimum deposits, and a limited number of products. The simplicity of the business model means that its costs are low. In some parts of the business, they are one-sixth the costs of a conventional bank. This means that ING Direct can offer relatively high interest rates on deposits, often much higher than its competitors.

However, the bank rejects customers who do not play by its low-cost rules. The company "fired" more than 3,500 customers in 2004. These customers made too many calls to customer service or asked the bank to make exceptions for them too often. These high cost-to-serve customers did not fit with ING Direct's low cost model and were unprofitable.

ING Direct must be doing something right. In its first five years of operation, the bank had 2 million customers and $30 billion of assets.

An example of the result of a profitability analysis is shown in Table 14.3 and Figure 14.8.[23] This analysis was performed by a pharmaceutical company on all prescription products sold by the firm in three sales territories. The customer unit was physicians. The analysis covered 1.5 years of prescriptions, so it is profitability analysis rather than a full LCV analysis. The margins were calculated on the prescriptions written, and the marketing costs (*MC* in the preceding profit formula) included sales calls, product samples, and direct mail. As can be seen from Table 14.3, of the 834 physicians covered, the profitability was highly variable, ranging from a high of $62,407.20 to a low of –$12,814.12. Figure 14.8 provides a visual perspective on these data. There are some high-profit physicians generating more than $20,000 in profits for the firm and a large number of low-profit customers, with more than 50 who are unprofitable. Clearly, a large percentage of the profits result from a relatively small number of the doctors.[24]

As a result of analyses such as these, the marketing manager has sufficient information to select which customers to keep or "fire." Criteria would include:

- Current profitability.
- Future profitability (LCV).
- Similarity of the customer's profile to other customers who are currently profitable.

However, you should be wary of indiscriminately "firing" unprofitable customers. First, as noted earlier, LCV calculations are based on assumptions that are often difficult to validate. For example, it is difficult to know which small customers will grow into large ones. It would not have been smart for a supplier to have cut off Microsoft as a customer back in the late 1970s. In addition, some customers may be particularly vocal in the community. While it may look like a sound financial decision to cut off an unprofitable doctor

Table 14.3

Descriptive Statistics on Customer Profitability for Physicians	
Number of Observations	834
Maximum	$62,407.20
Minimum	$-12,814.12
Mean	$7,026.04
Median	$3,536.68

Source: This article was published in *Journal of Interactive Marketing*, Winter, 1999, Francis J. Mulhern "Customer Profitability Analysis: Measurement, Concentration and Research Directions", pp. 25-40. Copyright © Elsevier 1999. Reprinted with permission.

Figure 14.8

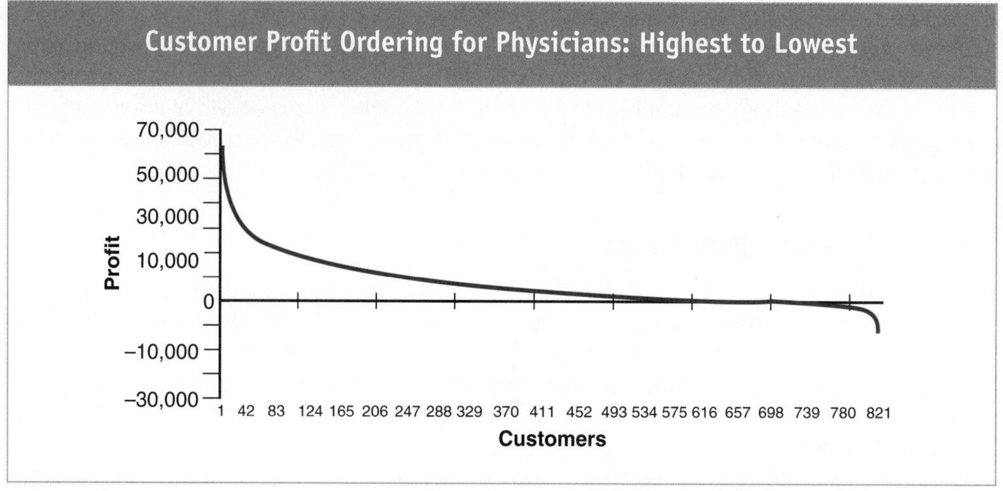

Source: Frederick F. Reichheld (1996), *The Loyalty Effect* (Boston: Harvard Business School Press), p. 39.

using the data in Table 14.3 and Figure 14.8, one of those doctors could be influential in the physician community. Second, it is important to attempt to make unprofitable customers profitable before firing them, either by looking for ways to increase revenue growth or by looking for ways to decrease the costs-to-serve. For example, customers with small savings accounts become unprofitable when they visit tellers in retail branches. However, these customers can become profitable if restricted to online or ATM banking. Still, many companies continue to serve unprofitable customers simply because they lack the CIF to perform a customer-level profitability analysis.

Application Fidelity Investments

Consider Fidelity Investments,[25] the world's largest mutual fund company. Fidelity realized that some customers were unprofitable because of the channels they used to interact with the company. When a customer who does limited business with Fidelity, and probably has limited potential, calls a service rep too frequently, the costs can easily outstrip any profits.

A few years ago, when such customers called, Fidelity's reps began teaching them how to use the company's lowest-cost channels: its automated phone lines and its Web site. It also made its site friendlier and more enticing to use. These customers could still talk to service reps, but the phone system identified their calls and routed them into longer queues, which meant the most-profitable customers could be served more quickly; for the unprofitable customers, the longer wait would be a disincentive to call.

Fidelity couldn't lose. If the unprofitable customers switched to lower-cost channels, they became profitable. If they didn't like the new experience and left, Fidelity became more profitable without them. But Fidelity found that 96 percent of those customers stayed, about the same retention rate as in the industry overall, and most of them switched to lower-cost channels. Over time, customer satisfaction actually increased for the smaller customers as they learned how to save time and get faster service through the lower-cost channels, increasing Fidelity's operating profit within 12 months.

Application The Wireless Industry

Customer complaints about their cell phone service suppliers are widespread.[26] However, many customers are not aware that the carriers do not treat all their customers the same. In general, because the companies have good data on customers' calling habits, if you spend more, you get better service, better deals, and more extras.

Many of the cellular companies have installed data analysis software that helps them predict which of their subscribers are the most likely to move to another carrier and thus need to be treated better. The software considers how many calls you make and receive, what percentage are long distance, the duration of the calls, the kind of phone you have, and how often you have contacted customer service. The software takes these variables into consideration and then predicts how likely you are to "churn." A score from the model of 85, for example, indicates that the probability of your switching is 85 percent.

When highly profitable customers call Sprint PCS to cancel their service, they are contacted immediately by someone from the customer retention department, where operators provide special incentives to stay. If you stay within your allotted minutes and do not generate additional profits for the company, you are not given anything, that is, you are "fired." At VoiceStream Wireless, the higher your bill, the less time you will spend on hold if you call customer service. Those customers with cheap calling plans are routed to the least-experienced representatives. Those on better plans may be offered special rates or new phones.

Customer Targeting for Retention

Once the customers that you wish to target have been selected, conventional direct-marketing approaches are then used to keep them. In the context of CRM, these direct-marketing channels are often referred to as one-to-one marketing. Special promotions, prices, perks, products, and other offers are made through telemarketing, direct mail (regular "snail mail," fax, e-mail), and personal sales calls.

Application | The Royal Bank of Canada

At least once a month, analysts at the Royal Bank of Canada (based in Toronto) use data mining techniques on the bank's 10 million customers according to a number of factors:

- Their credit risk.
- Their current and future profitability.
- Their stage of the family life cycle.
- Their likelihood of leaving the bank.
- Their channel preference (call center, branch bank, or the Internet).
- Their likelihood to purchase more bank products.[27]

Consider the following hypothetical customer. Her balance is low, her credit card payments are slow, and her deposits have recently become sporadic. All of these data point to her leaving the bank. Further analysis of her CIF shows that she has been a profitable customer and that she could potentially be even more profitable based on her past banking patterns and other products she holds. The latter include a car loan, a line of credit, and a checking account. The analysts infer that she is in a phase of her life where her borrowing needs are high. They also know she likes to use the Internet to pay her bills and check her balances. They conclude that she would be a good target for a particular package of banking services. The bank has found that people with these kinds of packages stay with the bank an average of three years longer than customers who do not and that they are more profitable to the bank. With this information, the marketing managers have a personalized strategy for her.

The marketing managers then enter this information about the customer into a central database that is fed to the desktops of all its personal bankers and customer service and call center representatives. She then receives a call from a personal banker offering her the package of services. Because she does not immediately take the offer, the call is followed up by a call center representative. Her reaction to the offer is logged into her row of the CIF for future reference.

Relationship Marketing Programs

Given the preceding discussion concerning customer targeting, it is important to describe marketing programs beyond discounts and other special perks that are part of the normal arsenal of marketing managers, and that have been described elsewhere in this book. Thus, this section of the chapter describes programs that have been specifically designed for retaining customers.

Customer Satisfaction

Clearly, one of the requirements of customer retention is satisfaction. Satisfied customers are much more likely to repurchase and become good customers than dissatisfied customers. Many studies have shown a positive relationship among satisfaction, loyalty, and profitability.[28]

Spurred by the quality movement of the 1980s, the introduction of several very public competitions (such as the Malcolm Baldrige Award for Quality), and well-publicized satisfaction surveys (such as the one done by J. D. Power for automobiles), many companies around the world are investing substantial sums in measuring customer satisfaction and exploring its impact on their businesses. As a result, this has become a big business for research firms. By one estimate, up to one-third of all revenues generated by U.S. marketing research firms are from customer satisfaction surveys and analyses.

expectation confirmation/disconfirmation model
a basic customer satisfaction model that presumes that levels of customer satisfaction with a product or service are determined by how well the product performs compared to what the customer expects

The basic customer satisfaction model is shown in Figure 14.9. The model is often called an **expectation confirmation/disconfirmation model** because it assumes that levels of customer satisfaction with a product or service are determined by how well the product performs relative to what the customer expected. In the center of the figure is perceived customer satisfaction or quality. The circle on the right is experienced quality, or how the product or service actually performed. To the left, the customer is presumed to form an expectation or prediction about the product's performance. This expectation is formed from a variety of sources of information, including advertising, word-of-mouth information from friends and relatives, and past experience with the product or product category. If the product meets or exceeds expectations, the customer is satisfied to different degrees. Obviously, if the product just meets expectations, satisfaction is less than if the product goes way beyond expectations. Any performance below expectations results in a dissatisfied customer.

Satisfaction can be measured in a number of ways. As in the multiattribute model shown in Chapter 4, the most common approach is to use a scale to compare satisfaction, along a number of product dimensions, with competition and expectations. Figure 14.10 shows several common scale types. FedEx has been known to use the 101-point scale, General Electric uses the 10-point scale, and most other companies use a 4- or 5-point scale. For example, a satisfaction question for an airline might look like the following:

"How satisfied were you with the food (relative to your expectations)?"
Very dissatisfied *Very satisfied*
1 2 3 4 5

After obtaining satisfaction measures on a number of attributes, the survey always contains an overall satisfaction question:

"Overall, how satisfied were you with the flight today?"
Very dissatisfied *Very satisfied*
1 2 3 4 5

Figure 14.9

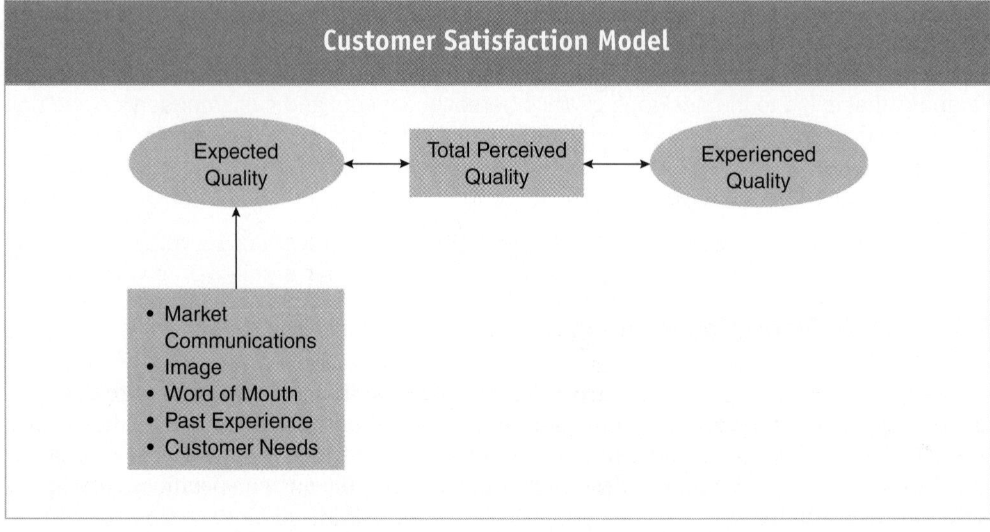

Figure 14.10

Customer Satisfaction Scales

101-Point Scale

0% Complete Dissatisfaction	————————	100% Complete Satisfaction

5-Point Scale

Excellent	Good	Satisfactory	Not Too Satisfactory	Poor
(Percentage Strongly Satisfied)			(Percentage Not Satisfied)	

Very Satisfied	Satisfied	Neutral	Dissatisfied	Very Dissatisfied
(Percentage Satisfied)				

4-Point/5-Point Scale

Much Better	Better	About the Same	Both Not Satisfactory

Much Better	Better	About the Same	Not as Good	Much Worse

10-Point Scale

Not Important at All									Extremely Important
1	2	3	4	5	6	7	8	9	10
1	2	3	4	5	6	7	8	9	10
Poor									Excellent

Source: AMACOM Resources for the Professional Manager in Print by Mack Hanan and Peter Karp. Copyright 1989 by AMACOM Books. Reproduced with permission of AMACOM Books in the format Textbook via Copyright Clearance Center.

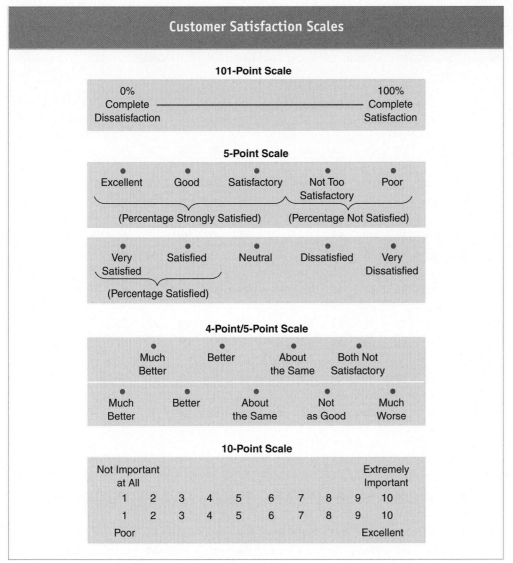

Most companies track these satisfaction measures over time and relative to competition in order to determine trends in different market segments or product areas. An important trend is that more companies are using customer satisfaction data in calculating senior executive bonuses. For example, the bonus plan developed by cable TV company Charter Communications defines six customer-satisfaction metrics that are measured in each of its key market areas on a monthly basis.[29]

Customer satisfaction measures for companies and industry sectors are tracked by the National Quality Research Center at the University of Michigan. Based on an index with a maximum of 100, the scores from the airline industry (through 2009) and for specialty retail stores (through 2008) are shown in Figure 14.11.[30] As can be seen by examining the column labeled "previous year % change," there are some notable shifts in these satisfaction scores based on company investments in customer service, communications, and word-of-mouth activities, particularly in the airline industry.

Customer satisfaction surveys for products and services sold via the Web can be conducted quickly and easily using a service introduced by CustomerSat.com. The Web site operator first designs the survey using a variety of questionnaire options provided at the CustomerSat.com site. The survey is then distributed by a pop-up window at the client's Web site. The frequency of the pop-up window can be adjusted to appear to every visitor or as few as 1 out of 100 visitors for sites that have heavy traffic. Reports based on the answers to the survey questions are generated and updated in real time for the client.

Figure 14.11

Some Sample ACSI Scores

Airlines

	Baseline	96	97	98	99	00	01	02	03	04	05	06	07	08	09	Previous Year % Change
Southwest Airlines	78	76	76	74	72	70	70	74	75	73	74	74	76	79	81	2.5
All others	NM	74	70	62	67	63	64	72	74	73	74	74	75	76	77	2.7
Continental Airlines	67	66	64	66	64	62	67	68	68	67	70	67	69	62	68	9.7
Airlines	**72**	**69**	**67**	**65**	**63**	**63**	**61**	**66**	**67**	**66**	**66**	**65**	**63**	**62**	**64**	**3.2**
Delta Air Lines	77	67	69	65	68	66	61	66	67	67	65	64	59	60	64	6.7
American Airlines	70	71	62	67	64	63	62	63	67	66	64	62	60	52	60	−3.2
US Airways	72	66	68	65	61	62	60	63	64	62	57	62	61	54	59	9.3
Northwest Airlines	69	67	64	63	53	62	56	65	64	64	64	61	61	57	57	0.0
United Airlines	71	70	68	65	62	62	59	64	63	64	61	63	56	56	56	0.0

Specialty Retail Stores

	Baseline	96	97	98	99	00	01	02	03	04	05	06	07	08	09	Previous Year % Change
Barnes & Noble	NM	NM	NM	NM	NM	NM	NM	NM	NM	NM	NM	NM	83	83		0.0
Costco	NM	NM	NM	NM	79	77	76	79	80	79	79	81	81	83		2.5
Borders	NM	NM	NM	NM	NM	NM	NM	NM	NM	NM	NM	NM	81	79		−2.5
SAM'S CLUB	NM	75	72	75	78	74	78	77	77	75	76	78	77	79		2.6
All others	NM	NM	NM	NM	NM	NM	72	73	73	75	73	75	76	78		2.6
Specialty Retail Stores	NM	75	72	75	79	76	73	74	74	75	74	75	75	76		1.3
Staples	NM	NM	NM	NM	NM	NM	NM	NM	NM	NM	NM	NM	77	78		−1.3
Lowe's	NM	NM	NM	NM	NM	NM	75	76	77	76	78	74	75	76		1.3
Office Depot	NM	NM	NM	NM	NM	NM	NM	NM	NM	NM	NM	NM	78	75		−3.8
Gap	NM	NM	NM	NM	NM	NM	NM	NM	NM	NM	NM	NM	75	75		0.0
OfficeMax	NM	NM	NM	NM	NM	NM	NM	NM	NM	NM	NM	NM	76	74		−2.6
Best Buy	NM	NM	NM	NM	NM	NM	NM	NM	72	72	71	76	74	74		0.0
TJX	NM	NM	NM	NM	NM	NM	NM	NM	NM	NM	NM	NM	74	73		−1.4
Circuit City	NM	NM	NM	NM	NM	NM	NM	NM	73	72	70	69	71	72		1.4

Source: American Customer Satisfaction Index, www.theasci.org. Used by permission.

Interestingly, a large amount of evidence indicates that merely satisfying customers is not enough to keep them loyal to your company or product. In other words, although Figure 14.10 implies that "excellent," "good," and "satisfactory" ratings all mean "strongly satisfied," there may be a real difference between those responses. Research by Xerox showed that totally satisfied customers (i.e., those choosing 5 on a 5-point scale) were six times more likely to repurchase Xerox products over the next 18 months than those that were only satisfied (i.e., those choosing 3 or 4 on the 5-point scale).[31] The largest differences in loyalty between completely satisfied and merely satisfied customers have been found in the most highly competitive industries, such as automobiles and many services.

The importance of looking at the most and least satisfied customers has recently been proposed as being an important predictor of firm performance. Net Promoter is a customer loyalty metric introduced by Reichheld in his 2003 *Harvard Business Review* article "The One Number You Need to Grow." Based on customers' responses on a 0 to 10 rating scale—"How likely is it that you would recommend our company to a friend or colleague?"—customers are grouped into one of three groups: "promoters" (9–10 rating, extremely likely to recommend), passively satisfied (7–8 rating), and "detractors" (0–6 rating, extremely unlikely to recommend). The percentage of detractors is then subtracted from the percentage of promoters to obtain the "Net Promoter score." A score of 75 percent or above is considered quite high. The Net Promoter score also provides insights into how to get more promoters and fewer detractors. These insights can then be provided to marketers for follow-up action. The most important proposed benefits of this methodology derive from its simplicity, but it has been criticized for not being applicable to many business settings.[32]

The relationship between satisfaction and loyalty is complex. One study identified four customer types based on their levels of satisfaction and loyalty:[33]

1. **Loyalist/Apostle.** These customers are completely satisfied, have high loyalty, and are very supportive of the company. Apostles help you get new customers through referrals.
2. **Defector/Terrorist.** They tend to be dissatisfied or somewhere in the middle, switch to competitors, and are unhappy with you. Terrorists spread negative word of mouth.
3. **Mercenary.** They can have high satisfaction but high switching rates as well. Their commitment to you is low. They are usually price- and promotion-sensitive, and rarely stay with you long enough for them to be profitable.
4. **Hostage.** These customers are stuck with you. They may be dissatisfied, but they are highly loyal because there may not be a viable alternative. A good example is cable TV service. When an alternative surfaces (e.g., satellite TV), they switch.

Thus, Apostles and Mercenaries can be highly satisfied but exhibit totally different loyalty patterns. Likewise, Apostles and Hostages are both highly loyal, but for different reasons. It is therefore critical to understand the context within which you are measuring satisfaction and loyalty.[34]

customer service
service that supplements or complements the main product or service purchased

Customer Service

An important component of customer satisfaction is **customer service**. Although we will discuss the marketing of services in the next chapter, all products, whether manufactured or services, have a service component. Automobiles and computers must be repaired. Customers have questions about how to set up a DVD player. Machinists need technical advice about how to operate a new lathe. The quality of these encounters can make or break a relationship with a customer. How many times have you sworn not to return to a restaurant or not to buy a product from a company that has delivered poor customer service?

Ritz-Carlton is famous for its high level of customer service including this hotel in Moscow, Russia.
Source: Alexei Boitsov/Getty Images, Inc-Liaison

Companies that market services know that the level of customer service delivered is equivalent to product quality. However, many companies in manufacturing businesses underestimate how important these service encounters are to customer loyalty. Although it is important that a personal computer works as advertised, for some consumers it is equally important that the company provides helpful responses to questions and does not leave them waiting on the telephone to speak to a representative.

In fact, many companies are reexamining their approach to customer service. Traditionally, a company would develop a product and then "throw it over the wall" to a separate customer service department. However, much of the information gleaned from service interactions with customers was not getting back to marketing managers. As a result, the term often used today is *customer experience management* rather than customer service, implying the companies are interested in managing the customer's interaction with the company at any number of different interaction points and using the feedback to improve products and processes.[35]

Thus, regardless of the type of product, as we noted earlier in this chapter, the relationship between buyer and seller is only beginning when the purchase is made. The points of contact between buyer and seller are not all equal in importance. Those that are critical to the relationship are called moments of truth.[36] It is important for you to understand which customer contacts are sufficiently critical to the long-term relationship to be considered moments of truth for your business.

The key to using customer service to develop these long-term relationships is to view service as a way of differentiating your product from the competition. Figure 14.12 illustrates this differentiation effort. Consider the core product to be the basic attributes of the product or service. For a manufactured product, these would be the physical characteristics. For example, for a car, color, weight, gas mileage, and similar characteristics constitute the core product. The expected product is the core product plus any expectations about the product or service held by the target segment. Thus, the expected car would also feature a certain level of reliability, service from the dealer, prestige obtained from driving it, and so on.

How, then, do you use customer service to differentiate your products? Today, whether you are in a high-tech or low-tech business, all competitors in a market either offer or have the potential to offer equivalent core products. Thus, it is difficult to achieve differentiation based on product features and attributes. Also, simply meeting expectations is insufficient for maintaining buyer loyalty over an extended period of time. To differentiate, you need to reach a third level (shown in Figure 14.12), the augmented product. In other words, you have to go beyond expectations by offering levels of customer service that competitors cannot match.

Figure 14.12

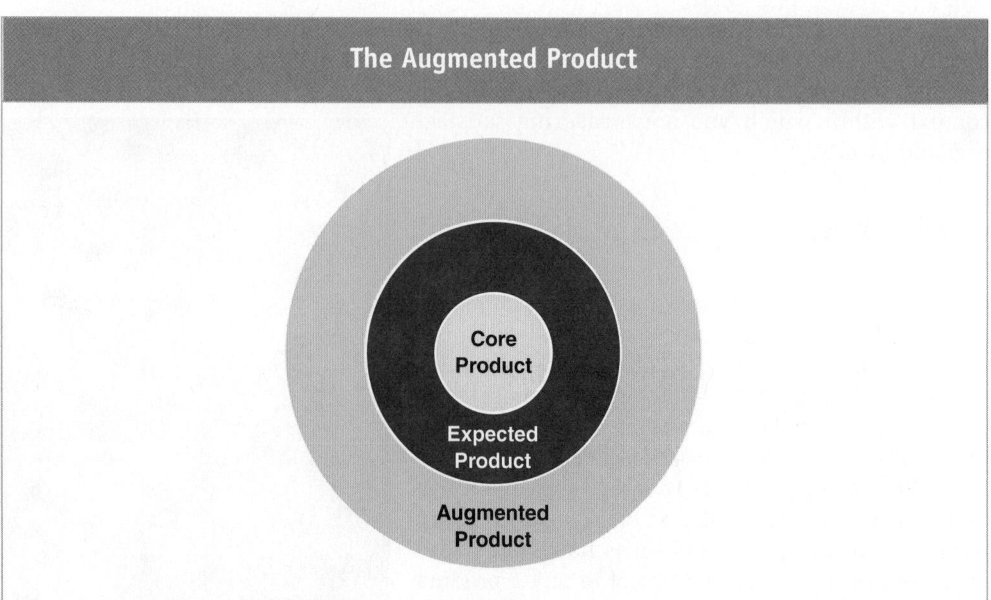

Source: Theodore Levitt (1980), "Marketing Success through Differentiation—of Anything," *Harvard Business Review*, January–February. pp. 83–91. Copyright © 1980 by the President and Fellows of Harvard College. Reprinted by permission.

Application Rackspace

Rackspace is a San Antonio-based Web-hosting company.[37] The company manages the technology "back end" of Web sites for clients who highly value reliability (e.g., e-tailers). In an industry not particularly known for great customer service, Rackspace has developed a reputation for a fanatical dedication to its customers (see www.rackspace.com).

However, this reputation was not obtained just through advertising. Prior to the adoption of a new vision for customer service, employees had believed that, as with any technical service, as long as the system was up and running, the customer service job was done. The new approach consisted of a number of initiatives. First, criticizing a customer became a firing offense. Second, employees were organized by teams of account managers, a billing specialist, and several tech-support specialists. Each team served a group of customers. The team approach enabled the customer's problems to be solved more quickly because the problems often involved what had been separate departments. Also, the team gets to know its customers well, which gives the latter a sense of security because they get to know the team members over time. Finally, each team is treated as its own separate business with responsibility for profits and losses. Each month, employees could earn bonuses of up to 20 percent of their monthly base salaries, depending on the performances of their teams by both financial and customer-based metrics.

Application Zappos

Tony Hsieh, the founder of Zappos.com, is considered one of the most innovative Internet marketers of all time.[38] Zappos started as an online shoe retailer in 1999, but the company has since expanded to selling a number of different product lines (see the company's home page in Figure 14.13) using multiple channels including catalogues and telemarketing. The company sold $1 billion worth of products in 2008.

What makes Hsieh and Zappos successful is a level of customer service that sets it apart from other Internet retailers. The basics of their service are free shipping and free returns.

Figure 14.13

Zappos Web Site

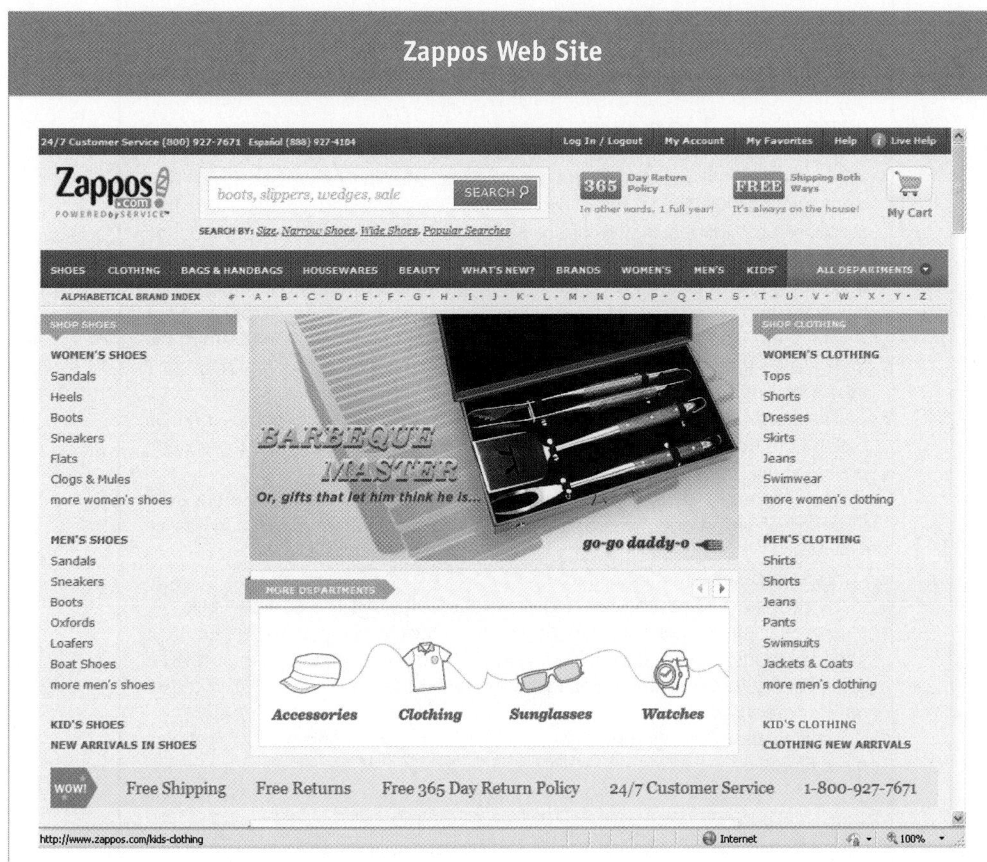

Source: © 2008 Zappos.com, Inc.

However, what really separates Zappos from the competition is the attitude of the customer service representatives. All new Zappos employees receive two weeks of classroom training. Then they spend two weeks learning how to answer customer calls. At the end of this program, each trainee is offered $2,000 to quit! Hiseh figures that this weeds out those who would probably leave soon anyway from those who will be committed to Zappos.

On the job, employees are not given scripts nor are their call times tracked like in many call centers. Customer service representatives are encouraged to make decisions on their own and are supposed to send a dozen or so personal notes to customers every day. They call it "P-E-C": Personal Emotional Connection with the customer.

The company has become so well known for its customer service that it has begun offering training programs for other companies. In 2009, the company began offering two-day, $4,000 seminars on how to recreate the Zappos corporate culture. The company is launching Zappos Insights, a Web site offering management videos and tips from its staffers at a cost of $39.95 per month.

A final illustration is shown in Figure 14.14. One of the largest complaints consumers have in the area of customer service is about automobile repairs. This figure shows how one dealer has managed to go beyond customer expectations and deliver outstanding customer service.

Figure 14.14

Illustration of Outstanding Customer Service

Last summer at a little before 4:00 P.M. on a blisteringly hot Saturday, a tow truck pulled up in front of our service area at Tasca Lincoln-Mercury.

Behind it rode a small red, well-used Mercury Tracer. In the truck was an entire family, looking despondent—their holiday on Cape Cod seemed in jeopardy. There they were, stuck in Seekonk, Massachusetts, with a broken car, and who knew for how long? The kids grew increasingly fidgety. "Can you do anything for us?" the dad asked, his tone of voice revealing his frustration and disappointment. "I know it's late in the day, but you're the only place around here open for service." His voice trailed off.

He was right; it *was* late in the day and we *were* the only place open. That was just the problem. Our guys had been working since 7:00 that morning—sometimes in the direct sunlight. The temperature had reached ninety-five degrees and hadn't dropped much yet. Only one more hour to go, and they could drive home and relax with their families and friends. The service assistant who talked with the new customers looked at his team. "Well?"

The team leader responded, "I don't know; it's pretty late in the day, and the men are all tired, and we don't even know what's wrong with it.... Okay, we'll take a look at it."

The word came back in less than twenty minutes. "Bad fuel pump—and we haven't got one in stock now. We just used the last one. Can't get more parts until Monday."

The kids really looked crestfallen now. A couple of the team members eyed them. "Hey," yelled one, "we got a used Tracer on the lot. We could cannibalize the pump."

"Let's go," yelled the team leader.

While they pushed one car and drove the other into the service bays, the service assistant explained the proposal to the family and asked for their approval to install a used part. They agreed. Twenty minutes later, their revived red Mercury Tracer sat happily idling in front of them. Time? 4:57. Time to go—for everybody.

I asked the team members later, "Would you have done it if it had taken more time?"

"Yeah," they said, "it was the look in those kids' eyes. We knew if we did it, it would make their day."

Source: Bob Tasca (1996), *You Will Be Satisfied* (New York: HarperCollins), pp. 95–96.

Some useful customer service principles are:[39]

- Service is the backbone of any business. If you do not satisfy the customer the first time, you may not get a second chance.
- Great service is measured by customer satisfaction. Profits will follow if your customers are highly satisfied.
- Compensation plans determine behavior. Thus, your compensation scheme should reward your workers for delivering high levels of service.
- Sales and service departments are complementary. Great service gives the sales department more to sell.
- The hours your service department is open sends signals about your dedication to customer satisfaction. You should be open when your customer needs you.
- Service technicians should work together to solve customers' problems.

One way to differentiate your product through customer service is with service guarantees.[40] Guarantees not only offer the customer some assurance about product quality but also reinforce the brand image at the same time. Some examples are Domino's Pizza's former promise that you will get your pizza delivered in 30 minutes or you do not have to pay for it, and Lucky Supermarkets' offer of "Three's a Crowd" service that guarantees the opening of a new checkout station when any line has more than three people. Although their effectiveness varies, such guarantees can differentiate a product from the competition.

Another way to demonstrate excellence in customer service is through service recovery. Unfortunately, products do break down and there are often tense moments as services are delivered (e.g., the waiter spills soup on your dress). Thus, a critical moment for a company is when the product or service does not perform up to expectations or fails to work properly. How you react in such situations is crucial for maintaining customer relationships.

Effective service recovery demands significant training and the right people to do the job. When service recovery is necessary, customers are typically unhappy because some aspect of the product or service has failed. The people dealing with the situation must be compassionate and good listeners, as well as effective problem solvers. In 1997, because of its highly selective screening process focusing on interpersonal and empathy skills, Southwest Airlines sorted through 105,583 job applications to fill 3,006 positions.[41]

Turning around a potential disaster can be a tremendous boost to loyalty. The British Airways anecdote earlier in this chapter was a lost opportunity. In a more positive vein, an IBM account team was having difficulty overcoming the hostility of a potential major buyer of mainframe processors. Although the potential buyer did own several IBM processors, the company was not interested in buying any more or in buying peripheral equipment such as tape and disk drives. The account team's basic strategy was to build a new level of confidence from the lower levels of the company's organization that were key influences in the buying decision. Although they were having some success with this approach, one of the breakthrough events that turned the account around was how they handled a failure of one of the installed IBM processors. A large number of IBM personnel worked around the clock to restore the system. Their efforts prompted a laudatory letter from the director of the company's information systems group and went a long way toward improving the relationship. Eventually, the team's efforts resulted in a larger order.[42]

Application EMC Corporation

EMC is the world leader in data storage systems.[43] Along with Cisco Systems, Oracle, and Sun Microsystems (now part of Oracle), it has been referred to as one of the "four horsemen" of the Internet. In 1988, the company had 910 employees, annual sales of $123 million, and a net loss of $7.8 million. In 2009, it had 40,000 employees and annual revenues of $15 billion. While excellent products certainly helped, it is generally acknowledged that its commitment to customer service has been the driving force behind its growth. The company has an astounding customer retention rate of 99 percent.

The company's major customers are banks, phone companies, automakers, oil companies, e-commerce companies, and other companies that stand to lose millions of dollars every minute their data systems are down. As an example of their commitment to service, in the winter of 1999, a bank in Wisconsin suddenly lost access to its data-storage facility. Within minutes, customer service engineers at EMC headquarters remotely retrieved the logs of the bank's system but could not locate the problem. The next step was to re-create the bank's system in a $1 billion facility that EMC designed just to simulate its customers' setups in such emergencies. Through mirroring the customer's facility, the engineers found the problem. A second example of the company's willingness to invest in customer service came at the 1996 Olympics in Atlanta. A number of large EMC clients had computer operations in the city's center. Unfortunately, the center was snarled with traffic and people attending the games. The manager in charge of managing EMC spare parts around the world stationed bicycle messengers at two dozen locations and stocked each one with EMC spare parts. As a backup, she hired two helicopters. Although they were never used, no one in the company felt it was a waste of money.

Web-based customer service has improved substantially with the advent of live chat and other similar services. An example of a company that provides such services is LivePerson.com.[44] A visitor to a site using the LivePerson service can choose among three different modes of customer service: a telephone number, e-mail, and live chat. If you choose the live chat, the pop-up screen shown in the figure appears and the dialogue begins. One LivePerson client claims that customers who used live chat during their shopping experience are three times more likely to buy from the site and two times more likely to return back to the site within 24 hours versus those that did not chat. Also, the average order for customers who chatted was 35 percent higher than customers who purchased from the site and did not chat.

Also, the reason these numbers are so high for this retailer is that they employ LivePerson's new product, LivePerson Sales Edition. This product is different from its flagship live chat solution because it enables sales agents (much different than customer service agents) to reach out to incoming Web site visitors that LivePerson's rules-based engine deems a top prospect and engage them in a sales consultation.[45]

Besides the use of the Web, improvements in technology have been leveraged by a wide variety of industries. Two examples are:

- Rolls-Royce uses live satellite feeds displayed on video screens to continuously monitor the health of some 3,000 jet engines for 45 airline customers.[46]
- Some hotels are using "smart" networks to connect individual rooms to network servers to keep track of guests' preferences and change room conditions automatically. For example, desired room temperatures can be set and frequently dialed numbers can be loaded into its guests' phones upon check-in.

Loyalty Programs

loyalty programs
also called frequency marketing, programs that encourage repeat purchasing through a formal program enrollment process and the distribution of benefits

One of the major trends in marketing in the 1990s is the tremendous growth in **loyalty programs** or, in general, frequency marketing. These are programs like Harrah's Total Rewards, which encourage repeat purchasing through a formal program enrollment process and the distribution of benefits. The best examples of such programs are the frequent-flyer programs offered by every major airline in the world, where miles are accumulated and then exchanged for free travel or merchandise. The innovator was American Airlines, which started its AAdvantage program in 1981. A newsletter that follows loyalty programs is *Colloquy*, www.colloquy.com.

These programs have migrated to many different industries. Some examples are:

- Cracker Barrel, a restaurant chain with a country flavor, has its Cracker Barrel Old Country Store Neighborhood program, where you earn one "neighborhood" point for every dollar spent at its stores. The points are redeemable at the stores.
- The retailer Pier 1 Imports has a Preferred Card program with three levels of benefits: basic (under $500 in annual spending), Gold ($500 to $1,000), and Platinum (more than $1,000 spent annually).
- Hallmark's Gold Crown Card program is targeted toward customers of their Gold Crown retail stores. Customers receive points for money spent and greeting card purchases, which are redeemable for certificates of different monetary value. These certificates are spendable only in the Gold Crown stores.

- The British pharmacy retailer or "chemist" Boots has its Advantage card program, launched in 1997, which enables shoppers to earn points toward free goods.
- A small Spanish grocery chain, Plus, differentiates itself from other grocery chains through its loyalty card program; more than 80 percent of its customers use the card.

Technology is changing the way these programs can operate. Most of them currently involve a special-purpose membership card or a co-branded Visa or MasterCard. The magnetic strip on the back of the card forwards data from the transactions to a separate information system, which tracks behavior and issues rewards. So-called smart cards have microprocessors built into them. These cards can store points accumulated from loyalty programs, which allows for more sophisticated multiple retailer programs to be developed. For example, in the United Kingdom, Shell has a program whereby points collected at Shell service stations can be converted into free gifts, flights, or movie tickets.

These frequency or loyalty programs can have several problems:[47]

- **Making the reward too high.** Restaurant chain Chart House's program, the Aloha Club, offered free around-the-world trips to any member who ate in all 65 Chart House restaurants. Unfortunately, the company underestimated the zeal of its 300,000 members. Forty-one members qualified, costing the company a considerable sum of money. Although the value of the program to the customer should exceed the cost of being a member, the programs should also be cost-effective.
- **Ubiquity.** There are so many programs that customers are rebelling against carrying all the cards. You should target your best customers with these programs and provide a compelling reason for joining.
- **What kind of loyal customers are you actually getting?** As we have noted in this chapter, it is possible to confuse loyalty with repeat purchasing. United Airlines has many repeat-purchasing customers in the San Francisco Bay area because of its Mileage Plus frequent-flyer program. At the same time, because United is the major carrier in the region, these customers are also "hostages" and are not necessarily attitudinally loyal to the company. Compare the failure of United's shuttle services in California with Southwest Airlines' tremendous success (although Southwest's frequent-flyer program is less attractive than United's).
- **Lack of inspiration.** Many programs are simply copies of other programs. To be successful, the program must have a differential advantage over competitors' programs.
- **Lack of communication with customers.** Loyalty/frequency programs need to have a significant communication component to retain customer satisfaction.
- **Insufficient analysis of the database.** A large amount of information about customer behavior is produced from these programs. To maximize the value of these programs, these data must be mined for better market segmentation, targeting, and new-product development. This is particularly a problem for supermarkets. Only a few of the chains with frequent-shopper programs have gone beyond offering discounts at the cash register to cardholders.

For a customer loyalty program to be effective, it must leverage the brand's value proposition. For example, airline loyalty programs that provide upgrades to airline travelers are very valuable and at the same time, cost airlines very little because the upgrades are based on the unfilled seats on a plane.

Loyalty programs are not just for consumer products and services. Verizon's Business Link loyalty program offered discounts, bonuses, and special benefits to targeted business customers based on call volume. About 80 percent of the eligible business customers enrolled. The results? The account defection rate was 30 percent less for enrollees than for non-enrollees. Friedrich Grohe, a Germany-based manufacturer of kitchen and bathroom fittings, has a loyalty program with 1,500 members in Germany. Members pay $130 per year and attend product training to earn points, which can be redeemed for advertising and trade show booths designed and built by Grohe.[48]

In general, loyalty programs seem to work best under the following conditions:

- The program supports and is consistent with the brand's value proposition.
- The program adds value to the product or service.
- Lifetime customer value is high.

Mass Customization

mass customization
a new marketing process whereby a company takes a product or service that is widely marketed and develops a system for customizing it to each customer's specifications

Customer retention and loyalty are also being affected by a marketing process called **mass customization**. As noted in Chapter 7, this is a process whereby a company takes a product or service that is widely marketed and perhaps offered in many different configurations and develops a system for customizing (or nearly customizing) it to each customer's specifications. This imparts a feeling that the product was made especially for the customer, an important affective (attitudinal) component of a buyer–seller relationship.[49] Because services can be and often are tailored to each customer, most of the attention to mass customization has been in the manufacturing sector, where a combination of information and flexible manufacturing technologies has enabled companies to personalize their products for customers. In the case of Nike, NikeID allows customers to build their own shoes and select the colors for just about every area of the shoe. Lands' End offers tailored clothing on its Web site, allowing one to choose a collar, sleeve style, pocket, etc.

Community Building

A challenge for marketing managers is to create in their customers a sense of affinity for their companies and brands. Even customers that are brand loyal do not necessarily feel a sense of "belonging" to the brand, a more emotional, dedicated sense of a relationship in the human sense. In such a situation, it may not take a significant activity on the part of a competitor to induce a brand switch.

community
a group of customers who share information between themselves and the company about their experiences with the product or service

As a result, many managers seek to create not just a set of customers who purchase their product, but a **community** of customers who share information between themselves and the company about their experiences with the product or service. The concept of a community is not new. High-tech products have formed user groups for years, where groups give the company feedback and give each other tips on how to better use the product. These user groups can be sponsored by the company or formed independently. For example, many have formed around the Macintosh computer. However, it is a new concept for consumer-product companies, where there are many customers and where individual interaction is difficult (see Figure 14.6).

Particularly since the expansion of the Internet, community building is normally high on the list of goals for the construction and enhancement of a Web site for all kinds of products and services due to the ease of interacting. Successful communities on the Internet offer participants:[50]

- A forum for exchange of common interests.
- A sense of place with codes of behavior.
- The development of congenial and stimulating dialogues leading to relationships based on trust.
- Encouragement for active participation by more than an exclusive few.

Such online communities offer real opportunities for enhancing the brand and creating long-term relationships because of the increased involvement offered. Customers do not feel simply like they are buying a product—they feel they are also purchasing entry into and participation with a similar group of people. In fact, with respect to Internet behavior, a study found that the more a person uses the community features of a site, the more that person tends to visit it and make purchases there. Users who contribute product reviews or post messages remain twice as loyal and buy almost twice as often as those who do not.[51]

Some examples of successful communities are:

- Microsoft's community, for its Xbox videogame console, invites both users and game creators to participate. There is a different discussion forum for each game, and there is a code of conduct for the forum.
- Adobe Systems' Web site allows customers to congregate virtually, trade industry gossip, share practical product tips, and create a buzz around the company's products. The company tries to promote the community as not only a place where you can learn how to use its products better, but also to help your career through networking. The company does not censor any views or opinions, in order to receive honest criticism.

- Pillsbury's Web site offers menu suggestions as well as cooking hints and tips. Users are encouraged to share their own recipes on the site's bulletin board, and children are targeted through contests.
- Ace Hardware's Commercial & Industrial division created an online community so the 325 licensed dealers of its paint, construction, and hardware products could exchange sales tips while ordering products. In one case, a dealer in Arizona asked peers for advice on selling a new kind of industrial paint that bonds well on metal. The resulting discussion led to $1.7 million in new sales for the product.[52]
- A Boston-based company named Communispace operates brand communities for companies like Kraft Foods. The communities are closed to a small group of around 300 (typically) women from whom Kraft generates new product ideas and general insights about what the group is thinking.

Other Ideas

The notion of building relationships with customers is often thought of as the job of the sales force or other personnel related to marketing. From the customer's perspective, the concept of customer service does not necessarily imply marketing. In many cases, it may simply be the need to communicate with the company, to personalize it.

A successful program built on this idea was launched by Southwestern Bell Telephone Company (now AT&T) in 1995.[53] The company began the Volunteer Ambassador program in which employees volunteer to establish relationships with designated customers. The objective was to put a face on the company and to let each customer know that Southwestern Bell cares about him or her and values the business. The ambassadors were drawn from a pool of nonsales employees, and each was assigned 5 to 10 customers they were expected to visit quarterly. The program started with 1,300 volunteers and expanded to 3,500 in two years.

A good way to get information about how to improve customer loyalty is to examine customers who defect. Marketing research studies often focus on your customers or potential customers and rarely are ex-customers analyzed. However, there may be more to learn from customers who have been lost than those who are loyal. The former can provide a number of ideas on how to improve the product or service, based on actual performance levels they deemed too low for them to continue as a customer.[54]

Privacy Issues

Because of the importance of detailed customer information (the CIF in Figure 14.5) to an effective CRM strategy, the issue of privacy again becomes important. All of the issues raised at the end of Chapter 13 in the context of direct marketing are obviously relevant here.

The issue of privacy is particularly important in online communities. Not only do you have to register to join; many of the communities host chat rooms where product users communicate with each other, creating personal contact. Thus, online communities should post links to the company's privacy policies. All of the communities noted earlier explicitly list their privacy policies. In addition, both the Xbox and Adobe communities are certified by TRUSTe, an independent initiative to build user confidence in joining communities and using the Web in general.

Metrics

Traditional metrics for measuring the effectiveness of marketing programs are market share, sales volume, ROI, and similar aggregate measures. However, the whole concept of CRM is based on the idea of one-to-one customer relationships. Thus, while aggregate metrics such as sales and market share are important and should always be collected, CRM demands that customer-level measures be taken as well.

Table 14.4 is a list of some of the kinds of measures that should be obtained in a CRM-based marketing system. Besides the traditional metrics noted earlier, a large variety of customer-based metrics exist. Following the table, the primary metrics are:

- The acquisition rate and cost, retention rate (opposite of churn).
- The survival rate (the percentage of customers in group that were obtained at the same time who are still customers).
- The probability of a customer being active or purchasing in a given time frame [*P*(Active)].
- The lifetime duration (expected length of time a customer will remain active).
- Win-back rate (customers who return who had previously defected).

The "popular" metrics are:

- Share of category requirements (what percent of all purchase volume in the category is your brand).
- Size of wallet (how much is spent on the whole category).
- Share of wallet (what percent of all purchase value in the category is your brand).

These can be calculated at both the aggregate and individual consumer levels. Finally, the "strategic" metrics have already been defined in this chapter or elsewhere in this book.

Thus, the marketing manager has a large number of measures to take from the market and to follow in order to gauge the efficacy of a customer relationship-oriented marketing program.

Table 14.4

CRM-Oriented Metrics
1. Traditional marketing metrics
a. Market share
b. Sales growth
2. Primary customer-based metrics
a. Acquisition rate
b. Acquisition cost
c. Retention rate
d. Survival rate
e. *P* (Active)
f. Lifetime duration
g. Win-bank rate
3. Popular customer-based value metrics
a. Share of category requirement
b. Size of wallet
c. Share of wallet
d. Expected share of wallet
4. Strategic customer-based value metrics
a. Past customer value
b. RFM value
c. Customer lifetime value
d. Customer equity

Source: V. Kumar and Werner J. Reinartz (2006), *Customer Relationship Management* (Hoboken, NJ: John Wiley & Sons), p. 91. Reprinted with permission of John Wiley & Sons, Inc.

Executive Summary

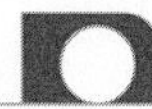

Key learning points in this chapter include the following:

- The buyer–seller relationship does not end when a sale is made; buyers expect sellers to deliver services after the sale.
- The economic advantages of customer loyalty through long-term relationships are clear: increased profits derived from profit margins produced over the term of the relationship, increased revenues from greater purchase volume or greater purchase frequency, lower costs of serving loyal customers, referrals to new customers, and price premiums (because loyal customers tend to be more insensitive to price).
- Customer relationship management, or CRM, is a strategic activity where the purpose is to develop and manage long-term relationships on a customer-by-customer basis.
- A complete CRM program consists of building a customer database, analyzing the database, selecting which customers to pursue and allocating resources to them, developing the specific relationship marketing programs, being concerned about customer privacy, and establishing appropriate customer-based metrics for evaluating the program's success.
- A key to long-term relationships is customer satisfaction. Completely satisfied customers are produced when companies go beyond customer expectations in the relationship.
- Outstanding customer service is provided by going beyond the physical product or service attributes to the augmented product (i.e., seeing that what you are selling is not just the product itself but the product and services you can offer to differentiate your product from competition).
- A popular way to maintain loyal customers is through loyalty or frequency programs. These programs reward customers for repeat purchases.
- Long-term relationships can also be established through mass customization in which the customer sees the company as providing a product or service tailored to his or her needs.
- Building a community around a brand to stimulate customer interaction enhances the brand and helps to foster relationships with customers.

Chapter Questions

1. Think of a recent example in which you were treated poorly by a company. Assuming you choose not to buy any more of that company's products or services, approximately what is the present value of the revenue that company has lost? (Assume the only lost revenue is from your purchases and not, for example, from your negative word-of-mouth.)
2. Consider the customer satisfaction model shown in Figure 14.9. Why is it important for marketing managers to measure customer expectations as well as actual satisfaction from consumption or usage?
3. Think of a company that has provided great customer service to you recently. What did it do? How did it go beyond what you expected? What do companies have to do to get employees to deliver such service?
4. Are loyalty programs more likely to be successful for certain kinds of products and services than for others? Given the proliferation of loyalty programs, how can you differentiate your program from competitors' programs?
5. Think about two contrasting products: one with which you are involved (e.g., a hobby, cars) and one you don't think about much when you purchase it (e.g., toothpaste, milk). How would you go about building community about a brand in one of the latter categories if you were the marketing manager?
6. Continuing question 5, how would you construct a database or CIF for the brand in one of the low-involvement categories?

Key Learning Points

The purpose of this chapter is to introduce the differences in developing strategies for services versus manufactured products. Key areas of learning are:

- The nature of services and the characteristics that distinguish them from manufactured goods
- The service quality model
- Measuring the quality of services
- Developing marketing strategies for services
- Marketing-mix decision making for service businesses
- How information technology affects the marketing of services

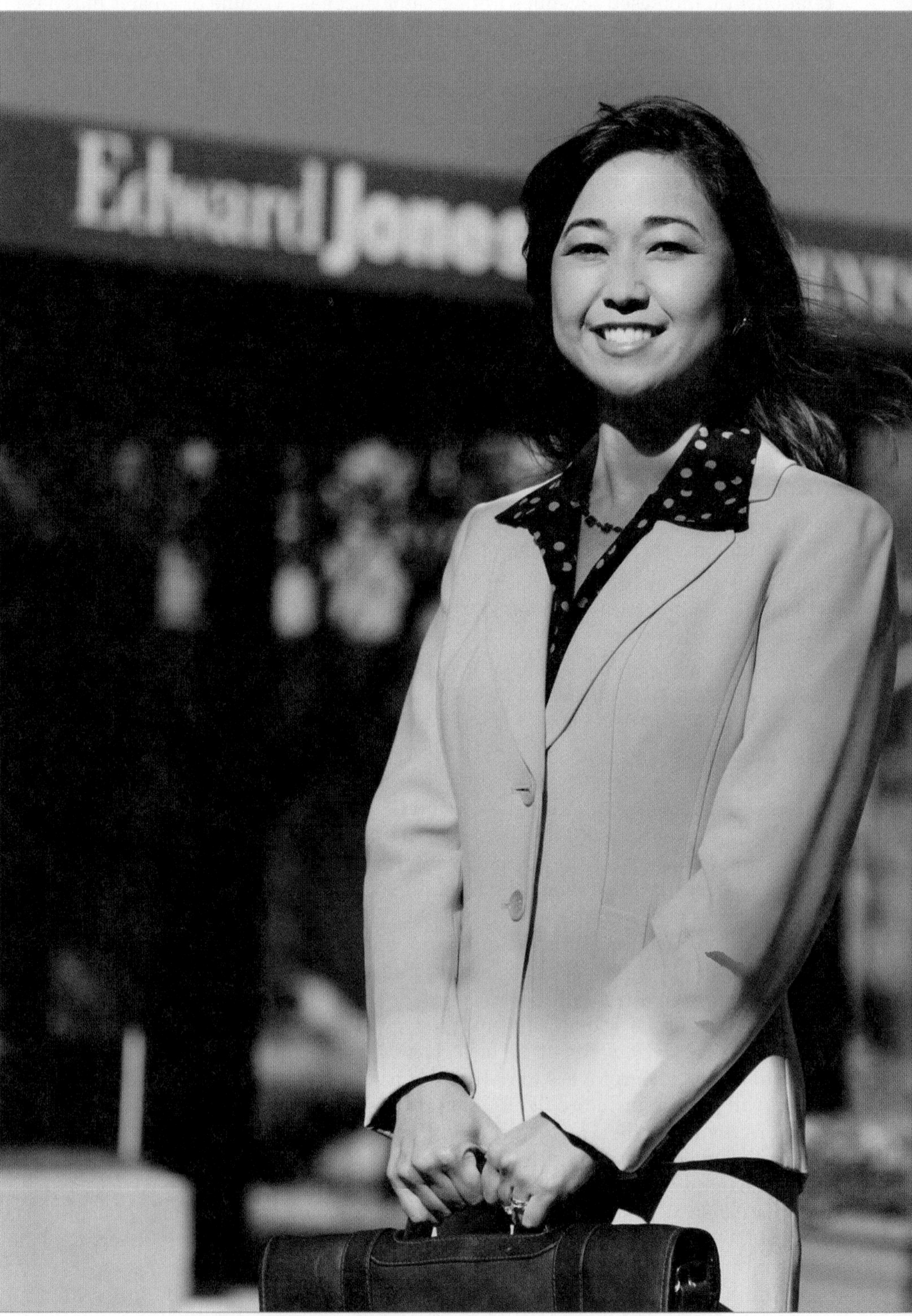

Edward Jones is a successful retail brokerage company due to its unique marketing strategy.
Source: Used by permission, courtesy of Edward Jones

Special Topic: Strategies for Service Markets

Chapter Brief

One of the largest investment brokerage firms in the United States in terms of number of offices is Edward Jones, based in St. Louis.[1] The company initially located its offices in rural and small towns but now has offices in metropolitan areas as well. In fact, the firm has more than 11,000 offices in the United States and through its affiliates in Canada and the United Kingdom. The company is so successful and innovative that it is one of the few firms with which the late eminent consultant Peter Drucker agreed to work. It is regularly rated one of the best companies to work for in the United States.

What makes Edward Jones so successful in an industry where it is difficult to differentiate and develop a unique value proposition? The competition for investment advice is keen, ranging from full-service brokers like Merrill Lynch, discount brokers such as Charles Schwab, online brokers including TD Ameritrade, and banks such as Wells Fargo. Any broker working for any company can give clients access to a wide variety of financial instruments (e.g., mutual funds, options, commodities, stocks, and bonds). A key aspect of Edward Jones's success is its organizational structure. Each office is managed by an individual investment representative (IR) who is autonomous and can therefore be as entrepreneurial as he or she wants. Each IR can segment his or her market, develop communication programs, and determine employee work hours. In short, the IR has complete control over the operation of the office.

However, the key to its success is a constant focus on helping customers achieve their financial goals by asking the following questions continuously: What is our business? Who is our customer? What does the customer value? The company's IRs focus on long-term relationships and long-term investments rather than seeking high short-term returns, which carry a high level of risk. IRs do not sell their clients initial public offerings (IPOs), options, commodity futures, or penny stocks (stocks with share prices less than $1). They also do not have their own company-branded mutual funds, as other firms such as Charles Schwab do, because they believe that such funds present IRs with a potential conflict of interest.

What the company does offer clients (depending on their goals) are stocks in stable companies with high capitalization. They also recommend highly rated bonds and mutual funds with sound track records, when appropriate. The IRs are rewarded for not churning customers' accounts (buying and selling often to generate commissions) through a trailing fee, an annual 0.25 percent commission for IRs who do not move clients' funds around from investment to investment. The company believes that its investment representatives should help customers understand their investments and feel comfortable with their investment decisions rather than focus on short-term returns. As a result, the average holding period for a mutual fund bought by an investor using Edward Jones's services is 13.1 years compared to the industry average holding period of 5.1.

The company's marketing strategy is well represented by a page from its Web site, shown in Figure 15.1. This page highlights the guiding principles of the firm. As you can see, the major principles focus on a traditional, conservative style of investing that serves its customers well in the long term. The theme "Making Sense of Investing" and the text focus on reliability rather than high risk. Thus, two key elements of the Edward Jones value proposition are local investment advice and security and the close customer relationships. These principles have helped Edward Jones grow its client list to 7 million people with $350 billion under management.

This illustration shows some of the key differences between services and manufactured products. Products such as automobiles and computers can be touched, examined, and tested by customers before they are purchased. They exist before they are sold. Services are intangible and do not exist until the customer buys them. As a result, services are marketed based on assertions of what they can do for the customer because the customer cannot usually verify that before purchasing. Image and perception are crucial components of services marketing. In addition, many services have a strong human component. Because of the customers' interaction with the delivery or production of the service, quality is a critical component of services marketing. As a result, it is easy to see why Edward Jones has been so successful. Its promise—peace of mind—resonates with its target customers and it stresses the importance of the human interactions with those customers.

Figure 15.1 Edward Jones Web Site

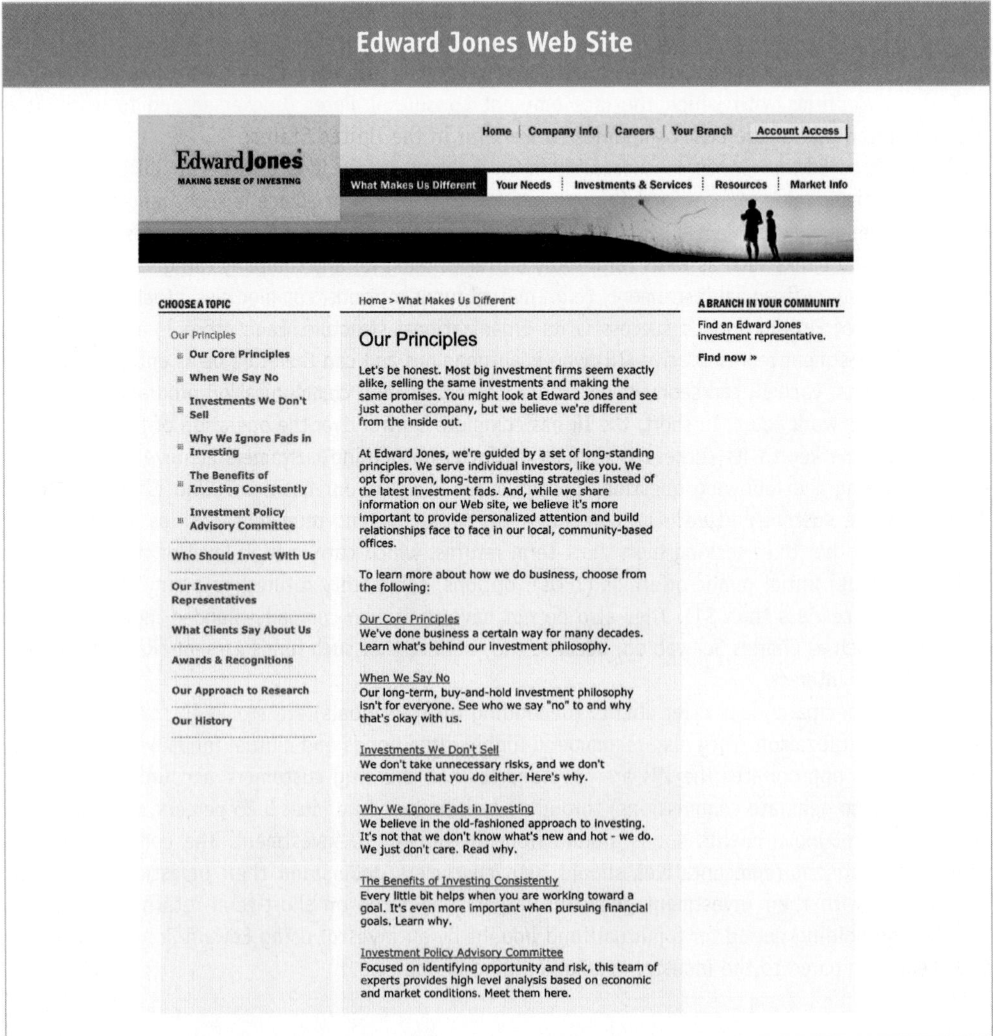

Source: Used by permission, courtesy of Edward Jones.

Figure 15.2

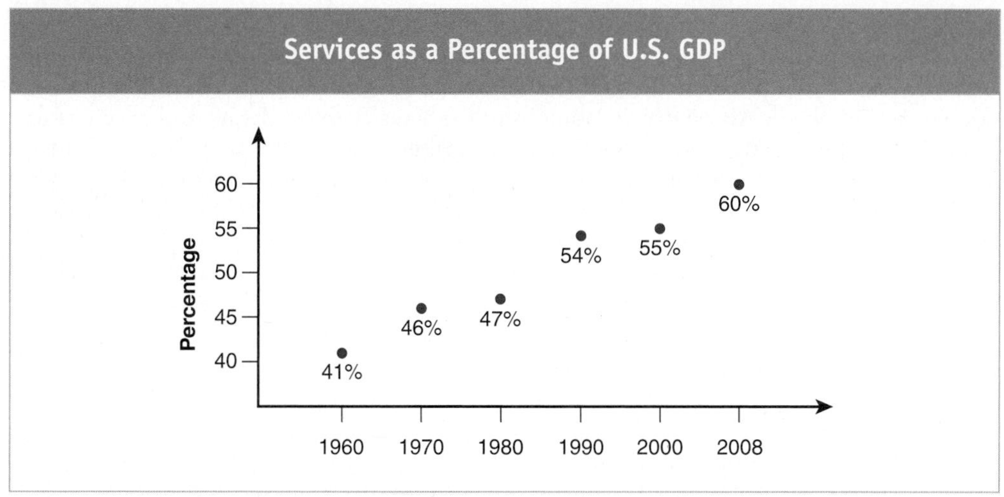

Source: Economic Report of the President, 2009, Table B-8.

Services now account for nearly 85 percent of all jobs in the United States[2] and increasing proportions of jobs in other industrialized nations. Countries like India have benefited significantly from the outsourcing of a variety of services from the United States and other English-speaking countries. Walmart, the largest company in the United States in 2009, is part of the services economy. Figure 15.2 shows the growth of services as a percentage of the U.S. gross domestic product; as of late 2008, services account for 60 percent of the GDP. Globally, services account for more than 80 percent of the GDP in Hong Kong and more than 70 percent in countries such as the United Kingdom, the Netherlands, and Australia.[3] Many companies worldwide, better known for their manufactured products, are generating serious revenues from services. For example:

- IBM, historically known for producing computers, now gets 60 percent of its revenues from services.
- The Finnish mobile phone company, Nokia, is aiming to shift its mix of products toward services such as music and maps.
- The copier company, Xerox, obtained 20 percent of its $17.6 billion in revenue in 2008 from copying consulting services showing customers (ironically) how to cut their copying costs. The company also purchased Affiliated Computer Services Inc., an information technology services company, in 2009 to get access to that company's clients for selling them printing services as well.
- Hewlett-Packard's third-quarter profit in 2009 increased by 14 percent due to an increased emphasis on technology consulting and information technology services boosted from its acquisition of Electronic Data Systems.[4]

In addition, with the growth of outsourcing noted in Chapter 1, companies are now purchasing services in many instances to replace products. For example, many large companies outsource their document preparation services to other firms. Software purchases are being replaced in some instances with software that is "hosted" (the ASP, application server provider, model described in Chapter 12) by other companies who charge a monthly service fee. Although services marketing is not completely different from the marketing of manufactured goods, it is important to understand the differences.

Walmart is an important part of the U.S. service economy.
Source: Kristoffer Tripplaar/Alamy Images

It is interesting that there is not always a clear distinction between physical products and services. For example, some products are bundled with a service component. Purchasers of the digital video recorder TiVo pay a price for the box and a monthly service fee for programming information and other features. Likewise, if you purchase a new digital camera, you will be asked if you are interested in an extended warranty. A cellular phone is distinct from the cellular service, with two different sets of companies involved. Alternatively, some services have both hardware and service components together. If you purchase a direct subscriber line (DSL) for high-speed Internet access, it involves an ethernet card in the PC, a special modem, some cables, plus the service itself.

The Nature of Services

How are services different from manufactured products?

A Classification of Goods

Economists have developed a classification of different types of product attributes that is useful for understanding the differences between manufactured products and services.[5] The three major types of attributes are:

1. **Search attributes.** These are characteristics, the quality of which can be assessed before purchase. These are typical of manufactured products; for example, a consumer can assess the picture quality of a TV or an industrial purchaser can determine the strength of an adhesive.
2. **Experience attributes.** These are characteristics, the quality of which can be assessed only after purchase or during consumption. These are typical of services. For example, the quality of an airline's service is unknown before the customer purchases a ticket and takes a trip.
3. **Credence attributes.** These are characteristics, the quality of which may not be determined even after consumption because the customer lacks the expertise to make an evaluation. An example of such products is wine: only the most knowledgeable consumers can tell the difference between a very good and an excellent wine. Another example is auto repair services: only the mechanic knows if the oil was changed.

Figure 15.3 displays goods and services on a continuum from search to credence attributes. As can be seen, manufactured goods are normally high in search attributes, and most services are characterized by experience or credence qualities. The major implication of this typology is that services are more difficult to evaluate before purchase than manufactured products. This leads to a different evaluation process by customers and a different marketing strategy by the firm.

Many services are performed by humans resulting in quality variance over time.
Source: Rob Walls/Alamy Images

Characteristics of Services

Some of the basic characteristics of services are:

- **Intangibility.** The intangible nature of services and this impact on assessing service quality has been mentioned. A further implication of intangibility is the difficulty of inventorying services. In many cases, when a service is not performed at a particular time, the revenue is lost forever and cannot be recaptured. An example of this is when a FedEx jet takes off with unfilled capacity. Although later planes may be filled, the lost revenue from the unfilled one is gone because the space cannot be held for later purchase. A similar situation exists with unfilled seats at a baseball stadium, slack time in an auto repair facility, and underused staff in an accounting firm. With respect to physical goods, TV sets not sold one day can still be sold the next.
- **Nonstandardization.** As noted earlier, many services are performed by humans. As a result, they can vary from purchase occasion to occasion. The haircut you get from a stylist in January

Figure 15.3

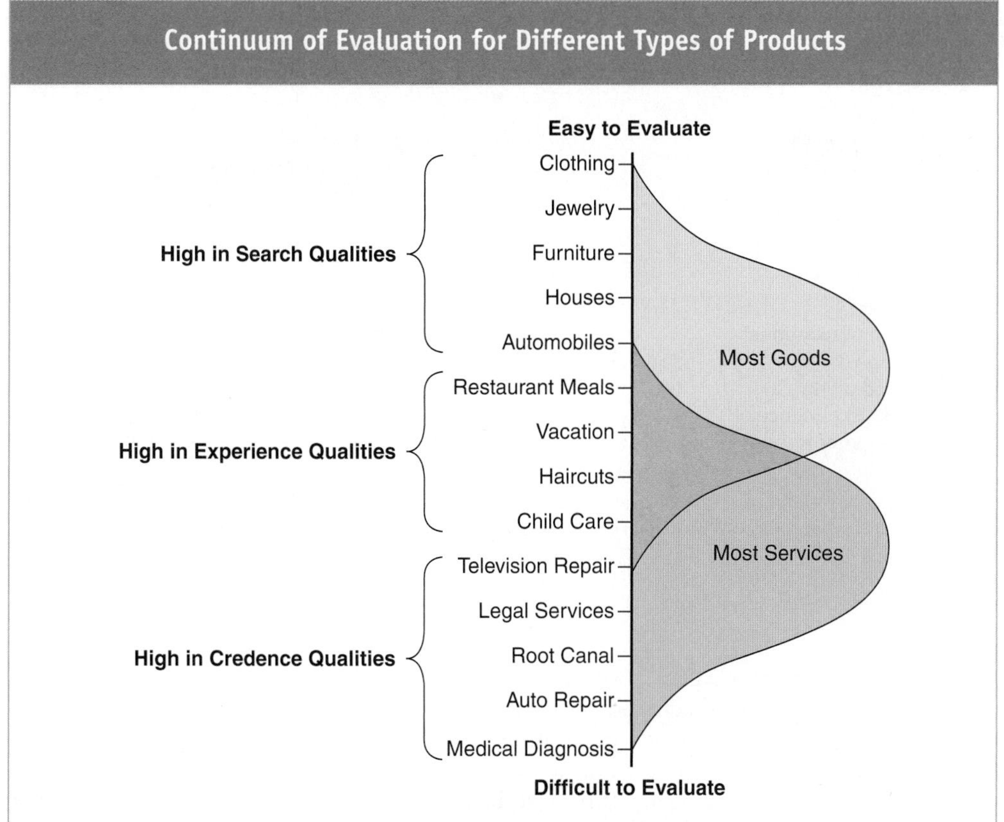

Source: Reprinted with permission from the American Marketing Association, published by the American Marketing Association, Valarie A. Zeithaml (1991), "How Consumer Evaluation Processes Differ between Goods and Services," in C. Lovelock (Ed.), *Services Marketing*, 2nd ed. (Englewood Cliffs, NJ: Prentice Hall), p. 40.

can differ from the haircut you get in February, even from the same person. The service on a United Airlines flight from San Francisco to Boston can vary from trip to trip. Therefore, it is much more difficult to control quality for services than for manufactured products. Compare this situation with the quality control mechanisms that exist for autos and similar products, in which there is much greater uniformity from product to product.

- **Inseparability of production and consumption.** In many cases, services are produced and consumed simultaneously; that is, the customer is part of the production process. However, it has been said that services are performed, not produced, and the customer is part of the performance. The customer's involvement in service delivery increases the difficulty of standardizing services. The service quality is determined by this interaction, not simply by the quality of the service provider's efforts. For example, the excitement of a classroom discussion varies with the preparation by both the instructor and the students. If the students or the instructor are unprepared, the quality of the service is diminished.

Service Quality

Because of the size of the service economy, services marketing has been one of the most heavily researched areas in marketing over the past 15 years. This research has produced a number of important findings in the area of service quality.

The Service Quality Model

How do customers determine whether they have received good service from a supplier? As noted earlier in this chapter, one characteristic of services is that because of their intangibility, perceptions play a greater role in assessing quality than they do with manufactured products. It is not an exaggeration to say that particularly with services, quality is how the customers perceive it.

Figure 15.4

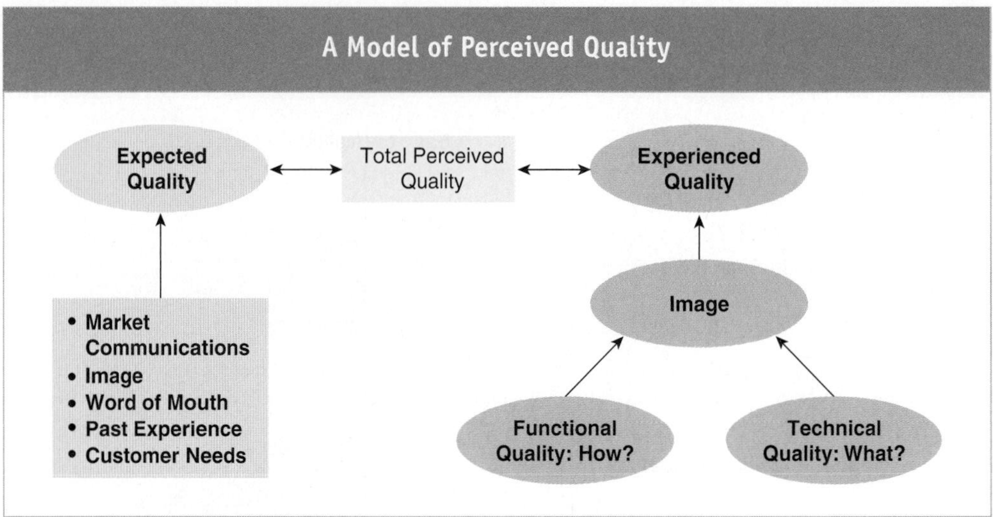

Source: Christian Grönroos (1990), *Service Management and Marketing* (Lexington, MA: Lexington Books), p. 41.

A model of service quality is shown in Figure 15.4 (this is an expanded version of Figure 14.9). As we have discussed earlier in this book, quality is defined in terms of customer perceptions. A customer's perception of quality is based on a comparison of the quality actually experienced to what he or she expected to occur when the service was delivered. The right side of the figure describes the customer evaluation process during and after the service contact. The left side depicts the customer's prediction of what the service contact will be like, or the expectation.

Expectations are based on a variety of information sources. A key source of information is the set of communications offered by the firm. These include advertising and brochures. Other sources of information include word-of-mouth communications from friends, relatives, suppliers, and others. Customer needs also affect expectations. If a software problem is important to the operation of a business, the customer will expect to get a quick answer. Past experience with the company plays a key role. If a customer called a toll-free telephone number to solve a problem and had to wait several hours to get through because all the lines were busy, this experience will create an expectation of a similar experience in the future. This source of information is important when the customer has had some experience with a service provider. However, because services are intangible and difficult to sample before purchasing, new customers rely more on the other sources of information to form their expectations.

The experienced quality (shown on the right side of Figure 15.4) results from an image or perception the customer forms after the service encounter. This perception of experienced quality is based on two components. The first component is the set of features or attributes of the service, or technical quality. In the computer software example, this would be the quality of the advice given. Functional quality is how the service is delivered or the quality of the actual interaction with the company. This could include the friendliness of the telephone service person, how many rings it took before someone answered, and so on. This dimension of service quality reflects the fact that customers take a broad view of the quality of a service encounter.

Let us return to the Edward Jones illustration. When a client is new, she forms an expectation of the quality of the investment advice she will receive from recommendations by friends (word-of-mouth), the image the firm has developed based on its communications, and her needs (e.g., the establishment of a retirement account). After taking the advice of a Jones broker, the client experiences a certain degree of service quality, based on the returns of the retirement fund as well as her interactions with the broker and the information she receives. The client compares her expectations with the experienced quality and forms a perception of the actual quality of the service. If the client is not new but seeking to add to her investments already managed by Jones, then the expected quality is also based on the firm's past performance.

Figure 15.5

Source: Valarie A. Zeithaml and Mary Jo Bitner (1996), *Services Marketing* (New York: McGraw-Hill), p. 119. Reproduced with permission of the McGraw-Hill Companies.

The Dimensions of Service Quality

Although there are many models of the different factors that affect service quality,[6] a parsimonious and well-known model contains the factors shown in Figure 15.5:[7]

- **Reliability.** This is the ability to perform the service dependably and accurately (i.e., deliver it as promised).
- **Assurance.** This is the service provider's employees' knowledge and courtesy and the confidence they instill.
- **Tangibles.** Services do have attributes (e.g., interest rate, price), and the quality of a service depends on customers' perceptions of these attributes. Tangibles also include facilities, written materials, and other physical evidence of the service.
- **Empathy.** This is the high level of attention given to customers.
- **Responsiveness.** This is the ability of the service provider to respond to the customer's needs on a timely basis.

This model is often referred to as the RATER model of service quality. The importance of these dimensions of service quality is that service firms can use them for the purposes of differentiation and positioning. These uses are described more fully later in this chapter.

Application The Broadmoor Hotel

For more than 40 consecutive years, the Broadmoor Hotel and Spa in Colorado Springs, Colorado, has received five-star ratings from *The Mobil Travel Guide*.[8] How does it ensure that the 1,600 employees maintain the superior service quality required to achieve that record of success?

- **Reliability.** This is achieved through exhaustive staff training. Before ever encountering a customer, a new Broadmoor employee attends a 2½ day training session where service expectations are set. For example, employees are trained to always give an estimated time for service, whether it is room service, laundry service, or estimating how long it will take to be seated at a restaurant (note the application of the model shown in Figure 15.4). Further training includes a 90-day on-the-job program and a five-module program once they become permanent employees.

- **Assurance.** The Broadmoor conveys trust by empowering its employees. For example, in a service recovery situation when a guest has a problem, employees are given discretionary resources to either solve the problem or mollify the customer. Assurance is also provided by employees attempting to address guests by their names whenever possible.
- **Tangibles.** This is, of course, a key part of the service offering. The Broadmoor offers first-run movies, boutiques, a cigar bar, an English pub, and three championship golf courses. The world-class spa features hydrotherapies, body treatments, massage therapies, and aesthetic treatments. Of course there are tennis courts, swimming pools, and many other tangible aspects of the service.
- **Empathy.** Employees are trained to see things from the customer's perspective. Employees follow the HEART model to take care of problems: *hear* what the guest has to say, *empathize* with him or her, *apologize* for the situation, *respond* to the guest's needs, and *take action* and follow up.
- **Responsiveness.** All department managers are expected to have sufficient staff to ensure the responsiveness that the hotel guests expect to receive. Management is also responsive to staff: managers award "star" cards on-the-spot to employees who demonstrate outstanding behavior toward guests. The hotel also seeks advice from guests concerning new amenities and features that can be added, such as water slides at the pool.

Gaps in Perceptions of Quality

Inevitably, a discrepancy will arise between the expectations formed about the service encounter and the experienced quality. As you might expect, customers who are upset with poor service tend to talk about it. As also might be expected, they talk more about negative experiences than positive ones.

loss aversion
a psychological phenomenon characterized by customers reacting more strongly to unexpectedly poor service than to unexpectedly good service

This asymmetry of the effects of negative and positive discrepancies is theoretically justified by the well-known psychological phenomenon called **loss aversion.**[9] Figure 15.6 is a graphic representation of loss aversion. Losses are situations in which the expectations of service quality were higher than the realized quality. Gains are the opposite situation. The curve to the left of the vertical axis demonstrates that losses are more negatively valued than gains are positively valued. In other words, customers react more strongly to unexpectedly poor service than they do to unexpectedly good service.

Figure 15.6

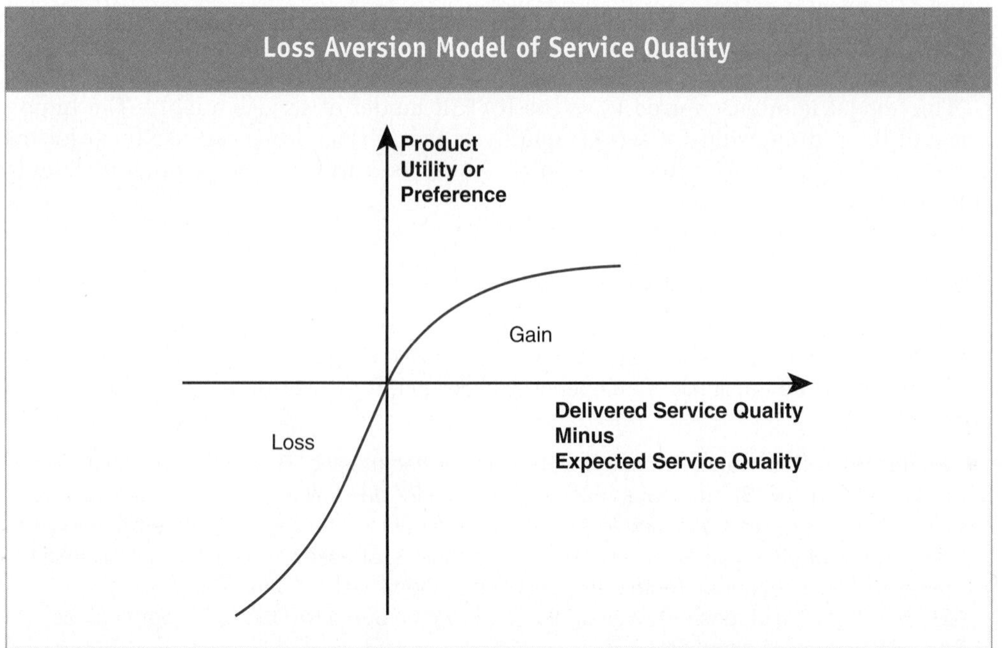

Negative gaps in perceived service quality can be remedied in two ways. The marketing manager can either lower expectations or raise service quality through improved service features (technical quality) or higher-quality interactions (functional quality). Because expectations are difficult to manage and lowering customer expectations is not usually in the best long-term interest of the service provider, raising service quality is usually chosen. However, a good example of the former is the author's dentist, who consistently overestimates the length of time it will take for the visit. Even though patients learn to expect that he will overestimate the length of the visit, it is still a nice bonus when it actually happens. Financial services firms such as Edward Jones had to lower investors' expectations in 2008–2009, when the bull stock market that had been raging since the early 2000s began to cool down.

Positive gaps in perceived service quality can also be a problem because customers' expectations adapt over time. When a positive gap exists, the service provider must increase quality just to keep matching expectations. Consider Singapore Airlines, which has consistently been recognized as the airline with the best service in the world. Of course, this is very pleasing to the company. However, it also creates potential problems because every passenger expects an almost magical experience. When that lofty expectation is not met, customers are disappointed even though the level of the service is still very high. A similar situation exists for popular restaurants and other services that generate strong word-of-mouth. Although this is a "problem" that most managers would love to have, it is still important to understand that customer expectations do drive their ultimate evaluations of quality.

We can categorize the major discrepancies between expectations and realizations into four general types of gaps:[10]

1. **The gap between customers' expectations and management's perceptions.** One key problem is that managers often think they know the bases on which customers form expectations, but often are incorrect. Companies can remedy this problem by conducting focus groups for managers to attend and presenting them with more formal research results.
2. **The gap between management's perceptions and service quality specifications.** Even when managers have a good understanding of how customers form expectations, they can find it difficult to apply their understanding to the design of the service operation. For example, knowing that computer software customers want quick response to phone calls is not enough. Defining acceptable response time takes discussions with customers.
3. **The gap between service quality specifications and service delivery.** Even if the previous gap is closed, marketing objectives will not necessarily be met. Simply setting the appropriate response time is still different from actually meeting the targets.
4. **The gap between service delivery and external communications.** As Figure 15.4 shows, communications with customers can have a powerful effect on expectation formation. As noted earlier, some of these are traditional communications such as advertising. Others are more personal; for example, how many times has a customer service person promised that a plumber or cable TV installer would be at your home at a particular hour and the person has been late?

Measuring Service Quality

Service quality cannot be measured in the way the quality of physical goods is measured. Manufacturers can use engineering or other physical metrics to assess quality as products come off the manufacturing line. By necessity, service quality is measured using a survey instrument administered to customers.

One of the most popular approaches to measuring service quality is the SERVQUAL instrument.[11] SERVQUAL is composed of questions about the five categories of service quality shown in Figure 15.5 (tangibles, reliability, responsiveness, assurance, and empathy). Each customer surveyed completes one 22-question survey measuring expectations and then one survey for each company or product to measure actual competitor performance. The SERVQUAL score for a service is the difference between the perception of the dimension and the expectation. A company can then determine its quality of

Table 15.1

Example of SERVQUAL Survey							
	Strongly Disagree						Strongly Agree
1. Excellent __________ companies will have modern-looking equipment.	1	2	3	4	5	6	7
2. The physical facilities at excellent __________ companies will be visually appealing.	1	2	3	4	5	6	7
3. Employees at excellent __________ companies will be neat appearing.	1	2	3	4	5	6	7
4. Materials associated with the service (such as pamphlets or statements) will be visually appealing in an excellent __________ company.	1	2	3	4	5	6	7
5. When excellent __________ companies promise to do something by a certain time, they will do so.	1	2	3	4	5	6	7
6. When a customer has a problem, excellent companies will show a sincere interest in solving it. __________	1	2	3	4	5	6	7
7. Excellent __________ companies will perform the service right the first time.	1	2	3	4	5	6	7
8. Excellent __________ companies will provide their services at the time they promise to do so.	1	2	3	4	5	6	7

Source: Reprinted with the permission of The Free Press, a Division of Simon & Schuster, from *Delivering Quality Service: Balancing Customer Perceptions and Expectations*, by Valarie A. Zeithaml, A. Parasuraman, and Leonard L. Berry.

service on each of the five dimensions by taking the average score across the questions for that dimension and calculating an overall score. A weighted SERVQUAL score can also be calculated by asking the customer to give importance weights (summing to 1) on each of the five dimensions. Table 15.1 shows four tangible and four reliability questions. Besides using SERVQUAL to calculate service quality perceptions, managers can use it to track competition, examine differences among market segments, and track internal service performance.

Of course, high scores on service quality surveys do not guarantee repeat customers. For example, in 1990 the U.S. General Accounting Office issued a report on a survey of 20 companies that had scored well in the 1988 and 1989 Baldrige quality competitions. One important result was that although responding managers said customer satisfaction levels had increased since then, customer retention remained almost unchanged.[12]

The Return on Quality

It normally takes a significant investment to improve service quality. For example, Florida Power & Light spent millions of dollars competing for Japan's prestigious Deming Prize. However, the ensuing lack of attention to controlling the costs of the quality improvements upset the state's ratepayers, causing the quality program to be dismantled.

return on quality (ROQ) an approach attempts to quantify financial returns on investments in improved service quality

As a result, several authors have developed a **return on quality (ROQ)** approach based on the following philosophy:[13]

- Quality is an investment.
- Quality improvement efforts must be financially accountable.
- It is possible to spend too much on quality.
- Not all quality expenditures are equally valid.

Figure 15.7

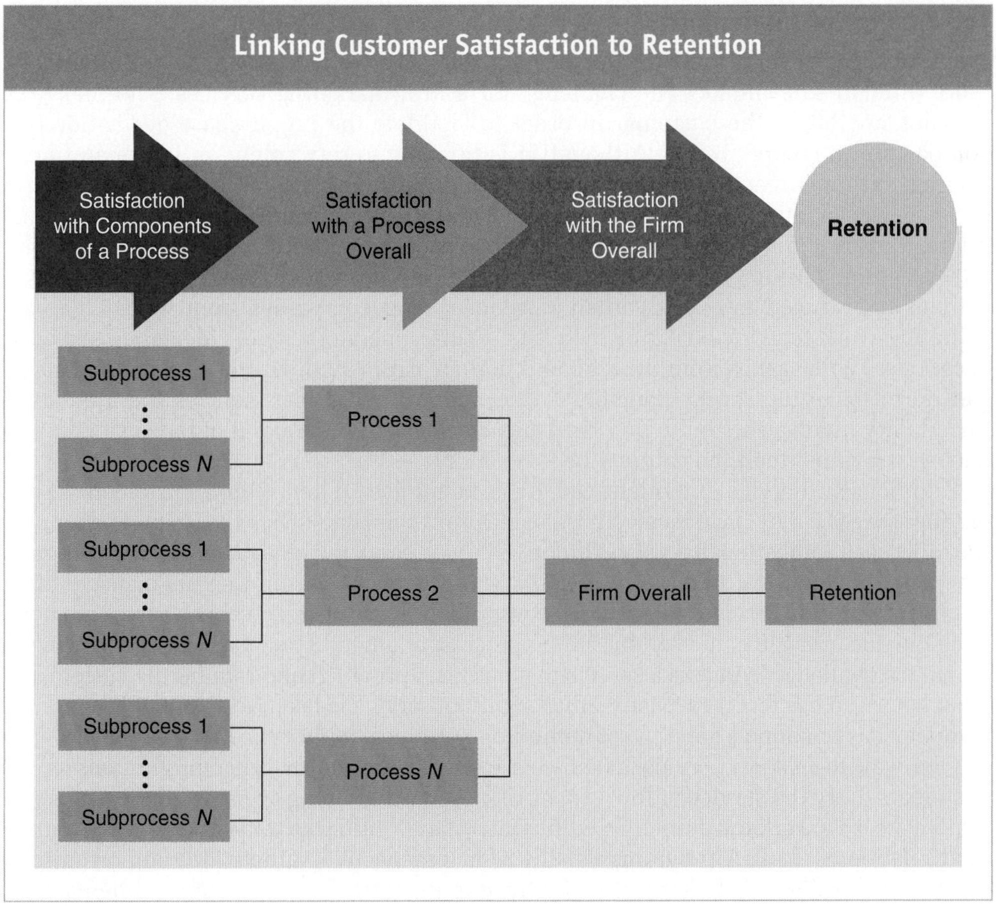

Linking Customer Satisfaction to Retention

Satisfaction with Components of a Process → Satisfaction with a Process Overall → Satisfaction with the Firm Overall → Retention

Subprocess 1 … Subprocess *N* — Process 1
Subprocess 1 … Subprocess *N* — Process 2
Subprocess 1 … Subprocess *N* — Process *N*
Process 1, Process 2, Process *N* — Firm Overall — Retention

Source: Roland T. Rust, Anthony J. Zahorik, and Timothy L. Keiningham (1994), *Return on Quality: Measuring the Financial Impact of Your Company's Quest for Quality* (Chicago: Probus).

The basic notion behind the ROQ approach is that managers are looking for improvements in actual customer behavior, such as increased loyalty, that generate a profit. The ROQ model is shown in Figure 15.7.

The key to the approach is to break down satisfaction levels with an overall process into satisfaction levels with components of those processes. This allows a more targeted approach to investing in service quality because the company can invest in the areas that will deliver the greatest return. This ultimately leads to higher overall satisfaction and greater customer retention.

Application | Marriott

For example, Marriott found that customers at full-service Marriotts wanted five things (processes): a great breakfast, fast check-in, fast check-out, clean rooms, and friendly service.[14] Managers at the company then examined each process to see which subprocesses needed the most attention. They gave each process the greatest leverage to increase customer satisfaction with the process and, ultimately, overall customer satisfaction. To improve breakfast service, the company speeded up service by hiring runners to bring the food to the servers. This allowed servers to be more attentive to customers. To improve check-in, the company established a system of allowing customers to register and get their room keys at the door, bypassing the front desk. For quicker check-out, the bill is slipped under the room door at 4 a.m. and the customer just has to sign it.

Strategic Issues

Marketing managers need to take the special characteristics of services into consideration when developing a marketing strategy.

The Problem of Intangibility

We have noted several times in this chapter that services are intangible and, therefore, more difficult to evaluate. The challenge for a firm marketing services is to make the product tangible to the customer in order to facilitate the prepurchase evaluation and comparison to competitors.[15] Although it is possible to rely solely on image and positioning, customer reaction is more uncertain and idiosyncratic.

There are many examples of attempts to make services more tangible. Professional photographers show prospective customers books of their work. Landscape architects invite potential customers to drive by other houses for which they have constructed gardens or trimmed trees. Advertising agencies send companies from whom they are soliciting work reels or books of their ads. Cruise operators send videotapes of happy vacationers with scenes from the ship and ports of call. Anything the marketing manager can do to make the service tangible to the potential customer reduces the amount of uncertainty involved with the purchase and increases the chances that the customer will choose you rather than the competitor.

Additionally, service providers can do a better job of reminding customers of the excellent service they have received. Hotel cleaning personnel leave the strip of paper over the toilet seat, indicating that the bathroom has been sanitized. An executive at a computer company sends a letter to an information systems manager, reminding the manager of all the free consulting services (e.g., evaluation of their accounts receivable system) the company obtains over the course of the selling process. Intangibility can also mean invisibility, where the challenge is to take a service that has been provided and remind the customer of what he or she has received. Many times excellent service is taken for granted because the company has not done a good job of reminding customers of that excellent service.

One way to make a service tangible is to use sampling or other promotions to get customers to try the service at low cost or risk. New advertising agencies often send speculative creative work to companies with which they would like to develop a more permanent relationship. MBA programs usually offer prospective students the opportunity to sit in on classes to get a better feeling for the quality of the instruction and students.

The Problem of Low Barriers to Entry

Many service industries are characterized by low barriers to entry. This is particularly characteristic of professional services. It is common for law firms, stock brokerage firms (e.g., Edward Jones), advertising agencies, consulting firms, and similar organizations to splinter, with several senior members of the original firm leaving to start their own firms. It is easy to obtain the credentials to become a travel or real estate agent and set up a business. Even telecommunications companies have started without any lines or repair personnel by merely purchasing excess capacity from existing companies and reselling long-distance and local services. New airlines often start up by renting used airplanes, purchasing landing rights at airports with unused capacity, hiring nonunion pilots and flight attendants, leasing maintenance services from other airlines, and using telephone or Internet-based reservation systems. Low barriers to entry create more competition, customer switching, employee turnover, and lower profits. The problem is exacerbated by the fact that many customers are loyal to the person in the company with whom they have had the most contact, rather than the company itself, and move with the employee to the new company.

Competition puts pressure on the company to develop a clear differential advantage and positioning in the marketplace. You can use the dimensions of service quality noted earlier in this chapter to differentiate your business from competition and effectively communicate or position the service:

- **Reliability.** An example of this positioning is shown in Figure 15.8 in the ad for AT&T. Note that tag line "Best coverage worldwide."—which implies reliable service anywhere in the world.
- **Assurance.** This aspect of service quality describes how the company inspires trust and confidence. The billboard for Charles Schwab shown in Figure 15.9 does just that by assuring you that you will save money on your taxes by investing in a Schwab financial product (an Investment Retirement Account).
- **Tangibles.** Figure 15.10 shows an ad for Embassy Suites Hotel touting a tangible difference between its service and its competitors: a complimentary cooked-to-order breakfast every morning.

Figure 15.8

AT&T Ad

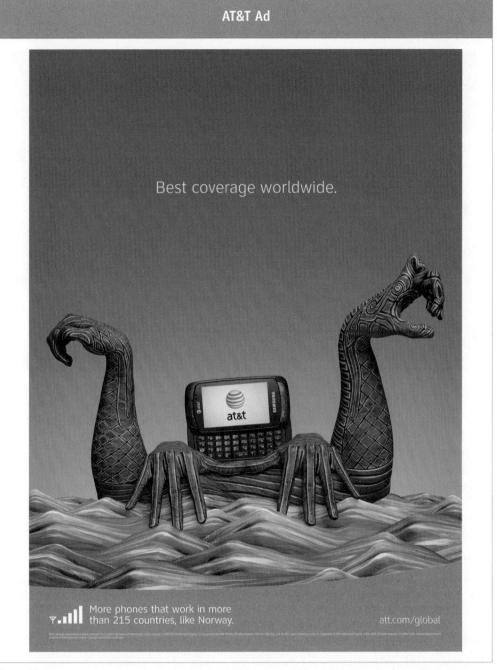

Source: Att.com.

An additional framework for thinking about differentiating services is the value chain shown in Chapter 1 in Figure 1.2. Service companies can attempt to differentiate themselves from competition by emphasizing the following value chain:

- **Inbound logistics.** In the case of services, inbound logistics focuses squarely on the quality of the employees. Because services are produced by people, product quality is directly related to staff quality and training.
- **Operations.** For service companies, the operation *is* the product. McDonald's quality is based on the extraordinary control and consistency maintained throughout its restaurants. For Edward Jones, the operation is the one-person brokerage site. FedEx's hub-and-spoke operation in Memphis is the key to its on-time record and high levels of customer satisfaction.
- **Marketing and sales.** As we have noted, because of the significant emphasis on image and positioning, strength in marketing is critical to success in service businesses. Because there are often few objective measures on which customers can

Figure 15.9

Charles Schwab Billboard

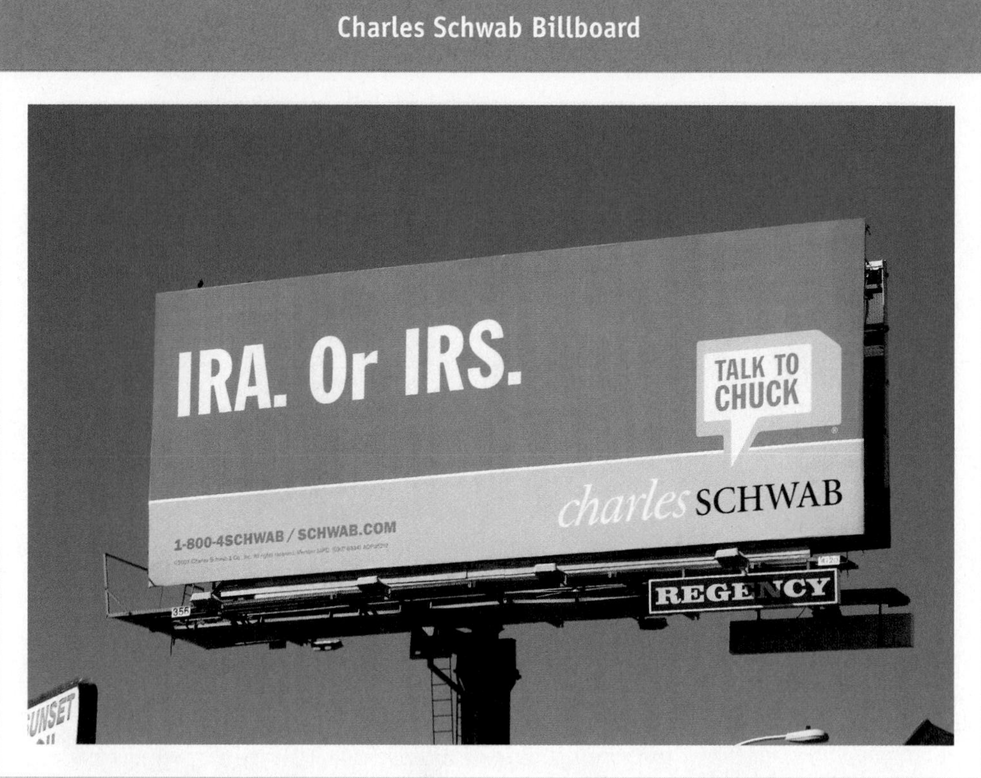

Source: Bill Aron/PhotoEdit Inc.

compare competitors (other than price), marketing success often leads to success in the marketplace.

- **Service.** Service quality brings customers back for repeat business. Marketing can gain trial, but only customer satisfaction creates repeat purchasing. As you saw in Chapter 14, a large part of service quality is customer relationship building because so much of service marketing depends on personal relationships. We discuss the topic of service quality in more detail later in this chapter.

Professional Services

Professional services firms (e.g., law, consulting, accounting firms, advertising agencies) deliver products that are almost entirely dependent upon the quality of the employees. Unlike travel, communications, and other services, the quality of the product delivered is a combination of a number of factors—not only the people involved but the underlying technology (quality of the digital cellular connection), equipment (aircraft used), and so on. While barriers to entry are high, intangibility of the product is still a problem as is the inseparability of production and consumption, to some extent, as clients have to participate in the creation of tax returns, consulting reports, and other products of professional service firms.

A high overall level of technical expertise is a given for a competitive services firm. Key dimensions for differentiation include specialized technical expertise (e.g., an accounting firm specializing in performing audits of universities), reputation, and integrity. For professional services, reputation is the key asset because it is the basis for positive word-of-mouth and reduces the amount of uncertainty inherent in service products. Reputation is the sum effect of the RATER dimensions: reliability, assurance, tangibles (expertise), empathy, and responsiveness. Reputation can also be viewed as the sum of the competitive strategy components of excellence in employee recruiting (inbound logistics), service operations, marketing and sales, and service quality. Integrity has entered the limelight with the demise of the once-powerful Arthur Andersen accounting firm.

However, technical expertise, reputation, and integrity usually only get a professional services firm into the client's evoked set. To win the account, the challenge is to make the firm's accomplishments tangible to the prospective client. As noted earlier, advertising agencies can create portfolios and reels of their creative work. Consulting firms tout

Figure 15.10

Embassy Suites Ad

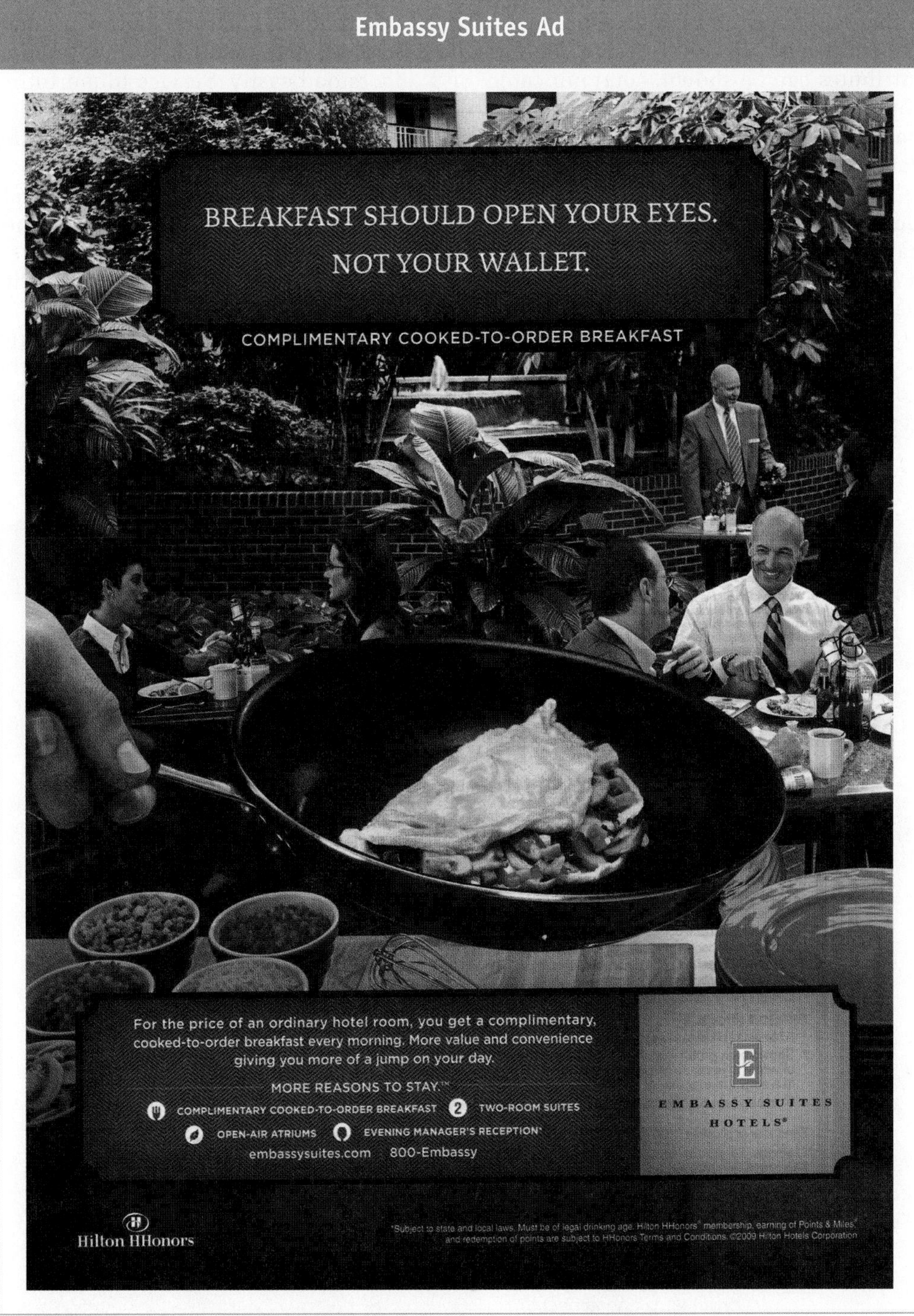

Source: Advertisement for Embassy Suites Hotels, Hilton Honors.

money saved through new processes instituted, law firms note significant cases won, and so on. In addition, expertise can be made tangible. For example, consulting firms often sponsor symposia in their areas of expertise. The usual strategy of brand-building works as well. An example of this is the consulting firm McKinsey, which is one of the most powerful brands in the world. Finally, as we discussed in Chapter 14, CRM is critical, particularly in a person-to-person business such as professional services.

Service Design

Because services are intangible, they are difficult to describe and, therefore, to design and redesign if a new service is desired. Perhaps the best way to understand this is to think of the design of a manufactured item. Physical goods can be blueprinted; that is, either on paper or using computer software, the physical nature of the product (width, length, circuitry design, etc.) can be described. As a result, physical product attributes can be shown, communicated, and understood easily. Service blueprinting involves creating a flowchart that describes the flow of activity from the time the customer first contacts the service provider to the time the customer receives the service.[16]

An example of a service blueprint is shown in Figure 15.11, a blueprint for a mail delivery service. The process or flow of the service begins when the customer calls the firm. The customer speaks with a customer service representative and then a variety of activities occur, culminating with the arrival of the package at its destination.

What is interesting about the figure is that the activities are broken down into three types. The first type, above the top line, is the parts involving customers: calling the company, giving the package for delivery, and receiving the package. The middle two types of activities describe customer contact points (what we called "moments of truth"

Figure 15.11

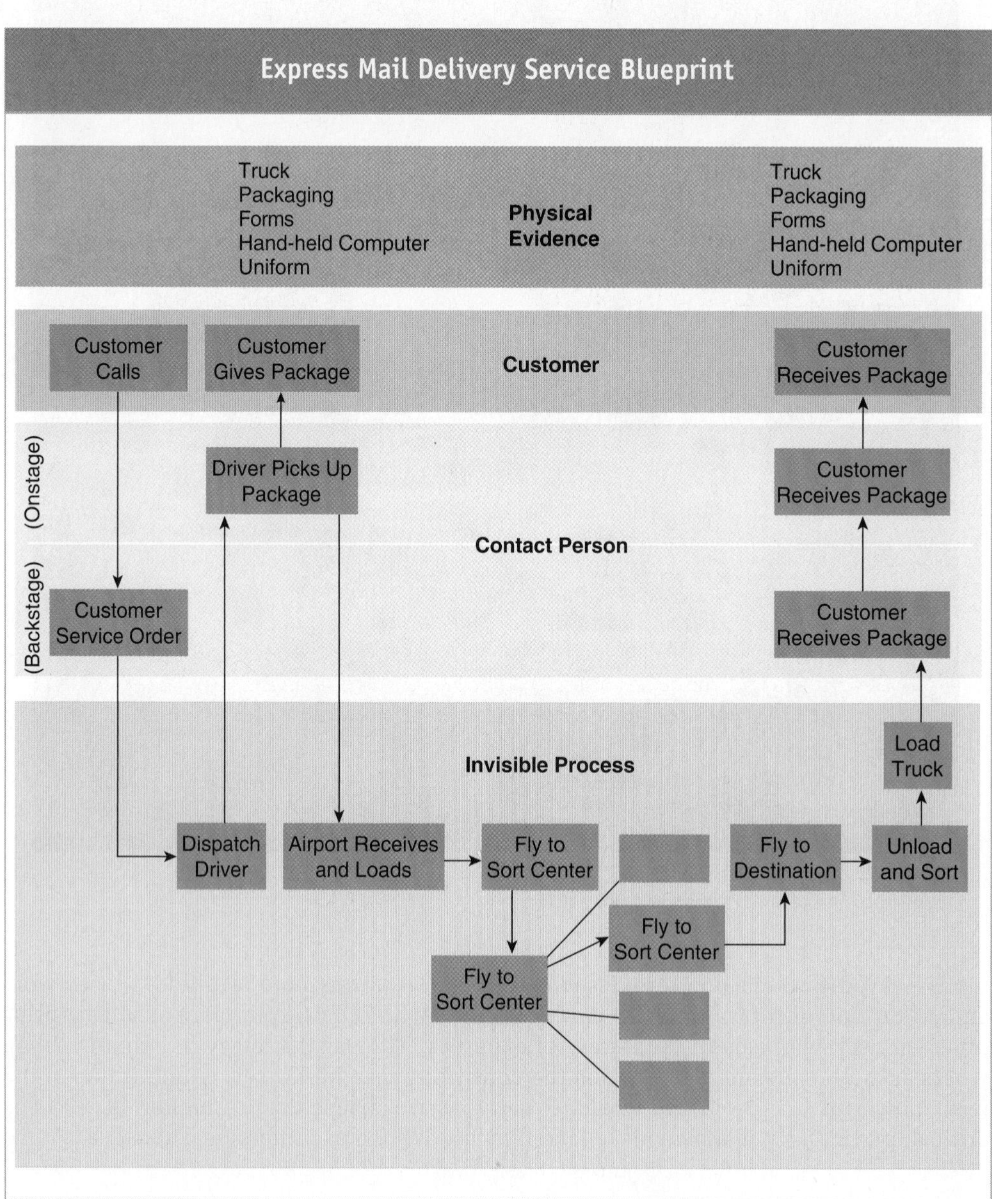

Source: Valarie A. Zeithaml and Mary Jo Bitner (1996), *Services Marketing* (New York: McGraw-Hill), p. 281. Reproduced with permission of the McGraw-Hill Companies.

in Chapter 14). Some of these contact points are observable to the customer, or "onstage." These include the customer interactions with the drivers picking up and delivering the package. "Backstage" contact points are those in which the contact is not face-to-face; in this instance, this is limited to the person taking the order. If there was a problem with the delivery, a backstage contact would be with a customer service representative handling customer complaints or problems. For this service, much of the activity is below the third line, invisible to the customer.

These blueprints or flowcharts are extremely valuable to service companies. Perhaps the most valuable aspect of blueprints is simply the exercise of creating one. The act of creating a service flowchart forces you to put yourself in the shoes of the customer and thereby develop better insights about the service encounter. As a result, the moments of truth become clear. In addition, the key areas for potential service failure and thus the need for backup and recovery systems are highlighted. In Figure 15.11, it is easy to see that each arrow involves a potential service failure, creating the need to think carefully about the process. When the customer calls the service center to place an order, how is she greeted? How many phone rings are acceptable? After the order is placed, the company needs a system to give the order efficiently and quickly to the dispatcher to get a driver to pick up the package. When the driver has the order and goes to the customer's home or place of work, how is the driver dressed? Is she or he polite and knowledgeable? These kinds of questions can be extended to the other boxes and arrows in the blueprint.

As a result, blueprints are useful tools for understanding the design of the service and for redesigning it. For example, FedEx and UPS have information systems in place, so the large space in the top half of Figure 15.11 between "Customer Gives Package" and "Customer Receives Package" could have a box labeled "Customer Tracks Package." Bar coding on each package enables the companies to know where every package is at a given time. Customers can input the package ID number using PC-based software or the companies' Web sites and obtain that location information for themselves.

Application | Singapore Airlines

Although Singapore is only 25 percent of the size of the state of Rhode Island, Singapore Airlines is one of the world's 10 biggest airlines, as measured in international tons–kilometers of load carried.[17] The airline became successful by concentrating on marketing. The goal of the airline's management was to create an international airline with a distinctly Asian personality. At the top of the priority list was an emphasis on customer service. The company used the island's main natural resource—the natural hospitality of its people—as a competitive advantage. Through comfortable seating, free drinks and movie headsets, and the hospitality of its flight attendants, Singapore Airlines has set the world standard for international air travel quality.

In 1991, the airline was facing increased competition and improved service quality from several Western and Asian airlines, including Cathay Pacific, Japan Airlines, Thai International, and Malaysia Airlines. The challenge facing the company was how to continue to maintain its outstanding reputation for customer service and technical innovation.

To better understand customer needs, the company undertook two activities. The first was a blueprinting operation. The result is shown in Figure 15.12. Although the format is somewhat different from that of Figure 15.11, it can be seen that the parts of the service operation visible to the customer are on the left part of the figure, and the internal aspects of the operation are on the right. This flowchart goes only up to the point where the customer is seated on the aircraft. In addition, the contact people are omitted.

A more thorough analysis of customer activities is shown in Figure 15.13. Note that these activities are divided into three parts: preflight, in-flight, and postarrival. Singapore Airlines used this flowchart in two ways. First, each block in the activity sequence was separately analyzed from a customer service, moment-of-truth perspective. Second, the airline evaluated each block to see where technological enhancements could improve its customers' experiences and provide additional ways to differentiate from the competition.

Figure 15.12

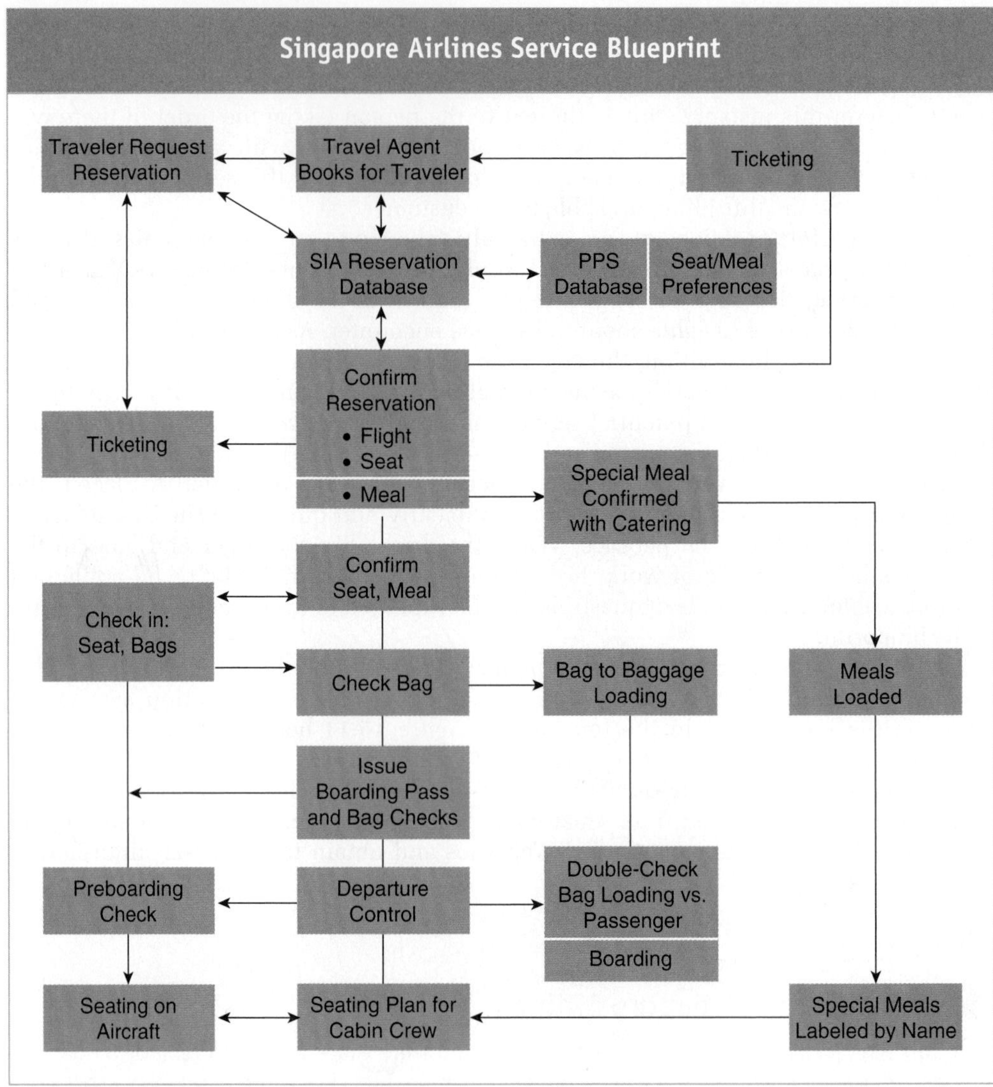

Source: Sandra Vandermerwe and Christopher H. Lovelock (1991), "Singapore Airlines: Using Technology for Service Excellence," IMD case No. IMD-5-0408, p. 20. Used by permission, courtesy of International Institute for Management, Switzerland.

Marketing-Mix Implications of Service Marketing

In general, decisions on pricing, channels of distribution, and communications are made using the same general principles described earlier in this book, whether the product is a manufactured good or a service. However, a few subtle differences must be acknowledged.

Channels of Distribution

Because services are intangible, the notion of physical distribution channels does not apply. However, the general principle of channels offering customers access to the product does. Because services are characterized by the inseparability of production and consumption, service organizations must be physically present when the service is delivered or engage others to be present. Recall the comparison of direct and indirect channels in Chapter 12. Any time the product leaves the producing company's hands and is put under the control of others, there is the potential for the independent channel member to do a less effective job of marketing the product than the producer would. This is an even greater problem with services because they are often delivered by people. Nonstandardization of services increases when the service is being delivered by people who do not work for your company.

Figure 15.13

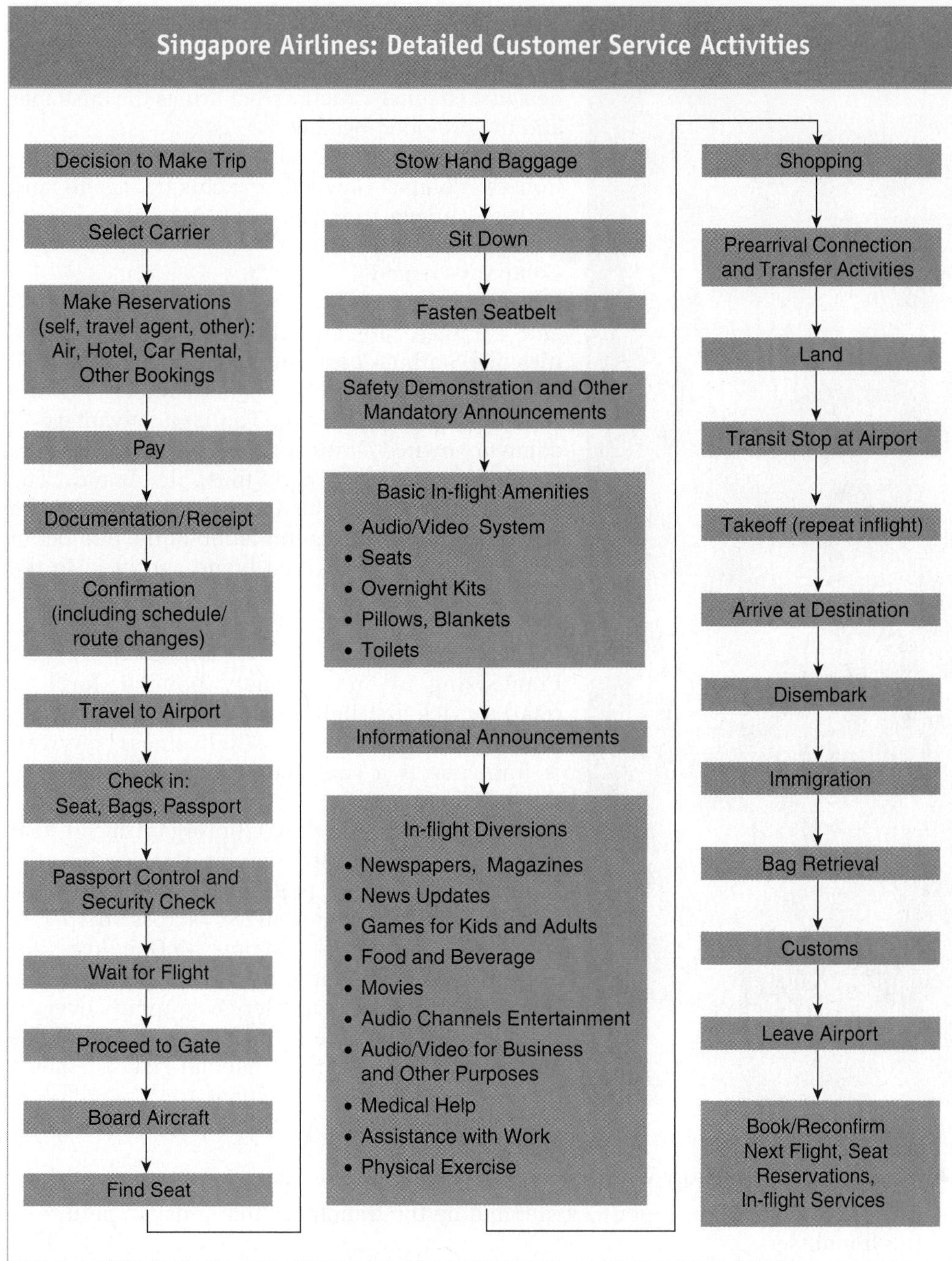

Source: Sandra Vandermerwe and Christopher H. Lovelock (1991), "Singapore Airlines: Using Technology for Service Excellence," IMDcase No. IMD-5-0408, p. 20. Used by permission, courtesy of International Institute for Management, Switzerland.

As a result, we can draw a distinction between the service principal (the company or person originating the service) and the service deliverer (the person or company that actually delivers the service to customers). As with physical goods, service deliverers or intermediaries can provide a number of benefits to the principal. Service deliverers can co-produce the service with the principal. For example, franchisees delivering automobile lubrication services (e.g., Jiffy Lube) execute the principal's concepts by operating the service centers and lubricating the cars (often other services are available as well). Service intermediaries also provide the customer with locations that make it easy to purchase services. Multiple Jiffy Lube outlets in a metropolitan area make it convenient for customers to purchase the lubricating services. These local retail outlets also promote the Jiffy Lube brand name and provide local presence for the service principal.

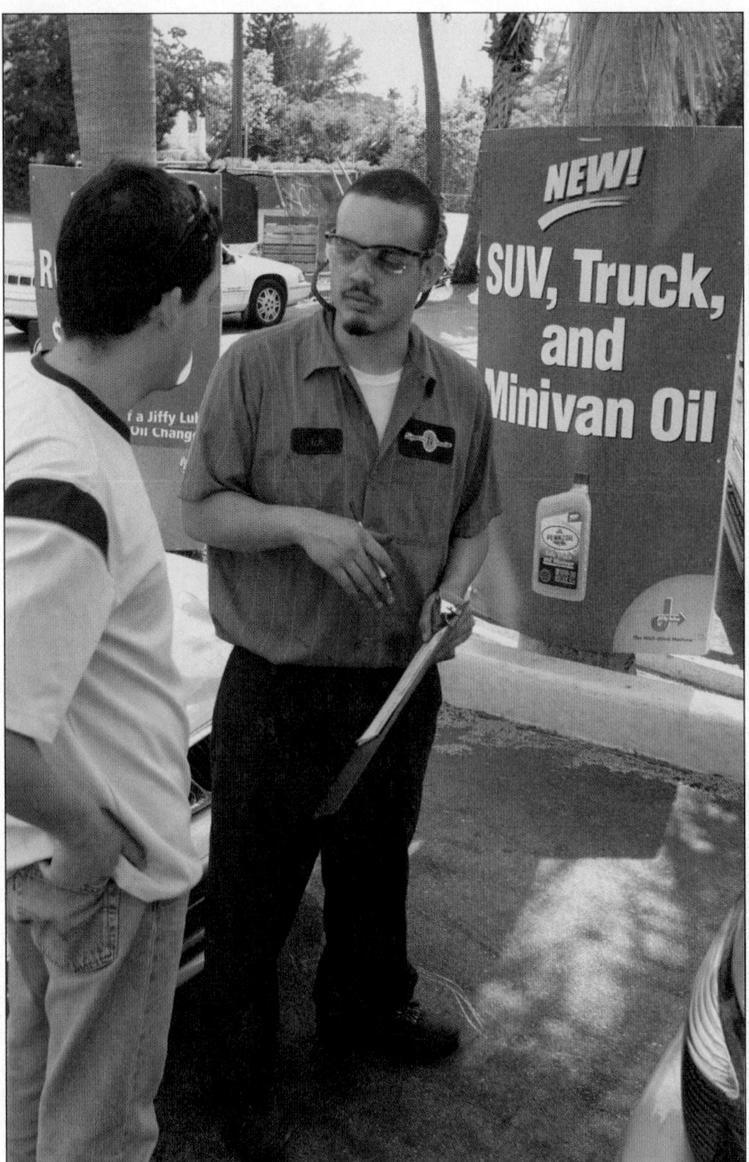

Channels for services must be designed to bring the customer and service provider together.
Source: Jeff Greenberg/Alamy Images

Because services are intangible, perishable, and generally not storable, services must be brought to the customer. That is, the service principal must design a channel structure that brings the customer and the provider together.

The four major approaches to service distribution are company-owned, franchising, agents and brokers, and electronic channels.

Company-Owned

Using the terminology developed in Chapters 12 and 13, these are also direct channels. Companies like Starbucks and McDonald's own some or a large portion (depending on the company) of the stores bearing their name. The large advantage of company-owned stores is that the firm controls the customer experience and, thus, the brand. The large disadvantage is the financial risk that must be borne and the resulting limitation of the number of outlets that one individual brand can have in the world.

Franchising

Franchising is an extremely popular form of retail service distribution covering a wide variety of consumer and business-to-business services. A franchise is a contractual agreement between the originator of the service concept (the franchiser) and an individual or organization that provides retail distribution for the service (the franchisee). It works particularly well when the service can be standardized across disparate geographic locations. Many McDonald's, for example, are independently owned. This permits the company to have greater geographic coverage than it would be able to have by owning all the stores as well as shared financial risk. Elements of a typical franchise agreement are:[18]

- The nature of the service to be supplied by the franchiser.
- The geographic territory within which the franchisee can market the service.
- The percentage of the revenue generated by the franchisee that must be paid to the franchiser.
- The length of the agreement.
- The up-front fee paid by the franchisee to the franchiser.
- The terms by which the franchisee agrees to operate and deliver the service.
- An agreement by the franchisee not to sell another company's services.
- The promotional support provided by the franchiser to help develop the franchisee's market.
- The administrative and technical support provided by the franchiser.
- The conditions under which the agreement can be terminated.

Agents and Brokers

Many service companies use independent agents or brokers to sell their services. Well-known examples are the insurance and travel industries. As the discussion in Chapter 12 showed, there are trade-offs with using these methods for distributing any kind of product. Major advantages include a wider distribution and the fact that agents and brokers know their local markets well. Disadvantages include the loss of control, because it is very difficult to determine what agents and brokers are doing and what they are saying about your product.

Electronic Channels

As discussed in previous chapters, the growth of the Internet has spawned many opportunities for distributing services. Travel services (e.g., Kayak, Expedia, Travelocity, Orbitz) is the largest segment of the e-commerce industry with more than $110 billion sold in 2008.[19] The financial services industry has also taken advantage of electronic channels through services such as home banking and stock brokerage. The advantage of electronic channels is their low cost and the ease of access (for those with Internet connections). For example, rather than using a large number of branch banks or automatic teller machines ("bricks and mortar"), customers of most major banks can now check their balances, move money between accounts, and pay bills using the banks' Web sites. Entertainment companies, particularly in interactive gaming and gambling, have also taken advantage of the Web. The implications of the Internet on services marketing are discussed more thoroughly later in this chapter.

Advertising

The role of communications in service delivery is shown in Figure 15.4. As we have discussed, a key element of service quality evaluation is the assessment of the service relative to expectations. Advertising plays an important role in setting customer expectations. Therefore, marketing managers for services must be careful not to promise what cannot be delivered. All communications targeted to customers should be examined in terms of how well they reflect reality. If you do not do this, the customer certainly will. The unique aspects of services discussed in this chapter have the following implications for advertising.[20]

First, service advertising should contain vivid information. Vivid information is more likely to hold the viewer's attention and excite the imagination. It also results in improved customer understanding of the service. Because service attributes are intangible, this improved understanding is critical to a customer's ability to evaluate the quality of the service and to compare it to other options. Vividness can be achieved through three different strategies: attempts to make the service tangible; concrete, specific language; and dramatization. A good example of the latter is the former series of American Express commercials featuring actor Karl Malden that demonstrated the value and security of American Express traveler's checks by showing the disasters that can befall travelers if they use a competitor's brand.

A problem faced by customers purchasing a service is developing alternatives from which to make the final choice. The reason that this can be difficult is inherent in the way services are distributed. When a service is delivered through a franchise operation, there is only one choice at a particular location, unlike the normal assortment available from retailers of physical goods. Although some (e.g., travel agents) do offer competing services, many do not. Thus, a major problem facing service companies is how to get your brand into the customer's choice set.

The relevant communications goal is to have the customer connect your brand with the product category. This can be done with repetition or through an approach called interactive imagery. Imagery involves having customers visualize a concept or relationship by integrating two items in some mutual or reciprocal action. This approach can be used to enhance vividness. The advertisement for Charles Schwab shown in Figure 15.9 is an example of this kind of imagery. In this ad, the company is attempting to provide the image of a company that provides assistance to customers who are seeking to reduce their taxes. The terse text on the billboard communicates this effectively.

Finally, service attributes are experience or credence attributes, not search attributes. Therefore, prepurchase evaluation of services is difficult. One way to approach this problem is to highlight the behind-the-scenes rules, policies, and procedures that make the service provider the best option to choose. This helps to make the service tangible to customers and gives assurance that it will be of high quality. Alternatively, a marketing manager can use the ad to show the service actually in use. The advertising for Embassy Suites in Figure 15.10 is an example of this approach. The picture of the omelette in the frying pan gives potential customers a sense of the quality of the breakfast.

Pricing

Customers find service prices difficult to determine and compare. You cannot put physical price tags on services. The fact that services can be delivered in many different configurations makes the task even more difficult. For example, try finding out a rate on a home mortgage. The combinations of terms (5, 15, 20, 30 years), amount of down payment, points you are willing to pay (percentage of the loan amount paid as a fee to the mortgage originator), and myriad other options are nearly infinite. Try the same exercise with life insurance policies. Therefore, it is important to simplify your pricing policy as much as possible to eliminate customer confusion.

More than with physical goods, price is often used as an indicator of service quality. This is because service quality is more difficult to ascertain. Thus, the pricing of services must be consistent with the overall strategy for the product. For example, if you decide to drop the price of your service but attempt to maintain a premium brand image through your communications and other elements of the service operation, customers will become confused or skeptical: if you are so good, why are you so cheap? Although consistency between the strategy and price is important for all products, in service businesses where purchasing is driven so heavily by perceptions, it is critical.

In service industries the role of the reference price is very important. As described in Chapter 9, a reference price is an internal standard against which observed prices are compared. Reference prices are based on both past experience in a product category (internal reference prices) and observed prices in the marketplace (external reference prices). Not only is price information more difficult to collect for services, but the large number of product alternatives can make price comparisons impossible. For example, for competing automobile insurance policies, the deductibles or other aspects of the policies are often slightly different, making exact price comparisons difficult. When a customer cannot use observed prices easily to make a purchase decision, internal reference price becomes more important as a way of simplifying the process.

To illustrate these two service pricing principles, several years ago, one of the authors decided to have the gutters of his house cleaned before the winter rains hit. Obtaining prices for such services is time-consuming because it entails waiting at home for the (uncertain) arrival of the service providers. Two companies gave bids, one much higher than the other. With little experience to draw upon, he calculated a reference price based simply on what seemed to be reasonable. Both bids were below this price, so they both remained in the running for the work. He then chose the higher of the two, figuring that the lower-priced company would skimp on the work somehow. Pricing policies in professional service firms have been changing in response to clients' interests in reducing their costs and risks. Advertising agencies, for example, are shifting from a fixed commission rate on advertising billings to a combination of fixed fee and incentives for achieving agreed-upon goals. Even some law firms have started to move away from the traditional model of billable hours to a more fixed-fee solution so clients have a better idea of what their total costs will be.[21]

Customer Relationship Management

While CRM is important for physical products as well as services, it is particularly critical for what are called *contractual* services where the contract or subscription must be renewed on a periodic basis. Examples of contractual services are health club memberships, cable TV and cellular phone contracts, and so forth. What makes these different is that once dropped, it is very difficult to get the customer back. The customer will have switched to another service supplier or dropped the service entirely. If it is the former, it takes a complete subscription cycle to have the opportunity to get the customer back. However, unlike the purchase decision for most services, the decision about renewing is known and visible to the service supplier. This is clearly an advantage because the company can time its renewal communications precisely.

It is crucial not to wait until the end of the subscription cycle to make the benefits of the service tangible to the customer. In addition, research has shown that customers form expectations about how much they will use a contractual service and make the renewal decision based upon a comparison of the expected to the actual. If the actual is less than expected, the probability of renewal decreases.[22] It is thus incumbent upon the contractual service provider to perform two activities during the subscription cycle:

1. Remind the customer continuously about the benefits of the service. For example, in the context of a health club, ensure that the staff comment positively to the client about the benefits of working out.
2. Track the customer's usage and develop a system to remind the customer to use the service if usage level is low. For example, low usage of a cellular phone would predict the high likelihood of nonrenewal. As a result, the service provider could develop special programs of discounts or new features to encourage additional usage.

Global Aspects of Services Marketing

As we have noted in this chapter, one feature of service businesses that distinguishes them from product manufacturers is that they involve interpersonal contact between the service provider and the customer. An implication of this is that, generally, service firms do not grow by producing more of the same service in the same place.[23] There are three basic growth strategies for service businesses:

1. **Multisite:** provision of the same service(s) in new locations.
2. **Multiservice:** provision of a new service at existing locations.
3. **Multisegment:** provision of a different class of service targeting a different market segment, at new or existing locations.

Many service and retail businesses have chosen the first option. McDonald's and Starbucks, for example, views global expansion as the key to their future growth. Most large professional service firms such as public accounting and law firms as well as advertising agencies have set up shop in different countries as their clients expand, or simply to build a global business.

Table 15.2 shows some of the difficulties in launching a service business in a different country. The two columns labeled "Target Market" and "Operating Strategy" are common to physical products as well, as we described earlier in this book. However, the "Service Concept" and "Service Delivery System" lists are unique to service products. For example, the notion of "fast food" was at one time a foreign service concept in most countries. In addition, the use of credit cards is a novel concept, because some cultures and religions dissuade people from going into debt. Also, fraud rates on credit card payments are higher in some countries than others. People have different expectations about the levels

Table 15.2

Issues Posed by Internationalization of a "Strategic Service Vision"

Target Market	Service Concept	Operating Strategy	Service Delivery System
• Culture	• Culture	• Labor market institutions	• Technology
• Industry structure	• Perceptions of value		• Premises
• Demographics	• Expectations	• Managerial practices	• Labor market norms and customs
	• Usage patterns	• Language	
	• Interactions with service providers		

Source: Gary W. Loveman (1993), "The Internationalization of Services," Harvard Business School case #9-693-103, Exhibit 2. Copyright © 1993 by the President and Fellows of Harvard College. Reprinted by permission.

Quality can be difficult to maintain when service concepts are expanded globally due to cultural and institutional differences.
Source: Picture Partners/Alamy Images

and quality of service. American retail petroleum companies like Chevron need to understand that in many countries, such as Brazil, customers expect service people to fill up their gas tanks and wash their windows without paying a premium for the gas. Finally, labor markets may not provide the level of quality needed to launch a new site. Thus, when McKinsey (the consulting firm) opened its branch in Bogotà in 1994, it was staffed largely by Spanish-speaking consultants from other countries.

Application Euro Disney

The Euro Disney resort complex opened on April 12, 1992, in Marne-la-Vallee, France.[24] Disney theme parks had built their reputations not only on the quality of the product but on the service delivery as well. Standards of service, park design and operating details, and human resource policies and practices were integrated to ensure that the Disney "play" would be performed at a uniformly high level at each location. The reason behind this outstanding level of service was the establishment of "Disney University," where new employees were oriented to Disney's strict service standards, received continuous communication and training, and gathered for frequent recognition and social events. Employees were called "cast members," as they wore "costumes," not uniforms and were "cast in a role," not assigned to a job. When on the job, they were considered to be "on stage," with the highest priority given to satisfying "guests." The cast members had to meet stiff dress and grooming requirements as well.

The largest challenge to Euro Disney managers was to match this traditional level of customer service. The company encountered significant resistance in the hiring process, which was criticized by applicants, the press, and French unions. The key resistance point was the standard for grooming, including a dress code, a ban on facial hair, a ban on colored stockings, standards for neat hair and fingernails, and a policy of "appropriate" undergarments. As a result, within the first nine weeks of operation, about 1,000 employees left Euro Disney, close to half voluntarily. In addition, the general conclusion was that the experience of visiting Euro Disney fell short of what people had come to expect from Disney. While some of this was due to attributes of the park, much of it was attributed to the fact that the "cast members" were acting like "real" people rather than "Disney" people. Adapting this people-oriented entertainment product to Europe was not as easy as the company thought it would be. Although the park is the most popular tourist attraction in Europe, receiving more visitors than the Louvre and Eiffel Tower combined, Euro Disney has had trouble making a profit and has had five CEO changes in nine years.

Disney had different cultural problems with its theme park in Hong Kong, which opened in September 2005. Since it opened, the park has had difficulty connecting with consumers. Although it attracted 5 million customers during its opening year, attendance fell 20 percent in the second year. Some of the complaints were about the relatively few number of attractions compared to other Disney parks. However, it has also introduced more Chinese characters to the park to supplement Mickey and Minnie Mouse. For example, a "live" Cai Shen Ye, the bearded Chinese god of wealth, walks around the park creating photo opportunities for guests. In addition, in 2008–2009, the year of the rat, Disney's own rodents, Mickey and Minnie, wore special red Chinese New Year outfits for the "Year of the Mouse." Shanghai is up next for Disney.

The Impact of Technology on Service Marketing

The rapid improvements in and diffusion of information technology and the use of the Internet have changed marketing in general and, specifically, services marketing, for three main reasons:

1. As mentioned earlier in this chapter, the use of the Internet has created a new channel of distribution ideally suited for certain kinds of services, particularly those involving travel and financial transactions and entertainment services.

2. Recall that an important feature of services is that because they are often delivered by people, their quality is variable both at one point in time and over time (i.e., they are nonstandardized). Computerization, substituting capital for labor, provides uniform service delivery at a quality level people cannot match.
3. As in all product categories, companies are looking for new ways to differentiate their products from competitors. Information technology and the Internet have provided powerful, tangible opportunities for such differentiation.

Application Travel Services

As noted earlier in this chapter, travel services is the largest category of e-commerce, with more than $100 billion of bookings in 2008.[25] In the United States, 46 percent of consumers report researching online for deals prior to traveling. Almost 40 percent of all airline reservations are made through the Internet. Most of the bookings are done through two kinds of sites: Internet travel companies and Web sites run by the airlines, hotels, and car rental firms themselves. Although it is cumbersome to book complicated air itineraries, fares for simple travel plans can be easily compared and, in fact, some airlines offer lower fares on the Web than through personal contact with airline or independent agents.

The major players in the online travel industry are the following:

- **Expedia.** Expedia Inc. had revenues of nearly $3 billion in 2009. It was started by Microsoft in 1996 and later sold to InterActiveCorp. In 2005, the company became a separately traded public company containing other travel companies formerly owned by InterActiveCorp such as Hotels.com, Hotwire, and TripAdvisor.
- **Travelocity.** This company is owned by Sabre Holdings. At one time, Travelocity was the number-one online travel company. However, a slowdown in innovation cost the company its lead in the market.
- **Orbitz.** Orbitz Worldwide was founded in 2001 by a group of American airlines: American, Continental, Delta, Northwest, and United. It was sold for $1.25 billion in 2004 to Cendant but has been an independent company since 2007. Its current revenues are about $800 million.
- **Priceline.** Priceline pioneered the "name your own price" format (see Chapter 9) through its reverse auction format. Revenues in 2009 were $2.2 billion. The company is famous for its long-running advertising campaign using the actor William Shatner.
- **Kayak.** Started in 2003 by the two founders of Travelocity and Orbitz, Kayak is currently the most popular travel site with more than 35 million visitors each month. It is a "mega" site, allowing users to search over all of the other travel sites. The site uses a technology called Rich Internet Application architecture (RIA), which allows it to look at more than 100 Web sites continuously. Other aggregators include Yahoo! Travel, SideStep, and Cheapflights.

However, the airlines' own sites still account for most online bookings. The discount airlines, Southwest, JetBlue, Virgin, EasyJet, and so on, do not sell through travel agents and motivate customers to use their Web sites by offering incentives such as extra credits in their loyalty programs. Southwest.com attracted more than 8 million unique visitors to its Web site in April 2005, with 14 percent of them resulting in sales. One of the advantages of Southwest's site is that a visitor does not have to go through the tedious process of registration. Most of the airlines have significantly boosted their bookings through their Web sites by moving the reservations part of the site to the home page.

Application Car-Sharing Services

An emerging service industry utilizing Web and other technologies are car-sharing services.[26] The industry leader is Zipcar with 325,000 members who pay an annual fee of $50 and rent cars for as little as $8 per hour, gas and insurance included. Typically, users apply for membership online, providing details such as their driver's license number. Cards that electronically open and lock the cars are mailed to approved applicants. Cars are then reserved through the company's Web site, indicating what kind of car is available at different locations. Other major competitors to Zipcar include Connect by Hertz, Mint Cars On-Demand, and I-Go.

While the industry is still relatively small, the service has a number of things in its favor. First, the primary market—city dwellers—is focused and potentially quite large, particularly taking a global view. The latter is particularly important in places like Hong Kong and Singapore that have high population density and commensurate high costs of operating and maintaining a car. Second, it is a good way to save money. This is particularly important during the tight economic conditions prevailing in the 2008–2010 time period. Third, in an era where "green," environmentally friendly products have become more popular, car sharing is a particularly good way to keep more cars off the road, conserve gas, and promote less air pollution.

Executive Summary

Key learning points in this chapter include the following:

- Most services can be characterized as having experience attributes (where product quality is determined only after usage) rather than search attributes (where product quality can be ascertained before purchase).
- The main characteristics of services are intangibility (lack of physical attributes), nonstandardization (because they are usually delivered by people), and inseparability of production and consumption.
- Service quality is defined by the service provider's reliability, responsiveness, assurance, empathy, and tangibles (service features or physical aspects of the service delivery).
- Service quality is assessed negatively when there is a gap between customer expectations and experienced quality.
- Service quality can be measured through the use of survey instruments such as SERVQUAL; the financial return on investments in service quality can also be evaluated.
- Some strategic issues in services marketing are making the service tangible to customers, combating low entry barriers, and using service blueprints to design services.
- Because of the people-intensive nature of most services, globalizing a service business requires special attention to culture, labor market, customer expectations of service, and other conditions.
- New technologies in services marketing affect channels of distribution, improved standardization of service offerings, and the establishment of competitive advantage.

Chapter Questions

1. Consider the three kinds of attributes described in this chapter: search, experience, and credence. Which of these are most appropriate for services? What are the implications for marketing managers?
2. Recall the last time you had an unsatisfactory encounter with a service provider. Given the dimensions of service quality discussed in this chapter, exactly where were the negative gaps between expectations and the actual service?
3. Pick two services, one consumer and one industrial. What can a company in each industry do to make its services more tangible to customers?
4. Develop a blueprint for the course registration process at your school or university. Where are the likely service failure points? Where can the school improve its service levels?

5. Suppose you have spent the first five years of your career working for Procter & Gamble as the assistant, associate, or brand manager for Crest toothpaste. You apply for a job as a senior marketing manager for United Airlines. What have you learned at P&G that is applicable to airline marketing? What do you need to learn about airline marketing to be effective beyond the fact that airlines are different from toothpaste?
6. As the U.S. economy continues to be increasingly dominated by services, is it necessary to change our thinking about marketing and marketing strategy? Would a marketing course be different between the United States and, say, China, which is a manufacturing-dominated economy?

Notes

Chapter 1

1. This illustration is based on Chuck Salter (2002), "On the Road Again," *Fast Company*, January, pp. 50–58; Christopher Helman (2003), "The Big Tune-Up," *Forbes*, April 14, p. 99; Unmesh Kher (2006), "The Segway Riddle," *Time*, August 6, p. 48; Mark Gimen (2006), "Reinventing the Wheel, Slowly," *BusinessWeek*, September 11, p. 56; Jake Wagman (2008), "Battle Over Segway Looms," *McClatchy-Tribune Business News*, February 15; Stu Woo (2008), "Segway Glides as Gasoline Jumps," *The Wall Street Journal*, July 16, p. B2; John Reed (2009), "GM and Segway Hope Puma Joint Venture Proves to Be the Cat's Whiskers," *FT.com*, April 8; and Nicole Perlroth (2009), "Drinking Water Act," *Forbes*, August 24, p. 34.
2. For readers who would like a more formal definition of marketing, the American Marketing Association's definition is as follows (http://www.marketingpower.com/content21257.php): "Marketing is an organizational function and a set of processes for creating, communicating, and delivering value to customers and for managing customer relationships in ways that benefit the organization and its stakeholders."
3. Those with a morbid interest in failed consumer packaged goods should visit the New Products Showcase and Learning Center, part of the consulting firm, New ProductWorks (http://www.arborstrategy.com/asg/newproductworks/the-collection.html), in Ann Arbor, Michigan.
4. See Franklin Houston (1986), "The Marketing Concept: What It Is and What It Is Not," *Journal of Marketing*, 50 (April), pp. 81–87.
5. Peter F. Drucker (1954), *The Practice of Management* (New York: HarperCollins).
6. Theodore Levitt (1986), "Marketing and the Corporate Purpose," *The Marketing Imagination* (New York: Free Press).
7. Of course, this must be done within local law. For example, pubic restaurants in the United States cannot deny service to any person on the basis of race.
8. William C. Taylor (2005), "Rebels With a Cause, and a Business Plan," *The New York Times*, January 2, p. BU-5; Jena McGregor (2007), "When the Boss Goes to Work in the Call Center," *BusinessWeek*, October 22, p. 94; and Michael Steen (2008), "ING Direct Quietly Extends Global Reach," *Financial Times*, January 4, p. 14.
9. Jena McGregor (2008), "Customer Service Champs: Ace Hardware," *BusinessWeek*, March 3, p. 50.
10. Jerry Kaplan (1995), *Startup: A Silicon Valley Adventure* (Boston: Houghton Mifflin).
11. David Pringle (2005), "In Mobile Phones, Older Users Say, More Is Less," *The Wall Street Journal*, August 15, p. A9.
12. Roland T. Rust, Debora Viana Thompson, and Rebecca W. Hamilton (2006), "Defeating Feature Fatigue," *Harvard Business Review*, February, pp. 98–107.
13. See Houston, "The Marketing Concept."
14. David Leonhardt (2007), "Lessons Even Thomas Could Learn," *The New York Times*, October 24, http://www.nytimes.com/2007/10/24/business/24leonhardt.html?_r=1&oref=slogin.
15. For some history of the brand management system, see George S. Low and Ronald Fullerton (1994), "Brands, Brand Management, and the Brand Manager System: A Critical-Historical Evaluation," *Journal of Marketing Research*, 31 (May), pp. 173–190.
16. Michael E. Porter (1985), *Competitive Advantage*, (New York: The Free Press).
17. Gary Hamel and C. K. Prahalad (1994), *Competing for the Future* (Boston: Harvard Business School Press).
18. See http://en.wikipedia.org/wiki/Blu-ray_Disc.
19. See Houston, "The Marketing Concept."
20. For some history of the brand management system, see Low and Fullerton, "Brands, Brand Management, and the Brand Manager System: A Critical-Historical Evaluation."
21. For a more detailed discussion of the product manager's responsibilities and the pros and cons of different organizational forms, see Donald R. Lehmann and Russell S. Winer (2005), *Product Management*, 4th ed. (Burr Ridge, IL: McGraw-Hill), Ch.1.
22. This example is adapted from Michael Hayes (1989), "Grasse Fragrances SA," IMD case #M369.
23. Beth Snyder Bulik (2005), "Intel's New Strategy Demands New Partner," *Advertising Age*, March 14, p. 4.
24. This example is based on Beth Snyder (1998), "Digital Revolution Leaves Motorola Playing Catch-up," *Advertising Age*, October 19, pp. 32–33; David Pringle (2002), "Mobile Phones Ring Up Worst Year Ever," *The Wall Street Journal*, February 12, p. B5; Ted C. Fishman (2005), "How Ed Zander Honed Razr's Edge," *Business 2.0*, June, pp. 47–49;

and Sara Silver and Joann S. Lublin (2008), "Will Splitting Motorola in Two Help?" *The Wall Street Journal*, March 27, p. B1.

25. See Lehmann and Winer, *Product Management*; and Donald R. Lehmann and Russell S. Winer (2009), *Analysis for Marketing Planning*, 7th ed. (Burr Ridge, IL: McGraw-Hill).
26. See Thomas L. Friedman (2006), *The World Is Flat: A Brief History of the Twenty-First Century* (New York: Farrar, Straus & Giroux).
27. www.eMarketer.com.
28. See, for example, Glen L. Urban (2005), "Customer Advocacy: A New Era in Marketing?" *Journal of Public Policy & Marketing*, Spring, pp. 155–159.
29. Professor John Deighton, Harvard Business School.
30. *eMarketer* (2008), March 18.
31. Jennifer Saranow (2006), "Savvy Car Buyers Drive Bargains with Pricing Data from the Web," *The Wall Street Journal*, October 24, p. D5.
32. Alex Markels (2001), "We Can Deliver Customers on a Global Basis," *Wired*, November, pp. 190–200.
33. *Fortune* (2004), "What China Eats (and Drinks and . . .)," October 4, pp. 1510–1513.
34. Jean Halliday (2008), "GM Roars Forward into Digital Ad Channels," *Advertising Age*, March 17, p. 4.
35. David C. Court, Jonathan W. Gordon, and Jesko Perrey (2005), "Boosting Returns on Marketing Investment," *The McKinsey Quarterly*, Number 2, pp. 37–47.
36. See, for example, James D. Lenskold (2003), *Marketing ROI* (New York: McGraw-Hill); and Donald R. Lehmann and David J. Reibstein (2006), *Marketing Metrics* (Cambridge, MA: Marketing Science Institute).
37. Michael Skapinker (2008), "Virtue's Reward?" *Financial Times*, April 28, p. 8.

Chapter 2

1. This illustration is based on data from www.beveragemarketing.com, www.beerinsights.com, and *BRANDWEEK*, as well as information given to the author from private sources.
2. Miller was bought by South African Breweries PLC (SAB) from Philip Morris in 2002 and renamed SAB Miller.
3. Jeremy Mullman (2008), "Miller Genuinely Daft: Changes Message—Again," *Advertising Age*, April 7, p. 1.
4. Rodney Ho (2000), "Floturn Forgoes Fat Profits to Boost Its Market Share," *The Wall Street Journal*, January 15, p. B2.
5. Sara Silver, Cassell Bryan-Low, and Amol Sharma (2007), "Motorola Profit Warning Generates Unease Over CEO Zander's Strategy," *The Wall Street Journal*, January 6, p. A1.
6. Costs can also decrease over time with increased volume. This is the experience curve phenomenon discussed later in this chapter.
7. Pepsi actually developed a new brand, Pepsi A.M., to compete with coffee and other beverages at breakfast. If the thought of drinking cola at breakfast does not excite you, you are not alone; the product was a failure.
8. http://money.cnn.com/magazines/fortune/fortune_archive/2007/06/11/100083454/?postversion=2007053109.
9. *INC. Magazine* (2007), "Dramatic Results: Making Opera (Yes, Opera) Seem Young and Hip," October, pp. 61–62.
10. This illustration is based on John Bowen (1998), "Pardon Me: Grey Poupon Is a Niched Brand," *BrandWeek*, April 27, p. 14.
11. A good reference on country selection is Christoph Lymbersky (2008), *Market Entry Strategies* (Hamburg, Germany: Management Development Press).
12. Susan P. Douglas and C. Samuel Craig (1995), *Global Marketing Strategy* (New York: McGraw-Hill), Ch. 7.
13. Purchasing power indices account for a country's per capita income and the prices of a standard market basket of goods.
14. See, for example, Geoffrey Moore (1991), *Crossing the Chasm* (New York: HarperCollins), Ch. 6.
15. David A. Aaker (2004), *Strategic Market Management*, 7th ed. (New York: Wiley).
16. Normally, the horizontal axis is in cumulative units of production. However, because the relevant units for the two industries are different, time is used instead.
17. See for example, Michael Porter (1980), *Competitive Advantage* (New York: Free Press). However, some writers feel that differentiation on any one dimension is difficult today, and as a result, it is a preferred strategy to try to offer higher-quality products and services that meet customer needs better than competitors' offerings. See Paddy Barwise and Seán Meehan (2004), *Simply Better* (Cambridge, MA: Harvard University Press).
18. Porter, *Competitive Advantage*.
19. Gideon Lichfield (2002), "Cement Plus Heavy-Duty Networking Equals Big Profits," *Wired*, July, p. 104.
20. http://www.nytimes.com/2006/01/19/fashion/thursdaystyles/19skin.html.
21. The discussions of both perceptual mapping and branding will be expanded in Chapter 7.
22. Interestingly, *position* is both a noun and a verb. A product's position is how customers perceive it relative to competition, as show in the perceptual map in Figure 3.7. Marketing managers position products by actively choosing the appropriate dimensions, differential

advantage, and communications and other elements of the marketing mix that affect customer perceptions.

23. http://blog.futurelab.net/2008/01/clorox_aims_to_show_that_green.html.
24. Sales histories of individual brands are called *brand life cycles.*
25. William Boulding and Markus Christen (2001), "First-Mover Disadvantage," *Harvard Business Review*, October, pp. 20–21.
26. Alternative pricing approaches for the introductory phase of the PLC are discussed in more detail in Chapter 13.
27. See Peter N. Golder and Gerard J. Tellis (1993), "Pioneer Advantage: Marketing Logic or Marketing Legend?" *Journal of Marketing Research*, 30 (May), pp. 158–170.
28. See, for example, Jim Collins (2000), "Best Beats First," *Inc.*, August, pp. 48–51; and Joan Indiana Rigdon (2000), "The Second-Mover Advantage," *Red Herring*, September, pp. 462–470.
29. For more on this interesting company, see www.lansdale.com.
30. Linda Grant (1996), "Stirring It Up at Campbell," *Fortune*, May 16, pp. 80–86.
31. This figure is from Johan A. Quelch (1994), "Heineken N.V.: Global Branding and Advertising," Harvard Business School case #9-596-015.
32. Andy Webb-Vidal, Hal Weitzman, and Jenny Wiggins (2005), "SAB Miller to Raise Its Glass to Loyalty," *Financial Times*, July 25, p. 18.

Chapter 3

1. This illustration is based on Andrew Tilin (2003), "Will the Kids Buy It?" *Business 2.0*, May, pp. 95–99; Jonathan Welsh (2008), "As Car Sales Slump, What's Still Selling," *The Wall Street Journal*, June 25, p. D1; John Murphy (2008), "Toyota Slashes Sales Forecast," *The Wall Street Journal Online*, August 28; Steve Miller (2008), "Motorhead vs. Mariah Is Easy Choice for Scion," *Brandweek*, August 25, p. 11; and Claude Brodesser-Akner (2008), "Despite Cash-Strapped Target Demo, Scion Stays the Course," *Advertising Age*, November 17, p. 10.
2. Del I. Hawkins and Donald S. Tull (1994), *Essentials of Marketing Research* (New York: Macmillan).
3. A more detailed discussion of how to choose a marketing research supplier is beyond the scope of this book. However, in the United States, a good place to start is the local chapter of the American Marketing Association.
4. See Donald R. Lehmann, Sunil Gupta, and Joel H. Steckel (1998), *Marketing Research* (Reading, MA: Addison-Wesley).
5. Special issue of *Marketing Management* on qualitative research, Summer 1996, p. 5.
6. Bobby J. Calder (1977), "Focus Groups and the Nature of Qualitative Marketing Research," *Journal of Marketing Research*, August, pp. 353–364.
7. For a humorous story about how Procter & Gamble heavily uses residents of Cincinnati (where its headquarters is located) to participate in focus groups, see Emily Nelson (2002), "Focus Groupies: P&G Keeps Cincinnati Busy with All Its Studies," *The Wall Street Journal*, January 24, p. A1.
8. Natalie Zmuda (2009), "Facebook Turns Focus Group with Splenda Product-Sampling App," *Advertising Age*, July 13, p. 18.
9. Jerry Zaltman (2003), *How Consumers Think: Essential Insights into the Mind of the Market* (Cambridge, MA: Harvard Business School Press).
10. Jim Rendon (2003), "Rear Window," *Business 2.0*, August, p. 72.
11. Stephanie Rosenbloom (2010), "In Bid to Sway Sales, Cameras Track Shoppers," *The New York Times*, March 19, p. A1.
12. Russell Adams (2008), "Campbell Soup Sacks NFL's Mothers," *The Wall Street Journal*, August 27, p. B6.
13. Ilan Brat (2010), "The Emotional Quotient of Soup Shopping," *The Wall Street Journal*, February 17, p. B6.
14. Gary S. Vassana and Duane Bachman (1994), "Fax Attracts," *Marketing Research*, 6 (Spring), pp. 19–25.
15. Martin Opperman (1995), "E-mail Surveys: Potentials and Pitfalls," *Marketing Research*, 7 (Summer), pp. 29–33.
16. Timothy L. Keiningham, Bruce Cooil, Tor Wallin Andreassen, and Lerzan Aksoy (2007), "A Longitudinal Examination of Net Promoter and Firm Revenue Growth," *Journal of Marketing*, 71 (July), pp. 39–51.
17. Keith J. Winstein and Suzanne Vranica (2008), "U.S. Drug Ads Questioned," *The Wall Street Journal*, September 3, p. B7.
18. C. Samuel Craig and Susan P. Douglas (2005), *International Marketing Research* (Chichester, UK: John Wiley & Sons, Ltd.).
19. Donald R. Lehmann and Russell S. Winer (2008), *Analysis for Marketing Planning*, 7th ed. (New York: McGraw-Hill), Ch. 6.
20. From http://cadlab6.mit.edu/2.009.wiki/anchor/index.php?title=Amount_of_disposable_diapers_landfilled_each_year_in_the_US
21. For a good overview of different methods, see J. Scott Armstrong (1985), *Long-Range Forecasting: From Crystal Ball to Computer*, 2nd ed. (New York: John Wiley & Sons).

Chapter 4

1. This illustration is based on "Club Méditerranée," Harvard Business School case #9-579-061; Andrew Jack (1997), "Club Med

Turns Its Back on the Idealism of the Past," *Financial Times*, February 24, p. 19; Andrew Jack (1998), "Redefining Sun, Sand, and Sangria," *Financial Times*, January 29, p. 14; Jane L. Levere (2002), " 'Wanna Play?' That's What Club Med Asks in Its New Campaign," *New York Times*, January 31, p. C8; Mike Beirne (2004), "Club Med to Travel 'Emotional' Route," *Brandweek*, December 6, p. 9; and Jo Johnson (2004), "Out of Huts and Into Boutiques," *Financial Times*, August 4, p. 6.

2. Organizational or industrial buying behavior is examined in Chapter 5.
3. We cover this topic more fully in Chapter 14.
4. For an interesting analysis of ethnic differences in behavior and tipping behavior in particular, see Michael Lynn and Clorice Thomas-Haysbert (2003), "Ethnic Differences in Tipping: Evidence, Explanation, and Implications," *Journal of Applied Social Psychology*, August, pp. 1747–1772.
5. Eduardo Porter and Emily Nelson (2000), "P&G Reaches Out to Hispanics," *The Wall Street Journal*, October 13, p. B1.
6. For an excellent reference on psychographic and other attitudinal segmentation schemes, see Eric J. Arnould, Linda Price, and George Zinkhan (2002), *Consumers* (Boston: Irwin/McGraw-Hill).
7. A visitor to SRI's VALS Web site, http://www.strategicbusinessinsights.com/vals/surveynew.shtml, can classify himself or herself into one of the groups.
8. Paul C. Judge (1998), "Are Tech Buyers Different?" *BusinessWeek*, January 26, pp. 64–68.
9. Karen Benezra (1998), "The Fragging of the American Mind," *Brandweek*, June 15, pp. S12–S19.
10. Everett M. Rogers (1995), *Diffusion of Innovations*, 4th ed. (New York: Free Press).
11. This is a similar number to those shown in Table 4.4.
12. If you want to find out the PRIZM designation for the ZIP code in which you live, go to http://www.claritas.com/MyBestSegments/Default.jsp.
13. Another way to say this is that if the index numbers are similar across the levels of the variable, then that particular variable tells us nothing to help us discriminate between those who go to the beach and those who do not.
14. The material in this section is based on William R. Swinyard (1996), "The Hard Core and Zen Riders of Harley Davidson: A Market-Driven Segmentation Analysis," *Journal of Targeting, Measurement and Analysis for Marketing*, June, pp. 337–62.
15. Many models of how consumers make decisions have been developed. A good overview of several classic models can be found in J. A. Lunn (1974), "Consumer Decision-Process Models," in J. N. Sheth, ed., *Models of Buyer Behavior* (New York: HarperCollins), Ch. 3. An alternative approach is in James R. Bettman (1979), *An Information Processing Theory of Consumer Choice* (Reading, MA: Addison-Wesley).
16. One of the enduring controversies in marketing is that many people believe that marketers can create customer needs. This is unlikely; although marketers certainly try and do influence how a customer satisfies those needs, the basic need must be established by the customer.
17. Abraham H. Maslow (1970), *Motivation and Personality*, 2nd ed. (New York: HarperCollins).
18. See David Godes and Dina Mayzlin (2004), "Using Online Communications to Study Word-of-Mouth Communication," *Marketing Science*, 4 (Fall), pp. 545–560.
19. It should be noted that the customer could choose not to choose, that is, conclude that none of the products in the evoked set satisfy the need and postpone the purchase decision.
20. This illustration is based on David Kiley (2007), "At Hyundai, Branding Is Job 2," *BusinessWeek*, May 21.
21. There are several ways to ask this question besides the approach used in the text, and different numbers of scale points can be used.
22. The numbers in the table are fictitious and are only meant to illustrate the multiattribute model.
23. Other data combination models or rules exist. For example, using a lexicographic rule, the customer selects one attribute as the most important and then chooses the brand that is rated the highest on that attribute. See William D. Wells and David Prensky (1996), *Consumer Behavior* (New York: Wiley), Ch. 12.
24. We will see this model of expectation formation and comparison to outcomes in Chapter 8, in the discussion about customer evaluation of service quality.
25. Frank Bradley (1991), *International Marketing Strategy* (New York: Prentice Hall), Ch. 5.
26. Philip R. Cateora (1993), *International Marketing*, 8th ed. (Homewood, IL: Irwin), Ch. 5.
27. See Rogers, *Diffusion of Innovations*.
28. Gail Edmonson and Constrance Faivre (2005), "Got 5,000 Euros? Need a New Car?" *BusinessWeek*, July 4, p. 49.
29. This illustration is based on Michael J. Enright (1993), "The Japanese Facsimile Industry," Harvard Business School case #9-391-209.
30. Actually, FedEx was prescient in seeing that fax machines would ultimately be a major competitor to its document delivery service. Because fast plain-paper fax machines are very inexpensive today, fax transmissions do indeed substitute for many former FedEx shipments.

31. Itamar Simonson (1989), "Choice Based on Reasons: The Case of Attraction and Compromise Effects," *The Journal of Consumer Research*, 16 (September), pp. 158–174.
32. From *Petfood Industry*, June 11, 2009.
33. This illustration is from Catherine Arnst (2006), "Hey, You Don't Look So Good," *BusinessWeek*, May 8, pp. 30–32; Christine Bittar (2001), "The Message and the Medium," *Brandweek*, July 16, pp. 33–38; Thomas M. Burton (2002), "Reining in Drug Advertising," *The Wall Street Journal*, March 13, p. B1; and Jim Edwards (2005), "Sleep, Diet Awaken as Pharma Regroups," *Brandweek*, June 20, p. S60.
34. We discuss changes in distribution channels in more detail in Chapter 12.

Chapter 5

1. This illustration is based on Geoffrey Adamson (2001), "netCustomer: A Global Startup," Stanford University Graduate School of Business case #EC-26; and personal conversations with the company's founder, Punita Pandey.
2. Frederick E. Webster, Jr. (1979), *Industrial Marketing Strategy* (New York: Wiley).
3. This illustration is based on conversations with ATX personnel; David Pearson (2004), "Life in the Fast Lane," *The Wall Street Journal*, January 12, p. R7; the company Web site, www.atxg.com; and "In-Vehicle Text-by-Voice Application Introduced by ATX to Automotive Market," *PR Newswire*, July 21, 2009.
4. This is not true for services, of course.
5. V. Kasturi Rangan, Rowland Moriarty, and Gordon Swartz (1992), "Segmenting Customers in Mature Industrial Markets," *Journal of Marketing*, October, pp. 72–82.
6. This illustration is based on Tom Geller (2007), "A Hard-Knock Laptop," *Business 2.0*, October, 2007, p. 42; and the Toughbook Web site, http://www.panasonic.com/business/Toughbook/laptop-computers.asp.
7. This section is based on two books by Geoffrey A. Moore, *Crossing the Chasm* (1991; New York: HarperBusiness) and *Inside the Tornado* (1995; New York: HarperBusiness).
8. SGI went into bankruptcy in 2009 and was purchased by Rackable Systems Inc., which later assumed the SGI name.
9. This illustration is based on Nikhil Hutheesing (1997), "Auto-Baan," *Forbes*, October 6, pp. 109–113; and David Orenstein (2000), "Dogged by History," *Upside*, May, pp. 138–148.
10. Robert D. Hof (2005), "PayPal Spreads Its Wings," *BusinessWeek*, May 23, pp. 105–106; Hoovers Online, and http://en.wikipedia.org/wiki/PayPal.
11. Other companies producing such reports include Marketresearch.com, Mindbranch, and the Fredonia Group.
12. See Justin Fox (2002), "America's Most Admired Companies: What's So Great about GE?" *Fortune*, March 4, pp. 65–67.
13. The original research is published in Geert Hofstede (1980), *Culture's Consequences: International Differences in Work-Related Values* (Thousand Oaks, CA: Sage Publications). The second edition based on new research was published in 2001.
14. To get a better picture of how the countries compare, you would have to plot the countries by all pairs of the five dimensions.
15. We devote more space to channels of distribution in Chapter 12.
16. From the 2009 Grainger Fact Book at www.grainger.com.

Chapter 6

1. This illustration is based on Michael E. Porter (1991), "Coca-Cola versus Pepsi-Cola and the Soft Drink Industry," Harvard Business School case #9-391-179; Mark Gleason (1996), "Coke, Pepsi Repel Thrust by Alternative Beverages," *Advertising Age*, September 30, p. S18; Betsy McKay (2001), "Facing Slow Sales, Coke and Pepsi Gear Up for New Battle," *The Wall Street Journal*, April 16, p. B4; Nanette Byrnes (2004), "Gone Flat," *BusinessWeek*, December 20, pp. 76–82; Betsy McKay (2008), "Soft-Drink Sales Volume Slipped Faster Last Year," *The Wall Street Journal*, March 13, p. B6; Stuart Elliott (2008), "Pepsi Shifts to a New Ad Agency," *The New York Times*, November 18; Valerie Bauerlein (2009), "Pepsi Sweats Over Gatorade," *The Wall Street Journal*, July 23; Yahoo!Finance; and http://online.wsj.com/article/SB10001424052748704479404575087123562176374.html.
2. Pepsi's restaurants are now owned by Yum! Brands.
3. It should be noted that Coca-Cola manufactures only the concentrate or syrup; its bottlers, some of which are company-owned, assume the costs of making the soft drink and distributing it.
4. Bruce H. Clark and David B. Montgomery (1999), "Managerial Identification of Competitors," *Journal of Marketing*, July, pp. 67–83.
5. Joe S. Bain (1968), *Industrial Organization* (New York: Wiley).
6. Richard Tomkins (1997), "Coca-Cola Strives to Rival Tap Water," *Financial Times*, October 27, p. 9.
7. Sarah Ellison (2002), "Is Less Risqué Risky?" *The Wall Street Journal*, May 20, p. B1.

8. Justin Scheck and Ben Worthen (2009), "Cisco, H-P Square Off in Hunt for Revenue," *The Wall Street Journal*, July 22, p. B8.
9. Alex Kuczynki (2002), "Brek Mints: A Hot War for America's Cool Mouths," *The New York Times*, April 24, Section 9, p. 1.
10. A good source for these methods is Vithala R. Rao and Joel H. Steckel (1995), *The New Science of Marketing* (Chicago: Irwin), Ch. 4.
11. See, for example, S. Ratneshwar and Allan Shocker (1991), "Substitution in Use and the Role of Usage Context in Product Category Structures," *Journal of Marketing Research*, August, pp. 281–295.
12. Michael Fielding (2004), "Damage Control," *Marketing News*, September 15, p. 15.
13. Ted Bridis, Glenn Simpson, and Mylene Mangalindan (2000), "How Piles of Trash Became Latest Focus in Bitter Software Feud," *The Wall Street Journal*, June 29, p. A1; Andy Serwer (2001), "P&G's Cover Operation," *Fortune*, September 17, pp. 42–44; and Tamar Audi and Peter Lattman (2009), "Hilton Is Sued Over Luxury Chain," *The Wall Street Journal*, April 17.
14. "Kraft Foods Works on Improving Its Recipe for Distributing Goods," *The Wall Street Journal*, August 3, 2004, p. A9.
15. Ira Teinowitz (1995), "Marketing, Ad Woes Choking RJR Brands," *Advertising Age*, June 26, p. 3.
16. A version of this approach is described by Kevin P. Coyne and John Horn (2009), "Predicting Your Competitor's Reaction," *Harvard Business Review*, April, pp. 90–97.
17. See, for example, Pierre Wack (1985), "Scenarios: Uncharted Waters Ahead," *Harvard Business Review*, September–October, pp. 73–89.
18. Ellen Neuborne (2003), "Know Thy Enemy," *Sales & Marketing Management*, January, pp. 29–33.
19. Sarah Lacy and Jay Greene (2005), "How to Face Off Against Microsoft," *BusinessWeek*, September 5, pp. 66–68.
20. A search on Amazon.com for "competitive intelligence" titles resulted in 50 different books.
21. See Michael Peel (2007), "Data Treasures for the Taking," *Financial Times*, August 16, p. 10.
22. Dave Fedewa, Ashish Kothar, and Ananth S. Narayanan (2009), "Squeezing More Ideas from Product Teardowns," *McKinsey Quarterly*, Number 3, pp. 84–85.
23. For a perspective on how to maximize the information from plant tours, see David M. Upton and Stephen E. Macadam (1997), "Why (and How) to Take a Plant Tour," *Harvard Business Review*, May–June, pp. 97–106.
24. This illustration is based on Pui-Wing Tam (2000), "Palm Puts Up Its Fist as Microsoft Attacks Hand-Held PC Market," *The Wall Street Journal*, August 8, p. A1.
25. This section draws on K. Sridhar Moorthy (1985), "Using Game Theory to Model Competition," *Journal of Marketing Research*, 22 (August), pp. 262–282; as well as material from Professor Devavrat Purohit of Duke University.
26. Named for the famous economist John Nash, popularized by the 2001 Oscar-winning movie *A Beautiful Mind*.
27. This simultaneous solution also assumes that both firms have complete information in that they both know the payoff matrix and that it is the same for both of them. Of course, they still do not know what the other is going to do.
28. Game theory can be extended to include more than two participants and games over an extended period of time with multiple moves.
29. F. William Barnett (1995), "Making Game Theory Work in Practice," *The Wall Street Journal*, February 13, p. A14.

Chapter 7

1. This illustration is based on Adrian B. Ryans (1992), "Logitech," Richard Ivey School of Business case #92-A012, University of Western Onatario; Alan Cane (2005), "Why Logitech Has Gone from Mouse to House," *Financial Times*, April 1, p. 8; Noah Robinson (2005), "Getting Into a New Game," *Business 2.0*, April, p. 58; and "Feel the Beat: Logitech Unveils Premium Drum Controller for Guitar Hero," *Leisure & Travel Week*, August 2, 2009, p. 50.
2. David A. Aaker (1991), *Brand Equity* (New York: Free Press).
3. Aaker's model is not the only conceptualization of brand equity. For example, the advertising agency Young & Rubicam has its Brand Asset Valuator (BAV) model discussed later in this chapter.
4. Suzanne Vranica (2004), "Aflac Duck's Paddle to Stardom: Creativity on the Cheap," *The Wall Street Journal*, July 30, p. B1; and Rupal Parekh (2009), "Brand Awareness Was Only Half the Battle for Aflac," *Advertising Age*, June 22, p. 27.
5. Maria Halkias (2005), "IKEA Standing Tall Among Rivals," *Knight Ridder Tribune Business News*, July 26, p. 1; Michelle Higgins (2009), "A Cheap Date, with Child Care by Ikea," *The New York Times*, June 11; and franchisor.ikea.com.
6. David A. Aaker (1996), *Building Strong Brands* (New York: Free Press).
7. Stuart Elliott (2009), "Tropicana Discovers Some Buyers Are Passionate About Packaging," *The New York Times*, February 23.

8. Another type of extension is called a *line* extension. This is normally a new flavor or model of the existing product.
9. Kenneth Hein (2008), "BK Boxers Leads Pack of Worst Line Extensions," *Brandweek*, December 15, p. 7.
10. Amy Merrick (2005), "Once a Bellweather, Ann Talor Fights Its Stodgy Image," *The Wall Street Journal*, July 12, p. A1.
11. Ibid.
12. Kenneth Hein (2002), "Run Red Run," *Brandweek*, February 25, pp. 14–15; and Scott Leith (2004), "Drinks Try to Sustain the Buzz: Limited-time Offerings Work Well for Pepsi," *The Atlanta Constitution*, October 30, p. G1.
13. *PR Newswire*, August 19, 2008.
14. Theodore Levitt (1983), "The Globalization of Markets," *Harvard Business Review*, May–June, pp. 92–102.
15. For more background, see John Quelch (1984), "British Airways," Harvard Business School case #9-585-014.
16. See Susan P. Douglas and Yoram Wind (1987), "The Myth of Globalization," *The Columbia Journal of World Business*, 22 (Winter), pp. 19–29.
17. See Arindam K. Bhattacharya and David C. Michael (2008), "How Local Companies Keep Multinationals at Bay," *Harvard Business Review*, March, pp. 85–95.
18. Jenny Wiggins (2009), "Worlds' Next Top Brands Set to Rise in the East," *Financial Times*, July 19.
19. Dexter Roberts, Frederik Balfour, Bruce Einhorn, Michael Arndt, Michael Shari, and David Kiley (2004), "China's Power Brands," *BusinessWeek*, November 8, pp. 77–84.
20. Douglas A. Holt, John A. Quelch, and Earl L. Taylor (2004), "How Global Brands Compete," *Harvard Business Review*, September, pp. 68–75.
21. From www.interbrand.com.
22. Roberts et al., "China's Power Bands."
23. Ginny Parker (2004), "Going Global Can Hit Snags, Vodafone Finds," *The Wall Street Journal*, July 16, p. B1.
24. Jennifer Gilbert (2001), "SAP Goes All Out," *Business 2.0*, June 12, pp. 34–35.
25. Diane Anderson (2005), "Cisco Reboots Image with $150M Effort," *Brandweek*, January 10, p. 4; and Charlotte Woolard (2008), "BtoB's Best Brands," *BtoB magazine*.
26. Scott Van Camp (2005), "What Yellow Did for Them," *Brandweek*, January 10, p. 14.
27. This illustration is based on David Weinstein (1994), "Intel Inside," INSEAD case #594-038-1; Ellen McGirt (2009), "Intel Risks It All (Again)," *Fast Company*, November, pp. 87–96; and data from Yahoo! Finance.
28. Jennifer L. Aaker (1997), "Dimensions of Brand Personality," *Journal of Marketing Research*, August, pp. 347–356.
29. Karen Lundegaard and Vanessa O'Connell (2002), "Audi Moves to Create a Personality in the U.S.," *The Wall Street Journal*, February 19, p. B7.
30. Susan Fournier (1998), "Consumers and Their Brands: Developing Relationship Theory in Consumer Research," *Journal of Consumer Research*, March, pp. 343–473.
31. Beth Kowitt (2009), *Fortune*, May 11, pp. 84–91.
32. Abbey Klaassen (2008), "Consumers Become Kindle Ambassadors," *Advertising Age*, September 8.
33. Piet Levy (2009), "Marketing in Aisle 5," *Marketing News*, May 30, pp. 12–15.
34. Nirmalya Kumar and Jan-Benedict E. M. Steenkamp (2007), *Private Label Strategy* (Boston: Harvard Business School Press).
35. A "fighting" brand is a brand marketed by a large multinational company but without much marketing support.
36. James Surowiecki (2004), "The Decline of Brands," *Wired*, November, pp. 205–209.
37. Tim Ambler (2003), *Marketing and the Bottom Line*, 2nd ed. (London: Financial Times/Prentice Hall), p. 63.
38. A good description of Interbrand's methodology is in "The Top 100 Brands," *BusinessWeek*, September 29, 2008, p. 56.
39. For further details on MDS methods, the reader is referred to marketing research textbooks such as Donald R. Lehmann, Sunil Gupta, and Joel H. Steckel (1998), *Marketing Research* (Reading, MA: Addison-Wesley).
40. Eric Pfanner (2008), "Calling Off on Dubious Eco-Friendly Claims," *Advertising Age*, July 18.
41. Dana James (2002), "Skoda Is Taken from Trash to Treasure," *Marketing News*, February 18, pp. 4–5.
42. Richard Milne (2005), "A Drive to Escape the Mass Market," *Financial Times*, August 19, p. 6.
43. Mark Bergen, Shantanu Dutta, and Steven M. Shugan (1996), "Branded Variants: A Retail Perspective," *Journal of Marketing Research*, February, pp. 9–19.
44. Deborah Ball (2007), "After Buying Binge, Nestlé Goes on Diet," *The Wall Street Journal*, July 23, p. A1.
45. Adrian J. Slywotzky (2000), "The Age of the Choiceboard," *Harvard Business Review*, January–February, pp. 40–41.
46. James H. Gilmore and B. Joseph Pine II (1997), "The Four Faces of Customization," *Harvard Business Review*, January–February, pp. 91–101.
47. Itamar Simonson (2005), "Determinants of Customers' Responses to Customized Offers: Conceptual Framework and Research Propositions," *Journal of Marketing*, 69 (January), pp. 32–45.

48. This illustration is based on Stephanie Fitch (2007), "The Keg That Scored," *Fortune*, October 15, pp. 70–73; and David Kesmodel (2009), "MillerCoors Tests a Draft-Beer Box for the Fridge," *The Wall Street Journal*, July 29, p. B8.

Chapter 8

1. This illustration is based on Wendy Bounds (1996), "Camera System Is Developed but Not Delivered," *The Wall Street Journal*, August 7, p. B1; Tricia Campbell (1999), "Back in Focus," *Sales & Marketing Management*, February, pp. 56–61; "APS Update: It's Not Dead Yet," *Retailing Today*, February 25, 2002; Geoffrey Smith (2002), "This Market Just Isn't Developing," *BusinessWeek*, May 13, pp. 90–92; James Bandler (2004), "Ending an Era, Kodak Will Stop Selling Most Film Cameras," *The Wall Street Journal*, January 14, p. B1; and Robert Tomsho (2009), "Kodak to Take Kodachrome Away," *The Wall Street Journal*, June 23.
2. See www.uspto.gov/web/offices/ac/ido/oeip/taf/top05cos.htm.
3. See Ashish Sood and Gerard J. Tellis (2008), "Do Innovations Really Pay Off? Total Stock Market Returns to Innovation," Marketing Science Institute working paper number 08-106; and Barry Jaruzelski, Kevin Dehoff, and Rakesh Bordia (2005), "Money Isn't Everything," *Strategy + Business*, Winter.
4. See C. Merle Crawford and C. Anthony Di Benedetto (2005), *New Products Management*, 8th ed. (Burr Ridge, IL: McGraw-Hill).
5. Deborah Ball, Sarah Ellison, and Janet Adamy (2004), "Just What You Need!" *The Wall Street Journal*, October 28, p. B1.
6. The person best known for studies in this area is Robert G. Cooper. Two articles he has written on this topic are R. G. Cooper and E. J. Kleinschmidt (1987), "New Products: What Separates Winners from Losers?" *Journal of Product Innovation Management*, 4, pp. 169–184; and Robert G. Cooper (1996), "New Products: What Separates the Winners from the Losers," in M.D. Rosenau Jr., A. Griffin, G. A. Castellion, and N. F. Anscheutz, eds., *The PDMA Handbook of New Product Development* (New York: Wiley), Ch. 1.
7. Andrew Pollack (2009), "Nasal Vaccine Holds Promise Against Swine Flu," *The New York Times*, July 31. Interestingly, it is sometimes better to be lucky than good. It turns out that because FluMist uses a different strain for inoculating against the swine flu that is easier to produce than those delivered by conventional shots, the company is the leading producer of the vaccine for the government.
8. This concept was first introduced by Hirotaka Takeuchi and Ikujiro Nonaka (1986), "The New Product Development Game," *Harvard Business Review*, January–February, pp. 137–146.
9. See, for example, Robin Cooper and W. Bruce Chew (1996), "Control Tomorrow's Costs through Today's Designs," *Harvard Business Review*, January–February, pp. 88–97.
10. Dan Swenson, Shahid Ansari, Jan Bell, and Il-Woon Kim (2003), "Best Practices in Target Costing," *Management Accounting Quarterly*, Winter, pp. 12–17.
11. Eric Von Hippel (2005), *Democratizing Innovation* (Cambridge, MA: MIT Press).
12. Rob Walker (2004), "Risky Business," *The New York Times Sunday Magazine*, November 28, p. 68.
13. http://www.digitalpodcast.com/podcastnews/2008/04/22/social-marketing-case-study-levis-project-501/.
14. See C. K. Prahalad and Venkat Ramaswamy (2004), *The Future of Competition: Co-Creating Unique Value with Customers.*
15. For some other examples, see *Conference Summary: Innovation and Co-Creation*, Marketing Science Institute, www.msi.org.
16. Prahalad and Ramaswamy, *The Future of Competition.*
17. David Robertson and Per Hjuler (2009), "Innovating a Turnaround at LEGO," *Harvard Business Review*, September, pp. 20–21.
18. See, for example, Anthony W. Ulwick (2002), "Turn Customer Input Into Innovation," *Harvard Business Review*, January, pp. 91–97. However, some researchers disagree. A new method called *empathetic design* obtains information from customers about potential new-product ideas, not from focus groups or more traditional methods, but through observing their behavior in natural environments.
19. Desiree De Meyer (2001), "Get to Market Faster," *Smartbusinessmag.com*, October, pp. 62–71.
20. For more information about concept testing, see Crawford and Di Benedetto, *New Products Management*, Ch.9.
21. Jack Neff (2000), "Safe At Any Speed?" *Advertising Age*, January 24, p. 1.
22. Erik Brynjolfsson and Michael Schrage (2009), "The New, Faster Face of Innovation," *The Wall Street Journal*, August 17, p. R3.
23. Ely Dahan and V. Srinivasan (2000), "The Predictive Power of Internet-Based Product Concept Testing Using Visual Depiction and Animation," *Journal of Product Innovation Management*, March, pp. 99–109.
24. Paul E. Green and Yoram Wind (1975), "New Way to Measure Consumers' Judgments," *Harvard Business Review*, July–August, pp. 107–117.
25. This section is based on John R. Hauser and Don Clausing (1988), "The House of Quality," *Harvard Business Review*, May–June, pp. 63–73.

26. G. Kalyanaram and V. Krishnan (1997), "Deliberate Product Definition: Customizing the Product Definition Process," *Journal of Marketing Research*, 34 (May), pp. 276–285.
27. The product used in this phase typically is specially produced and may not match the quality of the product after it reaches a large scale of production. For example, Knorr soup product test samples were produced in Europe, whereas the actual mass-produced product was made in a new, computerized plant in Argo, Illinois, which produced a product of different quality.
28. This illustration is based on De Meyer, "Get to Market Faster,"
29. *Business Wire*, May 24, 2004 located at http://findarticles.com/p/articles/mi_m0EIN/is_2004_May_24/ai_n6040172/.
30. Suzanne Bidlake (1998), "Winner Taco Wins over Europeans Searching for Snack," *Ad Age International*, April 13, p. 19.
31. J. H. Parfitt and B. J. K. Collins (1968), "Use of Consumer Panels for Brand-Share Prediction," *Journal of Marketing Research*, May, pp. 131–145.
32. Alvin J. Silk and Glen L. Urban (1978), "Pre-Test Market Evaluation of New Packaged Goods: A Model and Measurement Methodology," *Journal of Marketing Research*, May, pp. 171–191.
33. Glen L. Urban, Bruce D. Weinberg, and John R. Hauser (1996), "Pre-market Forecasting of Really-New Products," *Journal of Marketing*, January, pp. 47–60.
34. This illustration is based on V. Kasturi Rangan (1995), "Nestlé Refrigerated Foods: Contadina Pasta & Pizza (A)," Harvard Business Schools case #9-595-035.
35. This illustration is based on Susan Fournier and Robert J. Dolan (1997), "Launching the BMW Z3 Roadster," Harvard Business School case #9-597-002; and James T. Areddy (2007), "Starbucks, PepsiCo Bring 'Subopera' to Shanghai," *The Wall Street Journal*, November 1, p. B1.
36. *ICONOCAST*, February 2, 2001.
37. Stuart Elliott (2008), "For a New Brand, Pepsi Starts the Buzz Online," *The New York Times*, March 14.
38. Christopher D. Ittner and David F. Larcker (1997), "Product Development Cycle Time and Organizational Performance," *Journal of Marketing Research*, February, pp. 13–23.
39. Nick Bunkley (2009), "Automakers Start Rush for New Models," *The New York Times*, August 7, p. B4.
40. Abbie Griffin (1997), "The Effect of Project and Process Characteristics on Product Development Cycle Time," *Journal of Marketing Research*, February, pp. 24–35.
41. Faith Keenan and Spencer E. Ante (2002), "The New Teamwork," *BusinessWeek e.biz*, February 18, pp. EB 12–16.
42. At the time of this writing, Hewlett-Packard was slated to purchase Palm Inc. but had not yet completed the acquisition.
43. Bruce Nussbaum (2004), "The Power of Design," *BusinessWeek*, May 17, pp. 73–75.
44. This section is partially based on Geoffrey A. Moore (2004), "Darwin and the Demon: Innovating Within Established Enterprises," *Harvard Business Review*, July–August, pp. 86–92.

Chapter 9

1. This illustration is based on *The Economist* (2004), "The Meaning of iPod," June 12, p. 16; Jeff Leeds (2005), "Apple, Digital Music's Angel, Earns Record Industry's Scorn," *The New York Times*, August 27, p. A1; Ethan Smith and Yukari Iwatani Kane (2009), "Apple Changes Tune on Music Pricing," *The Wall Street Journal*, January 7; and Jim Dalrymple (2009), "Strong iPhone and iPod Sales Drive Apple Profits to $1.21 Billion," *Macworld.com*, April 22.
2. As we will discuss later in this chapter, Apple's pricing policies for the iPhone have not been without controversy.
3. In fact, the famous late management consultant Peter Drucker called cost-driven pricing a "deadly sin" in Drucker (1993), "The Five Deadly Business Sins," *The Wall Street Journal*, October 21, p. A16.
4. This notion was first introduced to us by pricing consultant Daniel A. Nimer.
5. Ibid.
6. We are purposefully vague for the moment about the definition of cost; this is explained later in this chapter.
7. Joel E. Urbany (2001), "Are Your Prices Too Low?" *Harvard Business Review*, October, pp. 26–27.
8. Vishy Cvs, Alexandru M. Degeratu, and Rebecca L. Ott-Wadhawan (2002), "Bank Deposits Get Interesting," *McKinsey Quarterly*, Number 2 (March).
9. Constance Gustke (2002), "Prices and Possibilities," *Progressive Grocer*, January 1, pp. 66–67.
10. Connie Ling and Wayne Arnold (1998), "Prospective Customers Compete to Buy Nokia's New Mobile Phone," *Asian Wall Street Journal*, September 21, p. 12.
11. For another take on the economics of the music business, see David Byrne (2007), "Survival Strategies for Emerging Artists—and Megastars," *Wired*, issue 16.01, December 18.
12. Remi Trudel and June Cotte (2009), "Does It Pay to Be Good?" *Sloan Management Review*, Winter, pp. 61–68.
13. A retailer may set the price of a product or service below cost. This is usually called a *loss leader* and is intended to bring in more

customers to the store by offering a deep discount on a popular item. For example, cranberry sauce is often used as a loss leader at Thanksgiving. We assume that a manufacturer would not do this intentionally.

14. The vertical bars indicate absolute value.
15. Gerard J. Tellis (1988), "The Price Elasticity of Selective Demand: A Meta-Analysis of Econometric Models of Sales," *Journal of Marketing Research*, 25 (November), pp. 331–341.
16. For a good description of this approach, see James C. Anderson, Nirmalya Kumar, and James A. Narus (2007), *Value Merchants* (Cambridge, MA: Harvard Business School Press).
17. An alternative way to phrase the question is to ask how much the customer would have to be paid to be indifferent between the preferred brand and the other brand.
18. Robert J. Dolan and Hermann Simon (1996), *Power Pricing* (New York: The Free Press).
19. This example is drawn from Ted Kendall (1990), "And the Survey Says...," *The Marketer*, September, pp. 47–48.
20. This illustration is based on Gery Khermouch (1998), "Sticking Their Neck Out," *Brandweek*, November 9, pp. 26–38.
21. P. K. Kannan, Barbara Kline Pope, and Sanjay Jain (2009), "Pricing Digital Content Product Lines: A Model and Application for the National Academies Press," *Marketing Science*, 28 (July–August), pp. 620–636.
22. Janice Revell (2001), "The Price Is Not Always Right," *Fortune*, May 14, p. 240.
23. Kenneth Hein (2009), "Study: Value Trumps Price Among Shoppers," *Brandweek*, March 2, p. 6.
24. For the rankings by category, see http://www.brandweek.com/bw/special-reports/brand-key/2009/index.jsp.
25. Joan O. Hamilton (1990), "Genentech: A Textbook Case of Medical Marketing," *BusinessWeek*, August 13, pp. 96–97.
26. Owen Thomas (2004), "SanDisk Plays it Cards Right," *Business 2.0*, May, pp. 60–62.
27. Drucker, "The Five Deadly Sins."
28. We will refer to this $0.99 price later in the chapter as a *reference* price, that is, a price that becomes a mental standard price for a product.
29. See for example, David Carr (2007), "Steve Jobs: iCame, iSaw, iCaved," *The New York Times*, September 10; and Joseph De Avila (2007), "Why Some Apple Fans Won't Buy the iPhone," *The Wall Street Journal*, September 12, p. D3.
30. Oliver P. Heil and Kristiaan Helsen (2001), "Toward an Understanding of Price Wars: Their Nature and How They Erupt," *International Journal of Research in Marketing*, June, pp. 83–98.
31. Akshay R. Rao, Mark E. Bergen, and Scott Davis (2000), "How to Fight a Price War," *Harvard Business Review*, March–April, pp. 107–116.
32. See, for example, Gurumurthy Kalyanaram and Russell S. Winer (1995), "Empirical Generalizations from Reference Price Research," *Marketing Science*, 14, issue 3, pp. G161–G169.
33. For more information on the signaling aspect of prices, see Amna Kirmani and Akshay R. Rao (2000), "No Pain, No Gain: A Critical Review of the Literature on Signaling Unobservable Product Quality," *Journal of Marketing*, April, pp. 66–79.
34. For some background on odd prices, see Mark Stiving and Russell S. Winer (1997), "An Empirical Analysis of Price Endings with Scanner Data," *Journal of Consumer Research*, 24 (June), pp. 57–67; and Manoj Thomas and Vicki Morwitz (2005), "Penny Wise and Pound Foolish: The Left-Digit Effect in Price Cognition," *Journal of Consumer Research*, 32 (June), pp. 54–64.
35. For more information about bundling, see Stefan Stremersch and Gerard J. Tellis (2002), "Strategic Bundling of Products and Prices: A New Synthesis for Marketing," *Journal of Marketing*, January, pp. 55–72.
36. For a good discussion of the legal aspects of pricing, see Thomas T. Nagle and Reed K. Holden (2002), *The Strategies and Tactics of Pricing*, 3rd ed. (Upper Saddle River, NJ: Prentice-Hall), Chapter 14.
37. The experiment affects only 2,000 of the 41,000 seats in the stadium that are the last to sell and where there are no season ticket holders. Ken Belson (2009), "Baseball Tickets Too Much? Check Back Tomorrow," *The New York Times*, May 18, p. D2.
38. Charles King III and Das Narayandas (2000), "Coca-Cola's New Vending Machine (A): Pricing to Capture Value, or Not?" Harvard Business School case #9-500-068.
39. David Streitfeld (2000), "Amazon Flunks Its Pricing Test," *San Francisco Chronicle*, September 28, p. B4.
40. Andrew Pollack (2009), "Drug Deals Tie Prices to How Well Patients Do," *The New York Times*, April 23.
41. The survey results can be accessed at http://www.whatpricedidyouchoose.com/.
42. Greg Kot (2008), "Turn it Up," *Chicago Tribune*, October 20, blog located at http://leisureblogs.chicagotribune.com/turn_it_up/2008/10/radioheads-in-r.html; and Wendy Davis (2008), "Freeloaders Didn't Hurt Radiohead Sales," *The Daily Online Examiner*, October 16.
43. Eric Newman (2008), "As Inflation Resurfaces, So Does Package Shrink," *Brandweek*, June 9, p. 5.

44. John A. Quelch and David Harding (1996), "Brands versus Private Labels: Fighting to Win," *Harvard Business Review*, January–February, pp. 99–109.
45. For a more general discussion of consumers' interests in "free" that includes both online and offline shopping behavior, see Chris Anderson (2009), *Free* (New York: Hyperion Books).
46. Jeffry R. Brown and Austan Goolsbee (2002), "Does the Internet Make Markets More Competitive? Evidence from the Life Insurance Industry," *Journal of Political Economy*, 110, issue 3, pp. 481–507.
47. Michael D. Smith and Erik Brynjolfsson (2001), "Consumer Decision-Making at an Internet Shopbot: Brand Still Matters," *Journal of Industrial Economics*, December, pp. 541–558.
48. Walter Baker, Mike Marn, and Craig Zawada (2001), "Price Smarter on the Net," *Harvard Business Review*, February, pp. 122–127.
49. Eric J. Johnson, Wendy W. Moe, Peter S. Fader, Steven Bellman, and Gerald L. Lohse (2004), "On the Depth and Dynamics of Online Search Behavior," *Management Science*, 48 (October), pp. 1350–1368.
50. Daniel Fisher (2009), "Cheap Seats," *Forbes*, August 24, pp. 102–103.
51. Scott McNealy (2001), "Welcome to the Bazaar," *Harvard Business Review*, March, pp. 18–19.
52. Geoffrey A. Fowler (2009), "Auctions Fade as eBay Offers Wholesale Items at Fixed Prices," *The Wall Street Journal*, May 26.
53. See Margaret C. Campbell (1999), "Perceptions of Price Unfairness: Antecedents and Consequences," *Journal of Marketing Research*, May, pp. 187–199.
54. Interestingly, it has been argued that consumers are clearer and more articulate about what they perceive as unfair prices than they are about fair prices. See Lan Xia, Kent B. Monroe, and Jennifer L. Cox (2004), "The Price is Unfair! A Conceptual Framework of Price Fairness Perceptions," *Journal of Marketing*, October, pp. 1–15.

Chapter 10

1. This illustration is based on Timothy L. O'Brien (2005), "Madison Avenue Wants You," *The New York Times*, September 25, p. BU 1; and Dave Moniz (2005), "Fewer Early Sign-ups as Army Struggles to Recruit Soldiers," *USA Today*, July 27, p. A6; and www.army.mil.
2. For a classic reference in this area, see Wilbur Schram (1955), *The Process and Effects of Mass Communication* (Urbana: University of Illinois Press).
3. See E. Katz and P.F. Lazarsfeld (1955), *Personal Influence* (Glencoe, IL: Free Press).
4. Electronic environments such as those discussed are called hypermedia computer-mediated environments. See Donna L. Hoffman and Thomas P. Novak (1996), "Marketing in Hypermedia Computer-Mediated Environments: Conceptual Foundations," *Journal of Marketing*, 60 (July), pp. 50–68.
5. Philip Evans and Thomas S. Wurster (2000), *Blown to Bits* (Boston: Harvard Business School Press), Ch. 3.
6. Ralph S. Alexander, ed. (1965), *Marketing Definitions* (Chicago: American Marketing Association), p. 9.
7. Direct marketing is also often considered to be a channel of distribution because it brings the product to the customer. We consider it to be a channel in this book; see Chapter 12.
8. Like direct marketing, personal selling is often considered to be a direct channel of distribution.
9. Lea Goldman (2002), "A Fortune in Firewalls," *Forbes*, March 18, pp. 101–108.
10. This background material is from http://home.swipnet.se/~w-33318/websolut/history.htm
11. Press Release, LG dated December 7, 2009.
12. http://en-us.nielsen.com/main/news/news_releases/2009/march/u_s_ad_spending_fell.
13. Normandy Madden and Andrew Hornery (1999), "As Taco Bell Enters Singapore, Gidget Avoids the Ad Limelight," *Ad Age International*, January 11, p. 13.
14. Stuart Elliott (2002), "Advertising's Big Four: It's Their World Now," *The New York Times*, March 31, Business Section, p. 1.
15. Jack Neff (2001), "Coupons Get Clipped," *Advertising Age*, November 5, p. 1.
16. See, for example, Demetrios Vakratsas and Tim Ambler (1999), "How Advertising Works: What Do We Really Know?" *Journal of Marketing*, 63 (January), pp. 26–43.
17. See, for example, Johanna S. Ilfeld and Russell S. Winer (2002), "Generating Web Site Traffic: An Empirical Analysis of Web Site Visitation Behavior," *Journal of Advertising Research*, September–October, pp. 49–61.
18. See George E. Belch and Michael A. Belch (1993), *Introduction to Advertising and Promotion* (Burr Ridge, IL: McGraw-Hill).
19. A good reference on copy testing procedures is Rajeev Batra, John G. Myers, and David A. Aaker (1996), *Advertising Management*, 5th ed. (Upper Saddle River, NJ: Prentice Hall), Chapter 14.
20. Believe it or not, a woman sold her forehead as ad space. She had the words "GoldenPalace.com" tattooed on her forehead for $10,000.
21. Jean Halliday (2005), "Ford Ups 'Targeted' Media Spending," *Advertising Age*, p. 8.

22. Kris Oser (2005), "Online Crisis Looms as Ad Demand Surges," *Advertising Age*, September 12, p. 1.
23. See, for example, *BusinessWeek Online* (2001), "Online Advertising: It's Just the Beginning," *Special Report: Internet Advertising*, July 12.
24. Joshua Rosenbaum (2002), "Annoying...but Effective," *The Wall Street Journal Online*, April 15.
25. Lorne Manley (2005), "When the Ad Turns Into the Story Line," *The New York Times*, October 2, p. BU-1.
26. Michael Schneider (2009), "Fox Wants Answers from Nielsen," *Variety*, May 18, http://www.variety.com/article/VR1118003924.html?categoryid=14&cs=1.
27. H. Rao Unnava and Robert E. Burnkrant (1991), "Effects of Repeating Varied Ad Executions on Brand Name Memory," *Journal of Marketing Research*, 28 (November), pp. 406–416.
28. Hubert A. Zielske (1959), "The Remembering and Forgetting of Advertising," *Journal of Marketing*, 23 (January), pp. 239–243.
29. See David Kiley (1998), "Optimum Target," *AdWeek*, May 18, pp. 39–42.
30. Mya Frazier (2005), "You Suck," *Advertising Age*, July 25, p. 1.
31. "Fighting Apple on Its Turf," *The New York Times*, August 30, 2009, P. BU6.
32. See John Philip Jones (1990), "Ad Spending: Maintaining Market Share," *Harvard Business Review*, January–February, pp. 38–48.
33. See Rita Koselka (1996), "The New Mantra: MVT," *Forbes*, March 11, pp. 114–117.
34. These data are from Darral G. Clarke (1985), "G.D. Searle & Co.: Equal Low-Calorie Sweetener (A)," Harvard Business School case #9-585-010.
35. John D.C. Little (1970), "Models and Managers: The Concept of a Decision Calculus," *Management Science*, 16, pp. B466–B485.
36. See J. Enrique Bigné (1995), "Advertising Budget Practices: A Review," *Journal of Current Issues and Research in Advertising*, 2 (Fall), pp. 17–31.
37. Brian Steinberg (2005), "Putting a Value on Marketing Dollars," *The Wall Street Journal*, July 27, p. B1.
38. Leonard M. Lodish, Magid Abraham, Stuart Kalmenson, Jeanne Livelsberger, Beth Lubetkin, Bruce Richardson, and Mary Ellen Stevens (1995), "How T.V. Advertising Works: A Meta-Analysis of 389 Real World Split Cable T.V. Advertising Experiments," *Journal of Marketing Research*, 32 (May), pp. 125–139.
39. Abbey Klaassen (2005), "Is Court TV Guarantee Birth of a New ROI Trend?" *Advertising Age*, June 13, p. 46.
40. Gert Assmus, John U. Farley, and Donald R. Lehmann (1984), "How Advertising Affects Sales: Meta-Analysis of Econometric Results," *Journal of Marketing Research*, 21 (February), pp. 65–74.
41. The vast majority of empirical research in this area has focused on consumer products and services. Thus, generalizing these findings to industrial products should be done with caution.
42. Geoffrey A. Fowler (2005), "Northwest Air Takes Japanese Ads to New Heights," *The Wall Street Journal*, October 13, p. B4.
43. David Kiley (2005), "Cable's Big Bet on Hyper Targeting," *BusinessWeek*, July 4, pp. 58–59.
44. David H. Freedman (2005), "The Future of Advertising Is Here," *Inc. Magazine*, August, pp. 70–77.

Chapter 11

1. This illustration is based on Jeremy Grant and Tim Burt (2002), "Carmakers Feel Pain Despite Incentives Drug," *Financial Times*, April 4, p. 16; Sholnn Freeman (2005), "GM, Ford Shift Gears on Pricing," *The Wall Street Journal*, August 2, p. D2; and BusinessWire report (2009), http://www.businesswire.com/news/home/20090901006373/en, September 1.
2. Scott A. Neslin (2002), *Sales Promotion* (Cambridge, MA: Marketing Science Institute). This book also has an excellent overview of research in the area.
3. www.promomagazine.com, October 2008.
4. Julie Pitta (1999), "Squeeze Play: Databases Get Ugly," *Forbes*, February 22, pp. 50–51.
5. Carl F. Mela, Sunil Gupta, and Donald R. Lehmann (1997), "The Long-Term Impact of Promotion and Advertising on Consumer Brand Choice," *Journal of Marketing Research*, 34 (May), pp. 248–261.
6. Hannah Kate Kinnersley (2008), "The Best Sites for Coupon Clipping," *The Wall Street Journal*, May 22, p. D2.
7. Bridget Goldschmidt (2009), "Economic Woes Spur Coupon Use," *Progressivegrocer.com*, September 10.
8. Kenneth Hein (2009), "Coupon Enthusiasts' Drive Up Redemption Rates," *Progressive grocer.com*, September 4.
9. Karen Talley (2009), "Sam's Club Tries Texting For Its Discount Coupons," *The Wall Street Journal*, September 30, p. B5B.
10. Timothy W. Martin (2009), "Coupons Are Hot. Clipping Is Not," *The Wall Street Journal*, February 25.
11. David Card (2001), "Online Couponing Is Cost-Effective for CPGs," Jupiter-Media Metrix Report, October 26.
12. David Kesmodel (2008), "The Coupon King," *The Wall Street Journal*, February 16.
13. Data provided by Information Resources Incorporated (IRI).

14. Private communications.
15. Gerry Khermouch (1997), "Read This. It's Free," *Brandweek*, June 16, p. 42.
16. Miho Inada (2009), "Tokyo Café Targets Trend Makers," *The Wall Street Journal*, August 24, p. B5.
17. Emily Nelson (2002), "P&G Promotion Is Too Successful, Angering Buyers," *The Wall Street Journal*, April 2, p. B1.
18. Shirley Leung (2002), "Happy Meals Angle for Little Girls' Loyalty with Well-Dressed Dolls," *The Wall Street Journal*, April 5, p. B1.
19. Gerry Khermouch and Jeff Green (2001), "Buzz-z-z-z-z Marketing," *BusinessWeek*, July 30, pp. 50–56.
20. For more information on slotting allowances, see Paul N. Bloom, Gregory T. Gundlach, and Joseph P. Cannon (1999), "Slotting Allowances and Fees: Schools of Thought and the Views of Practicing Managers," Report #99-106 (Boston: Marketing Science Institute).
21. Julie Forster (2002), "The Hidden Cost of Shelf Space," *BusinessWeek*, April 15, p. 103.
22. See Matthew G. Nagler (2006) "An Exploratory Analysis of the Determinants of Cooperative Advertising Participation Rates," *Marketing Letters*, 17:2 (April 2006), pp. 91–102.
23. This illustration is based on Jack Neff (2000), "Clorox Gives in on Glad, Hikes Trade Promotion," *Advertising Age*, November 27, p. 22.
24. The marketing manager may want to reward loyal customers and aid retention, particularly in the face of competitor promotions, by giving them a discount. However, if they would normally pay the regular price, this is a cost of the promotion.
25. Stephanie Thompson (2004), "Nestlé Warns Stores: Prove It or Lose It," *Advertising Age*, September 13, p.1.
26. Scott A. Neslin and Robert W. Shoemaker (1983), "A Model for Evaluating the Profitability of Coupon Promotions," *Marketing Science*, 2, pp. 361–88.
27. This illustration is based on John A. Quelch (1983), "Procter and Gamble (B)," Harvard Business School case #9-584-048. Note that retail promotions are omitted because such decisions are made by the retailers.
28. See also J. Jeffrey Inman, Russell S. Winer, and Resellina Ferraro (2009), "The Interplay among Category Characteristics, Customer Characteristics, and Customer Activities on In-Store Decision Making," *Journal of Marketing*, September, pp. 19–29.
29. Readers should not expect to get these kinds of results for every brand or kind of product.
30. Paule W. Farris and Robert D. Buzzell (1979), "Why Advertising and Promotional Costs Vary: Some Cross-Sectional Analyses," *Journal of Marketing*, 43 (Fall), pp. 112–122.
31. Robert M. Prentice (1977), "How to Split Your Marketing Funds between Advertising and Promotion," *Advertising Age*, January 10, p. 41.
32. Natalie Zmuda (2009), "Coke: Buy 1 Rival, Get Our Brand Free," *Advertising Age*, March 9.
33. Ilan Brat and Ann Zimmerman (2009), "Tale of the Tape: Retailers Take Receipts to Great Lengths," *The Wall Street Journal*, September 1.

Chapter 12

1. This illustration is based on Nick Wingfield (2009), "Microsoft to Open Stores, Hires Retail Hand," *The Wall Street Journal*, February 13; Karan Mehrishi (2009), "A Can of 'Windows,'" *4Ps Business and Marketing*, February 27–March 12, p. 62; and Vladisov Savov (2009), "First Two Microsoft Retail Stores Now Hiring," www.engadget.com, August 21.
2. The potential components of this value are described later in this chapter.
3. This illustration is based on John Deighton (2002), "How Snapple Got Its Juice Back," *Harvard Business Review*, January, pp. 47–53.
4. This illustration is based on Charles Fishman (2001), "Sweethearts and Wafers—and an Assortment of Nostalgic Candies—Connect Necco to Its Rich Past," *Fast Company*, February, pp. 137–145.
5. U.S. Department of Commerce, http://www.census.gov/retail/mrts/www/data/pdf/09Q4.pdf
6. eMarketer, February 6, 2008.
7. http://pressroom.grainger.com/phoenix.zhtml?c=194987&p=irol-factsheet#4
8. The companies also changed how the sales force is compensated. Their method, called multilevel selling, is covered later in this chapter.
9. Rob Wherry (2001), "Ice Cream Wars," *Forbes*, May 28, pp. 160–164.
10. This illustration is based on Haim Mendelson (2001), "Tesco Delivers," Stanford Graduate School of Business case #EC-32; Louis Lee (2003), "Online Grocers Finally Delivering the Lettuce," *BusinessWeek*, April 28, p. 67; *New Media Age* (2005), May 5, p. 17; and http://www.nomensa.com/news/industry-news/2009/10/tescos-online-sales-hit-1billion.html.
11. This illustration is based on Nick Wingfield (2009), "Netflix Boss Plots Life After the DVD," *The Wall Street Journal*, June 23; Farhad Manjoo (2009), "Box Tops," *Fast Company*, July/August, p. 57; and Rob Walker (2009), "Few Releases," *The New York Times Magazine*, October 25, p. 22.
12. John R. Hayes (1997), "Watch Out, Dell," *Forbes*, March 24, p. 84.

13. V. Kasturi Rangan, Melvyn A. J. Menezes, and E. P. Maier (1992), "Channel Selection for New Industrial Products: A Framework, Method, and Applications," *Journal of Marketing*, 56 (July), pp. 69–82.
14. Joseph B. Myers, Andrew D. Pickersgill, and Evan S. Van Metre (2004), "Steering Customers to the Right Channels," *The McKinsey Quarterly*, 4, pp. 37–43.
15. This illustration is based on V. Kasturi Rangan and E. Raymond Corey (1989), "Ingersoll-Rand (A): Managing Multiple Channels," Harvard Business School case #9-589-121; Lauren Keller Johnson (2005), "Motivating Cross-Boundary Thinking and Acting at Ingersoll-Rand," Harvard Business School Press; and www.ingersollrand.com.
16. Rowland T. Moriarty and Ursula Moran (1990), "Managing Hybrid Systems," *Harvard Business Review*, November–December, pp. 146–55.
17. Anne T. Coughlan, Erin Anderson, Louis W. Stern, and Adel I. El-Ansary (2001), *Marketing Channels*, 6th ed. (Upper Saddle River, NJ: Prentice-Hall), p. 200.
18. Pamela Sebastian Ridge (2002), "Big Tooth? Suit Says Dentsply Has a Monopoly," *The Wall Street Journal*, April 12, p. A13.
19. Coughlan, Anderson, Stern, and El-Ansary, *Marketing Channels*, Ch. 9.
20. This illustration is based on Kevin Kelleher (2004), "Giving Dealers a Raw Deal," *Business 2.0*, December, pp. 82–84.
21. Lisa Bannon (2000), "Selling Barbie Online May Pit Mattel vs. Stores," *The Wall Street Journal*, November 17, p. B1.
22. This is not always the case. An OEM channel may want a long-term relationship with a supplier because it gives the latter an incentive to invest in improving its own technology and bringing down its costs, which ultimately benefits the OEM. An OEM may also require an investment on the part of the supplier to tailor the product in some way, such as making a special adapter to fit into the product.
23. Some of the material in this section is based on Coughlan, Anderson, Stern, and El-Ansary, *Marketing Channels*.
24. For tips on how to develop channel arrangements in foreign countries, see David Arnold (2000), "7 Rules of International Distribution," *Harvard Business Review*, November–December, pp. 131–137.
25. This illustration is based on Joseph Kahn (1995), "P&G Viewed China as a National Market and Is Conquering It," *The Wall Street Journal*, September 12, p. A1; and Norihiko Shirouzu (1997), "P&G's Joy Makes an Unlikely Splash in Japan," *The Wall Street Journal*, December 10, p. B1.
26. *Progressive Grocer* (2009), May; www.ibisworld.com.
27. Suman Basuroy, Murali K. Mantrala, and Rockney G. Walters (2001), "The Impact of Category Management on Retailer Prices and Performance: Theory and Evidence," *Journal of Marketing*, October, pp. 16–32.
28. D. Gail Fleenor (2009), "Dairy Aisle Leadership: The Next Space Optimizer," *Progressive Grocer*, February 25, http://www.progressivegrocer.com/progressivegrocer/content_display/esearch/e3ia9c64386847182ff1c2991ecfc57ec13.
29. Some large supermarkets such as SuperValu, Kroger, and Walmart have their own distribution networks and do not use independent food wholesalers extensively.
30. "America's Largest Private Companies," *Forbes* November 16 (2009), pp. 146–148.
31. This illustration is based on Brett Nelson (2005), "Stuck in the Middle," *Forbes*, August 15, p. 88.

Chapter 13

1. This illustration is based on Michele Marchetti (2000), "Cisco Systems," *Sales & Marketing Management*, July, pp. 60–61; "America's 500 Largest Sales Forces," (2005), *Selling Power*, p. 64; Stephen Wildstrom (2009), "Meet Cisco, the Consumer Company," *BusinessWeek*, May 4, pp. 73–74; and *BtoB Online* (2009), October 26, interview with Susan Bostrom, Executive vice president and chief marketing officer, Cisco Systems.
2. Andris A. Zoltners, Prabhakant Sinha, and Sally E. Lorimer (2008), "Sales Force Effectiveness: A Framework for Researchers and Practitioners," *Journal of Personal Selling & Sales Management*, (Spring), pp. 115–131.
3. *DMA 2009 Statistical Fact Book* (New York: The Direct Marketing Association).
4. Natalie Zmuda (2009), "Direct Disconnect: Retailers Neglect Valuable Data Trove," *Advertising Age*, September 21, 2009.
5. *DMA 2009 Statistical Fact Book*.
6. These data are from *Selling Power* (2009), October.
7. *Sales & Marketing Management* (2000), September, p. 82.
8. Frank V. Cespedes (1994), "Hewlett-Packard Imaging Systems Division: Sonos 100 C/F Introduction," Harvard Business School case #9-593-080.
9. "MCI Communications Corporation: National Accounts Program," Harvard Business School case #9-587-116.
10. Kathleen Cholewka (2001), "Xerox's Savior?" *Sales & Marketing Management*, April, pp. 36–42.
11. "Reorganizing a Sales Force" (2000), *Sales & Marketing Management*, March, p. 90.

12. William A. O'Connell and William Keenan Jr. (1990), "The Shape of Things to Come," *Sales & Marketing Management*, January, pp. 36–41.
13. This illustration is from Sanjit Sengupta, Robert E. Krapfel, and Michael A. Pusateri (1997), "The Strategic Sales Force," *Marketing Management*, Summer, pp. 29–34.
14. Theodor Levitt (1986), "Relationship Management," in *The Marketing Imagination* (New York: The Free Press), Ch. 6.
15. In addition to the model used in this book, the interested reader can also consult Mark Johnston and Greg Marshall (2005), *Churchill-Ford-Walker's Sales Force Management*, 8th ed. (Burr Ridge, IL: McGraw-Hill).
16. Of course, the firm may have better investment opportunities that generate more than $1 in contribution margin. The method can be adjusted to set a hurdle rate for the return of a salesperson beyond a given opportunity cost of capital.
17. This illustration is based on Darral G. Clarke (1983), "Syntex Laboratories (A)," Harvard Business School case #9-584-033.
18. Thomas M. Siebel and Michael S. Malone (1996), *Virtual Selling* (New York: The Free Press). See also Dianne Ledingham, Mark Kovac, and Heidi Locke Simon (2006), "The New Science of Sales Force Productivity," *Harvard Business Review*, September, pp. 124–134.
19. This illustration is based on Todd Shapera (2001), "SFA Helps NuGenesis Customzie Relationships," *1to1*, May/June, p. 29.
20. This illustration is based on Peter Leach and Wendy Close (1999), "Card Games: How Lanier Worldwide Automated Its Sales Force," *Executive Edge*, February–March, pp. 50–54.
21. Ellen Byron (2001), "The Web @ Work: AstraZeneca," *The Wall Street Journal*, November 5, p. B6.
22. The Direct Marketing Association, www.the-dma.org.
23. For other approaches to analyzing lists, see Füsun Gönül, Byung-Do Kim, and Mengze Shi (2000), "Mailing Smarter to Catalog Customers," *Journal of Interactive Marketing*, Spring, pp. 2–16; and Nissan Levin and Jacob Zahavi (2001), "Predictive Modeling Using Segmentation," *Journal of Interactive Marketing*, Spring, pp. 2–22.
24. *The DMA 2009 Response Rate Report* (New York: The Direct Marketing Association).
25. This illustration is based on Jeff Borden (2008), "Eat My Dust," *Marketing News*, February 1, pp. 20–22.
26. The data in this paragraph are from Jeffrey Ball (2009), "In Digital Era, Marketers Still Prefer a Paper Trail," *The Wall Street Journal*, October 16, p. A13.
27. Dianna Dilworth (2009), "Strike Up the Brand with E-Mail," *DMNEWS*, March 9, p. 12.
28. Seth Godin (1999), *Permission Marketing* (New York: Simon & Schuster).
29. For more information on the DoubleClick/Abacus Direct incident, see David P. Baron (2001), "DoubleClick and Internet Privacy," Graduate School of Business, Stanford University case #P-32.

Chapter 14

1. This illustration is based on Joe Ashbrook Nickell (2002), "Welcome to Harrah's," *Business 2.0*, April, pp. 47–54; Mike Beirne (2002), "Dollars in the Desert," *Brandweek*, April 1, pp. 19–20; John Quelch (2005), "Ambidextrous Marketing," *The Wall Street Journal*, October 11, p. B-2; and data from *Yahoo! Financial* pages.
2. Matt Richtel and Andrew Ross Sorkin (2004), "AT&T Wireless for Sale as a Shakeout Starts," *The New York Times*, January 21, p. C1.
3. Andrea Petersen and Nicole Harris (2002), "Chaos, Confusion and Perks Bedevil Wireless Users," *The Wall Street Journal*, April 17, p. A1; and Matt Richtel (2004), "$41 Billion Deal, But What's in It for Consumers?" *The New York Times*, February 18, p. C1.
4. Theodore Levitt (1986), "Relationship Management," in *The Marketing Imagination* (New York: Free Press), Ch. 6.
5. Barbara Bund Jackson (1985), "Build Customer Relationships That Last," *Harvard Business Review*, November–December, pp. 120–128.
6. Chuck Pettis (1997), "A Customer's Loyalty for $200," *Marketing Computers*, September, pp. 67–70.
7. Some authors question the basic notion that long-term relationships always lead to greater profitability. See, for example, Grahame R. Dowling and Mark Uncles (1997), "Do Loyalty Programs Really Work?" *Sloan Management Review*, Summer, pp. 71–82. In addition, some authors draw a distinction between contractual (e.g., magazine subscriptions, health club memberships) and noncontractual relationships (e.g., catalogue buying) and argue that the economics of long-term customer relationships in the latter situation are not so clear. See Werner J. Reinartz and V. Kumar (2000), "On the Profitability of Long-Life Customers in a Noncontractual Setting: An Empirical Investigation and Implications for Marketing," *Journal of Marketing*, October, pp. 17–35.
8. A more comprehensive model of CRM that incorporates business strategy into the model has been developed by Adrian Payne and

Pennie Frow (2005), "A Strategic Framework for Customer Relationship Management," *Journal of Marketing*, October, pp. 167–176.

9. Rashi Glazer (1999), "Winning in Smart Markets," *Sloan Management Review*, Summer, pp. 59–69.
10. "Traceable" activity would be any marketing program in which the response can be directly related to the program. An example would be a catalogue mailing. Mass advertising would not be included, for example.
11. Erik Schonfeld (2001), "The Total Package," *Ecompany*, June, pp. 91–96.
12. This framework is due to Professor Florian Zettelmeyer.
13. Normandy Madden (2004), "Nestlé Broadens Efforts to Bond with Consumers," *Advertising Age*, May 24, p. 4.
14. See, for example, Michael J. A. Berry and Gordon S. Linoff (2000), *Mastering Data Mining* (New York: John Wiley & Sons).
15. See, for example, Paul D. Berger and Nada I. Nasr (1998), "Customer Lifetime Value: Marketing Models and Applications," *Journal of Interactive Marketing*, Winter, pp. 17–30. In addition, a good reference in this area is V. Kumar and Werner Reinartz (2006), *Customer Relationship Management* (Hoboken, NJ: John Wiley & Sons), Ch. 6.
16. Sunil Gupta and Donald R. Lehmann (2003), "Customers as Assets," *Journal of Interactive Marketing*, Winter, pp. 9–24.
17. For an examination of LCV in a channels context, see Rakesh Niraj, Mahendra Gupta, and Chakravarthi Narasimhan (2001), "Customer Profitability in a Supply Chain," *Journal of Marketing*, July, pp. 1–16.
18. This has sometimes been referred to as customer equity. See, for example, Roland T. Rust, Valarie A. Zeithaml, and Katherine N. Lemon (2000), *Driving Customer Equity* (New York: Free Press).
19. For a more detailed look at this acquisition/retention decision, see Robert C. Blattberg and John Deighton (1996), "Manage Marketing by the Customer Equity Test," *Harvard Business Review*, July–August, pp. 136–144.
20. "BrooksBrothers.com" (2000), *The Wall Street Journal*, September 24, p. R6.
21. Gary McWilliams (2004), "Analyzing Customers, Best Buy Decides Not All Are Welcome," *The Wall Street Journal*, November 8, p. A1.
22. William C. Taylor (2005), "Rebels With a Cause, and a Business Plan," *The New York Times*, January 2, p. BU-5.
23. Francis J. Mulhern (1999), "Customer Profitability Analysis: Measurement, Concentration, and Research Directions," *Journal of Interactive Marketing*, Winter, pp. 25–40.
24. For a similar result in customer profitability being concentrated among a few customers, see Niraj, Gupta, and Narasimhan, "Customer Profitability in a Supply Chain."
25. Larry Selden and Geoffrey Colvin (2002), "Will This Customer Sink Your Stock?" *Fortune*, September 30, p. 128.
26. This illustration is based on Peterson and Harris, "Chaos, Confusion and Perks Bedevil Wireless Users."
27. Meredith Levinson (2000), "Slices of Lives," *CIO Magazine*, August 15, www.cio.com/archive/081500_slices_content.html.
28. See the references in Eugene W. Anderson, Claes Fornell, and Donald R. Lehmann (1993), "Economic Consequences of Providing Quality and Customer Satisfaction," Marketing Science Institute Report #93-112 (Cambridge, MA).
29. Bhattiprolu Murti (2005), "Customer Satisfaction Figures Into Some Executives' Bonuses," *The Wall Street Journal*, October 28, p. B-3C.
30. These are from www.theacsi.org.
31. Thomas O. Jones and W. Earl Sasser Jr. (1995), "Why Satisfied Customers Defect," *Harvard Business Review*, November–December, pp. 88–99.
32. Based on Frederick F. Reichheld, "The One Number You Need to Grow" *Harvard Business Review*, December 2003.
33. Jones and Sasser, "Why Satisfied Customers Defect."
34. In addition, there are many different measures of loyalty, from survey-based measures such as purchase intentions to behavioral measures such as share-of-requirements, the percentage of all purchases of a product that are of a particular brand.
35. See, for example, Beth Snyder Bulik (2004), "Brands Spotlight Customer Experience," *Advertising Age*, April 19, p. 1.
36. Jan Carlzon (1987), *Moments of Truth* (Cambridge, MA: Ballinger).
37. Alison Overholt (2004), "Cuckoo for Customers," *Fast Company*, June, pp. 86–87.
38. This illustration is based on Jake Chessum (2009), "Get Happy," *Inc.*, May, pp. 67–73; and Christopher Palmeri (2010), "Now for Sale, The Zappos Culture," *Bloomberg Businessweek*, January 11, p. 57.
39. Bob Tasca (1996), *You Will Be Satisfied* (New York: HarperCollins).
40. James L. Heskett, W. Earl Sasser, and Christopher W. L. Hart (1990), *Service Breakthroughs: Changing the Rules of the Game* (New York: Free Press).
41. Chad Kaydo (1998), "Riding High," *Sales & Marketing Management*, July, pp. 64–69.
42. "International Business Machines (B): Applitronics Account Strategy," Harvard Business School case #9-581-052.
43. This illustration is based on Paul C. Judge (2001), "EMC Corporation," *Fast Company*, June, pp. 138–145; and data from www.emc.com.

44. Another company is netCustomer, described at the beginning of Chapter 5.
45. Peter Fuller (2002), "A Two-Way Conversation," *Brandweek*, February 25, pp. 21–27.
46. Stanley Reed (2005), "Rolls-Royce, At Your Service," *BusinessWeek*, November 14, pp. 92–95.
47. Rebecca Piirto Heath (1997), "Loyalty for Sale," *Marketing Tools*, July, pp. 40–46; see also Grahame R. Dowling and Mark Uncles (1997), "Do Customer Loyalty Programs Really Work?" *Sloan Management Review*, Summer, pp. 71–82; and Louise O'Brien and Charles Jones (1995), "Do Rewards Really Create Loyalty?" *Harvard Business Review*, May–June, pp. 75–82.
48. Laura Loro (1998), "Loyalty Programs Paying Off for B-to-B," *Business Marketing*, September, p. 49.
49. See B. Joseph Pine II (1993), *Mass Customization: The New Frontier in Business Competition* (Boston: Harvard Business School Press).
50. Gil McWilliam (2000), "Building Stronger Brands through Online Communities," *Sloan Management Review*, Spring, pp. 43–54. For additional information on building online communities, see Ruth L. Williams and Joseph Cothrel (2000), "Four Smart Ways to Run Online Communities," *Sloan Management Review*, Summer, pp. 81–91; Albert M. Muniz Jr. and Thomas C. O'Guinn (2001), "Brand Community," *Journal of Consumer Research*, March, pp. 412–432; and James H. McAlexander, John W. Schouten, and Harold F. Koenig (2002), "Building Brand Community," *Journal of Marketing*, January, pp. 38–54.
51. Shona L. Brown, Andrew Tilton, and Dennis M. Woodside (2002), "The Case for On-line Communities," *The McKinsey Quarterly*, January, www.mckinseyquarterly.com
52. Evan I. Schwartz (2001), "Real Community Is Possible," *Business 2.0*, March 6, p. 64.
53. Pat Long (1997), "Customer Loyalty, One Customer at a Time," *Marketing News*, February 3, p. 8.
54. Frederick F. Reichheld (1996), "Learning from Customer Defections," *Harvard Business Review*, March–April, pp. 56–69.

Chapter 15

1. This illustration is based on Paul Sweeney and Denise Lugo (2001), "The Choice: While Some Regionals Tout the Virtues of Merging, the Independent-Minded Still Flourish," *The Investment Dealers' Digest: IDD*, May 26, pp. 18–23; David Colis and Troy Smith (2007), "Edward Jones in 2006: Confronting Succes," Harvard Business School case #9-707-497; and www.edwardjones.com.
2. *Economic Report of the President*, 2009.
3. https://www.cia.gov/library/publications/the-world-factbook/index.html.
4. These examples are from William M. Bulkeley (2009), "Xerox Tries to Go Beyond Copiers," *The Wall Street Journal*, February 24; Richard Waters (2009), "Big Blueprint for IBM Services," *Financial Times*, March 3, p. 12; Andrew Parker and Andrew Ward (2009), "Services Hold Key to Nokia's Future," *Financial Times*, August 24, p. 13; Justin Scheck (2009), "H-P Gets a Boost From Services Unit," *The Wall Street Journal*, November 24, p. B1; and William M. Bulkeley (2009), "Print Outsourcing Gives Boost to Xerox, H-P," *The Wall Street Journal*, December 22, p. B5.
5. For some basic information on this classification scheme, see Philip Nelson (1970), "Advertising as Information," *Journal of Political Economy*, July–August, pp. 729–754.
6. See also David Garvin (1987), "Competing on the Eight Dimensions of Quality," *Harvard Business Review*, November–December, pp. 101–9; and Christian Grönroos (1990), *Service Management and Marketing* (Lexington, MA: Lexington Books).
7. A. Parsuraman, Valarie A. Zeithaml, and Leonard L. Berry (1988), "A Multiple-Item Scale for Measuring Consumer Perceptions of Service Quality," *Journal of Retailing*, 64, pp. 12–40; see also Valarie A. Zeithaml and A. Parasuraman (2004), *Service Quality* (Cambridge, MA: Marketing Science Institute).
8. Andrew J. Czaplewski, Eric M. Olson, and Stanley F. Slater (2002), "Applying the RATER Model for Service Success," *Marketing Management*, February, pp. 14–17.
9. Daniel Kahneman and Amos Tversky (1979), "Prospect Theory: An Analysis of Decision Under Risk," *Econometrica*, 47, pp. 263–291.
10. Valaria A. Zeithaml, A. Parasuraman, and Leonard L. Berry (1990), *Delivering Quality Service: Balancing Customer Perceptions and Expectations* (New York: Free Press).
11. Zeithaml, Parasuraman, and Berry, *Delivering Quality Service*, Appendix A.
12. Shelly Reese (1996), "Happiness Isn't Everything," *Marketing Tools*, May, pp. 52–58.
13. Roland T. Rust, Anthony J. Zahorik, and Timothy L. Keiningham (1994), *Return on Quality: Measuring the Financial Impact of Your Company's Quest for Quality* (Chicago: Probus).
14. Malcolm Fleschner and Gerhard Gschwandtner (1994), "The Marriott Miracle," *Personal Selling Power*, September, pp. 17–26.
15. See Theodore Levitt (1986), *The Marketing Imagination* (New York: Free Press), Ch. 5.
16. Valarie A. Zeithaml, Mary Jo Bitner, and Dwayne D. Gremler (2006), *Services Marketing*, 4th ed. (New York: McGraw-Hill), Ch. 9.

17. This illustration is based on Sandra Vandermerwe and Christopher H. Lovelock (1991), "Singapore Airlines: Using Technology for Service Excellence," IMD case #592-014-1.

18. Zeithaml, Bitner, and Gremler, *Services Marketing*, Ch. 14.

19. eMarketer (2008), "Where Have All the Online Travelers Gone?" August 25.

20. This section is based on Donna Legg and Julie Baker (1987), "Advertising Strategies for Service Firms," in C. Suprenant, ed., *Add Value to Your Service* (Chicago: American Marketing Association), pp. 163–168.

21. Simona Covel (2009), "Firms Try Alternative to Hourly Fees," *The Wall Street Journal*, April 2.

22. Katherine M. Lemon, Tiffany Barnett White, and Russell S. Winer (2002), "Dynamic Customer Relationship Management: Incorporating Future Considerations into the Service Retention Decision," *Journal of Marketing*, January, pp. 1–14.

23. This section is based on Gary W. Loveman (1993), "The Internationalization of Services," Harvard Business School case #9-693-103.

24. This illustration is based on Gary Loveman and Leonard Schlesinger (1992), "Euro Disney: The First 100 Days," Harvard Business School case #9-693-013; Alison James (2005), "Euro-Mickey Braces for Wild Ride," *Variety*, p. 22; Geoffrey A. Fowler (2008), "Main Street, H.K." *The Wall Street Journal*, January 23, P. B1; and http://en.wikipedia.org/wiki/Disneyland_Resort_Paris.

25. Sources include various Wikipedia sites, Yahoo! Finance, eMarketer, and Robert Levine (2008), "Globe Trotter," *Fast Company*, September, pp. 73–74.

26. This illustration is based on Alex Frankel (2008), "Zipcar Makes the Leap," *Fast Company*, March, pp. 48-50; Shivani Vora (2009), "Test-Driving Car-Share Services," *The Wall Street Journal*, June 11, p. D2; and Ken Belson (2009), "Car-Sharing Services Cut Cost of Ownership," *The New York Times*, October 22, p. 8.

Glossary

acquisition costs the incremental costs involved in obtaining any new customer (p. 408)

association/causal methods a sales forecasting method that tries to develop statistical models relating market factors to sales (p. 81)

B-to-B (business-to-business) marketing when a product or service is sold to an organization (p. 127)

brand equity the value of a brand name in communicating quality or other aspects of a product (p. 50)

brand positions customers' perceptions of one brand in relation to its competitors (p. 50)

brands a name, term, sign, symbol, or design (or a combination thereof) intended to identify the goods and services of a seller and differentiate them from the competition (p. 152)

breakdown method a major method used to determine the size of the sales force that is based on the forecasted sales level divided by an assumed average sales per salesperson (p. 384)

budget competition a level of competition that includes any product, related or unrelated, that could be viewed as substitutable in a budget (p. 155)

buy classes a set of descriptor variables used in industrial marketing segmentation that is based on the newness of the purchasing situation (p. 131)

buying center a group of individuals collectively involved in a purchase decision (p. 127)

cannibalization the amount of sales for a new element of a product line that is taken away from an existing element of the line (p. 200)

category management a process that considers product categories to be the business units that should be customized on a store-by-store basis in a way that satisfies customer needs (p. 367)

channel power the ability of one channel member to get another channel member to do what it otherwise would not have done (p. 359)

channels of distribution the system by which customers have access to a company's product or service (p. 341)

chasm the large gap that can exist between the early adopters of an innovation and the early majority (p. 134)

choiceboards online, interactive systems that allow individual customers to design their own products by choosing from an array of attributes, delivery options and prices (p. 202)

co-creation using people outside of the organization to help develop new product ideas (p. 222)

cohort analysis an analysis that develops age-related profiles of each generation to segment the market (p. 93)

commission a form of compensation based directly on a sale or some other activity (p. 389)

community a group of customers who share information between themselves and the company about their experiences with the product or service (p. 430)

compatibility an attribute evaluated by customers of new technologically-based innovations that refers to the compatibility of the innovation with existing systems, values, and beliefs or previously introduced ideas (p. 117)

compensatory model any model in which a low score on one attribute can be compensated for by a higher score on another (p. 114)

competitive advantage the strategic development of some basis on which customers will choose a firm's product or service over its competitors' (p. 44)

competitive pricing a pricing policy in which the objective is to maintain a competitive price by either pricing at the market average or copying a particular brand (p. 263)

competitor analysis an analysis in which the strengths and weaknesses of competitors and their current and likely future strategies are examined (p. 151)

competitor targets the brands or companies that offer the most likely competition for that customer (p. 36)

complementary pricing an approach to product line pricing that applies to products that are used together when one of the products is a consumable that must be replenished continually (p. 269)

complexity one factor of an innovation that is negatively related to its success (p. 117)

concept development making further refinements to a new product concept (p. 226)

conjoint analysis a popular marketing research method in new product development that uses theoretical profiles or concepts to determine how customers value different levels of product attributes (p. 255)

consumer franchise building (CFB) activities that build brand equity, including advertising, sampling, couponing, and product demonstrations (p. 335)

consumer-oriented promotions a marketing tool such as a coupon that targets consumers and is intended to generate a short-term change in a product's sales or market share (p. 286)

continuous replenishment program (CRP) a program wherein members of a supply chain partner with supermarkets, working together to attempt to accurately forecast demand, which is then used to generate inventory replenishment data electronically (p. 369)

control group in an experiment, a set of respondents or experimental units who receive the normal level of the manipulation and against which the experimental group is compared (p. 75)

core strategy designed by the marketing manager, a statement that communicates the reason to buy to a specific customer group (p. 36)

correlation method of forecasting an association/causal method of sales forecasting in which a correlation between two variables is used to indicate the strength of the association (p. 84)

counting methods sales forecasting methods that rely on customer data (p. 81)

couponing a price-oriented promotion that offers a discount off the price of a product and is accompanied by a physical or electronic document indicating the amount of the discount (p. 318)

cross-elasticity of demand the percentage of change in one product's sales caused by a percentage change in a marketing variable for another product (p. 156)

customer information file, or CIF a customer database including information on past and current purchasing, contact, response to marketing variables, and monetary value to the company (p. 411)

customer relationship management, or CRM develops programs that match the kind of relationship the customer wants with the company, whether it is relational or transactional (p. 407)

customer service service that supplements or complements the main product or service purchased (p. 423)

customer targets a more specific segment of customers (e.g., income over $40,000, small businesses with revenues under $10 billion), which the marketing manager wants to entice to buy the product or service (p. 36)

customer value what a product or service is worth to the customer in monetary terms; also called perceived value (p. 247)

customerization a process whereby a company takes a product or service that is widely marketed and perhaps offered in many different configurations and develops a system for customizing (or nearly customizing) it to each customer's specifications (p. 202)

data mining analyzing a customer information file for the best prospects to target (p. 414)

decline stage of the product life cycle where product category sales are decreasing (p. 55)

Delphi method of forecasting a judgment method of sales forecasting that relies on a jury of experts formed from a diverse population to provide individual estimates of forecasted sales, which then are collated and refined in order to produce a final number (p. 81)

descriptors variables that describe customers in terms of their inherent characteristics (p. 90)

differential advantage one of the three components of a core strategy, a statement of how a particular product or service is better than the competition (p. 44)

differentiation an approach to creating a competitive advantage based on obtaining an observable point of difference that customers will value and for which they will be willing to pay (p. 46)

direct channel is one where the product or service remains under the control of the company from production to customer (p. 353)

direct mail marketing a form of direct marketing that involves sending letters or catalogues to potential customers (p. 286)

direct marketing any communication form that sends messages direct to a target market with the anticipation of an immediate or very-short-term response; also, any method of distribution that gives the customer access to the firm's products and services without any other intermediaries (pp. 286, 396)

direct sales in the context of direct marketing, an approach that involves the use of friends and neighbors as the sales force in reaching potential customers (p. 286)

disintermediation the process by which companies are eliminating intermediate channels of distribution through the use of information technology (p. 354)

diverters in international marketing, middlemen who purchase products or arrange for their purchase and thereby divert the products away from normal channels (p. 367)

Do Not Call Registry gives consumers a choice about whether or not they wish to receive phone calls from particular telemarketers (p. 286)

dollarmetric method in estimating customer value, a method used in conjunction with survey-based methods that creates a scale that puts survey responses in monetary terms (p. 255)

early adopters one type of adopter in Everett Rogers's diffusion of innovations framework; buyers who are not the first to purchase an innovation but who follow innovators (p. 99)

early majority one type of adopter in Everett Rogers's diffusion of innovations framework that follows early adopters; buyers who are interested in new technology and gadgets but who wait to see whether an innovative product is just a fad (p. 100)

econometric models an association/causal method of sales forecasting that involves the use of large-scale, multiple-equation models most often used to predict the economic performance of a country or a particularly large business sector (p. 84)

economies of scale also called economies of size, the rationale that larger sales mean that fixed costs of operations can be spread over more units, which lowers average unit costs (p. 45)

efficient consumer response (ECR) a process seeking to reduce costs throughout the entire distribution system, resulting in lower prices and increased consumer demand (p. 369)

emotional appeals an approach to developing advertising copy that strives to tap an underlying psychological aspect of the purchase decision (p. 296)

ethnographic research in-depth study of consumer consumption through interviews and observing behavior (p. 71)

evoked or consideration set in consumer behavior, the set of products from which the customer will choose to purchase (p. 111)

executive opinion method of forecasting a judgment method of sales forecasting in which the marketing manager relies on his or her own opinion to predict sales, based on his or her experience and knowledge or consultations with internal or external experts (p. 81)

expectation confirmation/disconfirmation model a basic customer satisfaction model that presumes that levels of customer satisfaction with a product or service are determined by how well the product performs compared to what the customer expects (p. 420)

expectations are developed based on the information the customer has collected from the prior search activities (p. 114)

experience curve the notion that costs fall with cumulative production or delivery of a service and that, using the first few years of a product's life as a yardstick, the continued decline in costs is predictable (p. 45)

experiences the interactions that a customer has with a company (p. 26)

exponential smoothing method of forecasting a time-series method of sales forecasting that relies on historical sales data, like the moving averages method, but also uses exponentially declining weights based on past sales values (p. 83)

external validity the ability to generalize experimental results to the real world or, more generally, the target population (p. 75)

extrapolation extending a line based on existing data outside the range of the data (p. 84)

factor analysis a multivariate statistical procedure to reduce a set of variables to a smaller set called factors that retain most of the information of the original set (p. 106)

family life cycle the stages of life individuals pass through (p. 114)

field experiment an experiment that takes place in a realistic environment (pp. 76, 256)

flat-rate vs. variable-rate pricing strategy often used in services that offers customers a choice between a fixed price and a variable usage fee (p. 271)

focus group small groups of people, typically recruited through their membership in various target groups of interest, who are brought together in a room to discuss a topic chosen by the marketing manager and led by a professional moderator (p. 68)

forecast a prediction of a future quantity such as sales (p. 77)

frequency marketing also called loyalty programs, which encourage repeat purchasing through a formal program enrollment process and the distribution of benefits (p. 428)

generic competition a level of competition that includes all products or services that the customer views as fulfilling the need requiring satisfaction on a particular purchase or use occasion (p. 154)

global marketing a generic term encompassing any marketing activities outside a company's home market; also a standardization of the strategies used to market a product around the world (p. 185)

gray market a market in which trademarked goods are sold through channels of distribution that are not authorized by the holder of the trademark (p. 367)

growth phase in the product life cycle, the stage immediately following the introductory phase, in which product category sales are growing, competitors are increasing in number, and market segmentation begins to be a key issue (p. 54)

horizontal marketing marketing to different industries with the same product or service (p. 131)

house of quality a matrix used in new product development that illustrates how customer needs and engineering characteristics influence one another (p. 226)

hybrid system a modification of the multiple-channel system in which members of the channel system perform complementary functions, often for the same customer, thereby allowing for specialization and better levels of performance (p. 357)

incentive payments payments monetary awards for special performance (p. 390)

indirect channel is an independent party paid by a company to distribute the product; in this case, the channel member and not the company has direct contact with the end user or organization (p. 353)

industrial marketing marketing of a product or service to another organization, also called organizational marketing (p. 127)

industry a group of products that are close substitutes to buyers, are available to a common group of buyers, and are distant substitutes for all products not included in the industry (p. 152)

informational appeals an approach to developing advertising copy that focuses on the functional or practical aspects of the product (p. 294)

innovators one type of adopter in Everett Rogers's diffusion of innovations framework; the first buyers of an innovation (p. 99)

inquiry tests track the number of inquiries received from a print advertisement (p. 298)

integrated marketing communications (IMC) the concept that all elements of the marketing mix communicate messages that must be coordinated in order to reinforce what each is saying and to avoid customer confusion (p. 281)

internal validity the degree to which experimental results are caused by the experimental manipulation (p. 75)

introductory phase in the product life cycle, the stage in which the product or service is new; sales volume increases slowly because of a lack of marketing effort and the reluctance of customers to buy the product (p. 53)

investment pricing also called return on sales, a pricing policy that assumes you can set a price that will deliver the rate of return demanded by senior management; most often used when a product has a monopoly position (p. 262)

joint space a perceptual map that contains both brand spatial locations as well as consumer perceptions of their ideal brand (p. 195)

judgment methods sales forecasting methods that rely on pure opinion (p. 81)

laboratory experiment an experiment run in an artificial environment (p. 76)

laggards one type of adopter in Everett Rogers's diffusion of innovations framework that follows the late majority; buyers who are generally not interested in new technology and are the last customers to buy, if they ever do (p. 100)

late majority one type of adopter in Everett Rogers's diffusion of innovations framework; buyers who are conservative in terms of how much of an industry infrastructure must be built before they will buy an innovative product (p. 100)

lead users the first buyers of an innovation in industrial marketing situations; also called innovators (pp. 133, 220)

leading indicators an association/causal method of sales forecasting in which certain macroeconomics variables are used to forecast changes in the economy, based on the fact that changes in these variables occur before changes in the economy (p. 84)

lifetime customer value the present value of a stream of revenue that can be produced by a customer (p. 408)

logistics physical distribution of goods from one location to another (p. 341)

loss aversion a psychological phenomenon characterized by customers reacting more strongly to unexpectedly poor service than to unexpectedly good service (p. 442)

loyalty programs also called frequency marketing, programs that encourage repeat purchasing through a formal program enrollment process and the distribution of benefits (p. 428)

manipulation in an experiment, the marketing variable that is of central interest and is experimentally controlled by the researcher (p. 75)

marginal economic method a major method used to determine the size of the sales force, based on the macroeconomic concept that a resource should be allocated up to the point at which the marginal revenue obtained from an additional unit of the resource equals the marginal cost (p. 386)

market development funding any money a company spends to help channel members sell their products (p. 324)

market development strategy one possible strategy in segmenting the market; the decision to target customers who have not yet purchased the product or service (p. 39)

market penetration strategy one possible strategy in segmenting the market; the decision to target current customers of a product or service (p. 38)

market potential the maximum sales reasonably attainable under a given set of conditions within a specified period of time (p. 77)

market segmentation breaking mass marketing into segments that have different buying habits; also refers to the decision about which customer groups a company will pursue for a particular brand or product line (p. 89)

market share pricing also called penetration pricing, a pricing policy in which the objective is to gain as much market share as possible; often used as part of an entry strategy for a new product (p. 262)

market structure analysis an analysis in which the marketing manager seeks to better understand who the competition is and thus define the market (p. 151)

market survey method of forecasting a counting method of sales forecasting that relies on surveys to predict demand (p. 83)

market testing method of forecasting a counting method of sales forecasting that uses primary data collection methods, such as focus groups and in-depth interviews, to predict sales (p. 83)

marketing the set of activities designed to influence choice whenever an individual or organization has a choice to make (p. 4)

marketing concept the importance of having a customer focus (i.e., organizing the resources of the firm toward understanding customers' needs and wants and then offering products and services to meet those needs) (p. 6)

marketing mix the set of decisions about price, channels of distribution, product, communications, and customer relationship management that implements the marketing strategy (p. 37)

marketing plan a written document containing the guidelines for a product's marketing programs and allocations over the planning period (p. 21)

marketing research the function that links the consumer, customer, and public to the marketer through information used to identify marketing opportunities and problems, generate and evaluate marketing actions, monitor marketing performance, and improve understanding of marketing as a process (p. 60)

mass customization a new marketing process whereby a company takes a product or service that is widely marketed and develops a system for customizing it to each customer's specifications (pp. 29, 90, 202, 430)

maturity phase in the product life cycle, the stage in which the sales curve has flattened out and few new buyers are in the market (p. 55)

measurable response the estimation of the effects of a marketing program such as direct marketing (p. 396)

mission statement a general statement describing a company's major business thrusts, customer orientation, or business philosophy (p. 37)

modified rebuys a kind of purchasing situation faced by an organization in which something has changed since the last purchase (e.g., a new potential supplier or a large change in price levels) (p. 132)

moving average method of forecasting a time-series method of sales forecasting that uses the averages of historical sales figures to make a forecast (p. 83)

multiattribute model a popular model of decision making that requires information about how useful or important each attribute is to the customer making a brand choice (which involves assigning importance weights) and how customers perceive the brands in the evoked set in terms of their attributes (p. 112)

multi-channel marketing marketing using multiple channels to distribution simultaneously. (p. 355)

multidimensional scaling (MDS) develop perceptual maps based only on customer-based judgments of brand similarity (p. 196)

multiple-channel systems a channel of distribution that uses a combination of direct and indirect channels and in which the multiple channel members serve different segments (p. 355)

naïve extrapolation a judgment method of sales forecasting that takes the most current sales and adds a judgmentally determined x%, where x is the estimated percentage change in sales (p. 81)

Nash equilibrium in game theory, the most common form of equilibrium, which involves a list of strategies, one for each player, with the property that no manager wants to change its strategy unilaterally (p. 172)

network externalities the concept that, for many products and services, the value of owning them increases as the number of owners increases (p. 118)

new-task purchase a purchasing situation that is unusual or occurs infrequently in a given organization (p. 132)

new-to-the-company a product that has not been marketed by the company but has been marketed by another company (p. 213)

new-to-the-world a product that has not been marketed by any company previously (p. 213)

nonpersonal channels of communication mass-media communication channels, such as television, newspapers, radio, direct mail, and the Internet (p. 283)

objective the criterion by which the success or failure of the strategy is to be measured (p. 36)

observability the degree to which an innovation or its results are visible to others (p. 117)

on-the-air/recall tests measure advertising effectiveness through follow-up surveys after a TV advertisement is shown (p. 298)

one-to-one marketing also called mass customization, a marketing process whereby a company takes a product or service that is widely developed and develops a system for customizing it to each customer's specifications (p. 90)

organizational marketing marketing a product or service to another organization, also called industrial marketing (p. 127)

original equipment manufacturer (OEM) a channel of distribution for technology-based products; companies that purchase ingredients or components (e.g., hard disk drives) from manufacturers (p. 189)

packaging the design of the container for the product in which it is displayed in a retail environment (p. 179)

panel a set of customers enlisted to give responses to questions or to provide data repeatedly over a period of time (p. 74)

parallel importing the development of gray markets across country lines, often as a result of significant currency exchange rate or price differences between countries that make it profitable to purchase goods in one country and import them into another for resale (p. 367)

Parfitt-Collins model a simple market share forecasting model that uses an estimate of the eventual penetration rate, an estimate of the ultimate repeat rate, and an estimate of the relative product category usage rate of buyers of the new brand to determine eventual market share (p. 232)

payoff matrix in game theory, a graphic depiction of the rewards or costs to each player for each possible combination of strategies (p. 172)

penetration pricing also called market share pricing, a pricing policy intended to gain as much market share as possible; often used as part of an entry strategy for a new product (p. 262)

perceived risk in regard to their adoption of new technologies, the extent to which customers are uncertain about the consequences of an action (p. 118)

perceptual map a map, based on marketing research from customers, that measures perceptions of competing products on a variety of attributes (p. 49)

periodic discounting a pricing strategy that varies price over time in order to take advantage of particular time periods during which some customers are willing to pay a higher price (p. 271)

personal channels of communication communication channels that involve direct sales as well as face-to-face or word-of-mouth interactions between customers (p. 283)

personal selling the use of face-to-face communications between seller and buyer (p. 288)

physiological methods measured advertising response by taking physical measures, such as pupil dilation or eye tracking (p. 297)

point-of-purchase (POP) advertising a form of retailer promotion that includes information related displays and other company-paid advertising inside the store (p. 326)

position the communication of the value proposition to the customer, which differentiates the product from competition in the mind of the prospect (p. 194)

potential the maximum sales reasonably attainable under a given set of conditions within a specified period of time (p. 77)

premiums a product-oriented promotion in which free merchandise is provided with a purchase or some free or reduced-price item is made available (p. 323)

prestige pricing also called skimming, a pricing policy used when there is a strong price perceived quality relationship and the product is positioned at the high end of the market; often used when costs are not related to volume and gaining significant market share is not an objective (p. 262)

price bands or tiers price variations within a product category (p. 247)

price bundling an approach to product line pricing in which a set of products is offered to customers in a package, which is usually priced lower than the sum of the individual components (p. 268)

price discrimination the practice of charging different prices to segments of the market according to their price elasticity or sensitivity (p. 247)

price elasticity of demand the percentage change in a product's demand resulting from a 1% change in its price (p. 252)

primary information sources in market research, sources of information that are generated for the particular problem being studied by the marketing manager (p. 62)

primary needs biological or physiological needs that a person must meet in order to stay alive (p. 226)

prisoner's dilemma game a particular form of competitive game in which neither participant wants to change his or her current strategy because if one does and the competitor matches, both will be worse off (p. 173)

product features are the characteristics or attributes of a product or service (p. 179)

product category also called a product class, one particular product segment of a particular industry (p. 152)

product class or product category competition a level of competition in which products or services that have similar features and provide the same function are considered (p. 153)

product definition a stage in the new product development process in which concepts are translated into actual products for further testing based on interactions with customers (p. 226)

product design combines art, science and technology to create tangible three-dimensional goods (p. 179)

product form competition a level of competition in which only products or services of the same product type are considered (p. 153)

product life cycle (PLC) a sketch of the sales history of a product category over time; used as a strategic tool because the importance of various marketing mix elements and strategic options available to the marketing manager vary over the life cycle (p. 52)

product line a group of closely related products (p. 179)

product-line pricing a pricing strategy covering a set of related products (p. 268)

product line strategy a marketing strategy covering a set of related products (p. 199)

product-oriented promotions consumer promotions that give away the product itself or a closely related product (p. 321)

product positioning considering the alternative differentiation possibilities and determining what differential advantages are to be emphasized and communicated to the target (p. 37)

product types group of products that are functional substitutes (p. 152)

product variants also called product brands, different specific combinations of features within a specific product type (p. 152)

public relations communications for which the sponsoring organization does not pay, often in some form of news distributed in a nonpersonal form (p. 287)

pull one of two kinds of basic activities of channel management that requires motivating customers to ask for your brand by name (p. 341)

purchase set in consumer behavior, the set of products that the customer has actually chosen within a specified period of time (p. 111)

push one of two kinds of basic activities of channel management that requires getting channels to carry and sell the product (p. 341)

qualitative research market research that usually involves small samples of customers and produces information that by itself does not directly lead to decisions but is valuable as an input for further research (p. 67)

quantitative research market research that typically involves statistical analysis of data, where the intent is to provide descriptive results or explicitly test a hypothesis (p. 68)

reference price any standard of comparison against which an observed potential transaction or purchase price is compared (p. 263)

regression analysis an association/causal method of sales forecasting in which the time series extrapolation model is generalized to include independent variables other than simply time (p. 84)

relative advantage the concept that a customer will adopt an innovation only if he or she considers it to be an improvement over the current product being used to satisfy the same need (p. 116)

relationship customers customers who see the benefits of interdependency between the buyer and the seller (p. 407)

relationships meaningful relationships between an individual and his or her brand (p. 26)

repositioning seeking a new perceived advantage in order to improve on a product's current positioning (p. 50)

reservation price the maximum price someone is willing to pay for a product or the price at which the product is eliminated from the customer's budget (p. 249)

retailer promotions short-term financial incentives to purchase provided by retail channel members (p. 325)

return on quality (ROQ) an approach attempts to quantify financial returns on investments in improved service quality (p. 444)

return on sales pricing also called investment pricing, a pricing policy that assumes you can set a price that will deliver the rate of return demanded by senior management; most often used when a product has a monopoly position (p. 262)

salary a form of compensation in which a basic amount of money is paid to a worker on a regular basis (p. 390)

sales contests sales force competitions based on sales performance (p. 390)

sales force method of forecasting a judgment method of sales forecasting in which salespeople form their own forecasts of the sales in their territories and the marketing manager sums them up to provide an overall forecast (p. 81)

sales/minimarket tests advertising tests in controlled geographic areas (p. 298)

sales promotion communication activities that provide extra incentives to customers or the sales force to achieve a short-term objective; an action-focused marketing event whose purpose is to have a direct impact on the behavior of the firm's customers. (pp. 286, 314)

sales quotas specific sales goals that salespeople are required to meet (p. 389)

sales territory a group of present and potential customers assigned to a salesperson, often designed on a geographic basis (p. 384)

sampling a product-oriented promotion in which a product is given away for free (p. 321)

scanner panel a collection of supermarket/drug store purchasing data of individual households obtained from electronic scanners in the stores (p. 75)

scenario planning planning that involves asking "what-if" questions to produce forecasts of alternative outcomes based on different assumptions about advertising spending, price levels, competitor actions, and other variables (pp. 81, 167)

second market discounting selling excess production of a product at a discount to a market distinct from the main market (p. 270)

secondary information sources in market research, sources of information that already exist and were not developed for the particular problem at hand (p. 62)

secondary needs social or psychological needs that can remain unsatisfied without any immediate danger to life or health (p. 226)

skimming also called prestige pricing, a pricing policy used when there is a strong price perceived quality relationship and the product is positioned at the high end of the market; often used when costs are not related to volume and gaining significant market share is not an objective (p. 262)

solutions products or services that solve a particular customer's problem at a given point in time (p. 26)

solutions buy a purchase situation in which the organization is buying a system that solves a specific problem (p. 132)

straight rebuys routine purchases made by an organization from the same supplier used in the past (p. 131)

supply chain the organizations involved in the movement of raw materials and components that are part of a product's production process (p. 128)

target costing in new product development, an alternative approach to setting the price of a new product, in which the ideal selling price is determined, the feasibility of meeting that price is assessed, and costs are controlled in order to produce the product that can be sold at the target price (p. 213)

target market group of customers or segment on which the marketing manager has decided to focus a marketing strategy (p. 38)

telemarketing a form of direct marketing that uses the telephone as the mechanism for reaching potential customers (p. 286)

tertiary needs a type of customer need considered in new product development; the operational needs related to the engineering aspect of actually making the product (p. 226)

theater tests tests of prospective advertising copy that take place in a theater-like environment (p. 297)

time-series methods sales forecasting methods that rely on historical sales data (p. 81)

trade promotions sales promotions oriented toward the channels of distribution in an effort to get the channels to carry and promote the product, often including devices such as sales contests, quantity discounts, and training programs (pp. 286, 324)

transaction buyers buyers who are interested only in the particular purchase at hand, rather than a long-term relationship (p. 407)

trialability the ability of potential users of an innovative or new product to try it on a limited basis before adoption (p. 117)

value-added reseller (VAR) organizations that buy products from a variety of vendors, assemble them in packages, and resell the packages to specialized segments; part of the channel of distribution for technology-based products (p. 363)

value-in-use a method of estimating customer value that puts the benefits of the product in monetary terms, such as time savings, less use of materials, and less downtime (p. 247)

value pricing giving customers more value than they expect for the price paid (p. 269)

value proposition a one-paragraph summary of a product or service's differentiation strategy and positioning to each target customer group; in short, a statement of why the customer should buy that product or service rather than the competitor's (p. 37)

vertical marketing marketing to specific industries with products and services tailored to those industries (p. 131)

virtual selling the reengineering of sales in the 1990s, especially the impact of sales force automation and the salesperson's educated use of technological tools in working with prospective customers in a highly efficient way (p. 393)

virtual shopping a new technology incorporating computer graphics and three-dimensional modeling that allows marketing managers to observe how consumers choose between different brands using a virtual reality setting (p. 71)

workload method a major method used to determine the size of the sales force that is based on the ability to calculate the total amount of work necessary to serve the entire market (p. 385)

Name Index

Subject Index

D

E

F

Q

R

S